Law and Legal Interpretation

The International Library of Essays in Law and Legal Theory
Second Series
Series Editor: Tom D. Campbell

Titles in the Series:

Freedom of Speech, Volumes I and II
Larry Alexander

Law and Legal Interpretation
Fernando Atria and D. Neil MacCormick

Privacy
Eric Barendt

Comparative Legal Cultures
John Bell

Contract Law, Volumes I and II
Brian Bix

Corporate Law
William W. Bratton

Law and Democracy
Tom Campbell and Adrienne Stone

Legal Positivism
Tom D. Campbell

Administrative Law
Peter Cane

International Trade Law
Ronald A. Cass and Michael S. Knoll

Sociological Perspectives on Law, Volumes I and II
Roger Cotterrell

Intellectual Property
Peter Drahos

Family, State and Law, Volumes I and II
Michael D. Freeman

Natural Law
Robert P. George

The Creation and Interpretation of Commercial Law
Clayton P. Gillette

Competition Law
Rosa Greaves

Chinese Law and Legal Theory
Perry Keller

Constitutional Law
Ian D. Loveland

Human Rights
Robert McCorquodale

Anti-Discrimination Law
Christopher McCrudden

Medical Law and Ethics
Sheila McLean

Mediation
Carrie Menkel-Meadow

Environmental Law
Peter S. Menell

Criminal Law
Thomas Morawetz

Law and Language
Thomas Morawetz

Law and Anthropology
Martha Mundy

Gender and Justice
Ngaire Naffine

Law and Economics
Eric A. Posner

Japanese Law
J. Mark Ramseyer

Restorative Justice
Declan Roche

Constitutional Theory
Wojciech Sadurski

Justice
Wojciech Sadurski

The Rule of Law
Frederick Schauer

Regulation
Colin Scott

War Crimes Law
Gerry Simpson

Restitution
Lionel D. Smith

Freedom of Information
Robert G. Vaughn

Tort Law
Ernest J. Weinrib

Rights
Robin West

Welfare Law
Lucy A. Williams

Law and Legal Interpretation

Edited by

Fernando Atria and D. Neil MacCormick

Universidad de Talca, Chile and University of Edinburgh, Scotland

LONDON AND NEW YORK

First published 2003 by Ashgate Publishing

Reissued 2018 by Routledge
2 Park Square, Milton Park, Abingdon, Oxon OX14 4RN
711 Third Avenue, New York, NY 10017, USA

Routledge is an imprint of the Taylor & Francis Group, an informa business

© Fernando Atria and D. Neil MacCormick 2003. For copyright of individual articles please refer to the Acknowledgements.

All rights reserved. No part of this book may be reprinted or reproduced or utilised in any form or by any electronic, mechanical, or other means, now known or hereafter invented, including photocopying and recording, or in any information storage or retrieval system, without permission in writing from the publishers.

Notice:
Product or corporate names may be trademarks or registered trademarks, and are used only for identification and explanation without intent to infringe.

Publisher's Note
The publisher has gone to great lengths to ensure the quality of this reprint but points out that some imperfections in the original copies may be apparent.

Disclaimer
The publisher has made every effort to trace copyright holders and welcomes correspondence from those they have been unable to contact.

A Library of Congress record exists under LC control number: 2002043894

ISBN 13: 978-1-138-71557-8 (hbk)
ISBN 13: 978-1-138-71556-1 (pbk)
ISBN 13: 978-1-315-19747-0 (ebk)

Contents

Acknowledgements vii
Series Preface ix
Introduction xi

PART I   INTERPRETATION AND LAW: WHY IS INTERPRETATION IMPORTANT FOR LAW?

1. Ronald Dworkin (1994), 'Law, Philosophy and Interpretation', *ARSP*, **80**, pp. 463–75.   3
2. Joseph Raz (1996), 'Why Interpret?', *Ratio Juris*, **9**, pp. 349–63.   17

PART II   INTERPRETATION AND LEGAL REASONING: LAW AND MORALITY

3. M.J. Detmold (1989), 'Law as Practical Reason', *Cambridge Law Journal*, **48**, pp. 436–71.   35
4. Fernando Atria (1999), 'Legal Reasoning and Legal Theory Revisited', *Law and Philosophy*, **18**, pp. 537–77.   71
5. Michael S. Moore (1985), 'A Natural Law Theory of Interpretation', *Southern California Law Review*, **58**, pp. 277–398.   113

PART III   INTERPRETATION AND APPLICATION OF LEGAL RULES, VAGUENESS AND DEFEASIBILITY

6. Robert Alexy (1993), 'Justification and Application of Norms', *Ratio Juris*, **6**, pp. 157–70.   237
7. Klaus Günther (1993), 'Critical Remarks on Robert Alexy's "Special-Case Thesis"', *Ratio Juris*, **6**, pp. 143–56.   251
8. Zenon Bankowski (1996), 'Law, Love and Computers', *Edinburgh Law Review*, **1**, pp. 25–42.   265
9. Carlos E. Alchourrón (1996), 'On Law and Logic', *Ratio Juris*, **9**, pp. 331–48.   283

PART IV   LEGAL INTEPRETATION AND POLITICS

10. Roberto Mangabeira Unger (1996), 'Legal Analysis as Institutional Imagination', *Modern Law Review*, **59**, pp. 1–23.   303

11 Emilios A. Christodoulidis (1996), 'The Inertia of Institutional Imagination: A Reply to Roberto Unger', *Modern Law Review*, **59**, pp. 377–97. 327

PART V INTERPRETATION AND OBJECTIVITY

12 Charles M. Yablon (1987), 'Law and Metaphysics', *Yale Law Journal*, **96**, pp. 613–36. 351
13 Jes Bjarup (1988), 'Kripke's Case: Some Remarks on Rules, their Interpretation and Application', *Rechtstheorie*, **19**, pp. 39–49. 375
14 Stanley Fish (1989), 'Working on the Chain Gang: Interpretation in Law and Literature', in Stanley Fish, *Doing What Comes Naturally*, Durham and London: Duke University Press, pp. 87–102, 559–62. 387

PART VI INTERPRETING THE LAW

15 Jan M. van Dunné (1998), 'Normative and Narrative Coherence in Legal Decision Making', *ARSP-Beiheft*, **69**, pp. 194–205. 409
16 Jerzy Wróblewski and Neil MacCormick (1994), 'On Justification and Interpretation', *ARSP-Beiheft*, **53**, pp. 255–68. 421
17 Aleksander Peczenik (1988), 'Authority Reasons in Legal Interpretation and Moral Reasoning', *ARSP Supplementa (III)*, pp. 144–52. 435
18 Robert S. Summers (1978), 'Two Types of Substantive Reasons: The Core of a Theory of Common-Law Justification', *Cornell Law Review*, **63**, pp. 707–88. 445
19 Neil MacCormick (1999), 'Reasonableness and Objectivity', *Notre Dame Law Review*, **74**, pp. 1575–603. 527

Name Index 557

Acknowledgements

The editors and publishers wish to thank the following for permission to use copyright material.

Blackwell Publishing for the essays: Joseph Raz (1996), 'Why Interpret?', *Ratio Juris*, **9**, pp. 349–63. Copyright © 1996 Blackwell Publishers Ltd; Robert Alexy (1993), 'Justification and Application of Norms', *Ratio Juris*, **6**, pp. 157–70. Copyright © 1993 Blackwell Publishers Ltd; Klaus Günther (1993), 'Critical Remarks on Robert Alexy's "Special-Case Thesis"', *Ratio Juris*, **6**, pp. 143–56. Copyright © 1993 Blackwell Publishers Ltd; Carlos E. Alchourrón (1996), 'On Law and Logic', *Ratio Juris*, **9**, pp. 331–48. Copyright © 1996 Blackwell Publishers Ltd; Roberto Mangabeira Unger (1996), 'Legal Analysis as Institutional Imagination', *Modern Law Review*, **59**, pp. 1–23. Copyright © 1996 Modern Law Review Ltd; Emilios A. Christodoulidis (1996), 'The Inertia of Institutional Imagination: A Reply to Roberto Unger', *Modern Law Review*, **59**, pp. 377–97. Copyright © 1996 Modern Law Review Ltd.

Cambridge Law Journal for the essay: M.J. Detmold (1989), 'Law as Practical Reason', *Cambridge Law Journal*, **48**, pp. 436–71. Copyright © 1989 Cambridge Law Journal and M.J. Detmold.

Cornell Law Review for the essay: Robert S. Summers (1978), 'Two Types of Substantive Reasons: The Core of a Theory of Common-Law Justification', *Cornell Law Review*, **63**, pp. 707–88. Copyright © 1978 Cornell University.

Duke University Press for the essay: Stanley Fish (1989), 'Working on the Chain Gang: Interpretation in Law and Literature', in Stanley Fish, *Doing What Comes Naturally*, Durham and London: Duke University Press, pp. 87–102, 559–62.

Duncker & Humblot GmbH for the essay: Jes Bjarup (1988), 'Kripke's Case: Some Remarks on Rules, their Interpretation and Application', *Rechtstheorie*, **19**, pp. 39–49.

Ronald Dworkin (1994), 'Law, Philosophy and Interpretation', *ARSP*, **80**, pp. 463–75. Copyright © 1994 Ronald Dworkin.

Edinburgh Law Review for the essay: Zenon Bankowski (1996), 'Law, Love and Computers', *Edinburgh Law Review*, **1**, pp. 25–42.

Franz Steiner Verlag for the essays: Jan M. van Dunné (1998), 'Normative and Narrative Coherence in Legal Decision Making', *ARSP-Beiheft*, **69**, pp. 194–205. Copyright © 1998 Franz Steiner Verlag; Jerzy Wróblewski and Neil MacCormick (1994), 'On Justification and Interpretation', *ARSP-Beiheft*, **53**, pp. 255–68. Copyright © 1994 Franz Steiner Verlag; Aleksander Peczenik (1988), 'Authority Reasons in Legal Interpretation and Moral Reasoning', *ARSP Supplementa (III)*, pp. 144–52. Copyright © 1988 Franz Steiner Verlag.

Kluwer Law International for the essay: Fernando Atria (1999), 'Legal Reasoning and Legal Theory Revisited', *Law and Philosophy*, **18**, pp. 537–77. Copyright © 1999 Kluwer Academic Publishers.

Notre Dame Law Review for the essay: Neil MacCormick (1999), 'Reasonableness and Objectivity', *Notre Dame Law Review*, **74**, pp. 1575–603. Copyright © 1999 Notre Dame Law Review, University of Notre Dame. Reprinted with permission.

Southern California Law Review for the essay: Michael S. Moore (1985), 'A Natural Law Theory of Interpretation', *Southern California Law Review*, **58**, pp. 277–398.

Yale Law Journal for the essay: Charles M. Yablon (1987), 'Law and Metaphysics', *Yale Law Journal*, **96**, pp. 613–36. Reprinted by permission of the Yale Law Journal Company and Williams S. Hein Company from *The Yale Law Journal*, Vol. 96, pp. 613–36.

Every effort has been made to trace all the copyright holders, but if any have been inadvertently overlooked the publishers will be pleased to make the necessary arrangement at the first opportunity.

Preface to the Second Series

The first series of the International Library of Essays in Law and Legal Theory has established itself as a major research resource with fifty-eight volumes of the most significant theoretical essays in contemporary legal studies. Each volume contains essays of central theoretical importance in its subject area and the series as a whole makes available an extensive range of valuable material of considerable interest to those involved in research, teaching and the study of law.

The rapid growth of theoretically interesting scholarly work in law has created a demand for a second series which includes more recent publications of note and earlier essays to which renewed attention is being given. It also affords the opportunity to extend the areas of law covered in the first series.

The new series follows the successful pattern of reproducing entire essays with the original page numbers as an aid to comprehensive research and accurate referencing. Editors have selected not only the most influential essays but also those which they consider to be of greatest continuing importance. The objective of the second series is to enlarge the scope of the library, include significant recent work and reflect a variety of editorial perspectives.

Each volume is edited by an expert in the specific area who makes the selection on the basis of the quality, influence and significance of the essays, taking care to include essays which are not readily available. Each volume contains a substantial introduction explaining the context and significance of the essays selected.

I am most grateful for the care which volume editors have taken in carrying out the complex task of selecting and presenting essays which meet the exacting criteria set for the series.

TOM CAMPBELL
Series Editor
Centre for Applied Philosophy and Public Ethics
Charles Sturt University

Introduction

Interpretation is one of the central elements in legal thought and activity. Lawyers have always needed to ascribe meaning to general terms and face cases in which either the meaning of them is not perspicuous or circumstances are present that are special in some way. For legal theory, however, interpretation and legal reasoning were important but marginal subjects, in the sense that the central questions legal theorists wanted to discuss did not include interpretation as a topic. Thus some of the most sophisticated legal theorists of the twentieth century did not think it necessary to develop a complete theory of legal interpretation as part and parcel of a broader theory of law. As an illustration of this claim one could turn to Kelsen's *Pure Theory of Law* (1970) which explicitly discussed interpretation in the last (and shortest) chapter or Hart's *The Concept of Law* which, as Hart himself conceded some 30 years after its publication, 'said far too little . . . about the topic of adjudication and legal reasoning' (Hart, 1994, p. 259).

During the last decades, however, interpretation (together with the related issue of legal reasoning) has been at the centre of the theoretical reflection about law. What is it that lawyers and judges and laypersons do when they *interpret* the law? Does the process of legal interpretation show that there is some connection between law and morality? Is it constrained by what is interpreted, or is it always (or usually, or sometimes) 'unfettered discretion'? How much of what lawyers do is properly called 'interpretation'? Questions such as these have been hotly discussed at least since the publication of Ronald Dworkin's 'Is Law a System of Rules?' (1970), which has been reprinted so many times that it has not been included in this collection (see, for example, Dworkin, 1977a and 1977b).

Starting from questions of this kind, one could try to systematize the problems surrounding the issue of legal interpretation in current legal theory under six headings, which form the basic structure of the present collection. This arrangement makes the collection more manageable for the reader, but risks giving the impression that only the corresponding subject is being discussed in each essay. In this Introduction we want to discuss generally the relevance of these six topics, and indicate the important contributions made by each of the selected essays. Along the way this will allow us to mention some of the aspects in which arguments or positions discussed in one essay have broader implications for subjects other than that denoted by its respective heading.

Interpretation and Law: Why is Interpretation Important for Law?

That interpretation is central to the practice of law is something that can hardly be denied. But this does not settle the theoretical problem, *why* is interpretation so important? An answer to this problem cannot be limited to pointing out that legal rules are general rules and they are used to solve particular cases, because in many social practices the need to apply general rules to particular cases does not make interpretation as important as it is in law (consider the 'interpretation' of the rules of chess, for example) (cf. Atria, 2002, ch. 1). Hence there must be something special about law that makes it so dependent on interpretation. As Joseph Raz says in Chapter 2, this seems to suggest that there is something to be learned 'about the nature of law from the fact that interpretation plays such a crucial role in adjudication' (p. 17).

The two essays grouped under this heading provide two different answers to this problem. In his 'Law, Philosophy and Interpretation' (Chapter 1), Ronald Dworkin provides a useful restatement of the theory of law and interpretation he has developed over the last 20 years, particularly in and after *Law's Empire*. Dworkin's theory is particularly interesting when discussing the issue of legal interpretation, because he believes that there is an important sense in which interpretation is not something lawyers and judges sometimes do, but is in a way *constitutive* of law. Traditionally, one would think of interpretation as a specific activity directed to understand a rule or apply it to a particular case. This view seems to imply that there are (first) legal rules that have to be (second) interpreted and applied. Dworkin's thesis of law as an interpretive concept challenges this viewpoint.

In his essay Dworkin emphasizes the fact that interpretation is not a purely legal phenomenon. Reliance upon interpretation is common for practices that share one feature: they are 'regarded by those . . . who take them up not as pointless but as beneficial or worthwhile in some other way' (p. 9).

Now, the particular way in which a particular practice like history or law is valuable depends on the participant's opinions about the practice. Hence, for example, Dworkin explains that there is a significant difference between historical and legal interpretation, in that the latter is not guided by an 'explanatory purpose' (p. 14) as the former is – a difference that will resurface in Detmold's essay, based on the idea of law being practical as sociology is not (cf. p. 36). Legal interpretation aims to make law 'as just as it can be' (p. 14). In this way, Dworkin treats law as inextricably connected with political morality, which is the reason why MacCormick (1976) called him a 'pre-Benthamite'. But this seems to leave Dworkin open to the objection that law is 'subjective' in the same sense in which political morality is. To this, Dworkin has famously replied with his 'right answer' thesis.[1] In its current version, the right answer thesis cashes in on the performative contradiction that prevents any agent from saying *both* that there is no 'correct' answer to controversial questions of political morality (or morality, or law and so on) *and* that something (abortion, say) is right (or wrong). Any objectivity that law may have is founded on the objective nature of the basic truths of political morality, *as perceived by the participants*.

In *Law's Empire* this argument was presented as the distinction between external and internal scepticism: *internal*, interpretive scepticism is *substantive* scepticism, in the sense that it is the conclusion we could reach after having examined the reasons for and against a particular proposition or decision and rejected them all. *External* scepticism is scepticism about the interpretive process: it is not an interpretive claim; it is a claim about interpretive claims. Dworkin believes that we can ignore external sceptics because they do not engage with us. The only scepticism that should give participants to an interpretive practice cause for concern is internal scepticism.[2] But there is no reason to believe that it will be sensible to adopt a generalized internal sceptical position: sometimes we will have reasons to believe that one action, decision or proposition is true (or justified or whatever), and we will have reasons to reject the sceptical position on that issue. And sometimes we might be convinced of the non-existence of an answer that is correct or true or justified, and we will accept scepticism regarding this issue. Notice that if we adopt the internally sceptical position regarding an issue (for example, abortion), then, when asked, we will have to say that we take the position that there is no way of deciding whether it is right or wrong. This argument of Dworkin's, and the broader subject of the possibility of solutions to controversial questions (hard cases) being correct, is one subject that is discussed by many of the essays in this collection.

Dworkin's rejection of external scepticism, and his claim that only internal, *interpretive* scepticism is to be taken seriously, shows that interpretive practices are self-referential, in the sense that whether or not practices are interpretive is in itself an interpretive question. If we grant Dworkin's point, all the following questions should be understood as being interpretive: 'Is the law interpretive?', 'Are interpretations "objectively correct"?', 'Are there right answers to difficult questions?' and the like.

In his essay, 'Why Interpret?' (Chapter 2) Joseph Raz seems to get close to a Dworkinian theory of interpretation when he writes that *'[a]n interpretation successfully illuminates the meaning of its object to the degree that it responds to whatever reasons there are for paying attention to its object as a thing of its kind'* (p. 23). There appear, however, to be two significant differences between them. First, Raz seems to believe that his (quoted) claim at p. 23 warrants some sort of 'interpretive pluralism' that seems to be incompatible with Dworkin's right answer thesis. Having noticed that different people may have different reasons to understand history, he goes on to say that 'it is plausible to suppose that these reasons will lead to somewhat divergent interpretations of various historical events and processes. Hence pluralism' (p. 24). To establish pluralism, however, it is not enough that different interpretations are possible: one has to claim that they are all equally valid. And Raz indeed adds, '[i]t is possible for them to be good reasons, and they may be valid simultaneously' (p. 24).

Second, Raz differs from Dworkin in terms of the viewpoint from which his argument is formulated. Dworkin's theory of law is, and has always been, formulated from the 'internal, participants' point of view; it tries to grasp the argumentative character of our legal practices by joining that practice and struggling with the issues of soundness and truth participants face' (Dworkin, 1987, p. 9). Raz's is a *detached* perspective – that is, a perspective characterized by the fact that the observer, who is not a participant, *mimics* the attitudes of participants to understand their practices as they appear to them.[3] This helps to explain the notion of interpretive pluralism defended by Raz in this essay: If *I*, as a participant, believe that history is about 'predicting the future' (one of the possible reasons for historical interest in Raz's example at p. 24), I must also believe that those who think that history is about 'understanding God's message to man' are mistaken. But I might be observing an argument between two people holding these two views. If this is the case, I might report *their* disagreement about history as the confirmation that there is more than one plausible way of understanding the value of history.

Turning to legal interpretation, Raz claims that what makes legal interpretation important is that, in law, 'we value . . . continuity [and] authority, legal development and equity' (p. 25). The key to the question, 'Why interpret?' is provided, however, by the values of continuity and authority. Raz believes that law's immanent claim to be morally justified accords to these two values a pre-eminent role in answering this question because 'to understand the law we must understand the way the law understands itself' (p. 26). This is the reason why the answer to the title question is 'the moral respect we owe to [the law]' (p. 27). The two other values, legal development and equity, come in only at a second stage, when the question is not 'Why interpret?' but 'How should we interpret?'.

Raz's essay belongs with a number of his other pieces on legal reasoning and interpretation, a subject to which he has devoted a series of essays including the one offered in this collection (see, for example, Raz, 1994a; 1998a; 1998b). They naturally invite the question, 'How compatible are Raz's considerations concerning legal reasoning with his own theory of law, as deployed in works such as *Practical Reason and Norms* (1992), *The Morality of Freedom* (1986) and "Authority, Law and Morality" (1994b)?'. In another essay also included in this collection, Fernando Atria (Chapter 4) investigates this issue, claiming that they are at odds. The reason for this, in brief, is Raz's characterization of legal rules as exclusionary reasons (Raz, 1992, pp. 142–43). If rules are exclusionary reasons, it seems that, after having understood the meaning of a rule, all that is left for the institutions called to apply it is to act on the basis of that rule, excluding all conflicting considerations. In the terminology of Raz's theory of law, Atria claims, those conflicting considerations would be pre-empted by the exclusionary character of legal rules.

Interpretation and Legal Reasoning: Law and Morality

We have seen that one of the reasons why interpretation became such a fashionable topic for legal theory in the last decades was Dworkin's idea of *constructive* interpretation, of interpretation being, in a way, constitutive of the practices in which they are formulated and consequently of *legal* interpretation being, in some way, *constitutive* of law. But there is another reason that explains the increased interest in the related subjects of interpretation and legal reasoning, and it is that these topics became the battleground in which that very traditional and recurrent problem for legal theory was disputed: that of the existence of some form of necessary relation between law and morality.

In *The Concept of Law* (1994), Hart tried to provide a theory of law that could do justice to the normativity of law – as previous theories like those of Bentham and Austin had failed to do – while holding fast to the distinction that they (and others) had drawn between law and morality (MacCormick, 1981, ch. 2). This he achieved, or so it seemed, with his theory of social rules, and in particular (for law) with his seminal idea of the rule of recognition. The rule of recognition was conceived of as a social practice the existence of which could be ascertained independently from its moral worth, and its function was to set out the criteria for any *other* normative criteria to belong to the legal system. In this way, Hart was able to explain the fact that rules could be both valid *and* unjust. A legal rule exists as such when it fulfils the criteria specified by the rule of recognition, and there was no reason why those criteria *had* to include reference to moral value.

In a way, this point seemed to fit with the way in which legal systems work, in the sense that the criteria for something being a rule of (say) English law seems to be non-moral, pointing mainly to the occurrence of *facts* such as the queen giving royal assent to a piece of legislation that has been voted favourably by a majority of members of both Houses of Parliament and so on.

In this context, and with regard to legal reasoning and interpretation, one might concede (or remain agnostic concerning) Hart's point about rules being valid regardless of their intrinsic moral worth *and* claim that this is not enough to support the positivist's claim about the separation of law and morality. This is the position taken by Atria and Detmold in their essays in this collection, although they offer different reasons to support their claims.

In his 'Law as Practical Reason' (Chapter 3) Detmold takes as his starting point the *practicality* of law. From law's practicality follows the practicality of legal reasoning: 'legal reasoning is practical in the sense that its natural conclusion is an action' (p. 35). In applying rules to particular cases, judges need to cross what Detmold calls 'the particularity void', because:

> ... there is a radical logical difference between the most highly defined set of universals and a particular case; a radical difference between interpretation and the crossing of the particularity void. (p. 38)

The particularity void occupies a space between a hypothetical rule mandating one normative consequence (nc) to follow the occurrence of operative facts (op) and a particular case in which (op) and indefinite other facts are present.[4]

For Detmold, this is a void 'about which nothing can be said (anything I *say* will be universal)' (p. 55), about which 'only mystical, poetic things can be said or nothing'. Furthermore, '[j]udges enter this realm every day (if they only knew)' (p. 56). Respect for particulars demands that the particularity void be bridged, and to bridge the void the judge needs to address the particular *as particular*, not as simply an instance of a universal rule. In other words, the judge will have to make a *judgment* about the reasonable thing to do in the circumstances, in the concrete and particular case.

Does this not amount to a claim that the judge is never bound by law? Not for Detmold. Here we come to the point made before, of interpretation and legal reasoning as providing a different way of tackling the old problem of the relation between law and morality.[5] In principle, one could accept Hart's view on the rule of recognition, and with it the claim that the existence of a legal rule is something that is not necessarily linked to its moral value, *and* Detmold's claim that legal adjudication is necessarily a matter for practical (moral) judgement. Detmold points this out by distinguishing:

(1) apply what is reasonable
from
(2) apply what is reasonable to apply.

The judge is bound by law insofar as he or she is not supposed to discuss what is reasonable. A rule that fulfils the criteria set out by the rule of recognition specifies what is reasonable, and '[t]here is no question of redeliberating that question' (p. 52). But Detmold makes the point that this still leaves the judge in the dark, because 'what is reasonable to apply has not been decided by the legislature and cannot be decided ... no respect can be given to a decision that has not been made' (ibid.).

In a likeminded way, Fernando Atria's essay, 'Legal Reasoning and Legal Theory Revisited' (Chapter 4), deals with the relation between a theory of law and a theory of legal reasoning. Atria claims that a theory of law, in answering the question 'What is law?', specifies what counts as a normative premise for legal reasoning. We can then test the correctness of a theory of law by considering whether the picture of legal reasoning and legal interpretation permitted by a given theory is acceptable (see, further, Atria, 2002). Concerning legal positivism, Atria claims that it implies either rule-formalism or rule-scepticism. Reduced to its essentials, the argument is this: we can formulate the central problem of a theory of legal reasoning as an answer to the question 'What does the law require in this particular case?' or, identically, 'What is the legal obligation of the judge concerning this case?'. Positivism leads to formalism if it claims that rules apply to all cases that are covered by the semantic meaning of their operative facts, regardless of any other feature the particular case may have or lack. To avoid formalism, positivism could claim that the question 'What is the law?' is different from the question 'What is the law *for the case*?', so that from 'the law is: if (op) then (nc)' we could not immediately infer that (nc) is legally required in a particular case displaying (op), because the case may also display some other features that defeat the application of the rule. This, however, would imply rule-scepticism insofar as the link between the validity of a general rule requiring 'if (op) then (nc)' and a particular case displaying (op) would be severed: in order to apply a general rule to any particular case, the judge would have to make what Hart (1994, p. 135) called a 'fresh judgment' to the effect that the rule is not defeated. But, of course, this judgment is one for which, according to legal positivism, the judge has discretion. So judges have discretion in all cases (=rule-scepticism). Atria claims that this problem is visible in the theories of such authors as Neil MacCormick, Joseph Raz and H.L.A. Hart.

Instead of discussing the issue of interpretation and its relation to morality, as Detmold does, or to legal theory, as Atria does, Michael Moore, in 'A Natural Law Theory of Interpretation' (Chapter 5), defends a theory *of* interpretation – a theory that aims at explaining how interpreters should interpret the law. The theory of interpretation that Moore defends, however, is not neutral concerning issues about the linkage of law and morality. It is, in fact, as the title says, a 'natural law' doctrine of interpretation, a phrase that he explains as holding, first, that there is a right answer to moral questions, 'a moral reality if you like' (p. 122), and, second, 'that the interpretive premises necessary to decide any case can and should be derived in part by recourse to the dictates of that moral reality' (ibid.). A further point of importance stressed by Moore in other writings, and relevant here too, is the claim that there is a 'legal reality' that is connected to, but by no means identical with, moral reality. In the same way, however, in both cases there are true statements about law and morality that are true by virtue of the character of the subject matter they describe, rather than by virtue of conventions built into language or social usages that are prevalent here or there. In the view of such a robust metaphysical realism (not to be confused with legal realism!), the essence of a good interpretative practice is that it discloses the true meaning of the object in view, not that it constitutes such a meaning by virtue of being a good interpretation, as Dworkin seems to suggest.

In the essay, Moore examines the relevance that four notions have for interpretation: meaning, legislative intention, precedent and values. All these notions except legislative intention are taken up by Moore's theory in special ways.

Take meaning, for example. In the essay Moore defends a realist position with regard to the issue of the meaning of meaning.[6] Moore believes that our general conceptual terms, including terms like law, refer to real objects, and new discoveries about the nature of the objects in question do not involve a change in the meaning of the term in question but a better understanding of what it means. A prominent feature of Moore's work is to try, in this context, to figure out the idea of 'texts' as the subject matter of activity that is interpretative in the humanistic sense, rather than in the causal sense that would apply in the natural sciences. He puts this concisely in an essay written ten years later than the seminal essay reprinted here:

> There is a text, and thus interpretation in the desired sense, whenever (1) people have some good reason (2) to treat some phenomenon they do not yet know the meaning of, as meaningful, (3) in

the sense that such meanings give them either reasons for belief or reasons for action. (Moore, 1995, p. 8)[7]

This suggests that interpreting the meaning of a text connects back to the issue of the 'good reason' people have to treat the phenomenon as meaningful. In the case of law, the meaning concerns the organization of the polity and the use of law for the peaceful and just settlement of disputes. To the extent that a legislator's intention, or, more likely, the intention we impute to a legislature on the assumption that it seeks to maintain just conditions of social peace, point towards an interpretation of legislative texts, this would be relevant to elucidating their meaning. But this is not really to do with actual historically held intentions 'in the mind' of legislators or the legislature as a corporate entity. In truth, it leads us back to the issue of the values that the legislation is best understood as serving in the context of the whole complex of a legal system and the great body of precedents and prior elucidations that it contains. Legal realities are thus intertwined with moral ones, and the best interpretation is one that reveals the law in its character as a genuine and sound reason for action.

Interpretation and Application of Legal Rules, Vagueness and Defeasibility

In Chapter 9, 'On Law and Logic', Carlos Alchourrón introduces what he calls 'the master system' and the 'master book' as an attempt to capture a political ideal that, though impossible, has exerted a considerable influence in matters of institutional design and legal thinking over the last centuries, at least in Western countries. The central ideal is that the law works by the application of general rules to particular cases. Rules are applied to cases in a deductive manner: 'in this ideal model the set of rules are the starting points (axioms) for deriving the instructions to follow in each particular concrete situation' (p. 284).

When it comes to legal interpretation and legal reasoning, Alchourrón believes that, influential though this model has been, it is the source of at least two dangers:

> The first is the rationalist illusion of believing that the ideal is realized in some or in all normative systems. The second stems from not noticing that because there are other ideals that point in different directions it may not even be convenient to try to maximize its requirements. (p. 291)

There are, in other words, reasons why there cannot be a master book and reasons why, even if we could have a master book, it would not be worth having.[8] These reasons, in turn, map on to two different problems faced by judges when trying to apply general rules to particular cases.

The master-book ideal is *impossible to achieve*, because it is 'written in ordinary language', and this implies 'well-known difficulties derived from ambiguity and vagueness'. A judicial decision will satisfy the 'master-book' idea if the norm that is being applied has an unambiguous meaning for the legislator *and* has the same unambiguous meaning for the judge. In Alchourrón's view, this will make it necessary to 'compare the meanings attributed to a text by the interpreter and the meanings attributed to it by the legislator' (p. 292). This incorporates the problem of the attribution of intentions to corporate bodies. All these problems make the idea impossible.

But, even if it were possible, the master book would not be a sensible ideal to pursue because rules are *defeasible* (Baker, 1977; MacCormick, 1995). It is the idea of the defeasibility of legal rules that explains the dictum of the Roman jurist:

Neque leges neque senatus consulta ita scribi possunt, ut omnes casus qui quandoque inciderint comprehendantur, sed sufficit ea quae plerunque accidunt contineri. [Neither statutes nor *senatus consulta* can be written in such a way that all cases which might at any time occur are covered; it is however sufficient that the things which very often happen are embraced.] (D.1.3.10, Jul., *libro LVIIII digestorum*)

In other words, a conditional of the form 'if A then B' is defeasible when A is not a sufficient condition for B, but only under normal circumstances: under normal circumstances, if A then B. A *together with* 'normal' circumstances is sufficient for B (MacCormick, 1995). That legal rules are defeasible means that the legal requirement attached by a rule to the occurrence of some operative facts can be defeated when abnormal circumstances are present. We must keep apart, however, cases in which legal rules are defeated from cases in which the law has not been followed, and, to do this, Alchourrón proposes a 'dispositional analysis' of defeasibility:

> According to the dispositional approach a condition C counts as an *implicit exception* to a conditional assertion 'if A then B' made by a speaker X at time T when there is a disposition of X at T to assert the conditional 'if A then B' whilst rejecting 'if A and C then B'. (pp. 293–94)

It is then, because the master-book ideal is both impossible (because of the vagueness of natural languages) and undesirable (because legal rules cannot be drafted appropriately to solve all cases, but only those that are recurrent) that '[t]he formalist illusion of the purely deductive model has to be given up' (p. 297).

The issue of defeasibility is also the key to understanding Klaus Günther's distinction between 'justification' and 'application' of rules in his 'Critical Remarks on Robert Alexy's "Special-Case Thesis"' (Chapter 7). Writing in the tradition of discourse ethics, Günther believes that a norm is justified insofar as it satisfies the *universalization* requirement – that is, if it can be shown to be in the interest of all those who are affected. But, to know *who* are those potentially affected by a norm and *how* the norm affects them, one would have to be able to consider all possible cases to which the norm will be applied, and this is simply impossible. If a norm can be justified only after one has sustained in discourse the claim that it is in the interest of all those who can possibly be affected by the rule, then the conclusion can only be that no norm can ever be justified.

In order to avoid this conclusion, Günther separates the requirement of universalization from that of impartiality. Norms are justified, Günther claims, when under unchanging circumstances they can be shown to be in the interest of all those affected. But from the fact that a norm is justified it does not follow that it has to be applied to all cases, because sometimes circumstances might not be unchanged. In application discourses this issue is taken up, and the object of the discussion is the application of a justified norm. Conversely, in justification discourses the issue is that of showing a given norm (like 'thou shalt not lie') to be in the interest of all concerned, *ceteris paribus*; in application discourses the general issue is not under discussion (we do not discuss whether 'thou shalt not lie' is in the interests of all those concerned), and what is thematized is whether the particular case at hand (described as fully and exhaustively as possible) presents some special feature that would warrant departure from the justified rule (say, because some brutal dictatorship's secret police is asking about the hiding place of an innocent person, and we have to decide whether or not to lie in response).

However, Günther's distinction is open to two objections. First, it would seem that, since justified norms do not imply the duty to act according to them in any particular case, they are irrelevant. Second, it could be said, as Albrecht Wellmer has indeed said, that moral discourse is always application discourse: 'what is applied is the moral principle itself', a sufficiently abstract moral principle such as 'do good and avoid evil' (Wellmer, 1991, pp. 204–11).

As regards the first problem, Günther's answer has to show that justified norms are important *not only* because of their action-guiding function. Indeed, he claims that they also contribute to define our identities and self-image:

> Moral reasons, which are used for justification in concrete cases, shape the mutual relations between each of us as individuals and as members of a moral community. They represent the characteristic traits of our intersubjectivity, i.e. the general expectations according to which we want to treat each other and how we want to be treated. For example, we don't want to be treated as someone who could be betrayed for any reason. (p. 257)

Thus, justified norms are important even though they can be defeated in particular cases.

Regarding the second problem, Günther believes that the reason why justification discourses do not collapse into application discourses in the manner suggested by Wellmer is that, in each form of discourse, the nature of the arguments and their function is different:

> *In reality*, it may often seem as if justification and application discourses could not be separated analytically from one another. [But] this objection does not hold true; it arises as the result of the appearance that those arguments which are relevant in application discourses can also be relevant in justification discourses. (Günther, 1993, p. 124)

Similar problems are raised by Robert Alexy in his 'Justification and Application of Norms' (Chapter 6). Alexy asks whether an exception that has been found to a justified norm in a discourse of application is in need of justification. Günther believes that it would not, since the exception would have been found because of the need to find *coherence* in the system of justified norms. But, for Alexy, this seems to demote justified norms to the status of rules of thumb: 'With the rise of the discourse of application to a discourse of coherence, the discourse of justification would deteriorate to a mere discourse of *topoi*' (p. 246).

This leads Alexy to consider the basic difference between application and justification. He accepts Günther's characterization of that difference in terms of the goals of each form of discourse: discourses of justification are concerned with the validity of universal norms, while discourses of application are concerned with applying justified norms to particular cases in appropriate ways. But, Alexy asks, is it correct to think that particular cases do not appear in discourses of justification? In fact, 'situations of application' do appear in justification discourses. Alexy distinguishes two ways in which they can appear and claims that Günther is ambiguous between the two. On the one hand, they can appear as illustrations, as 'hypothetical' or 'exemplary situations', in brief as *standard cases* (pp. 247–48).[9] The *ceteris paribus* clause that Günther finds operating in justification discourses has the consequence, on this interpretation, of 'artificially excluding the consideration of different situations of application' (p. 248).

On the other hand, Alexy claims that, in justification discourses, application situations appear not only as standard cases but should be 'as manifold as possible', so that the only reason that should prevent participants to a discourse of justification from considering some situations of application is factual impossibility, in the form of 'limits of empirical knowledge, of historical experience, and of time' (p. 248). This interpretation would reduce (though certainly not eliminate) the theoretical importance of the distinction. Application situations, in this interpretation, would be fed back to justification discourses. Thus, Alexy concludes, 'any discourse of application necessarily includes a discourse of justification on which its result depends' (p. 249).

When it comes to legal reasoning, the distinction between application and justification helps the explanation of, and is explained by, institutional differences between legislative and adjudicative bodies because the institutional nature of law makes matters of form important as they are not in morality:

> [Application] discourse requires a constellation of roles in which the parties (and if necessary a government prosecutor) can present all the contested aspects of a case before a judge who acts as the impartial representative of the legal community . . . . By contrast, in justification discourses there are only participants. (Habermas, 1997, p. 172)

Here we can see how, in the context of an institutionalized system, many of Alexy's objections lose some weight: one could claim that judges, when conducting application discourses, should try to *mimic* the reasoning of legislative assemblies, but as a matter of fact they are not institutionally designed to serve as adequate fora for justification discourses. The idea of coherence allows the judge to apply a general rule to a particular case in a non-mechanical way because it allows the judge to avoid the conclusion that follows from the semantic meaning of the rule when it would be too inappropriate *without denying* the validity of the rule.[10]

Zenon Bankowski's essay, 'Law, Love and Computers' (Chapter 8), deals, in a way, with the same problem, but from an ethical perspective. The main issue he addresses is that of the 'moral implications of placing ourselves "under the governance of rules",[11] as we try to live our lives among our fellows. What does it mean for the individual and society to organise in this way?' (p. 269). That the answer to this question is not as self evident as one might think is shown by the anarchist challenge to law: 'Anarchists above all oppose law because they think that it takes away decisions that should rightly be my own: that instead of my deciding what to do, I let some external force do this for me' (p. 269). The ideal of legalism that lies behind the rule of law – that is, the ideal of decisions being taken according to pre-intimated rules seems to warrant this criticism. Bankowski makes this point using the analogy of a cash machine. A user has a card, the card is inserted into the cash machine and the PIN number is keyed in. The machine checks the status of the account vis-à-vis the amount presently requested and depending on that status, gives or refuses the money: 'The machine does not see you, the concrete human being with particular pressing needs and problems. It just sees (reads) the card' (p. 273).

As Bankowski is well aware, one could object that this is not what actually happens, for perhaps there is always a human bank teller taking the decision. But should the cash machine metaphor work here as an ideal – the ideal of rule-governed decision-making? Is not the whole point of having rules that one can stop thinking about the particular case in terms of all of its features and give a formally just decision based on some of the features of the case *and some only* – those that are picked up as relevant by the rule?

Bankowski then contrasts the logic of law with the logic of love, because the anarchist critique of law seems to be captured by the idea of 'All you need is love' (p. 275). Love is a 'mysterious force', one that 'makes people do so many things, good and bad but above all unpredictable' (p. 275). And this is the reason why 'all you need is love' cannot be true in modern, functionally differentiated societies. Law gives security and predictability while love is sheer contingency. Here we see the twist that Bankowski's argument puts on the traditional distinction, at the level of legal interpretation and legal reasoning, between what H.L.A. Hart called 'formalism' and 'rule-scepticism'. Formalists like Hayek believe that 'any relaxation from the strict following of the rules . . . means the eventual and total collapse of the rules', while for rule-sceptics (Bankowski here does not name names, but CLS authors seem to be good candidates) 'the slightest indeterminacy of meaning means that the rules are always applied creatively' (p. 276).

If we are to avoid both the machine-like formalism and the contingency of love, we need 'a way of knowing when to stop acting like the machine and not follow the set patterns'. But can this hold? Or is one 'either locked in the general rules or stuck in particularity?' (p. 279).

Maybe this is a question that cannot be answered because it is a question about what Detmold called the 'particularity void', about which, as we saw, only poetic or mystic things can be said. And Bankowski's essay seems to go hand-in-hand with that, because in the end he offers not an answer but a parable. The universal and the particular are linked in Bankowski's idea of *legality*:

> Here we come to the deep intertwining of both heteronomy and autonomy. Love transforms both. It shows how autonomy must find itself in dependence and need . . . . Autonomy needs love since otherwise it is mere caprice. . . . [Autonomy] does not mean [the autonomous subject] is the only person in the world; that everyone is only there to do his will. That form of 'autonomy' is really heteronomy since you are lost in your own comfortable world . . . . It is that love that transforms the system world of law into legality where law and love do not destroy one another. (pp. 281–82)

Legal Interpretation and Politics

In Part IV of the collection Roberto Unger and Emilios Christodoulidis discuss the issue of the political content of legal interpretation, in particular the issue of its potential for radical political change. Unger believes that 'a reoriented practice of legal analysis' can 'work, tracing divergent trajectories along which to advance, through cumulative institutional change, the democratic project' (Unger, 1996, p. 2).[12]

As in his 1983 CLS manifesto (Unger, 1983, pp. 6–7), Unger starts off his essay, 'Legal Analysis as Institutional Imagination' (Chapter 10), by finding deep-seated contradictions in different areas of substantive law. Here, he focuses on the contradiction between 'rights of choice [and] rules designed to ensure the effective enjoyment of these rights' (p. 303). The idea that the value of a right to choose is severely limited, if not negated, by lack of effective enjoyment of those rights has penetrated '[l]ittle by little and in country after country' (p. 303) into legal consciousness, and in so doing it has transformed contemporary law. Unger carefully examines this transformation by contrasting three moments of legal consciousness: that of nineteenth-century legal science, that of the 'rationalizing legal analysis', corresponding to the social-democratic compromise behind the American New Deal and the European welfare state, and that of tactical interpretation of legal doctrine.

For Unger, nineteenth-century legal science was animated by the idea of making 'patent the hidden legal content of a free political and economic order' (p. 313) which was based on a private order structured around such concepts as contracts and property and safeguarded by public-law arrangements and entitlements. Methodologically, this substantive vision expressed itself through conceptualism and formalism which constituted '[d]iscursive practices designed to police the boundaries between distributively neutral, good law and redistributive, bad law' (p. 314), all backed up (in the US) by the possibility of constitutional invalidation (see also Horowitz, 1992).

The conflict between rights to choose and effective enjoyment of those rights arose here insofar as:

> The impulse to contain moral hazard and to make people responsible for the uncompensated consequences of their activities had to be balanced against the need to encourage risk-taking behaviour in production and finance. (p. 315)

These conflicts could not be solved by 'probing more deeply into the system of categories and doctrines' (p. 1314), and a *decision* had to be adopted – a decision that from the point of view of the categories of legal science could not but look arbitrary. It was this basic dilemma that, according to Unger's analysis, led to the demise of 'explicit' Lochnerism – that is, 'the fetishist acceptance and constitutional entrenchment of a particular private rights-system against all efforts to redistribute rights and resources and to regulate economic activity' (p. 316). Nineteenth-century legal science was displaced by what Unger calls 'rationalising legal analysis – that is:

> ... the policy-oriented and principle-based style of legal analysis that, recognising the reliance of legal analysis upon the ascription of purpose, gave to the guiding purposes the content of general conceptions of collective welfare or political right. (p. 317)

The nineteenth-century idea of a fixed system of private and public rights implicit in the very definition of a free political order has therefore been abandoned and in its place rationalizing legal analysis is looking for a general conception of public interest. The need to find such a general conception is created by the dilemma facing rationalizing legal analysis – the dilemma of conceiving law either as embodying such a conception or as the result of strategic in-fighting between different interest groups.

In looking for a solution to this basic dilemma, rationalizing legal analysis finds itself pulled between two forces: its basic commitment to present law as the expression of some conception of the public interest leads rationalizing legal analysis to endorse rather than denounce, to correct rather than challenge the law. Yet by presenting the law as embodying a vision of public interest it allows that vision to come into conflict with prevailing practices and organizations. The conservative pull endangers the reformist pull, and the reformist pull endangers rationalizing legal analysis's claim to be interpreting existing law rather than engaging in legal reform by stealth. Rationalizing legal analysis's solution to this dilemma is essentially unstable, given by '[a]n implicit judgement of practical political feasibility' (p. 319).

It is this instability that explains the passage from the second to a third moment in modern legal consciousness, that of *conservative reformism*, a specially influential version of which is what Unger calls 'progressive pessimistic reformism'. Progressive pessimistic reformism is conservative in that it assumes that 'no institutional change is in the cards', but also pessimistic because it also assumes that 'in the politics of lawmaking, the self-serving majority will regularly dump on marginalised and powerless groups' (p. 320). Faced with these constraints, progressive pessimistic reformism adopts the face of rationalizing legal analysis, giving it an ironic twist: 'although the assumptions of [rationalizing legal analysis's] method may not be literally believable they serve a vital goal' (p. 321). Progressive pessimistic reformism pays dearly for its conservatism when major social problems require experimentalism about practical arrangements; then '[t]he tactic avenges itself against the tactician' (p. 321).

Unger's proposal is what he calls 'legal analysis as institutional imagination', which he conceives as being based on a distinction between mapping and criticism. While the former is 'the attempt to describe in detail the legally defined institutional microstructure of society in relation to its legally articulated ideals', criticism 'explore[s] the interplay between the detailed institutional arrangements of society as represented in law, and the professed ideals or programmes these arrangements frustrate and make real' (p. 322).

As Christodoulidis (Chapter 11) shows (p. 328), the strategy of mapping and criticism stretches back in Unger's work to the deviationist doctrine of his CLS manifesto. It contains Unger's belief that critical legal theorizing can vest 'in law the possibility to pursue radical politics' (p. 327), drawing a 'political logic of disruption . . . from within the institution' (p. 328).

But is this possible? This is Christodoulidis' question, and his answer is a rather sceptical one. He notices how concepts that are fundamental for Unger cannot be translated into law because of the kind of thing (the kind of complexity-reduction achievement, he would say) law is.[13] This he shows by pointing to the nature of 'solidarity rights', one of the categories of Unger's reconstructed system of rights as he formulated it in *Politics* (1987, pp. 508–39). The idea of solidarity is central for much critical legal thinking insofar as it underpins the fundamental notion of *community*. But solidarity cannot be fed into law and remain true to itself, or so Christodoulidis claims:

> . . . solidarity involves a 'reaching out' to the other person, an element of suppression of the self and sacrifice towards the other, and law by its very structure as a means of litigating competing claims, its operating of dispositive conflicts and the win-or-lose principle, violates the self-effacing moment underlying the encounter of solidarity. (p. 331)

So the claim here is that there are limits to what can be accomplished through law; solidarity is beyond them.

But what Christodoulidis has to say is not restricted to the special status of solidarity as a political ideal. He uses this example to make a more important claim, introduced by distinguishing between 'simple' and 'structural' inertia.

'Simple' inertia has been the main target of CLS. CLS's strategy has always consisted of two elements (see, for instance, Unger, 1983; 1987; Kelman, 1987, pp. 15–17): first, the recognition of a number of exceptions to settled rules in any field of substantive law as embodying a *counterprinciple*; and, second, the reorganization of that field of substantive law around the counterprinciple thus identified in such a way that what, at the beginning, was a number of exceptions became the guiding principle. This move is subversive because 'the system always will, initially at least, give a disciplining, non-random response to the random event' (p. 339). This is why it is important that the counterprinciples are retrieved from the law rather than exported from some normative theory (although, of course, the drive to retrieve *them* can only come from one's own values and commitments). Christodoulidis argues that there is ample space here for this subversive strategy, but in the end the radical programme of exploiting the 'self-transformative capacities of the practice of legal analysis' (p. 340) will get us just so far, because at some point it will confront not 'simple' but 'structural' inertia.

The strategy of exploiting the indeterminacy of rules, and the simultaneous presence of principle and counterprinciple, amounts to resisting the simple inertia of legal systems by 'feeding deviant, subversive counter-theses into law in ways that will resonate in the discourse and lead to cumulative change' (p. 340). The strategy, however, implies that 'whatever challenge is to register in law will only make a difference in the evolution of the system on the basis of its *alignment* to already existing reductions' (p. 340). This is where the unavoidable constraints of structural inertia start to bite: 'Challenges *to* the structure can only be accommodated *by* the structure as demands to draw new internal distinctions and boundaries' (p. 341). If Christodoulidis is right, the *structural* inertia of law prevents radical legal analysis from being radical enough.

Interpretation and Objectivity

Is interpretation 'objective'? Can judges ever be bound by rules according to their single correct meaning as revealed by interpretation? These are the main issues discussed by the essays in Part V. After having discussed the way in which American philosophers and legal theorists have answered questions such as these, paying particular attention to American legal realism, Charles Yablon, in 'Law and Metaphysics' (Chapter 12), considers the importance of one particular rule-sceptic argument – namely, the one deployed in Saul Kripke's *Wittgenstein on Rules and Private Language* (1982), which in turn contains Kripke's version of Wittgenstein's argument (presenting it 'as an attorney', says Kripke (1982, p. ix)).

For Kripke the attorney, the argument is as follows (his argument is so widely known that we can reduce it here to its essentials): there is no fact of any kind in my previous usage of a rule (for example, addition) which can uniquely determine my behaviour when I apply it to a novel case. So if I have not performed the operation '57+68' before, I have no answer to the sceptic who comes along and claims that, *according to my previous usage of the word 'plus'*, the solution should have been 5, because it is as compatible with my present use of it (according to which 57 *plus* 68 equals 125) as it is with the different function, *quus* (symbolized by $\oplus$, so that $x \oplus y = x+y$, if $x, y < 57$, $=5$ otherwise). The sceptic challenges 'whether any instructions I gave myself in the past compel (or justify) the answer "125" rather than "5"' (Kripke, 1982, p. 13).

We need not go into the details of Kripke's argument. It is important, however, to mention his solution to the problem, which is not to refute the sceptic, but rather to incorporate the sceptic's premises: 'if one person is considered in isolation, the notion of a rule as guiding the person who adopts it can have *no* substantive content' but 'the situation is very different if we widen our gaze from consideration of the rule follower alone and allow ourselves to consider him as interacting with a wider community' (Kripke, 1982, p. 89).

Yablon believes that Kripke's argument is 'extremely important' for lawyers (p. 370), in two different ways: first, because it proves that there is no 'superlative' fact that 'can provide a determinate meaning to legal rules' (ibid.). But Yablon notices that this does not imply that rule-based decision-making is in any way illegitimate. After all, Kripke's argument was presented using the rules of arithmetic and, even if we were to accept it, we would still use the rule of addition in our conventional ways both to add and to criticize those who failed to add. This leads Yablon to the second way in which Kripke's argument is important for lawyers: it clarifies 'the ways in which a rule may be indeterminate' (p. 371). Kripke's argument, says Yablon, allows us to distinguish 'Kripkean' indeterminacy from 'causal' indeterminacy. While the former means that 'no particular action can ever be justified as following or not following the rule', the latter means that 'a competent decisionmaker cannot arrive at a correct application of the rule in response to a particular case' (p. 371). Yablon believes that, according to Kripke, rules of addition would be rules that are indeterminate in the 'Kripkean' sense, but not in the 'causal' sense.

What does it mean to say that a rule is indeterminate in a Kripkean sense but determinate in a causal sense? Simply by replacing the labels we would get a rule such that 'no particular action can ever be justified as following or not following the rule' yet 'a competent decisionmaker can arrive at a correct application of the rule in response to a particular case'. But surely if no particular action can be justified as following, or not following, the rule then competent decision-makers would recognize this and be unable to arrive at a correct application of the rule?

Jes Bjarup in 'Kripke's Case' (Chapter 13) takes a more radical line against Kripke and Yablon – one that is more in line with the reception Kripke's book met at the hands of many Wittgenstein scholars. What according to Kripke was Wittgenstein's crucial point in the private-language argument of the *Philosophical Investigations* is, for Bjarup and those scholars, the illness Wittgenstein was warning us against. Kripke and Yablon, according to Bjarup, assume that interpretations mediate between a general rule and its application. But Wittgenstein himself claimed that 'there is a way of grasping a rule which is not an interpretation but which is exhibited in what we call "obeying the rule" and "going against it" in actual cases' (Wittgenstein, 1958 § 201). For Bjarup, Kripke and Yablon made the very mistake Wittgenstein wanted to correct – that is, 'the assumption that there must be an interpretation which mediates between an order or a rule on the one hand, and action in conformity with it, on the other hand' (p. 380). Rules do not apply:

> No interpretation of a legal rule, no rule for the application of a rule, can definitely determinate [sic], by itself, what counts as accord or conflict. This is so, because each interpretation generates the same problem, that is, has it to be applied? The answer to this problem is, I suggest, to consider reasons for action, rather than interpretations of rules. (p. 381)

On this basis Bjarup thinks that he can reject Yablon's distinction between 'Kripkean' and 'causal' indeterminacy, believing that the distinction falsely assumes that rules can be 'causal' in the sense that they can cause agents to act, when in truth 'it is not the rule that compels people' (p. 381).

The disagreement between Yablon and Bjarup is mirrored by the exchange between Stanley Fish and Ronald Dworkin. Fish's essay, 'Working on the Chain Gang' (Chapter 14) is part of an important exchange between the two that took place in the 1980s,[14] and in this collection should be read against the views Dworkin puts forward in his 'Law, Philosophy and Interpretation' (Chapter 1).

Fish notices how Dworkin, in presenting his theory of law as an interpretive concept, wants to 'avoid claiming either that in deciding a case judges find the plain meaning of the law "just there" or, alternatively, that they make up the meaning "wholesale" in accordance with personal preference or whim' (p. 387).

This might be the alternative Dworkin wants to avoid but, according to Fish, most of what Dworkin actually says about interpretation in general, and legal interpretation in particular, revolves around this very dichotomy. Fish claims that this is particularly noticeable as regards Dworkin's 'chain novel' metaphor. The chain novel argument relies on the distinction between 'mechanical' and 'free' interpretation insofar as 'it assumes that the first person in the chain is in a position different in kind from those who follow him because he is only creating while his fellow authors must both create and interpret' (p. 388). All the authors in the chain are 'free and constrained in exactly the same way' as any other. Whatever any author wants to write must be something that qualifies as a 'novel' and, as such, is both constrained and made possible by the relevant literary practice. The hypothetical 'free' act, which simply ignores or steps away from the practice altogether, would fail to be a novel at all. And at each stage of the evolution of the project it is possible to problematize, for example, the genre of novel to which this one should be ascribed. In doing so, one works from a different interpretation that necessarily colours what has gone before. In the same way, earlier interpretations will have previously established some parameters which it would be difficult to escape at a later phase, while still being engaged in the 'chain gang' at all.

This is the basis on which Fish seeks to refute Dworkin's view that the development of a branch of law – for example, concerning liability for nervous shock caused by a negligent act (one of the examples used by Dworkin in *Law's Empire*) – can become more dense over time so that the leeway for interpretative reconsideration is narrower for judges later in a decisional series than earlier. (On the face of it, Dworkin's view of common law interpretation seems intuitively plausible when we consider how substantial bodies of doctrine can build up through a series of satellite cases interpreting the theses derived from an original 'leading case'. But Fish's point is that this process goes on only so long as interpretative practice remains constant and, once somebody suggests a new interpretation of the doctrine or any part of it, the whole doctrine in question takes on a new character for that interpreter, and potentially for other participants in the practice if they adopt the new interpretation – and even, to an extent, if they do not.)

The importance of Fish's vividly argued critique of Dworkin lies in his insistence that Dworkin has not committed himself sufficiently wholeheartedly to the interpretative approach. Taken most rigorously, this approach cannot admit that there is already a text awaiting interpretation at any point in the practice. Taking something to be a text within a practice is already an interpretative position, even before one's more detailed interpretation of the always-already interpreted-as-a text object gets under way. If one finds it impossible after all to carry this project through, one will have to revise the initial interpretative move and abandon the supposed 'text' as an item alien to the practice of the interpretative community. If this is right, we are left with a choice between the more radical interpretivism advocated by Fish or one or other of the two positions rejected by Dworkin. In other words, one will have to move in the direction of Michael Moore's natural law version of metaphysical realism, such that interpretation is a way of revealing and bringing forth a meaning immanent in an actually pre-existing norm of law, or in the direction of some version of positivism that proposes criteria for the recognition of law and laws as propositions emanating from conventionally established sources. In either case, interpretation is an activity ontologically distinct from that which is interpreted. To Fish, either of these views is profoundly mistaken, and mistaken in fundamentally the same way. There can be no such dualism of text and interpretation.

Interpreting the Law

In Part VI we turn finally to theorists whose approach tries to give substance in various ways to the dualism rejected by Fish. In 'Normative and Narrative Coherence in Legal Decision Making' (Chapter 15) Jan van Dunné discusses the related notions of 'normative' and 'narrative' coherence as they have been defended by Neil MacCormick. While normative coherence has to do 'with the justification of legal rulings or normative propositions more generally in the context of a legal system conceived as a normative order', narrative coherence has to do 'with the justification of findings of fact and the drawing of reasonable inferences from evidence'. A norm coheres with others when they can be justified under higher principles or values, 'provided that the higher or highest-order principles and values seem acceptable as delineating a satisfactory form of life' (p. 410).

For van Dunné, the distinction between normative and narrative coherence follows from the Kantian dichotomy between norms and facts (p. 411). This dichotomy, however, should not be taken for granted, since there is a long and venerable tradition in which it is not accepted. This tradition stretches from the Roman jurists: *da mihi facta, dabo tibi ius*, to modern authors of the kind of H.H. Gadamer and Josef Esser who, van Dunné reminds us, used to say that 'we can only know the law through the case at hand' (p. 411).

The idea here is twofold: on the one hand, facts do not bring themselves under the judge's consideration: they have to be argued and proven, and more crucially structured in particular, rule-friendly ways. Any operative description of the facts will prejudge as to the applicable law. On the other hand, rules are given content in their application; hence it is through the consideration of cases that we will get to learn about the law. Hence 'the difference between normative and narrative coherence is distinctive at first sight only, and deceptive on closer scrutiny' (p. 416).

After showing the ways in which normative and narrative coherence merge, van Dunné discusses cases where the very way in which the facts were narrated implied a solution for the case, because the facts are presented in story form – 'a plot which asks for a certain (happy) end' (p. 415). Consideration of those cases allow him to conclude that narratives fulfil the role of 'the go-between in the relation of norms and facts' (p. 415). In 'normal' cases the narrative will be absorbed by the abstract description of the rule's operative facts. But in special cases 'storytelling is the crux, if one is to realize the bending of the hard and fast rule to suit the circumstances of the case and make a just and reasonable solution possible' (p. 416).

The relation between facts and norms is also discussed by Neil MacCormick in 'Reasonableness and Objectivity' (Chapter 19). Although MacCormick discusses only the concept of reasonableness in law, most of what he says about it can also be applied to many other open-ended concepts like 'due care', 'good faith' and the like.

MacCormick begins with Hart's view of the function of concepts such as 'reasonableness', in which they are assimilated to delegated legislation (see Hart, 1994, pp. 132–33). For MacCormick this view, although exaggerating the decisionist element in a judgment concerning what is reasonable (p. 536), correctly calls our attention to the fact that, by using a concept like 'reasonableness', the legislator recognizes 'the existence of a plurality of factors that must be evaluated in respect of their relevance to a common focus of concern' (p. 538), while at the same time recognizing that, in many instances, the way in which that plurality of factors is to be evaluated can only properly be ascertained in the light of full information about particular cases. The 'focus of concern' varies, and hence what is reasonable when we are talking about spouses' obligations to each other is not the same as when we are talking of the way in which public authorities must exercise their powers and so on.

The fact that the focus of concern can change from one sphere to the next does not mean that there is no common ground. Indeed, MacCormick claims that the central idea behind the concept of reasonableness can be explained on the basis of Adam Smith's 'impartial spectator':

> Reasonable persons resemble Adam Smith's 'impartial spectator'. (Indeed, it might be better to say that they themselves exhibit recourse to 'spectator' reasoning.) For they seek to abstract from their own position to see and feel the situation as it looks and feels to others involved, and they weigh impartially their own interests and commitments in comparison with those of others. (pp. 531–32)

It is this idea of detached impartiality that constitutes the nucleus of 'reasonableness' according to MacCormick. The way in which this central idea operates varies because (a) the topics to which reasonableness connects are variable, and (b) because the factors relevant to judgement vary according to the topic (p. 539). This last variable explains the fact that sometimes statutes offer a list of the relevant factors (see the case discussed by MacCormick at pp. 539–41). It also explains the sense behind the lawyers' idea that reasonableness is a question of *fact* because the behaviour demanded by a rule that requires reasonableness is something that changes with time: 'Precautions at work which were once treated as unusual or extravagant may come to be accepted as normal and proper' (p. 546).

All in all, MacCormick concludes, although in every judgement of reasonableness 'there is bound to be for each of us an element of the subjective' (p. 555), in something like the idea of an 'impartial spectator' we can bring our 'reflections beyond raw feeling' (p. 544), and give them thus some objectivity.

Aleksander Peczenik's essay 'Authority Reasons in Legal Interpretation and Moral Reasoning' (Chapter 17), deals with the role that the idea of authority and authority reasons play in moral and legal reasoning. He wants to claim that '[a]*t least in the Western-type society, the law is necessary as a relatively certain starting point of moral reasoning. But it is not a means to eliminate moral reasoning*' (pp. 442–43).

His reason for this claim has to do with the essentially gappy character of the legal reasoning involved in moving from general legal premises to particular decisions – another version of the 'particularity void'. Frequently there is a 'jump' involved between the premises that can be established and the conclusion to be justified. To some extent, the gaps can be covered by 'authority reasons', and these might be instances of legal authority – for example, precedents – or moral authority – what most people would think right. But these are in turn incompletely determinate in many contexts and for many reasons. In the last resort, it is 'autonomous' reasoning – that is, one's own sense of the rightness of the matter – that closes the gap. And the most ultimate of autonomous reasons are moral reasons expressing the commitments of a moral agent.

Peczenik's running example is that of the doctrine of 'adequate causation' in the (Swedish) law of torts. In order to have a right to compensation from the defendant, the victim must show both that the act in question is of a kind properly characterizable as engaging the defendant's liability and that the harm he or she suffered was 'adequately caused' by the defendant's action. The Air Transport Liability Act says that the owner of an aircraft is strictly liable for damage caused by the use of the aircraft. Flying very noisy military aircraft in a populated area has resulted in the death of silver fox cubs, bitten to death by their mothers when frightened by the noise. It appears that there is some causal connection between the cubs' death and the operation of the aircraft. But does this connection amount to 'adequate' causation under the governing unwritten principle of Swedish law? If one can hold that it is 'adequate', then the owner's (the state's) use of the aircraft has, in legal terms, caused the damage in question, and the state should be held liable to compensate the fox-farmers. But this is justifiable without any illicit 'jump' from premises to conclusion only if one can give good reasons why to treat the requirement of 'adequacy' as being satisfied here.[15] There are, in principle, two possibilities, of which one is a (heteronomous) authority reason and the other involves resort to autonomous reasoning. The former shows that, according to some authoritative agency or text, the facts at issue satisfy the authoritatively stated interpretation of the concept as it is used in the principle concerned. The latter shows why the interpreter holds it to be right to treat this case as covered by that concept, or holds that important values would be served by this decision.

Legal interpretation, it follows, is conducted as far as possible through reliance on authority rather than on autonomous reasoning, and the particular kinds of relevant authority are particularly legal. The ultimate appeal to autonomous reasoning on grounds of rightness or other values can be narrowed, but can never be cut off.

The terminology of 'authority reasons' deployed by Peczenik in this essay echoes, and probably has its origin in, the typology of reasons developed by Robert Summers in his influential 'Two Types of Substantive Reasons' (Chapter 18), which indeed he subtitles 'The Core of a Theory of Common-Law Justification'. The reasoning he has in mind concerns common law in a double sense, for not only is he concerned with reasoning in common law (Anglo-American) systems of law, but, in respect of these systems, he also concentrates on reasoning within domains where common law in the sense of case-law remains predominant ('Common law authority reasons consist primarily of appeals to precedent.') These are to be distinguished from those domains that the contemporary common law systems construct largely around bodies, even 'codes', of statute law, where the reasoning process involves much attention to statutory interpretation. Summers has subsequently made an enormous contribution to the understanding of the processes of statutory interpretation in a comparative perspective through his leadership of the *Bielefelder Kreis*, a group of jurists from several countries representing different types of legal system who tried to establish an illuminating common approach to understanding methods of interpretation and variations among these methods across their different systems (MacCormick and Summers, 1991; cf. MacCormick and Summers, 1997).

For Summers, there is a difference between what he calls 'substantive reasons' (which are somewhat comparable with Peczenik's idea of 'autonomous reasons') and 'authority reasons', 'factual reasons', 'interpretational reasons' or 'critical reasons'. To dwell for a moment on two of these, 'authority reasons' are essentially textual in character, where the source of some text about law or about legal rights or obligations makes it binding or persuasive in respect of a decision-making process. 'Interpretational reasons' concern the proper approach to interpreting a text which has authority in relation to, or at least relevance to, a context of decision. We may add that there is also interplay with 'institutional reasons', having to do with the nature of the institutions through whose agency the legal system is implemented and sustained.

Summers argues that common law decision-making does, and should, give primacy to 'substantive reasons'. That is, judges should not simply look to the authorities and the decision they appear to mandate, but should seek to achieve the best possible resolution of any dispute having regard to authorities, institutions and the rest. But they must finally take responsibility for expounding reasons that show one course of decision as preferable to any alternatives. Such reasons, he argues, typically have two kinds. Either they justify the decision in terms of a goal towards which it is oriented or they justify it in terms of its being right in the light of a 'sociomoral norm of rightness' (p. 456). In short, substantive reasons are either goal reasons or rightness reasons. Since institutional architecture often has a strong and legitimate bearing on the goals one should pursue or on how it is right to allocate decisional responsibility, institutional reasoning can play an auxiliary role in relation either to goal reasons or to rightness reasons.

Summers's essay belongs in the broad school of thought according to which justification involves an accumulation and 'weighing' or 'balancing' of reasons, with a view to establishing which decision or course of action is best supported by the strongest reasons. This being so, it is important to establish what sorts of reasons there are for (say) legal decisions, whether a convincing typology can be worked out, and whether any light can thereby be shed on the apparently mysterious process of 'weighing'. Do different reasons or types of reason have different weights or different justificatory force, and, if so, how do they interact or oppose or cancel each other out?

If the 'law as interpretation' approach is to be taken seriously, however, all these modes of reasoning or kinds of reasons may, in the end, simply come down to different forms of, or approaches to, interpretation. At first sight this seems odd, given that Summers and other like-minded thinkers treat 'interpretational reasons' as a subset of available legal reasons, not as an alternative name for the whole set. How are we to deal with this? Is interpretation one of the tasks of a lawyer, or the whole business of understanding law?

The final essay in the collection to be discussed, 'On Justification and Interpretation' (Chapter 16) by the late Jerzy Wróblewski[16] together with Neil MacCormick (who in the text acknowledges Wróblewski as the primary author of this piece) offers a possible approach to answering these questions. Typically, legal systems include an established body of legal texts, such as constitutions, enactments by legislatures printed in chronological order, or in the differently structured and more comprehensive form of 'codes', and books of precedents recording higher court decisions, as well as juristic commentaries on constitution, statutes, subordinate legislation, precedents and so on. Values like that of respecting the rule of law call for an approach to the decision-making between citizen and citizen or citizen and state that treats these texts with special deference. They demand an approach that holds to the need for decisions to be either based on some textual authority or on authority from an implicit principle to be found in the practice of the legal system based on these texts.

Sometimes – there is an echo of Bjarup's point here – acting on the rule stated in such a text is unproblematic and reliant on a direct movement from understanding to action. An honest and straightforward person keeps her promises usually without need for reflection either on the 'text' of the promise she made or on her community's explicit or implicit rules for the practice of promising. That is what being honest and straightforward amounts to. But there are occasions when even such a person has to resolve a doubt, perhaps because the promisee has asked for a performance other than the one she thinks due or because she wonders if a general exception to the normal bindingness of a promise applies here – for example, she has promised to lend someone her car, but now has reason to suppose it is to be used as the getaway car in a criminal enterprise.

Where doubts of this kind arise, Wróblewski argues, we are in the domain of interpretation in the strict sense (rather than some wide sense in which every act of understanding a text, however immediately and unreflectively, involves interpretation). We have to reflect on the question what the text really means, or means for present purposes, there being a real doubt between two or several possible readings of it that make a difference for the purpose in hand. This situation is typical in legal contexts, especially in more-or-less adversarial settings where different legal answers or decisions turn on the question which interpretation of a text is to prevail, there being at least ostensible reasons in favour of rival possibilities that make a real difference to the particular subject matter in contention.

To set this against the model of decision-making suggested in the essay, we should look at the authors' suggestion that justification involves working towards the thing to be justified, the *justificandum* or 'JM' starting from justificatory premises 'JP' and using justificatory reasoning 'JR' to establish the link between JP and JM. Often, one JP is a legal text. But often also, the meaning of a legal text is subject to doubt and debate, and the justification of any final decision depends on a prior resolution of the point in doubt or subject to debate. The whole justification depends therefore on internal 'fractional decisions', concerning choices among rival interpretations of a relevant text that have been put forward. These, for their part, have to be justified by reasoning with their own justificatory premises and methods. The essay sketches Wróblewski's theory supporting a 'semantic' typology for the elements of interpretive reasoning – an approach largely adopted by the *Bielefelder Kreis* in its large-scale work on comparative statutory interpretation. Thus, although the argument in Wróblewski's essay is fairly concise and abstract, its implications can be followed through in considerable detail in MacCormick and Summers's *Interpreting Statutes* (1991).

In the event, there is agreement with Peczenik (also a significant figure in the *Bielefelder Kreis*) that 'external' reasons – what Peczenik calls 'autonomous' reasons and Summers calls 'substantive reasons' – are decisive in any really problematic setting. Wróblewski characterizes these reasons as depending either on a static conception of the values served by a legal system, stressing the rule of law and respect for settled expectations against a dynamic approach concerned to keep the legal order in tune with perceived needs and values of a changing society, or bringing it better in tune with the demands of the right and the good propounded through a general theory of ethics and practical reason.

If sound, this suggests that issues of interpretation are indeed central to legal thought and activity. But this is because of the omnipresent significance of legal texts whose validity is determined by something other than interpretation. The need for explicit accounts to be given concerning favoured interpretations of these texts entails a need to adduce reasons for these interpretative decisions. These reasons are reasons that *lead* one *to* an interpretation. They are not necessarily reasons that *come from* an interpretation of some other text in any sense of that term, however extended. They are thus not necessarily reasons that are themselves 'interpretative' in kind, in the sense of themselves depending on some decision about the interpretation of some other text. Interpretation is surely best viewed as one critical moment of or element in legal reasoning, rather than as an undifferentiated name for the whole of it.

Notes

1. Originally defended in Hacker and Raz (1977) and 'Is There Really No Right Answer in Hard Cases?' in Dworkin (1985). Whether the thesis has remained the same or undergone substantive changes is not clear. See Dworkin (1996).
2. This seems to be basically Hume's argument against 'those who have denied the reality of moral distinctions'. According to Hume, 'The only way, therefore, of converting an antagonist of this kind, is to leave him to himself. For, finding that nobody keeps up the controversy with him, it is probable he will, at last, of himself, from mere weariness, come over to the side of common sense and reason' (Hume, 1777, s. I).
3. See Raz's discussion of 'statements from the legal point of view' in Raz (1992, pp. 175–77). For a similar perspective, which he calls a 'hermeneutic' perspective, see MacCormick (1981, pp. 37–40).
4. For the notions of 'normative consequence' and 'operative facts' as we are using them here, see MacCormick (1994).
5. M.J. Detmold's position concerning positivism was fully set out in Detmold (1984).
6. A position associated with philosophers such as S. Kripke and H. Putnam and, among legal theorists, defended by Stravropoulos (1996).
7. Compare for his general position on 'natural law' Moore (1992).
8. This is what Hart also believed: see Hart (1994, pp. 128f). But see also Atria's essay in this collection (Chapter 4).
9. However, see Agamben (1998, p. 22): 'if one asks if the rule applies to the example, the answer is not easy, since the rule applies to the example as to a normal case and obviously not as an example.'
10. The counterexamples L. Fuller levelled against Hart in Fuller (1958) can be satisfactorily explained from this point of view.
11. The reference here is to Fuller (1969, p. 106).
12. This book develops more fully many of the themes discussed in the essay included here.
13. For Christodoulidis' full argument showing the limits of law's capacity to 'contain' politics see Christodoulidis (1998).
14. Which also included pieces such as Dworkin (1982); Dworkin (1983); and Fish (1989).
15. For a full account of Peczenik's view on this and other issues, see Peczenik (1989).
16. A more extensive and fully elaborated – indeed highly elaborate – version of Wróblewski's thought is to be found in Wróblewski (1992).

References

Agamben, G. (1998), *Homo Sacer*, Stanford, CA: Stanford University Press. First published 1995.
Atria, F. (2002), *On Law and Legal Reasoning*, Oxford: Hart Publishing.
Christodoulidis, E. (1998), *Law and Reflexive Policies*, Dordrecht: Kluwer.
Baker, G.P. (1977), 'Defeasibility and Meaning', in P.M.S. Hacker and J. Raz (eds), *Law, Morality and Society*, Oxford: Clarendon Press.
Detmold, M.J. (1984), *The Unity of Law and Morality: A Refutation of Legal Positivism*, London: Routledge & Kegan Paul.
Dworkin, R. (1970), 'Is Law a System of Rules?', in R. Summers (ed.), *Essays in Legal Philosophy*, Oxford: Blackwell, pp. 25–60.
Dworkin R. (1977a), *Philosophy of Law*, Oxford: Oxford University Press.
Dworkin, R. (1977b), 'The Model of Rules I', in R. Dworkin, *Taking Rights Seriously*, Cambridge, MA: Harvard University Press, ch. 2. First published as 'Is Law a System of Rules?'.
Dworkin, R. (1982), 'Law as Interpretation', *Texas Law Review*, **60**, pp. 527–60.
Dworkin, R. (1983), 'My Reply to Stanley Fish (and Walter Benn Michaels): Please Don't Talk About Objectivity Any More', in W. Mitchell (ed.), *The Politics of Interpretation*, Chicago: Chicago University Press, pp. 287–321.
Dworkin, R. (1985), *A Matter of Principle*, Cambridge, MA: Harvard University Press.

Dworkin, R. (1987), *Law's Empire*, London: Fontana.
Dworkin, R. (1996), 'Objectivity and Truth: You'd Better Believe It', *Philosophy and Public Affairs*, **25**, pp. 87–117.
Fish, S. (1989), 'Wrong Again', in S. Fish, *Doing What Comes Naturally*, New York: Oxford University Press, pp. 101–19.
Fuller, L. (1958), 'Positivism and Fidelity to Law: A Reply to Professor Hart', *Harvard Law Review*, **71**, pp. 630–72.
Fuller, L. (1969), *The Morality of Law*, New Haven, CT: Yale University Press. First published 1964.
Günther, K. (1993), *The Sense of Appropriateness*, Albany, NY: SUNY. First published 1988.
Habermas, J. (1997), *Between Facts and Norms*, Cambridge: Polity Press. First published 1992.
Hacker, P.M.S. and Raz, J. (eds) (1977), *Law, Morality and Society*, Oxford: Clarendon Press.
Hart, H.L.A. (1994), *The Concept of Law*, 2nd edn, Oxford: Clarendon Press. First published 1961.
Horwitz, M. (1992), *The Transformation of American Law*, New York: Oxford University Press.
Hume, D. (1777), *An Enquiry Concerning the Principles of Morals*, London.
Kelman, M. (1987), *A Guide to Critical Legal Studies*, Cambridge, MA: Harvard University Press.
Kelsen, H. (1970), *Pure Theory of Law*, 2nd edn, Berkeley: University of California Press.
Kripke, S. (1982), *Wittgenstein on Rules and Private Language*, Oxford: Blackwell.
MacCormick, D.N. (1976), 'Dworkin as a Pre-Benthamite', reprinted as 'Taking the "Rights Thesis" Seriously', D.N. MacCormick (1982), *Legal Rights and Social Democracy*, Oxford: Clarendon Press, pp. 126–53.
MacCormick, D.N. (1981), *H.L.A. Hart*, Stanford, CA: Stanford University Press.
MacCormick, D.N. (1994), *Legal Reasoning and Legal Theory*, Oxford: Clarendon Press. First published 1978.
MacCormick, D.N. (1995), 'Defeasibility in Law and Logic', in Z. Banowski *et al.* (eds), *Informatics and the Foundations of Legal Reasoning*, Dordrecht: Kluwer, pp. 99–117.
MacCormick, D.N. and Summers, R. (1991), *Interpreting Statutes: A Comparative Study*, Aldershot: Dartmouth.
MacCormick, D.N. and Summers, R. (1997), *Interpreting Precedents: A Comparative Study*, Aldershot: Ashgate.
Moore, M.S. (1992), 'Law as a Functional Kind', in P. George (ed.), *Natural Law Theory: Contemporary Essays*, Oxford: Clarendon Press, pp. 188–242.
Moore, M.S. (1995), 'Interpreting Interpretation', in A. Marmor (ed.), *Law and Interpretation*, Oxford: Clarendon Press, pp. 1–29.
Peczenik, A. (1989), *On Law and Reason*, Dordrecht: D. Reidel.
Raz, J. (1992), *Practical Reason and Norms*, Princeton, NJ: Princeton University Press. First published 1975.
Raz, J. (1994a), 'On the Autonomy of Legal Reasoning', in J. Raz, *Ethics in the Public Domain*, Oxford: Clarendon Press, pp. 310–24.
Raz, J. (1994b), 'Authority, Law and Morality', in J. Raz, *Ethics in the Public Domain*, Oxford: Clarendon Press, pp. 194–221.
Raz, J. (1986), *The Morality of Freedom*, Oxford: Clarendon Press.
Raz, J. (1998a), 'Two Views on the Nature of the Theory of Law: A Partial Comparison', *Legal Theory*, **4**, pp. 249–82.
Raz, J. (1998b), 'Postema on Law's Autonomy and Public Practical Reason: A Critical Comment', *Legal Theory*, **4**, pp. 1–20.
Stravropoulos, N. (1996), *Objectivity in Law*, Oxford: Clarendon Press.
Unger, R.M. (1983), *The Critical Legal Studies Movement*, Cambridge, MA: Harvard University Press.
Unger, R.M. (1987), *Politics: A Work in Constructive Social Theory. Part One: False Necessity*, Cambridge: Cambridge University Press.
Unger, R.M. (1996), *What Should Legal Analysis Become?*, London: Verso.
Wellmer, A. (1991), *The Persistence of Modernity*, Cambridge, MA: MIT Press.
Wittgenstein, L. (1958), *Philosophical Investigations*, New York: Macmillan.
Wróblewski, J. (1992), *The Judicial Application of Law*, ed. Z. Bankowski and D.N. MacCormick, Dordrecht: Kluwer Academic Publishers.

Part I
Interpretation and Law: Why is Interpretation Important for Law?

[1]

Law, Philosophy and Interpretation*

Ronald Dworkin, Oxford and New York

Thank you very much for those splendid introductions. To those of you who have not experienced it, I must tell you it's a very great pleasure to be introduced and perhaps praised in the language you don't understand. Because then you can make up for yourself part of the introduction. In any case I am very grateful. You can imagine how pleased I was to be asked not only to give one lecture but a series of inaugural lectures. I am very grateful.

I shall give two lectures on general jurisprudence in two different cities. The first lecture, here in Tokyo, will emphasize the role of interpretation in law. The lecture in Kobe will be devoted mainly to questions about the interrelation between political philosophy and law – in particular the connection between law and democracy. This split gives me a convenient opportunity. If people ask me in the question period today why I didn't discuss a certain subject, I will say, "I shall discuss that in Kobe." If in Kobe people ask me why I didn't discuss a certain subject, I will say, "I talked about that in Tokyo last week."

---

* The form of a lecture has been kept.

In the beginning of today's lecture, I shall in some part simply be summarizing views that I have explained at greater length elsewhere. I do this, though perhaps some of you are familiar with those views, because others are not and I thought I had better begin with a brief summary of what I have argued before so I can then develop some new material in the main part of the lecture.

The general problem I want to discuss has two separate aspects. I begin by reminding you – though the lawyers among you won't need much to be reminded – that even experts often disagree about what the law is on some subject. They disagree, moreover, in a particular and special and deep way. Even when lawyers agree about what we might call the ordinary historical facts of the matter – even when lawyers agree about what happened on some occasion, about who did what to whom, and even when they agree about what words are written in the statute books and other books of law, and about what judges in past cases have written and said – they may still disagree about what the law is. I offer you two examples, both drawn from American law, to illustrate this.

The first is a famous case decided long ago called Riggs v. Palmer. That case arose when a young man, who knew that his grandfather had written a will leaving the young man all the grandfather's property, learned that the old man was about to marry again and make a new will, and murdered his grandfather to stop him from doing so. Of course, the young man was sent to jail. But then the question arose, "Was he still entitled to inherit the property of the man he had murdered?" There was no disagreement about the facts. Everyone agreed that the young man had murdered his grandfather. Everyone agreed about what was said in the statute dealing with wills. The statute said nothing about murderers: it did not say that if the heir murders the testator, the heir is disqualified from inheriting. Nevertheless, the lawyers disagreed about the right answer to that case, and the judges also disagreed. Two judges said that the law is that murderers may not inherit. And one judge, the dissenting judge, said, "No, that is wrong. The law is that the murderer can inherit the property."

I mention another famous case just to have another example. This is the case of Buick Motor Company v. McPherson. At one time, most American lawyers thought that if someone bought an automobile which was defective, that person could only sue the dealer, the automobile dealer, from whom he or she had bought the car. He could not sue the manufacturer of the motor car, they thought, because there was no contract between the purchaser and the manufacturer. In the Buick case, the plaintiff, who was injured because her automobile was defective, decided that she would sue the manufacturer, the Buick Motor Company which is part of General Motors, in spite of the widespread opinion that she would lose. Again the judges disagreed. The majority, in a famous opinion written by Judge Cardozo, said, in effect, "If we look at the previous decisions carefully, in the right way, then we see that, in spite of the general opinion among lawyers, actually the law does allow someone who has bought a defective automobile from a dealer to sue the manufacturer directly." The dissenting judge said, "No, if we look at the cases the right way, we will see the opposite. The law forbids a law suit directly by the purchaser against the manufacturer. The purchaser can sue only the local automobile dealer from whom she bought the car." Once again, there was no disagreement about what actually happened. Everyone agreed that the motor car was defective. Everyone agreed that there was no contract directly with the manufacturer. Everyone agreed about what was written in the past cases and, nevertheless, very learned, able, capable lawyers and judges disagreed about the correct statement of the law.

Now, that raises a problem of a philosophical kind, which we can describe in two different ways. We can describe it from what philosophers might call an epistemological perspective, as a problem of legal reasoning. When all the facts are settled, what is the right way to reason to a conclusion of law? We can also describe the problem (again to use a piece of philosophical jargon) as an ontological problem, that is, a problem about what must be true about the world – about what must have happened there – in order to make a proposition of law true or false.

But though these are different formulations, the underlying issue is the same one. Let me illustrate that point with a non-legal example. Suppose I ask whether Japan is a rich country. Someone might be puzzled about the epistemological issue: how would we go about discovering the right answer to that question? What would count as good evidence for deciding whether a country was rich? Or someone might be puzzled about an ontological issue. No one thinks that the proposition that Japan is a rich nation is true because Japan is a person with a lot of money in her pocket. We might therefore ask: what different kinds of facts – about the wealth of actual, individual people, for example – make it true that a nation is rich?

The same two kinds of questions, epistemological and ontological, are raised by the disagreements in law that I described and illustrated. We have, as I said, first the question of legal reasoning: what would count as a good argument that a murderer is not allowed, in law, to inherit from his victim? And second, equally mysterious, we have the ontological question: if it is a fact that murderers cannot inherit, what kind of fact is it? Is it a hard fact, like the fact that there are nine planets in our solar system? If not, is it the same kind of fact as the fact that Japan is rich – is it a summary of a large number of other, more basic facts about what particular people do or have done? Those are, to my mind, the central questions of jurisprudence. Those are the philosophical questions behind the familiar, traditional jurisprudential question "What is law?"

For a long time, not just in America and England where I teach but around the world, one family of answers to these questions, one general legal theory, has been very influential, which is usually called legal positivism. In America and Europe, the most influential philosophers in this tradition have been Hans Kelsen and John Austin and H. L. A. Hart. I can best summarize the answers that positivism gives to my two questions by beginning with the ontological question.

Positivism says that the propositions of law, like the proposition that the law forbids murderers from inheriting, can be true only in virtue of historical events – of particular people thinking or saying or doing particular things. John Austin said, as most of you know, "Law is the command of the sovereign." He meant that what makes a proposition of law true, when it is true, is an historical event of a particular sort, namely a sovereign, a person in undominated political power, issuing a command to that effect. That is the only thing, according to Austin, that can make a proposition of law true.

H. L. A. Hart has offered a much more sophisticated theory. He said that propositions of law are true, most fundamentally, in virtue of a sociological fact: that the general public (or at least the officials) of a community have accepted a general principle, which he calls a Rule of Recognition, stipulating procedures and conditions that make laws valid. "For example," said Hart, in effect, "in Britain the Rule of Recognition, a general principle accepted by everyone, is that whatever Parliament declares to be law is in fact law." It follows that a proposition of law is true, in Britain, if Parliament has enacted the rules that proposition describes.

To summarize: positivism's answer to the ontological question is "law is true in virtue of facts about what particular people – either sovereigns, as in the case of Austin, or people generally in the case of Hart – have decided or think. If you give that answer to the ontological question, then the answer you will give to the more practical, epistemological question is straightforward. According to the positivist, you discover what the law is simply by looking to history to find out what law has in fact been made by the historical acts that, according to the version of positivism in question, make law. So, in the case of that bad young man who murdered his grandfather, you simply look to the books to see whether the legislature has ever said – one way or the other – what the answer is.

But there is an obvious difficulty with all this. How does it explain how and why judges and lawyers disagree? You remember I said that all the lawyers and all the judges agreed, in Riggs v. Palmer and in the Buick case, about what the historical facts were, including the facts about what the legislators had done. But if positivism is right, if the only thing involved in the legal question is what past decision had been reached, how could there be a disagreement? The positivist answers that question this way. There is no disagreement in these cases about what the law is. That is an illusion. Judges may say they are disagreeing about what the law is, but they are not, since they agree about what the past decisions were. What then are they disagreeing about? They are disagreeing, according to positivism, about what the law should be. They are arguing with one another about how far they should change the law in the exercise of their discretionary power to do so.

Now, I shall just summarize my reasons for thinking that that is a very bad answer. Lawyers and judges think that they are disagreeing about what the law is. That is how they understand themselves. That is how it feels to be a lawyer or to be a judge. You feel that there is a hard problem to solve, and that this is the problem of what the law really is, not what it should be, which you may think a much easier matter. We need a theory of law, an answer to our questions, that does not lead us to the surprising conclusion that the disagreement that seems so genuine and so demanding is really illusory. That is the reason that I have tried to defend a different kind of answer than the answer positivism gives. This answer finds the nerve of law not in past official decisions alone but in the process of interpretation of past decisions, which I am now going to try to illustrate.

It is sometimes helpful to introduce a complicated idea by an analogy. So I am going to imagine a game for rainy afternoons when there is nothing else to do. Imagine ten people, novelists, who spend such an afternoon together and pass the time by arranging the following game. They draw lots – pieces of paper with different numbers on them. The writer who draws No. 1 writes the first chapter of a novel, a new original novel, and then she gives the chapter that she has written to the novelist who has drawn No. 2, and then novelist No. 2 reads the first chapter and writes a second chapter continuing the story, trying to make the novel as it develops as good as it can be. And then the first two chapters are given to the novelist who has drawn No. 3, and he writes another chapter, still continuing the story, trying to make it as good a story as it can be. This process continues until the novelist who has drawn No. 10 has completed his chapter. By this time they have produced a very thick novel. Novelist No. 10 had to read the whole story so far, and write a new chapter with new events but regarding that new chapter still as a continuation of the same story.

Now, I want to compare the development of law to that chain novel, as I call it. My idea put in a very crude way (I will try to do better later) is that when a lawyer or a judge has a new problem like the problem of the murdering young man or the problem of the defective Buick car, the lawyer or judge must read all the law up to that point as if it were the opening chapters of a novel and must understand that the decision he or she must reach in the new case must be one that continues the story in the most appropriate way.

Now, I hope it will be clear from my imaginary game that two different writers would write the same chapter in the story in different ways. So, too, different lawyers or judges will have different opinions about the best way to continue the story. They will have different opinions in part, not entirely but in part, because which way makes the continuing legal story better will depend on one's own moral and political convictions. So, if a judge is very conservative, that judge will decide the Buick case in a different way from the way a judge who was more radical would decide it. But still, in spite of that fact, if judges are in good faith trying to decide as interpreters rather than legislators, then for each judge there will, nevertheless, be a difference between two questions. The first is the question of interpretation. What is the best reading I can give to this legal history so far? How can I interpret or understand it to make the best story from a political standpoint so far? The second is the question not of interpretation but of legislation. If I could make the law fresh, with no responsibility to the past, the way a legislator can – if I could, in effect, start a new novel -how would I do it?

I claim that even though any judge's legal opinions will reflect his political conviction, nevertheless there will be a difference for each judge between interpreting the story so far and deciding how that judge would rule if there were no story so far. For example, suppose (I agree it's very unlikely) there is a Communist judge in the United States, and he is faced with the Buick case. Suppose he says, "I would like to establish the legal principle that anyone who sues a large capitalist company automatically wins." If he actually tries to interpret the history of American law to see whether that principle could be regarded as continuing the story, he would fail. The story of American law so far is very much not the story in which capitalism always loses: no responsible judge could think it was, and that fact underscores the difference between interpretation and original legislation. Or, as we might put it, the difference between interpretation and invention.

Very well. That concludes my attempt at a quick summary of the position that I have tried to defend in the past, particularly in the book mentioned in the introduction, *Law's Empire*. Now, I want to report to you various important objections that have been made to my position. I do so not just because any author likes an opportunity to reply to his critics, but because the objections seem to me to require an answer which is a more general and illuminating account of interpretation than just repeating what I said in *Law's Empire*. So, this afternoon, I want first to describe the objections and then to try to develop, with you, a more general theory of interpretation. You will see, I hope, what I mean.

Here are the objections that I would like to discuss with you. The first insists that I have misunderstood what interpretation is really about. This objection has been made by many people including literary critics. They say that in my view interpretation is always an attempt to make of a story the best it can be. I said that when the writers were writing the chain novel, each was trying to make the continuing novel as good a novel as it could be. I say that when judges decide a hard case, each should be trying to continue the story so as to make it the best story from the standpoint of political justice. Now, the objection is that interpretation aims to describe the object of interpretation as it really is, not to make it the best it can be. In my view, interpretation aims to improve the object of interpretation, whereas, according to the first objection, interpretation is not a matter of improving something but describing it accurately.

The second objection is related to the first. It says that my view of interpretation applied to the law has the undesirable effect of making law seem more attractive than it is. Suppose you were interpreting "Mein Kampf" or the Holocaust or the rise of Joseph Stalin to power. Would you be trying to make any of those stories look good?

There is something horrible, according to this second objection, about the idea of trying to rewrite history to make it as good as it can be. Sometimes it is important to show it to be as bad as possible.

The third objection is different from the first two; it is more philosophical. The third objection says: you can't believe, can you, that there is always a right answer to a question of interpretation. Interpretation is inherently a subjective matter. For every person there is a different interpretation. If two people look at the same painting or look at the same play or go to the same performance of a Noh drama, they will see different things. Because interpretation is not objective but subjective. So, if I am right that law is essentially a matter not of discovery of historical events but of the interpretation of these events, then law becomes, according to this objection, subjective rather than objective.

Those are the three objections that I believe require me (or us I should say) to think more generally about the phenomenon of interpretation. So with your indulgence, I am going to turn my back for a few minutes on law. I know this is a legal conference and you are all lawyers. But I am going to turn away from law for a while because, of course, we interpret over a very great range of phenomena and contexts. Let me just remind you of the different kinds of activities in which one way or another interpretation is a central idea.

There is law. But there is also literature and art and aesthetic interpretation. There is scientific interpretation. Scientists, we say, interpret the data. There is historical interpretation. Historians don't just describe the events of the past, they interpret them. And there is psychoanalytic interpretation. Sigmund Freud's most famous work, at least among the general public, was called the Interpretation of Dreams. I need hardly remind you, of course, that there is a much more mundane occasion of interpretation called conversation. Indeed that form of interpretation now going on before your ears, because those admirable translators speaking into your earphones are struggling to make sense of what I am saying. They are interpreting what I say, and interpreting it in a different language from the language that I myself am using.

Now, the fact that we have such a wide range of activities in which the idea of interpretation figures suggests a problem that, so far as I am aware, has not been taken up by philosophers, at least not in these terms. I mean the problem of offering an answer to the following question. Are all of these various activities interpretation in the same sense? If so, what is interpretation, if it can be understood so abstractly that the interpretation of dreams and the interpretation of statutes both count as occasions of interpretation?

If we can find some theory of interpretation so general as to cover all these different cases, or even most of them, then a further problem arises. How do we then distinguish between these different kinds or occasions of interpretation? We certainly do distinguish. Suppose behind me right now there suddenly appears a series of flashes of light. And I then asked you to interpret those lights. You wouldn't know even how to begin until you knew what kind or form of interpretation was appropriate. You would have to decide whether the lights were a natural phenomenon – some mysterious lights just appearing in the atmosphere, for example – or whether it was a coded message by someone signaling in dots and dashes, or whether it was a new art form composed of the play of light directed by some kind of artist.

So we have two problems that any general theory of interpretation must confront. The first is: what (if anything) makes all of these kinds or occasions of interpretation occasions of the same thing? And the second problem, equally difficult, is: what makes the difference between each form as deep as that example suggests it is? And when we develop, if we can, a general theory of interpretation answering those questions, we must design it so as to answer two other questions at the same time. The first is this. It is a feature of all these different kinds of interpretation that those who practice each of them – the scientists, the lawyers, the historians, the translators, the psychoanalysts – when they disagree with one another each thinks, at least on most occasions, that he or she is right and the others are wrong. That is: we typically think of interpretation as something that can be done better or worse, that an interpretation can be true or false. And that adds to the problem. Because there aren't many activities, if you think of all the different activities we engage in, which are in that sense truth-seeking or truth-claiming.

But once we understand that it is part of interpretation in this very general sense that it claims truth, then we see a fourth feature that the theory must also account for, which is this. A general theory of interpretation must leave at least room for skepticism, because it is also a feature of each of the kinds of interpretation I described that there are skeptics who say the whole field is a kind of nonsense. I gather there has been much discussion in Japan recently, for example, of the deconstructionist movement in literary theory, which is a kind of skeptical position. We are familiar in America with varieties of skeptical positions that say that law is nonsense, that there is no law. So a general theory of interpretation must explain not only why most practitioners view the enterprise as truth-seeking, as hoping to establish truth, but also why some practitioners see it in a skeptical way as devoid of truth.

Very well, that is the challenge. And I am going to offer a very quick response to it. This will not, of course, be a complete theory, not only because I don't have time to develop the details, but because it will fit only some of the contexts of interpretation I described. It is a partial theory, part of an even more general theory that I shall try to describe on some other occasion. But the part of the more general theory that I shall try to describe now is particularly important for us, because, though it does not fit all of the contexts, it does fit the class of these that includes law. I call this form of interpretation constructive interpretation.

You will already have noticed that interpretation takes place within organized social practices, and that the concepts we use in forming interpretations of different sorts take their sense, not from the natural world, but from these social practices. Consider, for example, the concepts that figure in aesthetic interpretation: the concepts of novel, fiction, poem, sonnet, drama. These concepts have their life in, take their meaning and sense from, human enterprises and activities. There must have been a time when people first began to think that inventing a story was creating something. Before that, it was simply telling lies; suddenly telling lies becomes a way of creating art. There must have been a moment at which a drawing of a buffalo on the wall acquired a new dimension of meaning as art. That was the moment at which it was absorbed into a distinct human enterprise. Of course, conversation and translation are also parts of a distinct human enterprise.

Now, all the practices and enterprises that I have named so far are regarded by those of us who take them up not as pointless but as beneficial or worthwhile in some other way. We regard them as having a purpose or point. We think that law serves a function for the community whose law it is. We believe art serves a different kind of function, that it brings a valuable dimension of experience into our lives. We regard history as having a different kind of narrative value, and so forth. That is, we don't regard these enterprises as just rituals. We regard them as something important, as something having value.

Now, with that background I can offer this account of constructive interpretation. Constructive interpretation arises when people engage in a practice of this kind, which they all regard as serving a purpose or a point but disagree as to what, exactly, the purpose or point is. In that event, participants will regard the extension or range of application of the concepts that make up the practice as sensitive to, determined by, the point.

Now, that is very abstract and I am going to illustrate it in various ways in a moment. But even at this level of abstraction you might see how this account might be thought to respond to the series of problems about interpretation I listed. I began with the problem of range. What is common to different kinds of interpretation? My answer would be that constructive interpretation is general because we have many practices or enterprises that meet the test I just described. That is, we think of them as serving a purpose but to some degree we disagree about what the purpose is. And we judge the range of application of the concepts tied to those practices as determined by the purpose we ascribed to the practice as a whole.

Since that is so, we now know how to distinguish one interpretive practice from another. Interpretive practices will differ because they serve different kinds of points. We may disagree about what the point of law is but we agree that the point of law is different from the point of poetry. Why can we be truth-seeking about the matters of interpretation? Because we are truth-seeking about the matters on which interpretation depends. Suppose we disagree with other lawyers, about some matter of legal interpretation, because our views about the point of law, or about justice so far as we think it is law's purpose to provide justice, differ from theirs. We will think our interpretation true (not just different) if and because we think our opinions about the point of law or about justice are true. We hold our views on these subjects as a matter of conviction, which means that we think they are true.

But you also see, I hope, why skepticism is always in the background. Because skepticism is always on offer whenever we are dealing with matters in which people feel deeply, as a matter of conviction, but disagree, and none of them can prove that they are right. I might think, with great passion, that the true point of literature is to celebrate God. But others think the value of literature is very different. I have no way to demonstrate that I am right, and therefore I am vulnerable to the challenge of the skeptic who says that no one is right, that there is no truth or falsity about such questions. So, as a formal matter, just in the abstract, the sketchy theory I have given you (which you might call the teleological or purposive theory of interpretation) has the right shape to answer to the various requirements I said that the theory of interpretation should meet.

Let's look in more detail at some examples of this theory at work, and since I promised that I would return to law sooner or later, I will return to it for my first example. How does this account of interpretation help us to understand the argument in Riggs v. Palmer, the case about the young man who murdered his grandfather, or the case of Buick v. McPherson, about the woman who sued the Buick Motor Company? Many views can be and are held about the purpose or function of law as a collective enterprise, of course. But in order to simplify this illustration, I shall suppose that there are only two that are held by anyone in a particular community. The first insists that law exists to provide certainty and strict guidance in order that collective life can be more efficient, so that people can plan their lives knowing what rules the police or the state will enforce against them. Now, if one took that view of the point of law – roughly speaking that law exists in order to allow society to function efficiently in spite of the fact that people disagree about justice and morality – then he would be drawn to a positivist approach to law. In particular, he would be drawn to the ontological view that law exists only in the form of explicit past decisions by political officials which can be read and known. He would be likely to think, in the case of the murdering heir, that the murderer should be allowed to inherit, because the statute is very clear about the formal tests a will must meet to be valid, and says nothing at all about murderers. It would defeat the purpose of law, on this view of that purpose, if we had to decide such moral questions as whether and when murderers should be allowed to inherit in order to know whether a particular will was enforceable. A judge disposed to positivism, because he held the view that the purpose of law was to promote predictability, would therefore think the law allowed the murderer to inherit, though he might also think that the law should be changed for the future, though by the parliament not by the judge. Similarly, in the Buick case, a positivist holding that view would be disposed to decide not to allow a suit against the manufacturer, for the simple reason that no past case had ever allowed such a suit, and the legislature had not said that this practice should be changed.

Now consider a different view of the point or purpose of having law. It holds that the positivist view I just described is too narrow. It acknowledges that law does serve the purpose of allowing people to plan their affairs, and that for that purpose predictability is desirable. But it adds that law should do more than that for a community. Law should also make government more coherent in principle; it should seek to help to preserve what we might call the integrity of the community's government, so that the community is governed by principles and not just by rules that might be incoherent in principle. And it insists that this latter purpose is so important that it might well, in particular cases, be more important than predictability and certainty.

Now, someone who takes that view might well think, in the case of the murdering heir, that it goes so far against general principles of morality and law to allow a murderer to profit by his terrible crime that we should understand the statute of wills as forbidding that, just for that reason. Even though nothing in the statute explicitly says that a murderer may not inherit, when we read that statute against the background of the law as a whole, with the aim that law should be coherent in principle, then we are led for that reason to decide that the law, properly understood, does not allow a murderer to inherit. That is what the court actually decided.

In the Buick case, which was, as I said, a very famous decision by Judge Cardozo, the court used a similar kind of reasoning. If we want the law to be coherent in principle, it said, then we must not understand it, so far as possible, not to make decisions that are morally arbitrary. If the defect in the automobile is the fault not of the dealer who simply sold it but of the manufacturer who created the defect, then what principle of morality could justify not allowing the person who was injured recovery against the institution that actually caused the damage?

I can now, I hope, begin to answer the questions I listed earlier. What are judges who disagree about the law, even though they agree about the facts, really disagreeing about? They are disagreeing (we may now say) about the correct interpretation of the story so far, and they disagree about that because interpretation is purposive, and they disagree about the best ascription of purpose or point to the general enterprise of law.

Let us test the generality of this account by considering other occasions of constructive interpretation. We might begin with literary interpretation. There are, of course, many schools of literary interpretation; there are heated arguments, no doubt in Japan as well as in the rest of the world, among advocates of different ways of understanding poetry or plays or novels. But again, to simplify, and just for purposes of illustration, I will contrast only a few views about the point of literature. As in the case of law, this simplification neglects many interesting subtleties, but I do it for the purpose of illustration.

The first of the few views I shall mention holds that the point of literature is moral instruction. It should aim to increase our sensitivity to genuine moral issues, to show us, in a compelling way, truths about conflicts and choices and tragedies that we see only inexactly and without the right depth apart from literature. That was the view, for example, of the very influential British critic, F. R. Leavis.

The second view is, in contrast, formalist. It holds that the point of literature is internal to aesthetics, that it consists in creating a kind of beauty or power that must be valued for its own sake, on its own terms, and not because it teaches us anything about morality (or psychology or history or anything else.) A third view is Marxist. It holds that the purpose of literature is to contribute to the historical triumph of the working class.

Now I suggest to you, though I can hardly hope to demonstrate it, that people who held one of these three views about the point or purpose of literature would be likely to interpret a complex play or poem very differently from the way in which a critic who held either of the other two views would do. On the surface it might be unclear what people who disagree (for example) about the correct analysis of the character of Shylock, in Shakespeare's play *The Merchant of Venice* are really disagreeing about. On this suggestion, the root of the disagreement might lie in sharp differences about the correct understanding of the point of valuing and interpreting art. A Marxist interpreter might be drawn to see Shylock as both oppressor and victim of Venetian capitalism. A Leavisite would be tempted to a more profound study that might emphasize, for example, the complexity of Shylock's relations with his daughter, Jessica. And a formalist might reject both views as too external, too little connected to the vocabulary, metaphor and other linguistic aspects of the play.

Now consider the most common form of interpretation: conversational interpretation. Philosophers have become puzzled about the following difficulty. It is impossible to understand what someone else is saying, what that person means, before you understand many other things about that person including, for example, what he believes and what he wants. Intentions, meanings, and beliefs are tied together in a system. How can the interpreters here today translate what I am saying into Japanese without knowing a great deal else about me? I say to you, "This is a glass of water." How do the translators know that I use the word "water" to refer to water, so that they should translate me by using the Japanese word for water? How do they know that "water" isn't just my own, perhaps cute or ironic, way of referring to vodka? They must be assuming, for example, that I think that what is in this glass (from which I have been drinking from time to time throughout the lecture) is water.

Now the puzzle is this. How can the translators decide what I think before they know what I mean by the words that I use? And how can they decide what I mean by those words until they know what I think? Philosophers led Donald Davidson, who built on the work of Williard Van Orman Quine, have proposed that we must think about beliefs, meanings and desires not one by one but as an interconnected system. We bring a variety of initial assumptions to any problem of translation, but our overall aim is to make overall sense of what the speaker is doing as well as saying. That is, we don't just translate sentence by sentence but we look to the person's entire behavior with the tentative assumption, at least, that the speaker is rational. So if I am giving a lecture and I drink from this glass, then if you assume I am rational, you might also assume that I wouldn't be drinking so much if I thought it was vodka. You are relying on that kind of evidence, as well as a thousand other assumptions about me, in order to translate my statement, "This is a glass of water." Any particular translation, you might say, is only the tip of the iceberg, because beneath the surface are thousands of other assumptions that contribute to making sense of the speaker's behavior as a whole.

I remind you of that problem in the philosophy of language, because I want to make the following claim. There are some occasions of personal interpretation in which our aim, our ambition, is not just like that. Ordinarily we try and make the most sense we can of someone's behavior to allow us to predict and mesh our lives with that person's. But on some occasions we add other requirements. Consider for example another interpretive occasion I mentioned earlier: psychoanalysis.

According to some students of psychoanalysis, doctors interpreting what a patient dreams or the jokes he tells or the linguistic mistakes he makes are not just trying to find an interpretation that helps explain the patient's behavior in the ordinary way. On this view, the doctor has a slightly different purpose: to find an explanation which will transform the patient's behavior – not simply explain it but transform it by supplying an explanation that the patient will internalize in such a way that the patient will be helped toward a cure. That is such a special purpose, on this view, that it justifies us in saying the point or purpose of the psychoanalytic interpretation of dreams or jokes is different from the point or purpose of conversational interpretation – of listeners trying to interpret a lecture in jurisprudence, for example. If so, then a jurisprudential critic would come to different conclusions about my intentions, in telling a certain joke in this lecture, than a doctor would in interpreting the same joke if I were her patient.

I have now supplied three examples, an example drawn from the law from literary criticism, and from the difference between psychoanalytic and conversational interpretation. These different examples are meant simply to illustrate the general thesis (and, I hope, suggest its power) that we must understand interpretation as tied to a practice and as governed by or sensitive to one's sense of the purpose, the telos, of that practice.

We may, finally, return to the beginning. You will remember that I mentioned a variety of objections to the interpretive account of jurisprudence that I summarized. The first objection was this. "You say that legal interpretation aims to make the best of the story so far, to make the best of a community's legal record. Whereas we say that interpretation means accurate reporting not rose-tinted-glasses reporting." Now, my answer is, "Interpretation is in principle purposive and, therefore, it is in principle an attempt to make the best of the object of interpretation." But that claim is easily misunderstood and that is why I included the second objection I mentioned.

The second objection (as you remember) argues that the interpretive method is a way of whitewashing, a way of making things look better than they should. Would you interpret the Holocaust in that way? But constructive interpretation aims to make the best of its object only in the special sense I described. It aims to make the best of it given the purpose or point of the general enterprise to which the occasion of interpretation arises. So consider the case of Hitler and Holocaust. That is historical interpretation. And the point of historical interpretation is rather similar to what I described as the normal point of conversational interpretation, that is, to provide a description of what happened that makes the most complete, coherent sense. We cannot entirely succeed in explaining the holocaust as the behavior of rational people. But still interpretation or historical interpretation requires us to do the best we can. And that means that we must attribute to the monsters who were in charge motives that make sense of what they did. And once we do this, then of course we are doing the best we can, given the purpose of this kind of interpretation. But the best we can means showing them for what they were, and that is as beasts.

Law is different. Why? Because the purpose of legal practice is not the explanatory purpose of historical interpretation. Lawyers are not trying to make their account of what happened the best possible explanation of the behavior of particular people. For one thing, the law we interpret is not the doing of any particular group of people. It is the doing of a society or a civilization over a long time, even centuries. So making the best of our legal tradition means something very different from making the best historical interpretation. It means, I think, making the law as just as we can. That is what accuracy means in legal interpretation.

I have said that we aim to make the object of interpretation the best it can be. But that is just a slogan summarizing the longer account I have now given you. It means making the best of it, given what we believe to be the right view of the point of the enterprise in question. Of course, as I said, lawyers will disagree about what it means, in detail, to make the law as just as it can be. Your own view will reflect your more concrete views about the purpose of the law, and also about what justice is. So, to go back to what I said earlier, if you think the purpose of law is certainty, then you make the law best by making it most certain. If you think as I do, that the point of law is to make our governance a governance of principle, then you will think making the best of it has a more substantive character. It means making it the best from the point of view of law's integrity.

Now, almost in closing, I take up the third of the three objections. The third objection is in a way the most powerful of the three, because, I think, it will seem right to many of you. It claims that interpretation, as I have explained it, is subjective, so that once we agree that law is a matter of interpretation it makes no sense to say, as I do, there is one best answer even in hard, disputed cases like Riggs v. Palmer and the Buick case. Interpretation depends too much on how things look from the particular point of view of the single interpreter to suppose that there is one best answer to the interpretive questions posed in those cases. Now, that is a deep objection and I am not going to explore it in full detail, you will be pleased to hear, this afternoon. But I do want to make some observations I believe pertinent.

First, once we understand the full range of interpretation, the full range of activities that have that interpretive character I have been trying to describe, then we will see that there are some theaters or departments of interpretation where we do naturally assume that there are right answers. One example is conversational interpretation. Your understanding what I say in a foreign language, indeed your understanding what each of you say to the others in your own language, is a much more complex matter than is commonly thought. Such understanding draws on many kinds of normative assumptions including assumptions about rationality. Yet most of us think that we get it right almost all the time. Now, of course, that is special. There are evident reasons why conversational interpretation has that character. I mention this only because I want to deny there is anything inherent in the enterprise of interpretation that makes it distinctly subjective.

My second observation is this. If my general account of interpretation has been correct, or anything close to correct, then whether interpretation is subjective or objective depends on the character of the underlying claims about the purpose of the enterprise. If I am right that interpretation in law is sensitive to one's view about the purpose of law, and the purpose of law has something to do with justice, then legal uncertainty is simply derivative from moral or political uncertainty. If we are skeptics about law, if we want to say, "Oh, there is no right answer in any really hard case," this must be because we are skeptics about political morality. If we think there is a right answer to questions of justice, then we will think there are right answers to questions of law, even the most complicated ones about which law professors and judges disagree.

That may seem a surprising point for me to make, because it is a very popular idea, particularly among American law students, that morality is subjective, that there is no truth or falsity about profound moral issues, that it is just a matter of opinion. I am going to say more about that question in other lectures in this series, and I will be discussing its impact on the work of the United States Supreme Court (for example, on the question of abortion) at the Tokyo Seminar at the American Center. For now, however, I want only to say this.

I have never met any student who actually believes the moral skepticism that students so commonly announce. I don't mean to say that students are hypocrites. But I do think that they often fail to understand the contradiction inherent in their position. Many of the people I have in mind say to me there is no right answer to these very difficult questions confronted by the Supreme Court, for example. I say, "Why is that?" And I explain about interpretation and how interpretation connects law and political morality. Then the students say to me, "Uh-huh, we told you so. Because now you say law depends on justice and everyone knows justice is just subjective." Then I say, "Do you have an opinion about the morality of abortion?" And every student has an opinion. Many of them say, "Abortion is murder." Most of them say, "Anti-abortion legislation is tyranny." I say, "Do you really believe those opinions?" They say, "Yes, I will march this afternoon carrying banners that proclaim them." I say, "But you say there is no right answer in matters of politics, it is just a matter of opinion." And they think and then they say, "Ah, but that is my opinion."

Well, the contradiction is evident, isn't it? It is certainly logically possible to take up a fully skeptical position about abortion, or any other matter of political or social justice. But then you have to give up your own opinion. And most people confronted with that choice will give up bad philosophy rather than intensely held convictions.

I am at the end. I won't bother you with much of a summary. I do want, however, because this is the first Kobe lecture and the Kobe lectures will be devoted to jurisprudence, to make a final reference to the subject. I have been emphasizing the contribution that philosophy – for example, the philosophical study of interpretation – can make to law. It is my view, in fact, that law is in large part philosophy. But I also hope – and this is more imperial – that these remarks might suggest the contribution jurisprudence can make to philosophy, and beyond philosophy to intellectual life in general. I said earlier that philosophers have insufficiently studied the phenomenon of interpretation. I believe interpretation is a very important subject, and that considering its character at a general level, though in much more subtlety and detail than I did, will illuminate very important issues in, for example, the study of art and literature. I also think that lawyers who work professionally with interpretation have a great deal to contribute to that general theory. Indeed, I go so far as to suggest that lawyers are better equipped than members of those other disciplines self-consciously to reflect on the nature and character of interpretation. But you will now be saying, "How like an American professor of jurisprudence to claim that his subject is at the center of the universe!"

So, I'd better stop. Thank you.

Author's Address(es): Professor Ronald Dworkin, University College, Oxford, 17 Chester Row, London SW 1, UK (January-July); New York University Law School, 40 Washington Square South, New York, N.Y. 10012, USA (August-Dezember)

[2]

Why Interpret?

JOSEPH RAZ*

Abstract. My article is about legal interpretation, but not about the question: how to interpret the law. Rather its aim is to make us consider seriously the question: Why is interpretation central to legal practices? After all not all normative practices assign interpretation such a central role. In this regard the law contrasts with morality. The reason for the contrast has to do with the status of sources in the law. There are no "moral sources" while legal sources are central to the law. Legal interpretation is primarily—I will suggest—the interpretation not of the law, but of its sources. To understand why interpretation is central to legal practices requires understanding the role of sources in the law: the reasons for having them, and hence also the ways in which they should be treated. I will show how reflections about these topics connect with some traditional jurisprudential puzzles, such as the relations between law and morality. Are there gaps in the law? Is the law or its interpretation objective or subjective?

I.

We—legal theorists—write a lot about interpretation. Mostly we inquire into the methods of interpretation used or to be used in law. But we do not often ask why interpret at all? You may think that interpretation is so deeply established in law that there is no point in raising the question. Interpretation is here to stay. That is indeed so, but it is an objection to the question only if it is understood as a sceptical question: Would it not be better if legal practices were not bound up with interpretation as they are? That, however, is not my question. Mine is a quest for understanding: What can we learn about the nature of law from the fact that interpretation plays such a crucial role in adjudication?

Let me mention five issues raised by the importance of interpretation in legal practice:

First, law is often compared to morality, and the relations between law and morality is one of the persistent puzzles which preoccupy legal philosophy.

---

* This is a slightly revised text of a talk to a plenary session of the IVR International Congress at Bologna, 1995. I am grateful to Jeremy Waldron, Kent Greenawalt, David Leebron, Jules Coleman and Liam Murphy for comments on a draft of this paper.

Interpretation[1] is not essential to morality or to our moral practices, but is essential to our legal practices. Why this difference? Can it illuminate in any way the question of the relations between the two?

Second, it has become a common tenet of our understanding of the law that it is meant to provide common standards for the guidance of the people of a political society. Political societies are societies in which acknowledged authorities are empowered to act for the society, and in particular to decide how the people in that society should behave in matters where there may be disagreements on principles or conflicts of interest among members of the society. This aspect of the law suggests that it typically consists of publicly proclaimed standards which are meant to be available to those subject to them so that they can be guided by them. But interpretation is possible only when the meaning of what is interpreted is not obvious. Therefore, if interpretation is central to the law it must be doubtful whether the law can be available to its subjects.

Third, some theories of law claim that the law is necessarily incomplete, that there are legal propositions which are neither true nor false. For example, according to these theories there are modes of conduct regarding which it is neither true nor false that they are lawful, and there are other gaps in the law, gaps regarding rights, status and so on. Theories which emphasise the incompleteness of the law usually argue that courts have a dual function: to apply law and to create new or revise old law.[2] The prevalence of interpretation, however, seems to belie this view. Interpretation straddles the divide between the identification of existing law and the creation of a new one. Where interpretation is concerned that distinction does not apply. Rather than sometimes identifying the law as it is and sometimes making new law the courts seem always to interpret it.

Fourth, just as the validity of the distinction between identifying existing law and making a new one is inconsistent with the role of interpretation so is the widespread belief that the law is necessarily incomplete. Were it incomplete the courts would not be able to decide cases by interpreting the law. In fact—so some claim—all cases can be decided by legal interpretation and therefore the law is complete.

Fifth, and last, contrary to the view of many who believe that while moral matters are perhaps subjective, the law is objective, the fact that what is law is a matter of interpretation shows—according to some—that, since any object of interpretation allows for multiple interpretations, the law is subjective, that law, like beauty, is in the eye of the beholder.

---

[1] Contrary to the suggestions of some writers. See Walzer 1987.
[2] Strictly speaking incompleteness of the law implies only that apart from their duty to apply law courts have also the duty to settle disputes not settled by law. It takes additional arguments to establish that the courts can also make new law, and a separate argument still to show that they have authority to revise existing law. But such arguments are commonly advanced by theorists who accept the incompleteness of the law.

These problems, and others like them, are not new. Various accounts of legal interpretation have been offered, each with its own solution to some of these problems. Some of these accounts may be true. It is quite likely that all of them contain some grains of truth. However, we cannot have confidence in any of them until we understand why interpretation is so central to the law, for only then will we be in a position to evaluate the different accounts of legal interpretation.

My aim here is the modest one of doing what I have started to do: to raise the question and convince you that it is a distinct question, not to be confused with the commonly discussed question of how should one interpret the law. As I've just said I do not believe that the question "How to interpret?" can be answered without an answer to the question "Why interpret?"

Legal theorists have tried to advance our understanding of legal interpretation by comparing it with interpretation in other spheres.[3] Such analogies can be very helpful in two respects: First, in exploring the nature of interpretation in general they help us avoid mistakes derived from assigning features specific to interpretation in one field to interpretation as such. Second, by comparing and contrasting interpretation in the law and elsewhere they help us understand what is specific to legal interpretation, the ways it differs from interpretation in other spheres. I too will draw analogies with interpretation in other fields, first to illustrate a few general features of interpretation and then to reflect on the special nature of legal interpretation.

II.

The general features of all interpretation which help understand how to deal with the question "Why interpret?" are trivially obvious: First, every interpretation is of an object. Second, there can be good and bad (or better and worse) interpretations. Some interpretations are correct or incorrect (rather than good or bad). The general point, however, stands: Interpretations can be objectively evaluated regarding their success as interpretations. Third, there can be competing yet good interpretations of the same object. Often what passes for several interpretations does not amount to an affirmation of interpretive pluralism. Several interpretations may illuminate several different aspects of the same work. For example, one may concentrate on the iconography of a painting, the other on its formal structure. Both can be integrated in a single more complete interpretation of the painting. Interpretive pluralism is manifested by the fact that several competing interpretations can all be good interpretations. For example, that both Glenn Gould's and Wilhelm Kempff's interpretations of Beethoven piano sonatas can be excellent. Fourth, interpretations are judged good or bad by their ability to make people understand the meaning of their object.

---

[3] Fish (1989) and Dworkin (1985) have been particularly influential in their use of analogies between law and literature.

I say that these features are trivially obvious even though some of them have been, and are being, keenly contested. Some people, for example, dispute that any interpretation can be truly said to be good or bad. They dispute that the success of interpretations is an objective matter. But features of concepts can be trivially obvious and in dispute at the same time. It is trivially obvious that the statements: "I now realise that I was wrong in thinking that Richter's is the best interpretation of Liszt's Sonata in B-minor. In fact Brendel's is better," are meaningful English statements. It is trivial—in other words—that it is part and parcel of the practice which constitutes the concept of interpretation that the success of interpretations is an objective matter. Those who dispute the objectivity of interpretations do not, or at any rate should not, deny that. As an analysis or description of the practice of interpretation their denial of the objectivity of interpretation flies in the face of obvious features of our practice. But it may be right, and it certainly should be taken seriously as a denial of the very possibility of our practice. Of course in a sense the practice exists, we interpret and we judge interpretations to be more or less successful. But for our practice to make sense and to have a point it has to be coherent, and its presuppositions have to be true. Claims that interpretations are not, and cannot be, objective challenge either the coherence or the presuppositions of our practice, and claim that the practice of interpretation cannot really make sense, or cannot really have a point unless it is changed to be a practice of subjective opinions: unless the practice we now have, which understands interpretations as objective, is reformed.[4]

It has to be admitted that the reforming nature of some philosophical accounts is not always clear. Some are motivated by a global, metaphysical world view, for example, by some form of physicalism. In trying to impose that picture on various philosophical issues, like that of the nature of interpretation, they sometimes vacillate between attempts to understand the phenomena in light of their metaphysical picture, claiming that the phenomena readily fit their picture and need no reinterpretation (such claims being sometimes accompanied by blindness to the very basic features of our practices), and claims that our concepts need reforming to conform to some allegedly true metaphysical doctrine; and there are other variants on these themes. For example, the objectivity of interpretation is sometimes challenged not in the cause of reforming our practices, but in denial that our practices treat interpretation as objective. Such denials are sometimes based on gross misunderstandings of our practices (e.g., equating statements like "Brendel's interpretation is better than Richter's" with "I (the speaker) like Brendel's performance better than Richter's").

[4] Some may claim that they do not challenge our practice, rather that our understanding of the practice is their target. But that is a mistake. The practice includes commonplace observations like "How can you say that the film is about the condition of modernity? It is pure entertainment and nothing more." This is what it is for it to be an objective practice, i.e., a practice which admits of judgements of the success of interpretations, and regards them as either true or false.

Sometimes, however, philosophical denials of truisms like the four I mentioned are motivated by suspicion that claims that interpretation is "objective" are not mere reports of aspects of our practices (e.g., that it is possible to like Richter's recording better than Brendel's, yet think that Brendel's is the better interpretation, or that considerations which may force one to admit that one was mistaken in judging Richter's to be the better interpretation may have no bearing on the correctness of the assertion that one likes his performance better). Philosophers sometimes suspect talk of objectivity to be deeply committed to a metaphysical picture which they reject, and therefore they deny that interpretation is, or can be, objective, not minding one way or another whether our practices establish its objectivity. As these remarks make plain I have little sympathy with this philosophical temperament. Metaphysical pictures are, when useful at all, illuminating summaries of central aspects of our practices. They are, in other words, accountable to our practices, rather than our practices being accountable to them.

I do not deny that some of our concepts may be incoherent. But while dogmatic conceptual conservatism is misguided, moderate conceptual conservatism is in place. Moderate conservatism postulates for any concept a presumption that that concept is coherent. In this article I will proceed on the basis of that presumption, and will find no reason to think that it is rebutted in the case of "interpretation."

In itself moderate conceptual conservatism does not resolve the tensions between various aspects of our concepts. And these tensions are the main difficulty in our attempt to develop an account of interpretation as a coherent activity. Particularly troubling is the tension between the objectivity of interpretation and interpretive pluralism, given the last of the mentioned features, namely that interpretations are judged by their success in elucidating or illuminating the meaning of their object.

Why should the fact that there can be several good interpretations of the same object be thought to be in tension with the objectivity of interpretation? There is no conflict or tension between pluralism and objectivity as such. There is, for example, no conflict between the existence of a plurality of distinct values and their objectivity. The conflict results from the fact that an interpretation is good only if it illuminates the meaning of its object. But as the meaning of the object is one how can there be many good yet competing interpretations? If interpretations are subjective then the problem does not arise. In that case the meaning is in the eye of the beholder, and anything goes.

III.

The way out of this *impasse*, the way to reconcile the existence of a multiplicity of competing interpretations with objectivity turns on the point which is often put metaphorically by saying that "the meaning of the object is not in the object." The helpful suggestion in the metaphor is this: If interpretation depends in part on something outside its object then possibly there are a plurality of such additional objects, and they will account for the plurality of good interpretations. Subjectivism, with its claim that any interpretation goes is but one extreme way of understanding the metaphor. According to it the way an interpreter sees the object of interpretation at any time, as expressed in the interpretation, *determines* its meaning. That is why all interpretations are equally good. But the metaphor itself allows for more sensible accounts which identify other factors as those which in part determine the meanings of objects, and thus their proper interpretations.

This having been said I cannot but add that the metaphorical contrast between the internal and the external has often been the grave of good sense. First, there are those who take it to be an explanation rather than an obscure picture in need of an explanation. Second, sometimes the element "external" to the object, and relevant to its interpretation, is said to be the conventions of interpretation or of meaning prevailing among one group of people or another.

The triumphalism which often accompanies this suggestion, and the implication that conventions were overlooked in pre-post-modern analysis is somewhat surprising. Since the decline of magic no one has ever doubted the dependence of language and other carriers of meaning on conventions. But in any case this suggestion would not do for it misconceives the relations between meaning and conventions of meaning. The existence of conventions of meaning in a certain population indicates that they all regard the same things as having the same meaning. Such conventions are necessary for communication, and indirectly they are necessary for anything to have meaning at all. But conventions are not grounds justifying one interpretation rather than another. Admittedly we can correctly say that "sister" means female sibling, and add that everyone understands "sister" to mean female sibling. That everyone so understands it *shows* that this is its right meaning but it is not *a reason* for it being the right meaning.

Contrast, the following interpretive exchange about Shaw's play *Pygmalion*:

Interpreter: It is a play about transformations, and especially about the transformation of Eliza from a wild teenager into a mature woman.

Sceptic: Why do you say that? Why not prefer a more romantic interpretation?

Interpreter: Because my interpretation makes better sense of the relationship between Higgins and Eliza.

Here the reason supporting the interpretation "it makes better sense of a relationship between two characters"—assuming for the sake of argument that it is a good reason, and adequate to its task—not only shows that this is a good interpretation of the play. It not only points to a presupposition of this being the meaning of the play, it explains what makes it the meaning.

And it makes it intelligible that it is the meaning of the play. It is what I'll call a constitutive reason: the facts which make the interpretation correct, and therefore the facts the understanding of which (whether conscious or not) enables one to understand the interpretation. *Since interpretations are successful to the extent that they illuminate the meaning of their objects they should be supported by constitutive reasons which show how they do so.*

Though time will not allow exploring the matter, this web of precepts: that interpretation is of *meaning*, that it not only establishes what the meaning is, but makes it transparent, that is *intelligible*, and that therefore interpretation is backed by *constitutive* reasons—marks the kind of interpretation we are interested in, the kind of interpretation which advances understanding and which is the special repository of art criticism, the humanities and the social sciences. *For so far as we know there is meaning in the world only where it was invested with meaning by human beings.*

This fact probably accounts for the tenacity of the view that interpretation consists in retrieving the author's or the agent's intention. For if interpretation is of meaning and meaning is the result of human agency does it not follow that it is the result of human intentions and therefore that the successful retrieval of those intentions is the mark of a good interpretation? As we know this inference is invalid. Intentional action creates more (as well as—quite often—less) than is intended. What counts is what we express in our actions, and what the products of our actions express.

Shifting from talking of the meaning of actions, practices or their products to what they express does not solve the puzzles of interpretation. However, since what we express is not necessarily what we mean to express it shows at least one way in which the meaning of what we do is not exhausted by what we intend it to mean. Yet from a broader perspective concentration on what actions or their products express commits the same fallacy that the intentionalist is guilty of. Both understand interpretation as a process of retrieving the meaning invested in the object by its creator.

Subjectivists by contrast stand at the other extreme. In holding that meaning is in the eye of the beholder they regard the receiver rather than the creator as the sole origin of meaning. Common sense suggests that both are wrong. The anthropocentric aspect of meaning and interpretation means that they are responsive to facts about human nature, as historically constituted, and to human interests. Neither of these are under the voluntary control of anyone.

So here is my summary preliminary statement of the key to interpretation: *An interpretation successfully illuminates the meaning of its object to the degree that it responds to whatever reasons there are for paying attention to its object as a thing of its kind.* This summary statement requires much careful unpacking, too long to undertake here. I will, however, return to it and modify it at the end of this article.

Think, by way of illustrating my point, of different reasons people may have, or believe they have, for understanding history. Some may view it as divinely ordained, and may study it to understand God's message to Man as it reveals itself in history. Others may believe it to be deterministically dictated by physical/biological/economic factors and they may turn to history in order to predict the future. Others still may be interested in history as a repository of stories and characters they can identify with, regarding history as the font of their own identity. It seems plausible to suppose that these different reasons for historical interest: to understand God's message to man, to predict the future and to make/discover one's own identity—it is plausible to suppose that these reasons will lead to somewhat divergent interpretations of various historical events and processes. Hence pluralism.

I am not using this example as an argument for pluralism. It is merely an illustration of the way different reasons for paying attention to history would lead to different interpretations of history. Hence it is no objection that it is unlikely that all three reasons I mentioned are valid ones. It is possible for them to be good reasons, and they may be valid simultaneously. This is all one needs to be able to use them—as I did—to illustrate the way a diversity of reasons can lead to interpretive pluralism, which is, of course, entirely consistent with the objectivity of interpretation: Reasons in general, and interpretive reasons are no exception, are objective factors, about which we can be right or wrong.

There are other ways in which the dependence of interpretation on reasons for paying attention to its object leads to interpretive pluralism. Given any single reason for paying attention to the object of interpretation there may be several different interpretations which satisfy the reason in some way and to some degree so that none of them is better than any of the others. This is another topic it is impossible to explore further here.

IV.

With these general remarks in mind we can turn to the issues of legal interpretation. Interpretive pluralism understood by reference to the variety of reasons people have to be interested in the object of interpretation offers not only the possibility of a plurality of interpretations of any one object in any of the areas where interpretation is a central mode of understanding: law, the arts, sociology and history in particular. It also opens the possibility that there are reasons which determine the nature of interpretation in one of them and are alien to the others. What then can we say about the reasons for the centrality of interpretation to legal reasoning?

Clearly there are *prima facie* reasons to think that they differ from the typical reasons which prevail in other areas. While law is like art in that typically it is made to be interpreted,[5] history, again typically, is not made to be interpreted.[6] This helps explain how the reasons for historical interpretation differ from reasons for artistic interpretation. Works of art can be created specifically in order to provide an object for the exercise of interpretive imagination. It would be a bizarre motive for a person to perform an act of historical interest with the sole aim that it be the object of interpretive imagination. In this respect law is of course like history and unlike art. There are other fairly obvious ways in which legal interpretation differs from art interpretation. It may be a matter of the taste of a particular period, but at least in some cultures novelty in art interpretation is valued in itself. The great interpreters are—other things being equal—those who can make us see the work interpreted in a new light. Think of Peter Sellars' interpretation of *The Magic Flute* set under a spaghetti junction in Los Angeles, or Jonathan Miller's *Rigoletto* set in Chicago in the 1920s. The very fact that we can talk of Sellars' *Magic Flute*, or Miller's *Rigoletto* makes the point. There is no analogy for this in law.

In legal interpretation we value—other things being equal—continuity. We also value authority, legal development and equity.[7] Continuity, authority, legal development and equity provide the four *foci* of legal interpretation. But it is continuity and authority which hold the key to the question of my article, to the question "why interpret?" and in reflecting on them we may come closer to an understanding of the issues to which the question gives rise.

There is little need to belabour the role of authority in the law. The law is an *institutionalised* normative system, and in being institutionalised it is based on recognising the authority of institutions to make, apply and enforce laws.

Is not continuity merely a by-product of the legal role of authorities? Not at all. The importance of continuity in the law is manifested most of all by two central features. First is the fact that legislation and precedents remain binding long after their authors lost power. The life of the law is not bounded by the life of the law makers. This endows the law with a considerable measure of continuity. Second, there is the role of legal doctrine. Legal doctrine provides a glue which binds different legal regulations together. It

---

[5] See on the relations between art and its interpretation Raz (1995). Cf. also Danto (1981, 1986). For example, in the latter book Danto observes that "indiscernible objects become quite different and distinct works of art by dint of distinct and different interpretations, so I shall think of interpretations as functions which transform material objects into works of art" (Danto 1986, 39).
[6] Some historical events are caused with the intention that they will be understood in certain ways by some people: members of the government, those eligible to vote in the next general election, workers in manufacturing industries, etc. But few are caused with the intention that they will be interpreted in certain ways by the general public, now and in the future. When this happens we say—usually disapprovingly—things like: "The president is now concerned only with his place in history."
[7] I am using "equity" in a narrow sense to refer to considerations which affect the way rules are applied in particular circumstances, sanctioning deviations from "the letter of the rules," which are not meant to lead to a modification or development of the rule.

smoothes and polishes the law, regularises what would otherwise be deviant, irregular aspects of legislation or precedents. Of course, these features are no barrier to legal upheaval in countries which undergo fast political change or suffer political instability.

What the law is, and how stable it is, are ultimately contingent on the circumstances of the country concerned. But these two features which in one form or another are present in all legal systems create a systematic bias in favour of continuity which is inherent in the law. They also show how continuity transcends and conflicts with authority: The first point shows how continuity extends the life of laws beyond the period during which they are to be respected through respect for the authority which issued them. The second point, the role of doctrine, shows how continuity can conflict with the power of legal authorities, and set limits to it.

These observations point to the inherent importance of continuity and authority in the law. They do not justify their importance, nor do they explain the function they perform. Nor do they show why they rather than legal development and equity help explain why so much legal reasoning is interpretive. To do all of that it is necessary to reflect on the essential role of the law in society—in as much as it is capable of being ethically justified. There can be no doubt that it is inherent in law that it aims to be ethically justified, and that every legal system claims to be by and large ethically justified. Since to understand the law we must understand the way the law understands itself, that is the way its officials and others who accept its legitimacy understand it, we must understand it as it would be understood by people who see it as ethically justified, at least in the sense that it is ethically right to obey it,[8] and therefore we must understand it as if it were so justified.

It follows that a general theory of legal interpretation, that is a theory which claims general validity, and is not merely an account of interpretation in one country or one family of countries, is necessarily based on the assumption that the law is justified, at least in the sense that it is justified to obey it. Its application depends on the assumption being correct, which it may not be. In that sense there is no theory of interpretation which is strictly speaking universal. The universal theory of interpretation is not a theory of how to interpret all law in any legal system. Rather, it is a theory of the interpretation of justified law only.

Can there be a general theory of legal interpretation, even one confined to justified legal systems? To be sure, the specific goals pursued by the law of any country are many and diverse, and that remains the case even if we restrict our concern to ethically justified systems only. But diverse as they are they share certain general characteristics: I hope that you will bear with me if I venture to offer a very brief and simplified sketch of a couple of points which emerge from this line of exploration.

---

[8] One may consistently believe that it is morally justified to obey a law which is morally defective, and in need of reform.

First, all the measures adopted by law are measures which at the time and place at which the laws which embrace them were made were right for the law to embrace, or at least it is justified to treat them as if this condition is satisfied. If the condition is not satisfied then the laws embracing these measures will not be justified or it would not be justified to obey them (i.e., to treat them in practice as if they are justified, i.e., as one would treat laws which are justified), as we assume that it is. This condition means that— other things being equal—the justification for treating laws as valid derives from the authority of their makers. The laws pursuing the goals should be understood in a way which accurately reflects the intentions of the lawmakers in making them. The reasoning behind this principle is simple: The very notion of practical authority is that of a person or body deliberately deciding how things should be done. The normal justification of authority assumes that people are better able to conform to reason by following the decisions made by the authority. It follows that the law laid down by authority is that it meant to lay down, the law it intended.

Second, while the initial validity of a law normally derives from the authority of its maker this cannot explain its continued existence beyond the point where that authority's rule runs. Take a law made at the beginning of this century. No account of legitimate authority can yield the conclusion that we are now subject to the authority of the long defunct maker of that law. Yet the law it made may well still be valid, and following it may be ethically justified. I suspect that the considerations which account for this fact include the ethical importance of continuity. Continuity is ethically welcome for a variety of reasons, one being the need to provide people with common standards for the guidance of the members of the political society. This requires that the standards be relatively stable.

V.

This thumbnail sketch, oversimplified as it is, is I think along the right lines and helps in seeing the role of our question "why interpret?" in an account of interpretation. Interpretation is of an object and is in place when there is reason to be attached to the object. When it comes to the law, that is to morally legitimate law, the thumbnail sketch shows that that reason is the *moral respect* we owe to the object of interpretation. This is not the general reason for interpretation: The reasons for our concern with the interpretation of history, and with the meaning of historical events are not due to respect for history. Nor is art interpretation motivated by *moral* respect for works of art. In as much as legal reasoning is interpretive it is so because of moral respect for the law, and for its sources.

Authority and continuity: The two factors which explain the reasons for the importance of interpretation are systematically related: To the extent that the law arises out of respect for legitimate authority legal reasoning must establish the law as laid down by authority, that is it must rest on an interpretation of the decisions of legal authorities which accord with the intentions of those authorities. To the extent that the law arises out of the need to secure continuity legal decisions are binding even when their authors no longer have authority. The content of these decisions is established by interpreting them as they were interpreted when the reasons for paying them attention were based on respect for the authorities which took them.

Authority and continuity provide the key to the question why interpret and as such they also guide us in how to interpret: We should interpret in ways responsive to the reasons we have for interpreting. But there are—as I have already indicated—other factors which though they provide no help with the question "why interpret?" are crucial to the question "how should we interpret?" These are the role of the courts in the development of law and equity.

Since to be justified the law must be just to the people it is applied to, equity has an inescapable separate role in the application and enforcement of the law. Just as justice requires the presence of a relatively stable framework of familiar principles by which individual and social life are governed, so it requires that the application of the principles to specific cases should be mediated by equity, to make sure that no injustice results from their application. For it is impossible to have general rules the application of which may not on occasion lead to injustice if not mitigated by equity. Equity is not always manifested through interpretive reasoning. Jury decisions in common law jurisdiction, which are rendered without making their reasons public, are an example of a mechanism which allows for the operation of equity, allowing it to take place not through interpretation.[9] However, equity can also be manifested in the way courts or others interpret authoritative decisions when confronted by the specific circumstances of a case litigated before them.

The moral need for equity to inform interpretation, combined with the tendency of institutions to develop routines, i.e., to develop a common law—broadly understood—generate the fourth major factor fashioning interpretation: the role of courts in the development of the law. Here too, just as with equity, different jurisdictions have different traditions regarding the ways the courts contribute to the development of the law. But that they have such a role is pretty universal.

The need to consider changing and developing the law to improve it, to adapt it to changing conditions, and to do justice to the litigants in the case before the court is a major influence on the way the law is interpreted. It is not, however, part of the answer to the question "why interpret?" On the

---

[9] Juries are expected to reason about the law, even though their reasoning is not made public. This means that in discharging their duties they do interpret the law. However, the absence of a requirement to make their reasons public enables them to rely on considerations of equity outside an interpretative framework.

contrary. So far as that question is concerned considerations of equity and the role of the courts in developing the law are considerations which militate against assigning interpretation a major role in legal reasoning. In themselves they would suggest that legal reasoning in the courts should have the same character as legislative reasoning. If these considerations were the dominant considerations dictating the character of judicial reasoning then it would have been the same as the reasoning on which legislation in parliaments or subsidiary legislative agency is based.

This point is worth pondering. It illustrates how the question "why interpret?" is distinct, and should not be confused with the question "how should we interpret?" It shows how factors which play a major role in determining the character of legal interpretation: equity and the role of the courts in developing the law, play no role in explaining why interpret. The reasons for conducting so much of legal reasoning as an interpretive reasoning are respect for authority, and the case for continuity, and especially the first. The need for continuity plays a similar role in legislative reasoning, without giving it interpretive character. It is only in combination with the courts' respect for authority that it supports interpretive reasoning.

So the factors which determine the character of legal interpretation divide into two: authority and continuity which provide the reason for interpretation as well as contributing to the determination of its character, and equity and the development of the law which in themselves are no reason to interpret at all, but given that we have reason to interpret they contribute to the determination of its character. Moreover, the two types of factors are forever in conflict: Authority and continuity militate towards a broadly speaking conservative attitude in interpretation, equity and legal development—towards an innovatory attitude. This tension—in one form or another—is typical of all interpretation. Understanding it, and its sources, is at the centre of understanding what makes interpretation what it is.

VI.

The conflict between the conservative and the innovatory factors in legal interpretation takes us back to some issues left behind earlier in this article. First, my preliminary statement of the nature of successful interpretation (see page 355 above) was cast in terms of the reasons one has for paying attention to the object of interpretation as a thing of its kind. It may seem that this characterisation leaves no room for any considerations to govern the conduct of interpretation which are not also reasons for interpreting in the first place. According to this understanding one cannot maintain that equity and legal development are reasons which guide the interpretation of the law while denying that they provide reasons for interpreting the law.

I think that both the objector and I are correct on this matter. We simply need a further distinction to reconcile the two opposing claims. Given that authority and continuity provide reason to pay attention to the law, equity and legal development become additional reasons to pay it attention in a certain way, or in the light of certain considerations. They are secondary reasons for interpreting the law, dependent on the primary reasons, in that had there not been the primary reasons which determine the need to interpret the law, the secondary reasons would not have been reasons for interpreting it at all. But given that there are primary reasons for interpretation, they attract, or generate, additional, secondary reasons for interpretation. My earlier characterisation of a successful interpretation refers to all the reasons for paying attention to the object of interpretation, be they primary or secondary. In the discussion of legal interpretation, however, I drew the distinction between the conservative reasons which motivate interpretation in the first place, and the innovatory reasons which are secondary reasons for interpretation.

The conflict between the two groups of consideration takes us back also to the five issues about the nature of law with which I started, and to which I will briefly return in these concluding remarks. The dependence of law on authority explains why much of legal reasoning is interpretive, whereas moral reasoning is not. Morality is not based on authority. The dependence on authority leads to the need to interpret the decisions of authority and that is the basic object of legal interpretation. The other factors I mentioned: continuity, equity and legal development, are all factors in the interpretation of authoritative acts and decisions. One often neglected question is what is legal interpretation an interpretation of? Is it an interpretation of the law, of legal texts, or legal acts? No doubt all of these are subject to interpretation on one occasion or another, and no doubt often it does not matter which is being interpreted. But some clarity is gained by being clear as to what is the primary object of legal interpretation. If authority and continuity provide the answer to the question "why interpret?" then the decisions of legal authorities are the primary objects, and through interpreting them we gain understanding of the content of the law, which they create.

This reveals what some would regard as a paradox: If legal reasoning establishes what the law is by interpreting authoritative decisions, this can only mean that its purpose is to reveal the intention of the authorities which took these decisions. It follows that there is no room in legal interpretation for equity or for considerations of legal development. This apparent paradox accounts for some misguided theories of law: Some emphasise the innovatory aspect of interpretation and—under the influence of moral subjectivism —tend towards subjectivist pluralism in their understanding of law. Others, restrict legal interpretation to its conservative elements, which are usually crudely understood in theories such as originalism. Others still, realising rightly that interpretation is neither wholly conservative nor wholly innovative deny that the distinction between identifying existing law and creating a new one is coherent, or that it plays a central role in the functioning of courts of law. But no one has succeeded in offering an account of interpretation which does not rely—openly or surreptitiously—on that distinction in explaining legal interpretation. Nor can such an account be found. The distinction between identifying the law and changing it is basic to the law, and central to any coherent understanding of judicial decision-making. It is equally important to realise that both aspects—the conservative and the innovatory—are present in legal interpretation just as they are present in the interpretation of *Hamlet*, or of *Don Giovanni*. It is equally crucial to understand that the two elements introduce a tension into the factors which direct judicial decisions, a tension which expresses itself in the problems I mentioned at the outset: How can the law form a stable guide for people's actions if it is subject to innovatory interpretation? How can there be a fact of the matter as to what the law is if there can be a plurality of valid interpretation?

These are good questions which require carefully balanced answers. The question arises out of the fundamental conflict in legal interpretation I have diagnosed. Their answers lie in recognising the inescapability of this conflict in the law. It arises from the fact that due to the basic nature of human societies law and adjudication must fulfil several functions, and therefore even an ideal law cannot fulfil all of them in an ideal fashion.

Balliol College
Oxford
OX1 3BJ
United Kingdom

References

Danto, A. 1981. *The Transfiguration of the Commonplace*. Cambridge, Mass.: Harvard University Press.
———. 1986. *The Philosophical Disenfranchisement of Art*. New York: Columbia University Press.
Dworkin, R. 1985. How law is like literature. In R. Dworkin, *A Matter of Principle*. Cambridge, Mass.: Harvard University Press.
Fish, S. 1989. *Doing What Comes Naturally*. Durham, NC.: Duke University Press.
Raz, J. 1995. Interpretation without Retrieval. In *Law and Interpretation: Essays in Legal Philosophy*. Ed. A. Marmor. Oxford: Clarendon.
Walzer, M. 1987. *Interpretation and Social Criticism*. Cambridge, Mass.: Harvard University Press.

Part II
Interpretation and Legal Reasoning: Law and Morality

[3]

LAW AS PRACTICAL REASON

M. J. Detmold[*]

Law is practical. Legal reasoning is practical reasoning. We could make nothing of a judge who having listened to counsel's arguments and reflected about the law governing his case thought that the state of knowledge that he had achieved was the natural termination of his enterprise and submitted his conclusions to the editors of Halsbury's Laws of England rather than performed the action of giving judgment. The parties would be outraged, and rightly. And if the judge continued to do such a thing he would be dismissed. Legal reasoning is practical in the sense that its natural conclusion is an action (in the judge's case the action of giving judgment) rather than a state of knowledge. This is taking "practical" in a strong sense. By this definition thought is practical whose natural conclusion is an action (or decision against action): its strongest contrast is with theoretical thought whose natural conclusion is knowledge. But it also contrasts with hypothetical thought about action (say, my thinking it would be good to play cricket again). I do not call this practical because it does not conclude in an action or decision against action (others do; for example John Finnis in *Fundamentals of Ethics*[1]; my reasons for differing in this matter will emerge). A judge's practical reasoning towards the action of giving judgment has priority for our understanding of law over that vast range of practically idle things that lawyers do, from the construction of digests like Halsbury to casual reflection about the rule in Shelley's case (of course there is one sort of doing involved in both these, but not legal doing). It is important here to be clear about this priority. It is a priority of practicality, not a priority of judges or lawyers.

Joseph Raz has pointed out that:

> there is something inherently implausible in adopting the lawyers' perspective as one's fundamental methodological stance. There is no doubting the importance of the legal profession and of the judicial system in society. It is entirely appropriate to make them the object of a separate study and to regard legal theory as that study. It is, however, unreasonable to study such institutions exclusively from the lawyers' perspective. Their importance in

[*] Reader-in-Law, University of Adelaide.
[1] Oxford, 1983.

society results from their interaction with other social institutions and their centrality in the wider context of society. The law is of interest to students of society generally, and legal philosophy, especially when it inquires into the nature of law, must stand back from the lawyers' perspective, not in order to disregard it, but in order to examine lawyers and courts in their location in the wider perspective of social organisation and political institutions generally.[2]

But an analytical priority given to what judges (and attendant lawyers) do is justifiable not as the priority of judges in the philosophical analysis of law but as the priority of practicality. Sociology is theory not practice (except in the Marxist way that what we think about the world changes the world); that is, sociology is reasoning that contemplates no particular action (except an occasional rather distant one such as joining a political party to change a theoretically revealed evil). It is obvious that sociology itself as theory must accord priority to practice: if those humans it studies are not doing what it says they are doing it fails in its own terms. And if it is a difficult and philosophically contestable thing to say what humans are doing (even to say what humans think they are doing) then so much the worse for sociology.[3] But Raz is right to see something wrong in a court-centred legal theory. Law is for citizens before judges (judges are for citizens, not citizens for judges) and there is something very wrong in a theory which overlooks this. One of my purposes in this essay is to show how the practicality of judging (by judges) connects necessarily to the practical judgment[4] of the particular citizens concerned. With this connexion the practicality of legal reasoning becomes the whole practicality of law in society. In the first part I examine the place of reason in law; in the second the essential particularity of practical reasoning; in the third, I draw both together to offer a theory of the practicality of law.

I Reason and Law

Law is a certain sort of practical reason. Coke's exceedingly controversial words in *Dr Bonham's* case[5] propose a relation between reason and law:

> The common law will control acts of parliament, and sometimes adjudge them to be utterly void: for when an act of parliament is against common right and reason, or repugnant, or impossible

---

[2] "The Problem about the Nature of Law" (1983) 31 U. of Western Ontario L.R. 202 at 211–212.
[3] See my *The Unity of Law and Morality* (London, 1984) pp. 37–38.
[4] This connexion makes it difficult (I think impossible) to accommodate the conventional spelling distinction between judgment (of judges) and judgement; so I abandon it.
[5] 8 Co. Rep. 107a at 117b–118b.

to be performed, the common law will control it, and adjudge such act to be void.

But between reason and law there is a very complex relation. When a judge determines the law to be such-and-such he does so by reason; but the reason is different in different cases. In order to begin to understand the relation between reason and law it is necessary to identify and distinguish four types of law-determining process:

1. The decision of particular cases according to law or right. Such decisions are never just the automatic application of a pre-existing norm to the particular case. They have an element of creativity in them which justifies us in regarding them as a type of law-determining process. We shall call this first type *the adjudicatory process*.

2. The giving of an advisory statement as to some general proposition of law or right. This may be for purposes of confirmation, exhortation, warning, or simple advice. It may be substantive, as when a penalty is increased, the better to exhort and warn. It may simply be informative advice. Or it may be to forestall some of the inconveniences of necessarily retrospective adjudication. The Supreme Court of Canada has this latter power in relation to constitutional law; and it has been mooted as a power for the High Court of Australia, where it has been held to be a non-judicial power.[6] It should be noted that the declaratory judgment of administrative law is not usually a case of this sort of law-determination, since it is usually the adjudication of a particular case and clearly judicial. We call this quasi-legislative type of law-determination *the advisory process*.

3. The explanation, exposition, particularisation, interpretation or amplification of some pre-existing law or right. This process spells out the detail of or enlarges upon the meaning of pre-existing law or right. It is a more creative process than simple advice which might just reproduce undisputed law; and is really a sub-legislative function. It must also be distinguished from adjudicative "interpretation". It is common to say that modern courts exercise an interpretative function in respect of Acts of Parliament. But what they do is really adjudication. Adjudication is the decision of particular cases. This is not the same thing at all as the sub-legislative interpretation of a term in a law. Suppose there is a law referring to motor vehicles. This covers the class of motor vehicles. An interpretation of the term, say, to include motor cycles preserves the same logical character. What we can now say is that the law covers, *inter alia*, the class of motorcycles. There is as yet no adjudication; just sub-legislative interpretation. No matter how highly we define the term (say: vehicles with

---

[6] *In re the Judiciary and Navigation Acts*, (1921) 29 C.L.R. 257.

characteristics a, b, c, . . . n) we still have a class, the class of vehicles with characteristics, a, b, c . . . n, and not yet a case of adjudication. Adjudication is the application of the class of the law (however finely defined) to a particular case; to pursue our example, the decision that a particular contraption is or is not close enough to the central case to be called "vehicle with characteristics a, b, c . . . n". We may suppose that a b c . . . n is the ultimate refinement of definition (of course no single human life would be long enough to construct this refinement); there still remains the question of the application of the defined class to the particular (later in this essay we call this question the particularity void). It is common to call the process of refining a definition particularisation; but actually this is a corruption of the term, for the most highly refined definition is still universal (a, b, c . . . n are all universal properties and relations): there is a radical logical difference between the most highly defined set of universals and a particular case; a radical difference between interpretation and the crossing of the particularity void (as we shall put it). Adjudication is the decision of the particular case, and it contrasts radically with the (sub-legislative) progressive definition of a term in a law. In the modern common-law legal systems there are no strong examples of the sub-legislative interpretative process, but it is occasionally to be found in what the courts do, and perhaps in certain types of delegated legislation. It is not common for the courts to interpret in this sub-legislative way, though it perhaps appears to be so. Meaning *is use*, not some mental entity established prior to use; so that when a court applies, say, the statutory term of our example, "motor vehicle", to a particular contraption the meaning of "motor vehicle" is found only in its application or use.[7] Occasionally a court might make a sub-legislative interpretation of a term (say that "motor vehicle" means *inter alia* "motor cycle"). In which case the term it applies in its adjudication (the term it uses) would be "motor cycle" or "motor-vehicle-including-motor-cycle". Such a thing is not as common as it seems; and is obiter dicta anyway, since all that was necessary for the decision was the application of the word "motor vehicle" to the particular contraption. If this last point is thought strange, think what the case would be like if it concerned the first motor cycle ever constructed, when no word for the contraption was yet in the language. There is now no possibility of sub-legislative interpretation, but the case is no different: it is now as always the case of the application (by adjudication) of "motor vehicle" to the particular contraption. Despite the current thoroughly glib use of the word

---

[7] This Wittgensteinian idea I have developed in *Courts and Administrators* (London, 1989). See particularly pp. 69–73.

"interpretation" to describe the courts' adjudicative application of Acts of Parliament, there is no better word for the true sub-legislative type, and so we shall call this sub-legislative type *the interpretative process*.

4. The making of novel law. The first three processes are creative processes. But they determine the law essentially from some sort of pre-existing base in law or right. Where there is no such base, or where the base is irrelevant to the process, we have what we shall call *the legislative process*. Something very fundamental occurs when a legal system admits legislation in this sense. To apply, advise about, or interpret pre-existing law or right is justified simply in reason: the fact that pre-existing law or right is not self-executing is sufficient rationally to require these processes. But legislation is strictly novel with no necessary rational relationship to prior law at all. The King coming under law in English constitutional history was a denial of his legislative power (the assertion of *common*, that is pre-existing, law); but the English Revolution was two revolutions, and this very denial of the King's power brought the establishment in the Parliament of legislative power in the fullest sense. What is the justification for so revolutionary a thing? This is *the* fundamental question of political philosophy, and we shall offer no answer to it except to say that in a democracy part of the answer is that legislation is justified as an expression of the will of the people. Certainly, the contrast between legislation and our first three types of law-determination is the fundamental contrast in political philosophy between will and reason. But even with the strongest example of the legislative process, the modern Act of Parliament, there is a tendency to its corruption. For example, some Australian Parliaments have repealed the common law doctrine that courts searching for the meaning of a statute (*i.e.*, how to apply it) should not look to Hansard or parliamentary papers.[8] The common law doctrine is of course precisely consistent with the idea that legislation is a pure act of will. On the new conception whereby we look at Hansard, what do we say is the legislation, statute or Hansard? Some may think that the Members' speeches and attached papers are interpretations of Parliament's legislation. Perhaps occasionally they are that; but most often the statute is the expression of the reasons that led to it; that is, it would be truer to say that the statute is an interpretation of those reasons. So which is legislation and which interpretation? We only have the legislation of Parliament (as opposed to the hopelessly vague idea of the informal legislation of occasional ministers and of the bureaucrats who write their papers) if the statute is the base point, *i.e.* absolute in itself

---

[8] For example, the (Victorian) Interpretation of Legislation Act 1984, s.35.

(though subject to subsequent processes including judicial ones). Now, we should not underrate the extent to which the Westminster constitutional systems have been corrupted to the position that the lawmakers are actually the departments of state. But I suppose the more palatable account of the idea behind the Australian repeals is to say that Hansard and the papers are to be aids to judicial law application. This is confused. For the question is, which law is it that is to be applied? The tendency of the Australian repeals is to degrade the purely legislative process of Parliament to the third of our law-determining processes, whereby an Act becomes in part a sub-legislative interpretation of a prior base, namely ministers' speeches and attached papers.

Now, the first three of these types of law-determining process are processes of reason in the sense that reason is intrinsic to them; and they contrast with the fourth legislative type which is a process of will having no reason intrinsic to it. This point is best explained by looking at the fourth type first.

The point is not that the legislative process has no relationship to reason. We may, of course, presume that legislators make their legislation for reasons. And secondly, their act of will is to be accepted or recognised only in so far as it is (legally) reasonable to do so (constitutional law is this process of legal reason). But this double relationship to reason is extrinsic to the act of will. When we look at a modern Act of Parliament we see nothing but a set of absolute norms (this is the sense in which the Australian repeals of the Hansard–excluding rule are a corruption of legislation). The thing itself is a pure act of will: there is no reason intrinsic to it. By contrast when we look at modern precedent decisions of courts we may see what can at first glance look like a similar set of absolute norms. But by the common law theory of precedent the norm of a precedent is tied rationally to the facts of its case. Thus if a new set of facts arises which is rationally distinguishable from the precedent facts the norm of the precedent is not applied, *notwithstanding that by its (normative) terms it is applicable.* A simple illustration of this is the following: suppose that the norm that we find in *Donoghue* v. *Stevenson* is "persons are liable for their negligence to their neighbours". When the case of a barrister arises the norm is not simply applied, *though as a norm it is applicable* (a barrister is a person, his client a neighbour). Since the case of a barrister is rationally distinguishable from the case of a manufacturer, *Donoghue* v. *Stevenson* is distinguished. Its norm is taken with reason intrinsic. A statutory norm on the other hand is tied to no particular set of facts. Thus there would be no question of distinguishing the case of the barrister if the above-stated norm had been enacted in a statute. If the norm is in its terms applicable it must be applied unless there is a question as to its validity. And though the judgment of validity is a matter of reason, it is extrinsic to the norm. This distinction between extrinsic and intrinsic reason is fundamental to any conception of law as practical reason.

Reason is not so obviously intrinsic to the advisory and interpretative processes as it is to the adjudicative. One problem is that the result of an advice or an interpretation may look like simple legislation. Suppose there is legislation:

A: No motor vehicle shall be taken into a park,

and the following interpretation is given of it:

B: No motor car or motor cycle shall be taken into a park.

Or suppose that norm A is for some reason obscure, controversial, or not well-known, and that the following is offered as an advisory opinion:

C. No motor vehicle shall be taken into a park.

The trouble with both B and C is that they take the same form as A (and C looks identical). They might have been enacted in the first place by Parliament as A was. Instead of enacting A, Parliament might simply have enacted B. But these looks are deceptive. This enacted B is logically a quite different thing from B as an act of interpretation. The difference is simply that the latter is only explicable as an act of interpretation by virtue of a *rational* (interpretative) relationship to A. And its derivative and rationally dependent constitutional status would follow. If A were later discovered to be not what was thought, the necessity in reason to amend B immediately follows: this is the sense in which reason is intrinsic to B, the process of interpretation. And it will be obvious that a similar analysis applies to the advisory process. If an advice is given (C) as to A and A is subsequently found to be different from what was thought the reason intrinsic in C requires its amendment.

To revert now to Coke's theory, which as a theory of the relation between reason and law is a theory of intrinsic reason. But first a word of explanation about our four categories of law-determination. Perhaps there is a temptation to say that only adjudication and legislation are of fundamental importance in the modern common-law legal systems (the courts, we have seen, generally do not advise or sub-legislatively interpret). But to say such a thing would be a strong example of a distorting court-centred jurisprudence; excluding from primary concern the extraordinarily important case of a solicitor's advice to his client. Anyway, all four law-determining processes are necessary to provide a complete conceptual basis for the analysis of Coke's theory. Now, Coke's theory. There is proposed by him a relation between reason and law (law being something that has been determined by one or more of the law-determining processes). It is obvious that the relation of reason to something intrinsically reasonful (we cannot say "reasonable", because that implies a favourable recommendation) is different from its relation to something which is not. The law-determining process with which Coke's reflections are concerned is that of Parliament. So, the first question must concern the nature of Parliament's law-determining in Coke's time. If it is intrinsically reasonful there will be much care needed in translating Cokes' theories about the relation between reason and law to the modern Act of Parliament. For that, we have seen, is not an intrinsically reasonful thing.

In *The High Court of Parliament and its Supremacy*,[9] C. H. McIlwain proposed the following theses:

> (a) England after the Norman Conquest was a feudal state, *i.e.*, its political character is better expressed by the word feudal than by the word national. (b) As a consequence, her central assembly was a feudal assembly, with the general characteristics of feudal assemblies. (c) One of those characteristics was the absence of law-*making*. The law was declared rather than made. (d) The law which existed and was thus declared was a body of custom which in time grew to be looked upon as a law fundamental. Rules inconsistent with this fundamental law were void. Such a law was recognised in England down to modern times. (e) Another characteristic of the times was the absence of a division of labour between different "departments" of government and the lack of any clear corresponding distinctions in governmental activity, as "legislative", "judicial", or "administrative". (f) Parliament, the highest "court" of the Realm, in common with the lower courts, participated in these general functions of government. It both "legislated" and "adjudicated", but until modern times no clear distinction was perceived between these two kinds of activity, and the former being for long relatively the less important, we may say roughly that Parliament was more a court than a legislature, while the ordinary courts had functions now properly called legislative as well as judicial. (g) "Acts" of Parliament were thus analogous to judgements in the inferior court, and such acts were naturally not treated by the judges in these courts as inviolable rules *made* by an external omnipotent legislative assembly, but rather as judgements of another court, which might be, and were at times, treated as no modern statute would ever be treated by the courts to-day.

Declared law is law determined in one or more of our first three types of process (McIlwain's book is full of examples of all three).

---

[9] Yale, 1910, pp. vii–viii.

The idea of declaration implies logically some pre-existing source, which is the distinguishing-mark of our first three types: McIlwain's contrast between declared law and made law (our fourth type) is clear enough (though we must be careful with it: our first three types of law-determination make law, too—they make it with a relation of reason to some pre-existing source). Its function of declaring law rather than making it in a completely novel way makes the medieval parliament, McIlwain argued, more like a court than a modern legislature. In particular, we can say, all its determinations are to be taken as intrinsically reasonful.

The argument is clearly established. Indeed it was anticipated by a number of scholars including Jenks, as J. W. Gough shows.[10] There is scholarly contest at the edges of the argument. For instance, McIlwain maintained that it was at the time of the civil war that Parliament first clearly undertook a law-making role; but Jenks disagreed, holding that the critical first steps towards that role were taken by the Reformation Parliament in the time of Henry VIII, a view which McIlwain later accepted.[11] And there is contest as to when it can be said that Parliament's modern exclusively legislative (fourth type) role was established. On this matter Maitland argued that it was not until the 19th century that Parliament gave up governing particularly (adjudication) in favour of the (legislative) laying down of general rules.[12] And Gough replied that Maitland had forgotten that the 19th century Parliament was very much concerned with saying what (particular) railways should be built.[13] But the evidence for McIlwain's central thesis is beyond doubt. Our question is what is the implication of this for Coke's conception of the relation between reason and law?

A crude interpretation of Coke's theory is to see it as a forerunner of the modern American doctrine of judicial review. Gough, quite rightly, refutes this interpretation;[14] and also refutes the implication of the same in McIlwain's *The High Court of Parliament* (an implication not easily attributable to McIlwain himself). "Americans", Gough writes:

> approach the English seventeenth century with a different bias. They are familiar with the principle of a limited legislature, and disposed to regard the idea of fundamental law, embodied in the American Constitution, as one of the most precious safeguards of political history. Hence, so far from belittling or seeking to explain away the references to fundamental law with which they

---

[10] *Fundamental Law in English Constitutional History* (Oxford, 1955) p. 5.
[11] *Constitutionalism Ancient and Modern*, 2nd edn (Cornell, 1947) p. 170–178.
[12] *Constitutional History of England* (Cambridge, 1908) p. 382ff.
[13] *Op. cit.*, note 10 at p. 24.
[14] *Ibid.*, chapters 1–3.

meet in studying the seventeenth century, they are apt to greet them with enthusiasm, sometimes misplaced, as forerunners of their own constitutional principles.[15]

The reason that Coke is no forerunner of Marshall is simply that there is a radical difference between the questions that each had to face. When Coke thought of an Act of Parliament he thought of it as something to which reason was intrinsic, that is as an example of one or all of our first three processes, but not the fourth (we should say thought of it primarily as that: for it had begun the process of transformation into a legislature of our pure fourth type). That was its logical status, and to the extent that it failed to be reasonable relative to its prior base it failed to be what it purported to be (void or null for what it purported to be; just as a judicial precedent in modern times is liable to be overruled or not followed (void or null) by virtue of its lack of reason). For Marshall on the other hand an Act of Congress was purely legislative, and when it failed (as when it was unconstitutional) it failed in extrinsic constitutional reason: it did not fail in what it purported to be, namely, a pure act of will. The difference between the two things is substantive as well as logical, and may be represented by the following pair of norms:

A. Accept what is reasonable.
B. Accept what it is reasonable to accept.

Since it is obvious that it is often reasonable to accept something unreasonable (reasonable to say that an unreasonable statute is nevertheless constitutional) it is obvious that there is a quite fundamental difference between Coke's doctrine (A) and judicial review (B); between intrinsic and extrinsic reason.

Gough does not appear clearly to understand this difference. He writes:

> How, then, does Professor McIlwain's theory stand in the light of what we have seen? I think we must, in the first place, dismiss the notion that law was only declared and not made. This may have been true of the early Middle Ages, but in the later Middle Ages, or in Tudor times, it was certainly no longer so. It remains true that parliament often, perhaps generally, continued to be thought of as primarily a court, and this may have impeded the recognition of the fact that it was at the same time becoming more and more of a legislature,[16]

and he is here thinking in terms of our fourth (legislative) type of law-determination, where the question of reason is extrinsic. But the distinction between declaring and making is too stark: our first three

---
[15] *Ibid.*, p 3.
[16] *Ibid.*, p. 27.

types of law-determination are cases of making as well as declaring (making reasonably if intrinsic reason holds a place, as it does in Coke's doctrine). Gough's failure to see his way right through the problem emerges in what he says about one of his principal examples of early law making, the Statute of Uses (1536). Of the analysis of that statute which Montague CJ offered in *Wimbish* v. *Taillebois*[17] Gough writes:

> Yet strained and unnatural though Montague's interpretation seems to us, there was obviously no question of the court trying to set aside the Statute of Uses, or pronounce it void for contradicting common 'law' or reason.[18]

The implication here is that there is a fundamental opposition between what Montague did and Coke's idea of voidness. But they are complementary parts of the same doctrine of intrinsic reason. Montague's interpretation of the statute is actually a strong example of the approach to something intrinsically reasonful. It would have been flatly contrary to the reason of the middle ages for an act of parliament to expropriate property (property was sacrosanct in reason). So the statute could not have been seen as that. Montague sees it in this way:

> When the statute of 27 H.8 was made, it gave the land to them that had the use. And, sir, the Parliament (which is nothing but a court) may not be adjudged the donor. For what the Parliament did was only a conveyance of the land from one to another, and a conveyance by Parliament does not make the Parliament donor; but it seems to me that the feoffees to uses shall be the donors, for when a gift is made by Parliament, every person in the realm is privy to it, and assents to it, but yet the thing shall pass from him that has the most right and authority to give it. . . . So here it shall be said the gift of the feoffees by Parliament, and the assent and confirmation of all others. For if it should be adjudged the gift of any other, then the Parliament would do a wrong to the feoffees in taking a thing away from them, and making another the donor of it. . . . And here the land is by act of Parliament removed from the owners, that is to say the feoffees, to the *cestuy que use*, and the statute would do wrong if it should not adjudge them the donors, for they have the greatest authority to give it, and the Parliament is only a conveyance, and therefore it shall be adjudged the gift of the feoffees by Parliament. . . .[19]

Prior law for Montague and for all English judges up to his time was not just the common law but it included natural reason (right) and

---

[7] I Plowden, 38.
[18] *Op. cit.*, note 10 at p. 27.
[19] *Op. cit.*, note 17 at p. 59.

the law of God. In *Partridge* v. *Strange & Croker*,[20] we find him saying the following (of another statute, 32 H8 C9):

> This statute was made in affirmance of the common law, and not in alteration of it, and all that the statute hath done is, it has added a greater penalty to that which was contrary to the common law before. . . . For to construe the statute that he, who is in possession, shall not make a lease . . . except he had been in possession . . . for a year before, would be a hard law, and contrary to all reason and equity: and such an exposition of the statute was never intended by the makers of it. . . . And that which law and reason allows shall be taken to be in force against the words of statutes.

Natural reason and the law of God ordained the sanctity of property. Thus it was necessary to see the Statute of Uses (and 32 H8 C9) as a *reasonable* working out of that prior state. And this is what Montague did when he said that the Statute of Uses was a conveyance. Now this (the conveyance process) is not quite like any one of our first three law-determining processes (perhaps we should see it as a fourth type), but it clearly shares with them the same logical character: it is an expression or working out of some prior right or law, and that character is intrinsic to it. Had Montague not been able to see it as that, then it would have failed to achieve the status it sought and Coke's idea of voidness would have come into play.

One of Coke's own examples is instructive here: he cited various precedents in *Dr Bonham*'s case, one of which was *Thomas Tregor*'s case from the eighth year of Edward III:

> And therefore in 8E. 3.30 a.b. Thomas Tregor's case on the Statute of W.2.c.38 & *artic. super chartas*, c.9. Herle saith, some statutes are made against law and right, which those who made them perceiving, would not put them into execution.[21]

It is a strange thing in our constitutional history that there should be so many trivial interpretations (both conceptual and political) of such as Coke, a jurist both profound and courageous. One of them is Pollock's interpretation of the passage on *Tregor's* case:

> plenty of modern statutes have been inoperative in practice, not because the common law controlled them, but because they were in fact unworkable.[22]

Now, it is true that Coke interpolated in his quotation from Herle the words "against law and right"; but it is also clear, as McIlwain shows,[23] that he did not regard this as changing their sense. So what is the sense of the words? McIlwain gets close:

---
[20] 1 Plowden, 77 at p. 88.
[21] *Supra* note 5 at p. 118a.
[22] *First Book of Jurisprudence*, 5th ed (London 1923) p. 266n.
[23] *Op. cit.*, note 9 at p. 288.

One very striking thing about the whole case is the fact that Coke is apparently citing these words of Herle—"There are some Statutes made which *he himself who made them* does not will to put into effect"—as proof of the power of the *judges* to disregard the statute concerning the college of physicians which was under discussion in Bonham's Case. What possible relation can there be between the opinions of the *judges* and the opinions and desires that *the makers of the law* begin to entertain subsequent to the passage of the Act? . . . When Herle says that the *makers* of the statutes often will not to enforce them, is it certain, as is usually assumed, that he means the *"legislature"* exclusively? Is it not possible that Coke was as nearly right when he cited the statement to prove the right of the *courts* to review "legislation"? But would it not be still nearer to the truth to say, in view of the close relations of judges and Parliament, of the fusion of functions judicial and legislative which we have found in both the High Court of Parliament and the inferior courts, and above all in view of the manifest absence of any clear distinction between a judgement and a law, between judicature and legislation, in the time of Edward III,—in view of all this, would it not be better to say that Herle would probably have considered an alteration of a statute by a subsequent statute, and a modification of it, or even a refusal to enforce it, by the *courts*; as actions not essentially different in character?[24]

The judicial process is a process of intrinsic reason. And so, at the time, in the way we have been arguing, was the process of Parliament. Hence the identity between court and Parliament that McIlwain finds. Coke's words ("those who made them perceiving, would not put into execution") actually express the point more perspicuously than McIlwain's. A person does not will the conclusion of a process of reason about prior right except in so far as it is reasonable. When its lack of reason appears the will supporting the conclusion slips away and the prior right reasserts itself. And it is thus with the old parliaments. Their statutes obtain to the extent of their intrinsically reasonful relation to prior law and right. Perhaps we who are familiar with the wholesale legislative overturning of old ideas, find it hard to understand this. But this is because we are familiar with Parliament *the legislator*. The nearest that we have to the old idea in the law these days is when a judge talks of an earlier judge as "going too far" or "speaking incautiously" or "per incuriam". The point is not to say that the judge has willed something which later reason holds void; it is that the perceived unreasonableness limits what is willed.

The most common trivial interpretation of Coke's words in *Dr Bonham*'s case is that he was merely expressing ordinary principles

---

[24] *Ibid.*, pp. 289–291.

of statutory interpretation. So held C. K. Allen[25] and Gough[26]; and Holdsworth wrote of the cases relied on by Coke that they were:

> decisions that the courts will ... interpret statutes *stricti juris* ... that is, so as to give them a meaning in accordance with established principle ... These are principles of interpretation which would be accepted at the present day.[27]

But it is literally possible for a proposition with meaning to be null as an expression of reason (as an expression of something to which reason is intrinsic). For example, the law "all judges shall give judgment standing on their heads" is meaningful but null in point of intrinsic reason. Whereas in the modern matter of the interpretation of purely legislative acts (adjudicative interpretation: as we have seen, the word "interpretation" is used loosely in that context), if a statutory proposition is meaningful there is a quite early point beyond which interpretation cannot go and remain interpretation. How far could the judges strike *by interpretation* at the just-stated law? And for another example, if Dicey's famous statute requiring the execution of blue-eyed babies were held to apply only to babies whose whole eyes were blue (that is, to none), though it might be pretended that that was interpretation, it would not be. In truth, it would be a simple case of extrinsic reason (judicial review) refusing to recognise the statute; that is, holding it to be invalid; and concealing the fact. And that also is quite different from the nullity of an intrinsically reasonful act. The difference we shall express again.

A. Refuse to accept what is unreasonable (Coke).

B. Refuse to accept what it is unreasonable to accept (judicial review).

It is well-known that Coke also said of the power and jurisdiction of Parliament that it was:

> so transcendent and absolute as it cannot be confined for cause or persons within any bounds.[28]

There are trivial political explanations for what is conceived to be an inconsistency between this passage and the other doctrines of Coke that we have been discussing in this section (for example, Holdsworth[29]). But there is no such inconsistency. There is no inconsistency between the absolute finality of a court's settlement of the particular case it adjudicates and the non-final, non-absolute

---

[25] *Law in the Making*, 4th edn (Oxford 1946) p. 369.
[26] *Op. cit.*, note 10 at p. 355.
[27] Holdsworth, *History of English Law*, ii, p. 443.
[28] 4 Inst, cap 1, 36.
[29] *History of English Law*, iv, pp. 186–187.

intrinsic reasonfulness of the general pronouncements it makes in the course of that settlement. Nor is there any suggestion that the absoluteness of a particular adjudicative settlement has any connexion to the absoluteness of a modern Act of Parliament (true legislation). McIlwain[30] and Gough[31] are subtler. The jurisdiction of Parliament was absolute for Coke (they held) in the indisputable fact that it was the highest and final court: it could not be "confined" by any further proceeding. Such a doctrine only applies to Parliament's adjudication, its settlement of single cases. Obviously when the Parliamentary process in question is interpretative or advisory (our second and third types) there is possible any number of further proceedings; but when a single case is settled by the adjudication of the highest court there is nothing further in the legal system. Gough gives an apt example. Coke writes of the attainder of Thomas Cromwell:

> And albeit I find an attainder by parliament of a subject of high treason being committed to the tower, and forth-coming to be heard, and yet never called to answer in any of the Houses of Parliament, although I question not the power of the Parliament, for without question the attainder standeth of force in law: yet this I say of the manner of the proceeding, *Auferat oblivio, si potest; si non, utcunque silentium tegat*: for the more high and absolute the jurisdiction of the Court is, the more just and honourable it ought to be in the proceeding, and to give example of justice to inferior Courts.[32]

Now, this takes us to the fundamental point of constitutional law. The jurisdiction of the highest *court* is necessarily self-validating. If an administrator claims jurisdiction over me I can argue in a court that he does not have it: his decision is not self-validating. However, if the highest court makes a decision over me there is no place for me to argue that that decision is beyond jurisdiction. That is the meaning of the common law proposition that the superior courts have a self-validating jurisdictional power.[33] And it is this ultimate jurisdictional power in the old parliaments that Coke is talking about in this matter of absolute and transcendent jurisdiction. The attainder of Thomas Cromwell settled his case finally. But general utterances in the course of that settlement, perhaps interpretations of prior law and right, would be, like the general utterances of the modern superior courts, and the other general (universal) things that the old parliaments laid down, intrinsically reasonful in their relation to pre-existing law and right, not final and absolute. This is the sense in

---

[30] *Op. cit.*, note 9 at p. 129.
[31] *Op. cit.*, note 10 at pp. 42–43.
[32] 4 Inst, cap 1, 37.
[33] *Scott* v. *Bennet* (1871) L.R. 5 H.L. 234. This remarkable case and its doctrine of the ultimacy of adjudication is discussed extensively in *op. cit.*, note 7.

which the true successors of the old parliaments are the superior courts. But we have to be careful in this comparison: the superior courts are not, as the old parliaments were, in the process of becoming legislatures in the true sense (or are they? but with what democratic justification?).

Parliament was a court. Parliament is now a legislature. The (Diceyan) doctrine of the omnipotence of Parliament is based upon a fundamental failure to understand history. It is a simple *non sequitur* to reason from the ultimacy of an intrinsically reasonful process (with all the qualifications that that particular nature implies) to the ultimacy of a purely legislative process. That latter ultimacy denies reason altogether: reason is neither intrinsic nor allowed to hold extrinsically. When history transformed Parliament from an intrinsically reasonful court to a legislature that point was overlooked; that is to say, the (rational) necessity to replace the lost intrinsic reason with extrinsic reason was overlooked. These points could hardly be clearer than they are in Willes J's well-known words in *Lee v. Bude & Torrington Railway*:[34]

> Acts of Parliament . . . are the law of this land; and we do not sit here as a court of appeal from Parliament.

Of course not! We must distinguish again:

A. Accept (from Parliament) what is reasonable.
B. Accept (from Parliament) what it is reasonable to accept.

Only if the courts acted on the intrinsically reasonful A would they presume to be a court of appeal from Parliament. Appeal is concerned with rightness or reasonableness (in administrative law it is contrasted with review on this very point). Only A raises the rightness or reasonableness of Parliament's Acts. The extrinsically reasonful B is a different matter entirely: it is obviously often reasonable to accept unreasonable legislation. The fact that Willes J. found it necessary to deny A but not necessary to deny B shows that the idea of extrinsic reason (what it is reasonable *to accept*) entirely eluded him. The (Diceyan) doctrine that whatever Parliament enacts is the law is nothing; neither history (for it has not caught up with the history that transformed Parliament from a case of intrinsic reason to extrinsic) nor reason (for intrinsic reason has been lost and no extrinsic reason has replaced it).

Many philosophers of law overlook the difference between A and B. One of them is Joseph Raz. In "The Problem About the Nature of Law", Raz argues that the "inclination to identify the

---

[34] (1871) L.R. 6 C.P. 576 at p. 582.

theory of law with a theory of adjudication and legal considerations with all those appropriate for courts is based on a short-sighted doctrine overlooking the connection of law with the distinction between executive and deliberative considerations."[35] He accepts that courts make their decisions on the basis of both moral and legal considerations. But that very fact, he says, shows that it is wrong to take a theory of adjudication to be a theory of law; a theory of law must at least distinguish between these legal and moral considerations. The distinction for Raz turns upon the concept of an "authoritative positivist consideration". The need for this concept in a theory of law:

> is clearly seen by contemplating its negation. There are forms of arbitration in which the arbitrator is instructed merely to judge the merits of the case and to issue a just judgment, without being bound to follow any authoritative positivist standard. We can imagine a purely moral adjudication taking the same form. Positivist considerations are those the existence and content of which can be ascertained without resort to moral argument. Statutes and precedents are positivist considerations whereas the moral principles of justice are not. A moral adjudicator will rely in his deliberation on the existence of positivist standards but he is not bound to regard them as authoritative. But one does not have a court of law unless it is bound to take as authoritative some positivist standards such as custom, legislation or precedent.[36]

It is true that if there were no considerations that judges were bound to take as authoritative without moral test they would not be judges in law but simply moral adjudicators. And Raz is surely also right to hold that the point of having, say, a legislature in the first place is to settle something. If legislation did not in some way settle the question it addressed, the community would in truth have no legislation, for it would in its institutions still be deliberating the legislative question (the community would be just like a person who could never make up his mind: Raz draws heavily upon analogy with personal decision). The point is presented by Raz as one of "paramount importance to social organisation,"[37] and it is, but it is perhaps even stronger than that. It may be logical. Just as in the case of a man who never made up his mind we would be logically precluded from saying he had made a decision, so for a community which redeliberated legislative questions we would be logically precluded from saying any legislation (any law) existed (and does not this logical point prove the case for legal positivism?).

But Raz mistakes the question that legislation settles. Suppose a

---
[35] *Supra* note 2 at p. 217.
[36] *Ibid.*, at pp. 213–214.
[37] *Ibid.*, at p. 216.

statute is passed: Where A, B and C, persons shall do X. By moral deliberation this statute settles the question implicit in what it says, should all persons do X where A, B and C? Raz says:

> Since law belongs to the executive [*i.e.* non-deliberative] stage it can be identified without resort to moral arguments, which by definition belong to the deliberative stage.[38]

This does not follow at all. The legislature has decided that all persons shall do X. And this must be accepted without resort to further moral argument. But the only court that would fail here would be a court that acted on:

A: Apply only what is reasonable.

The true principle of judicial action in relation to true legislation (our fourth type of law-determination) is, we have seen,

B: Apply only what it is reasonable *to apply*.

And this second principle preserves the sense of legislation in a community. There is, consistent with it, a legislative question which has been settled, namely, what is reasonable. There is no question of redeliberating that question. But what it is reasonable to apply has not been decided by the legislature and cannot be decided. This is so even if our legislation is taken to contain a second norm:

All persons shall do X and all courts shall apply this first norm.

We may accept that the legislature has now deliberated upon and decided: first, that the first norm is reasonable, and, second, that it is reasonable to apply the first norm. But not a third thing, that it is reasonable to apply the second norm. The question that remains is whether it is reasonable to apply the second norm. And so on. Nor is the issue avoided if the second or any subsequent norm is self-referring. There would remain the question whether the now self-referring whole entity is to be accepted. This is just as the question whether the Cretan is a liar remains unresolved—no matter how much we believe him—by the Cretan's statement "I am a liar." No matter how much we believe him: no matter how much respect we give to Parliament. The point is a logical one: no respect can be given to a decision that has not been made.

The distinction between what it is reasonable to legislate and what legislation it is reasonable to apply obtains even in a legal system in which the courts judge it reasonable (right, required, the law) to apply any legislation at all (as Dicey believed was the case with the legal system of the United Kingdom). The question of application is,

---

[38] *Ibid.* at p. 217.

even in such legal systems, a distinct, logically required, question which the courts and not the legislature answer (affirmatively, so it is said, every time).

If we think again of Raz's comparison with personal decision the importance of the difference between A and B will become apparent. I make a decision to go to Nottingham, Raz supposes (this is one of his examples of personal decision). For that decision to subsist it must be the case that I do not reconsider it (though I may actively consider subsidiary questions such as where to stay and so on). This analogy is very misleading for there is out of account in the sphere of personal decision just what it is that makes it important in law to distinguish A and B, legislation and adjudication. I decide to go to Nottingham and I can immediately set about executing that decision because there is no question but that it is *my* decision. What if it were your decision to go to Nottingham. Of course *I* wouldn't go! Nor even if it were your decision that it is reasonable that everyone go to Nottingham. And even if it were your decision that *I* go to Nottingham I wouldn't go unless there were some mediation connecting your decision to me: I am not your slave. There are various things in the personal sphere (a contract, for example) which might provide that mediation. In law the mediation is adjudicated upon and completed by the courts. Our contract under which you claim I must go to Nottingham if you direct me would be adjudicated upon by a court, and if against me I must go to Nottingham. The whole law of contract bears witness to the distinction between A and B: the court decides upon the *application* of contracts (B: Apply what contracts it is reasonable *to apply*); not whether what they stipulate is reasonable (A: Apply what contracts are reasonable) (though there are obviously some minor qualifications to this). The application of statutes is similar. The statute of our example has (reasonably) decided: where A B C, persons shall do X. This might just be your decision (yours and certain other citizens), just like your decision to send me to Nottingham. It might be a reasonable statute, and even if not it can be accepted as having decided what is reasonable (total respect for what it *does* decide). But for me to do X requires some particular connexion of me to the statute (some mediation as in the contract case). Thus B rather than A. Reasonable *application* to me rather than reasonableness. A and B can be distinguished on the ground that they are simply different questions governed by different reasons.[39] But the fundamental distinction now seems to be that a particular connexion to me is necessary before any norm can justly

---

[39] *Op. cit.* note 3 at pp. 251–259.

be applied to me. The reasonableness of the norm (A) is no warrant for B. The distinction between A and B is fundamental to freedom.

It is also fundamental in the practicality of law. Where law is seen as essentially theoretical, *i.e.* as something to be known, the distinction between A and B gets no hold. Something known is the law regardless of whether it might be assessed in point of reasonableness or in point of whether it should be applied to a particular person. When law is seen as practical there is raised a question of practical reason. A particular action is contemplated and the question is one of reason about that action (B . . . reasonable *to apply*). By contrast, A, though it mentions the action ("*apply* what is reasonable"), raises no question of practical reason about it. It is this action and the accurate focusing of reason upon it that raises the distinction between A and B. A theoretical view of law (some versions of legal positivism) has seemed attractive in the interests of freedom; for one's freedom appears to be the greater when the law is something to be known prior to action (thus, it is thought, we can calculate clearly and act the more freely). This always has been the most plausible argument for any legal positivism. But the great destructions of freedom (all the fascisms) are built upon a denial of the distinction between A and B: humans are conscripted or obliterated in the service of what is reasonable (what glory or destiny the tyrant or state holds reasonable); whereas it is states that are conscripted in the case of what it is reasonable to apply to citizens (for then they are accountable to their citizens' rights).[40]

II THE PARTICULARITY OF ADJUDICATION

My deciding to go to Nottingham is one thing. Your deciding it in respect of me is another. And yet another is whether it is reasonable for anyone (or all) to go there. This last is not practical until the determination of the will of at least one person is effected or at least contemplated. It is universal and not practical; whereas the first two are particular and practical (the first connecting to my action in going to Nottingham; the second to yours in, say, forcing me to go). What is the connexion between these things? How does a universal decision become practical?

Suppose I am seeking to acquire judicial office by exam. I am given a problem to solve consisting of facts A B and C. I work it out and conclude, the defendant must pay damages. My conclusion is universal: *a* defendant in circumstances A B and C must pay damages.

---

[40] *Op. cit.*, note 7, where the argument is that the proper function of the courts in administrative law is to preserve citizens' rights against the state, because individuals' rights (which determine *particular* applications of law) are absolute against the state.

But am I right? I check my reasoning and conclude I am right. I finish the exam, content. But being rather introspective, I go to my books after the exam to make sure. Yes, the defendant must pay damages. I am sure. I am now sure that I have an answer to the (universal) question: where A B C must the defendant pay damages? But it is not a practical answer. My will is not determined to any action, for there is no particular A B or C, nor any (particular) defendant to act against. Some would say that my conclusion was theoretical. This is not strictly true because it is a practical sort of question that I have considered (it is not a question of mere knowledge): it is better to say my conclusion is hypothetical. My answer will become practical when it becomes particular. But is this just a matter of waiting until a particular comes along which fits my universal judgment?

I was right. I pass the exam, am appointed, and my first case turns out to be exactly the case of my exam: A B and C are proved and the plaintiff seeks damages. Let us in this (philosophical) analysis hurry over all the pleading, proof and argument to the point where I sit alone in my chambers and commence to contemplate judgment. Where A B C the defendant must pay damages. I know this is right. I have done that reasoning. What more is there? Is not my will coiled appropriately, ready to be unleashed? Yes. But what is required to unleash it? Why does it not just unleash itself? The six weeks or so between my exam and the case are nothing (in another case, D E F, suppose I work out my judgment and it is six weeks before I give it; bewigged and berobed, I sit myself in the place of judgment and notwithstanding the six weeks delay my will does just unleash itself). But not here. What is it that gives me pause in the A B C case? It is not that I doubt my conclusion. I remember my reasoning very clearly. It is not that I wish to go off to Halsbury to see if there is something I've overlooked (though I might do that, stalling for time). I know I've overlooked nothing. It is just that I now have a radically different problem. A particular, practical problem, which universal hypothetical (theoretical) reasoning does not solve. And the whole problem is that no reasoning can solve it. It is particular, about which nothing can be said (anything I *say* will be universal). I am strictly at a loss, and if I keep on thinking I will give no judgment at all. This moment of indecision (a whole realm) is a recurring theme in literature. Think of Hamlet, whose inaction was tragic (true to an unconsoling, unanswering world) not a simple flaw in character. Think of the confrontation between Pierre and Davoût in *War and Peace*. The moment of indecision is what saved Pierre from being shot as a Russian spy on Davoût's orders (Russian spy=A B C; so the relevant rule of action, for Davoût is, execute where A B C):

> Davoût looked up and gazed intently at him. For some seconds they looked at one another, and that look saved Pierre. Apart from conditions of war and law [A B C] that look established human relations between the two men. At that moment an immense number of things passed dimly through both their minds, and they realized they were both children of humanity and were brothers.
>
> *War and Peace* Book XII, Ch X

I, the judge, and Davoût, at the moment of practicality entered the unanswering void of particularity, the realm of love, about which only mystical, poetic things can be said (children of humanity, and such like); or nothing (Hamlet: "the rest is silence"). Judges enter this realm every day (if they only knew).

Before proceeding I wish to recall the question of Finnis's wider definition of practicality in *Fundamentals of Ethics*. Finnis includes hypothetical practical thought (terminating in practical knowledge) in his conception of practical as well as thought terminating in action (or a decision against action). With this definition he excludes the particularity void. Thus he says:

> [A certain] argument would work *in just the same way* if the question were not hypothetical but required of you a choice here and now . . .; thus its being hypothetical does not remove its radically practical character.[41]

Of course the matter is not just a definitional one: Finnis has deep reasons for this, which we shall later discuss. In part I we identified two problems of particularity: the adjudication of particular cases (the crossing of the particularity void, as we now call it) and the greater refinement in definition of a certain class. Hart said:

> Different legal systems, or the same system at different times, may either ignore or acknowledge more or less explicitly such a need for the further exercise of choice in the application of general rules to particular cases. The vice known to legal theory as formalism or conceptualism consists in an attitude to verbally formulated rules which both seeks to disguise and to minimize the need for such choice, once the general rule has been laid down. One way of doing this is to freeze the meaning of the rule so that its general terms must have the same meaning in every case where its application is in question. To secure this we may fasten on certain features present in the plain case and insist that these are both necessary and sufficient to bring anything which has them within the scope of the rule, whatever other features it may have or lack, and whatever may be the social consequences of applying the rule in this way. To do this is to secure a measure of certainty or predictability at the cost of blindly prejudging what is to be done in a range of future cases, about whose

---

[41] *Op. cit.*, note 1 at p. 17. My emphasis.

composition we are ignorant. We shall thus indeed succeed in settling in advance, but also in the dark, issues which can only reasonably be settled when they arise and are identified.[42]

And so we have, according to Hart's argument, institutions to settle these issues by greater refinement of definition. This is like Raz's idea of adjudication, being (when it is not mere execution) sub-legislation: the progressive refinement of the categories of law according to experience. But this is not true particularisation. Sub-legislative interpretation is really (as we saw in part I) just specification. It doesn't matter for the problem of the particularity void how highly-defined A B and C are. We might have set out a very large number of very detailed facts and our problem would be exactly the same (though somewhat disguised). How to act in respect of a particular? How to cross the void? This is one important thing that we learn from example. Sometimes example is thought of as greater, though somewhat indeterminate, specification. Many things cannot be stated definitively; for example, how to dance the eightsome reel. But they can be taught by example. And it is often thought that the example is just greater, unarticulated, specification. It is this, but not just this. The first thing that its particularity teaches, and what it constantly teaches, is the overcoming of the particularity void.

The particularity void is simply respect for the particular. Respect for the particular is not respect for any (universal) quality or relation attaching to the particular, not respect for A B or C or any further refinement of them. It is respect for the particular itself. Respect for any particular is respect for the mystery of the existence of the world: the world might be simpler, *i.e.* any particular might be the whole world, and the mystery of existence would be the same.[43] But there is a certain bleakness in this conclusion. A judgment in respect of A B and C cannot be a practical judgment because it cannot cross the void. Of course it can justify *a* judgment in the matter: a theoretical/hypothetical, whatever you call it, judgment right up to the void. But the final rationality of practical judgment seems in doubt here. Neil MacCormick has attempted to reassert that rationality against certain theories of particularity[44] by reconsidering the idea of justification. He sees that the act of justification is incapable of solving the problem for it immediately raises the question, why justify?; and the answer, like that to the original question, will be ultimately particular, not universal; so it will have its own particularity

---

[42] *Concept of Law* (Oxford, 1961) at p. 126.
[43] *Op. cit.*, note 3 at p. 17.
[44] In "Universalisation and Induction in Law", in *Proceedings of Conference on Reason in Law* (Bologna, 1984), where he considers three theories of particularity: Adam Smith, *Theory of Moral Sentiments* (1759), R. S. Summers, "Two Types of Substantive Reasons" 63 Cornell LR 707 (1978), and my *The Unity of Law and Morality* (London, 1984).

void. MacCormick seeks to derive the desired universality by the postulation (following Adam Smith) of the ideal impartial spectator:

> By abstracting from one's particular involvement and confronting an issue either in universalised terms or as it would appear to an ideal impartial spectator, we objectify the issue. One poses it as anyone's question, open to anyone's answer. Exactly what made Smith the most persuasive of the particularists turns out to be in truth a surrogate for universalisation in his theory.[45]

But anyone's question is anyone's void. What MacCormick and Smith have not shown is how the impartial spectator's judgment is not also incorrigibly particular; why he does not also confront the particularity void. There are two questions of universalisation in practical judgment. If I judge p the two questions of universalisation concern I, the self, and p. The first question is whether I am to be universalised to all moral agents judging p. That is one question of universalisation and objectivity, and that one Smith's theory approaches. But the other, which it does not deal with, is whether p is universal or incorrigibly particular. Wittgenstein thought of two god-heads: "the World and my Independent I".[46] Being god-heads both are particular, resisting universalisation. But I don't make any judgment about I: the self is not in the world, as Wittgenstein showed.[47] Thus it is p which opens the particularity void and casts doubt on the truth of all practical judgments, subjective or objective.

In this essay I want to pursue the idea that the negotiation of the particularity void depends upon the particular in respect of which my action is contemplated speaking for himself. Suppose again that I am a judge and I am contemplating judgment against a particular citizen. If my respect is such that I allow him to speak for himself then I respect him as an end in self. And is that not precisely respect for his particularity? Is not his being particular his being an end in self?

Not quite. I have used the word "particular" so far (rather than, say, "individual") to indicate my view that ultimately other humans are just particular arrangements of the matter of the universe (other humans: it is meaningless for me (I) to say it of myself). This austere ontology is Wittgensteinian: "My attitude towards him is an attitude towards a soul. I am not of the *opinion* that he has a soul."[48] This in my view is the state of nature that political philosophers have searched for. There are no souls in nature awaiting discovery under some super microscope. But the bleak loneliness of such a world is an inducement to love (Wittgenstein's "attitude"), and in love the soul

---

[45] *Ibid.*, at p. 14.
[46] *Notebooks 1914–1916* (Oxford, 1961) 74e.
[47] *Tractatus*, 5.632–5.633.
[48] *Philosophical Investigations* (Oxford, 1953) 178e.

of the other is attributed. Thus from the state of nature by love emerges politics in which humans are souls or, as we are putting it, ends in selves.[49] Particular arrangements of the matter of the universe become particular ends in selves[50] capable of speaking for themselves.

Now, I am a judge contemplating action against a particular citizen. My contemplated action is connected to his action (what he did to warrant judgment). And it is by our hypothesis connected to his being an end in self. What is the connection between these two things, that is between his action and his being an end in self (between practicality and particularity)?

Action is purposeful. If I knock a glass from a table in the course of a muscular spasm I perform no action. And, similarly, if you by overriding strength force my hand the action of knocking the glass from the table is not mine. But if there is a purpose in my movement (attract attention, demonstrate the law of gravity . . .) there is an action I have performed. And, of course, there are many intermediate cases; for example, when I knock the glass in great anger, or drunkenness. Any philosophy of action must be a philosophy of purposes (ends). Now, law being a practical enterprise, it is concerned to guide, influence or control the *actions* of citizens. This is not the only way to achieve peace. We might cut off the hands of potential pickpockets, whose subsequent omissions in the matter are not then actions of obedience to the law. Or we might double the strength of bank-vaults (or their defensive soft-ware); and we would not say that a decrease in the number of bank robberies has been achieved by law. Or we might achieve our ends by the force of war. We have in these cases simply modified the world; not influenced, guided or controlled the actions of citizens. More borderline cases occur when citizens are tranquillised; or put in great terror to the point where the law's sanction, so-called, is not just a reason for rational action but, rather, an overwhelming domination of the person. Is compliance in these circumstances a case of the action of citizens? Or is it, rather, a modification of the world (a modification of certain brain-states in citizens)? These cases are borderline, but the point is still clear: law concerns not peace as such, nor the bringing-about of a certain peace, but the actions of citizens in peace.

Action is necessarily particular. And this in two senses. First, an action must be in relation to a particular or set of particulars. Thus I might generate the purpose, intention or end to drink burgundy; but until a particular bottle comes my way there is no question of my

---

[49] This whole process I have examined in more depth in *op. cit.*, note 7.
[50] Note that the particularity void pre-exists the other soul; as can be seen if you really think hard about (say) chopping down a tree.

performing the relevant action. This sense is, of course, quite obvious; the second, perhaps, not quite so. For there to be an action there must be a particular purpose or end of a particular agent. It may in some vague way be a purpose or end of humankind to drink wine; but unless it is particularly the purpose of a particular person it will not feature in any description of anyone's actions. Thus in the matter of obedience to the law, the law must be a particular end or purpose of a particular citizen if he is to *act* in obedience to it. A statute for example, must in some sense be his statute (taken into his ends).

Suppose it is a statute which provides the law for my case as a judge (where A B and C judgment against the defendant). Now, if we are able to say that the statute is the defendant's own statute has not the crossing of the particularity void been authorised in the only way possible; that is, by the authority of the particular himself? Of course the statute does not have to be his statute in any immediate way. He may not even know about it. But if the statute is authorised by *his* community or constitution (the community or constitution taken into his ends) that may be enough.

Usually these questions are not explicitly raised, for the simple reason that, generally speaking, only citizens are brought to answer charges before courts, and citizens are precisely those of whom it can be said: the laws, including the statutes, are their laws. The point should not be misunderstood. Because someone breaks a law it does not follow that he disowns the law. Most convicted criminals do not do this, but, rather, maintain their basic allegiance to their legal system notwithstanding even an inclination to offend again when the opportunity arises. What charges them is their community, and since it is their community its laws are their laws in the fundamental sense. Of course some law-breakers do disown the whole legal system that charges them. And thus the laws are not their laws: they are external to the law and strictly speaking at war with the community in the Hobbesian sense (there are many problems with the analysis of particular reasoning in war which we shall not here consider). But occasionally the accused's particular connexion to the statute can be raised. Consider this well-known case from Jennings:

> Parliamentary supremacy means, secondly, that Parliament can legislate for all persons and all places. If it enacts that smoking in the streets of Paris is an offence, then it *is* an offence. Naturally, it is an offence by English law and not by French law, and therefore it would be regarded as an offence only by those who paid attention to English law. The Paris police would not at once begin arresting all smokers, nor would French criminal courts begin inflicting punishments upon them. But if any Frenchman came into any place where attention was paid to English law, proceedings might be taken against him. If, for

instance, a Frenchman who had smoked in the streets of Paris spent a few hours in Folkestone, he might be brought before a court of summary jurisdiction for having committed an offence against English law.[51]

Now, what will the Frenchman say, hauled up from Folkestone to the magistrates? Quite simply: "It is not my law. You may punish me if you like but it is not for an offence against law. I have broken no law. You don't even pretend that I should in Paris have looked to your law rather than my own." Were the trial to proceed it would not be the trial of the Frenchman; it would be an argument (you may call it a trial) between Englishmen as to what to do with this Frenchman, who necessarily is thought of not as an end in self, but as a means to (English) ends. The status of this (French) means to an end in such a proceeding is no greater than that of, say, an (English) dog the impounding of which Englishmen are arguing about in court (it is of course an abuse of words to talk of an impounding case as the trial of a dog). Now, this point must be insisted upon: if the Frenchman is treated as human rather than dog then he is an end in self, and if he is an end in self the fact that the laws are not his laws (*his* end) is critical. There is no authority to cross the particularity void. Only if the laws are his laws may they justly (respectfully) be applied to him.

It is highly possible that English courts would follow Jennings and apply the statute. This would not be to apply the laws to the Frenchman. It would be to apply them in respect of him (as with the dog) to others: we may take it that our statute authorising the arrest of the Frenchman at Folkestone and his imprisonment applies *to* the English officials involved). This would be to achieve peace (in relation to the Frenchman) by force rather than the guidance of action. It would not treat the Frenchman as an end in self. It would cross the particularity void in respect of him by force. It would be a simple act of war not law.

Jennings thought that his case was an illustration of the omnipotence of Parliament. And it may be, even if it is admitted that the statute cannot be applied to the Frenchman. There is nothing in this part of our argument which suggests any limit at all to what Parliament may enact for its citizens. Who are citizens is a question limiting the application of the statute (B, what it is reasonable to apply) not a limit on A, what it is reasonable to enact. Thus Raz's requirement that the reasons for legislation not be reconsidered is absolutely satisfied. But accepting that, its application is not the simple execution of it. Nor would it be if the statute contained a section stating that it

---

[51] *The Law and the Constitution*, 3rd edn (London, 1943) p. 149.

only applied to citizens (in our example adding a fourth universal to A B and C); for the question would still be: who can *that provision* be applied to? This last reflection shows that citizenship is always a matter for the courts not the legislature; and citizenship is always a matter of the determination of particular connexion (the connexion which enables one to say: this is my statute) not the application of a universal quality.

Jennings's case is a very good example of the difference between

A. Accept (apply) what is reasonable,

and

B. Accept (apply) what it is reasonable to accept (apply).

It might be highly unreasonable to ban smoking. Thus if the question before the courts were the intrinsically reasonful A the legislation would in the case even of a citizen be invalid (null in intrinsic reason, as we put it earlier). But the question is B, and for citizens it is reasonable (in a democracy) to accept the legislation notwithstanding its unreasonableness. So it is reasonable to apply the unreasonable ban on smoking. On the other hand the legislation might be highly reasonable, and if its reasonableness were the judicial test it would be applied to the Frenchman without further question. But the question is B not A. And it is unreasonable (unreasonable if the particularity void is respected) to apply this reasonable statute to one to whom it is foreign: the reasonableness of A B C gives no authority to cross the particularity void. In extreme cases the two questions, A and B, merge. Dicey's statute requiring the execution of blue-eyed babies may be said to be so wicked (so unreasonable) that it is foreign to any human enterprise, and therefore the statute of no-one. Likewise the case of Jews at Auschwitz. It is important to see here that the argument does not turn upon killing, or wholly upon even wickedness. Socrates before his execution was invited to escape. But he said no. He had no law but Athenian law (where else might he go at his age?). Thus the law that authorised his death was his law. It was reasonable, Socrates judged, to accept his lawful execution. Socrates himself authorised the law and the crossing of the particularity void to his own death.[52]

III THE FULLNESS OF PRACTICAL REASON

Wittgenstein's two god-heads were "the World and my independent I."[53] A god-head is a point of mystery, a point where there is a void

---

[52] Having one's law as a deep end in this way is a very complex thing. In *op. cit.*, note 7 I have argued (particularly in chapter 7) that law becomes the law of particular citizens not by original contract but by a much more complex particular consensual connexion.

[53] *Loc. cit.*, note 46.

of reason. The god-head, world, is simply the world's particularity. Reason led Davoût to the acceptance of the norm: execute all Russian spies. But the void of reason (the particularity void as we called it in part II) stood between this norm and the particular Pierre. Wittgenstein's second god-head is I, or the self: Davoût might also have said to himself, "it is reasonable to execute the enemies of France, but why should *I* do it?:"

> 'man disobeying
> Disloyal, breaks his fealty, and sins,
> Against the high supremacy of Heaven,
> Affecting godhead'
> *Paradise Lost*, Bk III

There is thus a second particularity void: one for the god-head I, as well as the god-head, world; one for subject as well as object.

It is this subject void which defines the modernist predicament; which activates, amongst other things, Critical Legal Studies. The crisis of modernism, the very idea of modernism is of a self without transcendent connexion:[54] Without God, I am god-head and tragic hero. For non-modernists (those who have God as their friend) the fullness of practical reason comes from its connexion to God. John Finnis's last chapter in *Natural Law and Natural Right*[55] is an argument towards that fullness. First the *idea* of God:

> the originators of natural law theorizing, who did not suppose that God has revealed himself by any such act of informative communication, believed none the less that through philosophical meditation one can gain access to the transcendent source of being, goodness, and knowledge. Nor is this belief of Plato and Aristotle irrelevant to their development of a teaching about practical reasonableness, ethics, or natural right, in opposition to the sceptics, relativists, and positivists of their day. For at the foundation of such teachings is their faith in the power and objectivity of reason, intelligence, *nous*. And there is much reason to believe that their confidence in human nous is itself founded upon their belief that the activity of human understanding, at its most intense, is a kind of sharing in the activity of the divine nous.[56]

If human practical reason leads to a certain conclusion about action then its participation in divine reason would seem authority enough to cross both particularity voids: on the simple precept that my reason is God's reason, I may do it (whatever it is). Of course I may get it wrong. But that is an ordinary human possibility: it is no category

---
[54] R. M. Unger, *"The Critical Legal Studies Movement"* (1983) 96 H.L.R. 563 at p. 561. See also *op. cit.* note 7, Postscript 3.
[55] Oxford, 1980.
[56] *Ibid.*, at pp. 392–393.

mistake. Yet still particularity holds out. Why I? Why this it? There is required here a category leap: the particularity void cannot be crossed by reason. In the end, according to this reasoning, it is only God as particular (as my particular friend), rather than God as the (ideal) conclusion of a philosophical meditation, who can make the whole fullness of practical reasoning. Finnis notices the deep uncertainty of Plato and Aristotle in their knowledge of God's nature and relation to the world;[57] and holds that only a revealed and particular (therefore loving) God can cover that void (that void which we can see as a particularity void).

> Without some revelation more revealing than any that Plato or Aristotle may have experienced, it is impossible to have sufficient assurance that the uncaused cause of all the good things of this world (including our ability to understand them) is itself a good that one could love, personal in a way that one might imitate, a guide that one should follow, or a guarantor of anyone's practical reasonableness.[58]

It is friendship with the particular God which overcomes the subject void: my rebellion to god-head is quelled. And it overcomes the object void too in a way that is not merely definitional. Finnis's broad definition of practicality (we earlier saw) is one which ignores the object void. I set out more fully a passage I quoted briefly earlier:

> But as the argument unfolds, we can see that it *works*, *i.e.* induces understanding and knowledge of what is a full and proper human existence, precisely by getting you to "imagine yourself in a situation where you would be . . .", and asking "Would you settle for this?"
> True, the argument gets you to acknowledge something which can indeed be expressed in a proposition about human nature. But it does this by getting you to consider a question which, though hypothetical, is none the less practical. (For the argument would work *in just the same way* if the question were not hypothetical but required of you a choice here and now between the alternative lives (forms of life); thus its being hypothetical does not remove its radically practical character.)[59]

A "full and proper human existence" conceived in friendship with a particular God is particularity enough. The wonderfully incisive definition of practicality that Finnis offers (the proposition "I think X" is practical if the "I think" is not transparent to X)[60] focuses practical thought in the subject, which is not god-head when it is the friend of the particular God. The object void is then not noticed. I,

---
[57] *Ibid.*, at p. 397.
[58] *Ibid.*, p. 398.
[59] *Supra*, note 41.
[60] *Ibid.*, at p. 3.

the friend of the particular God, see no object void. God is particularity enough.

For modernists the two particularity voids remain, and the main problem in the philosophy of (modernist) practical reason is to give an account of their crossing which can stand in their reasoning as Finnis's account of the particular God does in his. Only then comes the fullness of practical reason.

. . .

The common law is the ordinary law in two main senses. The term came into our law from canon law:

> The term *common law (ius commune, lex communis, commun dreit, commune lei)* is not as yet a term frequent in the mouths of our temporal lawyers. On the other hand, *ius commune* is a phrase well known to the canonists. They use it to distinguish the general and ordinary law of the universal church both from any rules peculiar to this or that provincial church, and from those papal *privilegia* which are always giving rise to ecclesiastical litigation.[61]

These two senses of ordinary, not a local peculiarity and not a privilege, passed into the secular law of England to give it its name:

> From the ecclesiastical it would easily pass into the secular courts. A bishop of Salisbury in 1252 tells the pope how, acting as a papal delegate, he has decided that the common law makes in favour of the rector of one church and against the vicar of another. The common law of which he speaks is the common law of the catholic church; but this bishop is no other than William of York, who owes his see to the good service that he has done as a royal justice. In connexion with English temporal affairs we may indeed find the term *ius commune* in the Dialogue on the Exchequer; the forest laws which are the outcome of the king's mere will and pleasure are contrasted with the common law of the realm. A century later, in Edward I's day, we frequently find it, though *lex communis (commune lei)* has by this time become the more usual phrase. The common law can then be contrasted with statute law; still more often it is contrasted with royal prerogative; it can also be contrasted with local custom: in short it may be contrasted with whatever is particular, extraordinary, special, with "speciality" *(aliquid speciale, especialte).*[62]

The king's mere will: something not intrinsically reasonful in the sense used in part I of this essay, that is, something which as *mere* will has no intrinsically reasonful relation to prior law or right. Modern statutes, we have seen, are mere will, too, in this way. They

---
[61] Pollock and Maitland, *The History of English Law*, 2nd ed (Cambridge, 1898) p. 176.
[62] *Ibid.*, p. 177.

are not intrinsically reasonful and (which is the same thing) they are not common. Of course, the law of the *recognition* of statutes (or of the King's will) is common law: "apply what it is reasonable to apply" is common law (or to be more precise the elaboration of what it is reasonable to apply is common law). This is B, distinguished from A "apply what is reasonable" in which (latter) reasonableness qualifies the thing applied (legislation) not the act of application (common law). Legislation was the fourth of our law-determining processes. The other three processes (adjudication, advice and interpretation) have creative elements as well; so some care is needed in identifying the sense in which they are common. A special response to a legal problem, an advice or a clarification, is not *itself* common, but the reason of the common law being intrinsic to these processes (in the way stated in part I) they are quickly submerged in the commonality ("The assizes of Henry II had worked themselves into the mass of unenacted law, and their text seems already to be forgotten:" Pollock & Maitland).[63] Adjudications, too, are made and therefore special. No one has ever pretended that adjudications were simply found (as though judges consulting their books were consulting a speaking oracle); but the common law, that which governed the adjudication, was found not made. It had to be: if it were made it would be special not common. It would be the law of judges not the law of commons (a term we might now translate as people). The common law is quite clear here. It is the modern jurisprudence with its ideas of prospective overruling and judicial law-making which are confused.[64] To say in this way that law is found not made is no licence for conservatism in the common law. Quite the opposite, really. Judges tend to be conservative in temperament. If they make the law they will therefore tend to make it conservatively. If, on the other hand, they find the law in the people, and the people change, the law changes.[65]

. . .

A common law judge finds the law in the people. Our judge faced, like Davoût, with the object particularity void found in the consent of the object citizen an authority to cross that void. But why judge-subject and citizen-object? It is as though we are thinking of law as something that exists for judges as subjects (the extreme of the judge-centredness in jurisprudence that Raz rejected). Law (and judges) exist for citizens, not vice-versa. Thus the citizen-object void is more truly the citizen-subject void. And the fullness of law as practical

---

[63] *Ibid.*, p. 176.
[64] *Op. cit.*, note 3 at pp. 201–204.
[65] A way in which this might translate into a programme of judicial reform in administrative law I have offered in *op. cit.* note 7.

reason is achieved when the law that judges apply is law that has crossed the citizen subject void; when law is in a true sense the citizen's law; when law is common law.

What is it, then, for law to be citizen's law? One answer is to state the conditions under which law is taken into citizens' ends.[66] Another is to ask whether there is law other than as citizen's law? Hart distinguished internal attitudes to law from external,[67] and this provided the central element in his concept of law; but there was a curious ambivalence here. What was internal to what? Was citizen internal to rule; or rule internal to citizen? Most of what Hart says suggests the former. For example:

> It is important to distinguish the external statement of fact asserting that members of society accept a given rule from the internal statements of the rule made by one who himself accepts it.[68]

It is as though the rule is constituted by those internal to it. But for our present purposes the more interesting idea of internality is not that when citizen is internal to law, but that when the rule or the law is something that the citizen has taken as his own end, as Socrates did the law of Athens. Then the law is internal to the citizen. It is this second idea of internality which is needed to complete our account of the practicality of law.

Let us compare a citizen who has law internal to him with one who treats law externally. Suppose a judge applies law to an external person (let us say he committed a criminal offence the penalty for which was gaol). The first thing to notice is that since the criminal is external he cannot be punished. But as I don't want here to get into the intricacies of the theory of punishment, I had better say the second thing. The judge is given no authority to cross the object particularity void. The law is not the external person's end (it has not crossed his subject void); so if he is to be treated as a particular end in self the law cannot be applied to him. To treat him as end in self is to treat him as subject. Treating him as subject, this law to be applied to him is no common law because it is not his law. The judge's practical reason is incomplete. If he thinks about it he is brought to a halt as Davoût was. He might cross the particularity void by force (or habit, or uncaring brutishness) but not by law. In one sense by law. The judge may think himself bound by law (as Davoût was by French law before he saw Pierre as particular). But that is a special law, a law for the judge. It is not common law. On

---

[66] *Op. cit.* note 7, which is concerned to state those conditions. See particularly chapter 7.
[67] *Op. cit.* note 42.
[68] *Ibid.* at p. 244.

the other hand, for the judge to apply law to an internal citizen (one for whom the law is an end) the matter is quite different. There is then (as we suggested in part II) authority to cross the particularity void. As we have seen, the fact that a citizen has broken the law does not mean law is not his end (internal to him). Some criminals do abandon the law and their community entirely (or they have never had it in them). Others do not, recognising that the law and their community is deeply theirs, and therefore something wronged by their crime (the sense here is of their having wronged themselves by breaking *their* law). Only these may be punished, because only those who have wronged themselves may be punished (though hardly by the bestial institutions which we run today in the name of punishment).

The difference between internal and external citizens in practical theorising about law has been noticed by John Finnis, who asks of Hart's conception of the internal attitude:

> But is there any reason not to apply to the philosophical concept of the "internal viewpoint" those philosophical techniques applied by Hart in his philosophical analysis of "law"—viz the identification of a central or standard instance among other recognizable but secondary instances?[69]

And answers:

> we are led to adopt the position Hart was concerned to reject when he advanced his list of possible sufficient motivations for allegiance to law: the position that law can only be fully understood as it is understood by those who accept it in the way that gives it its most specific mode of operation as a type of reason for acting, viz those who accept it as a specific type of moral reason for acting. Once one abandons, with Hart, the bad man's concerns as the criterion of relevance in legal philosophy, there proves to be little reason for stopping short of accepting the morally concerned man's concerns as that criterion . . . Analytical jurisprudence rejoins the programme of philosophizing about human affairs, the programme whose conditions have been identified by Aristotle: We hold that in all such cases the thing really is what it appears to be to the mature man [the *spoudaios*].[70]

The internal citizen's concerns are the criterion of relevance in legal philosophy, but we must be careful here to see that "internal" does not mean the simple opposite of bad (it is the bad man's concerns that are rejected). To the extent that we respect humans as ends in selves the question is not one of their having or not having a good in the sense of ideally true human attitude: it is true particular choice

---

[69] "Revolutions and Continuity of Law" in *Oxford Essays in Jurisprudence (2nd series)* ed. Simpson (Oxford 1973) p. 74.
[70] *Ibid.*, at 74–75.

not ideal truth which is fundamental in that sort of respect. Of any particular human the question of his internal attitude to law is: is the law in fact deeply his (an end chosen by someone who is true to himself, rather than a fickle day-to-day convenience)? *Spoudaios*, Aristotle's word, has an ambivalence here, which it is essential to clarify. The normal translation of the passage in Aristotle[71] is that things are what they seem to the *good* man.[72] This thoroughly subverts Aristotle's purpose; and is anyway highly implausible, for a couple of lines further on Aristotle resumes with the more conventional words for good, *arete* and *agathos*. He is able to resume with these words because he has avoided (at least sought to avoid) the obviously question-begging form—good is what appears so to the good man— by saying good is what appears to the *spoudaios*. Good is one meaning of *spoudaios*, but its basic meaning is serious, as contrasted with childish or fickle; hence Finnis's "mature". What Aristotle is seeking to do with this word is apparent from his argument a few lines earlier: "the same things do not seem sweet to a man in the grip of fever." Thus sweet is what appears so to the healthy man, rather than the question-begging, sweet is what appears so to the sweet-perceiver. And maturity, seriousness of purpose, provides independent criteria for the perception of good just as general health does for the perception of sweetness. But only in practical, particular, perception. If the mature man was an ideal of goodness, the circularity that Aristotle sought to avoid would reassert itself, though it would be obscured. Suppose good is A. How do we know? Because the mature man tells us so. Who is the (ideal) mature man? The one mature enough to perceive A! And the same for B, C, etc. But the mature man is not an ideal. Aristotle's argument is not of the form: truth is what appears to the truth-perceiver. In the matter of law the mature man is every particular citizen who takes law as a deep and particular end of his. Such a person is mature (serious) by virtue of his taking some long-term thing as an end. He is mature in law by virtue of his taking law as a long-term end. Law for such a person is common law in the fullest sense. The immature (childish) person takes no long-term thing as an end. The immature (childish) person in law takes no law as a long-term end. There is no question here of our saying that a mature person *ought* to take law as an end (imposing an ideal on him). A long-term end of one sort of mature person might be the accumulation of pleasure. He might treat law as a day-to-day means to that end (use it when it aids the accumulation; avoid it when it doesn't). He would be external in law, but mature in another way

---

[71] *Nic. Eth.* 1176a 17.
[72] JAK Thomson, Penguin, p. 298; John Warrington, Everyman, p. 224.

(immature in law, but mature in hedonism). And the long-term end of another might be revolution. The point is to say that the fullness of practical reason *in law*, and its central case, is achieved only in so far as a legal system has (and recognises that it has) serious citizens (those mature in the matter of law; those who have law as common law). And that a legal system disposed to take the judicial maxim as:

    A. Apply to citizens what is reasonable,

rather than one disposed so to respect the particularity void that it regards its citizens as subjects within the judicial maxim:

    B. Apply to citizens what it is reasonable to apply to them as ends in self,

is a legal system of crippled practicality; of peripheral theoretical concern; and not one of common law.

[4]

FERNANDO ATRIA*

LEGAL REASONING AND LEGAL THEORY REVISITED

(Accepted May 20, 1999)

ABSTRACT. This article deals with the relation between a theory of law and a theory of legal reasoning. Starting from a close reading of Chapter VII of H. L. A. Hart's *The Concept of Law*, it claims that a theory of law like Hart's requires a particular theory of legal reasoning, or at least a theory of legal reasoning with some particular characteristics. It then goes on to say that any theory of legal reasoning that satisfies those requirements is highly implausible, and tries to show that this is the reason why not only Hart, but also writers like Neil MacCormick and Joseph Raz have failed to offer a theory of legal reasoning that is compatible with legal positivism as a theory of law. They have faced a choice between an explanation of legal reasoning that is incompatible with the *core* of legal positivism or else strangely sceptical, insofar as it severs the link between general rules and particular decisions that purport to apply them.

KEY WORDS: application of law, appropriateness, clear cases, deductive reasoning, legal positivism, legal reasoning, open texture

When H. L. A. Hart wrote *The Concept of Law*, legal reasoning as such was not in the philosophical agenda. Consequently, he later acknowledged that in *The Concept of Law* he had "said far too little about the topic of [...] legal reasoning" (1994, p. 259). This aspect of Hart's book was soon subject to criticism because it appeared to some (most notably, Dworkin 1967) that the implications of Hart's theory for legal reasoning were clearly at odds with what lawyers and judges saw themselves as doing. What was needed, in consequence, was a "companion" to *The Concept of Law*, an examination of the way in which a powerful explanation of the nature of law such as Hart's could further the understanding not only of what the law is, but also of how the law works, or, better, how

---

* Licenciado en Derecho (Universidad de Chile, 1994); Ph.D. (University of Edinburgh, 1999); Assistant Professor of Law, Universidad de Talca (Chile). I am indebted to Zenon Bankowski, Neil MacCormick, Kevin Walton, Claudio Michelon and Burkhard Schafer for thoughtful criticism of previous versions of this article. They have, of course, no responsibility for the mistakes that remain.

people work with the law: a theory of the application of the law (i.e. legal reasoning). We are now told that *Legal Reasoning and Legal Theory* was supposed to be such a companion (MacCormick 1994, p. xiv). Before considering that book, let me explain where the tension between legal reasoning and legal theory lies, and to do so we shall consider H. L. A. Hart's "open texture" thesis.

HART ON OPEN TEXTURE

For our purposes, a full exposition of Hart's open texture thesis is not needed here: suffice it to say that he tried to strike a middle way between what he called "rule formalism" and "rule scepticism", and that to do this he borrowed from F. Waismann (Waismann 1951) the idea of open texture. According to the text-book exposition of this thesis, the argument was that, since meaning is use, concept-words cannot have any meaning whatsoever without there being clear instances to which they apply. To be able to recognise those examples as instances of the relevant concept-word(s) is to know the meaning of the latter. By the same token, however, in many instances the application of those concept-words to some event will not be completely obvious, and disagreement between competent users will arise. In these circumstances, failure to use the relevant concept-word to refer to those events is not evidence of ignorance of their meaning (as failure in the clear cases is), since these events are said to be in the *penumbra* of meaning of the relevant concept-word(s), where different opinions might exist between competent users as to whether or not a particular concept-word applies. To make an often-quoted passage even more often quoted,

If we are to communicate with each other at all, and if, as in the most elementary form of law, we are to express our intentions that a certain type of behaviour be regulated by rules, then the general words we use [...] must have some standard instance in which no doubts are felt about [their] application. There must be a core of settled meaning, but there will be, as well, a penumbra of debatable cases in which words are neither obviously applicable nor obviously ruled out (Hart 1958, p. 63).

So understood, Hart's is a thesis about the limits of certainty that general classificatory terms can have in natural languages: "[open texture is] a *general feature of human language*; uncertainty at the borderline is the price to be paid for the use of general classifying terms in *any form of communication* concerning matters of fact" (1994, p. 128; my italics). It is an inescapable feature of natural languages as we know them, and hence is part of the human predicament: if we are to communicate with each other using natural (rather than artificial) languages, then it is pointless to strive to achieve complete certainty: *there is nothing we can do to exclude open texture*, at least insofar as we also want to use general classificatory terms:

> my view was (and is) that the use of *any* language containing empirical classificatory general terms will, in applying them, meet with borderline cases calling for fresh regulation. This is the feature of language I called 'open texture' " (Hart, quoted by Bix 1993, p. 24).

On this first reading of it, the open texture thesis is one about language, and only derivatively about the law. "Open texture" is not a feature of law but, as Hart explicitly says in the quoted passage, one of natural languages. Needless to say, since (or: only because) legal rules are expressed in natural languages, the open texture of the latter communicates, so to speak, to the former. Thus it is not surprising at all to hear from Hart that, for example, "whichever device, precedent or legislation, is chosen for the communication of standards of behaviour, these, however smoothly they work over the great mass of ordinary cases, will, at some point where their application is in question, prove indeterminate" (Hart 1994, pp. 127–128).

Immediately after presenting the notion of open texture, and in an apparent effort to cheer the reader up, Hart explains that uncertainty at the borderline is certainly nothing to be afraid of. But in the course of this consolation the nature of the open-texture thesis switches: it becomes a thesis no longer about one of the inescapable features of natural languages as we know them, but about the *convenience* of having open-textured (i.e. not completely certain and predictable) rules. It ceases to be a feature of language to become one of the law.

Of course, there is no reason why you cannot argue that X is the case and then go on to argue that X is also desirable, which is the usual way in which the relevant passages on *The Concept of Law* seem to have been read. But Hart did something more: when arguing about the desirability of open texture, and contradicting his statements quoted above (and many others) Hart conceded that *it is possible*, for us now and here, to eliminate the uncertainty at the borderline, i.e. "to freeze the meaning of the rule so that its general terms must have the same meaning in every case where its application is in question" (1994, p. 129).

He even explained to us how:

To secure this we may fasten on certain features present in the plain case and insist that these are both necessary and sufficient to bring anything which has them within the scope of the rule, whatever other features it may have or lack, and whatever may be the social consequences of applying the rule in this way (1994, p. 129).

And if we were to follow his advice,

we shall *indeed succeed* in settling in advance, but also in the dark, issues which can only reasonably be settled when they arise and are identified (1994, p. 130; my italics).

If we *can indeed succeed* in settling in advance the outer limits of the law, it follows that the explanation of the fact that these limits are uncertain must be in the reasons why it is not convenient for us to do so, i.e. in the reasons why these cases "can only *reasonably* be settled when they arise and are identified". In other words, if we can eliminate the uncertainty at the borderline, then it is simply wrong to say that the reason why the law is uncertain is because the uncertainty at the borderline cannot be eliminated; the reason why the law is uncertain in hard cases is *not* some inescapable feature of general classificatory terms in natural languages, but the very different one that it is *unreasonable* to try to settle "in advance, but also in the dark" issues we cannot yet identify.

Following this second line of argumentation, Hart explains that he is dealing not with a limitation on the levels of certainty imposed on human beings by the language they (we) happen to have, but with the very different issue of striking a right balance between two competing social needs, i.e.

the need for certain rules [...] and the need to leave open, for later settlement by an informed, official choice, issues which can only be properly appreciated and settled when they arise in a concrete case (1994, p. 130).

And furthermore, this tension is one that "*in fact*, all systems, in different ways" solve reaching some kind of compromise (ibid.

Italics added). Open texture then is not an external limit language imposes on the levels of certainty human beings can achieve, but the *consequence of a normative decision*, i.e. a decision about how best to balance the requirements of certainty with those of appropriateness.[1]

It is important to emphasise that, as we have seen, what a hard (clear) case is varies according to each of these interpretations of the open-texture thesis. In the first interpretation, a case will be hard when the facts are such that they do not fit naturally and uncontroversially one or more of the general classificatory terms of the relevant rules, i.e. when it is what could be called a "semantic" hard case (when, e.g. the rule forbids you to go into the park with a vehicle and you want to use a toy car in it). On the second interpretation, however, the point is not uncertainty at the borderline. As we can "indeed succeed" in having clear and certain rules (regardless of the features of natural languages), a case will be hard because what is an issue is *not the classification of particulars in the world*, but the very different one of whether or not *this* case was one of those left "open, for later settlement by an informed, official choice" even if it is covered by the semantic meaning of the rule in question (was the case of the veteran's wanting to use a military truck in a memorial in the park settled when the "no vehicles" rule was issued or was it "left open"?). Since the only reason why it makes sense to begin to discuss whether or not this case is covered is that it *could* be covered, in this explanation a hard case in fact presupposes that the particulars in the world can be classified under the rule's general classificatory terms.

Bearing these considerations in mind, we go back to the tension between law and legal reasoning, to the challenge mentioned by MacCormick: a Hartian explanation of legal reasoning has to be seen to flow from, or at the very least to be consistent with, the central claims Hart made in the "mother" theory. I hope it is not very controversial to say that one of the central tenets of Hart's theory of

---

[1] Some stipulations will be of use here: (a) I will call "certainty" (or: "predictability") the first of the social needs Hart distinguished and (b) "appropriateness" the second; (c) I will talk of "application" when referring to the problem of whether or not a rule should be applied to a particular case, and (d) of "meaning" when referring to that of grasping a rule's meaning.

law was that at a conceptual level law is independent from morality, that is, what the law ought to be is not the same than what the law is.[2] These two questions are, in Hart's view, not only different, but logically different: it is possible to establish what the law is without inquiry into what the law ought to be; no conclusion about what the law is follows from arguments about what the law ought to be. At the same time, Hart saw that any theoretical elucidation of the nature of law must explain why and how it is possible for competent lawyers, judges and lay persons to disagree not only about what the law ought (morally) to be, but also (and much more importantly in this context) about what the law actually is. Now, the explanation of the latter kind of disagreement cannot be grounded upon the existence of disagreement about what the law ought to be, since if that were the case the law as it is would not be conceptually different from the law as it ought to be (that is, it cannot be the case that we disagree about what the law is *because* we disagree what the law ought to be, if these two questions are conceptually different). Hence we got Hart's *open texture* thesis.

The importance of this thesis is that it performed the role of supplying a morally neutral explanation of legal disagreement, thus allowing us to explain disagreement about what the law is in a way that was not parasitical on disagreement about what the law ought to be. This was, therefore, the explanation (at least the *kind* of explanation) required by Hart's theoretical assumptions, if his theory was to have any consistency. But Hart noticed (or so I claimed) that the idea of open texture, important as it might be, did not explain the whole of the fact of legal disagreement when looked at from a legal reasoning-perspective, i.e. clarification of the meaning of words is not always the kind of information that would be useful to lawyers and judges and lay persons when they are discussing what the law

---

[2] There is some discussion as to the precise content of what is sometimes called "the separability thesis" (*see*, among others, Füßer 1996; Coleman 1996). This has to be kept in mind, since my argument would not affect some versions of the thesis. Consider Shiner's (admittedly "crude") version: "the existence of law is one thing and its merit or demerit another" (Shiner 1992). I do believe (along with most positivists, natural lawyers, and realists of different denominations) that in this sense the thesis is true. I think, however, that I can bypass this debate because in any plausible reading that thesis must mean, for legal positivists, that the fact that the law ought to be different is not enough to establish that it is different.

is in concrete cases. Hart realised that in many of these cases what was discussed was not whether a particular *x* was an instance of a general *X*, but rather whether or not a particular (otherwise clear and unambiguous) rule was, in a legal sense, meant to be applied to the facts that configured some concrete case. Hence he offered, in the same pages of *The Concept of Law*, a second explanation of the fact of legal disagreement, one based on the claim that there is a built-in tension in law between (what I called) predictability and appropriateness.

Now, it is in my view a crucial point that the legal theory-implications of this second explanation are at odds with the central claim of Hart's book identified above. In the first explanation, what made a case hard was a "value-free" feature, i.e. the open texture of the relevant words. This is why Hart was free to say that in clear cases the application of rules does not require the decision maker to exercise a "fresh judgement" (1994, p. 135). From the universe of cases courts will have to solve from now on, some of them are (or will eventually be) marked by the fact that they belong to the penumbra of meaning of the relevant words; the identification of those cases as hard will not imply, therefore, that evaluative ideas about what the law ought to be will be smuggled in at the moment of ascertaining what the law is. When the "mark" of open texture is discovered the court will have reached the outer limits of the law: it can then discuss about what the law will be after the court's decision, in the light of what the law should be, only because there is no law on the matter. Notice that nothing guarantees that this will be uncontroversial. There can be disagreement on whether skateboards and push-chairs are "core" or "penumbra" instances of the word "vehicle". That is to say, I think Raz is correct when he says (Raz 1985, p. 218) that it is false "that all factual matters are non-controversial" and that "all moral propositions are controversial". What is important here is not that according to the open texture thesis the application of the law is non-controversial, but that any *legal* disagreement will not be *moral* but *factual* (or verbal, or conceptual) disagreement: are push-chairs and skateboards, *as a matter of fact*, vehicles?

The second explanation (legal disagreement as the consequence of the tension between predictability and appropriateness) does not work so nicely, though it represents more faithfully the reality of legal reasoning. In it, the "mark" that singles a case out as hard is an evaluative feature: the case is (will be) marked as hard if predictability's requirements are overridden by those of appropriateness, i.e. if the solution offered by the rule is inappropriate enough for the demand of predictability to be defeated in the case. Notice that, in this view, to "discover" the "mark" that would allow us to classify a case as clear or hard is to exercise a "fresh judgement", as it is to answer the question of how pressing the inappropriateness of a norm ought to be for the demand for predictability to be overridden, the answer of which will depend on the relative importance those values are taken to have. From this standpoint the question of what the law is cannot be differentiated from that of what the law ought to be. In other words, *for the court* the question "*is* this pram a vehicle?" is linked to the question "*ought* this pram be considered a vehicle?" (consider the common judicial way of posing this kind of problems: "should skateboards be considered as vehicles *for the purpose of this law*?").[3]

If this is correct, there is no way in which we can say that there is a *logical* distinction between these two questions. To see why, it seems useful to divide Hart's view on hard cases up into two parts: one that contains a test about what makes a hard case hard, and another that explains what is going on once a case is recognised as such. We have seen that two answers can be found in *The Concept of Law* for the first problem, the test that makes a case hard. The answer to the second problem is that in hard cases there is no settled law, hence the courts have to exercise discretion. Now I believe (though I will not argue for this here)[4] that the first, non-moral test for the first problem, i.e. the *open texture* thesis understood as a thesis about language rather than about the law, has to be rejected, and something along the lines of the tension between predictability and appropriate-

---

[3] The fact that Hart himself sometimes (e.g.: 1967, p. 106) phrased the question in these terms (as one of ascertaining whether a particular x is an instance of a general X for the purpose of a given law) shows that he failed to notice that he was offering two explanations. If his open texture thesis (understood as a thesis about language) is true, then there are core instances that are recognisable as such regardless of the purpose of any law: *see* Schauer 1991, p. 212ff.

[4] See my "Games and the Law: Two Models of Institution" in ARSP (July 1999).

ness must be placed there instead. If we then retain the original second part, i.e. the claim that in hard cases courts have discretion, the incompatibility between what we would then get and the *core* of Hart's philosophy of law (as identified above) is evident: In this modified version, Hart's view on hard cases would be: (i) a case is hard when the application of the (*prima facie*) law is deemed objectionable (i.e. when the *prima facie* solution is such that the demand for appropriateness is stronger than the demand for certainty); (ii) when a case is hard, the law is unsettled, and the courts have discretion. In short: when the application of an otherwise clear legal rule to a case that belongs, so to speak, to its *core* of meaning produces an objectionable result, *it is the law* that there is no law on the subject. What the law *is* for the case depends upon what the law (i.e. the balance between predictability and appropriateness) *ought* to be for the case. When the (*prima facie*) law *ought to be* different, it *is* different. *lex iniusta non est lex*!

Now, is this "ought" a moral "ought"? It might appear that the answer is obviously yes: the point is why is predictability important, and why should we care about appropriateness. As Raz has claimed, they cannot but be moral, since "there is no other justification for the use of an autonomous body of considerations by the courts" (Raz 1993, p. 318). But we should be careful here. Hart is indeed careful not to talk of these values as moral values, at least in *The Concept of Law*. And in "Positivism and the separation of law and morals" he is explicit in denying that this is a moral ought: "we should remember that the baffled poisoner may say, 'I ought to have given her a second dose'" (Hart 1958, p. 70). Hart also points out that "under the Nazi regime men were sentenced by courts for criticism of the regime. Here the choice of sentence might be guided exclusively by consideration of what was needed to maintain the state's tyranny effectively" (ibid.).

So Hart believed that the solution to the conflict between appropriateness and predictability can be based upon purely instrumental considerations. But the obvious question is, what are these considerations instrumental for. In the poisoner's case, they are instrumental to achieve a goal previously and independently given, i.e. to kill the woman. In Nazi Germany, they "might" have been instrumental to the independently given goal of maintaining the state's repressive apparatus.

That the goal is *previously given* means, obviously, that there cannot be an instrumental "ought" before the goal has been specified. Therefore, when the application of the law is at issue, that goal cannot be something like "to follow the law", since the court is trying to establish what the law is for the case (it would be equivalent to saying that the goal for the poisoner is to administer the poison, a goal that is useless as a guidance for the problem of *how much* poison "ought" to be administered). The important point is, how can the court establish what the goal is?

Notice that the answer is not to be found in another rule of the system, because of the same reason why Hart argued that "canons of interpretation" could not succeed in eliminating uncertainty (1994, p. 126): because those rules would also be subjected to the problem.

Still, is this a moral "ought"? I hope we can see now that we do not need a positive answer to this question (positive though I think the correct answer is). Hart's answer to the rule-sceptic was to claim that the application of rules to a majority of cases does not call for "fresh judgement", with the obvious implication that the decision-maker did not have discretion to solve those ("core") cases. But this is an answer that works only if the first version of the open texture thesis is accepted, since only this version does not make the characterisation of a case as clear or hard dependant upon the very kind of judgement that is supposed to be absent from one kind of cases. In the second version, however, since the distinction itself is based on such a judgement, Hart is left with no answer to the rule-sceptic. However controversial or uncontroversial the decision to characterise a case as "clear" or "hard" might be, it is a judgement for the making of which the court has discretion.[5]

---

[5] We could go further into this point, though for the argument presented in this article that is quite unnecessary. Hart's claim that the "ought" in question might be an instrumental "ought", instrumental in achieving some (independently given) goal seems to leave him rather close to Dworkin: since what the goal is and how best to achieve it will determine how the balance between predictability and appropriateness has to be solved in the particular case, what the law is for this case will depend on the identification of that goal, and the chosen goal will have an impact upon the content of the rules (remember that we cannot know whether

In brief, the fact that the law *ought* to be different sometimes *makes it be* different. In order to refer to what Hart called "fresh judgement" without giving the impression that too much argumentative weight is placed upon its being a *moral* problem, I will use broader expressions, like Hart's quoted "fresh judgement", or "evaluative judgement" and the like.

The tension between legal theory and legal reasoning is explained, at least in part, by a difference in perspective between the two: when building a legal theory, what is at the centre of attention is a set of questions like "what is the law?" "when are we entitled to say that a legal system is valid (exists)?" "how can we know whether a particular rule is part of this or that (or of any at all) legal system?" (*see* Raz 1980, p. 1f, for a useful typology of the questions a legal theory must answer to be a "complete" legal theory). At this level it is hard to deny the difference between the law that is and the law that ought to be. The mere fact that many people can sensibly think the law of their land to be unjust, that is, different from what it ought ideally to be, shows that there is such a distinction.

But when the focus of the enquiry is shifted to legal reasoning, this clear difference is upset. It is still possible to apply a law that is different from the law that ought to be, and many times judges decide one thing while at the same time they think that a different decision ought to have been but for the content of the applicable law.[6] But we have seen that in order to apply the law, the judge has to decide how best to balance the values of predictability and appropriateness in the instant case. The obvious fact that judges are sometimes compelled to decide a case in a manner they think is not (morally) the best shows that the law does indeed pre-empt some substantive issues that would otherwise be prompted by the case. But the equally obvious fact that a law does not exclude *all* the substantive considerations (e.g. the consideration that the man

---

the case is clear or hard until we have solved this tension). This seems a different way of saying that the law is an interpretive concept (see Dworkin 1986, p. 46ff).

[6] Hence the italicised last phrase at the end of the paragraph eight paragraphs back was, in a way, a rhetorical excess. But it was only exaggerated, not plainly false: sometimes laws that produce unfair or unjust results when applied to a particular case are not laws for that case, and that suffices to put in question of the separability thesis, according to which from the fact that a legal solution is morally objectionable it does not follow that it is legally mistaken.

who shed blood in the streets of Bologna was a barber, and that he was shaving a customer), even when it *prima facie* appears to do so (Thus, for example, the Bolognese statute said that the words had to be taken literally, without interpretation: see the case in Pufendorf 1688: 5.12.8, pp. 802–803 [547]) shows that there is more to the ascertaining of what the law is than getting the meaning right. And it is somewhat ironic that Hart himself gave such an accurate description of what this something else is, that is, the solution of a tension between the values of predictability of judicial decisions and their appropriateness to the particular case at hand. To repeat: what the law *is* for the case cannot be known before deciding how the competition between predictability and appropriateness *ought to be* resolved.

One could, I suppose, insist on the idea that this is not a problem, and to do so one would have to argue that an answer to the question "what is law"? does not have any consequences for an answer to that of "what is the law for this case?". If it could be argued that an answer to the first question does not imply an answer to the second, this article's argument would be conceptually mistaken. And indeed, it has been claimed that "it has been a central presupposition [of analytical jurisprudence] that there is a clear distinction between the philosophical question, "What is law?" and the lawyer's question, "What is *the* law for this or that matter?" (Marmor 1995, p. v).

Now, there is an obvious sense in which these are two different questions, i.e. in the same way that the question "What is cancer?" is different from the question "Does this person have cancer?". But this is not to say that an answer to the first question does not imply (at least part of) an answer to the second, in the same way in which the answer to the first of Marmor's questions implies (at least part of) an answer to the second (indeed, to say that x has consequences for y assumes the existence of a [more or less] "clear distinction" between x and y).

One could claim, however, that the relation is not that close. Consider Hans Kelsen's position:

This determination [of a lower-level norm by a higher-level norm] however, is never complete [...]. Even a meticulously detailed command must leave a number of determinations to those carrying it out. If official A orders official B to arrest subject C, B must use his discretion to decide when where and how he will carry out the warrant to arrest C; and these decisions depend upon external circumstances that *A* has not foreseen and, for the most part, cannot foresee (Kelsen 1934, p. 78).

That a judicial decision is based on a statute means in truth simply that the decision stays within the frame the statute represents, means simply that the decision is one of the individual norms possible within the frame of the general norm, not that it is the only individual norm possible (Kelsen 1934, p. 80. The passage remains unaltered in the second edition of *The Pure Theory of Law*).

One could understand Kelsen here as saying that the *Pure Theory of Law* will never be able to answer "the lawyer's question" if that question is "When, where and how should *B* arrest *C*?". But this is not to say that the answer to the first question is not an answer to the second: in Kelsen's example, a complete answer to the first question (something like "a legal system is the set of all the laws enacted by the exercise of powers conferred, directly or indirectly, by one basic norm")[7] implies an answer to the second ("for this case, the law is that *C* should be arrested by *B*, though the law does not specify precisely where, when or how").

It is not clear to me whether Marmor was claiming that for analytic jurisprudence the two questions were different in the sense that an answer to one did not imply an answer to the second, or only that they were different, without any further claim. In the latter sense, he is surely right but it would not be an objection to my main argument in this article; in the former, it would indeed be an objection but (I would claim) it would not be true as regards "analytic jurisprudence" nor would it be correct in its own terms.

DEDUCTIVE REASONING, CLEAR CASES AND LEGAL ARGUMENTATION

The challenge for a complete Hartian (-like) theory of law (that is, a Hartian (-like) theory of law *and* legal reasoning) is, then, to harmonise these two perspectives, that of legal reasoning and that of legal theory. I want to consider now in some detail what is probably the most sophisticated attempt to meet this challenge, i.e. Neil MacCormick's *Legal Reasoning and Legal Theory*.

---

[7] This is Raz's version of what he calls Kelsen's "criterion of identity" (*see* Raz 1980, p. 95; and Kelsen 1934, p. 59ff).

That MacCormick's is an attempt to meet this challenge is clear from the new foreword of the paperback edition, where he says that "the analytical positivist approach to legal theory espoused by Hart is open to challenge, and has been challenged, for an alleged inability to give a satisfactory account of legal reasoning, especially reasoning-in-adjudication. This book took up that challenge" (MacCormick 1994, p. xiv). In particular, I take his argumentation concerning the role of deductive reasoning in law as constituting the best available analysis of clear cases in the tradition of legal positivism.

This is the reason why, before considering MacCormick's argument, it is necessary to address the issue of syllogistic (or deductive) reasoning in Herbert Hart's theory of law. Hart himself sometimes showed little sympathy for the idea that legal decisions can be reached in a deductive manner: he argued that "logic is silent on how to classify particulars" (Hart 1958, p. 67). Commenting upon this and related passages from Hart's work, Marmor claims that nothing could be farther from Hart's mind than the idea of the application of a rule to a clear case being a matter of logic or analyticity.[8] Defending Hart, Marmor has claimed that "it is easily discernible that whatever it is that connects a rule to its application cannot consist of logic [...]"[9] and he then argues,

as Hart put it, "logic is silent on how to classify particulars" but it is precisely this classification to which his distinction between core and penumbra pertains. In other words, we must keep separate what might be called "rule-rule" and "rule-world" relations; logic [...][10] pertain[s] only to the former, not to the later kind of relation(Marmor 1994, p. 128).

And he concludes by saying that "neither Hart nor any other legal positivist must subscribe to the view that the application of legal rules is a matter of logical inference" (ibid., at 128).

---

[8] As we shall see, MacCormick does not mention the idea that the judicial syllogism is analytic. Of course it is, but this is not to say that it is "analyticity" (or "logic") what connects a rule to its application. I will argue that what connects a rule to its application is logic *plus* the distinction between *core* and penumbra. For this reason, I will follow MacCormick in not discussing this at all in terms of analyticity.

[9] Following the previous note, "and analyticity" omitted.

[10] "And analyticity" omitted.

Marmor is right when he claims that the distinction between core and penumbra is not a matter of logic, but let us ask the question: "why is the core/penumbra important for Hart?" And the answer is: because, *in addition* to the existence of a core and penumbra of meaning for most (all) concepts, Hart claimed (at least in the traditional interpretation of the open texture thesis) that a state of affairs constitutes a clear *legal* case when in some of its descriptions it is encompassed by the *core* meaning of some applicable rule, and hard otherwise. It is with this further claim that a space for logic and deductive reasoning appears: to put it in Marmor's terms, *once* the relation rule-world has been settled, once the particulars of the case have been recognised to be in the core of meaning of the relevant words, then all that is left is to perform a syllogism.[11] This is so because when the relation "rule-world" has been established then a relation between rule-rule has to be established, i.e. a relation between a general rule (like "it shall be a misdemeanour, punishable by fine of £5, to sleep in any railway station") and a particular one ("the defendant should pay £5") has to be established. Logic does not answer the question of whether a Cadillac is a vehicle; this is something that follows from the very meaning of "vehicle", in such a way that not to see this is to show plain ignorance of English. But *once* that question is answered, logic (in the positivist view) must be able to answer the question of whether that Cadillac is to be allowed in the park.[12]

---

[11] There is a significant difference in the way in which logical language is used by logicians and lawyers: for the latter "syllogism", "deduction" and "logic" are, broadly speaking, synonyms, while for the latter they are quite different (however related) things. *See* Kneale and Kneale (1962). I will follow the lawyers' usage.

[12] To see that Marmor's claim that Hart does not "subscribe to the view that the application of legal rules is a matter of logical inference" (Marmor 1994, p. 128) is simply false all one needs to do is to read the passages in which Hart talked about *hard* cases, in order to see what is their implication for *clear* cases: "human invention and natural processes continually throw up such ["penumbral"] variants on the familiar ["core"], and if we are to say that *these ranges of facts* do or do not fall under existing rules, then the classifier must make a decision *which is not dictated to him* [...]" (Hart 1958, p. 63); "If a penumbra of uncertainty must surround all legal rules, then their application to specific cases *in the penumbral area* cannot be a matter of logical deduction, and so deductive reasoning [...] cannot serve as a model for what judges, or indeed anyone, should do in bringing

A Theory of Legal Argumentation or a Theory of Legal Reasoning?

Neil MacCormick began his *Legal Reasoning and Legal Theory* with a forceful argument for the importance of syllogistic reasoning in law, that is, for the idea that *modus ponens* alone can render, in some cases, fully justified legal decisions. With this claim he faced the challenge of those (he did not give references at this point) who would like to deny this:

> If this denial [of the possibility of legal reasoning being deductive] is intended in the strictest sense, implying that legal reasoning is never, or cannot ever be, solely deductive in form, then the denial is manifestly and demonstrably false. It is sometimes possible to show conclusively that a given decision is legally justified by means of a purely deductive argument (1994, p. 19).

The importance of this claim should be by now evident. If it can be shown that in *some* cases at least legal reasoning *can* be *solely* and *strictly* deductive in form, then all that will remain to be done is to specify (as MacCormick tries to do in chapter 3 of his book) the presuppositions and limits of deductive reasoning. Once we know these presuppositions and limits, we would be free to say that those cases in which some of those presuppositions fail (or those cases that are beyond such limits) are *hard cases*, where there is no difficulty at all to accept that the question of what the law is for the case (or better: will be) can be linked to that of what the law ought to be for it. This is the reason why MacCormick's argument, if successful, could be used to defend a positivist theory of law like Hart's.

Before examining MacCormick's argument with some detail it would pay, I believe, to pause for a while on what precisely it is that MacCormick is claiming when he says that the *Daniels* decision was justified in a deductive manner.

This is important because MacCormick's thesis is open to an interpretation that would make it trivial. Indeed, we shall see that MacCormick himself sometimes seems to understand his argument in this way.

For a start, consider Robert Alexy's theory of legal interpretation as set out in his *A Theory of Legal Argumentation* (1989). In it, he

---

particular cases under general rules. *In this area* men cannot live by deduction alone" (ibid., at 64; all the italics here are mine).

begins by distinguishing what he calls "internal" from "external" justification:

Legal discourses are concerned with the justification of a special case of normative statements, namely those which express legal judgments. Two aspects of justification can be distinguished: *internal justification* and *external justification*. Internal justification is concerned with the question of whether an opinion follows logically from the premises adduced as justifying it; The correctness of the premises is the subject-matter of the external justification (Alexy 1989, p. 221).

For Alexy, the problem of internal justification *is* that of deductive reasoning: "problems associated with internal justification have been widely discussed under the heading 'legal syllogism' " (Alexy 1989, p. 220). Now the important point here is that no decision is fully justified if it has not been externally *and* internally justified. For the external justification, non-deductive reasoning is typically needed. Once the premises have been (externally) justified (using whatever criteria is used to justify premises: consequential reasoning, purposive interpretation, authority reasons, etc), then it is possible to say that the decision is fully justified if it follows in a formally valid manner from those (externally) justified premises.[13]

Notice that for Alexy (unlike MacCormick) the requirement of the justification being deductive has nothing at all to do with the fact of the case in which it occurs being clear or hard. The difference will usually lie on the fact that the (external) justification of the premises will normally be more controversial in hard cases than in clear ones; but however controversial the external justification of the premises is, once they have been justified, then the internal justification takes over in the same way for one case or the other. Thus, in the context of a theory of legal argumentation, aimed at establishing "how fully to justify a legal judgement" (Alexy 1989, p. 2), deductive reasoning is to be used in every case.

---

[13] Example: In Hart's case of the electrically propelled toy car and the "no vehicles in the park" rule, the premise "a toy car is a vehicle" would have to be justified according to the requirements of external justification. But once that question is settled, all that is left is to *deduce* from the statement (thus justified) "this toy car is a vehicle" and the rule "no vehicles in the park", the conclusion that this toy car is not allowed into the park.

We can now see how MacCormick's thesis can be trivialised by taking it to mean only that a form of deductive reasoning is somehow important for legal reasoning. In any case syllogistic reasoning can play a part. To see this imagine the mother of all hard cases, then settle (according to your moral or legal intuitions) the controversial aspects of it and on you go! You are now ready to solve the case with "syllogistic reasoning playing a role".

These are the reasons why I believe this is not a correct interpretation of MacCormick's claim. But if this interpretation is incorrect, then how are we to understand MacCormick's argument? To answer this question we can turn to Joseph Raz's distinction between what he calls the "narrow" and the "wide" versions of the sources thesis (Raz 1985, pp. 214–215). The wide sources thesis "claims that the truth or falsity of [pure and applied] legal statements depends on social facts which can be established without resort to moral argument" (Raz 1985, p. 214). In these cases, all that is needed to solve the case is to find the applicable rule(s), and establish the relevant facts, while the narrow sources thesis is silent concerning applied legal statements. I believe that MacCormick's claim, as his analysis of *Daniels* makes clear, is precisely that sometimes the justification of a legal decision can be purely and wholly deductive in form, and it can be presented as a syllogism which features as major premisses only legal rules (and as minor premisses only statements of fact): "all of the major premisses involved in the argument [in *Daniels*], not all of which were expressly stated, are rules of law for which contemporary authority can be cited" (MacCormick 1994, p. 29) or, as he claims just a couple of pages below,

It will be observed that in the above analysis of the argument each stage in the argument is a valid hypothetical argument the premisses of which are *either* statements of propositions of law which at the material time were true for legal purposes, *or* findings of fact which are also for legal purposes taken to be true, or intermediate conclusions derived from such premisses (MacCormick 1994, p. 32; my italics).

Thus MacCormick's argument is not one about what makes a legal justification a good and complete one, as Alexy's was, but about the existence of some cases that can be solved in a deductive manner using as premisses only statements of propositions of law and findings of fact. About, I believe we could now say, the truth of the wide, and not only the narrow, version of the sources thesis.[14]

Actually, later in the book MacCormick seems to acknowledge that in the first sense (judicial syllogism as internal justification) "moments" of deductive reasoning exist even in hard cases, which are characterised by the fact that "deduction comes in only after the interesting part of the argument, settling a ruling in law, has been carried out" (MacCormick 1994, p. 197).

In Alexy's terms, the internal justification starts off only after the external justification has taken place, since only after the external justification (what MacCormick at 197 calls "settling a ruling in law") the major premises to be used by the internal justification will be found. MacCormick's claim in chapter 2 of *Legal Reasoning and Legal Theory*, then, amounts to saying that in some cases no external justification is needed beyond that provided by what he calls "the fundamental judicial commandment": "thou shalt not controvert established and binding rules of law" (MacCormick 1994, p. 195). These are the cases that in jurisprudential jargon are called "clear" cases, the cases that Hart distinguished on the basis that in them, rules can be applied without courts being required to make what he called "a fresh judgment" (Hart 1994, p. 135): I take "without the need for fresh judgement" to mean here "without premises needing external justification (beyond MacCormick's judicial commandment)".[15]

This might seem an instance of labouring the obvious, and indeed I think it is. My only justification for it is that MacCormick himself sometimes equivocates between the trivial (deduction has a role to play in legal justification) and the important (some cases can be decided following a strictly syllogistic line of reasoning) claims. I

---

[14] To go back to Hart's example (*supra*, n. 13): if I want to drive with my FIAT Regatta through the park in order to enjoy the view while I am driving (or to save a couple of minutes from my journey, etc), it would still be true that, in Alexy's terms the premise "this FIAT Regatta is a vehicle" calls for (external) justification. But the whole point of Hart's distinction between *core* and penumbra was that any challenge to the statement: "this FIAT Regatta ... etc" would be regarded as lack of mastery of the word "vehicle", to clarify which only conceptual or verbal considerations (if any) are useful.

[15] For the meaning I am ascribing to the phrase "fresh judgement" *see supra*, at 7.

will come back to this point later on in this article (*infra* at 18f), but for the time being suffice it to compare the two following statements by MacCormick:

[S]ome people have denied that legal reasoning is ever strictly deductive. If this denial is intended in the strictest sense, implying that legal reasoning is never, or cannot ever be, *solely deductive in form*, then the denial is manifestly and demonstrably false. It is sometimes possible to show conclusively that a given legal decision is legally justified by means of a *purely deductive argument* (MacCormick 1994, p. 19, my italics).

[D]eductive reasoning from rules *cannot* be a self-sufficient, self-supporting, mode of legal justification. It is *always* encapsulated in a web of anterior and ulterior principles and values, even though a purely pragmatic view would reveal many situations and cases in which no one thinks it worth the trouble to go beyond the rules for practical purposes (MacCormick 1994, p. xiii, my italics).

Daniels v Tarbard

We are now ready to examine MacCormick's example of a case in which a purely syllogistic justification of the decision is possible. His example was *Daniels and Daniels v R. White & Sons and Tarbard* (1938 4 All ER 258). Though MacCormick has made this case famous, it seems appropriate to give a brief description of its facts: Mr Daniels bought a bottle of lemonade (R White's lemonade) in the defendant's (i.e. Mrs Tarbard's) pub. He took the bottle home, where he and Mrs Daniels drank from it. As a consequence, they both became ill, because (as was proven later) the lemonade was heavily contaminated with carbolic acid. Mr and Mrs Daniels sued the owner of the pub and the lemonade's manufacturer. While the latter was absolved from liability, the former was held liable and ordered to pay damages to the (first) plaintiff. MacCormick's claim is that the court's decision follows in a deductive manner from these facts plus the legal rules as they were in 1938.

As a matter of fact (of logic, rather), however, MacCormick could not have shown that the court's reasoning in *Daniels* was strictly deductive without using the relationship of material implication, "$\supset$". "$\supset$" is used instead of "if *in any case* ... then ... " (1994, p. 29).[16] But legal rules do not rule for *all* cases, even if their

---

[16] MacCormick probably does not mean material implication in its technical sense. In symbolic logic, $(p \supset q)$ "is true if "not-p or q" is true. But "not-p or q" is

language may induce one to think they do. They do not rule "in all cases, if ... then ...", but "if in normal cases ... then ...". This point should not be particularly controversial against MacCormick, who has always believed that legal rules rule for "normal" cases, establishing what is to be "presumptively" the case (MacCormick 1974: 71; see also MacCormick 1995). Furthermore, MacCormick explicitly rejects in his book the move made by some authors, of explaining defeasibility on the basis of moral disagreement about the issue of whether or not the law should (moral "should") be applied. He thinks that in those kinds of cases what is at issue is not whether there are moral reasons to break the law, but what the law actually is:

[A] positivistic description of the system as it operates *cannot* answer a particular kind of question which may be raised *internally* to a legal system: the question as it might be raised for a judge in a hard case: "Why ought *we* to treat every decision in accordance with a rule valid by our criteria of validity as being sufficiently justified? and that is a question which can be, and from time to time is, raised [...]. For my part *I should be reluctant to treat such questions as being non legal simply because of a definitional fiat* [...]. To treat such arguments as ideological-but-not-legal (which is what Kelsen and, in effect, Hart do) on *a priori* grounds seems to me unsatisfactory" (MacCormick 1994, p. 63; only the fourth italics are mine).

To put it in the words used above: if rules are understood as referring to *normal* cases, then they simply cannot be applied without having previously established that the case is *normal*. It is still possible to say (with Kelsen and Hart) that as a matter of law all cases are normal (or, what amounts to the same thing, that legal rules are, according to the law, to be applied to *all*, instead of *normal*, cases), but this implies a definitional *fiat* that begs the question: the *fiat*

---

true in any one of the following cases: (1) p is true and q is true; (2) p is false and q is true; (3) p is false and q is false [...S]o long as p is false, no matter what q is, "p implies q" is true; and so long as q is true, no matter what p is, "q is implied by p" is true (Cohen and Nagel 1934, p. 127). This is because "*material implication is the name we give to the fact that one of a pair of propositions happens to be false or else the other happens to be true*" (ibid. at 128). But MacCormick wants to say, I believe, that $(p \supset q)$ means something else, to wit, that *because* of p then q. MacCormick mentions this problem, and claims that "nothing turns on that" (MacCormick 1994, p. 28n). I take him to be offering a stipulation of the meaning of "$\supset$", so that it means "if in any case p, then (because of p) q" (notice the important "*if in any case*").

of saying that according to the law legal rules are to be applied to all cases (or that according to the law all cases are normal), however absurd the result might turn out to be. Only after this *fiat* will the decision not to apply the law because of these absurd outcomes become an "ideological-but-not-legal" one. MacCormick is reluctant to endorse this solution, and hence he is committed to claim that, as a matter of law (and not as a matter of ideology or morals) legal rules apply to normal cases (indeed, this is the view that MacCormick presently endorses: cf. MacCormick 1974, 1995).

But if MacCormick accepts that laws are to be understood as referring to *normal*, instead of *all*, cases, then it is difficult to see how can he claim that that the decision in *Daniels* was *strictly* and *solely* deductive. Lewis J held Mrs Tarbard liable "with some regret, because it is rather hard on Mrs. Tarbard, who is a perfectly innocent person in the matter" (*cit.* in MacCormick 1994, p. 21). He thought the application of the law to be inappropriate for the case. It is easy to see why: Lewis J assumed that in a civil liability case it is normally the case that if the defendant is "a perfectly innocent person in the matter" judgement should not be passed against him or her. In other words, the "innocence" of the defendant is usually a relevant substantive consideration. Because in the court's understanding the rules excluded this consideration, their application to this particular case produced some inappropriateness: they demanded judgement to be passed against a "perfectly innocent person". But this inappropriateness was not, in Lewis J's view, important enough for the need for predictability to be waived.[17] In other words, he took the rules as being formal enough to trump the inappropriateness of finding against a "perfectly innocent" party, this consideration not being strong enough to make the case "abnormal". This "fresh judgement" was, for Kelsen and Hart (as MacCormick says) not required by the law: it was "ideological-but-not-legal". But MacCormick sensibly rejects this position as based upon a definitional fiat that effectively begs the question.

---

[17] It must be borne in mind that I have legislated above (at n. 1) the meaning of "predictability", in such a way that it encompasses all the values that stand for a formalistic application of a legal rule. Predictability in its non-stipulated sense is normally the most important of them (hence the stipulation), but it need not be the only one.

LEGAL REASONING AND LEGAL THEORY REVISITED 559

Hence, for MacCormick this "fresh judgement" is *legal*, i.e. what *the law is* for the case cannot be known before it is made. Therefore MacCormick's syllogism will not be formally valid unless it is stated as a premise. This can clearly be seen when attention is paid to MacCormick's translation of the court's decision into logical notation:

(16) If a seller has broken a condition of a contract which he was required to fulfil, the buyer is entitled to recover damages from him equivalent to the loss directly and naturally resulting to him from the seller's breach of the condition;

(15) In the instant case, the seller has broken a condition of the contract which she was required to fulfil;

(17) ∴ In the instant case, the buyer is entitled to recover damages from her equivalent to the loss directly and naturally resulting to him from the seller's breach of the condition (MacCormick 1994, pp. 31–32).[18]

This is translated as (the left column is MacCormick's, while the right one contains my translation of MacCormick's logical notation back to English, according to his stipulations on pp. 23 and 28f, which I will use thereafter):

(16) $y \supset z$ (16) In any case, if y then z;
(15) y (15) In the instant case, y;
(17) ∴ z. (17) Therefore in the instant case z

MacCormick is clearly correct in claiming that (17) follows from (16) and (15). But the point is that (16) is not a correct description of the law as it was at the time, and we have already seen

---

[18] MacCormick's complete syllogism is considerably longer (cf. 1994, p. 30ff). The objection I am presenting now could, however, be directed against any of its parts, therefore it is enough for me to quote a section of the reasoning. It is also worth noticing that though MacCormick now believes that a judicial syllogism like *Daniels's* should be represented using predicate rather than propositional logic, I have retained MacCormick's original representation of it (*see* MacCormick 1994, p. xv; MacCormick's change of mind was prompted by White 1979).

that MacCormick elsewhere in the book (and in other writings, most notably, 1974, 1995) agrees with this. If we correct (16) by introducing the idea of "normal cases", we would get

(16′) In normal cases, if y, then z;
(15) In the instant case, y;
(17) Therefore in the instant case, z.

And this is not a valid deductive argument: to be one it needs a further premise:

(18) The instant case is a normal case

MacCormick's preferred option (that legal rules establish what is "presumptively" to be the case) makes this problem even more noticeable. For consider:

(16″) If y, then presumptively z;
(15) In the instant case, y;
(17) Therefore in the instant case, z.

Again, (17) does not follow. What does follow is

(17″) Therefore in the instant case, presumptively z.

But (17″) does not, of course, justify a legal decision. It does not tell anybody what the law is for the instant case: it only states what the law "presumptively" is.

What MacCormick calls "the pragmatics of law" (1994, p. xiii; 1995) would not be of much use here. "A rule that ends with 'unless ...' is still a rule", of course, but it cannot be applied unless the exceptional circumstance is not present. The rule might be such that the "default" position is that the exception does not exist, but even in this case the justification would, from a logical point of view, be incomplete (i.e. invalid) if this circumstance is not asserted. For consider,

(16''') In any case, if *y*, then *z*, unless the court is satisfied of *w*;

(15''') In the instant case, *y*;

(17''') Therefore in the instant case, *z*.

Again, (17''') fails to follow. For the argument to be formally valid, a premise like the following is needed:

(19) *w* has not been proven (or: "the court has not been satisfied of *w*").

Following Hart, we have already seen that "*w*" here stands for a fresh judgement to the effect that the inappropriateness of the application of the rule to the particular case is important enough for the demand for predictability to be waived. As a premise, therefore, (19) is neither a rule of law nor a statement of fact, but an evaluative judgement: "in this case the result offered by the rule is not inappropriate, or at least not to a significant extent". In other words, even in as clear a case as *Daniels* and even assuming that the court has the obligation to apply the law, no decision can be reached in a syllogistic manner using only rules of law and statements of fact as premises. The fact that the absence of *w* need not be argued, important as it is from a pragmatic point of view (no external justification is needed to regard it as absent) is immaterial from a logical point of view.[19]

In short, the only way in which MacCormick's claim could succeed is assuming the definitional *fiat* he (rightly, in my view) rejects in chapter 3.

---

[19] Cf. MacCormick 1994, p. 29, where MacCormick rightly points out that to the premises stated by Lewis J a further one should be added, one "which is so trivially obvious that its omission from the express statements of Lewis J is scarcely surprising – namely that the transaction described in (i) above was intended by each of the parties to be a purchase by Mr. D. From Mrs. T. and a sale by her to him". Maybe the premise that states the normality of the instant case (or that the presumption in favour of the solution offered by the rule according to its meaning is not defeated in the instant case) is equally trivially obvious in many cases, but as MacCormick recognises the fact that a premise is "trivially obvious" does not mean that it is not required for the formal validity of the inference, though it might very well mean that the court is justified in not stating it.

Now, it could be argued that I have missed the point, that the fact that the rule should be applied to the particular case at hand is one of the presuppositions (and it thus constitutes a limit) of deductive justification. In *Legal Reasoning and Legal Theory*, MacCormick says that one of the presuppositions of legal reasoning is that

> every judge has in virtue of his office a duty to apply each and every one of those rules which are "rules of law" whenever it is relevant and applicable to any case brought before him. And that formulation reveals a second presupposition, without which the term "duty" would lack identifiable reference: that it is possible for the judge to identify all those rules which are "rules of law" (MacCormick 1994, p. 54).

Hence, the counter-objection would continue, if it is doubted whether the rule should be applied to *this* particular case, then we are going beyond one of the limits of deductive reasoning, while MacCormick's thesis was meant for those cases in which those presuppositions are satisfied. But this cannot be an answer to my objection to MacCormick's claim, since I am assuming that the court has to apply the law; what I am contesting is that in finding what the law is for the case, the court will necessarily have to assume that the case is "normal" if rules like those in *Daniels* are to be applied as they were in that case. This, again, could be used to defend MacCormick's position only if one were to adopt the solution that MacCormick is reluctant to adopt, i.e. if one were to claim that the rule applies to *all* cases as a matter of law, however justified (from an "ideological-but-not-legal" point of view) the court might be in not applying it to the particular case. Only given that assumption MacCormick could say that the process of finding a solution is (or can in some cases be) deductive: given the relevant rules as they were in 1938, and the facts of *Daniels* as they were proven in court, the conclusion could be reached in a deductive manner. By the same token, however, he would have to say that given Pufendorf's report of the Bolognese law (and the facts as he told them), we could reach the conclusion that the barber had to be punished in the same deductive manner. What we would add in the latter case would be an "ideological-but-not-legal" argument to the effect that punishing the barber is too absurd for the court to do it. MacCormick's argument cannot succeed without this *a priori* distinction between the legal and the ideological, a distinction that he himself thinks is unjustified.

Since MacCormick himself rejects this distinction we need not discuss it here.[20] What interests me here is to point out the incompatibility of MacCormick's legal theory with his account of legal reasoning.[21] We know that *Legal Reasoning and Legal Theory* was meant to be a Hartian explanation of legal reasoning. Hence, it had to claim that *some* cases were in a Hartian sense clear, that is, their outcome could be determined according to the rules alone (that is the gist of Hart's criticism of rule-scepticism). If those cases are completely determined by the rules, it must be possible to reconstruct the justification of a solution to them according to the deductive model. That is to say: if it is the case that

the life of the law consists to a very large extent in the guidance both of officials and private individuals by determinate rules which, unlike the applications of variable standards, do *not* require from them a fresh judgement from case to case (Hart 1994, p. 135)

then in those cases the court's decision can be represented in a syllogistic way, in which the only presupposition needed (along with statements of fact and of legal rules) is that the law ought to be applied, in which no premise containing a "fresh judgement" is needed for the formal validity of the inference. This is the significance of MacCormick's argument in Chapter 2 of *Legal Reasoning and Legal Theory* as an analysis of clear cases according to Hart. But in the following chapters, in which he undertook to build up a theory of legal reasoning, he was driven to positions which are incompatible with the claims of the (legal) theory.

Thus, when discussing the issue of clear and hard cases, he starts by noticing that "in truth there is no clear dividing line between clear cases and hard cases" (MacCormick 1994, p. 197). There is a spectrum of cases, ranging from the hardest to the clearest, and

---

[20] *See* my "Games and the Law" cit. supra at n. 4.

[21] I am referring here to MacCormick's legal theory as it can be found in *Legal Reasoning and Legal Theory*. His position is nowadays different: "[I] no longer accept nearly as much of his [i.e. Hart's] theses about law as I did in 1978" (1994, p. xv). My own comments about *Legal Reasoning and Legal Theory* are not to be seen as a criticism of MacCormick's legal theory, since (I would claim) his later work can accommodate most of the claims made here, but about the tension between the perspectives of legal theory and legal reasoning, a tension that permeates his argument as originally presented in 1978.

across that spectrum "it could never be judged more than vaguely at what point" interpretative doubts could become significant enough for the court to have discretion. Now instead of offering (like Hart with his open texture thesis in its first interpretation) a value-free test to distinguish a clear from a hard case, he finds the explanation of this uncertainty at the divide between clear/hard cases in "differences in the dominant style of different periods in the history of legal systems" (1994, p. 198). Later on we are told that "when we talk of differences between judicial styles [...] what we are talking about is or includes the degree of readiness which a judge manifests to permit that presumption [i.e. the presumption that "obvious meaning should be preferred"] to be overridden" (1994, p. 207).

In this view, how pressing the absurdity of the result produced by the application of the rule to the particular case should be for the judge to permit the presumption in favour of the obvious meaning of the words to be overridden is not something the rule can settle; it is a problem generated by the conflicting demands of predictability and appropriateness; a case cannot be decided before deciding whether it will be treated as a "normal" case (and given – and excluding – this decision a deductive justification could be reconstructed) or as one in which substantive considerations show that the case is abnormal, that is, is one in which the presumption must be overridden.

To emphasise: if what makes a case clear rather than hard (and vice-versa) is a judgment about the right balance between two values (i.e. a fresh judgment), then at least some (I would say: all, but all I need for the argument to stand is to say "some") hard cases *are* hard because they *ought to be* so.

The only reason, I submit, why MacCormick thinks he can claim *both* that the decision in clear cases can be justified in a syllogistic manner (using as premisses only statements of fact and of legal rules) *and* that rules apply only to normal cases (or that they establish only what is to be "presumptively" the case) is that he (as we already saw) equivocates between the two different claims identified above concerning what we could call the "deductive element" in legal reasoning.

MacCormick's argument was originally presented against those who held the thesis that "legal reasoning is [n]ever *strictly* deductive" (1994, p. 19). We are told that if this denial "is intended in the strictest sense, implying that legal reasoning is never, or cannot ever be, *solely* deductive in form, then the denial is manifestly and demonstrably false. It is sometimes possible to show *conclusively* that a given decision is legally justified by means of a *purely deductive argument*" (1994, p. 19). Later in the book, however, chapter 2 was supposed to have been directed against "those who deny that deductive logic is *relevant* to the justification of legal decisions" (1994, p. 45), and in the new foreword to the 1994 paperback edition the argument has definitely changed: now it is presented against "recurrent denials by learned persons that the law *allows scope* for deductive reasoning, or even logic at all" (1994, p. ix). In the same piece MacCormick seems to reject his own claim that "it is sometimes possible to show conclusively that a given decision is legally justified by means of a purely deductive argument" when he now claims that "deductive reasoning from rules *cannot* be a self-sufficient, self-supporting, mode of legal justification. It is *always* encapsulated in a web of anterior and ulterior reasoning from principles and values [...]" (1994, p. xiii; all the italics in this paragraph are mine).

In my opinion, the quotations from the new foreword reflect MacCormick's present view of the "centrality of deductive reasoning for legal reasoning" and they have to be understood in the light of Alexy's distinction between external and internal justification. So understood, the claim refers to the possibility of translating a given decision in syllogistic terms as being usually the clearest and safest way to check whether or not the decision was fully justified, whether or not issues requiring external justification had arisen (and if they had, whether or not they were settled according to the requirements of the external justification).

But in this sense chapter 2 does not answer the challenge to legal positivism it was designed to answer. If it is to provide an answer, it has to be taken as meaning that sometimes it is possible for legal decisions to be fully justified through a syllogistic chain of reasoning that uses only statements of fact and of legal rules as premises. Only in this sense the thesis would imply, if correct, the rejection of the argument presented up to now. Only in this sense could it help Hart to show that in some cases no fresh judgement is needed for courts and officials to apply the rules. But for this argument to work, an *a priori* distinction has to be made between the legal and the ideological. Since MacCormick is unwilling to make this *ad hoc* distinction, the argument fails to prove that sometimes legal decisions can be "purely" and "solely" deductive in form.

* * *

The reasons for considering in some detail MacCormick's argument were, as stated above, not only concerned with the intrinsic value of it; it also helps us illustrate the contemporary predicament of legal theory: depending upon the perspective adopted at the beginning, one can reach, following natural and plausible steps, incompatible conclusions. When MacCormick adopted the perspective of legal theory, that is, the perspective of an enterprise directed to understanding what law is, when a legal system exists and the like, he was driven to the Hartian view that sometimes rules are there, so to speak, and can sometimes be "straightforwardly" applied.

When he adopted the perspective of legal reasoning, that is to say, one that tries to understand how the law is applied (to my knowledge, his book is still one of the few, not to say the only one, self-avowedly positivist work in which the discussion of decisions given in *actual cases* plays a crucial methodological role) he could not live up to that: the conclusions for legal reasoning that would follow from the "legal theory" thesis are just too implausible, too *ad hoc*.

I want to claim that this is not a problem of MacCormick's alone. This problem appears in one way or another in the work of many of the most sophisticated authors writing today on legal theory. I want to end this article by showing that this is also the case concerning the place of legal reasoning in Joseph Raz's recent work.

LEGAL REASONING, RULES AND SOURCES

Contrary to what one could guess, Raz believes that "commitment to the sources thesis does not commit one to formalism or to the autonomy of legal reasoning" (Raz 1993, p. 317).[22]

---

[22] Raz here means by 'formalism" the thesis that "the art of legislation, and more generally law-making, is that of moral reasoning. But legal reasoning is

In 1985, however, Raz presented an argument that could easily lead one to believe that the sources thesis implied indeed some form of autonomy for legal reasoning. There Raz distinguished between two interpretations of the sources thesis:

> Let us distinguish between what source-based law states explicitly and what it establishes by implication. If a statute in country A says that income earned abroad by a citizen is liable to income tax in A, then it only implicitly establishes that I am liable to such tax. For my liability is not stated by the statute but is inferred from it (and some other premises). Similarly, if earnings abroad are taxed at a different rate from earnings at home, the fact that the proceeds of export sales are subject to the home rate is implied rather than stated. It is inferred from this statute and other legal rules on the location of various transactions.
>
> The two examples differ in that the statement that I am liable to tax at a certain rate is an applied legal statement depending for its truth on both law and fact. The statement that export earnings are taxed at a certain rate is a pure legal statement, depending for its truth on law only (i.e. on acts of legislation and other law-making facts). The sources thesis as stated at the beginning can bear a narrow or a wide interpretation. The narrow thesis concerns the truth conditions of pure legal statements only. Pure legal statements are those which state the content of the law, i.e. of legal rules, principles, doctrines, etc. The wide thesis concerns the truth conditions of all legal statements, including applied ones. It claims that the truth or falsity of legal statements depends on social facts which can be established without resort to moral argument (1985, pp. 214–215).

Using Raz's language, legal reasoning is reasoning about which applied legal statements are true (or valid). Under the *narrow* interpretation, therefore, the sources thesis is silent concerning legal reasoning, since it is silent concerning applied legal statements. Since in 1993 we find him categorically saying that the sources thesis does not commit one to the autonomy of legal reasoning, we would be forced to understand that as an endorsement of the narrow, as opposed to the wide, interpretation of the sources thesis.

But actually, for Raz the wide and the narrow versions of the sources thesis stand together, at least if moral facts are not contingent:

> All the arguments so far concern the narrow sources thesis only. Nothing was said about its application to applied legal statements. I tend to feel that it applies to them as well, since they are legal statements whose truth value depends on reasoning about the law as it is. As such it is free from any infection by moral reasoning. One can reason morally about legal reasoning but not in it, not as part of it" (Raz 1993, p. 314).

contingent facts as well as on law. If one assumes that contingent facts cannot be moral facts, then the sources thesis applies here as well. That is, what is required is the assumption that what makes it contingently true that a person acted fairly on a particular occasion is not the standard of fairness, which is not contingent, but the "brute fact" that he performed a certain action describable in value-neutral ways. If such an assumption is sustainable in all cases, then the sources thesis holds regarding applied legal statements as well (1985, p. 218).

In brief: the narrow version, together with the claim that moral facts are not contingent, imply the wide version and the wide version implies the autonomy of legal reasoning. Since Raz wants to say today that the sources thesis does not imply the autonomy of legal reasoning it would seem as if he owes us an explanation of how moral facts are contingent.

I believe, in fact, that the narrow version cannot fulfil the role Raz expected the sources thesis to fulfil. Indeed, what are we to make of Raz's statement (1985, p. 218) that "all the arguments so far concern the narrow sources thesis only"? The "arguments so far" were advanced to claim that only if the law complies with the sources thesis can it have authority. The reason for this was that authority-capacity required the two non-moral features of authoritative directives, and that they in turn required the sources thesis. Let us focus upon the second feature, i.e. that authoritative directives can be identified and their content ascertained without using evaluative considerations (the first one was that an authoritative directive was supposed to reflect someone's view on the balance of applicable reasons). Why was this condition required? The answer is: because if it were not met the would-be directive would fail to be able to fulfil its function, and subjects would fail to be able to be benefited by the existence of the authority: the subjects "can benefit by [the authority's] decisions only if they can establish their existence and content in ways which do not depend on raising the very same issues which the authority is there to settle" (Raz 1985, p. 203). Only if this condition is met would an allegedly authoritative directive be able to comply with the normal justification thesis. But at the end of the article we are told that the "arguments so far" concern the narrow version only, with the obvious implication that authority-capacity requires only the *narrow* sources thesis. This means that the argument turns out to be that the law can have authority-capacity even if the wide sources thesis is untenable, that is, even if subjects can *never* get *any* "applied legal statement" without raising all the moral considerations that were pre-empted by the authoritative directive, *even if the authority is fully legitimate.*

In other words: if we accept Raz's claim that "all the arguments presented [in the first four sections of 'Authority, Law and Morality'] concern the narrow sources thesis only" the authoritative nature of law ceases to be an argument for the sources thesis. For consider: Raz claims that "a decision is serviceable only if it can be identified by means other than the considerations the weight and outcome of which it was meant to settle" (Raz 1985, p. 203). Serviceable for what? For the parties to be able to *act* upon the decision rather than their own judgement. But to be serviceable in these terms what is required is the *wide* sources thesis, i.e. that (provided that the authority is legitimate), subjects can stop thinking about the substantive problem behind the authoritative directive and simply do as it commands.[23] If this cannot be done no authoritative directive can ever comply with the normal justification thesis.

But the distinction between the narrow and the wide interpretations of the source thesis was not mentioned by Raz in 1993. Is Raz's "The Autonomy of Legal Reasoning" a rejection of it? We are not given an answer to this question.

Instead Raz offers two different reasons why legal reasoning is not autonomous from moral reasoning: the first has to do with the fact that, "if our sole concern is to work out what ought to be done in order to obey the intentions, purposes or goals of the law-makers, we will often find ourselves faced with conflicting directives" (Raz 1993, p. 315). In this case, a choice is necessary, and the choice cannot be guided by source-based considerations. It follows that they have to be moral considerations.[24] But this in turn is not compatible with the thrust of the authority-based argument for the

---

[23] NB: the argument is silent regarding what should the subjects do. It does not claim that they should follow the authoritative directive, only that if that were the case it would be possible for them to do it. If it is possible for subjects to comply with the directives, then this implies (at least following Raz's theory of authority) that it is possible for them to take them as protected reasons, i.e. as reasons for action that also exclude other conflicting reasons.

[24] Raz claims that non source-based considerations cannot but be moral considerations, "for there is no other justification for the use of an autonomous body of considerations by the courts" (Raz 1993, p. 318). Therefore the question of the

sources thesis. Recall that the argument was that if the authoritative directives *claim* legitimate authority, it follows that they *can* have authority. If they can have authority, it follows that they must posses the non-moral conditions for having authority, one of which was that the subjects must be capable of establishing the directives' "existence and content in ways which do not depend on raising the vary same issues which the authority is there to settle" (Raz 1985, p. 203). But now Raz seems to be claiming that when applying source-based material our "sole concern" is not to apply the directives thus recognised, but to decide "what ought to be done in order to obey the intentions, purposes, or goals of the law-makers". Raz seems to be claiming that our *sole concern* should be that of second-guessing the authority, going beyond the meaning of the directive to check whether or not that meaning is a correct reflection of the authority's "intentions, goals and purposes". But we should not second-guess the authority, if the sources thesis is true.[25]

Let me pause for a while on the meaning of the "should" that appeared in the last sentence. Since we are considering whether or not legal reasoning is autonomous from moral reasoning, it seems appropriate here to understand this "should" in its moral sense. Last paragraph's last sentence, so understood, assumes that the authority is legitimate.

Needless to say, in many situations this will not be the case. Sometimes the authority will be a *de facto* authority and courts will have no reason at all to follow its directives. But this is immaterial to the discussion of the autonomy of legal reasoning, since,

---

autonomy of legal reasoning can only be the question of its autonomy from moral reasoning.

[25] Raz could claim here that I missed the point, which is the fact that the law displays "plurality of conflicting values [...] due to the fact that [it] is a product of human activity" (Raz 1993, p. 315n). But consider a case like Fuller's men sleeping in the station (see Fuller 1958). Here it might well be the case that there is a "plurality of conflicting values" (select the pair of your choice: predictability against appropriateness, keeping railway stations clean against fairness, or whatever), but the fact is, the source-based material does offer a solution: fine the first man and acquit the second. The problem created by the "plurality of conflicting values" will only be seen by the court if the court does precisely what it is *not* supposed to do, i.e. if it "raises the very same issues which the authority is there to settle" (cf. Raz 1985, p. 203). No conflict is evident if the court follows the law as identified according to the sources thesis.

from Raz's point of view, this is a moral question ("how, all things considered, should the courts decide the case?"), which is different from the legal question ("how, according to law, should cases be decided?"). The fact that courts sometimes have the moral duty to disregard authoritative directives does not show anything about legal reasoning, since that is a question about whether or not the law ought to be applied, while legal reasoning deals with the question of what is the law for the case (Raz 1993, p. 312). If this is the only way in which moral reasoning and legal reasoning are connected, the latter could still be autonomous from the former.

But Raz wants to deny this, since he wants to claim that "legal reasoning is an instance of moral reasoning". Therefore he has to show why legal reasoning is moral reasoning, even when the question of whether or not the law should (morally) be applied is not taken into account. To do this he distinguishes between "reasoning about the law" and "reasoning according to law". The first (i.e. "reasoning about the law") "is governed by the sources thesis" (Raz 1993, p. 316), hence if we restrict our view to it an autonomous form of legal reasoning will appear. But we should not leave the second aspect of legal reasoning, i.e. "reasoning according to law" aside, and once we pay attention to it, Raz tells us, we shall realise that it is "quite commonly straightforward moral reasoning" (Raz 1993, p. 317). That reasoning according to law is different from reasoning about the law is shown by that fact that

The law itself quite commonly directs the courts to apply extralegal considerations. Italian law may direct the courts to apply European community law, or international law, or Chinese law to a case [...]. In all these cases legal reasoning, understood to mean reasoning according to law, involves much more than merely establishing the law (Raz 1993, p. 317).

This might be so, but that does not show that legal reasoning is a form of moral reasoning. The most it could show is that Italian legal reasoning is a form of European legal reasoning (not that this makes any sense). So let us consider whether legal references to morality rather than to Chinese law would fare better for Raz. Would the fact that here and there a legal system may contain references to morality show that legal reasoning is a form of moral reasoning?

I hope the answer to this question is evident: insofar as particular rules make references to morality, then "reasoning according to law" is more than "reasoning about the law". But this argument is not enough to prove that "legal reasoning is an instance of moral reasoning" any more that the fact that sometimes engineers should consider aesthetic considerations makes engineering-reasoning an instance of aesthetic reasoning.

In brief, Raz does not want to draw the implications of his legal theory for legal reasoning. He tries to show that the sources thesis does not commit one to the thesis of the autonomy of legal reasoning, and to say so he has to make space for something to be left after the existence and content of the source-based material has been established. In the end, he can only come up with the small space provided by the fact that sometimes the law instructs courts to apply extralegal considerations and he offers this as a ground for the grand thesis that legal reasoning *is* moral reasoning. My argument all along has been that this latter claim is indeed true, and because this is the case anything like the sources thesis cannot but be false.

To make this point clearer, let me consider a more recent effort by Raz to show that the sources thesis does not commit one to what (in 1993) he called "formalism". In "On the Nature of Law" (Raz 1996) he tried to defend his legal positivism against the charge that it misrepresents legal reasoning. The "standard objection", he says, to it when its implications for legal reasoning are drawn, is that

> would we not expect two clearly separate stages in legal reasoning: an interpretive-factual stage and a (purely) moral one? First one would establish what authoritatively laid down law says on the issue at hand, and then either it does not provide a determinate disposition of the issue, or if one wants to determine whether the way it disposes of the issue is morally acceptable, one would move to the second purely moral stage in the argument. In fact we do not find that legal reasoning divides in that way. Legal reasoning displays a continuity through all its stages (Raz 1996, p. 19).[26]

To show how this objection actually reinforces rather than refutes his views on the nature of law, Raz invites us to consider interpretation

---

[26] Raz incidentally airs some doubts as to what he sees as the tacit assumption of this objection: "I believe that this point is overstated, and that legal reasoning is not all of a kind" (at 19). The objection, however, does not need to assume that "legal reasoning is all of a kind". Indeed, I believe (though I cannot defend this point here) that insofar as he defends the wide sources thesis it is *Raz*, and not the objector, who would be committed to the doubtful thesis that legal reasoning is all of a kind. But I will not pursue this issue.

in the arts. A good interpretation of a play or of a piano sonata is, he tells us, an interpretation that combines *tradition* with *innovation* in the right way, and because of this reason there cannot be a general theory of interpretation: "innovation defies generalisation. A theory of originality, in the sense we are considering, is self-defeating" (Raz 1996, p. 20). What the objection points to, says Raz, is that a theory of legal reasoning would be required to explain how best to combine "the two aspects of legal reasoning. On the one hand legal reasoning aims to establish the content of authoritative standards, on the other hand, it aims to supplement them, and often to modify them, in the light of moral considerations" (Raz 1996, p. 19). But how this combination should be achieved is not something that any theory can answer, hence the fact that positivism cannot offer a such a "self-defeating" theory does not show it to be a defective theory of law.

Let us go along with Raz's thesis that there cannot be a theory of interpretation because "tradition" and "originality" defy generalisation. *Before* he can use this argument to support legal positivism, however, he has to show why "originality" is important in legal reasoning. Instead of explaining this, however, he shows how this is the case when what is being interpreted is a piano sonata or a play and then immediately (and rather surprisingly) he claims "*hence* its [i.e. interpretation's] importance in law" (Raz 1996, p. 20).[27] I do not want to express here an opinion on the subject of the similarities and differences between artistic and legal interpretation, but it cannot go unnoticed that, from *Raz's* point of view there is a crucial difference: *law has authority*. That the law has authority implies, we must remember, for Raz that

courts will not entertain moral argument about the desirability of regarding a certain fact (e.g. a previous enactment) as a reason for a certain action but will once the existence of the relevant fact has been established through morally-

---

[27] The whole paragraph says: "The same is true of interpretations of plays or of other literary works. A work can be understood and (in the case of a play) performed as a celebration of the natural world, or as a utopian reflections on social ideals. Or it can be seen as an exploration of the rift between generations or alternatively as a crisis of adolescence and immaturity. Here again, different, even contrasting interpretations can be consistent with the original. Interpretation is the activity which combines reproduction and creativity. Hence its importance in law" (Raz 1996, p. 20).

neutral argument hold it to be a reason which they are bound to apply (Raz 1980, p. 214).

And this in turn must mean, if anything, that courts are not supposed to "combine originality with tradition" when they are applying the law, they are simply supposed to identify the existence and content of the directives and then apply them. In short, Raz's claim that legal reasoning has two dimensions can help him only if he begs the whole issue, which is precisely that the sources thesis does not allow for legal reasoning to display those two dimensions.

Indeed, why should legal reasoning be interpretive? Raz answers:

The explanation lies in the authoritative nature of law: When trying to establish the legal status of an action, we need to ascertain whether any of the authoritatively binding rules and doctrines bear on it and if so how. That means establishing what has been done by the authorities, what decisions they have taken and what they mean" (Raz 1996, p. 19).

But, unless Raz wants to claim that ascertaining the meaning of an authoritative directive (or its existence as such) is impossible without considering the moral reasons it purports to adjudicate (in which case that authoritative directive would paradoxically lack "authority-capacity"), the *mere* fact that legal reasoning is about identifying the existence and ascertaining the content of authoritative directives does not imply that legal reasoning must have two aspects. If we remember the importance Raz placed on the non-moral conditions for authority capacity (*see* Raz 1985) I suppose we could be tempted to say that *precisely* because legal reasoning is about what authoritative directives there are and what they mean it cannot be moral reasoning.

Towards the end of the article we are reminded that

the prominence of interpretive reasoning in legal reasoning results from the fact that in law the two aspects of legal reasoning, that is establishing the content of authoritatively endorsed legal standards and establishing the (other) moral considerations which bear on the issue, are inextricable interwoven (Raz 1996, p. 22).

But were not these "other" considerations pre-empted by the authoritatively laid down directives? Had we not been told before (in *Practical Reason and Norms*) that from the legal point of view legal rules are standards "all of which the primary organs [*i.e.* courts] are bound to act on to the exclusion of *all* other conflicting reasons" (Raz 1992, p. 143, my italics)?

If the sources thesis is correct, legal reasoning cannot display these two aspects, because legal rules would pre-empt all the considerations that would constitute the second aspect. It can, of course be the case that once the content and existence of those directives has been established the different question of whether or not they ought (morally) to be applied can be entertained, but this could not be legal reasoning: it would be moral reasoning *simpliciter*. And here we go back to the objection Raz tried to answer. He thought that he could answer the objection simply by pointing out that no theory can solve the problem of how best to combine tradition and innovation. But if I am correct, he has to explain why does legal reasoning displays those two aspects to begin with.

Responding to an objection raised by Gerald Postema (Postema 1996), Raz has recently made another important concession to defend the sources thesis *and* to deny that it implies some form of "autonomy" for legal reasoning: he now "reject[s] any thesis of the autonomy of legal reasoning, at least if that includes anything more than reasoning *to the conclusion that the content of the law is such-and-such* [... N]o such reasoning can by itself support any judicial decision in common-law countries" since there courts can resort to a number of "devices to ensure that the law as applied to the case is not unjust" (at 4).

Here the wide version of the sources thesis seems to be clearly abandoned. But this concession has another important consequence. According to Raz, "by the sources thesis courts have discretion when required to apply moral considerations" (Raz 1979, p. 75). Hence what we are effectively being told here is that courts (at least in "common law countries") is that courts *always* have discretion. One wonders how can this fit with Raz's own theory of authority.

Indeed, when presenting that theory, in *The Morality of Freedom*, Raz did answer an objection that seems similar to the point under discussion here. The objection claimed that "in every case authoritative directives can be overridden or disregarded if they deviate much from the reasons they are meant to reflect". This could be one way of describing the position of common law judges according to Raz. But in *The Morality of Freedom* Raz saw that such a concession "defeats the pre-emption thesis since it requires every person in every case to consider the merits of the case before he can decide to accept an authoritative instruction", thus denying that authoritative directives "can serve the mediating role assigned to them above" (Raz 1986, p. 61). In this way Raz might be able to defend the sources thesis, but at the cost of giving up his theory of authority. And if the theory of authority is given up, there seems to be little reason not to confine the sources thesis to an updated version of Ihering's *Begriffshimmel*.[28]

REFERENCES

Alexy, R., *A Theory of Legal Argumentation*. Translated by Neil MacCormick and Ruth Adler (Oxford: Clarendon Press, 1989).

Bankowski, Z., Ian White and Ulrike Hahn, *Informatics and the Foundations of Legal Reasoning* (Dordrecht: Kluwer, 1995).

Cohen, M. R. and E. Nagel, *An Introduction to Logic and Scientific Method* (London: Routledge and Kegan Paul, 1934).

Coleman, J., "Authority and Reason", in George, ed. (1996).

Dworkin, R., "Is Law a System of Rules?" (1967), in Summers, ed. (1968).

Dworkin, R., *Law's Empire* (London: Fontana, 1986).

Flew, A., ed., *Logic and Language* (Oxford: Basil Blackwell, 1951).

Fuller, L., "Positivism and Fidelity to Law: A Reply to Professor Hart", *Harvard Law Review* 71 (1958): 630–672.

Füßer, K., "Farewell to Legal Positivism", in George, ed. (1996).

George, R., ed., *The Autonomoy of Law* (Oxford: Clarendon Press, 1996).

Hart, H. L. A., "Positivism and The Separation Between Law and Morals" (1958), in Hart (1983).

Hart, H. L. A., "Ihering's Heaven of Concepts and Modern Analytical Jurisprudence" (1970), in Hart (1983).

Hart, H. L. A., *Essays in Jurisprudence and Philosophy* (Oxford: Clarendon Press, 1983).

Hart, H. L. A., *The Concept of Law* (Oxford: Clarendon Press, 1994).

Ihering, R., *Scherz und Ernst in der Jurisprudenz* (1900).

Kelsen, H., *Introduction to the Problems of Legal Theory* (Oxford: Clarendon Press, 1934).

Kneale, W. and M. Kneale, *The Development of Logic* (Oxford: Clarendon Press, 1962).

MacCormick, N., "Law as Institutional Fact", in MacCormick and Weinberger (1986).

---

[28] Ihering 1900; *see* Hart 1970.

MacCormick, N., *Legal Reasoning and Legal Theory* (Oxford: Clarendon Press, 1994).
MacCormick, N., "Defeasibility in Law and Logic", in Bankowski et al., eds. (1995).
MacCormick, N. and O. Weinberger, *An Institutional Theory of Law* (Dordrecht: Kluwer, 1986).
Marmor, A., *Interpretation and Legal Theory* (Oxford: Clarendon Press, 1994).
Marmor, A, ed., *Law and Interpretation* (Oxford: Clarendon Press, 1995).
Patterson, D. M., ed., *Wittgenstein and Legal Theory* (Boulder, Co: Westview Press, 1992).
Postema, G. J., "Law's Autonomy and Public Practical Reason", in George, ed. (1996).
Pufendorf, S., *The Jure Naturae et Gentium Libri Octo* (Oxford, Clarendon Press, 1934 (1688)).
Raz, J., *The Authority of Law* (Oxford: Clarendon Press, 1979).
Raz, J., *The Concept of a Legal System* (Oxford: Clarendon Press, 1980).
Raz, J., "Authority, Law and Morality" (1985), in Raz (1994).
Raz, J., *The Morality of Freedom* (Oxford: Clarendon Press, 1986).
Raz, J., *Practical Reason and Norms* (Princeton: Princeton University Press, 1992).
Raz, J., "On the Autonomy of Legal Reasoning" (1993), in Raz (1994).
Raz, J., *Ethics in the Public Domain* (Oxford: Clarendon Press, 1994).
Raz, J., "On the Nature of Law", *Archiv fur Rechts- und Sozialphilosophie* 82 (1996), pp. 1–25.
Schauer, F., *Playing by the Rules* (Oxford: Clarendon Press, 1991).
Shiner, R. A., "The Acceptance of a Legal System", in Patterson, ed. (1992).
Summers, R. S., ed., *Essays in Legal Philosophy* (Oxford: Blackwell, 1968).
Waismann, F., "Verifiablity", in Flew, ed. (1951).
White, P., "Review (of Neil MacCormick's *Legal Reasoning and Legal Theory*)", *Michigan Law Review* 78 (1979), pp. 737–742.

Faculty of Law
Universidad de Talca
P.O. Box 747
Talca
Chile
(E-mail: fatria@pehueuche.utalca.cl)

[5]
A NATURAL LAW THEORY OF INTERPRETATION

Michael S. Moore

I. THE ROLE OF ORDINARY MEANING 288
   A. THE MEANING OF "MEANING" 288
      1. *The Nature of a Theory of Meaning* 288
      2. *Conventionalist and Realist Theories of Meaning* . . 291
   B. COMMON SKEPTICISMS ABOUT WORDS HAVING MEANINGS 301
      1. *Functionalism* 302
      2. *Contextualism* 304
      3. *Vagueness* 307
      4. *General Epistemological Skepticism* 309
   C. THE MORAL CASE FOR ORDINARY MEANINGS 313
      1. *The Relevant Values by Which to Adjudicate Between Competing Theories of Interpretation* 313
         a. *The rule of law virtues* 313
            i. *Separation of powers* 314
            ii. *Equality and formal justice* 316
            iii. *Liberty and notice* 316
            iv. *Substantive fairness* 317
            v. *Procedural fairness* 317
            vi. *Utility and efficient adjudication* 318
         b. *Consequentialist virtues* 318
      2. *The Prima Facie Desirability of Looking to the Ordinary Meanings of Words in Legal Texts* 320
   D. THE MORAL CASE FOR THE REALIST THEORY OF MEANING 322
      1. *Natural Kind Terms of Ordinary Speech* 322
      2. *Specially Defined Statutory Terms* 328
II. THE ROLE OF INTENTION 338

	A. THE MEANING OF "INTENTION"	338
	1. *Semantic Intentions*	340
	2. *Further Intentions*	344
	3. *Legislative Intentions*	348
	B. COMMON SKEPTICISMS ABOUT INTENTIONS	349
	1. *The Intentions of Individual Legislators*	350
	2. *Legislative Intentions*	350
	C. THE MORAL CASE AGAINST INTENTIONALIST INTERPRETATION	352
III.	THE ROLE OF PRECEDENT	358
	A. THE MEANING OF "PRECEDENT"	359
	1. *Common Law Precedent*	359
	2. *The Precedent of Prior Interpretations of Texts*	363
	B. COMMON SKEPTICISMS ABOUT PRECEDENT	366
	1. *Conventionalist Theories of Precedent*	366
	2. *Realist Theories of Precedent*	369
	C. THE MORAL CASE FOR PRECEDENT IN INTERPRETATION	371
	D. THE MORAL CASE FOR THE REALIST THEORY OF PRECEDENT	373
IV.	THE ROLE OF VALUES	376
	A. THE MEANING OF "VALUE"	377
	B. COMMON SKEPTICISMS ABOUT VALUES	379
	C. THE MOPAL CASE FOR A LIMITED ROLE FOR VALUES	381
	1. *In Finding Ordinary Meanings*	381
	2. *In Finding the Holding of a Case*	383
	3. *In Finding Purpose*	383
	4. *In Preventing Injustice*	386
	D. THE MORAL CASE FOR USING REAL VALUES	388
	1. *In Interpreting Statutory Texts*	388
	2. *In Interpreting Constitutional Texts*	393
V.	CONCLUSION	396

A NATURAL LAW THEORY OF INTERPRETATION

MICHAEL S. MOORE*

Interpretation is a quite fashionable topic these days in legal academia. There is, for example, the well-known debate between "interpretivists" and "noninterpretivists" in constitutional law.[1] This debate is but a special instance of the more general debate between those who urge that courts can be objectively right in their interpretations of any legal text—common law rules and statutes as much as constitutions—and those who urge the contrary.[2] Even more generally, this interest in interpretation by legal academics stems from certain philosophical traditions with which some members of these debates claim allegiance. There are essentially two such philosophical traditions. First, there is the *Geistwissenshaften* tradition, which sees all social science, including law, as studying phenomena that have meaning and thus all social scientific reasoning, including legal reasoning, as an *interpretive* enterprise.[3] Second, there is the skeptical tradition in epistemology, which urges that all knowledge—natural science as well as

---

* Robert Kingsley Professor of Law, University of Southern California Law Center. A.B. 1964, Oregon University; J.D. 1967, S.J.D. 1978, Harvard University. Versions of this Article were presented to the USC Law Faculty Workshop, to the law faculties at Tel Aviv University and Hebrew University, Israel, as one of my David Ben Gurion Lectures, to the Association of Law and Social Philosophy, Korean Chapter, as one of my lectures on legislation, Seoul, South Korea, as well as to the Interpretation Symposium of the Southern California Law Review. My thanks go to the many individuals at each of these presentations whose comments have made the paper better. This Article will appear as part of my forthcoming book, THE SEMANTICS OF JUDGING, to be published in 1986 by the Oxford University Press as part of the Clarendon Series in Legal Philosophy.

1. Tom Grey originated the distinction. *See* Grey, *Do We Have an Unwritten Constitution?*, 27 STAN. L. REV. 703 (1975). The debate has continued in these terms in J. ELY, DEMOCRACY AND DISTRUST 1-14 (1980); M. PERRY, THE CONSTITUTION, THE COURTS, AND HUMAN RIGHTS (1982); Grey, *Origins of the Unwritten Constitution: Fundamental Law in American Revolutionary Thought*, 30 STAN. L. REV. 843 (1978); *Symposium: Constitutional Adjudication and Democratic Theory*, 56 N.Y.U. L. REV. 259, 259-544 (1981).

2. For a quite contemporary example of this larger debate, see Brest, *Interpretation and Interest*, 34 STAN. L. REV. 765 (1982); Fiss, *Objectivity and Interpretation*, 34 STAN. L. REV. 739 (1982). The concern with objectivity in judicial interpretation, of course, antedates considerably contemporary legal academia's fascination with interpretation. Much of the literature of American legal realism should be seen as an attack on the possibility of objectivity in judicial interpretation of legal texts.

3. For two accessible introductions to this tradition, see G. VON WRIGHT, EXPLANATION AND UNDERSTANDING (1971); P. WINCH, THE IDEA OF SOCIAL SCIENCE AND ITS RELATION TO

social science—is bound up with interpretation by an observer.[4] Legal academics attracted to either of these two traditions in philosophy not only have a built-in interest in interpretation, but they also approach the problem of interpretation in law with skepticism.

My interest in a theory of interpretation, the topic of this Article, is somewhat oblique in regard to the interests of the literature referred to above. I am not a skeptic in epistemology generally, nor do I believe that the social sciences have a special epistemological status because of their focus on intentional ("meaningful") behavior.[5] My belief that lawyers need a theory of interpretation thus does not stem from such philosophical concerns. Nor do I think it helpful to discuss the objectivity of legal reasoning either in general or in constitutional law, in terms of the objectivity of "interpretation." For what is called interpretation in such debates[6] embraces the whole of legal reasoning, whereas I think there is a part of legal reasoning, but only a part, that can use-

---

PHILOSOPHY (1958). For a summary of the quite diverse strands in contemporary thought, agreeing with the *geistwissenschaften* tradition that social science uses concepts categorically distinct from those used in natural science, see M. MOORE, LAW AND PSYCHIATRY: RETHINKING THE RELATIONSHIP (1984). Two legal academics whose interpretive theories are affected by this tradition are Robert Cover and Owen Fiss. *See* Cover, *The Supreme Court, 1982 Term—Foreword: Nomos and Narrative*, 97 HARV. L. REV. 4 (1983); Fiss, *supra* note 2.

4. The contemporary philosophical skeptics most influential with legal theorists appear to be N. GOODMAN, WAYS OF WORLDMAKING (1978); H. PUTNAM, REASON, TRUTH, AND HISTORY (1981); R. RORTY, PHILOSOPHY AS THE MIRROR OF NATURE (1979). Although each will in some sense disavow that he is a skeptic (in the sense, for example, that P. UNGER, IGNORANCE (1975), will avow that he is a skeptic), each of these authors nonetheless finds philosophical realism untenable, thus implying that it is ultimately up to us as interpreters to decide what exists. Tom Grey tells me that if he may be placed at all, his own views are skeptical in the sense of this tradition. For a rather explicit influence in the theory of legal interpretation, see Levinson, *Law as Literature*, 60 TEX. L. REV. 373 (1982).

5. I argue there are no ontological or categorical boundaries that separate social from natural science in Moore, *Determinism and the Excuses*, 73 CALIF. L. REV. (forthcoming, 1985), and in M. MOORE, *supra* note 3.

6. *See* Fiss, *supra* note 2. This broad use of "interpretation" is also found in the work of Ronald Dworkin, who seems to use the word to cover all aspects of legal reasoning. *See* Dworkin, *The Forum of Principle*, 56 N.Y.U. L. REV. 469 (1981) [hereinafter cited as *Forum of Principle*]; Dworkin, *Law as Interpretation*, 60 TEXAS L. REV. 527 (1982) [hereinafter cited as *Law as Interpretation*]. Fiss and Dworkin adopt such a broad concept of interpretation because they fail to distinguish the question of how one should pedigree a text as authoritative, from the question of how one should interpret a text that is conceded to be authoritative. Dworkin fails to make this distinction, in turn, because of two idiosyncratic ways of looking at law: first, Dworkin conceives of law in terms of *propositions* rather than in terms of those *sentences* that judges must take as authoritative. Second, Dworkin's idea of law focuses on those singular propositions of law that decide particular cases ("This contract is valid," for example). To distinguish law from interpretation requires that one focus instead on those general standards ("All contracts contrary to public policy are void," for example) from which singular propositions are derived. Dworkin, *How to Read the Civil Rights Act*, N.Y. REV. OF BOOKS, Dec. 20, 1979, at 37.

fully be labelled the activity of "interpretation." Despite my own eschewing the terms of the present debates in law and in philosophy that go under the name of "interpretation," my hope is that the partial theory of legal reasoning that I wish to defend herein will illuminate the larger debates I have mentioned; the theory will do this if, as hoped, it illuminates legal reasoning itself.

Legal reasoning—reasoning done by judges in deciding particular cases—is special in ways demanding that any complete theory of adjuciation include some subtheory called a theory of interpretation. Legal reasoning has a text to deal with in the same way that theology, dream theory, or literary criticism deal with various texts. All such "hermeneutic" enterprises are distinct from the normal scientific enterprise of explaining phenomena, natural or social, in that they depend upon the existence of a text that requires interpretation.

Perhaps the distinction between all hermeneutic forms of reasoning, on the one hand, and normal scientific reasoning, on the other, becomes clearer through a nonlegal example. Consider dreams.[7] The classical Freudian account of the manifest content (the remembered part) of dreams asserts that there is a preconscious wish to sleep that is being challenged by an unconscious wish of a sexual sort that demands expression during sleep. Because it is repressed, the latter wish would wake us up if it were directly expressed. Thus the "dream work" takes place, distorting the manifest content in different ways from the latent dream thoughts (the unconscious undistorted wish).[8]

There are two quite different ways to understand the Freudian account just sketched, each carefully distinguished by both Freud and later Freudians.[9] One can understand Freud to be *explaining* dreams in the same way any scientist explains any phenomena, in terms of its causal antecedents. In such a case the preconscious wish to sleep, the unconscious wish from childhood, the latent dream thoughts, and the dream-work, are all really existent states or processes that occurred at a time prior to or simultaneous with the manifest dream and that caused

---

7. I explore the Freudian account of dreaming in some detail in Moore, *The Nature of Psychoanalytic Explanation*, 3 PSYCHOANALYSIS & CONTEMP. THOUGHT 459 (1980), *reprinted in expanded form in* MIND AND MEDICINE: EXPLANATION AND EVALUATION IN PSYCHIATRY AND THE BIOMEDICAL SCIENCES, 8 PITTSBURGH SERIES IN THE PHILOSOPHY AND THE HISTORY OF SCIENCE (L. Lauden ed. 1983).

8. For citations and a more detailed summary, see *id.* at 10.

9. *See* Jones, *Dream Interpretation and the Psychology of Dreaming*, 13 J. AM. PSYCHOANALYTIC A. 304 (1965) (explicating the difference between Freud's interpretive and his explanatory enterprises).

the dream to occur as it did. Alternatively, one can understand Freud as *interpreting* dreams and not explaining them at all. In such a case the unconscious wish from childhood, etc., does not cause the dream and did not necessarily exist simultaneously with or prior to the dream; rather, if such states or processes exist at all, they are *present* wishes of the dreamer which free association and other techniques have led the dreamer to see in himself as he fits the dream in with a picture of what sort of person he is. Freud, of course, thought he was giving both a scientific explanation and a therapeutic interpretation whenever he gave an account of a patient's dream in therapy. For our purposes it is enough to see the distinction between the interpretive and the explanatory enterprises.

In the interpretive enterprise of Freud, the role of the text is central. Freud notes that dreamers will remember their dreams differently if they relate them at different times. He therefore found it important to give a "rule of recognition" for locating the text: treat all descriptions of the dream as part of its manifest content. Similarly, other interpretive enterprises are marked by their concern with finding the text. In literary criticism one must decide whether, for example, Max Brod did an acceptable job of piecing together the manuscript for Kafka's *The Trial*, or whether some other text should be the object of one's interpretations of that novel. Likewise in theology one must have some way of validating the Bible (or some translation of it) as accurate before one engages in the logical exegesis of its provisions. Legal reasoning is similarly a textbound enterprise. Lawyers also demand a "rule of recognition" that tells them which statements, of all the statements there are in any natural language such as English, are authoritative and should be taken as part of the law.

Such concern with finding a text, and then interpreting it, marks off law, dream interpretation, theology, and literary criticism from scientific enterprises. In each of these areas there is a nonexplanatory, interpretive aim that makes such disciplines distinct from natural and social sciences. Anyone concerned with legal reasoning should thus have an interest in interpretation, an interest that is not necessarily dependent on the skeptical philosophical traditions mentioned earlier.

We may pinpoint the role of a theory of interpretation within a larger theory of legal reasoning in the following way.[10] Imagine a

---

10. I sketch such a role for interpretaion within a theory of legal reasoning in Moore, *The Need for a Theory of Legal Theories: Assessing Pragmatic Instrumentalism*, 69 CORNELL L. REV. 988, 1002-10 (1984).

judge deciding a single issue in a case—for example the issue of whether a frozen, eviscerated chicken is or is not a "manufactured product" for purposes of granting an exemption from Interstate Commerce Commission certification for the interstate carriers of such items.[11] Suppose that the judge decides that no certificate is required. A full deductive justification for the decision[12] would include a statement of law, a statement of fact, *and* a statement interpreting the law so that it applies to the described facts. Such statements in the example just given would be, respectively:

1. (Statement of Law): If an item is not a manufactured product, then its carriage does not require a certificate.
2. (Statement of Fact): These items were frozen, eviscerated chickens.
3. (Interpretive Statement): If an item is a frozen, eviscerated chicken, then it is not a manufactured product.

With these three premises, the legal conclusion in the case—that carriage of these items does not require a certificate—can be deduced as a matter of standard deductive logic.[13]

I take a theory of interpretation in law to be a theory that tells judges (and lawyers who argue to judges) how to derive premises of the third sort. One can see the partial nature of such a theory of interpretation by seeing what else is needed for a full-fledged theory of legal reasoning. First, a judge must have a theory of law proper, which tells how to derive statements of the first sort for use in the judge's reasoning. The judge needs, in other words, some rule of recognition that explains how to derive a text ("the law"). Second, the judge must have some theory about facts that determines which of the indefinitely large number of descriptions of "what happened" should be used in deciding the case. Third, a judge needs the theory of interpretation noted above. And fourth, a judge needs a theory about logic and its place in legal reasoning. He needs this last theory even to legitimate this admittedly controversial way of schematizing legal reasoning.

A full-fledged theory of legal reasoning (of "adjudication") will include each of these four subtheories. Some of the debates about legal reasoning should be seen as debates about one or another of these sub-

---

11. ICC v. Kroblin, 113 F. Supp. 599 (N.D. Iowa 1953), *reprinted in* W. BISHIN & C. STONE, LAW, LANGUAGE AND ETHICS 117-31 (1972).
12. *See* N. MACCORMICK, LEGAL REASONING AND LEGAL THEORY (1978) (exploring deductive justification for particular legal decisions).
13. For the deduction, see Moore, *The Semantics of Judging*, 54 S. CAL. L. REV. 151, 171-72 (1981).

theories and its content. The debate between legal positivists and natural lawyers, for example, should be seen as a debate within the theory of law proper, positivists urging that the pedigree of statements of law can be solely a matter of fact while natural lawyers urge that value judgments are necessary to pedigree any proposition as an authoritative ("legal") proposition. The older debate between formalists and legal realists should be seen mainly as a debate about whether there is any value-free way to derive interpretive premises in law, the formalists urging that there is and the legal realists urging that there is not. (Other parts of the legal realist assault on the possibility of value-free adjudication is within the theory of fact, of logic, and of law proper.)

A theory of interpretation, as I am using the phrase, therefore plays a discrete role within an overall theory of legal reasoning. A theory of interpretation answers the question of how a judge should derive the interpretive premises needed to connect the law to the facts of the case to be decided. This theory of interpretation does not answer the equally important questions of where the authoritative text is found (the business of a theory of law), where the judge gets a description of the facts (the business of a theory of fact), or what the judge does with all of these statements (the business of a theory of logic).

"Interpretation," as I wish to use the word, thus names one discrete subactivity within the activity of legal reasoning. It is not a synonym for legal reasoning itself. There is a narrow use of "interpretation" that must also be put aside if we are to be clear on what we will be talking about. I do not intend by the word to distinguish between finding the meaning of a law, and applying that law to the facts of some case. "Interpretation," as sometimes used, names that activity of finding synonyms for legal words before one applies them to the facts.[14] As so used, one might then distinguish hard cases, where

---

14. This narrower use of "interpretation" distinguishes the interpretation of the law from its application. For a judicial use of this distinction, see, *e.g.*, Dahnke-Walker Milling Co. v. Bondurant, 257 U.S. 282, 294-95 (1921) (Brandeis, J., dissenting) ("[I]n every case involving a statute, the state court must perform . . . two functions essentially different. First the Court must construe the statute; that is, determine its meaning and scope. Then it must apply the statute, as so construed, to the facts of the case.") (footnote omitted). Several contemporary legal theorists also use such a distinction. *E.g.*, Schauer, *An Essay on Constitutional Language*, 29 UCLA L. REV. 797, 806-07 (1982).

As I use the word "interpretation," it covers both the activity denoted by interpretation in this narrow sense and application. Interpretation in the narrow sense only includes that part of what I call interpretation that those such as Brandeis and Schauer would call "finding the meaning" of an expression. That is, interpreting in the narrow sense is only finding a set of synonyms that brings out the meaning of the legal text. Missing from this narrow view of interpretation is the process of applying those synonyms to the facts of the actual case. When that second step, application, is

some interpretation of the law is required before it is applied to the facts, from easy cases, where no interpretation is required. As should be apparent from the foregoing, "interpretation," as I use the word, has no such distinction built into it. Whatever one must do to connect the law to the facts in the manner earlier sketched is what I mean by "interpretation," and a theory of interpretation is a theory of how this activity should proceed.

Partly because courts and scholars have not distinguished the theory of interpretation from an overall theory of legal reasoning in which interpretation (properly so called) is only a part, the theory of legal interpretation is in poor shape. Those introduced to the law for the first time (such as in the University of Southern California Law Center's Law, Language, and Ethics course) are rightly shocked that something as obviously basic to legal reasoning as interpretation should be so poorly worked out by either judges or scholars. Reading several opinions convinces such legal novices that the "rules" of interpretation stated by the courts are just so much rhetoric, a legal realist conclusion on which Karl Llewellyn was so persuasive many years ago.[15] The court-articulated rules are *either* so vague as to give no guidance—witness the vague injunctions of seeking to effectuate "legislative intent"— *or*, where such rules do have some bite, they are ignored by courts whenever it is convenient to do so.

Legal scholars have done little better. The older literature on interpretation is both vacuous and boring.[16] The more recent literature, although done by the best and the brightest in contemporary legal scholarship, is handicapped by one of two factors mentioned earlier: (1) most of that literature fails to distinguish interpretation as *one* activity within legal reasoning and, rather, equates interpretation with all of legal reasoning; or (2) much of the literature proceeds from skeptical

---

thought to be obvious because there is no need to find a set of synonyms for the legal text, courts will say that the meaning is "plain" and that no interpretation is needed. *See, e.g.,* Caminetti v. United States, 242 U.S. 470, 485 (1917) ("Where the language is plain and admits of no more than one meaning the duty of interpretation does not arise and the rules which are to aid doubtful meanings need no discussion.").

15. Llewellyn, *Remarks on the Theory of Appellate Decision and the Rules or Canons About How Statutes Are to Be Construed,* 3 VAND. L. REV. 395 (1950).

16. *See, e.g.,* Frankfurter, *Some Reflections on the Readings of Statutes,* 47 COLUM. L. REV. 527 (1947). These characteristics of the older literature on interpretation lead James Landis to remark that "passing acquaintance with the literature of statutory interpretation evokes sympathy with the eminent judge who remarked that books on spiritualism and statutory interpretation were two types of literary ebullitions that he had learned not to read." Landis, *A Note on "Statutory Interpretation,"* 43 HARV. L. REV. 886, 886 (1930). For a more recent review of the older literature, see Weisburg, *Calabresi as Judicial Artist,* 35 STAN. L. REV. 213 (1983).

traditions that dictate skepticism about the very possibility of there being anything that could be called a theory of interpretation. Because of this state of affairs, there is hardly any detailed debate over the proper content of a theory of how legal texts should be construed. The natural law theory of interpretation that this Article articulates, is my attempt to stake out a position in a debate that is itself poorly staked out.

I call the theory of interpretation I wish to defend a natural law theory of interpretation because of two propositions that characterize it: (1) that there is a right answer to moral questions, a moral reality if you like; and (2) that the interpretive premises necessary to decide any case can and should be derived in part by recourse to the dictates of that moral reality. In short, real morals, not just conventional morality or "shared values," have a necessary place in the interpretation of any legal text.

I have argued for each of these propositions elsewhere,[17] and while I shall recapitulate portions of the argument below, my main aim in this Article is to go beyond these two propositions. A full-fledged theory of interpretation should not only say *whether* real values should and must enter into interpretation, but also *how* they enter in, and what else interpretation involves besides value judgments. Surely in this post-legal-realist age it is implausible to urge that interpretation in law is *nothing* but the value judgments of the deciding judge, in no way affected by the existence of a text that is the judge's duty to apply. But identifying just how value judgments are mixed with other kinds of judgments—notably linguistic judgments about the meanings of words and legal judgments about the holdings of prior cases construing the relevant text—has remained an elusive task for the few theorists who have attempted it. In defending a natural law theory of interpretation, I hope to better our understanding of these matters.

The Article proceeds as follows. The four succeeding Parts each deal with one of what I take to be the four plausible ingredients of any theory of interpretation: ordinary meanings, intentions, precedent, and values. With each of these possible ingredients I shall seek to do four things. First, I shall analyze what we are talking about when we talk about the meanings of words, about the intentions of a legislature, about the holding of a prior case, or about values. None of these ideas are very clear, and the first thing I shall seek to do is clarify them. In

---

17. For a discussion of the existence of moral reality, see Moore, *Moral Reality*, 1982 WIS. L. REV. 1061; for a discussion of the need for moral reasoning in the interpretation of legal texts, see Moore, *supra* note 13.

the course of this clarification I shall in each case distinguish a philosophically realist[18] conception from a conventionalist conception; about values, for example, I shall distinguish a moral realist's conception of a value judgment's truth from a conventionalist's conception. The conventionalist would argue there are no really true value judgments but only value judgments that are "true" relative to the conventions of some society.

Second, I shall deal with certain skeptical arguments about meanings, intentions, holdings, or values, that deny existence to these four things in their realist guise, or in their conventionalist guise or, for some skeptics, in either guise. Further, I shall defend the optimistic (nonskeptical) position that judgments about the meanings of words, about people's intentions, about the holding of a case, and about morality, are indeed capable of being "really" true (the realist position). I shall also argue that one can at least intelligibly talk about there being convention-dependent judgments about meanings, intentions, holdings, and values (the conventionalist position).

Third, I shall examine the moral case for including each of these ingredients in an overall theory of interpretation. This will involve examining arguments about: whether and to what extent ordinary meanings of words may be relied on in legal interpretation; what weight should be assigned either to the enacting legislature's intentions or to the prior interpretations of the courts; and what role value judgments should play in interpretation.

Fourth and finally, to the extent that each of these *possible* ingredients are *proper* ingredients in a theory of interpretation, I shall examine whether the realist or the conventionalist conceptions of these things should be used. My natural law theory of interpretation urges the realist conception in each case. Judges should guide their judgments about the ordinary meanings of words by the real nature of the things to which the words refer and not by the conventions governing the ordinary usage of those words; judges should seek their own best theory of what a prior court did and not rely on what that court said it was doing; and judges should seek answers that are really correct when they rely

---

18. What I here call "philosophical realism" (and shall hereafter call simply "realism") is a metaphysical position having nothing to do with the collection of ideas named "legal realism." As Jerome Frank himself admitted, it was a blunder on his part to employ the phrase "legal realism" "because, among other things, 'realism' in philosophical discourse, has an accepted meaning wholly unrelated to the views of the so-called 'legal realists.' " J. FRANK, LAW AND THE MODERN MIND, *Preface to the Sixth Printing* ix (1949).

on values in interpretation and should not feel obeisant to the conventional moral judgments of their society.

The performance of these four tasks with respect to each of the main possible ingredients will spell out a theory of interpretation. Given the role of real values in the theory, it will be a natural law theory of interpretation. Beyond that, however, the completed theory will provide a four-part recipe to judges on how to interpret legal texts, a recipe calling for attention to ordinary meaning and precedent as much as to the more obviously value-laden judgments of purpose and justice. I shall conclude with a reminder that this four-part, natural law theory of interpretation is part and parcel of a more general philosophical realism.

I. THE ROLE OF ORDINARY MEANING

A. THE MEANING OF "MEANING"

1. *The Nature of a Theory of Meaning*

To say that the meaning of words is an *ingredient* in a theory of interpretation of those words may seem to be a trivial truth. After all, to interpret language is to find its meaning, so how could that meaning not be an ingredient in a theory of interpretation? Yet, the thesis that the meaning of words is an ingredient in a theory of interpretation is not trivial in this way. For the meaning spoken of here is not the meaning that a theory of interpretation seeks to uncover. The latter meaning is the output of a theory of interpretation, its final product. The meaning spoken of herein is different. The relevant meaning is the meaning words possess in natural languages such as English. Such meanings exist antecedently of any interpretive enterprise in law, and thus a theory of interpretation in law is free to incorporate such ordinary meanings or not. Many legal theorists have urged not only that such meanings are not a necessary ingredient in constructing the legal meaning of some word or phrase; but also that these ordinary meanings are to be shunned when the law constructs its own special vocabularies. To say, therefore, that the ordinary meanings of words is an ingredient in a theory of interpretation is a proposition that requires argument, which I propose to give in this Part of the Article. Preliminarily, however, this and the succeeding subsection seek to clarify what meanings are and to address certain skepticisms denying that meanings are anything at all.

A theory of the meaning of words in natural languages is part of a theory of communication.[19] A theory of communication for linguists and philosophers of language is a theory about how one person can convey some proposition to another. It is a theory about how certain propositional attitudes are created in an audience by an utterer who has similar attitudes and utilizes certain conventions of speech to communicate them.[20]

Although each of these distinctions has some controversy surrounding it, it is common to divide a theory of communication into four subparts: logic, syntax, semantics, and pragmatics.[21] In this way one sees the patterns of speech of a linguistic community as being governed by four different kinds of rules: those regularities of inference we assign to logic; those regularities of vocabulary, or of formation, or of transformation of sentences, we call the syntax of a language; those regularities of ordinary usage we assign to the meanings of words or sentences (studied by semantics); and those features of usage we assign to the particular contexts of uttering a sentence upon a particular occasion (studied by pragmatics). The argument supporting this subdivision of the theory of communication is no different than the argument for any scientific theory: the hope is that these subdivisions will yield the most fruitful systemization of the complex linguistic abilities of natural language users. Such subdivision succeeds if it makes possible the development of powerful, systematic expositions of various parts of the regularities in human speech patterns. By restricting one's attention to those few units of speech we call "logical connectives," for example, a very powerful and comprehensive systemization is possible for that subpart of communication we call logic.

Of primary interest to us here is the distinction between semantics and pragmatics. The semantics of a natural language studies sentence meaning, whereas pragmatics studies what is often called utterance

---

19. On the embedding of a theory of meaning within a larger theory of communication, see M. PLATTS, WAYS OF MEANING (1979).
20. Such an overall theory of communication is Paul Grice's ultimate concern in his well-known works. *See* Grice, *Meaning*, 66 PHIL. REV. 377 (1957); Grice, *Utterer's Meaning and Intentions*, 78 PHIL. REV. 147 (1969). *See also* S. SCHIFFER, MEANING (1972). As M. PLATTS, *supra* note 19, points out, one need not adopt the Grice/Schiffer view that propositional attitudes can explain meaning, even if one does grant that ultimately the theory of meaning must be part of an overall theory allowing one to explain the propositional attitudes.
21. The beginnings of this four-fold subdivision of the theory of communication are found in Morris, *Foundations of the Theory of Signs*, 1 INT'L ENCYCLOPEDIA UNIFIED SCI. 77 (1938). Morris distinguished syntax (which he felt dealt with the relations between expressions) from semantics (which dealt with the relations between expressions and objects in the real world) from pragmatics (which he felt dealt with the relations between expressions, objects in the real world, and contexts of use).

meaning.[22] The distinction thus to be pursued here is that between the meaning of a sentence and the meaning of an utterance of that sentence on some particular occasion.

Sentences are types of utterances. If I utter some sentence S, "the cat is on the mat," I have made an utterance on a particular occasion. This utterance is an event, an act of speech, that occurs at a particular time and place like any other event. Sentence S, however, is a type of utterance that many people have made in a wide variety of different contexts. The sentence is an abstract entity, a type, that does not exist at any particular time or place.

To speak of the sentence meaning of S is to speak of the meaning the type of utterance has, abstracted from any particular occasion of utterance. Katz and Fodor have us imagine what they call the "anonymous letter" situation wherein we receive a one-sentence letter "with no clue whatsoever about the motive, circumstances of transmission, or any other factor relevant to understanding the sentence on the basis of its context of utterance."[23] The sentence meaning of S is defined as what we know about the meaning of S in such a contextless situation. Utterance meaning, contrastingly, is what we take S to mean when uttered by someone in some particular situation. The context may show us, for example, which cat is referred to, which mat is referred to, and the time at which the "on" relation is being said to exist.

Utterances are instances or "tokens" of sentences. Utterance meaning is thus a function of two things: (1) the sentence meaning; and (2) the context in which the sentence was uttered. Utterance meaning should thus be more specific, more determinate than the sentence meaning of which it is partially a function.

Semantics studies the meaning of sentences, whereas pragmatics studies what the context contributes to utterance meaning. The distinction between semantics and pragmatics is of interest to lawyers because

---

22. For the distinction between sentence meaning and utterance meaning, *see* Moore, *supra* note 13, at 247-48. The notion of pragmatics explicated in the text was first introduced into modern discussions in Morris, *supra* note 21. It was originally worked out in Bar-Hillel, *Indexical Expressions*, 63 MIND 359 (1954). Indexical expressions are expressions whose reference changes from context to context, such as the word "I." Bar-Hillel attempted to work out some notions of pragmatics based on such expressions, context-sensitive as they are. For more recent extensions of this context sensitivity as the general criterion of pragmatics, *see* J. KATZ, PROPOSITIONAL STRUCTURE AND ILLOCUTIONARY FORCE (1980) and R. MONTAGUE, FORMAL PHILOSOPHY 63-66 (1974).

23. The example is from Katz & Fodor, *The Structure of a Semantic Theory*, 39 LANGUAGE 170, 174 (1963). The quoted language is from Katz's later discussion of the idea, in J. KATZ, *supra* note 22, at 14.

of the controversy as to which of the features is more important to a theory of interpretation. If one's theory is that a statute should be seen as an utterance by a legislature seeking to communicate in the usual way to some intended audience of citizens and judges,[24] then the use of all the tools of a full-fledged theory of communication would be called for. A theory of interpretation in law would then want to rely on both the sentence meaning and the context of an expression's utterance in order to recapture the intended message of the speaker. If, on the other hand, one thinks of statutes as unlike ordinary communications and more like the anonymous letter, so that one's interpretive efforts are not aimed at recapturing the speaker's intent, then only part of the theory of communication is relevant to legal concerns. One might, for example, guide one's interpretive efforts in law by applying standard deductive logic, ordinary English syntax, and some theory about the meaning of words and sentences in English, but exclude pragmatics. On this latter kind of interpretive theory, the context in which the legislature was "speaking" (legislative history), and the kind of effects it intended to achieve by such "speech" (legislative intent), are irrelevant, and thus that part of a theory of communication aimed at understanding such things is also irrelevant.

In a later subsection of this Part, I shall argue that no theory of interpretation in law can ignore the ordinary meaning of the words used in laws, and thus any theory of interpretation must contain as a subtheory a theory of meaning. In Part II of this Article I argue that no court should ever be concerned with any very rich notion of a speaker's intent ("legislative intent"), and thus, that a theory of interpretation in law has little need for a theory of pragmatics.

2. *Conventionalist and Realist Theories of Meaning*

Very broadly speaking, there are two kinds of theories of meaning one might incorporate into a theory of interpretation for legal texts: conventionalist theories and realist theories.[25] A conventionalist theory

---

24. Munzer and Nickel question whether the Constitution should be viewed as an utterance and, thus, whether one should be seeking the utterance meaning of that document. *See* Munzer & Nickel, *Does the Constitution Mean What It Always Meant?*, 77 COLUM. L. REV. 1029, 1044 (1977).

25. Because the labels "conventionalist" and "realist" are not well established in the legal or philosophical lexicon, I should say something about those theorists exemplifying each. As noted in the text, conventionalists are of one of two types. First, there are those who think that we assign certain things to be paradigm examples of our general words and that these paradigms are examples of such words because of the conventions that we establish by fiat. *See* Flew, *Divine Omnipotence and Human Freedom*, in NEW ESSAYS IN PHILO. THEOLOGY 144, 149-53 (A. Flew & A. MacIntyre eds. 1958); Flew, *Philosophy and Language*, in ESSAYS IN CONCEPTUAL ANALYSIS 1 (A.

is properly so called because it regards the relationships between symbols and things to be essentially arbitrary, a "mere matter of convention." How we divide up the world, and what names we attach to the subdivisions we ultimately adopt, are merely matters of convention.[26] We could have carved up the world differently, and we could have

---

Flew ed. 1956); Flew, *Farewell to the Paradigm Case Argument—A Comment*, 18 ANALYSIS 34 (1957); Urmson, *Some Questions Concerning Validity*, in ESSAYS IN CONCEPTUAL ANALYSIS 120 (A. Flew ed. 1956); Williams, *More on the Paradigm Case Argument*, 39 AUSTL. J. PHIL. 276 (1961).

The other and more popular kind of conventionalism is represented by the tradition stemming from John Locke's notion that for each meaningful word there is some associated abstract idea, definition, or concept that determines what things are properly labelled by that name. *See* J. LOCKE, AN ESSAY CONCERNING HUMAN UNDERSTANDING, (A. Fraser ed. 1894). Locke's general notion, that to give the meaning is to give a definition, has two strands in contemporary philosophy. There is first the tough-minded theory distinctive of logical positivism, the criterial theory of meaning, according to which one can construct for every word a definition in terms of necessary and sufficient conditions for the correct application of that word. *See, e.g.*, Carnap, *The Elimination of Metaphysics Through Logical Analysis of Language*, in LOGICAL POSITIVISM 60 (A. Ayer ed. 1959). More plausibly, concepts have been taken to include the looser criteriological theories of meaning stemming from the later Wittgenstein. *See* L. WITTGENSTEIN, PHILOSOPHICAL INVESTIGATIONS (G. Anscombe trans. 3d ed. 1958); Fodor, *Meaning, Convention and The Blue Book*, in THE BUSINESS OF REASON (J. MacIntosh & S. Coval eds. 1969); Lycan, *Non-Inductive Evidence: Recent Work on Wittgenstein's "Criteria,"* 8 AM. PHIL. Q. 109 (1971); Rorty, *Criteria and Necessity*, 7 NOUS 313 (1973); Wellman, *Wittgenstein's Conception of the Criterion*, 71 PHIL. REV. 433 (1962).

According to the criteriological theory, the meaning of a word is again given by a set of criteria, not by standard examples. These criteria constitute a kind of checklist one applies to an object to ascertain whether that object is meant by the particular word or not. The checklist notion comes from the idea that one checks off the properties of an object and sees whether those properties fit the criteria given for the meaning of the word. Still, the relation between the word and its checklist is looser on the criteriological theory than on the criterial theory, inasmuch as the criteria in the former theory do not constitute necessary and sufficient conditions. Rather, some loose assemblage of the conditions will be sufficient for the correct application of the word, and some large, but not necessarily total, absence of the conditions will be sufficient to apply the negation of the word.

The realist theory of meaning is illustrated by the works of Saul Kripke and Hilary Putnam. S. KRIPKE, NAMING AND NECESSITY (1972); H. PUTNAM, MIND, LANGUAGE, AND REALITY (1975). Others who have explicated the theory include L. LINSKY, NAMES AND DESCRIPTIONS (1977); M. PLATTS, *supra* note 19; Goosens, *Underlying Trait Terms*, in NAMING, NECESSITY, AND NATURAL KINDS 133 (S. Schwartz ed. 1977); Moore, *supra* note 13, at 204-11; and Schwartz, *Introduction*, in NAMING, NECESSITY, AND NATURAL KINDS (S. Schwartz ed. 1977).

"Realist" may be something of a misnomer here inasmuch as one can be a metaphysical realist and not subscribe to the kind of essentialism I have labeled the realist theory of meaning. For discussion of the latter possibility, see, *e.g.*, P. SMITH, REALISM AND THE PROGRESS OF SCIENCE (1981), wherein Smith asserts his realism but denies the Kripke/Putnam essentialism. Still, I find the realist label helpful because, if one subscribes to the theory of meaning developed in the text, one is necessarily a metaphysical realist. There may be alternative routes to realism, but they are less direct and, to my mind, less plausible.

26. One should not call a theory of meaning conventionalist just because it regards the particular name that is chosen for an object to be a mere matter of convention. Surely all theories of meaning must concede this much. Rather, what makes a conventionalist theory of meaning conventionalist from my viewpoint is its regard for the subdivisions of nature as themselves conven-

given the subdivisions different names. That we have not done so is simply a contingent happenstance, not a metaphysical necessity. We do not change such conventions any more than we change the conventions regarding the side of the road on which to drive: we need to have an agreement on one side or the other to permit safe driving but one side of the road is as good as the other for this purpose.

One important feature of conventionalist theories of meaning is that meaning will "run out" in our attempt to describe the world. "Fact is richer than diction" was the fetching aphorism J. L. Austin used to express this thought.[27] For example, we have (on a conventionalist theory of meaning) a set of conventions that give the word "death" a meaning. Suppose, for example, we took the meaning of "death" to be, "cessation of heart function, cessation of breathing, and loss of consciousness." We then come across a person who has lost consciousness and who has stopped breathing (until put in an artificial lung), but whose heart is still beating. Our conventions, in such a case, may yield no answer to the question of whether this person is properly described as "dead." New facts outrun the indicators derived from past usage precisely because past usage dealt with past situations that recurred often enough to develop the conventions that have developed about "death."

Another important feature of conventionalist theories of meaning is their implications for when there is a change of meaning for a word. With regard to "death," imagine that we come across a "drowned" person whose heart has ceased beating, whose breathing has stopped, and who has lost consciousness; we also discover, however, that this individual is revivable if certain procedures are undertaken quickly enough upon removal from cold water. On the conventionalist theory of meaning that makes cessation of heart and lung function and loss of consciousness sufficient to be called dead, we should say that such a person is dead. If we decide not to say this in various contexts it will only be because we have decided to *change the meaning* of the word "death." After the discovery of such revivable individuals, and after our decision

---

tional. *See, e.g.,* Putnam, *The Refutation of Conventionalism,* in SEMANTICS AND PHILOSOPHY 215, 227 (M. Munitz & P. Unger eds. 1974):

> In one respect, it is a triviality that language is conventional. It is a triviality that we might have meant something other than we do by the noises that we use. The noise "pot" could have meant what is in fact meant by the word "dog," and the word "dog," could have meant what is in fact meant by the word "fish."

Putnam believes that conventionalism is either trivial in this foregoing sense, or that it is false.

27. Austin, *A Plea for Excuses,* 57 ARISTOTELIAN SOC'Y PROC. 1 (1957).

not to call them "dead," we will have stipulated to a new meaning of "death" having to do with revivability.

A realist theory of meaning shares none of these features of conventionalist theories. A realist theory asserts that the meaning of "death," for example, is not fixed by certain conventions. Rather, a realist theory asserts that "death" refers to a natural kind of event that occurs in the world and that it is not arbitrary that we possess some symbol to name this thing. (It may be arbitrary *what* symbol we assign to name this class of events, but it is not arbitrary that we have *some* symbol to name it). Our intentions when we use the word "death" will be to refer to this natural kind of event, whatever its true nature might turn out to be. We will guide our usage, in other words, not by some set of conventions we have agreed upon as to when someone will be said to be dead; rather, we will seek to apply "dead" only to people who are really dead, which we determine by applying the best scientific theory we can muster about what death really is.

Further, on a realist theory of meaning fact will not outrun diction. Continuing with the example of "death": finding out that not all persons who have lost consciousness and who have stopped breathing, have also had their hearts stop, will not leave us "speechless" because we have run out of conventions dealing with such novelties. Rather, either "dead" or "not dead" will have a correct application to the situation, depending on whether the person is really dead or not. Whether a person is really dead or not will be ascertained by applying the best scientific theory we have about what death really is. Our present scientific theory may be inadequate to resolve the issue, but a realist will assert that there are relevant facts about whether the person is or is not dead even if we presently lack the means to find them. A realist, in other words, believes that there is more to what death is (and thus what "death" means) than is captured by our current conventions.

Finally, a realist theory of meaning will not view a change in our conventions about when to apply a word as a change in its meaning. If we supplant "heart stoppage" with "revivability" as our indicator of "death," we will do so because we believe revivability to be a part of a *better* theory of what death is than heart stoppage. We will not have changed the meaning of "death" when we substitute one theory for another, because by "death" we intended to refer to the naturally occurring kind of thing, whatever the true nature of the event turned out to be. Our linguistic intentions are constant, on the realist theory, even if our scientific theories change considerably.

There are two conventionalist theories of meaning that, at one time or another, have gained wide acceptance in this century. Perhaps the most straightforward of these is what in the 1950's was called the paradigm case theory.[28] On this theory a word such as "vehicle" takes its meaning from being conventionally assigned to be the name of certain standard examples (or paradigm cases). One might imagine some linguistic community looking at cars, buses, and trucks and deciding to lump those particular things together into one class. Those particular cars, buses, and trucks would henceforth be the governing standard for a vehicle, much as the iridium bar in Paris is the standard for a meter. Any one of the cars, trucks, or buses that was assigned to be a paradigm example of "vehicle" is necessarily a vehicle. Anything that is not one of these standard examples may nonetheless be a vehicle if it is "similar enough" to the standard examples of vehicles.

In philosophy the paradigm case theory was for a time thought to be a route to defeating skepticism in epistemology.[29] A would-be skeptic who doubts whether some blue Buick were a vehicle would need to be reminded only that such a Buick is a paradigmatic example of a vehicle and that such a thing *must* be classed a vehicle because of the very meaning of the word. Paradigm examples become, in some such way, a certainty-guaranteeing device because the skeptic could not doubt at least some truths, namely, those connections between certain things and certain words that are true by the conventions of the very language that the skeptic himself is speaking.

Echoes of such a certainty-guaranteeing function for the paradigm case theory may be found in law as well. When Justice Potter Stewart proclaimed that he could not define "obscenity," but that he knew it when he saw it,[30] he was implicitly claiming the knowledge of a speaker of English who knows the standard examples that give "obscenity" its meaning. More generally, H.L.A. Hart relied on this theory in making out his famous notion of a "core" of settled meaning for ordinary words like "vehicle" that are used in legal rules.[31] Such a core, Hart believed, consisted of the "standard instances" that any competent users of the language would recognize. For Hart, too, such standard instances provided a bulwark of certainty in the application of words like "vehicle"; outside such core, one was in the fuzzy area of the

---

28. The paradigm case argument is discussed in Moore, *supra* note 13, at 281-92.
29. *See, e.g.*, L. WITTENSTEIN, *supra* note 25; Urmson, *supra* note 25.
30. Jacobellis v. Ohio, 378 U.S. 184, 197 (1964) (Stewart, J., concurring).
31. Hart, *Postivism and the Separation of Law and Morals*, 71 HARV. L. REV. 593 (1958).

penumbra where one had to argue by analogy to the standard examples.

The other conventionalist theory eschews the word/thing relationship of the paradigm case theory in favor of a word/word relationship. According to the criterial theory, the meaning of a word consists not of things but of other words. The meaning of "bachelor," for example, consists of the equivalent phrase, "unmarried male person." The criterial theory is so called because such equivalent phrases give the *criteria* for the correct application of a word such as "bachelor."[32]

The criterial theory allows one to apply words to things in the world with certainty, but the connection is less direct than the paradigm case theory. On the criterial theory one would find a set of properties that form the criteria for "vehicle" and then check individual items for whether or not they possessed those properties. One might think that all and only vehicles possess the properties of being self-propelled, mobile, wheeled, and on land. If so, one would apply the word "vehicle" by using these criteria as a kind of checklist: one would look at a blue Buick, see that it satisfied each of the criteria, and conclude that necessarily it was a vehicle.

The criterial theory of meaning has also long served the function of guaranteeing a certain starting point for knowledge in both philosophy and law. To the would-be skeptic about knowledge, one could claim that some sentences were necessarily true—analytically true—because they were guaranteed to be true by the very meaning of the words employed in the sentence.[33] "A bachelor is an unmarried man" has long been paraded as such a sentence; the claim is that the very meaning of "bachelor" guarantees that such a sentence is true. In law such analytic truths are ways of defining Hart's core of settled meaning: anything that satisfied a sufficient criterion for a thing to be a vehicle necessarily was a vehicle; anything that lacked a necessary criterion for being a vehicle necessarily was not a vehicle; anything that neither satisfied a sufficient condition, nor lacked a necessary condition, was in the penumbra of uncertain application of the word "vehicle."

---

32. *See* L. WITTGENSTEIN, *supra* note 25; Fodor, *supra* note 25; Lycan, *supra* note 25; Rorty, *supra* note 25; Wellman, *supra* note 25. It is important to note that the criticisms following in the text apply both to the criterial theory of meaning of logical positivism and to the criteriological theory of meaning of the later Wittgenstein.

33. Both G. HARMAN, THOUGHT (1971) and M. WILLIAMS, GROUNDLESS BELIEF (1977) analyze the role of analytic truths as certainty-guaranteeing devices in logical positivism's answer to skepticism.

Popular as they have been, these two conventionalist theories fail to capture the meaning of "meaning." For the very certainty the conventionalist theories would generate show that they are not adequate theories of what we mean by "meaning." Consider again my example of the person submerged under cold water for some time, whose heart and lung functions have stopped and who has lost consciousness. Before much was known about brain functioning and about the revivability of such persons, they were considered dead. They were so considered because the conventional criteria for "death" accepted by all competent speakers of English were satisfied. The thought experiment that tests the adequacy of the criterial theory of meaning is to imagine what we would say of their judgments about such persons in light of what *we* know about revivability and brain functioning. Would we say:

> those persons were dead, by the then accepted meaning of "dead"; of course we would not consider them dead, but that is by our new idea of death. Since we have changed the meaning of "death," we are not talking about the same thing as they were, so we cannot say that they were wrong and we are right.[34]

I doubt that we would say any of this. We will not allow erroneous judgments to insulate themselves in this way (by claiming that they are true by convention). People in the past were *wrong* about when someone was dead. They and we meant the same thing by our usages of the word "death," namely, to name the natural kind of event that death (really) *is*. They got it wrong and we, by our present knowledge, are closer to the truth. Such cross-temporal judgments are possible only if the criterial theory of meaning is wrong; for only if the conventions they used in applying the word "death" are *not* necessarily true is there room to disagree with their applications of the word "death."

It may seem that in our haste to disagree with our ancestors about when someone is dead we are merely forcing our meaning of "death" onto them. Yet this is not so. The argument is that their linguistic intentions in using "death" were the same as our linguistic intentions in using the word. Both we and they intended to refer to the *thing*, the naturally occurring kind of event, that death is. If *they* knew what we know about revivability of persons submerged in cold water, they would also say that such persons are not dead. They would say this

---

34. A conventionalist who believes that the meaning of a word such as "dead" is given by a set of criteria should say all of this. *See, e.g.*, N. MALCOLM, DREAMING (1959).

because they, like we, intended to refer to a thing whose nature is partially known; and they, like we, would change the conventional indicators of when someone is dead whenever a better scientific theory comes along that demands that we do so. Given such linguistic intentions of previous users of "death," it cannot be said that we are merely foisting our meaning of the word onto them.

A similar argument can be directed against the paradigm case theory, with equal force. Imagine that some ancient "drownings" were among the paradigmatic examples that allegedly gave "death" its meaning. What would we say of those "drownings" if it turns out that the victims in fact were revivable? If the paradigm case theory were right, we should say that such persons were dead—necessarily dead because those events were paradigmatic examples of "death." Yet we would not say any such thing. Those ancient drowning victims were not dead, not really, no matter how much their supposed deaths were used as standard examples of when someone was dead. Again, such disagreement is possible because "death" is *not* conventionally assigned certain standard examples that *must* be included as instances of deaths. Rather, "death" names a natural kind of event, for them no less than for us; they and we accordingly can disagree meaningfully about whether someone is dead, even though the conventions prevalent during the times at which we speak are different.

As should be obvious, the defect of both conventionalist theories of meaning is a virtue of the realist theory. The realist theory yields results that are compatible with our sense that we can disagree with others who govern their words with different conventions. We can disagree with others because our conventions are not necessary truths about the meaning of "death." Rather, their conventions and ours are scientific theories about the true nature of death. As scientific theories about the same thing, they can compete with one another. We can claim, as we surely do, that our theory is better than theirs, something we could not claim if we were simply comparing our arbitrary conventions in the use of "death" with their different, but equally arbitrary, conventions.

There are, to be sure, conventionalists who would seek to appropriate these virtues of the realist theory for their own "deep conventionalist" theories. A deep conventionalist is one who thinks that conventions come in layers, that one can distinguish the conventions that define deep *concepts* from those that define more specific (and often competing) *conceptions* of those concepts.[35] A deep conventionalist will think that there are some "epistemically essential" facts about death, facts without which those in our linguistic community would not be talking about death.[36] For such a conventionalist, these deep conventions defining a concept of death allow us to argue meaningfully about disputed conceptions of when someone is dead; these deep concepts also allow one not to run out of meaning as one runs into situations not covered by one's own conceptions.

Deep conventionalists might think, for example, that everyone in our linguistic community regards permanent loss of consciousness as necessary for death.[37] It is this conventional agreement about a concept of death, they will then say, that accounts for our sense that we can meaningfully disagree with our ancestors about what death is. The surface indicators of heart stoppage and cessation of lung function were formerly the *conceptions* of when someone was dead; we have a different *conception*, one in terms of brain functions. Yet the real nature of death is not what allows meaningful disagreement here or allows us to discard one conception in favor of another when we learn more facts; rather, the deep conventionalist accounts for this in light of a yet deeper agreement in concepts.

Deep conventionalism is false, however, and for the same reason as its more shallow cousins. We only need to make more radical our thought experiments in order to falsify deep conventionalism as a theory of meaning. Imagine that it turns out in ways difficult to imagine that our conscious awareness survives death; the body dies and decays but the mind lives on. Would we say that no one dies, that there is no such event as death? Or would we say that death has a very different

---

35. Works by deep conventionalists about language include R. DWORKIN, TAKING RIGHTS SERIOUSLY (1978); P. SMITH, *supra* note 25; Gallie, *Essentially Contested Concepts,* 56 PROC. ARISTOTELIAN SOC'Y 167 (1956); and, in a little backsliding, H. PUTNAM, *supra* note 4, at 116-19.

36. P. SMITH, *supra* note 25. Smith wants to say that there are epistemically necessary conditions attached to our concepts such that, to us, it will seem that all surface indicators of a thing's existence will be hostage to some deeper essence of that thing. For Smith, however, it is not some theory about that deeper essence that renders provisional all surface indicators for a thing's existence; rather, it is a shared belief we have that the thing has an essence. This, with suitable substitution, is really a notion of a concept underlying a conception.

37. A deep conventionalist need not think that the conceptions are underlain by a concept. He might, as does Gallie, think that the concept is not given by some property or set of properties, but rather, by some single authoritative exemplar. *See* Gallie, *supra* note 35. The text's argument can be adjusted to work as well against such a paradigm case, deep conventionalism as against some criteria-based, deep conventionalism. The examplar, after all, may simply not be an example of the kind that speakers think that it is an example of, and science or ethics may eventually be able to show this.

nature than we had thought? It strikes me that the religious traditions that imagine a "life after death" are not speaking the nonsense they would have to be speaking on a deep conventionalist theory of meaning. "Death" as they use it refers to that natural kind of event, even if its nature turns out to be outside the basic *concept* of death of our linguistic community. Put more simply: There is no conventional agreement we can reach about what death must be that can be insulated from the falsification possible from an advancing science.

The meaning of words like "death," therefore, is not to be found in some set of conventions; meaning is neither a set of standard examples, nor a set of properties conventionally assigned to a symbol. The meaning of a word like "death" is only to be found in the best scientific theory we can muster about the true nature of that kind of event. By assuming that there are such true natures of natural kinds of things, the theory of meaning presupposed by our usage is aptly termed a *realist* theory of meaning.

Whether the realist theory of meaning is a correct theory of the meaning of other words (besides natural kind words) that occur in natural languages is a matter of some debate. I have argued elsewhere that it is the correct theory of meaning of words typically used in evaluative speech acts, for example, words such as "justice" or "responsible."[38] I shall argue shortly that it is also the correct theory of the meaning of words given special statutory definitions, such as "bird" and "malice." But does the theory apply to the names of artifacts, such as "sloop"?[39] Does it apply to conjunctions, such as "and"?[40] To dis-

---

38. Moore, *supra* note 17.

39. Hilary Putnam has argued that we form indexical intentions about things that are artifacts no less than about things that are instances of a natural kind. *See* H. PUTNAM, *supra* note 25, at 243-45. Others have disagreed. *See* SCHWARTZ, *supra* note 25; Schwartz, *Natural Kinds and Nominal Kinds*, 89 MIND 182 (1980); Schwartz, *Putnam on Artifacts*, 87 PHIL. REV. 566 (1978). I myself have urged some reservations to the extension of the essentialist theory of meaning to the names of artifacts. *See* Moore, *supra* note 13, at 214-18. Presently, I'm not so sure that something like Putnam's account may not be correct.

40. *See* Munzer, *Realistic Limits on Realist Interpretation*, 58 S. CAL. L. REV. 459, 461 (1985), wherein Munzer does not find it even "remotely plausible" to consider conjunctions as anything like natural kind words. What if, however, one regarded those conjunctions that are the rough English equivalents of the logical connectives to be unpacked in their meaning by the notion of logical truth? One then might be a realist about the correct meaning to be assigned to those conjunctions, based on the best theory as to the nature of logical truth that one can muster. In doing this, one might regard the systemizations of Aristotle through Frege to be competing theories about the nature of a thing we call logical truth. On such a view of logic, unpacking the meaning of certain conjunctions may not be as implausibly like unpacking the meaning of natural kinds as Munzer seems to think.

positional terms?⁴¹ To the names of mental states?⁴² To the theoretical terms of science?⁴³ To what are often called functional words, such as "vehicle," "pet," or "carburetor"?⁴⁴

These are not questions I shall pursue here. I later argue that judges should use the realist theory of meaning whenever the ordinary meaning of a legal text is relevant. The correctness of this argument is not put in question if it can be shown that there is no realist theory of meaning for certain classes of words. The *reach* of the argument, of course, would be affected.

B. Common Skepticisms About Words Having Meanings

Before addressing the role meaning should play in legal interpretation we should address the question of what role meaning *can* play.

---

41. I examine the case for considering dispositional words to be the names of natural kinds in Moore, *supra* note 13, at 221-23. For a contrary view, see Goosens, *supra* note 25.

42. Putnam rather clearly supposes his natural kinds analysis to apply to the names of mental states, inasmuch as such examples figure prominently in his papers outlining the realist theory of meaning. *See* Putnam, *Brains and Behavior*, and *Dreaming and Depth Grammar*, in MIND, LANGUAGE, AND REALITY 304, 325 (1975). Given Putnam's own functionalist view of mind, that would seem to commit him to a view that the realist theory of meaning is appropriate even if there is no hidden nature of a structural kind to mental states, but only an elaborate, theoretical, functional specification of such states.

43. I discuss the application of the realist theory to theoretical terms in science, in Moore, *supra* note 13, at 223-32.

44. Functional words are often lumped as a kind of artifactual words, which perhaps they are. Functional words are worth separate consideration, however, because of the possibility of building a functionalist theory about the hidden nature of such things. According to Richard Hare, a functional word is one that, "in order to explain its meaning fully, we have to say what the object it refers to is *for*, or what it is supposed to do." R. HARE, THE LANGUAGE OF MORALS 100 (1952) (emphasis in original). *See also* Cragg, *Functional Words, Facts, and Values*, 6 CAN. J. PHIL. 85 (1976). Munzer, in his commentary on my paper, finds it implausible to extend a natural kind analysis to functional words. Munzer, *supra* note 40. His resistance, however, may stem from an inadequate idea about what the "hidden nature" must be in order for the realist theory of meaning to be appropriate. I agree with him that it does not "seem plausible to think that people might discover some underlying structures for vehicles by dissecting them in the way that biology might discover something about frogs by dissecting them." Munzer, *supra* note 40, at 467. Yet, just as for words that name states of mind, it may be the case that the hidden nature to be discovered is that of a functional organization and not that of some structure. Functional organizations are discoverable. *See* M. MOORE, *supra* note 3, at 26-30.

Recognizing that functional characteristics might be the hidden nature necessary here, Munzer wants to assert that "the uses of vehicles by human beings vary somewhat as do the functional characteristics that vehicles exhibit." Munzer, *supra* note 40, at 467. This, however, assumes that the functions to be assigned to certain objects will necessarily be the average uses to which those objects are put by their average human users. Yet, the function of a thing need not be as conventional as this but might in fact be its contribution to a larger system. This, as I and others have urged, seems to be the essence of functional assignments, about which one may have better and better theories.

For there are certain common skepticisms about words having meanings (or at least meanings specific enough to pose any real constraint on interpretation) that, if true, would render academic any moral case for relying on meanings in interpretation.

1. *Functionalism*

There is, to begin with, the skepticism that focuses on the consequences of a speaker using words in certain contexts. In ethical philosophy, for example, it was once common to analyze what were called "moral words" as having evaluative functions and not descriptive ones. Words with conventional evaluative force, such as "just," were thought to be used to express the speaker's emotions, to incite emotions in others, to prescribe what others should do, and so forth.[45] Similarly, in the philosophy of mind, words such as "pain" were taken to *signal* or express the speaker's pain in the sentence, "I am in pain," but not to describe anything;[46] action concepts were taken to have ascriptive functions in our language and therefore no descriptive functions.[47] All of these theories have been pretty much abandoned in philosophy and all for the same reason: that a speaker can use words to do a variety of things besides describe the world is true, but a harmless truth with regard to word meanings. For there is nothing that prevents a speaker who is using action concepts to ascribe responsibility to someone, from also describing some class of events, namely, human actions. Similarly, speakers who are using "pain" to express a sensation may also and at the same time describe a felt sensation. Likewise, it is not impossible to use "just" to both express a commendatory emotion and to describe an institution as possessing a certain quality. In each case words may have descriptive meanings as well as conventional force.[48]

---

45. These are the familiar emotivist/prescriptivist views of ethics linked to the names of A. J. Ayer, Charles Stevenson, and Richard Hare. For citations and discussion, see Moore, *supra* note 17, at 1079-86.

46. L. WITTGENSTEIN, *supra* note 25.

47. Hart, *The Ascription of Responsibility and Rights*, 49 PROC. ARISTOTELIAN SOC'Y 171 (1949).

48. For a good discussion of the separation between a theory of meaning and a theory of force, see M. PLATTS, *supra* note 19, at 53-67. As Platts notes, any theory of meaning that is parasitic upon the notion of truth will sharply distinguish the force of an expression from the conditions under which the expression is true, i.e., its meaning. Even those such as Jerrold Katz, who wish to combine a theory of force with a theory of meaning into some overall semantic theory, J. KATZ, *supra* note 22, will nonetheless admit that the fact that there is conventional force attached to an utterance is no argument that the utterance also does not have determinant truth conditions. Conventional forces attach to the words "murderer" and "justice." That does not mean, however, that one may not describe an institution as being just, or describe a person as being a murderer. We can perform both assertorial and other speech acts at the same time.

Although most philosophers have moved beyond this naivete about speech acts, legal theorists have been slower to learn the lesson. Many words used in legal standards have certain legal consequences attached to their authoritative use by a judge. For a judge to say that someone *owns* something, for example, is to give that person that bundle of rights, privileges, powers, and immunities that we usually refer to as the incidents of ownership. From this fact some legal theorists, particularly those influenced by American legal realism, conclude that words such as "own" have no meaning; rather, their usage is governed by moral judgments ("policy arguments") about when the legal consequences of ownership should attach to someone with respect to some thing.[49]

If any of this were correct, then meaning would have no role to play in a theory of interpretation. Words used in legal rules would only be labels for certain legal results; the words themselves, having no "descriptive content" (i.e., meaning), could not provide even part of a *reason* for reaching those legal results. In such a case there would be no point to enjoining judges to look to the meanings of words used in legal rules, for it is the judges' decisions that *give* those words what meaning they have.

This view about meaning cannot possibly be correct. In law no less than in ordinary speech it cannot be the case that words have no descriptive content just because they are used as the triggers for certain legal consequences. A legal theory might urge that words used in legal rules *ought* to be so treated. But this requires moral argument, to the effect that a judge in each case should give the words he must interpret any meaning that yields the best results, no matter how far removed such meaning might be from the meaning the word has in ordinary speech or in prior case law. Not only is this not a very plausible moral argument (and I shall so argue in the next subsection), but also it *is* a moral argument, not some unquestionable, conceptual truth about the supposed vacuity of the meanings of words.

---

49. See Cohen, *Transcendental Nonsense and the Functional Approach*, 35 COLUM. L. REV. 809 (1935); Cohen, *The Problems of a Functional Jurisprudence*, 1 MOD. L. REV. 5 (1937). For discussions of Cohen's functionalism, see R. SUMMERS, INSTRUMENTALISM AND AMERICAN LEGAL THEORY 53 (1982); Golding, *Realism and Functionalism in the Legal Thought of Felix S. Cohen*, 66 CORNELL L. REV. 1032 (1981). As Summers notes, most realists "held a functionalist theory of meaning. For them, the very meaning of the law translates, in rough-and-ready terms, into what officials actually do in its name—its effects." R. SUMMERS, *supra*, at 53.

2. Contextualism

Another alleged conceptual truth that denies that words have meaning, also quite popular with legal theorists, goes under the name of "contextualism."[50] A contextualist believes that words cannot be considered in isolation from the context of their utterance. Meaning, a contextualist will believe, can meaningfully be attributed to utterances but not utterance-types (sentences). Such contextualism will necessarily deny any place to word meanings in a theory of interpretation.

Such extreme contextualism is plainly false. If it were true we would not know how to put sentences together to express our thoughts on particular occasions. We must know, for example, that words such as "improvement" do not mean just about anything.[51] If words were such chameleons, we would not be able to use them to communicate.

It is true that the context of an utterance may make certain parts of a text more determinate than would sentence meaning (the null context). Take the sentence, "I saw the shooting of the youngest son of Jones." In the null context we are not wholly ignorant of what this sentence could mean, for each of these words has meaning even when abstracted from any context. Still, in four respects, knowing something

---

50. Felix Cohen was also a contextualist. *See* Cohen, *Field Theory and Judicial Logic*, 59 YALE L.J. 238, 240-41 (1950):

> Perhaps, if we look closely enough, a sentence never means exactly the same thing to any two different people. For no two minds bring the same apperceptive mass of understanding and background to bear on the external fact of a sound or a series of marks. Indeed, I doubt whether any sentence means exactly the same thing to me the first time I hear it that it makes the tenth or the hundredth time.

Lon Fuller was a somewhat more cautious contextualist, urging that any word in a legal rule had to be judged in light of its place within a larger linguistic structure and the purpose behind the utterance of the word. *See* Fuller, *Positivism and Fidelity to Law—A Reply to Professor Hart*, 71 HARV. L. REV. 630 (1958). *See also* Williams, *Language and the Law* (pt. V), 62 LAW Q. REV. 387, 392-93 (1946).

Even good judges have succumbed to the lure of contextualism. *See, e.g.*, Pacific Gas & Elec. Co. v. G.W. Thomas Drayage and R. Co., 69 Cal. 2d 33, 38, 442 P.2d 641, 643-44 (Traynor, J.) (1968):

> Words . . . do not have absolute and constant referents. . . . The meaning of particular words or groups of words varies with the ". . . verbal context and surrounding circumstances and purposes in view of the linguistic education and experience of their users and their hearers or readers (not excluding judges). . . . A word has no meaning apart from these factors; much less does it have an objective meaning, one true meaning."

Traynor was partly quoting Corbin, *The Interpretation of Words and the Parol Evidence Rule*, 50 CORNELL L.Q. 161, 187 (1965), who was also a contextualist.

51. This is a paraphrase of Fuller, who asserts that the word "improvement" was "almost as devoid of meaning as the symbol 'X.'" Fuller, *supra* note 50, at 565. I discuss Fuller's contextualism in Moore, *supra* note 13, at 274-77.

of the context will make the meaning of this sentence *as uttered* by someone more clear to us.

First we need to know who is speaking in order to know to whom "I" refers. "I" is an indexical word, a word that changes its reference depending on context;[52] for such words that context that allows the audience to ascertain who is speaking is essential for understanding the meaning of the utterance.

Second, we need to know who Jones is, and the sentence by itself will not tell us. Fixing the reference of proper names has been the subject of considerable debate in philosophy, the issue being, to what extent reference is a matter of causal ancestry or, rather, of fitting some loose set of descriptions.[53] However one comes out on that debate, fixing the reference of "Jones" will require some context—here, the intent of the speaker.[54]

Third, the definite description, "the youngest son of Jones," is ambiguous as to whether it refers to some particular person who is the youngest son of Jones at the time of utterance, or to any person who at some later time (e.g., the time of Jones' death) meets the description.[55]

---

52. Indexical words are discussed in Bar-Hillel, *supra* note 22.

53. One side of the debate is represented by John Stuart Mill and Saul Kripke, who believe that proper names name something directly, without the mediation of any essential descriptions. Kripke's notion is that we baptize individual objects with certain names to which speakers, via a chain of continued reference, continue to refer even though they do not know as much about the object baptized as those who did the baptizing. *See* S. KRIPKE, *supra* note 25.

The other side of the debate is represented by Frege, Russell (insofar as he was not talking about what he called logically proper names), Wittgenstein, and John Searle. Their views are that one fixes the reference of proper names via some set of descriptions. Thus, "Aristotle," for example, would be fixed in its reference by a set of descriptions such as "the teacher of Alexander." For citations and discussion, see L. LINSKY, NAMES AND DESCRIPTIONS (1977); P. SMITH, *supra* note 25.

54. Thus, even Kripke makes plain that a chain of intentions by each speaker is required in order to maintain reference to some particular Jones by the name "Jones." S. KRIPKE, *supra* note 25. The only theory of reference to my knowledge that avoids any recourse to the intention of a particular speaker is a version of the description theory according to which there is some unique description associated with each proper name. If this is one's theory, then the meaning of a proper name and its reference is fixed by the sentence type and not by the intentions of the speaker. This, however, seems to be just what is wrong with Russell's theory of proper names, insofar as he thinks them paraphraseable into certain definite descriptions.

55. Keith Donnellan introduced the fruitful distinction between definite descriptions that are used to genuinely refer to particular entities and definite descriptions that have what Donnellan calls only an "attributive" use. Donnellan, *Reference and Definite Descriptions*, 75 PHIL. REV. 281 (1966). In the attributive use, the definite description picks out whoever fits the description, rather than using the description as simply a device to pick out a known individual. The distinction is a familiar one in law, too; thus, for example, the "unborn widow" rule in the law of perpetuities takes the phrases in wills such as "my widow" not to occur referentially, but only attributively. It

In order to say whether the definite description genuinely refers to a particular person or only describes a type of person that may or may not be instantiated can only be answered by recourse to context, in this case the intention of the speaker.

Fourth, the predicate "shooting" is also ambiguous. It may mean that Jones' son was shot, or that he was the one shooting. To know which is meant is again to know something of the speaker's intention.[56]

We might, following Tom Grey,[57] lump together these four uses of nonsemantic knowledge as the "essential context." They are essential in that one needs these minimal contextual features in order to fix the reference of the singular terms, to determine whether they are referring terms at all, and to fix unambiguously the extensions of the general predicates. Notice, however, how minimal is the needed context: we need to know who is speaking, whether and to whom the speaker intends to refer with the definite descriptions and proper names, and to which set of things the speaker intends to refer with the general predicates. To say that such context is essential is not to say that one needs much information here beyond sentence meaning alone. Nor is it, of course, to deny that there is such a thing as sentence meaning (and thus word meanings) that contributes to the meaning of the utterance. If contextualism were so limited, it would be a harmless enough truth about how one finds the meaning of an utterance containing either singular terms or ambiguous predicates.

Two further points:

(1) Unlike wills, contracts, and defamatory utterances, statutes and constitutional texts rarely contain indexical expressions such as "I," or singular terms such as "Jones" or "youngest son." Legal texts more typically are what are called "eternal sentences," sentences whose truth (and thus meaning) do not depend on the context of the utterance.[58] "Snow is white," for example, does not require us to fix the reference of any singular terms. Such sentences assert that anything, if it is snow, is white. Similarly, laws universally prohibit or permit cer-

---

is this interpretation that allows the possibility of there being an unborn widow, a person not alive at the time of the instrument who nonetheless becomes a wife and then a widow.

56. *See* Moore, *supra* note 13, at 181-88 (discussing the ambiguity of general predicates and the tools available to clarify them).

57. Grey, Supplement: The Unwritten Constitution, (1984) (unpublished manuscript). I am indebted to Grey for not only providing me with a preliminary copy of his paper, but also clarifying my own thoughts on this matter of essential context, via conversations and correspondence.

58. W. QUINE, WORD AND OBJECT (1960).

tain actions such as killing and do not require context to determine reference to particular objects.

(2) Even where legal texts do have ambiguity of reference, it is not conceptually necessary that one resort to context to determine reference. One may wish to regard statutes as sentence types, and *not* as utterances, so that even the essential context drops away as a relevant aid to interpretation. I urge the latter position in Part II, so that one should disambiguate general predicates, not by the speaker's intention but, rather, by the morally best purpose one can muster for the legal rule. Even if I am wrong in this latter normative argument, however, there is a moral argument that should be made the other way in favor of contextualism; the latter does not win by default because of some alleged conceptual necessity that we look to the context of an utterance in order to be able to attribute any meaning to words.

3. *Vagueness*

A third and more common sense skepticism than either functionalism or contextualism proceeds from the various attributes of language that are often lumped together as "vagueness."[59] With regard to constitutional interpretation in particular, the argument is often made that the great clauses of the United States Constitution, such as "due process of law" or "equal protection of the law," are too vague to be of any real guidance to judges.[60] This leads some constitutional scholars to urge that such phrases should not be interpreted at all, leaving only the more specific clauses (e.g., President must be 35) for use by courts in constitutional adjudication.[61] More generally, vagueness in the language of all legal texts leads many lawyers to be skeptical that too much weight is given to word meanings, at least in the many cases that they see as occupying Hart's "penumbral" area.

I myself have argued earlier that these pervasive features of natural languages are probably sufficient to undercut any literalist theory of interpretation, such as the plain meaning rule purports to be.[62] In the earlier article I sought to show that vagueness, ambiguity, and related features of natural languages not only prevented *all* cases from being decided on the basis of ordinary meaning alone, but also prevented *any* cases from being decided this way. That, however, is not to deny that

---
59. *See* Moore, *supra* note 13, at 193-200 (discussing three kinds of vagueness).
60. *See, e.g.*, J. ELY, *supra* note 1.
61. *See, e.g.*, Lester Roth Lecture by Judge Robert Bork (Oct. 25, 1984).
62. *See* Moore, *supra* note 13, at 271-72.

judges, like all native speakers of English, have linguistic knowledge about the meanings of words that can be a *part* of their overall theory of interpretation. As an ingredient in a judge's overall theory of interpretation, such linguistic knowledge will doubtlessly help more in some cases than in others. The argument of this Section is intended to establish only that, where there is some such knowledge, it must be reckoned with in interpreting legal texts.

This conclusion may be a little less modest than it seems. The indeterminacy in meaning that vagueness creates depends on what theory of meaning one follows. For vagueness is a conventional feature of language use; we enter the vague penumbra of a word when our conventions surrounding its correct use either run out or begin to conflict with one another. If one's theory of meaning is a realist one, however, running out of conventions is not the end of the road for word meanings' contribution to interpretation.[63] Reverting to "death" again, one might not know what to say by the older conventions governing the use of the word when confronted with a case in which consciousness is permanently lost but heart and lung functions continue without artificial means. Our conventional use of the word "death" has not been rich enough to develop a further convention with which to settle such cases. On a conventionalist theory of meaning we would say that "death" is vague and that we just must decide, as a matter of policy, whether to call Karen Quinlan dead or not. On a realist theory, however, our conventional indicators determining the use of the word "death" are only our temporary approximations to the best theory we can muster about what death is—temporary because such conventions are hostage to further scientific work showing us more about death, and approximate because even by our own best theory now. heartbeat, etc., are known to be inaccurate. "Death" is not vague, on a realist theory of meaning, because the word names that natural kind of event whose nature it is the business of science to progressively reveal to us. One does not thus "run out of meaning" in the way one can "run out of conventions." True, we may not know the best theory about death that will allow us to decide whether Karen Quinlan-like cases are instances of death; but on a realist theory of meaning anyone seeking the meaning of "death" is bound to keep looking and theorizing about what death is and not simply throw up his hands once linguistic conventions peter out. That we may not *know* whether the meaning of "death" is such that the word

---

63. I press this argument against the alleged vagueness of moral words, in Moore, *supra* note 17, at 1149-52.

includes in its extension events like those that happened to Karen Quinlan does not entail that meaning itself has run out; only that our present knowledge of it has.[64]

Hence, any skepticism based on vagueness is hostage to some conventional theory of meaning being true. Eliminate that conventionalist presupposition (as I have argued above that we should do in language theory, and as I shall argue below that we should do in legal interpretation), and one eliminates the skepticism about meaning that vagueness generates for many legal scholars. In Part III, I argue that this argument also holds for the great phrases of the Constitution, such as "equal protection of the laws." Such phrases are vague only if one's theory of meaning is conventionalist; to the realist whose realism extends to moral language as well as to scientific language such phrases have a very definite meaning that it is the business of a progressively better moral theory to reveal.

4. *General Epistemological Skepticism*

The fourth and last form of skepticism about meaning that I shall consider here is the kind that proceeds from a more general skepticism in epistemology. The philosophical roots of this skepticism are those mentioned in the introduction: either one says that all of *social* science is an interpretive enterprise, or one says that *all* knowledge about the world is an interpretive enterprise. In either case, the skeptical conclusion is that the world or human action has the meaning that we, the interpreters, place on it; it does not have any *objective* features that give it a meaning that we, the observers, discover. That judicial interpretation of legal texts is thus a helplessly subjective enterprise, a masked assertion of raw power by judges, is only a special case of this thesis about all interpretive activities.

In contemporary philosophy this skepticism stems from hermeneutics and its analytic admirers, such as Richard Rorty.[65] Owen Fiss[66]

---

64. A deep conventionalist will of course run out of meaning later than will the ordinary, run-of-the-mill conventionalist. Yet such a conventionalist will still run out of meaning eventually precisely because he is a conventionalist: events that could happen, or thought experiments that are conceivable, will outstrip the ability of conventionalists' conventions to deal with them. Thus, when Dworkin urges that there will be a right answer in every case, despite the vagueness of legal language, because in mature legal systems there will both be deeper concepts and deeper principles, he asserts what to me is wildly implausible. *See* Dworkin, *No Right Answer*, in LAW, MORALITY, AND SOCIETY 58 (P. Hacker and J. Raz eds. 1977).

65. R. RORTY, *supra* note 4. *See generally supra* note 4.

66. *See* Fiss, *supra* note 2.

has called its legal devotees, such as Sanford Levinson,[67] the "new nihilists." Actually there is nothing very new about such subjectivist musings in either philosophy or law. Grounding human knowledge has been the central quest of Western philosophy since Descartes, and grounding legal interpretation in some objective fashion has been the "preoccupation" of American jurisprudence in the twentieth century.[68] There has been no paucity of subjectivists in these debates in either philosophy or law.[69]

To a skepticism about meaning grounded in a more general philosophical skepticism, there is little I can say here. This is not the place for a frontal assault on epistemological skepticism. I have elsewhere attacked the particular skepticism that flows from some supposed categorical differences between the natural and the social sciences, the latter being inevitably "interpretivist" because of the *meaning* found in human behavior.[70] A more general defense of philosophical realism must await another time. I will, however, close this subsection by sketching such a defense, at least by my present lights.

For a philosophical realist there are two rejoinders to skeptics such as Sanford Levinson and to Richard Rorty, who stands behind him. One is to accuse the subjectivist of a kind of conceptual schizophrenia: when writing they propound subjectivist epistemology, but when it comes to daily living they make judgments and decisions as we all do: presupposing the existence of tables, chairs, and right answers to hard moral dilemmas and legal cases. They are skeptics in their explicitly philosophical moments, and realists *when it counts* in daily living.[71]

The second rejoinder is this: There is a version of the liar's paradox in explicitly skeptical assertions. Just as we puzzle about the Cre-

---

67. Levinson, *supra* note 4.
68. H.L.A. HART, THE CONCEPT OF LAW (1961).
69. A good example of a legal theoretician who was both a philosophical skeptic and (as a consequence) also a skeptic about word meanings is Jerome Frank. *See* J. FRANK, *supra* note 18.
70. M. MOORE, *supra* note 3.
71. Sanford Levinson quotes a rather revealing admission of just this kind of conceptual schizophrenia by Richard Rorty:

> I suspect that civilization reposes on a lot of people who take the normal practices of the discipline with full "realistic" seriousness. However, I should like to think that a pragmatist's understanding of knowledge and community would be, in the end, compatible with normal inquiry—the practitioners of such inquiry reserving their irony for after hours.

Letter from Richard Rorty to Sanford Levinson (April 28, 1982), *quoted in* Levinson, *supra* note 4, at 401 n.117. In Tom Grey's language, Rorty would appear to be a "giggler," Grey's word "for people who take skeptical positions, giggle in self-congratulation, and go on as before." Grey, *The Hermeneutics File*, 58 S. CAL. REV. 211, 226 (1985).

tan who says, "All Cretans are liars," so we puzzle about the skeptic who says, "Really now, there are no objective truths." We wonder in such cases what the skeptic is doing by his own lights: babbling subjectivist propaganda at us, not because it's really true, but only because we mistakenly think so and accept it as true? But why should the skeptic even care about making us believe it? Because he believes it? But on what good grounds could he believe it when *what* he believes is that there can be no good grounds for any belief?

If one looks closely at the contemporary debate about interpretation in law, one will find both of these rejoinders to the "new nihilists."[72] But they are much, much older; they form the classical ripostes to skepticism that realists in philosophy have used for centuries.[73] Both essentially come to the same thing: they point out an inconsistency between what the skeptic explicitly asserts (skepticism) and the realist presuppositions of both that assertion and of all the assertions the skeptic makes in daily life.

Charging the skeptic with inconsistency between his assertions and his presuppositions may not seem to establish realism. It may only seem to show that the skeptical position cannot be coherently articulated, leaving realism to be established in its own right. Yet a positive argument for realism can be constructed in two steps, each of which is only a development of the two replies to the skeptic. The first step is to show in detail that our practices with regard to thinking about and describing the world are realist in their metaphysical presuppositions. One does this, for example, by showing that the very language we employ commits us to a realist metaphysics: we use singular terms to pick out ("rigidly designate") real objects that exist and would exist "through all possible worlds," and we use general predicates to "indexically refer" to natural kinds of things or events, whatever their hidden natures might turn out to be.[74]

---

72. *See, e.g.*, Graff, *"Keep Off the Grass," "Drop Dead," and Other Indeterminancies: A Response to Sanford Levinson*, 60 TEX. L. REV. 405 (1982). For a similar response to the skeptical arguments of Stanley Fish, see Knapp & Michaels, *Against Theory*, 8 CRITICAL INQUIRY 723 (1982). The familiarity of these responses leads Putnam to his rather impatient rejection of relativism: "That (total) relativism is inconsistent is a truism among philosophers. After all, is it not *obviously* contradictory to *hold* a point of view while at the same time holding that *no* point of view is more justified or right than any other?" H. PUTNAM, *supra* note 4, at 119 (emphasis in original).

73. *See, e.g.*, I. SCHEFFLER, SCIENCE AND SUBJECTIVITY (1967).

74. The code words in the text are those of Saul Kripke and Hilary Putnam, whose works are cited *supra* note 25.

It is crucial at this stage to distinguish the realist metaphysics to which we adhere, from the coherence epistemology we also practice. However much we are holistic, coherence theorists in our procedures for *justifying* particular judgments as true, we are nonetheless implicit correspondence theorists when it comes to the meaning of truth itself. Our realist theory of *truth*, in other words, is not to be confused with the coherence theory of *justification* made quite plausible to us by philosophers such as Willard Quine.[75]

The second step of any positive argument for realism is the trickiest: it is to deny the skeptic any vantage point from which to be skeptical. Here one develops the liar's paradox analogy into a dilemma for the skeptic. If the skeptic is telling us that skepticism is the only true way of viewing our relation to the world, then he has presupposed a (realist) theory of truth whose possibility he has just denied. If he is telling us that skepticism is "true," but only relative to our practices and conventions it is "true," then he is wrong; if the first step of my argument is right, realism is "true," i.e., presupposed by our practices and conventions. In short, if the skeptic is right, he is wrong; and if he is wrong, obviously, he is wrong. To eliminate redundancy, the skeptic is wrong. Realism is both true, and "true" relative to our conventions.

What the skeptic needs to escape this dilemma is precisely what he denies the realist, namely, a vantage point that is free of all convention and that allows one to see the world unmediated by human theory. A skeptic needs such a stance if, *by his own metaphysics*, he can assert the truth of his skepticism. He needs to be able to step out of the human condition for just a peek at the universe to be able to say how it is (namely, that there is no way that it is). Yet no skeptic can do this, for no one can. Thinking is inconceivable for us if not done from the vantage point of some particular conceptual scheme. If that is one's conception of God, then God is (as some theists seem to accept) inconceivable. A realist needs no such God-like aspirations in order to assert his realism. He can admit that we view the world only through our own conceptual categories, because he can deny that there is any harm in that. A realist's conceptual categories are not distorting lenses through which to see an undistorted world; rather, they constitute a *theory* as to how that undistorted world really is. There are certainly

---

75. Quine himself is often ambiguous on the metaphysics of his epistemological position. Quine's coherence theory of justification is quite compatible with the correspondence theory of truth, however, whatever Quine's own ambiguities may have been. *See* Moore, *supra* note 17, at 1106-36.

other systems of thought that view the world differently, but they are competing theories about the same thing.

I doubt that any of this is convincing except to those who were initially convinced of the correctness of philosophical realism. Still, it is perhaps worth sketching what form a full response to Levinson, Rorty, Gadamer *et al.* would take. I feel somewhat comforted by the fact that the philosophical skepticism relied on by some legal theorists is no less sketchily defended. A sketch surely can answer a sketch. In any case, the full portrait must await another occasion.

C. The Moral Case for Ordinary Meanings

If one has been convinced thus far by the argument that there are such things as ordinary meanings, we can begin to argue for their proper place in the interpretation of legal texts. I shall present here the "course-grained" arguments for paying attention to ordinary word meanings, course-grained because I take them to establish that in legal interpretation there must be a place for ordinary meaning, no matter what one's theory might be as to what such meanings are. In the succeeding subsection I make the finer-grained argument for the use of the realist theory of meaning, as opposed to the conventionalist theories in legal interpretation.

1. *Relevant Values by Which to Adjudicate Between Competing Theories of Interpretation*

a. *The rule of law virtues.* The place to start in any normative discussion about what should go into a theory of interpretation is that basic set of values that justifies the judiciary having a limited role in a democracy such as ours. We should start, in other words, with those values that mandate that judges should not dispense justice in some ad hoc, case-by-case basis. Such values are often called the "rule of law virtues," and a system for resolving disputes that possesses such virtues we honor with the phrase, "legal system."[76]

We should start with the set of rule of law virtues because these values inform the entire theory of adjudication—which is, after all, a theory of the proper role of the judiciary. A theory of interpretation, being a part of that larger theory of the judicial role, should be guided

---

76. Some of these "rules of law virtues" are obviously culled from L. FULLER, THE MORALITY OF LAW 33-94 (2d ed. 1969); *see also* R. SARTORIUS, INDIVIDUAL CONDUCT AND SOCIAL NORMS (1975).

in its construction by the same values that generally define the job of judging.

Broadly speaking, there are six basic values that justify judges in a democratic society in refusing the Solomonic role of dispensing justice in individual cases and that justify the judge in accepting a humbler, more constrained mode of decisionmaking than that which they adopt when they view themselves as persons and not as functionaries of some kind. These values are separation of powers, equality, liberty, substantive fairness, procedural fairness, and utility. Although the application of these values to the judicial role is familiar ground to many lawyers, I shall briefly restate each before I apply them to the use of ordinary meanings in legal interpretations.

i. *Separation of powers*: The separation of powers slogan is in fact a label for three different political ideals. All three share the common conclusion that the legislature should make the laws and the courts merely apply them. Each of these ideals reached this conclusion a bit differently, however.

There is, first of all, the checks and balances notion. If one believes Lord Acton's famous dictum, that "power corrupts and absolute power corrupts absolutely," one will seek to limit the power of each branch of government by some functional division of the powers of governance. No particular functional division is required to allay this fear of concentrated government power; to succeed, a functional division need only be: (1) clear enough in its assignment of functions to the various branches of government, and (2) equal enough in its distribution of powers.

The second ideal often labelled "separation of powers" stems from certain ideas about the relative institutional competence of courts vis-à-vis legislatures. This ideal bids us to look to the structural features of each institution and ask what job each can do best. The comparatively short tenure of legislators, their representation of parochial interests, their investigative powers, and the unlimited scope of the choices they may consider, for example, are often argued to be features making it appropriate that legislators, and not the courts, make major social choices. Analogously, one points to the life tenure of judges (in the federal system, at least), their insulation from the pressures of politics, and their limited consideration of only those social choices presented to them by the accidents of the court calendar, as features making it appropriate that they not make the major social choices that govern our society but instead make (on one version) smaller, incremental policy choices[77] or (on another version) decisions of principle but not of policy.[78]

The third political ideal justifying a limited role for judges is quite distinct from these considerations of institutional appropriateness or fear of concentrated power. The third separation of powers ideal stems from the democratic notion that the people's voice should count in matters of social planning. When representatives are elected by the people, the major social choices those representatives enact are entitled to be respected by a court just because the people's representatives have spoken. Because legislatures represent the majority's wishes better than courts do, democracies' legislatures should have their wishes carried out by a judge even if that judge disagrees with the wisdom of such wishes. This third political ideal we might call the principle of democracy.

When interpreting a constitution, of course, the principle of democracy gets considerably muddier in its implications. For now there are two texts that can claim the respect due democratic promulgation. Still, the principle would maintain that the wishes of a constitutional convention are entitled to the respect of a court, even if a later consensus has spoken on the same issue in a contradictory way.

The three political ideals inherent in the separation of powers together justify limitations on the judicial role that are of particular importance in constructing a theory of interpretation. The separation of powers ideals mandate that a judge take interpretation seriously as a large part of his job. The interpretation of the social decisions of constitutional conventions or legislatures cannot be ignored as it might if the judge were left to decide cases by his own lights. The trick, as we shall see, is for the judge to construct a theory of interpretation that defines his interpretative task so as to maximally satisfy these ideals; for it takes considerable argument to decide what exactly is the "social decision" emanating from the democratic process that a judge is bound by his office to respect.

---

77. The familiar metaphors of Holmes and Cardozo. *See* Southern Pac. R.R. v. Jensen, 244 U.S. 205, 221 (1916) ("Judges do and must legislate, but they can do so only interstitially; they are confined from molar to molecular motions."); B. CARDOZO, THE NATURE OF THE JUDICIAL PROCESS 113 (1921) (judges "fill the open spaces in the law").

78. For the principle/policy distinction, see R. DWORKIN, *supra* note 35, at 22-28; *see also* Wellington, *Common Law Rules and Constitutional Double Standards: Some Notes on Adjudication*, 83 YALE L.J. 221 (1973).

ii. *Equality and formal justice*: The second rule of law virtue justifying a limited judicial role is equality. The distinctively legal ideal of equality is embodied in the ideal of formal justice, that like cases be treated alike. Formal justice is not the need for certainty and predictability in law—these are separate ideals animating the rule of law. Rather, the good of treating like cases alike is the good of equality, something we recognize early in childhood as a good independent of any other substantive goal.

A long-noticed feature of the ideal of equality is that one must specify in what respects two cases must be similar before they are entitled to equal treatment. For no two numerically distinct cases are exactly equal in all respects (qualitative identity). In order to apply the ideal of equality we must supplement it with ideals spelling out what respects are relevant. It might thus seem that the goal of equality does not provide any real constraint on judges, but this would be a mistake. If a case in the past has been decided in a certain way, the ideal of equality constrains a judge in a way he was not constrained before. The judge must either decide the case in front of him the same way, or articulate a defensible theory of why the differences between the two cases justify different treatment. Given the requirements of consistency and coherence as the judge continues to identify or distinguish cases with one another, his decisional processes are constrained in a way they would not be if he were not bound to take seriously the demands that persons receive equal treatment by the law.

It might seem that this limitation on the judicial role mandated by the ideal of equality will have little to do with a theory of interpretation. This would be true with regard to interpretation in brand new legal systems. But within any legal system with a bit of history, previous interpretations will exist that a judge should take into account in order to treat people equally. The trick, again, is to figure out just what those prior interpretations mean, a bit of the theory of interpretation I develop in Part III.

iii. *Liberty and notice*: The third rule of law virtue is liberty. Liberty is enhanced in a legal system if citizens can know before they act what consequences the law will attach to their behavior. Absent such knowledge they may be chilled in the exercise of their rights, such as those of speech and religion. More fundamentally, absent such knowledge they may simply be unable to carry out complex social arrangements that are dependent on legal sanctions being predictable in their application.

Liberty constrains the judicial role by asking judges to decide in a way that maximizes the predictability of their decisions. In terms of a theory of interpretation, that theory is best that yields decisions that surprise citizens least. Such a theory will provide, as I argue in Part IV, that some weight should be given to prior interpretations in earlier cases; it also will provide, as I argue shortly herein, that some weight be given to the ordinary meanings of words appearing in legal texts.

iv. *Substantive fairness*: Substantive fairness, the fourth rule of law virtue, is furthered by a legal system that does not in fact surprise the legitimate expectations of its citizens. The good that is achieved here is distinct from the maximizing of liberty for future decisions; rather, it is fairness that is furthered when people's present expectations about certain issues are not overturned by a court's decision. The good is fairness, not liberty. The constraint such an ideal places on judges is to tie them to decisions that do not flout established expectations on how legal issues will be resolved. In terms of a theory of interpretation, if citizens form expectations around some items more prominently than others, such items prima facie are to be included in the theory of interpretation in order not to frustrate these expectations.

v. *Procedural fairness*: Procedural fairness, the fifth rule of law virtue, is achieved by a legal system if it has processes of adjudication that are themselves fair. Suppose that judges could reach better and quicker results if they did not listen to arguments of opposing counsel and did not have to rationalize their "hunches" with bothersome opinions. The ideal of procedural fairness would constrain them from this kind of decisionmaking because it does not allow citizens fair access to the adjudicatory process. Such access is good—procedurally fair—quite apart from any argument that it produces better outcomes; even if it does not, it is good to allow citizens a way to participate in those government agencies (courts) that have such an immediate say in their lives.

Lon Fuller argued that such "participatory adjudication" requires that there be a *standard* around which parties can meaningfully argue.[79] If this is right, then procedural fairness constrains judges to make decisions with reference to standards to which the parties themselves have access. In terms of a theory of interpretation, this means one should frame the theory so as to allow litigants the maximal access to the interpretive tools needed to argue for their point of view. Secret

---

79. Fuller, *The Forms and Limits of Adjudication*, 92 HARV. L. REV. 353 (1978).

or hidden materials are worse, on such a view, because they deny the access litigants need to argue their case. Any theory of interpretation making such materials relevant to a judge's decision would accordingly offend the ideal of procedural fairness.

vi. *Utility and efficient adjudication*: The sixth rule of law virtue is utility. Adjudication is an expensive process. If the good that it achieves can be obtained at a lesser cost, utility is enhanced. Lesser costs are achieved if judges do not feel free to start with the legal equivalent of Cartesian doubt but instead take some things as settled. Decisionmaking is more efficient, in other words, by not reinventing the wheel every time a case is decided.

The constraint this demand for efficiency places upon the judicial role generally is to let what has been settled remain so. This is true whether the settling was done by a legislature, constitutional convention, or an earlier court. Respecting the outputs of all legitimate sources of law narrows what is left to be argued about. The trick, of course, is to decide what it is that prior courts, conventions, or legislatures have settled. This a theory of interpretation must provide. A theory of interpretation will be better, in the sense of enhancing utility, to the extent it makes both clearer and broader what has been settled by the past decisions of courts or legislatures. One thing the ideal of utility clearly demands of a theory of interpretation is that it pay some attention to prior interpretations, as I argue in Part III.

These six rule of law virtues together demand that judges give up some of the decisional freedom we each have as persons when deciding what, all things considered, it is best to do. These virtues together demand that judges justify their decisions with reference to legal texts, which is why legal reasoning is more like dream interpretation, literary criticism, and theology than unconstrained moral reasoning.[80] The theory of interpretation judges develop should be sensitive to the very values that justify their having a theory of interpretation at all. These are the six values I have just sketched.

b. *Consequentialist virtues*: In addition to these six values, however, another set of moral concerns should animate and guide the development of a theory of interpretation. These are the concerns about

---

80. I here make my moral realist assumption that moral reasoning treats the general rules and principles that have evolved as no more of a text than is constituted for scientists by the scientific laws and theories that have been discovered. Moral reasoning as I understand it does not involve the kind of textual exegesis involved in law, literary criticism, and theology. Like science, it makes use of general standards, but these standards are not authoritatively laid down. Indeed, they are not laid down at all but are discovered.

what sorts of *results* a theory of interpretation produces. Any theory that tends to generate better substantive outcomes than another's—"better" on the merits of particular controversies, not better in the sense of furthering the rule of law virtues—is to be preferred on this ground alone.

I realize that introducing such consequentialist considerations into the mix of proper values in judging competing theories of interpretation may appear to swamp the entire enterprise. One of the forms of skepticism mentioned in the introduction is to say that the desire for particular outcomes in particular cases will always outweigh any *systematic* values lying behind any theory of interpretation, with the result that interpretation will proceed in whatever way produces the desired outcomes in particular cases.[81] If this were true, we would have no coherent *theory* of interpretation even though, by necessity, adjudication would always involve interpretation.

There are two reasons not to fear this premature sinking of the boat (before it is launched, so to speak). One is some belief in the power of the rule of law virtues. Democracy, liberty, equality, fairness, and utility are not moral lightweights in anyone's moral theory. If some theory of interpretation demonstrably furthers these ideals over its competitors, then it takes considerable moral argument (extraordinarily good consequences in some particular case) to properly urge a judge to ignore that theory in the attempt to achieve an outcome otherwise thought to be good. Such occasions for a proper deviation from the theory of interpretation should be rarer than this kind of skepticism can admit.

Second, what the theory skeptic ignores is the possibility that there may be some systematic connection between certain theories of interpretation and the production of better outcomes. A theory of interpretation that can accommodate changes in the application of words

---

81. A good example of judges allowing their desire to reach a particular result to sway their theory of interpretation is provided by Keeler v. Superior Court, 2 Cal. 3d 619, 470 P.2d 617, 87 Cal. Rptr. 481 (1970). In *Keeler*, a majority of the California Supreme Court obviously did not want to decide that the killing of a fetus was the killing of a human being, inasmuch as that would make abortion murder. They accordingly adopted an "original understanding" interpretive theory and construed the California Penal Code section in question by virtue of its 19th century legislative history. See generally Llewellyn, *supra* note 15, for a particularly malicious, if effective, juxtaposition of contradictory interpretive maxims; such maxims contradict each other just because the courts have their eye on results rather than on the interpretive theory itself.

without necessitating a change in their meanings, for example, is a better theory of interpretation because it obligates courts to reach results that are more in tune with our current ideas of what is true or best. Such consequentialist considerations may thus systematically incline one towards one theory of interpretation over another. And, in the best of all possible worlds, they will incline one in favor of that theory of interpretation that most furthers the rule of law virtues as well. It is far from obvious that there is any theory of interpretation that can do both of these things. This Article, nonetheless, takes a stab at articulating such a theory.

2. *The Prima Facie Desirability of Looking to the Ordinary Meanings of Words in Legal Texts*

We are now in a position to assess the proper role of ordinary meaning in legal interpretation. The ordinary meanings of the words used are the place to start in constructing the meaning of a legal text. This does not mean that such ordinary meanings cannot be modified or supplanted entirely by the technical meanings given the words by prior case law, by the purpose a statute serves, or by an all-things-considered moral judgment about the injustice of the rule under an ordinary language interpretation. One will need some priority rules for dealing with those situations where the various ingredients in a theory of interpretation conflict. The only point to be established here is the proposition that, prima facie, the meaning of a legal text is its ordinary meaning.

This is thus not a defense of the much scorned plain meaning rule. The plain meaning rule claims much more for ordinary meaning than is claimed for it here. For that rule urges that the ordinary meaning can be so plain in some cases that a court need look to nothing else in carrying out its interpretive task.[82] This is (plainly) a mistake, but one can assert that ordinary meanings are the place to start in the interpretation of legal texts without making it.

Most of the rule of law virtues just identified are furthered by paying attention to the ordinary meanings of words. The deference to the legislature, demanded by the separation of powers ideals, is furthered when a court gives words their ordinary meanings. For that is presumptively how a speaker of a natural language would intend them to

---

82. *See, e.g.*, Tennessee Valley Auth. v. Hill, 437 U.S. 153 (1978); Caminetti v. United States, 242 U.S. 470 (1917). *See generally* Murphy, *Old Maxims Never Die: The "Plain Meaning Rule" and Statutory Interpretation in the "Modern" Federal Courts*, 75 COLUM. L. REV. 1299 (1975).

be understood. As is commonly said, the best evidence of what the "legislature intended" is to be found in the ordinary meanings of the words that it used.[83] (I shall go further than this in Part II, arguing that the *only* thing the legislature can have intended is that the words used name some particular thing or kind.) For a judge to give *no* weight to the ordinary meanings of the words used even in the absence of countervailing factors such as technical statutory definitions, precedent, or purpose, would be to free the judiciary entirely from any obedience to legislative mandate. Indeed, in an important sense a judge would be abdicating the interpretive process entirely and ceasing to be adjudicating disputes under law.

Other rule of law virtues are furthered by reliance upon ordinary meaning in interpretation. For the ordinary meanings of words form the conceptual inheritance of all native speakers of the language. Therefore, keeping legal meanings close to ordinary meanings enhances predictability in the application of law and, hence, liberty. Further, people have expectations about what words mean and will be taken to mean by the courts. Such expectations, and the reliance upon them, are protected by a theory of interpretation that endeavors to keep legal meaning and ordinary meaning close. Further, procedural fairness is also furthered by the use of ordinary meaning because every speaker of the language has access to ordinary meanings, to a greater degree than to other interpretive aids such as legislative reports, for example. Ordinary meaning interpretation keeps the tools of interpretation as close to the people as possible.

Using the ordinary meanings of words does not necessarily advance the goals of equality (formal justice) or utility (efficiency). To further these ideals, other ingredients must be added to a theory of interpretation. A role must be found for precedent such that technical legal meanings may supplement or even supplant ordinary meanings. This I shall take up in Part III. Also, using ordinary meanings does not always produce the best results. (Again, the merits of how a case should come out must be seen as separable from the goodness of following a theory of interpretation in reaching that result.) Indeed, one must always check, and sometimes overrule, ordinary meanings by purposes and more general value judgments in order to achieve acceptable results. Despite all of this, ordinary meanings remain the place to start in legal interpretation.

---

83. *See, e.g.,* J. ELY, *supra* note 1, at 25.

D. THE MORAL CASE FOR THE REALIST THEORY OF MEANING

1. *Natural Kind Terms of Ordinary Speech*

If ordinary meanings are to be used in the interpretation of legal texts, we must still settle whether a realist or a conventionalist conception of what meaning is should be used by a court. It is true, as I argued in an earlier Section, that the realist theory of meaning is *the* theory presupposed by the intentions with which we speak in everyday life. Although I shall build on this latter fact in this subsection, one cannot take it as establishing that we *must* use the realist theory in law. We could use one of the conventionalist theories, as courts at least sometimes purport to do. To say that it is the realist theory to which we should turn when we turn to ordinary meanings at all, thus requires some moral defense. One cannot settle it by noting that the realist theory is right (and the conventionalist theories wrong) in its ability to account for the intentions with which we ordinarily speak.

To get the argument started, imagine two cases, both involving the ordinary meaning of "death." In the first an organ transplant statute allows a doctor to cut out various organs of accident victims provided two things are true: (1) the victims have consented to such removal by signing the required form on the back of their driver's licenses; and (2) they are dead. Suppose further that the statute gives no definition of "dead," although we know that currently and at the time the statute was passed almost everyone regarded simultaneous cessation of heart and lung functions, together with loss of consciousness, to be an adequate definition of the word.

Now suppose the case comes up described earlier, where a victim who has been submerged in cold water for some time has lost consciousness, is not breathing, and has no heart beat. A doctor, finding the requisite consent form, wishes to cut out the victim's heart for a transplant. Suppose now the victim's relatives rush to court for a temporary restraining order, urging that the victim is not really dead. Accompanying them is another doctor, who wishes to testify that the victim can be revived if certain procedures are done quickly enough. Should the judge admit the testimony in the hearing on the temporary restraining order or exclude it as irrelevant to the proper meaning of "death" as used in the statute?

In the second case, the relevant statute governs the disposition of property upon death. Suppose a wealthy woman is struck by a mysterious malady that renders her unconscious, but does not stop either the heart beat or the lung functions. After she is in this state for some time, a state agency files suit to have the person declared legally dead so that the property can pass to the named beneficiaries in her will. To prove that the victim is dead, the state proposes to introduce testimony to the effect that the brain functions have irreversibly stopped so that she can never regain consciousness. Should the judge deciding the issue admit the testimony or exclude it as irrelevant to the proper meaning of the word "death"?

I think the judge in both cases should admit the testimony for each of the reasons earlier addressed as to why ordinary meaning should be looked to at all. To begin with, if we argue for ordinary meanings on the grounds that they are the best evidence of what the legislature intended, we should look to the best theory of the linguistic intentions that accompany language use to unpack that ordinary meaning. Most ordinary speakers intend by their use of the word "death" to name a natural kind of event whose nature it is the business of science to reveal as we learn more about it. They do not intend that their usage of the word be guided by either standard examples conventionally assigned to that word or by conventional definitions. The respective legislatures using the word "death" in the above statutes should be held to have the same linguistic intentions as other language users, namely, realist ones that allow organ transplants and property dispositions only when someone is really dead.[84]

Applying the liberty and fairness values is perhaps a little trickier here. For one might argue that what most people *know* about the words they use are some standard examples and some conventional definitions, even if their deeper semantic intentions are the realist ones previously referred to. One might accordingly urge that notice of how a statute will be applied is best given if the statute is construed by those very same conventional features that most people rely on in their daily use of the word. Abandon those conventional features, the argument would conclude, and you will surprise most citizens. Analogously, one might urge that reliance is based on conventions more than on scientific theories about the hidden nature of things, and that access is easiest

---

84. *Cf.* R. DWORKIN, *supra* note 35, at 131-49 (arguing that the Constitution drafters intend that their beliefs and intentions are not to be taken as authoritative by the courts). Brest, *The Misconceived Quest for the Original Understanding*, 60 B.U.L. REV. 204, 234 (1980) (legislators or constitutional conventioneers might have an "interpretive intention"). If I am right, speakers' normal "interpretive intentions" are to disavow any authority over the particular applications of the words they use.

through conventions, even if these are not the ultimate touchstones of meaning.

The problem with this argument is that it ignores the priority ordinary speakers give to their deeper semantic intentions whenever these conflict with conventional features guiding ordinary usage. Ten years ago people might well have been surprised to have learned that a man who has no heart beat, lung function, or consciousness because he has been under water for thirty minutes, is nonetheless alive. But their surprise would not have been as to the legal interpretation of "dead" but as to the facts about death itself. Once they too learned the facts about revivability, imagine their surprise at a legal decision that refused to even look at the facts about revivability as it authorized the cutting out of a "dead" person's heart. Most people would not only be surprised but shocked by any such conventionalist interpretation of "death." They would be shocked because they can fairly expect their courts to give "death" the meaning they themselves would give it: as the name of a natural kind of event about which we can learn all sorts of surprising facts without changing the meaning of the word at all. The possibility of factual surprise is something people must live with as they exercise their liberty, but an intolerable surprise is a court's giving ordinary words an interpretation that people themselves would eschew the moment they learned the true facts. In such a case their liberty is enhanced, not impeded, by use of the realist theory.

People may well form expectations of how laws will be interpreted because of their reliance on the conventions surrounding the usage of words in ordinary English. The heart recipient, for example, might well have felt assured of a new heart upon learning of the accident. Yet surely the recipient would not feel *cheated* by the law when told the heart's owner is still alive, and would not claim that some legalistic trick had created an artificial interpretation of the word "death." We expect no more and no less of the law than that it reflect accurately the ordinary meaning of the word "death"; the law in using such a word need not hold out a promise of certainty or stability that ordinary language itself does not possess. There is thus no substantive unfairness in applying the realist theory to words like "death."

It may seem that one can construct more telling examples of unfair surprise. Imagine the doctor who relied upon the conventional indicators of death and who cut the heart out of a (conventionally) "dead" person who was really quite alive. Suppose such a doctor is then prosecuted for murder for (really) killing a human being by cutting out the victim's heart. The doctor surely has a valid claim of unfair surprise, even if the victim really was a "human being." The doctor cut out the heart, one might say, relying on the conventional indicators of when some body is a corpse and when it is a person. Such a doctor does have a valid claim of surprise, but that does not weigh against application of the realist theory of meaning to both"death" and "human being." Applying such a theory will prohibit the *acts* the doctor did, yet will allow the doctor to avoid prosecution for murder because of the lack of requisite *mental state*. The doctor did not intend the death of a person or know that cutting out the victim's heart was causing such a death.[85] When the doctor does learn the correct facts about death, upon repeating his action he will not have this excuse, and he *should* be prosecuted. One can thus apply the realist theory of meaning in a thoroughgoing manner here without leading to any substantively unfair results.

The access point is the most difficult one for a realist because the conventions that govern usage are more readily available to ordinary speakers than is the scientific theory that determines the correct extension of a word. This difficulty for the realist, however, is but one counter placed against (but easily outweighed by) the benefits of the theory.

Aside from enhancing the rule of law virtues more than its conventionalist competitors, the realist theory of meaning also seems likely to produce better results in the long run. This is because the realist theory encourages judges to admit all testimony about the nature of

---

85. True, the hypothesized defendant did intend to cut out the heart of some body, and it is true that that body was a person. Still one cannot infer from this that the defendant intended to cut the heart out of a person. If one intends to cut something *X*, and *X* is a person, this does not mean that one intended to cut a person. This is because words forming the objects of mental states do not "rigidly designate" things. Except for what are called "*de re*" constructions of mental states, words used to describe the objects of mental states exhibit peculiar properties exempting them from the theory of meaning described in the text. *See* Moore, *Intentions and Mens Rea*, in THE LEGAL PHILOSOPHY OF H.L.A. HART (R. Gavison ed. 1985).

It is interesting whether a court should treat the mistake by the defendant in the text to be a mistake of fact or of law. That is, is the mistaken belief that the victim was a corpse a mistake of fact (about revivability, etc.) or a mistake in legal conclusion (about the meaning of "human being" as used in the Penal Code)? One of the interesting implications of the realist theory of meaning argued for in the text is that this distinction between mistakes of fact and mistakes of law cannot be made parasitic on some supposed distinction between facts and meanings. According to the realist theory of meaning, there is no distinction between meaning and evidence, or between criteria and symptoms. A mistake is simply a mistake about some victim being a certain kind or not. The criminal law recognizes something like this in its allowance for mistakes of law to excuse when those mistakes are about a material element of the offense. *See* MODEL PENAL CODE § 2.04 (Proposed Official Draft 1962). Although the criminal law categorizes such mistakes as mistakes of law, in legal effect they are treated just like mistakes of fact.

things like death. The realist theory encourages decisions based on the latest theories about what death is. Judges cannot shut their ears to such findings in the guise of ruling evidence irrelevant to the (conventionally proper) meaning of the word "death." Without the realist theory judges may believe they are changing the meaning of the word "death" if they admit the testimony and render their decisions based on it; such a change of a definition may (on a conventionalist theory of meaning) seem like a job for the legislature.[86] By contrast, the realist theory allows the admission of the testimony without burdening judges with showing why they are justified in overruling some established meaning. The realist theory allows judges to do exactly what they should do, namely, find what the meaning of "death" is by finding out more about death.

Such use of later theories of death is better because the theories are better. The brain dead notion has supplanted the heart stoppage notion because the former is part of a better theory of death. Use of that better theory in law produces better results because we all think of "death" with our built-in realist metaphysics when we are deciding when someone should be declared legally dead. Statutes that prohibit murder, allow transplants of organs, regulate burial, regulate life support systems, and transmit property by will or by intestacy, are best applied when someone is really dead.[87] Each of these are instances

---

86. Courts presupposing a conventionalist theory of meaning feel unduly constrained in their freedom to ascertain all relevant evidence regarding the presence or absence of a condition such as death. *See, e.g.,* Tucker v. Lower, No. 2831 (Richmond, Virginia, Law and Equity Court May 23, 1972), wherein the court rejected "the invitation offered by the defendants to employ a medical concept of neurological death in establishing a rule of law," and stated that application for "such a radical change" in the law should be made "not to the courts but to the legislature wherein the basic concepts of our society relating to the preservation and extension of life could be examined and, if necessary, reevaluated." *Id.* at 8-10, *quoted in* Capron & Kass, *A Statutory Definition of the Standards for Determining Human Death: An Appraisal and a Proposal,* 121 U. PA. L. REV. 87, 99-100 (1972). *But see* Lovato v. District Court, 198 Colo. 419, 432, 601 P.2d 1072, 1081 (1979), in which the Supreme Court of Colorado did not "believe that in the absence of legislative action we are precluded from facing and resolving the legal issue of whether irretrievable loss of brain function can be used as a means of detecting the condition of death." *Id.* The Court quite properly held that, at least in the absence of a legislative definition of death, it was not only entitled but had a duty to use the best scientific evidence available in order to ascertain when the natural condition of death occurs. *Id.*

87. There is of course an analysis of "death," according to which the word should be construed differently in each statute in which it appears because the purpose of each such statute is different. *Compare* Dworkin, *Death in Context,* 48 IND. L.J. 623 (1973) (arguing just such a position) *with* Capron, *The Purpose of Death: A Reply to Professor Dworkin,* 48 IND. L.J. 640, 645 (1973) (favoring a single definition of death for all statutes). Contrary to Munzer's commentary on my paper, nothing in the text requires that I take a position on whether one should have a uniform definition of death in each of the legal contexts in which the word appears. Rather, my

where the best theory of the true nature of death produces, we think, the best legal results. For we do not want (conventionally) "dead," but really alive, donors to lose their hearts or kidneys any more than we want the plug to be pulled or property to be taken from "dead" but alive persons, any more than we want prosecutions for murder to be carried out where the victim was conventionally "alive" but really already dead before the defendant acted. We are hopelessly realist in our metaphysics so that it is easy to say that these results would be worse and their opposites better. The consequentialist argument for the realist theory of meaning is that use of such a theory will generate results we will think to be better because we are realists about such facts as when someone is dead.

Using the realist theory of meaning can thus blunt much of the legal realist assault on words in legal rules being given their ordinary meanings. For the legal realist assumes that the conventions of language change much more slowly than do the changes in society that called for a change in the law. One thus has to override those old conventions in interpretation, ignoring the conventional meaning in favor of social policy. About the conventions of language they may well be right—it does take time for insights of a scientific or moral sort to seep into the conventions by which people guide their ordinary usage. But this criticism loses much of its force when ordinary meaning is seen not as a set of conventions that tie a judge's hands to the past but, rather, an invitation to participate in the development of the best (current) theory of the nature of the things to which words refer. On the realist theory, there is no need for a judge to change the meaning of "death" before he can rule admissible new or controversial evidence about the true nature of that class of events.

Everyone, I think, knows that no judge is going to refuse to hear evidence that someone is really alive despite all the conventional indicators of death being satisfied. At least, a judge is not going to do this when the issue is whether to unplug the life support systems or cut out the patient's vital organs. Yet, as I have argued, if one were applying

---

argument here is only that, *if and to the extent* ordinary meaning of the word "death" is relevant to its legal meaning in each of the contexts in which the word appears, the realist rather than any conventionalist theory of that ordinary meaning should be used. It may well be, for example, that the need for fresh organs might incline one to a somewhat different definition of "death" for purposes of organ transplantation than for other purposes, although I doubt it. If so, one would be construing the word "death" by the purpose such a statute serves. My argument in the text, however, is only that, insofar as ordinary meaning governs, the realist theory is the best theory of that meaning. My argument says nothing about ordinary meaning being overruled by purpose, which it may well be in some circumstances.

the ordinary meaning of "death," and if one were strictly conventionalist in what ordinary meanings might be, then the judge should refuse to look beyond those conventional indicators in applying the relevant legal rules. A conventionalist might concede that no judge would do this, but urge that this is because of other ingredients in a theory of interpretation. More specifically, a conventionalist might urge that it is because all judges check ordinary meaning against the *purpose* of a rule that they would not allow the cutting out of the heart of a (conventionally) "dead" person.

Yet this conventionalist response plainly will not do. For how should the judge formulate the purpose against which to check conventional meaning? Presumably, the conventionalist would say that the purpose of the rule allowing transplants did not include the carving up of live persons. Yet this of course is to use a realist notion of death in formulating the purpose behind the rule. Saving conventionalism as a theory of ordinary meaning, only to abandon it when formulating the objects of purposes with which one will override ordinary meaning, seems an unnecessarily circuitous route to realism. Better to admit straightforwardly: the judge should interpret "death" using the realist theory, and not be constrained by the conventions of ordinary usage.

2. *Specially Defined Statutory Terms*

It may seem that the argument just developed has force only as applied to the natural kind terms of ordinary speech. Yet many terms used in laws—including the most important ones like "possession," "contract," "malice"—are not natural kind terms. One might think, accordingly, that it makes no sense to urge that a realist theory of meaning should be applied to such terms when their meaning cannot come from some hidden nature of a natural kind. It may seem that the meaning of such words can only come from a set of conventions—here, not the conventions of ordinary speech but, rather, the legal conventions that explicitly define such terms of art in law.

With such explicitly defined terms it may seem that their meanings must be a matter of convention for two reasons. The first is that technical legal words such as "malice" do not, at least in their legal usages, name natural kinds. Arguably "malice" in ordinary speech does label a natural kind, some kind of emotional state of ill will; legal malice, however, is a term of art, explicitly defined. Because legal malice is not a natural kind, it may seem that it can have no hidden nature and, accordingly, no theory of that hidden nature that renders provisional and approximate all conventional definitions. For such terms of art in law, the argument would conclude, all there can be to their meaning is their definition.

Secondly, the explicit definition that gives meaning to terms of art in law is a *legislature's* definition and thus is entitled (one might think) to respect because of the political ideals mentioned earlier. Such respect is given, the argument would conclude, only by a court treating the definition as having stipulated the necessary and sufficient conditions for the use of "malice" in the law. Even if, in other words, there were a hidden nature to legal malice, a court should guide application of "malice" by the explicit, legislative definition and not by the best theory as to that hidden nature.

One can separate these two arguments by changing examples for the moment. The late W. Barton Leach created a case that is helpful here, *Regina v. Ojibway*.[88] In *Ojibway*, the defendant was prosecuted under the Small Birds Act, section two of which prohibited the killing of any small birds. The question for decision by the court was whether a pony with a downy pillow on its back was a "small bird" within the meaning of the Act. The defendant, it seems, had shot the pony when it broke its leg. The court of course construed the word "bird" to include a pony with a pillow on its back and thus held the defendant liable under the statute.

The court in its opinion recognized that a bird in law is not necessarily the same as a bird in fact. Indeed, section one of the Act explicitly defined "bird" as a "two-legged animal covered with feathers." Such explicit definition, by the second argument earlier given, correctly induced the court to regard "bird" as a term of art in law, governed solely by its definition.

If the definition gives criteria for "bird" that are necessary and sufficient, then anything that: (1) is an animal, (2) has two legs, and (3) is covered with feathers, is a bird. The pony is a bird because: (1) it is an animal; (2) it has two legs (any thing that has four legs necessarily has two legs); and (3) it was covered with feathers, namely, the downy pillow on its back. (The court pointed out that surely it did not matter if the animal were naturally or artificially covered with feathers, as a bird whose feathers had been stripped from it and glued back on would still be a bird). Moreover, the animal in question was a *small* bird, because, although large for a bird, it was small for birds of its kind

---

88. *Judicial Humour—Construction of a Statute*, 8 Crim. L.Q. 137 (1966).

(horses), and for attributive adjectives like "small,"[89] size must be considered with reference to the kind of thing we are talking about.

Counsel for the defendant raised four arguments that the court felt obliged to deal with: first, that this bird emitted neighing sounds; second, that persons could ride it; third, that it had shoes on its feet; and fourth, that since it would not have been a bird if the pillow had been removed prior to its shooting, so it should not be considered a bird in this case. The court easily dismissed the first three of these arguments, pointing òut that the statutory definition of "bird" does not make relevant the sounds a creature makes, to what use humans put it, or how it dresses. As for the fourth argument, about removal of the pillow prior to shooting, the court answers with a rhetorical question. "Is a bird no less a bird even if it has lost its feathers?"

I have gone into such detail in redescribing Bart Leach's marvelous opinion because it illustrates the poverty of the conventionalist theory of meaning even as applied to explicitly defined legal terms. There are two lessons to be drawn from *Ojibway*. The first is that, try as we might, we cannot get away from ordinary English with our explicit definitions in law. For the definition must eventually do its defining in terms we antecedently understand, i.e., in English. This, as I have shown in detail elsewhere,[90] is also true of "malice," which is further removed from ordinary English than is "bird." This means that any judge applying the definition must bring to it an antecedent understanding of what a bird really is. The *Ojibway* judge does not do this, but instead makes plausible enough constructions of "two legs" and "covered with feathers." It is true that an animal with four legs has two legs; and it is true that an animal artifically covered with feathers is covered with feathers. One has to know what a bird is to know that such interpretations of these ordinary words are not meant by section one of the Act. A conventionalist judge regarding "bird" as a legal term of art is stripped of this knowledge and thus is free to decide that a pony with a feather pillow meets the definition.

The second lesson to be drawn here is that no judge should take such explicit legislative definitions as providing necessary and sufficient conditions for "bird," for "malice," or for any term of art in law. The *Ojibway* judge attempted this by excluding as irrelevant evidence of the horseshoes being on the bird, of the horse-like sound that it made, or of

---

89. See Moore, *supra* note 13, for discussion and citations on attributive (Quine calls them syncategorematic) adjectives.
90. *See id.* at 235-42.

the fact that one could ride it just like a horse. The exclusion of such evidence was necessitated by the conventional definitions which gave the judge a set of conditions *sufficient* to deduce that the animal was a bird. If a sufficient condition is satisfied, logically the satisfaction of no other condition is necessary for the proper application of "bird," and the judge so held in excluding all other evidence.

But the judge in *Ojibway* cannot quite pull off this tenaciously conventionalist stance. For the fourth argument of the defendant's attorney cannot be written off as irrelevant to the explicit criteria for legal birdhood: if the pillow had been removed from the pony (or a fortiori never placed upon it), then it would not have been covered with feathers. Since being covered with feathers is treated by a conventionalist judge as a necessary condition of birdhood, this animal would not have been a bird. Refusing to countenance such a possibility, this conventionalist judge abandoned conventionalism and replied that a bird is no less a bird without its feathers. "Bird," in other words, refers to the natural kind of thing that birds are; the word is not to be taken as governed by its legislative definition to the exclusion of the true nature of the natural kind.

To avoid absurdity, the judge should have done from the beginning what was done in the end: regard the explicit legislative definition just as the conventional definitions of words in dictionaries would be regarded. These are conventional glosses on the meaning of words, handy things to say when you are trying to teach children, foreigners, or judges what sort of thing the word "bird" picks out. These conventional glosses cannot, without absurdity, be taken to provide necessary and sufficient criteria for the correct application of the word.

The upshot is that explicit legislative definition of a word does not mean that a judge should ignore the true nature of the kind of thing to which the word refers in an attempt to be faithful to the legislative definition. Rather, a judge should recognize that the knowledge about the natural kind of things birds are is necessary even to apply the definition in the right way, and that there may well be cases when it is necessary to ignore the definition when it runs counter to the true nature of the thing the definition was attempting to pick out. On the latter point: a judge would be fulfilling, not flouting, the separation of powers political ideals by guiding the application of the term by the true nature (as it best can be understood) of the thing the legislature was talking about, rather than treating the legislature as if it had the ability (no lexicographer ever has) to fully define a natural kind term.[91]

A conventionalist may well grumble at this point that the *Ojibway* example is a special one because the Act explicitly defined a term that is nonetheless very plausibly taken to refer to a natural kind of thing. "Malice," it might be urged, is a horse of a different color because it cannot be taken to name the emotional state we in ordinary speech designate with the term. This is true enough, and we should return to a consideration of "malice." It is worth noting before we do so, however, that *Ojibway* is not such an untypical example. Explicit legislative definitions of "death," for example, should not be treated differently than "bird" in *Ojibway*. The legislature should be taken to be saying that "death" names a natural kind of event, even where the legislature has attempted an explicit definition of that kind of event.[92]

"Malice" forms a convenient example with which to examine the argument between realism and conventionalism as theories of meaning

---

91. In one of the pioneer statutes in the early 1970's, Kansas defined death on the basis of *either* the absence of spontaneous respiratory and cardiac functions, *or* the absence of spontaneous brain function. KAN. STAT. ANN. § 77-202 (1970). Such a disjunctive test makes sense only if the meaning of "death" is *not* equated with the legislative criteria. Otherwise, the legislature would have given alternative definitions of death, and there would in fact be two kinds of death in the state of Kansas. This, however, no court has been silly enough to adopt. *See, e.g.*, State v. Shaffer, 223 Kan. 244, 574 P.2d 205 (1976), in which the criminal defendant contended that the statute was unconstitutionally vague by allowing two separate definitions of death. The court rejected the argument on the grounds that there is no constitutional requirement that a single standard be used. *Id.* at 249, 574 P.2d at 209. In other words, one can measure the unitary phenomenon of death in a variety of ways. For an interesting collection of materials on various proposed and enacted definitions of death, see M. SHAPIRO & R. SPECE, BIOETHICS AND LAW (1981).

92. I take it that this is what the courts must do in Kansas, considering the disjunctive definition of the Kansas legislature. *See supra* note 91. In judging the authoritativeness with which a court should treat a legislature's definition of "death," one must keep in mind what the legislature was trying to do. Was it simply trying to aid a court in picking out the kind of thing that is death, or was it trying to bind the court by some conventional standards of what will be regarded as death? For a helpful discussion of this distinction, see Capron & Kass, *supra* note 86, at 102, in which the authors distinguished four levels at which a definition of death might be taken: "(1) the basic concept or idea; (2) general physiological standards; (3) operational criteria; and (4) specific tests or procedures." Capron and Kass go on to argue that most legislatures should undertake to give definitions in terms of standards but not in terms of the basic concept of death (what I would call the essence of the kind of event that death is). If this is in fact what legislatures do attempt in their statutory definitions, it serves rather than flouts the separation of powers ideals *not* to treat the legislative definitions as the giving of necessary and sufficient conditions that must be followed by courts as they interpret the word "death."

It is worth noting that, because "death" names a natural kind of event, and because there is a danger that courts will be unduly deferential to legislative definitions, the President's Commission has recently recommended that death be left to medical expertise and not be given statutory definition. *Report of the President's Commission, Defining Death: The Medical, Legal, and Ethical Issues in the Determination of Death, excerpted in* CONTEMPORARY ISSUES IN BIOETHICS 301-05 (T. Beauchamp and L. Walters eds. 2d ed. 1982).

for legal terms of art. For "malice" in criminal law has a history that shows us realist and conventionalist theories at work. There are many courts and commentators who believe that "malice" is simply a stand-in term, an abbreviation. In the common law of homicide, "malice" simply labels a disjunction of four states: an intentional killing that is not provoked by the victim; an intentional infliction of grievous bodily harm on another, which results in death and was not provoked; a grossly reckless killing manifesting extreme indifference to human life (or, in the old language, evincing an abandoned and malignant heart); or a killing done in the course of perpetrating a felony inherently dangerous to human life.

"Malice" on a conventionalist theory of its meaning is exhausted by these four disjuncts. They are all there is to malice. They together form a set of conditions individually sufficient, and jointly necessary, for the correct application of "malice" in the law of homicide. Such conventionalism surfaced recently in the outcry that followed the United States Supreme Court's decision in *Mullaney v. Wilbur*.[93] The Court in *Wilbur* held that a state could not constitutionally presume that a killing was with "malice aforethought" by placing the burden of proof of provocation on the defendant; because proof of provocation negated malice, and because malice was part of the case in chief, the burden of proof on provocation had to be on the prosecution. A conventionalist will respond, as Justice Powell did two years later,[94] that "malice" simply means (in one of its disjuncts) "intentional and not provoked"; and that therefore it is silly to suppose that the prosecution is proving anything except intentionality and the absence of provocation when it proves "malice" and that, lastly, these two elements can easily be separated, the burden of proof on the first going to the prosecution and the burden of proof on the second going to the defendant.

A realist about malice, however, will think that "malice" names more than the complex disjunction of states just described. He will think that malice picks out some thing in the world that was *not* picked out by ordinary speech; it is because ordinary speech had no label for this thing that the law needed to invent a symbol for it. The thing in question is not a natural kind, in the sense at least in which intentions, emotional states, or mental states generally are natural kinds. For lack of a better name, I would call malice a "moral kind," and the function of the word in the criminal law is to name this moral kind.

---

93. 421 U.S. 684 (1975).
94. Patterson v. New York, 432 U.S. 197 (1977) (Powell, J., dissenting).

I have elsewhere described the kind of moral reality this view of things presupposes, and I will not here recapitulate that defense.[95] What I shall do here is to make plausible that at least some of our use of "malice" in the criminal law has this morally realist presupposition built into it. Consider the California Supreme Court's line of cases that developed the idea of diminished capacity. Although there are different strands to this development, of relevance here are cases like *Poddar*[96] and *Conley*,[97] which held that an intentional, unprovoked killing was nonetheless not malicious if it was done by someone so crazy or intoxicated as to be "unable to comprehend the duties imposed upon him by law" or "unable to conform his behavior to the requirements of law."

In adding these requirements to California's definition of "malice," the California Supreme Court was adopting a realist theory of meaning. It was saying in effect that "malice" denoted a state of most culpable killing, sufficiently culpable that it should be distinguished from those killings punished only as manslaughters. It treated the explicit legislative and common law definition of "malice" as partial attempts to state a theory of when a person who has killed another is in this most culpable state. The traditional theory is built on there being an absence of provocation, of heat of passion, or of extreme emotional disturbance. As a (moral) theory of such matters, there is room for improvement. If, as the California Supreme Court apparently thought, there are some forms of intoxication or mental disease (not amounting to insanity) that significantly alter the culpability of unprovoked, intentional killers, then such states should be included in one's developing theory of malice.

The California legislature has recently overruled the California Supreme Court on these matters, prohibiting evidence of diminished capacity to show lack of malice.[98] One way to take this overruling is as a slap on the wrist to an improperly functioning court: by refusing to treat the explicit, legislative definition of "malice" as giving necessary and sufficient conditions, the California high court overstepped its judicial bounds. There is, however, an alternative to this conventionalist reading of the legislature's action. The legislative redefinition of "malice" took place because of the light sentence Dan White received for

---

95. Moore, *supra* note 17.
96. People v. Poddar, 10 Cal. 3d 750, 518 P.2d 342, 11 Cal. Rptr. 910 (1974).
97. People v. Conley, 64 Cal. 2d 310, 411 P.2d 911, 49 Cal. Rptr. 815 (1966).
98. S. 54, 1981-82 Leg., 3d Regular Sess., 1981 Cal. Stat. 5756.

the unprovoked and intentional killings of two well-known public figures.[99] The Dan White sentence highlighted a moral fact for the legislature, as for many of us: Dan White deserved more punishment, even if he was somewhat diminished in his capacities. The legislature disagreed with the court on just what are those most culpable mental states deserving the punishment for murder. The legislature need not be seen as chiding the court for attempting to articulate the correct theory of malice; rather, the legislature may have been saying that the court simply got it wrong on the (moral) merits about the role of intoxication and mental disease vis-à-vis culpability. Had it gotten it right, it would not have been overruled by the legislature, no more than are courts who seek to articulate the best theory of death despite explicit legislative definition of the term.

A similar realism about malice has surfaced in the debates of courts, scholars, and legislators about the desirability of retaining the felony-murder rule. In considering whether the killing of another in the course of committing a felony should be regarded as a kind of malicious killing (and thus murder), there are two ways a court might think about it. A conventionalist about "malice" will regard the term as an abbreviatory device whose meaning is fully exhausted by statutory definitions or examples. On such a theory of meaning, a legislature that defines "malice" to include felony-murder will be seen as giving a sufficient condition for malice so that a court must find malice whenever it finds that a killing has occured in the course of an enumerated felony. A realist, by way of contrast, will take the legislative definition differently. A realist will take "malice" to name something real, something whose existence may be *inferred* from *some* killings done in the commission of a felony but not something that can be *identified* in *all* killings done in the course of committing a felony.

Illustrative of these approaches are the opinions of the Michigan Supreme Court in its recent abolition of the felony-murder rule.[100] The majority opinion is explicitly conventionalist about "malice": one of the four kinds of killings sufficient for a finding of malice under prior Michigan law was a killing done in the course of a felony.[101] This was

---

99. Dan White murdered Mayor George Mascone of San Francisco and used as a defense that his capacity was diminished by his eating junk food.
100. People v. Aaron, 409 Mich. 672, 299 N.W.2d 304 (1980).
101. Under the common law, which we refer to in defining murder in this state, each of the four types of murder . . . has its own mental element which independently satisfies the requirement of malice aforethought. It is, therefore, not necessary for the law to imply or for the jury to infer the intention to kill once the finder of fact determines the

true because the law was taken to have given necessary and sufficient conditions as the definition of "malice." As a consequence, the majority regarded itself as free to *re*define "malice" only because "malice" had been defined by the common law and not by the Michigan legislature; had the definition of "malice" been legislative in its origin, due deference to the legislature would have required that "malice" not be redefined by the court.[102] One of the concurring opinions, in contrast, takes the prior law definition of "malice" not to be supplying a sufficient condition for malice. Rather, such definition is construed as describing situations in which malice may typically (but not always) be inferred from the intent to commit an underlying felony. Killing in the course of a felony may be evidence of malice, but it is not malice itself.[103] Malice itself is a state of culpability measured primarily by an intent to kill (or some close substitute). The concurrance said, " 'malice aforethought is the intention to kill, actual or implied, under circumstances which do not constitute excuse or justification or mitigate the degree of the offense to manslaughter.' "[104]

Malice, so regarded, is something real whose existence "may be permissibly *inferred* from the facts and circumstances of the killing, but it can never be *established as a matter of law* by proof of other facts," such as felony-murder.[105] A realist thus does not need to make the (here) tortuous argument that the legislature has never defined "malice," because he can concede as much without conceding that such definitions give sufficient conditions. Rather, a realist will see legislative definitions (and enumerated examples too,[106] for that matter) as attempts to pick out that category of most culpable killing for which punishment for a murderer is appropriate. A court is properly deferential when it joins with the legislature in that attempt, not when it construes the legislature to be doing something else.

---

existence of any of the other three mental states because each one, by itself, constitutes the element of malice aforethought.

Id. at 715, 299 N.W.2d at 320 (footnotes omitted).

102. *Id.* at 717-21, 299 N.W.2d at 321-23.

103. *See id.* at 735-43, 299 N.W.2d at 329-33 (Ryan, J., concurring in part, dissenting in part).

104. *Id.* at 737, 299 N.W.2d at 330 (quoting People v. Morrin, 3 Mich. App. 301, 310-11, 187 N.W.2d 434, 438) (1971)) (Ryan J., concurring in part, dissenting in part).

105. *Id.* at 736 n.5, 299 N.W.2d at 330 (quoting People v. Richardson, 409 Mich. 126, 144, 293 N.W.2d 332, 340 (1980)) (emphasis in original).

106. The court in *Aaron* also had to deal with the fact that the Michigan legislature had enumerated certain felonies as the basis for first-degree felony murder. A conventionalist court will feel itself bound by such examples as necessarily being examples of malice; a realist court will regard them as it regards a legislative definition—as picking out situations that often (but not always) give rise to an inference of malice, but not constitutive of malice itself.

Much of this I think was noticed years ago when H.L.A. Hart discovered that legal words such as "contract" or "*mens rea*" were, as he called it, defeasible.[107] Hart explicitly urged that it is "absurd" to look for necessary and sufficient conditions for the use of such words. Why it is absurd has been the center of a protracted discussion since Hart's early article. His own arguments, about the open-endedness of adding negative conditions, have long been known to be inadequate.[108] Yet as a description of legal words, Hart's thesis is very attractive: our use of legal words is defeasible in the sense that our present indicators for the correct use of the words are never necessary or sufficient, but are always subject to potential defeat or replacement by new conditions that we had not previously imagined. To flesh out the point, one might pursue Hart's example, the word "contract," and trace through the history of Williston's attempt to make consideration a necessary condition. Try as he did, Williston could not get around the cases where courts said there was a contract although no consideration. Section ninety of the *Restatement (First) of Contracts* explicitly invites a further moral theory on when it is fair to hold persons to their promises, a theory of which "offer, acceptance and consideration" are only partial articulations.[109]

If my morally realist thesis is right, we are in a position to see why Hart was correct to describe legal words like "malice" or "contract" as defeasible. Legal words are defeasible in the same way that natural kind words are defeasible: namely, both have conventional glosses as to their meaning, but such glosses are provisional and hostage to a deeper theory about the nature of the thing to which the words refer. It does not matter a whit that the kinds of conventional glosses differ (linguistic versus legal conventions), or that the kinds of things to which ordinary and legal words refer may be different (natural and moral kinds), or that the kinds of theories one may use are different (scientific versus moral theories). It only matters that, as we use both such kinds of words, their meaning is given by the best theory we can think of as to the nature of the things referred to. Our deepest semantic intentions are in each case the same: to guide "death," "bird," "malice," and "contract" by the best theory we can muster. To find the meaning of

---

107. Hart, *supra* note 47.

108. *See* Baker, *Defeasibility and Meaning*, in LAW, MORALITY, AND SOCIETY 26 (P. Hacker & J. Raz eds. 1977). *See also* Moore, *supra* note 13, at 237-42.

109. *See* G. GILMORE, THE DEATH OF CONTRACT 62-65 (1974). Because Gilmore's account is based on Corbin's later recollections, one might question whether the history Gilmore recites is accurate.

all such words is, accordingly, not a matter of finding some antecedently stipulated convention; the task is the more creative one of discovering how the world is constituted.

II. THE ROLE OF INTENTION

The intentions with which a person speaks are distinct from the meanings of the words spoken. A speaker's intentions may constitute what the speaker meant by uttering a certain sentence on a certain occasion; they cannot possibly be identified with the sentence meaning earlier discussed.[110] This being so, intentions of legal "speakers" are a separate, possible ingredient in a theory of interpretation. In this Part I shall examine the nature of intentions and their relevance to legal interpretation.

As about meanings, there are four questions one might pursue about intentions: First, what an intention is; second, whether any such things can properly be said to exist; third, whether intentions have any prima facie role to play in a theory of interpretation and, if so, what that role is vis-à-vis ordinary meanings; and fourth, if they do exist and should have a role in interpretation, whether a realist or a conventionalist conception of an intention is the appropriate one to use. The discussion that follows is organized around each of these questions, although I ignore the fourth inasmuch as I conclude that no concept of legislative intention is appropriate to legal interpretation.

A. THE MEANING OF "INTENTION"

The discussion of legislative intention is complicated by the fact that we must deal with a group of persons, each of whom may have different intentions. Since there are plenty of problems to be addressed that have nothing to do with the necessarily composite nature of a legislature's intention, it will be helpful to organize the discussion in such a way as to keep this factor in abeyance for a while. I accordingly have organized the discussion around Paul Brest's recent reconstruction of an example of H.L.A. Hart's.[111]

Brest bids us to imagine that one of us is the town mayor, who, in response to a minor accident between a 1973 blue Ford and a jogger in the town park, enacts an ordinance forbidding vehicles in the park. We

---

110. *See* Moore, *supra* note 13, at 246-56 (separation of meaning from speakers' intention).
111. Brest, *supra* note 84. The example is originally from Hart, *supra* note 31.

are each one person, so we have no problems of multimembered legislatures as we reconstruct our intentions.

It is I think useful at this juncture to introduce three kinds of intentions the town mayor plausibly may be supposed to have: (1) An intention to pass this ordinance. Its passage and its wording, in other words, were no accident. This action of passing the ordinance was intentional. (2) An intention to accomplish certain effects in the world by passing this ordinance. The intention with which the mayor passed the ordinance was, for example, to promote safety for pedestrians in the park. The first question, whether an action was intentional, is distinct from the question of what the further intention was with which it was done. These are not the same kinds of intention, as the criminal law recognizes with its distinction between the *specific* (further) intention with which an action is done, and the *general* intention to do the prohibited act at all.

We have two nicely distinguishable intentions the mayor may have had in enacting the ordinance. Because enacting an ordinance is a kind of speech act, we might think that the mayor must have had a third kind of intention, what I shall call a semantic intention: (3) An intention by the word "vehicle" to mean either some definition of the word, or to include as clear examples of vehicles certain particular things in the world. For example, the mayor intended the word to cover the 1973 blue Ford that ran into the jogger the week before she enacted the ordinance.

The first of these intentions is plainly an intention the mayor had if she enacted this ordinance. For enacting an ordinance, like the act of rape, is not something one does by accident. Some actions are "intentionally complex"; that is, to be actions of a certain type they must be performed intentionally.[112] Telling an untruth, for example, cannot constitute *lying* unless the teller knows the falsity of the statement.

The mayor, thus, intentionally passed this ordinance. Saying this of course will not aid in construing this ordinance in the least. For aid in interpreting the ordinance a court must look to either the further intentions with which it was passed or the semantic intentions the mayor had with regard to the language used in framing the ordinance.[113] I shall discuss each of these latter two kinds of intentions separately, dealing with the semantic intentions first.

---

112. *See* G. ANSCOMBE, INTENTION §§ 47-48 (2d ed. 1963).

113. I call these two intentions the perlocutionary and the locutionary intentions of speakers, respectively, in Moore, *supra* note 13, at 256.

1. *Semantic Intentions*

There are two competing conceptions of the semantic intentions that we might attribute to speakers of natural languages, what I am going to call the *rich* and the *spare* conceptions. The rich conception supplies a speaker's mind with a rich variety of intentions that at least look like they will be of aid in supplementing ordinary meanings as a court interprets the language of the ordinances. The spare conception attributes very limited intentions to a speaker's mind, so limited that they will give no help in construing language beyond what one can find in the meanings of the words used themselves.

Rich semantic intentions are of two kinds (paralleling the two kinds of conventionalist meaning theories examined earlier): (1) Brest's mayor may have intended the use of the word "vehicle" to apply to certain particular things, such as the obnoxious 1973 blue Ford; or (2) the mayor may have intended the word to be synonymous with some broader definition of "vehicle," such as "self-propelled, mobile, on land." In either case, the mayor's rich semantic intentions hold out the promise of giving what the conventions of language can give: either standard examples (paradigm cases) of vehicles, or a definition of the word "vehicle." Of course, the mayor's examples or definitions may be different from those of the conventions of ordinary speech; indeed, to be helpful at all, they need to be not only different, but also more specific.

Spare semantic intentions, by contrast, are intentions to have the words one uses name a determinate class of things. What exactly is in the class and what properties would be abstracted to define that class are not (on the spare account) matters about which one has any intentions. One rather thinks that there is some theory that could be developed by someone that will show that all members of the class share some common nature. In the case of "vehicle," which names neither a natural nor a moral kind, the nature will be in the functional characteristics that are necessary to consider anything a vehicle. But on the spare account, the individual speaker does not form intentions that determine these matters. Such a speaker intends only to name a class, the membership of which is assumed to share a common nature. The speaker *may* have some thoughts about this nature or some pictured exemplars of the membership of the class. But (on the spare account) the speaker very well may not have such thoughts or such pictured exemplars and, even if he does have them, he does not regard them as fixing the meaning of the word "vehicle" as he has used it. On the spare account of semantic intentions, fixing the meaning of the word "vehicle" by authoritative examples or definitions simply is not his business, and he knows it.

As should be apparent, where one comes out between conventionalist and realist theories of meaning will determine where one comes out on the rich or the spare account of semantic intentions (and vice versa). My argument for the realist theory of meaning was based on the spare account of semantic intentions being true, and the rich account being false. The essential notion was that people intend in their use of words like "death," "bird," "malice," or "vehicle," to refer to kinds of things they believe really to exist in the world. People assume such kinds have hidden natures of a natural, moral, or functional kind and that, therefore, their own or anyone else's exemplars and definitions cannot authoritatively fix the meanings of the words they employ. People's spare semantic intentions designate a kind or a class; they realize that it simply is not up to them to specify the nature of that kind or class.

The evidence for there being such spare intentions, and no rich ones, was what we say when we find out surprising facts about death, malice, or vehicles. Do we say, "you're now talking about something else because you've abandoned my (or the conventional) indicators of the proper use of the word?" Or do we say, "we've learned more about what death, malice, or a vehicle really is?" I think we say the latter, betraying our spare semantic intentions.

In any case, if one bought my realist argument earlier, one should buy it here, for it is the same argument. If it is right, then people do not have semantic intentions different from the *right* way to apply a word. They do not because their only semantic intention is to apply it the *right* way, whatever that turns out to be. Semantic intentions thus drop out entirely as helpful tools in interpretation.[114] For their content is empty of anything that could help us as we look for the true nature of death, malice, or vehicles.

Suppose I am wrong about this and that speakers really have quite a variety of examples they picture to themselves when they use words

---

114. With the caveat that where reference is ambiguous there may be recourse to the intention of the speaker in order to fix the kind of kind to which reference is made. See *supra* text accompanying notes 51-58 for the discussion of "essential context."

like "vehicle," that they really do recite a definition or two to themselves when they write "vehicle" into the ordinance. I now want to argue that even this richer mental life is pretty poor in terms of its implications for interpretation. Let us return to Brest's example and suppose that the mayor had two semantic intentions when she used the word "vehicle": the intention to include the pesky 1973 blue Ford in the extension of "vehicle"; and, after looking up a dictionary definition of "vehicle," the intention to define vehicle as "a self-propelled, mobile thing that runs on the ground." Will this help when the mayor comes to interpreting the ordinance?

Suppose with Brest that the driver of a 1975 white Chevy sedan is caught driving through the park. Did the mayor have a semantic intention to prohibit this? Brest thinks that the answer is yes, noting "you will surely conclude that you intended to prohibit the 1975 Chevy."[115] Yet this is not the case. From the two semantic intentions given, one cannot conclude anything at all about the mayor's intent with regard to the 1975 white Chevy. Take the first semantic intention supposed, the intention to prohibit the 1973 blue Ford. From this statement of the mayor's intention, and the truth that a 1975 white Chevy is in many respects very much like a 1973 blue Ford, one may *not* infer that the mayor intended to prohibit the 1975 white Chevy. That would be like the following inference:

        1. I intend to eat my salad.
        2. My salad is very much like your salad.
Therefore: 3. I intend to eat your salad.[116]

In short, the mayor had no intention with regard to the white Chevy even assuming the supposed intention with regard to the blue Ford.

Equally problematic is any inference about the mayor's intentions that flows from the supposed semantic intention to prohibit things that are self-propelling, mobile, and used on land. From a statement of this intention and the truth that the white Chevy is a self-propelled, mobile thing used on land, it does not follow that the mayor intended to prohibit the white Chevy. To see this latter point, imagine that the mayor unequivocally does not want to prohibit buses in the park because they give greater access to the park, but the mayor overlooks the inconsistency between her intention not to prohibit buses and her semantic intention supposed above. If one could infer that the mayor intended to

---

115. *See* Brest, *supra* note 84, at 210.
116. I examine the problems with inferences of this sort in some detail in Moore, *supra* note 85.

prohibit the white Chevy because of her semantic intention, one could similarly infer that she intended to prohibit buses because both the white Chevy and buses meet the intended definition. Yet the mayor plainly does not intend to prohibit buses; in fact, when she thinks about it she intends not to prohibit them. Likewise, the mayor does not intend to prohibit the white Chevy; at least one cannot infer this intent from the supposed semantic intention.

Neither of the supposed semantic intentions allow one to infer anything about the mayor's intention with regard to the 1975 white Chevy. Absent other evidence, a court should conclude that the mayor had no intentions one way or the other about the white Chevy. Of course, a sensible court would construe the word "vehicle" to include the white Chevy. That is because the meaning of the word "vehicle" is such that the white Chevy is within its extension. It is not because the mayor had any intentions with regard to this object, because she did not (even supposing she had the two semantic intentions mentioned earlier).

If the supposed semantic intentions help this little with regard to the 1975 white Chevy, imagine how little help they will be when the mayor must confront the more *recherché* interpretive problems Brest poses: "Does the ordinance prohibit use of the park by . . . a moped, a baby carriage? Does it forbid the local distributor of a crash-proof car from dropping it into the park from a helicopter as a publicity stunt?"[117] The semantic intentions hypothesized will not help at all in resolving these cases either, for no intentions about them can be inferred from the intentions the mayor did (by hypothesis) have. The short of it is that the mayor's semantic intentions, even on the rich conception, are almost totally useless as interpretive tools because so little can be inferred from them.[118]

An intentionalist interpreter might wish to respond at this point that one need not use intended examples as the basis for inferring *further intentions*; rather, we might regard such intended examples as paradigm cases for the application of some statutory or constitutional

---

117. *See* Brest, *supra* note 84, at 209-10.
118. This is a conclusion Wittgenstein came to in rejecting his own earlier "picture" theory of meaning; although pictured exemplars of our general predicates seemed to fix the latter's sense unambiguously, in the end the picture tells us nothing. *See* L. WITTGENSTEIN, *supra* note 25, §§ 115, 295, 352, 422-26 (3d ed. 1958). *See generally* Engel, *Wittgenstein's Foundations and Its Reception*, 4 AM. PHIL. Q. 260 (1967).

words and reason by analogy from those examples to presently disputed cases.[119] This "loosened" intentionalism can be richer in its implications because it gives up on any attempt to infer *intentions* about the case at hand from the rich semantic intentions the legislature (by hypothesis) had.[120]

Yet this loosened intentionalism is so loosened that it is in danger of losing any claim to being an intentionalist mode of interpretation. Suppose Brest's mayor again pictures the 1973 blue Ford when using the word "vehicle." How is the interpreting judge to know which characteristics of the 1973 blue Ford are the ones that are to count when examining the 1975 white Chevy for "similarity" or analogy? I would say: by the characteristics of the 1973 blue Ford that make it a vehicle! In which case the word "vehicle" is interpreted by its ordinary meaning,[121] not by any intentions.

2. *Further Intentions*

Unlike the rich semantic intentions just discussed, a much more plausible case can be made that further intentions regularly accompany speech acts and can be of help when one is interpreting those acts. If Brest's mayor was not just babbling for no reason, presumably she was trying to achieve something by prohibiting vehicles in the park; whatever else the mayor was trying to achieve (beyond keeping vehicles out of the park) is her further intention. An example of a further

---

119. For an example of this kind of loosened intentionalism, see Christie, *Objectivity in the Law*, 78 YALE L.J. 1311, 1334-35 (1969). Christie urges that one should interpret a statute by what he believes to be the paradigm cases covered by the general language. With regard to the word "vehicle," Christie asserts:

> A party who asserts that a statute requiring motor vehicles to pay a road tax is applicable to go-carts or to farm tractors must state what he claims to be the paradigm case covered by the statute. In this instance, the paradigm case would presumably be the family motor car, although of course the bus or long haul truck might equally be paradigm cases under the statute. If a party were unable to supply any such paradigm cases, he would be forced to conclude that the statute was unintelligible.

Id. at 1334-35. More recently Bob Bennett has urged that one construe constitutional texts by analogical reasoning to the paradigm examples intended by the drafters of those texts. Bennett, *Objectivity in Constitutional Law*, 132 U. PA. L. REV. 445, 480-85 (1984).

120. More precisely, the loosened intentionalism can claim greater implications from the rich semantic intentions of the legislator just because such implications are outside the "intend" operator. As is well known to logicians, one cannot preserve standard rules of inference inside a mental state operator. *See* Moore, *supra* note 85.

121. Alternatively, one might construe the word "vehicle" in such a statute by virtue of the purpose behind the statute or by virtue of previous case decisions under such a statute. The point of the text is not that ordinary meaning necessarily governs, but only that any of the other ingredients in a theory of interpretation will in fact govern once one loosens intentionalism to allow analogical reasoning from intended examples. For a clear-headed discussion of this, see Bennett, *supra* note 119, at 461-75.

intention would be to promote safety for pedestrians in the park by the prohibition of vehicles. If that was the mayor's further intention, an interpreting judge who wishes to achieve the results the mayor wanted has some help in deciding about 1975 white Chevys, mopeds, and baby carriages. Keeping out the first two, the judge may think, enhances the safety of the park for pedestrians, while keeping out the latter does not.

There are two questions that recur in law about intentions generally. Pursuing these will allow us to sketch a realist and a conventionalist conception of further intention before we move on to consider its place in a theory of interpretation. The first question asks what sort of a thing an intention is. The second question asks how one fixes the object or content of an intention.

What kind of things are intentions? In criminal law there is a longstanding debate about whether "intention" should name the foresight that a harmful consequence would ensue from one's act, or whether one must have had that consequence as one's reason for acting before one can be said to have intended it. About the criminal law's equivalent of further intention—"specific intent"—there is much less debate. One has as one's further (specific) intention some harm if and only if one desired that harm, one believed that the actions undertaken would have at least the possibility of causing that harm, and one's action was caused by such a belief/desire set. An intention with which an action is done, on such an account, is just that desire or motive that causes one to act.[122]

How do we fix the objects of intentions? There are three problems here. First, there is the possibility that for any given action one has a "chain" of intentions for which one acted. The mayor, for example, may have sought safety in the park for pedestrians not for its own sake, but in order to encourage greater use of the park by citizenry. The mayor may well have had both intentions, not only one or the other. Second, even without having some chain of intentions, the mayor may have had mixed intentions. The mayor may have passed the antivehicle ordinance in order to accomplish both increased safety for pedestrians and decreased noise levels in the park. Such intentions are not related to one another as means/ends, as chains of intentions are; rather, they involve coordinate intentions that jointly caused the action of passing the ordinance. Third, with regard to any particular intention there is the problem of fixing the description of its object. One might

---

122. The causal account of reasons for action, and thus of intentions, is explored in M. MOORE, *supra* note 3.

describe the mayor's intention as "promoting the safety of pedestrians"; but one might also describe it more generally as "promoting safety," or more specifically, as "promoting the safety of pedestrians from speeding cars." Here one should not say that the mayor has all of these intentions; rather, one must specify which description of the object of the mayor's intention is correct.[123]

These two sets of questions about intentions will allow us to illuminate a realist idea and a conventionalist idea of intentions. A realist will say that what further intentions one has is a fact as real as the facts about the state of one's digestion;[124] that, accordingly, there really are states of belief and desire that exist, and these states really cause the actions that are their expressions. Further, the realist maintains that there is a right answer to whether intentions are hierarchically ordered as means to ends or whether they act on a coordinate basis in causing behavior; that, similarly there is a right answer as to how one should describe the objects of a person's intentions, an answer that depends in large measure upon that person's conscious or repressed linguistic abilities to describe those objects.[125]

A conventionalist about minds in general, and about intentions in particular, will deny all of this. For a conventionalist there really are no states of belief or desire within a person that cause behavior; there is no real hierarchical ordering or mixed causation; nor is there any one correct way to describe the objects of a person's intentions. Rather, ascribing intentions "behind" behavior is an interpretive task that

---

123. These different questions about the objects of intentions are not very precisely distinguished in the literature on interpretation. *See, e.g., Forum of Principle, supra* note 6, at 490. Dworkin distinguishes a concrete from an abstract intention. He is, however, quite unclear as to whether or not such abstract intention is a further intention in some chain of reasons or is a more abstractly formulated object of a particular intention. The distinction makes a difference because Dworkin would simply be wrong in his assertion that an individual might have both intentions, *id.* at 497, if what he is talking about is generalizing to a more abstract level the object of any particular intention. Because one intends to steal some yellow Ford, an observer is not licensed to infer that one intends to steal some colored object. One is entitled to formulate the objects of an individual's intention only with descriptions that are in some sense important to that individual; one is not free to generalize, as one does in other contexts, to larger classes of things which may not be at all what an individual intends. See Moore, *supra* note 85, for a discussion of these and other matters in fixing the object of intention.

124. *Compare* Moore, *The Moral and Metaphysical Sources of the Criminal Law*, 27 NOMOS (1984) (defense of a realist's view about mental states) *with Law as Interpretation, supra* note 6, at 54) (denying that the choice of the description of the object of an intention can "be made by any further reflection about what an intention really is").

125. One can deal with the possibility of unconscious intentions and other mental states, in terms of repressed linguistic abilities. Indeed, I have argued elsewhere that this notion of an extended memory is one of Freud's crucial insights. *See* M. MOORE, *supra* note 3.

makes sense only because the interpreter and his audience share some conventions about how the story should go.[126] There is, on this account, no fact of the matter about the mayor's intentions. If we say that the mayor intended to further safety in the park, it is because we can see peace in the park as a consequence of the vehicle prohibition that it would be intelligible for someone in our culture to want. Any society has norms of intelligibility built into its understanding of itself that rule out many consequences as unintelligible ends of actions. Soaking one's elbow in the mud all afternoon is not, in our society, intelligible as an intrinsically good end.[127] Any society will also have more specific norms of intelligibility that surround offices and roles, like that of a mayor. Some ends, such as personal reelection or pleasing one's spouse, may be generally intelligible ends, but they are not *institutionally* intelligible ends and so may be ruled out in formulating the objects of the mayor's intentions.

A conventionalist will believe that what we do when we describe the mayor's further intentions is simply tell an intelligible story about the mayor's action. We "set" the action of enacting the ordinance in a context that makes sense to us because we can empathize with the ends we select as the mayor's intentions.

To name names, the conventionalist view I have described is fairly attributable to the *verstehen* tradition in sociology and history, to the "empathetic understanding" approach of Collingwood and his admirers, and to more contemporary hermeneutics.[128] In psychoanalysis one sees such a conception at work in those who find intentions *in* dreams that nonetheless play no causal role in the dream's production.[129] In law one sees such a conception at work when judges purport to find the legislature's intention "in the words of the statute alone."[130] Such intentions are ends judges find intelligible and intelligibly served by the rules in question; they are not, however, the real psychological states of any legislators, a fact judges sometimes acknowledge.

---

126. *See*, for example, G. VON WRIGHT, *supra* note 3, for one such conventionalist view of intentions and other intentional states.

127. On intelligibility of ends, see Watt, *The Intelligibility of Wants*, 81 MIND 553 (1972).

128. This tradition is traced briefly in G. VON WRIGHT, *supra* note 3. For a further discussion of this tradition see Moore, *supra* note 3.

129. *See, e.g.*, Steele, *Psychoanalysis and Hermeneutics*, 6 INT'L REV. PSYCHOANALYSIS 389 (1979). For a general discussion of the notion of an intention *in* something, see Gustafson, *On Unconscious Intentions*, 48 PHIL. 178 (1973).

130. The judicial practice of finding the intention in the words of a statute is discussed in Moore, *supra* note 13, at 258-62.

3. *Legislative Intentions*

Having distinguished two conceptions of an individual's further intention, we now should explore the idea that a group of people, such as a legislature, can have an intention. Because we now face two levels at which one can be a realist or a conventionalist—at the level of individual intentions and at the level of group intentions—things get a little messier. I think it useful to distinguish four conceptions of "the legislature's intention," two realist and two conventionalist.

There is first a pure realism about legislative intent. This is the rather crazy position that legislatures can have an intention just as a person can have an intention or just as any possessor of a mind can have an intention. The pure realist thinks of the legislature as having a kind of group mind that quite literally can have intentions like any other mind. Saying this would also seem to commit one to a legislature's experiencing sensations such as pain, moods and emotions such as elation and anger, and the entire panoply of the mental life of a person. Few of us are willing to stomach the ontological commitment to group minds, so the pure realist conception is mentioned only to put it aside.

A more moderate realism is one that urges that real mental states of individual legislators be taken into account by being compared to one another, and when enough of these many intentions are similar enough, they may be said to be the intention of the legislature. Such a position makes no commitments to legislatures having minds, but is nonetheless realist in that it takes seriously the idea of constructing a legislature's intention out of intentions that individual legislators really had. For reasons that I and others have gone into elsewhere,[131] this moderate realist notion of legislative intent cannot possibly work. The number of cases in which it is true, as a matter of psychological fact, that a majority of legislators actually had the same intention in passing a bill is practically *nil*.

A pure conventionalist position about legislative intent would use the same methods in constructing the intention of the legislature as it uses in constructing an individual's intention. That is, one would self-consciously anthropomorphize the legislature by treating it as a single person. One might look at the words of the statute alone and seek to infer the intelligible consequences a single person might have intended by its passage. Alternatively, one might look at all committee reports,

---

131. *Id.* at 265-70.

statements on the floor, or statements made elsewhere by individual legislators and treat all of them as statements made by one person; these items, together with the ordinary meanings of the words employed in the statute, would then all be treated as *evidence* (of a no doubt often conflicting kind) of the further intention with which the legislature passed this bill.[132] In either case, one abandons any search for the actual mental states of individual legislators that caused them to vote as they did, and one abandons the effort to combine these mental states in some way. Instead, the pure conventionalist relies exclusively on the conventions of intelligibility that exist in any society and that surround any institution within any society; these conventions allow the pure conventionalist to make up some intelligible story about what intentions are to be attributed to a particular piece of legislation.

A more moderate conventionalism focuses not on the general norms of intelligibility that exist in a society, nor even on the norms that make some ends institutionally intelligible for a legislator *qua* legislator to have. Rather, moderate conventionalism focuses on whatever conventions are built into our actual legislative practice. Gerald MacCallum,[133] for example, echoed more recently by Ronald Dworkin,[134] urged that there is a developing practice of regarding committee reports as containing authoritative expressions of the legislature's intention. The point is not that because of such a convention a majority of individual legislators actually read the committee reports and adopt the views expressed therein as the consequences they intend the bill to have. If the legislative practice worked this way, we could satisfy the moderate realist conception of legislative intent. Rather, the idea is that the committee reports will be *taken* as authoritative of the intention of the legislature, so that a legislator voting on a bill ignores them at his peril. Such practices operate as a convention of interpretation, in other words, not as a convention around which actual intentions crystallize. The conception is therefore a conventionalist conception of legislative intent.

B. Common Skepticisms About Intentions

Before addressing any normative arguments about the place of legislative intent, it is worth pausing to summarize what is left of the

---

132. Bice, *Rationality Analysis in Constitutional Law*, 65 MINN. L. REV. 11, 26-33 (1980) (urging that one should anthropomorphize the legislature to find an intention behind the statute).
133. MacCallum, *Legislative Intent*, 75 YALE L.J. 754 (1966).
134. *Forum of Principle, supra* note 6.

idea of legislative intent that is worth arguing about. One is entitled to be skeptical of whether this label designates anything useful, but let me recapitulate the argument step by step. Skepticism can proceed at either of the two levels earlier distinguished: about there being (or there being any useful) intentions of individuals and about there being (or there being any useful) intentions of the legislature as a whole. I will take each in turn.

1. *The Intentions of Individual Legislators*

It is an illusion to think that one will find any rich semantic intentions of legislators when they vote. Speakers of language do have spare semantic intentions determining the reference and the extensions of the words they employ, but they do not have the intended examples or definitions an intentionalist interpreter would like. Moreover, even if speakers did have such rich semantic intentions, these would not provide much help in applying the language used to cases that differed in any way from the examples considered by the speaker. There is nothing here to aid a judge in interpreting legal language, and the persistent appeals to these kinds of intentions in building a theory of interpretation should be ignored.

An individual speaker does have further intentions, and so will at least some individual legislators when they vote on a bill. Skepticism about there being such (really existing) mental states of belief and desire causing behavior is misplaced. I have elsewhere defended the realist conclusion that "the state of a man's mind is as much a fact as the state of his digestion" against three forms of mind skepticism[135] and will not recapitulate the argument here. The problems presented by intentions being hierarchically ordered, mixed, and possessed of objects that have varying descriptions, are real enough problems; but they are only problems of evidence, of verifying just what intentions a person has on a given occasion. The surmountability of these problems is shown by the law of crimes, torts, and contracts, where we presuppose the existence and discoverability of the real intentions of individuals all of the time.

2. *Legislative Intentions*

Skepticism is warranted when we move from the further intentions of individuals to those of a group of such individuals. One cannot, as I

---

135. *See* Moore, *supra* note 124.

argued, make out either of the realist conceptions of legislative intent. There just are not the group minds or shared intentions that could give these conceptions of legislative intention any application.

The norms of intelligibility that breathe life into the pure conventionalist conception surely do exist in our society, or in any society of human beings we would recognize as being composed of persons. We are limited in our ability to empathetically understand states of affairs as good in themselves or as good in certain institutional contexts. Even so, this conception of legislative intent is sadly indeterminate in the outcomes it would allow. If one restricts one's gaze to the words of the statute alone in order to divine the intention "in" it, our norms of intelligibility are sufficiently wide to admit several plausible intentions behind the passage of any legislation. It is intelligible for a mayor (*qua* legislator) to have sought safety for joggers in the park in enacting the antivehicle ordinance. It is equally intelligible for the mayor to have sought the abatement of noise and fumes, or increased use of public transportation, etc. To say that many consequences of the antivehicle ordinance would be unintelligible as ends sought by its passage is true enough; but it is equally true that there are many consequences of its passage that are intelligible social goals, and a judge seeking to find *an* intention in the language of a statute alone is bound to be disappointed by the plurality he will find there.

If the judge adopts Scott Bice's "black box" approach (the other pure conventionalist possibility)[136] and treats all legislative materials as if they emanate from a single speaker, the result again will be indeterminacy. The same reasons that prevent the moderate realist from finding sufficient similarity between the intentions of individual legislators will prevent this pure conventionalist from finding *an* intention this conflicting mass of material will evidence. There is no one intention the divergent views of the different legislators will point to. If one anthropomorphizes the legislature into one person, we will have a "person" badly in need of psychotherapy because of the conflict in his intentions. Finding *an* intention in a legislature in this way is no more possible than it is to find *an* intention in a badly conflicted neurotic. There are many intentions warring with one another in such an individual, and there often is no single answer to the question, "What does he really want or intend?"

A pure conventionalist might point out that indeterminacy is not a conclusive objection to his approach, because legislative intent is only

---

136. *See* Bice, *supra* note 132.

one ingredient in a theory of interpretation. His pragmatic injunction might well be that one should use this one ingredient whenever it helps. This response has a point because the pure conventionalist approach is not totally vacuous; it will rule out unintelligible interpretations even if it does not uniquely determine one intelligible interpretation. Any argument against using this approach at all thus should be a normative argument, to which I shall shortly turn.

The same is true about the moderate conventionalist approach to legislative intent. Although one might quibble about whether courts really do adopt a convention that accords the preeminence to committee reports and floor statements that Dworkin assumes, the real question is whether they *should* adopt such a convention. That is a moral question to which I now turn.

C. THE MORAL CASE AGAINST INTENTIONALIST INTERPRETATION

What values lie behind the longstanding judicial tendency to pay at least lip service to the idea that interpretation is aimed at uncovering legislative intent? Of the rule of law virtues earlier identified, several may appear to speak in favor of intentionalist interpretation. One is the fear of untrammeled judicial power if judges can fill in the indeterminacies of ordinary meaning with their own ideas about sound social policy. Adding committee reports and floor statements to the materials they must construe seems to add an additional constraint ("checks and balances") on the feared power "to do what they want." Second, there is the sometimes-expressed notion that mandatory recourse to legislative materials makes the law's prospective applications more certain so that people can better predict the law's interventions on their behavior. This ability to plan enhances liberty, the second value thought to be served here. Third, it is often said (by me among others) that one can never rely solely on one's linguistic knowledge in interpreting the words that appear in legal rules. To avoid absurd interpretations one must always check one's linguistic intuitions against one's idea of the purpose of the rule in question. One thus must look to some version of legislative intent. Fourth, there are those political ideals of democracy and institutional competence that are allegedly served by deference to the legislature's own interpretation of its language.

None of these values, I shall now argue, is in fact served by adopting a convention mandating that courts look to legislative materials in interpreting statutory or constitutional texts. Take the first, the diminution in judicial freedom produced by requiring recourse to legislative materials. This would indeed constrain judicial power, but that is not enough to justify imposing this interpretive constraint. Many requirements could be thought of to constrain judges' interpretive freedom much more than this. For example, "when in doubt, the statute is to be interpreted by the decisional law of England."[137] What is needed is a justification for why *this* interpretive constraint is a good one; it cannot be because it is the most constraining, because it is not.

The liberty argument for requiring recourse to legislative materials is almost as bad. The problem is that legislative materials compare poorly with the words of statutes themselves, their ordinary meanings, values, and even case reports, in their accessibility to the public. Even well-equipped lawyers' libraries do not contain legislative materials as they do statute books and case reports;[138] nor are such materials to be found in us as individuals via our cultural inheritance, in the ways ordinary meanings and values are. To say, therefore, that courts should interpret by reference to legislative materials because citizens can also do the same, is to ignore other ways of making the law determinate that give *better* notice to citizens of what is expected of them.

These same considerations militate against use of legislative materials and in favor of values and meanings (and perhaps precedent) when one considers the related values of substantive and procedural fairness. With regard to the latter, the lack of citizens' and even lawyers' access to legislative materials may prevent individuals from as effectively participating in the interpretive process as they would if the standards were all in the public domain in the way meanings, values, and precedent are. With regard to substantive unfairness, it is usually absurd to claim that people rely on legislative materials in planning their behavior. A well-known instance of this claim was presented in *Keeler v. Superior Court*,[139] in which murder charges against a defendant who had killed a fetus were ordered dismissed by the California Supreme Court because it was thought substantively unfair to try him. The unfairness stemmed from the fact that one hundred years before the defendant "stomped the fetus out of" his estranged wife (his

---

137. *Cf.* CAL. CIV. CODE § 22.2 (West 1982).
138. *Cf.* Schwegmann Bros. v. Calvert Distillers Corp., 341 U.S. 384, 396 (1951), in which Justice Jackson argued against recourse to legislative aids because of this factor: "Aside from a few offices in the larger cities the materials of legislative history are not available to the lawyer who can afford neither the cost of acquisition, the cost of housing, or the cost of repreatedly examining the whole congressional history."
139. 2 Cal. 3d 619, 470 P.2d 617, 87 Cal. Rptr. 481 (1970).

words), a law revision commission of the California Legislature had concluded that "human being" as used in the California Penal Code did not include fetuses. As the dissent in *Keeler* pointed out, it is simply absurd to think that Keeler consulted the legislative history before his deed. It may of course be the case that citizens like Keeler do not give the law a thought in planning their behavior, but for those who do, what the law demands of them is more easily discovered in code books, case books, and their knowledge of meanings and values, and not in volumes of legislative history that even lawyers have trouble finding.

The third of the four values earlier mentioned, giving a sensible construction to texts, is certainly a *desideratum* of any theory of interpretation. Moreover, one does need some notion of purpose with which to check ordinary meanings so as to avoid all the well-charted horrors of literalism.[140] The mistake of the argument is to assume that we need *this* idea of purpose, that is, the further intention(s) expressed in the documents comprising legislative history. One might, as I argue in Part V, use "purpose" here in the sense Max Radin once used it,[141] as the *function* some statute serves in an ideally just and well-ordered society. One might, in other words, use real values to save ourselves from the horrors of literalism, not those values that were expressed in the legislative materials. A proponent of the use of legislative materials thus needs an argument why we should favor his legislative idea of purpose over the moral realists' idea of purpose. The argument that occurs to me actually cuts the other way: to save a statute's ordinary meaning from leading to really absurd or unjust consequences, we cannot look to anything else *but* real sensibility and justice. In particular, the legislature's formally expressed purposes will be just as riddled with absurd extensions as is the language chosen for the statute. If a judge is going to save the legislature from itself by asking Fullerian safety-valve questions about the language, he must do the same with the legislature's formally expressed intentions. This is done only by constructing the morally best purpose for a statute, and construing it by reference to that purpose. This is not done by giving a literal interpretation of the legislature's formally expressed intention and using that as a check on the literal interpretation of the legislature's language. If anything would be absurd, this literalist check on literalism would be, as I have argued elsewhere.[142]

---

140. *See* Moore, *supra* note 13, at 277-81.
141. Radin, *Statutory Interpretation*, 43 HARV. L. REV. 863, 876 (1930).
142. *See* Moore, *supra* note 13, at 280-81.

The main reason the rhetoric of legal interpretation is so riddled with obeisances to "legislative intent" stems from the fourth of the values I mentioned, the political ideals of democracy and institutional competence. Consider in this regard the argument of James Landis in favor of a court using legislative materials in construing a statute.[143] Landis pointed out that the tenure of legislators is comparatively brief, that they represent parochial interests, that they have greater investigatory powers than courts, that they had unlimited choice about what issues to deal with, and that they were more numerous, thus bringing more minds to bear on any problem. From these institutional features Landis concluded that the legislature's choice, as reflected in the legislative materials, should be respected by a court when it interprets legislation.

Consider also the argument of the majority opinion in *Keeler*, wherein Justice Mosk argued that the court could not disregard the legislative materials showing a fetus not to be a human being as that phrase is used within the California Penal Code; the court could not do this, Mosk felt, because that would be tantamount to the court creating a new crime—feticide—where there had been none before. Because of the legislative history, Mosk felt the people's elected representatives *had spoken* on the issue and a court, owing such choices obedience, could not contradict them. The creation of crimes is the prerogative of the elected legislature. The court would in effect be creating a new crime because the interpretation of the old statute to cover fetuses was barred by the legislative choice not to include fetuses.

The problem for each of these arguments—from institutional appropriateness and democracy, respectively—is that they beg the only interesting question to talk about. It is surely a good thing, as Landis and Mosk argue, to respect the choices of the people's representatives, given that they are elected and given that they have the institutional features that they do. But the interesting question is, what is it that those representatives have chosen? There is an assumption in the pro-legislative-intent literature that legislative materials such as that relied upon in *Keeler* contain the choice of the legislature. But surely that is a point that must be argued for. Surely it is open to someone such as Max Radin to argue (as he did in his debate with Landis)[144] that the job of a legislature is to pass statutes, not to form intentions; accordingly, the choice of a legislature that ought to be respected is limited to

---

143. Landis, *supra* note 16.
144. *See* Radin, *supra* note 141.

the statute itself, exclusive of the hopes, fears, and intentions that gave rise to its passage. Moreover, as has become increasingly apparent over the years as legislators take heed of courts looking to legislative materials, taking any position but Radin's tends to corrupt the legislative process. Legislators who cannot muster the votes to defeat a measure may nonetheless win in emasculating it by creating their own version of its legislative history. Similarly, legislators who have only the votes to reach a political bargain at the level of vague generalities may seek to undercut that bargain by inserting their own favored interpretation into the legislative history.[145] In light of such practices courts should regard the statute itself as the only bit of "legislative history" that has any authority; for it is the only thing that they can be certain had the votes to be passed, the only item there is that can count as the "legislature's choice."

Suppose it could be shown that a practice has built up within the legislature to regard one particular item—for example, the committee report—as the best expression of what a bill will achieve. Suppose further that the legislators, to the extent they read anything at all, read the committee report and then vote on the bill. In such a case it may seem that the committee report and the statute itself have equal dignity as constituting the choice the legislature has made that is entitled to respect. Whether this is so depends upon how we picture the mental states of the various legislators as they read the report. If they take it as speaking for them on what the law should accomplish, the report crystallizes a sameness of intention that satisfies the moderate realist conception of legislative intention. More likely, however, is an alternative possibility: the legislators regard the report as an expression of some committee members' hopes for the bill and as a prediction by that committee as to how the bill will be interpreted by the courts. In such a case, they neither form an intention that the bill accomplish these ends, nor vote for it because of that intention. If they do not form these intentions, the report can hardly be said to represent the legislature's choice. In such a case the report represents the intentions of some

---

145. In National Small Shipments Traffic Conference v. Civil Aeronautics Bd., 618 F.2d 819 (D.C. Cir. 1980), Judge J. Skelley Wright also noted this problem:

> We note that interest groups who fail to persuade a majority of the Congress to accept a particular statutory language often are able to have inserted in the legislative history of the statutes statements favorable to their position, in the hope that they can persuade a court to construe the statutory language in light of these statements. This development underscores the importance of following unambiguous statutory language absent clear contrary evidence of legislative intent.

Id. at 828.

members of one committee (or perhaps only of the committee's staff who drafted the report).

Even if one assumes the contrary, that legislators do crystallize their intentions around committee reports, much of Radin's point remains secure. It is like the old adage about footnotes in law review articles: anything worth saying at all is worth saying in the text.[146] Anything in the committee reports that was so well agreed upon by a majority of legislators could have been written into the statute itself. That it was not thought important enough to include in the text is a good reason for a court also to regard it as of little importance.

My conclusion is that the text has a better claim to being called the "choice of the legislature" than do any legislative materials. The political ideals of democracy and of institutional competence are thus better served by a court working from the text alone and not from some "second text" unofficially adopted by some supposed, silent consensus of legislators. That being so, and liberty and fairness also being better served by looking to the other ingredients in the theory of interpretation, I conclude that legislative intent has no role to play in interpretation.

This conclusion has been defended solely by using the rule of law virtues as our normative guidelines. This conclusion is supported by the other set of considerations relevant here, namely, the kinds of effects an intent-oriented theory of interpretation produces. Such a theory produces worse effects than its competitors because it imposes *old* ideals upon us. In constitutional law this consideration is so compelling that it swamps all the others in importance. Better that we fill out the grand clauses of the Constitution by our notions of meaning (evolving, as we have seen, in light of our developing theories about the world), by our notions of morals, and by two hundred years of precedent. What the founders intended by their language should be of relevance to us only as a heuristic device to enable us to think more clearly about our own ideals. The dead hand of the past ought not to govern, for example, our treatment of the liberty of free speech, and any theory of interpretation that demands that it does is a bad theory.

This argument applies to statutory interpretation as well, although with somewhat diminished force. For guiding one's statutory interpretations by legislative materials will be to judge by ideals as old as those

---

146. An admonition that, because of the author's weakness of will, is only sometimes adhered to in this Article.

materials. In the *Keeler* case, for example, a 1970 decision was predicated on an 1850 statute, recodified in 1872. Using nineteenth-century ideas of personhood to decide whether a fetus is a person is not a good idea in the twentieth century. We have thought more about the problem, and we know more factually and morally than those who drafted the commission report concluding that fetuses were not human beings. And even if we do not know more than they, we are as entitled to live under our ideals of personhood as we are to live under our ideals of free speech. For old statutes, thus, the consequentialist arguments against looking to framers' intent are as strong as they are for the Constitution.

The meanings of words, the direction of precedent, and the nature of goodness are all items about which we can have developing theories. Our admittedly imperfect knowledge of each of these things can get better. A theory of interpretation built out of these materials thus can accommodate change and development in our law by court interpretation. A theory emphasizing the enacting body's intention, on the other hand, is glued to the past. Change can only come by constitutional or legislative amendment. Even apart from the rule of law virtues, an intentionalist theory should be disfavored on this ground alone.

III. THE ROLE OF PRECEDENT

Few legal texts in any mature legal system stay very long in a virginal state with regard to interpretation. Most legal interpretation is thus of texts that have already been interpreted by previous court decisions. Any complete theory of interpretation must at least take account of this fact; even if the theory urges that the proper business of the courts is to be faithful to the text to the exclusion of their own prior understandings of that text, that conclusion denying any role to precedent requires a defense. In this Part I shall examine that proposition, and reject it. Again, however, before reaching the merits of such a proposal much preliminary analytic work must be done. Outlining what a doctrine of precedent is, spelling out different (realist and conventionalist) conceptions of it, and inquiring whether there can be such things as the "holdings of cases" or the "weight" to be attached to their holdings are the preliminary analytic matters undertaken in the next two Sections.

A. The Meaning of "Precedent"

1. *Common Law Precedent*

In arriving at some idea of what a doctrine of precedent is, I shall first analyze it in its traditional setting, that of common law adjudication. I shall then ask what modifications must be made in adapting such a doctrine to statutory or constitutional interpretation where a court must interpret not only its own prior decisions but also the text of which those decisions are themselves interpretations. I take the common law situation to be simpler, and therefore begin with it.

There are two ideas that any doctrine of precedent must make sense of: (1) the idea that a single case has a *holding* and, analogously, that a line of cases stands for some proposition of law; and (2) that such holding has *weight*. There are conventionalist and realist conceptions of each of these matters.

A conventionalist conception of the holding of a case will think of the holding as being a matter of historical fact. Just as there are two kinds of conventionalist theories of meaning, so there are two kinds of theories of the holding of a case, each claiming the primacy of one or another of two historical facts. There is what Goodhart and Simpson have called the "classical theory" of precedent, according to which the holding of any court is that proposition of law announced by the court in its opinion as the holding of the case.[147] One might call this the "yellow marker" theory of the holding, in honor of those numerous law students who treat cases this way, skimming the opinions they read to extract the single-sentence holding, which is then underscored in yellow.

The second conventionalist theory is the legal realist theory first enunciated by Herman Oliphant in 1927.[148] According to this view, the holding of any case is to be found in what the court *did* on the facts of the case before it. One ignores what the court *said* it was doing and gleans the holding solely from what the court did to the litigants before it on the facts of their particular case.[149]

---

147. The classical theory of precedent is discussed in Goodhart, *Determining the Ratio Decidendi of a Case*, 40 YALE L.J. 161 (1930); Goodhart, *The Ratio Decidendi of a Case*, 22 MOD. L. REV. 117 (1959); Simpson, *The Ratio Decidendi of a Case and the Doctrine of Binding Precedent*, in OXFORD ESSAYS IN JURISPRUDENCE 148 (A. Guest ed. 1961).

148. Oliphant, *A Return to Stare Decisis*, 14 A.B.A. J. 71 (1927).

149. There are well-known problems with each of these conventional conceptions of the holding of a case that I shall take up when I discuss skepticism about precedent in the succeeding

A philosophical realist, by way of contrast, will not treat the holding of a case as being a matter of historical fact, or at least not exclusively so. There are two realist positions here worth distinguishing, although I think one preferable to the other. What I shall call the pure realist theory will assert that the holding of any case is not to be found in what a court did or said or any combination of these. A pure realist will treat these doings and sayings in the same way he treats standard examples and definitions in ordinary speech: as conventional glosses on, heuristic devices to learn about, and even provisional theories of, meanings—but not the meanings of words themselves. Analogously, a pure realist would treat a previous court's actions and statements as evidence of the moral category that court was trying to describe and apply to the dispute before it. One would attribute, on such a view, spare semantic intentions to the deciding court. It was neither trying to give necessary and sufficient conditions defining the relevant category, nor was it trying to have its actions treated like some paradigm case in later courts' further elaboration of the category involved. Rather the deciding court was seeking to describe the best moral kind that decided the case before it, and all other cases it could imagine, in the right way.

To bring this down to earth, imagine Cardozo deciding *MacPherson v. Buick Motor Co.*[150] A conventionalist would say that Cardozo

---

Section. Because two of these problems introduce two mixed theories of precedent, I shall mention each of them briefly here. First, a serious problem for the classical theory is the well-known fact that succeeding courts simply do not treat the proposition stated by a deciding court as authoritative. Rather a succeeding court may characterize what a previous court describes as its holding as mere dicta or may reformulate the holding of the case more broadly or more narrowly. This problem with the classical theory generates a kind of mixed theory, according to which the holding of a case is that proposition of law stated by the court *and* that is necessary to the decision in the case. *See, e.g.*, J. GRAY, THE NATURE AND SOURCES OF THE LAW 261 (2d ed.1921); *see also* H. BLACK, HANDBOOK ON THE LAW OF JUDICIAL PRECEDENTS (1912).

Yet another kind of mixed theory is generated by a second kind of problem, namely, a problem with the legal realist view of precedent. This problem stems from the embarrassment of riches one faces when purporting to state the facts of some preceding case. For surely not *all* facts present in the preceding case were material to the decision by that court, e.g., plaintiff's hair color; and even if they were, one still must pick some description of each fact from the large number of equally accurate descriptions. This leads some, such as Goodhart, to attempt a mixed theory according to which the holding of a case consists of those facts *described as material* by the deciding court, and its decision thereof. *See supra* note 147. Goodhart's theory is discussed in detail in Montrose, *Ratio Decidendi and the House of Lords*, 20 MOD. L. REV. 124 (1957); Montrose, *The Ratio Decidendi of a Case*, 20 MOD. L. REV. 587 (1957); Simpson, *The Ratio Decidendi of a Case*, 20 MOD. L. REV. 413 (1957); Simpson, *The Ratio Decidendi of a Case*, 21 MOD. L. REV. 155 (1958).

150. 217 N.Y. 382, 111 N.E. 1050 (1916). Cardozo, doubtlessly because of his freewheeling approach to precedent, has been the example, or stalking horse, of many thinkers considering the doctrine of precedent. *See, e.g.*, H.L.A. HART & A. SACKS, THE LEGAL PROCESS (tentative ed. 1958) [hereinafter cited as THE LEGAL PROCESS]; E.A. LEVI, AN INTRODUCTION TO LEGAL REASONING 8-27 (1949).

should be seen as either stating explicitly a new definition of duty in tort law, or at least generating a decision that succeeding courts should treat as a standard example of when there is a duty of manufacturers to remote purchasers in tort. A pure realist, however, will see Cardozo as attempting to articulate and apply the right moral category for the duties we each owe each other not to invade another's bodily and emotional integrity. His statements in his opinion were only his provisional theory about the nature of that concept. In fact, he had a *better* theory later when in *Palsgraf*[151] he came closer to a view of the duties we owe to each other. Even his treatment of MacPherson and of Buick, on this view, is provisional: if the best moral theory of the duties we owe to each other shows that Buick really did not owe a duty to MacPherson, then when the next MacPherson sues the next car manufacturer the decision should go the other way. And deciding in favor of Buick the second time will be to follow (not overrule) *MacPherson v. Buick Motor Co.* because it will be to apply the moral category that was the basis of the earlier decision.

The pure realist conception of a case's holding admittedly runs counter to our intuition of what holdings are. For on such a view the only binding effect of a prior decision is that it identifies a moral category a subsequent court should apply, but apply in light of that subsequent court's own best theory of the nature of that moral kind. We do in fact expect more teeth to a theory of precedent than this and, as I shall argue later, we should. For the values of equality, liberty, fairness, and utility that stand behind the doctrine of precedent are real values too, and they are poorly served by conceiving of the holding of a case as the identification of a moral kind without regard to how that kind was previously articulated or applied.

Accordingly, I wish to distinguish what I shall call a moderate realist conception of the holding of a case. A moderate realist finds the holding of any case to be what the court did to the litigants before it based on those facts of the case that are morally relevant. A moderate realist, in other words, adopts the legal realist conception of the holding, but meets the indeterminacy problems[152] by adding that the materiality of facts, and the appropriate level of their description, is provided by (real) moral kinds. The holding of *MacPherson*, for example, is a decision against all manufacturers of all kinds of products in favor of all persons foreseeably hurt by those products (adopting for

---

151. Palsgraf v. Long Island R.R., 248 N.Y. 339, 162 N.E. 99 (1928).
152. *See supra* note 149.

purposes of discussion the later Cardozo view of duty as the right view). Unlike the pure realist, the moderate realist treats what the preceding court did as a historical given that partially fixes its holding; a case just like *MacPherson* in all morally relevant respects must yield a decision against the manufacturer if the holding of *MacPherson* is to be followed. A moderate realist might not follow *MacPherson*, but if he does not do so that will be because he has overruled it. A pure realist, by way of contrast, has no need for a doctrine of overruling because the holding of the preceding case is not fixed by the legal action taken in that case.

The second idea any doctrine of precedent must make sense of is the idea of *weight*. By "weight," I do not mean to designate the reach or scope of application of a precedent. That is a function of its holding.[153] By "weight" I mean the authority that is granted a prior case once it is conceded that its holding is applicable to some later case. As with the idea of the holding of a case, there are competing conventionalist and realist conceptions of the weight to be given an earlier holding.

A kind of crude conventionalism will give absolute weight to prior holdings. One will say, as the House of Lords once did,[154] that the court has no authority to overturn one of its own decisions, that "that is a job for the legislature." One hears occasional echoes of such an idea from time to time in this country when courts profess their inability to overrule a doctrine "of such long-standing."[155]

---

153. Although the concepts of weight and holding are analytically distinct, there may well be some systematic relation between them. One might think that the closer a second case is to a prior case in morally relevant ways, the more compelling it is that the prior case be followed. On such a view the weight to be given a prior case decreases as the logical space from its holding increases. How broadly the holding is formulated will thus affect how much weight is to be given that case vis-à-vis some later case. Such a view is how I would understand Ronald Dworkin's metaphor about prior cases having a "gravitational force" for later cases. R. DWORKIN, *supra* note 35.

Whether this view of the relation between weight and holding is correct is an interesting question. To resolve it would require some deep delvings, into: whether equality is a scalar phenomenon, such that it makes sense to talk about there being degrees of unequal treatment and such that morally some equality is better than none; whether moral realism is compatible with a scalar view of equality, given that the moral kinds that are determinative of when one case is really like another will have to be "fuzzy." In any case, however one comes out on the relation between the weight of a case and the breadth of its holding, it will be useful to distinguish these two dimensions of precedent.

154. London Tramways v. London County Council, 1898 A.C. 375.

155. *See, e.g.*, Reimann v. Monmouth Consol. Water Co., 9 N.J. 134, 155, 87 A.2d 325, 334 (1952) (Heher, J., dissenting):

[T]he fundamental principles of the common law are immutable except through the exercise of the legislative process. . . . It is not the judicial province to effect a change of private rights under the common law by the substitution of a new rule of action or stan-

Despite the judicial rhetoric, few if any courts really adhere to such an idea of weight, as the House of Lords illustrated by overruling its holding that it has no authority to overrule its own prior decisions.[156] If we do not give absolute weight to the holdings of prior cases, one faces the much trickier task of articulating some idea of relative weight to give decisions. A realist should not have much difficulty here: the values that stand behind the doctrine of precedent vary in strength depending on the kind of case that is involved. Predictability and reliance, for example, are often said to be of more significance in criminal cases than in civil ones. The weight to be attached to the holding of a case or line of cases, accordingly, will vary depending on the kind of case involved. Further, the substantive values that call for overruling a prior case will vary from case to case. The decision on overruling will thus be a balance between the values behind stare decisis and the values served by overruling a case in a particular situation. In some such way a realist can easily make sense of the idea that cases have various precedential weights attached to their holdings.

A conventionalist has a quite different conception of weight. Dworkin's theory, essentially conventionalist in this regard, urges that judges build the most coherent account they can of the law as a whole.[157] One thus may overrule a particular case, or even line of cases, on a showing that it does not fit the most coherent ordering of all law. One overrules a case, on this account, not because it is morally wrong but because it is inconsistent with a whole mass of other cases that it is also a judge's job to follow. The particular weight to be attached to any individual holding thus will vary depending on how well that case fits in with the law as a whole. In some such way a conventinalist can make sense of the idea of cases having varying precedential weights attached to their holdings.

2. *The Precedent of Prior Interpretations of Texts*

How do matters change when we take the various conceptions of holding and weight and apply them to cases that reinterpret a preexisting text? With regard to the idea of a holding of an interpretive case,

---

dard of liability. The Constitution invests the courts with the power of exposition alone. The modification of common law rules of liability comes within the legislative domain.

156. In the practice statement issued by the House of Lords in 1966 without regard to any particular case, the House proposed to modify its existing practice of being bound to follow its past decisions and to "depart from a previous decision when it appears right to do so." 3 All E.R. 77 (1966). The practice statement is discussed in Cross, *The House of Lords and the Rules of Precedent*, in LAW, MORALITY, AND SOCIETY 145-60 (P. Hacker & J. Raz eds. 1977).

157. R. DWORKIN, *supra* note 35.

the answer is: not very much. It is true that the holding of a decision interpreting a statute is partly determined by the language of the statute in question. To use the example mentioned in this Article's introduction of the noncertified carrier hauling chickens interstate, we know that part of the holding of the case was that some class of things are *not manufactured products*. We know this much about the holding just because the interpreting court must justify its decision as following deductively from the statutory language, "not a manufactured product." Its interpretive premise, whatever else it says, must use this phrase if it is to connect the statutory language to some description of the facts.[158] This is, to be sure, more than we know initially about the holding of a common law decision where there is no canonical language from which the decision must follow. Still, this is not very much help in fixing the holding of a case interpreting a statute; for one still has the crucial job of deciding how the things that were classified as not being manufactured products are themselves to be described: was it the fact that they were chickens, or animals, or killed, or dressed, or frozen, or eviscerated that was crucial? We will have the same theories about this as discussed above.[159]

The more interesting question is how one might conceive of the *weight* of precedent when dealing with decisions that interpret statutes or constitutional texts. For now there is an extreme position that is the opposite of the "absolute weight" notion we encountered with regard to common law precedent. This is the position that it is the text (or the

---

158. For the role of interpretive promises in deduct justifications of decisions, see *supra* text accompanying notes 12-13.

159. That is, the classical theorist will urge that we take the court's statement of these matters as a kind of authoritative, partial definition of the statutory language so that, if the court in its opinion described the things in the truck as eviscerated chickens, it is eviscerated chickenhood that gives a partial definition of the statutory phrase, "not manufactured products." Alternatively, a legal realist will urge that we take what the court did to be the holding, and thus would say that these things (no matter how described) are paradigmatically not manufactured products.

The pure realist will say that the holding is still the natural, moral, or functional kind the court was attempting to articulate, except now we know the label for that kind because the statute gives it to us. There is, accordingly, very little that interpretive cases tell the pure realist; such cases are only previous (but in no way binding) attempts at unpacking the nature of the kind of thing that certain labels name. A more moderate realist will again take what the court did to these litigants as having some binding force for future decisions but will state the holding of an interpretive case to be that premise that connects all the morally relevant features of the case to the statutory language (and connects no morally irrelevant features to that language). What are now conceived to be morally relevant features will be determined by one's own best theory as to the nature of manufactured products within the meaning of the rule containing that phrase. This differs from common law adjudication, where one has no canonical text fixing the category around which one's theory must be built and according to which one judges morally relevant likenesses and dissimilarities.

original understanding of a text) that is authoritative, that the courts are powerless to change the legal meaning of that text, and that, accordingly, there can be *no* precedential weight attached to interpretive decisions.

Although there have been grumbles of this sort by various Justices of the Supreme Court, our practice is again not this extreme (nor, as I argue in Section C, should it be). Cases interpreting texts are not deprived of precedential force just because of the authoritativeness of a text. What the presence of a text does do, however, is alter the idea of *weight* in more subtle ways.

A conventionalist of the Dworkin, coherence type needs to take into account the special authority of the statutory or constitutional text itself. For given the presence of the text, it is no longer adequate to say that the weight of a prior decision is in direct proportion to its fit in the most coherent reordering of all decided cases. Weight, consequently, has two dimensions: how well a decision coheres with past decisions and how well the decision fits the meaning and purpose of the text it purports to interpret. Needed to flush out this added dimension of weight will be some idea of a decision having *textual support*, i.e., how well a decision fits the meaning and purpose of a text. Munzer and Nickel[160] describe textual support, which they call an "ancestral relation to the text," in terms of four variables: (1) how *text-focused* a decision is, meaning that the decision must justify itself explicitly in tems of the text; (2) how *available* the decision is, meaning how likely it is to be offered in support of deciding new cases as they arise under the text; (3) how *authoritative* the decision is, meaning not how correct it is, but rather, how much it would be acquiesced in by the various branches of government; and (4) how *firm* the decision is, meaning how unlikely it is to be questioned by the deciding court. A decision meeting all of these criteria becomes, for Munzer and Nickel, as authoritative as the text itself. Presumably one could extend this to say that to the *degree* any decision meets these conventional criteria it has precedential weight for future cases construing the same textual provision.

A realist conception of weight again would think of weight as being a function of the strength of two competing sets of values: on the one hand, the values favoring the following of the decision in question, which will still include the values of equality, liberty, fairness, and utility, and on the other hand, the values served by overruling that deci-

---

160. *See* Munzer & Nickel, *supra* note 24.

sion. Now, however, the values served by overruling any particular case are not simply the moral values on the merits; they must include those values that underlie one's use of ordinary meaning and purpose as well, to the extent that the precedent case flouts the correct view of the meaning or purpose of the relevant text.

B. COMMON SKEPTICISMS ABOUT PRECEDENT

1. *Conventionalist Theories of Precedent*

One is entitled to a healthy skepticism about the conventionalist conceptions of the holding of a case or of its precedential weight. For some conventionalist conceptions of these ideas would ask the impossible from courts; others are not at all faithful to basic features of the ways in which our courts actually practice precedent. Consider first the holding of a case. According to the classical theory, one looks for some stated proposition in a court's opinion to find its holding. The problem with the classical theory is that it does not describe the way we practice precedent. Subsequent courts reformulate the holding of a case, making it broader or narrower than that stated by the deciding court. Subsequent courts also regard decisions as having holdings even if there is no stated holding in the opinion—indeed, even if there is no opinion at all. Cases in which there is no majority opinion in which to find the stated holding are also regarded as having precedential force.[161] To these may be added the well-established practice of discounting whole portions of an opinion as "dicta," no matter how essential the deciding court thought the portions to be in its reasoning.

These practices of courts have made themselves felt in the way law is taught in American law schools. Our case method of teaching is much more legal realist than it is classical. Students are dissuaded from using their yellow markers to extract the one sentence "meat" of an opinion and instead are taught to look at the facts of the case and the court's decision to decide for themselves what the holding must

---

161. *See supra* note 147, wherein all of these arguments are deployed against the classical theory of precedent. What Goodhart failed to perceive was that these same objections could be marshalled against his "material facts" theory, the mixed theory according to which one should ignore any *stated* holdings and yet one should look to the facts that the deciding court *stated* to be material as one frames for oneself the holding. As Julius Stone has pointed out, this mixed theory is also descriptively inaccurate; subsequent courts do not take at face value an earlier court's assertion of which facts were material to its decision; still less do later courts feel bound to accept the narrowness or the breadth of the description of those facts that the deciding court happened to use. J. STONE, LEGAL SYSTEM AND LAWYERS' REASONINGS (1964); Stone, *Ratio of the Ratio Decidendi*, 22 MOD. L. REV. 597 (1959) [hereinafter cited as *Ratio*].

have been. They are taught to regard the deciding court's opinion as only its theory about what the court's decision represents. They are not taught to see the statements in an opinion as authoritatively laying down that holding much as a legislature *lays down* rules in canonical language.

The classical theory thus cannot account for our practices with regard to precedent. But here the conventionalist must shift to the other horn of a dilemma. The legal realist view of precedent, while much more faithful to our practices, is woefully incomplete in its ability to determine what the holding of any case actually is. Saying that the holding of a case is the decision of that case on its facts does not help in the least in probing the level of generality at which those facts are to be described, or which facts are material. By any such conception of the holding, there are as many holdings to any case as there are descriptions of its facts—not an infinite number, perhaps, but large enough to make the legal realist theory untenable as a conventionalist doctrine of precedent.[162]

This problem is not alleviated by saying that there is always a *line* of cases for which one seeks the holding. Any set of decisions, no matter how large, will yield an indefinitely large number of generalizations that would have those decisions as instances. There is no unique proposition extractable from a line of cases once one leaves the language of the deciding courts to the side. Particular data "underdetermine" the generalizations that may truthfully be made about it.[163]

---

162. *See supra* note 161; *see also* Cohen, *The Ethical Basis of Legal Criticism*, 41 YALE L.J. 201, 216 (1931). The mixed theory of both Gray and Black discussed *supra* note 149, according to which one finds the holding of a case by finding the proposition of law stated by the court that was necessary to the decision, suffers these same defects. For there is no proposition necessary to the decision of any case, as both Stone and Cohen point out. This defect is shared by the legal realist and this mixed theory for the same reason: the materiality and the level of generalization of the facts are not determined by any conventions. Any generalization that accurately describes the facts of a case could be the proposition from which the decision flows deductively. But no one such proposition is necessary. The exploding coke bottle cases, for example, could have as part of their holding a description of the things for which manufacturers are liable, as "coke bottles," "soft drink bottles," "hour glass shaped bottles," "consumer products," "products," and so on.

163. I take the underdetermination point to be much more serious for the legal realist theory of precedent than it is as a problem about induction in science. For in law, unlike science, we are not predicting the outcome of cases, however much the legal realists may have thought the contrary. A doctrine of precedent is to give the deciding judge reasons for deciding his case one way or the other, not reasons to predict that he will decide one way or the other. The underdetermination thesis tells the judge that he has an indefinitely large number of generalizations that equally well fit all past cases, and some of these will decide his case one way, some another. The judge cannot wait and see which set of generalizations is falsified or verified by his decision. Rather, he must make his decision. Even if he sits back and predicts his decision, he still has to make it.

The underdetermination thesis not only undercuts any legal realist conception of the holding of a case, but also renders problematic any conventionalist account of the different weights to be attached to particular cases. The thesis means that there will be an indefinitely large number of general theories that fit all the decided cases equally well. Any particular case, accordingly, cannot be assigned some conventional weight in proportion to the degree of its fit within a theory; for there are many theories, in some of which a case will be more central than in others. And a conventionalist has no way to pick between such theories.[164]

Conventionalists emerge from this bath in skeptical acid with most of their clothes removed. They can articulate some idea of the weight to be attached to the holding of a case only if they take one of the extreme positions, which either give no weight or controlling weight to previous court interpretations; they have severe problems in making sense of the idea of precedents having some weight that varies from case to case. Conventionalists have even more difficulties in saying what the holding of a case is. If the radical indeterminacies of the legal realist theory are to be avoided, they must urge that we *ought* to take the holding of a case to be that proposition of law stated by the court as its holding. If the court says in the chicken example that it is the chickenhood and the eviscerated nature of the objects in question that counted in its construction of the statutory phrase "manufactured product," then the holding is just that interpretive premise of its reasoning: "For all items, if they are eviscerated and a chicken, then they are not manufactured products." Recognizing that this is not faithful to the way we practice precedent, it must instead be seen as a proposal for us to mend our ways. As such, I assess its moral merits in Section D.

---

164. *See* Schauer, *supra* note 14, at 814-18 (application of the underdetermination thesis against the suggestion that one could derive a theory purely by virtue of its fit with legal standards or examples that have already been established as authoritative). As Schauer notes, it is somewhat unclear where Dworkin's theory of adjudication should be classified. *Id.* at 815 n.77. Dworkin himself has urged on occasion that there can be no conventional test for what is the best theory from which all more particular rules and case decisions can be derived. *See* R. DWORKIN, *supra* note 35, at 40, 64-68. Yet, I have classified Dworkin as a conventionalist here because of his repeated and strong suggestions that a case's weight is in proportion to its fit within a theory that is itself derived from conventions within the legal system. Dworkin's theory of weight, thus, is an essentially conservative theory inasmuch as it is derived from the degree of fit within a theory that itself is derived from past institutional data. The other dimension of weight that Munzer and Nickel articulate is not radically indeterminate in this way. Their idea that a decision has precedential weight if it is "text-focused, available, authoritative, and firm," is no doubt somewhat vague in its applications; but vagueness here may be a virtue: the *more* of these things a decision has, the *more* weight it is entitled to in the continued elaboration of the meaning of some provision. *See* Munzer and Nickel, *supra* note 24, at 26.

2. Realist Theories of Precedent

The most obvious form of skepticism about realist theories of precedent is to doubt the existence of the moral kinds on which the theories depend. Because I have made my defense of this elsewhere,[165] I shall put this form of skepticism aside. Another, more interesting skepticism would attempt to use against the realist the underdetermination argument just developed against the conventionalist. The argument would be that generalizations in morals are subject to the underdetermination thesis, even granting the existence of a moral reality; that, accordingly, while we may have much particular moral knowledge, our knowledge of general moral principles is every bit as shaky as our inductively derived scientific laws or the underdetermined holdings of legal cases; and that, accordingly, a moral realist can find the holding of a case no better than can the conventional legal realist.

There are in fact two related skepticisms buried here. These are fruitfully untangled with regard to induction by Nelson Goodman's distinction between the old and the new riddle of induction.[166] The old riddle of induction was to ask how the universally generalized statements that scientific laws purport to be could possibly be derived from the singular sentences describing particular observations. What could possibly justify generalizing from "this raven is black" and "this one is too," to "*all* ravens are black," Hume asked. We have not seen all ravens, so how can we assert the truth of a universal statement having observed the apparent truth of only some of its particular instances?

The new riddle of induction is different. Even if we can justify universalizing singular statements about ravens into universally generalized statements, how do we justify picking one description of the particular facts we observe over another? Why not describe our observations as "this bird is black" and universalize over that description? All birds are not black, and we will eventually find this out. But there are an infinite number of ways in which we could describe what we saw when we looked at some black bird, particularly if we allow ourselves the freedom to invent new descriptive categories.[167] No finite amount of observation could rule out all of the possible descriptions there are other than "ravens;" thus, the second riddle about induction.

---

165. *See* Moore, *supra* note 17.

166. N. GOODMAN, FACT, FICTION, AND FORECAST (3d ed.1977).

167. *See* (or *hear*) the lawyer Wallace Steven's poem, "Thirteen Ways to View a Blackbird," in THE COLLECTED POEMS OF WALLACE STEVENS 92 (1954).

Both the old and the new skeptics about induction have their analogues about moral knowledge. An old riddle about morals is how one can justify moving from singular statements about what it is right or wrong to do in particular situations, to a universally generalized one—from "this lie is wrong" to "all lies are wrong." Kant thought he found the answer in the general form a judgment must take if it is to be a *moral* judgment,[168] an answer echoed more recently by Richard Hare, who purports to find in any descriptive use of language a presupposition that singular statments are universalizable;[169] but many are skeptical of such formal routes to justifying generalization in morals.

A "new" (but really quite old) riddle about morals is how one picks the relevant description of the situation over which one can universalize. Why "lying" in the above example? Why not "lying to a friend" instead? "New skeptics" will assert that even if generalizing over all people is justified by some ideal of equality, that ideal itself is essentially an "empty" one because one must specify what attributes are morally relevant before one can decide what equality requires.[170] Such "new" skepticism is but a special case of the old notion that a decision to universalize singular statements does not tell you what descriptions you will put in those singular statements, a criticism as familiar to Kant as it is to us.[171]

A conventionalist about science and morals as well as about law will be unable to get around these riddles in either science or morals. There will be no answer as to why there is an entitlement to universalize any singular statement, or why some descriptions of the facts can be favored over others. One only has one's own conventions ("I just do both these things") to look to. A scientific realist, however, will believe that there really are natural kinds of things in the world so that the descriptions of those kinds can be projected onto unexamined instances because such instances will share the essential nature of that kind. A realist will believe that reality itself gives warrant for these natural descriptions, and for projecting them, and that this is the only warrant that can or should be asked for. Analogously, a moral realist will think that we generalize as we do in morals because it really is right that we treat cases consistently and people equally; it is because there really are moral qualities in the world that we favor some descriptions over

---

168. I. Kant, Groundwork of the Metaphysics of Morals (Paton trans. 3d ed. 1958).
169. R. Hare, Freedom and Reason (1973).
170. Westin, *The Empty Idea of Equality*, 95 Harv. L. Rev. 537 (1982).
171. For a general discussion, see M. Singer, Generalization in Ethics (1971).

others as we frame the singular judgments from which we generalize our moral principles. A conventionalist again has no answer to these puzzles except to point to convention—that individuals do such things in their own moral practice—although it is this very convention that is puzzling to him.

Underdetermination may be an epistemological problem for a realist. This is because the realist, no less than anyone else, is always working with a finite set of data with which a large number of theories will be compatible. Thus the realist can be no more certain than anyone else that the theory (moral or scientific) with which he accounts for the observed data is the right theory, i.e., that it will equally well account for the not yet observed cases. But underdetermination is only an epistemological problem; it does not impugn the realist's metaphysics. Being uncertain that one has the right moral category—one that captures all and only the cases it ought to capture—is quite compatible with certainty that there is some such moral category. Only if the realist gives up his realist metaphysics (which is almost defined by its separation of what there is from how we know about it) does he have problems because of these riddles. There are appropriate moral categories to be used in framing the holding of a case even if the realist, no less than anyone else, has problems finding what they are.

C. THE MORAL CASE FOR PRECEDENT IN INTERPRETATION

Henry Monaghan has complained recently that "stare decisis is a moribund mode of constitutional interpretation" and has urged its revitalization as an ingredient in our theory of interpretation.[172] It is easy enough to state the prima facie desirability of having precedent play some role in the interpretation of statutory and constitutional texts; for a number of the rule of law virtues earlier sketched are served if courts give some weight to their own past interpretations. Equality, in its guise as formal justice, is served by a court treating like cases alike. Liberty is advanced by the enhanced predictability such consistent interpretation makes possible. To the extent that people do rely on court precedent, substantive fairness is served as well by attaching some weight to past decisions. Finally, efficiency may be furthered by some doctrine of precedent operating; for the doctrine of precedent forecloses

---

172. Monaghan, *Our Perfect Constitution*, 56 N.Y.U. L. REV. 353 (1981). A similar complaint is voiced by Bennett, *supra* note 119.

some issues from being reargued and redecided, encourages settlements, and generally allows more focused litigation.[173]

The trick is to specify how much weight to give precedent vis-à-vis other ingredients in a theory of interpretation. The two extremes are easily discounted. It would be wrong to claim absolute weight for a court's past interpretations because other values may simply outweigh the rule of law virtues that argue in favor of following precedent. For interpretive cases, as well as common law cases, the absolutist position that a court can never go back on its own interpretation is simply untenable, as virtually all courts today recognize.

The other absolutist position is equally untenable. Frankfurter's sometimes expressed view that the only correct rule of decision is "the Constitution itself and not what we have said about it" assumes that the political ideals underlying a court's allegiance to a text overshadow any possible values standing behind precedent. Yet this is not true either. Even in constitutional cases deciding matters of the greatest public moment, the values of equality, liberty, fairness, and utility are not to be ignored. Even a realist, who thinks that all interpretation should aim at describing the nature of the moral or natural quality named by legal texts, can and should admit that the rule of law virtues are real values too and that, accordingly, how prior courts have decided like cases has some moral force behind it. This is the reason I think the pure realist view about the holding of a case to be untenable: it ignores the equally real values behind following a past decision, even if it was wrongly decided. The pure realist view is vulnerable to Monaghan's charge[174] that "perfectionist" interpretive schemes can have no role for stare decisis. The more moderate realism defended herein is not vulnerable to such a charge, "perfectionist" though such a natural law theory avowedly is.

Distressing as it is for those of us who prefer crisp intellectual positions, the only defensible position here is that the past interpretations of a court are entitled to "some weight" when it continues its interpretation of some text. I shall next argue that any conventionalist theory of precedent founders on this idea of giving "some weight" to past decisions.

---

173. For arguments and suggestions in this regard, see THE LEGAL PROCESS, *supra* note 150, at 574-89.

174. Monaghan, *supra* note 172.

D. THE MORAL CASE FOR THE REALIST THEORY OF PRECEDENT

Once one rejects the extreme positions that are all too easily stated by a legal rule, the idea of precedent having "some weight" becomes very troublesome for a conventionalist. For a convention needs to be framed in a way that accords cases just the weight they are due by the competing sets of values that favor following or overruling any particular case. Given the case-by-case variation in the strengths of these two sets of values, unless the convention adopted is just "get the value mix right," a conventionalist will not get the value mix right in deciding the precedential weight of various cases.

Consider in this regard the Dworkin and Munzer/Nickel criteria for weight. Suppose, with Dworkin, one said that precedential weight was proportional to the degree of support that a decision had by the best theory of the law considered as a whole. Put aside underdetermination problems. By Dworkin's test the weight of a decision will not be proportional to the conservative values that are served by following it, discounted by the substantive values that urge that it should not be followed. Dworkin's coherence conventionalism is too conservative: it makes weight a function of *past* institutional data alone.[175] The substantive values that call for overruling—not in the name of some other part of the law but in the name of those moral values themselves—find no place in such a coherence account of weight.

Munzer and Nickel's criterion is subject to the same objection. Even if one adds their requirements that a decision be text-focused, available, authoritative, and firm to Dworkin's requirement that the decision also fit a coherent theory of prior decisions, one still has a criterion for weight that does not give room for substantive values. For their criteria all concern conventional features: whether the prior interpretation pertains to the language of the text itself; whether the interpretation has been or would be offered by responsible folk in deciding

---

175. It is arguable that Dworkin recommends that judges sacrifice coherence for goodness. See R. DWORKIN, *supra* note 35, at 37-38, 122-23. How conservative Dworkin's theory ultimately is depends upon what kind of institutional support the substantive principles urging the overruling of any particular case must have before they can be used by a judge to assign that case low weight. If Dworkin were to allow substantive moral principles without any institutional support—"raw background rights," so to speak—to be balanced against the conservative values urging the following of precedent, then the theory is not conservative. (It also would not be conventionalist.) Dworkin at least sometimes seems to believe, however, that it is only substantive principles that themselves have institutional support that can be used to urge overruling, which makes for a too-conservative conventionalism about weight.

cases interpreting the text; whether the interpretation has been or would be acquiesced in by the various branches of government; and whether it is likely to be overturned. These factors by their nature cannot capture the correct weight to be given to prior interpretations because they do not reflect in the least the substantive values that call for overruling. Only if the various officials who offer, acquiesce, or do not overturn the interpretation themselves have the *right* idea of what weight to give to a prior case will Munzer and Nickel's criterion give that case the right weight.

Can the conventionalist do better in formulating some rule that will assign to prior interpretations their correct weight? A little reflection shows how unlikely this is. After all, the right weight to give a prior decision is a function of the two sets of values mentioned before. What formal criterion *could* compete successfully with the obvious alternative of having judges apply those values directly in assigning precedential weight to past decisions? To capture the wide variations in the strength of the rule of law virtues that stand behind precedent, and to capture the varying strength of the values that argue for overruling a case, requires a test that uses those very values. No convention can capture this complex moral decision; for the very richness of variation of the relevant moral facts will outstrip the ability of any convention to capture them.

A realist theory of precedent is also preferable to any conventionalist theory in regard to the holding of a case, as well as to its weight. It will be recalled that the only conventionalist theory that escapes crippling indeterminacy problems is the classical theory whereby one extracts the interpretive holding for which a case stands from the language used by the court. Although this is not an accurate description of how we in fact find the holding of a case, the conventionalist might contend that it should be. It is this moral claim that I wish to examine here.

One of the main values served by following a doctrine of precedent at all is equality, the treating of like cases alike. The obvious question one always must ask here is how the *relevant* likenesses and dissimilarities are to be judged. The sort of conventionalist under consideration here would say that the relevant similarities are those stated by the precedent court. That is what his conception of the holding of a case commits him to. If the holding to be followed is what is stated by the precedent court to be its holding then that set of categories stated by the precedent court is the one to be used by a later court in trying to act *like* the first one. If the precedent court deciding a products liability case *said* its holding was about coke bottle manufacturers, then the relevant likeness is coke bottle manufacturers; the holding does not then apply to bottlers of beer, who can be treated differently in their liability to consumers without offending equality.

This is a preposterous idea of equality. Real equality is given only when *morally relevant* likenesses and dissimilarities are used as the benchmark for like treatment. What the precedent court said was the reach of its holding cannot be allowed to be the reach of its holding without offending one of the main ideals that gives precedent its point, namely, equality. At most, such language is the precedent court's own theory about the morally relevant features of the situation. To truly treat like cases alike later courts must second guess this theorizing by the earlier court; a second court must decide for itself what the morally relevant likenesses are that argue for like treatment, and what the morally relevant differences are that argue for different treatment. This is, of course, precisely what courts do when following or distinguishing the holdings of prior cases.[176]

Another ideal with which the classical conception of a holding is difficult to square is that of the separation of powers. It does not fit our picture of a court to have it issuing canonical statements like a little legislature. Courts are to decide disputes, not issue edicts. If "some law" arises from that legitimate process of deciding disputes, all well and good. But this is judicial lawmaking in increments, not by enunicated rules. The separation of power ideal that motivates this restricted view of judicial law-making is that of institutional appropriateness. Courts deciding individual cases do not have the information before them (nor the means to get it) to issue rules in the linguistically precise form of a statute. They do not know precisely what the reach of the rule should be when deciding cases. Attaching precedential weight to their precise statements may thus put a burden on them that they are not equipped to meet. Leaving it to later courts to work out on their

---

176. It might be thought that the ideal of equality is different when cases arise as interpretations of texts, because for intepretive cases there is a text that gives the court a conventional standard by which to judge relevant likenesses and differences. Yet the presence of the text does not license a conventionalist standard by which relevant likenesses are to be judged. That standard, admittedly derived from the text in question, nonetheless must be interpreted in light of the best theory about that text's ordinary meanings, *see supra* text accompanying notes 69-109, and in light of certain value considerations, *see infra* text accompanying notes 177-217. To render equality under a text is thus not a matter of convention either, but is rather a matter of treating alike cases that are really alike in the relevant respects.

own what precisely the holding of a case is places less of that burden on those that decide it.

For these reasons neither the conventionalist conception of the holding of a case, nor that of its weight, adequately further the normative ideals dictating that we have some doctrine of precedent. To say what the holding of a case is or what weight it has is a matter on which moral knowledge is necessary if the values of equality and the separation of powers are to be well served. Such knowledge, when combined with the historical knowledge of what earlier courts did with the facts of the cases before them, produces one ingredient in a theory of interpretation.

IV. THE ROLE OF VALUES

Since the heyday of legal realism it has been no secret that values enter into the interpretations of texts by judges. A natural law theory of interpretation will say that values can and should enter into the decision of every case and that real values, not just conventional mores, are the values that should be looked to by judges. In this Part I shall defend both of these natural lawyer's assertions. But as mentioned in the introduction, a theory of interpretation should do more than allow one to be categorized as a natural lawyer or not. A complete theory about interpretation should allow one to say *how* values enter in, and with what they must combine to produce the interpretation of some text.

There are four kinds of judgments a judge must make when deciding upon the correct interpretation of any legal text: first, a judgment about the ordinary meanings of the words used in the text; second, a judgment about what interpretation is suggested by prior case law interpretations of the text; third, a judgment checking both the ordinary meanings and the technical meaning suggested by precedent against what the judge takes to be the purpose of the provision in question; and fourth, a judgment checking ordinary meaning, precedent, and purpose against an "all things considered" value judgment about the best result in this case.

The role of values in this four-part interpretive scheme is: first, sometimes (but not always) to aid in the determination of the ordinary meanings of words; second, to enter into the determination of what is the holding of a prior case or line of cases; third, to enter into the formulation of the purpose behind a text; fourth, to determine the all things considered judgment about which interpretation will yield the best results in the particular case; and fifth, to determine the correct balance of each of the preceding four factors. An instance of this last kind of value judgment is where a judge must decide whether to overrule ordinary meanings, past holdings, or even purpose in the name of more important substantive values.

Before spelling this scheme out in more detail and defending it, both undertaken in Section C below, two preliminary matters will occupy us. These are, first, what is referred to when one speaks of values; here I shall again (as about meanings, intentions, and precedent) distinguish the realist from the conventionalist position about values. Second, I address the question of whether either conventional ("shared") values or real values exist, again adopting the view that they both do, so that one must argue about which sort of values should be utilized in interpretation. I shall take each of these matters in turn.

A. The Meaning of "Value"

Our ordinary ways of thinking, as recognized in our ordinary ways of speaking, mark the distinction between real value judgments and conventional ones. There are three indications of this that we all recognize. The first is the ability we feel we have to make value judgments that disagree with value judgments of most or even all members of our society. There may be a nearly universal taboo placed on incest in our society, for example; one can describe that agreement of individual value judgments as a conventional value judgment against incest. Despite our recognition of this conventional value judgment, we understand the person who says,"I think incest is good." If the only kind of value judgments were conventional ones, it would be much more difficult than this for moral radicals to make their unconventional value judgments understood.

Second, there is a lack of any logical relation between the statement, "bullfighting is wrong," and the statement, "most people (in England?) think (feel, believe) that bullfighting is wrong." These are not equivalent statements, as we all readily recognize. The first says nothing about people's mental states of belief or feeling; it talks about bullfighting. The second says nothing about the wrongness of bullfighting; it only describes the mental state of a group of people. There simply is no relation between the truth values of the two statements.[177]

---

177. Apart from our clear linguistic intuitions, one can see the lack of any logical or semantic connection between the two types of statements in the following way. Suppose the first statement (about bullfighting) *did* imply the second (about what most people believe about bullfighting).

Third, we have a linguistic device that we use when we wish to indicate that we are making a conventional moral judgment and not a real one. We use quotation marks in writing, and inflection in speaking. As in, "she is *so* 'good.'" In saying such things, we do not mean we think the person (Marie Osmond?) is really good; only that many people, applying certain conventional standards, would think so. The existence of such a semantic device would be unnecessary if there were not these two kinds of value judgments.

None of these three points establish that there are objective values, or even that the ethical relativist is wrong in the assertion that all value judgments presuppose certain conventions. These three points do establish that we each *think* there is a difference between what is really good and what is "good" according to some shared conception of goodness. Even the most skeptical of thinkers about morality can concede as much and still maintain their skepticism.[178]

Not only are there two quite different judgments that we make about values, real and conventional, but there are also quite a few variations on what passes for a conventional value judgment. These have been nicely brought out in the taxonomies of John Ely[179] and Paul Brest,[180] who in their survey of the sources of value in constitutional interpretation have described many of the variables with which one could subdivide conventionalist positions. One might, for example, look to the *time* at which a consensus about a certain value exists—the

---

Because the second statement contains the first as a subordinate clause, it also must imply another belief statement, namely: "most people think that most people think that bullfighting is wrong." There are two things wrong with this continued implication: first, it leads to an infinite regress of beliefs, as G.E. Moore noted long ago, G. MOORE, ETHICS (1912); second, such a second implication presupposes that we are inordinately self-conscious so that every time we think a thought we are also conscious of thinking the thought.

Suppose, alternatively, we took the second statement (about what most people believe) to imply the first (about bullfighting). We then face formal contradictions everywhere we discovered differences in what groups of people believed. If the statement, "most people in England believe bullfighting is wrong," implies "bullfighting is wrong," and if the statement, "most people in Spain think that bullfighting is not wrong," implies "bullfighting is not wrong," then *we* are committed to the contradiction that bullfighting is both wrong and not wrong.

The only relation between the two statements is a pragmatic one. A speaker who utters, "I believe bullfighting is wrong," is committed to also uttering, "Bullfighting is wrong," and vice-versa. It is a presupposition of normal (i.e., sincere) conversation that a speaker says what he believes and believes what he says. Such pragmatic connections do not affect the semantic difference between the two types of utterances.

178. For a recent example, see J. MACKIE, ETHICS (1977).
179. See J. ELY, *supra* note 1.
180. Brest, *The Fundamental Rights Controversy: The Essential Contradictions of Normative Constitutional Scholarship*, 90 YALE L.J. 1063 (1981).

time of the enactment of the text, the time of the court's decision, the future, or some vague combination of all of these such as the once prevalent idea that there are some values enduring from the past whose direction of change can be discerned, so-called "enduring values on the march." There is also the dimension of the degree of holistic restructuring that one is willing to do in regard to the conventional moral judgments of a group of people, ranging from Lord Devlin's "Gallup poll" conventionalism (taking popular moral judgments on particular matters at face value) through Harry Wellington's more cautious, differential conventionalism about principles versus ideals, to Dworkin's willingness to disregard entirely any particular popular moral judgment in the name of the best theory of popular moral sentiment, taken as a whole.[181] Despite these and other important differences between what might be meant by "conventional moral judgment," I shall lump them all together for purposes of contrasting conventionalism about values with realism. I do this because all conventionalist theories of value suffer a common defect, namely being hostage, in some way and to some degree, to popular (rather than to the right) moral judgments.

B. Common Skepticisms About Values

It is common in the debate about the role of values in adjudication to blend existential arguments with moral arguments. Consider in this regard John Ely's argument that neither real nor conventional values have a place in constitutional interpretation. Mixed with Ely's moral argument that having judges seek real values can be dangerous, is Ely's skeptical argument that real values (Ely's "natural law") are so hopelessly vague that they determine no real life dilemmas.[182] Mixed with Ely's moral argument that it makes no moral sense to rely on conventional morality (Ely's consensus morality of the majority) in order to determine the content of some minority's rights, is Ely's skeptical argument that conventional values are so vague that "one can convince oneself that some invocable consensus supports almost any position a civilized person might want to see supported."[183] Before coming to the

---

181. DEVLIN, THE ENFORCEMENT OF MORALS (1965); R. DWORKIN, *supra* note 35; Wellington, *supra* note 78. One should see in the difference between Devlin and Dworkin on what constitutes popular morality, the familiar difference we have seen before (about meanings, intentions, and precedent). Devlin and Dworkin represent two kinds of conventionalists: the conventionalist who urges that conventions are to be found at the level of particular judgments (Devlin), and the conventionalist who believes that agreement is to be looked for at the level of general standards (Dworkin).

182. J. ELY, *supra* note 1, at 48-54.

183. *Id.* at 67.

moral arguments for the place of values in interpretation, one must have some confidence that there is something here worth arguing about.

Ely quotes Roberto Unger in making out his vagueness skepticism about there being real values. According to Unger:

> [A]ll the many attempts to build a moral and political doctrine upon the conception of a universal human nature have failed. They are repeatedly trapped in a dilemma. Either the allegedly universal ends are too few and abstract to give content to the idea of the good, or they are too numerous and concrete to be truly universal. One has to choose between triviality and implausibility.[184]

From this dilemma Ely concludes that even if physical laws can be found "out there," "moral law will not."[185]

The vagueness of moral concepts (or of the natural concepts a naturalist in morals believes to underlie moral concepts) hardly even counts as an argument against moral realism.[186] Against conventionalism, the Unger-Ely skeptic has a point: a conventionalist has only social conventions to rely upon for moral insight, so that if they "run out" because of vagueness there is a serious problem. But a realist has no such problems; for a realist, moral insights are not limited to the conventions surrounding the use of some word. A moral realist will recognize that we have much knowledge of a particular kind with which we build a better and better theory of what justice, fairness, friendship, generosity, etc. might be. Our judgments about the injustice of some horrible (but novel) modes of punishment, for example, are not guided by applying the conventions we may have up to now adopted about what is cruel or inhumane; we may know that some completely novel punishments are inhumane and develop our theory accordingly. A conventional feature of language, such as the vagueness of "cruel" or of "inhumane," is simply beside the point for a moral realist.

The other horn of Unger's purported dilemma is equally ill-fated against the realist. For a realist, universal agreement about the truth of some proposition will hardly be confused with the actual truth of that proposition. So what if there is no universal assent to man's nature or the moral qualities that that nature may support? There are lots of

---

184. R. UNGER, KNOWLEDGE AND POLITICS 241 (1975); J. ELY, *supra* note 1, at 52.
185. J. ELY, *supra* note 1, at 52.
186. *See* Moore, *supra* note 17, at 1101-02, 1149-52.

people who disagree about whether the earth is round too. Intersubjective agreement is hardly the same as objectivity.[187]

The Ely-Unger dilemma is obviously better suited to be the basis for skepticism about the existence of conventional values. For a conventionalist does need to frame conventions so that: (a) they would be agreed to by most people, and (b) they would be determinate enough to decide some specific cases. Yet even here, my suspicion is that popular judgment would agree on many specific matters as it agrees on the "motherhood" generalizations. Describe a brutal murder in detail to people, and you will get wide agreement on its being wrong; describe a helpless infant gurgling out its young life face down in a mud puddle while an indifferent, and therefore passive, adult looks on, and you will get wide agreement on the minimal social obligation to help. This being so, it remains at least possible to assign to judges the task of examining conventional morals as well as real ones; that they should not do so I myself argue in Section D, but this is a different argument than that they *cannot* do so.

These remarks about value skepticism are intended only to get at one form of that skepticism pervasive in current legal theory. There are many other forms of skepticism about values that are philosophically more sophisticated. Since I have dealt at length with those on another occasion,[188] I will leave skepticism. Assuming there are both real and conventional values, how should a judge use them in interpreting texts?

C. The Moral Case for a Limited Role for Values

1. *In Finding Ordinary Meanings*

The best way to understand the role of values in interpretation is via the four kinds of judgments just outlined. The first is the judgment about meaning. Values have no role to play in articulating the meaning of many words. "Tiger," for example, is such a word. One's realist metaphysics do not dictate that one seek some *moral* nature to tigers, but only that a natural kind word like "tiger" names a natural kind. In such cases, the search for ordinary meaning does not involve a value judgment.

In other instances to find the meaning of some word or phrase will be to rely entirely on one's best moral theory. A legal rule may: Enforce a promise against its maker "when the interests of justice are

---

187. *See id.* at 1088-96.
188. *Id.*

served thereby"; award custody to that parent who will serve the "best interest" of a child; read into all contracts an implied covenant of "good faith"; guarantee to all "equal protection of the laws" and the process that is "due" them; disqualify from citizenship those lacking in "good moral character," or deport those guilty of a crime involving "moral turpitude." When a legal rule uses such words and phrases as these, finding their ordinary meanings is no different than finding out more about the things and qualities to which they refer. If one applies a realist theory of meaning, there is simply no difference between finding the meaning of "good character" and finding the best theory of the virtues. Even a conventionalist would have a difficult time distinguishing linguistic from moral judgments here; for a conventionalist would have to be able to distinguish linguistic conventions about the use of "good character" from moral conventions about what constitutes good character.

For other words some moral knowledge must be applied if one is to find their ordinary meanings, but morals will not be the whole story. Consider (yet again) the word "death." It is plausible to suppose that the best theory of what death is will include some judgments about what attributes are valuable in a person. Consciousness, for example, would be a good candidate for such an attribute. If this is so, a realist court seeking the meaning of "death" would have as part of its job the articulation of those attributes so valuable that loss of their possession entails death.

Statutorily defined words will also vary in the need for moral knowledge to find their meanings. The example of "bird" from *Regina v. Ojibway* shows that sometimes the meaning of such words will be found in a scientific theory about the hidden nature of such things. The example of "malice" from the law of homicide illustrates the fact that sometimes the meaning of such words will be found in a moral theory about the nature of such things as culpability. There is thus no necessity that either statutorily defined words or ordinary words have their meanings unpacked by moral theory, although this is often enough the case.

The moral case for using values to unpack ordinary meanings in the various ways just described is the same as for looking to such meanings at all. Nothing but some kind of moral theory, conventional or realist, can be used to give meaning to phrases like "best interest." If there is a case to be made for looking to ordinary meanings, as I argued there was in Part I, such a case applies to these words as well.

For words that are defined by the statutes that use them, the argument is a bit different. One might think that when the legislature gives a definition of "bird" or "malice" its definition should be treated as stipulating necessary and sufficient conditions for the application of that word in certain legal contexts. One might think this because of the deference due the legislature stemming from the various separation of powers considerations. Yet there is an alternative, and better, way of giving deference to the legislative judgment here; that is to assume that the legislature did not attempt a task that no lexicographer could undertake for ordinary words, namely, giving definitions that are necessary and sufficient criteria. A rational legislator would not want his definitions to be so taken because legislators know they do not know exactly what the dimensions of their own aims are when they legislate.[189] Their definitions should be seen as similar to dictionary definitions—as providing a gloss, a learning device, and (perhaps) the beginnings of a theory about the nature of the thing to which the word refers. A rational legislator would not want more than this from his definition, or else he ends up with the absurdity of pillow-backed ponies being classified as birds. Similarly, with words like "malice" deference to the legislature does not require that a court abjure from seeking what it elsewhere seeks: the true nature of the thing to which the word refers. That the task here involves moral knowledge is no reason to change the nature of that task.

2. *In Finding the Holding of a Case*

The moderate realist position about precedent defended above commits one to using a good deal of moral knowledge in formulating the holding of any case or line of cases. For once one decides to look to what the precedent court *did*, and not what it *said*, then one must frame for oneself the material facts and the morally correct level of generality in their description in order to state the holding of some prior case. The very point of following precedent, to treat like cases alike, requires that the judgment of what is and is not relevant be done in light of one's best moral theories.

3. *In Finding Purpose*

Once a judge determines the ordinary meanings of the words that make up a text and modifies that ordinary meaning with any statutory definitions or case law developments, there is still at least one more

---

189. H.L.A. HART, *supra* note 68, at 127-29.

task. A judge must check the provisional interpretation reached from these ingredients with an idea of how well such an interpretation serves the purpose of the rule in question.

The necessity for asking this question of purpose Lon Fuller made familiar to us in his famous 1958 debate with H.L.A. Hart.[190] True, Fuller made the argument for purposive interpretation only against what he took to be Hart's plain-meaning approach based on standard instances. But Fuller's argument is much more general than that. It applies against any kind of ordinary meaning or any kind of preestablished legal meaning (case law or statutory) ever being a sufficient basis on which to decide a case. One can get consequences contrary to the purpose of some statute no less with legislative definitions, or with an ill-considered line of prior interpretations by the courts, as with ordinary meanings. In all such cases a court must reserve to itself the power to overrule these formal ingredients in interpretation, enabling a decision the court thinks will better serve the rule's purpose. And as I have argued elsewhere,[191] if one ever asks this question of purpose, one will always ask it. A judge will always, as a consequence, be making the value judgment between the values that argue for following antecedent meaning, ordinary or legal, and the values that argue for effectuating the rule's purpose. In addition, as I now propose to show, even the judgment ascertaining the purpose of some legal rule is a value judgment.

The purpose behind some rule is not a psychological state of any individual or group of individuals. Nor is it some conventionalist's anthropomorphic reconstruction of the state of mind a legislature would have if it were but one person. Rather, the purpose a statute serves is the *function* it serves in our society.[192] A rule's function is partly a matter of fact but largely a matter of value. The factual part comes when one looks at a rule and asks what its likely consequences are in society. This is a matter of knowing causal connections, a matter of scientific fact. The passage of a statute has many likely consequences in this world, just as does any event. To honor one of these as *the* purpose (function) of the statute one must have some principle of selection. The principle we use everywhere in our function assignments is to ask whether the likely consequence we are considering as a rule's func-

---

190. *See* Fuller, *supra* note 50.
191. *See* Moore, *supra* note 13, at 277-81.
192. I discuss five senses in which the word "purpose" has been used in formulating a theory of legal interpretation. *Id.* at 262-63.

tion itself causally contributes to an end state of some system that we think to be good and worth preserving or achieving.[193] In the case of human hearts we say that their function is the circulation of blood. We pick this consequence of the heart's activity as its function over other consequences, such as making noise in the chest cavity, just because this consequence itself causally contributes to physical health, a desirable end state for the human body. Analogously for statutes, we pick as their function that likely consequence of their passage that itself causally contributes to a better society. The ultimate end state toward which all statutes should contribute, as Max Radin reminded us long ago, is justice.[194]

In formulating the purpose for a statute or other text there is admittedly something of a circle to be traversed by the interpreting judge. For the prediction of the likely consequences of a statute's passage depends in part upon the interpretation placed upon it. Yet this interpretation is dependent in part on what the likely consequences of the statute are (for remember, it is only these likely consequences that are eligible to be considered the statute's purpose and that this can influence the statute's interpretation). This is not a vicious circle, however, because there is a place to get on. A judge starts with ordinary and antecedent legal meanings in order to give the rule a provisional interpretation; under that interpretation purposes may be sought. If the judge can find none that serve the ultimate ends of a just society, he must start again with a bit more strained reading of the words of the text. Less ordinary meaning, or a more strained reading of statutory definitions and precedent, will be traded off against a better purpose. At some point the judge will reach equilibrium between the rule of law virtues supporting ordinary meanings and following precedent and the substantive good at which the purpose he is finding should aim. If the strain on meaning is harsh enough, a judge may "overrule" the ordinary meaning by acknowledging that this is a term of art in the law, guided by the law's special purposes and not by ordinary meaning. Analogously, if the strain on precedent is great enough a judge will not reconstrue the holdings of prior interpretations but will explicitly overrule them. In each such instance the judge checks the provisional interpretation yielded by the formal ingredients of meaning and precedent with the value-derived notion of the rule's purpose.

---

193. I defend this normative view of function assignments against considerable literature the other way in M. MOORE, *supra* note 3.
194. See Radin, *supra* note 141.

The values needed to assign purposes to statutes in this way are nothing less than a worked-out blueprint of the good and just society. For only in light of such an end state can a judge meaningfully pick between those many likely consequences of a statute's passage and assign some subset of those as its purpose(s). The moral case for any interpreting judge's using his values to find purposes in this way is that there is no real alternative. The judge cannot look to the actual intentions of the legislature because it did not have any. Some conventionalist's reconstruction of the intelligible purposes a legislature could have had is not helpful because there will either be too many intelligible ends, or too many in conflict, to pick a small set. To use purpose at all (as a judge must do to save any interpretation from the silliness of literalism), necessitates the construction of a theory of a good society and the search for purposes that contribute to that.

4. *In Preventing Injustice*

Often unnoticed by those extolling the virtues of purposive interpretation is that another kind of value judgment is needed to round out a complete theory of interpretation. This is the judgment that not only checks meaning and precedent, as does purpose, but also checks purpose itself. Consider a case the Supreme Court decided a century ago, *United States v. Kirby*.[195] Kirby was a county sheriff who had stopped a riverboat that was carrying the United States mail. He had done so in order to arrest a federal mail carrier, who was on duty; the sheriff had a warrant outstanding for the carrier's arrest for murder. Despite the obvious good sense of arresting a wanted murderer wherever he could be found, Kirby was prosecuted under a federal statute making it a crime to "obstruct or retard the passage of the mail, or any driver or carrier."[196]

By the ordinary meaning of the words "obstruct or retard," Kirby both obstructed and retarded the United States mails. Furthermore, the purpose of the statute may plausibly be taken to be the promotion of the free flow of mail. Such a purpose would be furthered somewhat by preventing interferences such as that by Kirby. Yet obviously other values are important here. Society was surely bettered by getting a suspected murderer off the street (or the river) even if the mail was a bit slower. And surely Kirby reasonably relied on just such a judgment being morally correct. It would make society worse, and it would be

---

195. 74 U.S. (7 Wall.) 482 (1869).
196. *Id.* at 483.

unjust to Kirby, to interpret the statute not to cover his kind of case. Yet the only way *not* to include his case is to recognize that there is a general "safety-valve" question of justice that must be asked in all interpretation.[197] As described by the Court in *Kirby*, "[a]ll laws should receive a sensible construction. General terms should be so limited in their application as not to lead to injustice, oppression, or an absurd consequence."[198]

The argument in favor of a court asking this last safety-valve question is to prevent injustice. Because any system of rules interpreted solely by the meanings of words, their prior interpretations, and the purpose of the rules in which they appear, will produce instances of such injustice, the case for adding this last question is just to prevent it. As I have argued elsewhere, if one *ever* asks this general safety-valve question, one *always* asks it, even when one's answer to it is to go along with ordinary meaning, precedent, or purpose.[199] There is no way of limiting this general value question, as the Supreme Court has at times suggested, to "rare and exceptional circumstances."[200] It may be rare that one overrules meaning, precedent and purpose, but it cannot be rare that one asks the question to see if one should do so.

Asking this safety-valve question of justice is the final way that values enter into the interpretative activities of a judge in every case. As with the safety-valve question of purpose, there are two different kinds of value judgments needed here. First, there is the judgment of

---

197. This is not quite true in criminal law. An alternative vehicle for saving the legislature from itself in criminal law is the general balance of evils test for justified criminal actions. *See* MODEL PENAL CODE § 3.02 (Proposed Official Draft 1962). Under such a provision, one would concede that Kirby's arresting of the mail carrier was an "obstructing" and a "retarding" of the passage of the mail, as those terms are used in the federal statute, but exempt Kirby from punishment because his (otherwise criminal) act was justified. By using this route, one's interpretation theory need not include the safety-valve question of justice because that question will be asked anyway after the statute has been interpreted.

There is an analogous criminal law doctrine that arguably makes the purposive safety-valve question equally superfluous. In some jurisdictions a criminal defendant is excused from punishment if punishing him would not serve the purpose of the statute he violated. Again, one could leave the purpose question out of one's interpretive theory because one knew that just that question would be asked anyway at the level of excuse.

We should see both of these criminal law doctrines as partial legislative recognition of the importance of asking *somewhere* the safety value questions of purpose and justice. That such questions are sometimes formally allocated to issues external to interpretation seems of little importance.

198. 74 U.S. (7 Wall.) at 486.

199. *See* Moore, *supra* note 13, at 279-81.

200. Tennessee Valley Auth. v. Hill, 437 U.S. 153, 187 n.33 (1978); *see* Moore, *supra* note 13, at 280 n.281.

what, all things considered, would be the just outcome in this particular case—obviously a judgment of values. Secondly, a judge must balance the good achieved by doing justice in this particular case against the values that stand behind following meaning, precedent, or purpose, to the extent that any of these other ingredients incline the judge to an interpretation other than the one that maximizes justice between these two parties. This balancing of values is also (and equally obviously) a value judgment.

D. THE MORAL CASE FOR USING REAL VALUES

The last question remaining is this: given that values must and should enter in as judges discover ordinary meanings and the holdings of cases, and given that values also enter in as they check meaning and precedent with purpose and justice, what kind of values should be relied on by the interpreting judge? Consistently with the realism about meanings and precedent earlier defended, I think that real values should be used, not the conventional values that happen to be prevalent in society. Because the argument is a bit different for constitutions than for statutory texts, I shall consider each separately.

1. *In Interpreting Statutory Texts*

The rule of law virtues earlier outlined usually should incline one towards the use of real values in interpretation, and not conventional ones, wherever recourse to values is warranted. Consider first the three separation of powers principles. With regard to the checks and balances notion, it may seem that conventional values have a constraining influence on judges that real values do not and, thus, that mandating use of conventional values limits judicial power and does not leave judges free to pursue their own personal values. One should see in any such thought moral skepticism rearing its head once again. For if one believes that the truth of a moral judgment is just as much a matter of fact as is the truth of a scientific judgment, then to enjoin a judge to seek the moral truth is just as constraining as it is to enjoin a judge to decide cases on the basis of factual truths. Certainly, a judge must use his best judgment about what *is* the moral truth in some situations, but in that harmless sense a judge must also "use his own best judgment" to find any facts, including social facts about conventions. That a judge must judge in no way implies that he is unconstrained in his judgments.

The real fear about untrammeled judicial power, if judges seek real values in their decisions, is the fear that they will give insufficient weight to the other ingredients in interpretation. The fear is that they will ignore ordinary or statutory meanings, precedent, or even a rule's purpose, in their rush to serve moral truth. Yet this fear is not really a fear about use of real (versus conventional) values; it is a fear that judges will (really) get it wrong by giving insufficient weight to the values that stand behind meanings, precedent, and purpose. The corrective, in such a case, is not to enjoin judges to make conventional value judgments, but only to make better, real ones.

If one considers institutional appropriateness, it might be thought that judicial institutions are better set up to engage in moral truth seeking than are the legislatures and that, accordingly, courts should seek such real values while legislatures should reflect popular moral judgment. While this familiar sort of argument may have something to be said for it, it is surely overstated. The institutional structure of courts allows them to be capable articulators of popular values as well as of real ones, provided one's idea of "popular values" is more like Dworkin's coherence view than Devlin's Gallup poll morality.[201] And legislatures, as I shall argue shortly, are better seen as attempting to lead society to the right moral views rather than being mere reflectors of prevailing moral views. Accordingly, it is difficult to make much, in this context, of institutional differences between courts and legislatures.

The real issues emerge when we consider the principle of democracy. For shared values seem in some sense to be "more democratic" than real values. The trick is to say whether this is so in any very potent sense of "democratic." Consider three variations of this conventionalist argument. The first would be quite potent if it were true. It would view statutes as being enacted to further popular values. The proper legislative role, on this view, would be to represent the value judgments of one's constituents. If each legislator does this, and does it well, statutes should be virtual embodiments of shared values. The judicial role, the argument would conclude, would be to interpret statutes in light of those same shared values that motivated their passage. Doing so furthers democracy in that it defers to the democratic legislature.

The problem with this argument lies in its theory of the legislative role. Legislators should not view their jobs, even in a democracy, as simply representatives of popular views.[202] Legislators are admired for

---

201. *See supra* note 181 and accompanying text.
202. I argue for this in Moore, *The Limits of Legislation*, USC CITES Fall-Winter 1984, at 23 and in Moore, *The Limits of Legislation*, SEOUL L. REV. (forthcoming 1985).

actions "on principle" and not simply for actions reflecting their constituents' views (often perjoratively considered to be a knuckling under to "political expediency"). Legislators should bring to their job their own moral insights into how this society can best be structured. If they cannot be persuasive enough, despite the platform their office offers them, we can vote them out. But we are entitled to more active moral leadership from legislators than the passive, representational theory of the legislative role allows.

If this is right then the judicial role should be tailored accordingly. A court should view the legislature as seeking to enact its vision of the good society. A court should see itself, accordingly, as a partner in seeking to articulate the details of that society's structure. This means interpreting statutes by the same values as the legislature itself was seeking—real ones, not necessarily widely shared ones. Only then can a court be praised for furthering democracy by deference to the elected legislature.

I suspect that most of the plausibility of the "shared values are more democratic" theme does not stem from the argument just considered. Rather, shared values themselves are thought to be democratic just because they are *shared*, not because the democratic legislature enacts statutes with reference to them. Consider, accordingly, a second view according to which a person's value judgments on particular issues are like his "vote" on those issues. Consensus values are accordingly democratic because they represent the popular will. They are to be viewed as a kind of *informally* enacted supplement to the *formal* consensus reached in passing a statute and are to be used by courts in interpretation accordingly.

The problem with this view lies in its enactment idea of moral judgments. Many people have moral views about how to raise children and what is best for them; that is not to say that such people regard their moral views on such issues as judgments to be summed by the court in interpreting a statute—for example, a statute awarding custody of a minor child to that parent who will most further the best interest of the child. Popular moral judgment does not usually include the second-order judgment that first-order moral judgments should be relied upon by some legal institution such as a court. A conventionalist cannot claim that popular moral judgment is the informal analogue of a statute, because moral consensus does not constitute even an *informal* enactment of that consensus into law.

The real claim of the conventionalist here is a third claim: shared values are most democratic simply because they represent what most people most prefer on moral issues. The interpretive implication of this third claim does not depend on formal or informal enactment of such shared values. Courts should use shared values, on this view, just because it is good to have most people's values guide the interpretation of the laws that govern their lives. This third democratic claim thus reduces to a kind of preference utilitarianism; what most people most prefer ("shared values") should be used in interpretation because doing so will maximize the net sum of satisfied preferences. As such, the claim is subject to the standard arguments against utilitarian views: there are values higher than utility that everyone, including a court, should seek. Considering people's preferences as determinative of these values does not give such values their true weight. A child has a right under a "best interest" statute to a creative and stimulating environment, no matter how much there may be a consensus (in rural Iowa, at least)[203] that such things are not all that important.

There simply is no very persuasive argument from democracy that requires a court to look to conventional values rather than real ones in its interpretation of statutes. On the other hand, there is a good reason on equality grounds to look to real values and not merely conventional ones: doing so promotes real equality and not merely the appearance of equality. Interpreting statutes by the right values ensures that cases that are truly alike are treated alike. Conventionalist interpretation will settle for less; for a conventionalist, it will be enough that cases that the public *accepts* as alike are treated as alike, even if a court can see a moral difference. The goodness of equality does not reduce to the satisfactions of majority preference, and, accordingly, a court seeking real equality in its interpretations must look to real values and not conventional ones (preferences) as it determines the morally relevant dimensions of a problem.

Two of the rule of law virtues, democracy (properly conceived) and equality, speak for realist interpretation. The third value here, liberty, undoubtedly speaks the other way; for predictability is probably enhanced by a court's use of shared values. That they are widely shared should provide better "moral notice" of what the law requires than would my own realist interpretive scheme.[204] One simply must balance which is more important here.

---

203. *See* Painter v. Bannister, 258 Iowa 1390, 140 N.W.2d 152 (1966) (Iowa Supreme Court awarded custody to Iowa grandparents over the child's natural father on the grounds that a stable environment in rural Iowa was worth more than a more Bohemian, if creative, environment in California).

204. See People v. Sobiek, 30 Cal. App. 3d 458, 106 Cal. Rptr. 519 (1973), in which the court

I suspect that for many the determinative arguments about values between a realist and a conventionalist do not lie in the above debates about the implications of the various rule of law virtues. For such persons the more motivated arguments are consequentialist in character. My own consequentialist intuition is that realist interpretation has a better chance of yielding better results in decided cases; the main counter by the conventionalist is that realist judges pose grave dangers of serious moral mistakes being imposed on hapless litigants and on the rest of us.[205]

My intuition here is a simple one: you get better results if you ask judges to seek them explicitly rather than if you tell them to do something else. An example of this is Learned Hand's decision in *Repouille v. United States*.[206] Hand had to interpret the naturalization statute, which allowed citizenship to those of "good moral character." Repouille applied for citizenship, despite having killed one of his children, a retarded, crippled, helpless child that drained family resources from Repouille's other children. Hand denied Repouille citizenship, relying on what he took to be the conventional moral judgment that euthanasia, no matter how tragic the circumstances, manifested bad moral character.

My simple intuition is that Hand would have done better if he had judged the moral question himself, let his emotions grapple with the choice Repouille had faced. One hears this in every regretful line of Hand's opinion, dryly reciting the conventional judgment that all mercy killings are bad. Had Hand taken the responsibility for deciding whether *this* mercy killing of Repouille really constituted a morally bad

---

refused to quash the indictment of a partner who had allegedly stolen partnership property, the defendant claiming unfair surprise because the statute defines theft as taking the property "of another." The court responded to the fairness argument in terms of the notice given by shared values: "'common social duty' would have forewarned respondent that circumspect conduct prohibited robbing his partners and also would have told him that he was stealing 'property of another.'" *Id.* at 468, 106 Cal. Rptr. at 525.

205. Michael Perry also notes this argument, which he calls the "possibility of serious judicial misadventure." M. PERRY, *supra* note 1, at 123-25. One thing this debate between the realist and the conventionalist is *not* about is whether reaching really better results is better. If you grant (1) that there are objective truths about moral questions, and (2) that the result that maximizes the net sum of satisfied preferences of people is not always the best result, then a result that is really better *is* better, even if most people's morals are offended by it. The real debate here is whether enjoining judges to seek moral truth will in fact yield those morally better results, or whether it will instead lead us further from them.

206. 165 F.2d 152 (2d Cir. 1947). Hand's other opinions on similarly freighted moral issues are helpfully collected in H. SHANKS, THE ART AND CRAFT OF JUDGING (1968).

act, he could not have allowed himself the comfort of a wooden recitation of a conventional moral norm. Forcing Hand to decide whether the act was really bad would have forced him, in Edmund Cahn's words, to have been "in session with himself, prepared to answer for the consequences."[207] With sensitive moral beings, you get better judgment with such personal involvement than you do when a judge can claim the dispassionate air of the sociologist of other people's morals.[208]

My simple intutition of course depends on our not having moral lepers on our benches. No one would urge that judges should feel themselves free of the constraints of conventional morals if the result of their doing so will be morally awful. But I doubt that that is the likely result, given the present occupants of the bench. The danger of the wildly erratic judge with the bit in his teeth, charging down some morally outrageous path, is the real myth here. The worst we get from bad judges is conventional moral judgments of a wooden-headed sort. The best judges are capable of giving us more, and there is no reason not to ask for it.[209]

2. *In Interpreting Constitutional Texts*

Conventionalism is something like the official theory of what sort of values are to go into interpretation of the federal Constitution. The grand phrases of Earl Warren ("the standards of decency that mark the progress of a maturing society")[210] or of Felix Frankfurter ("the canons of decency of English-speaking peoples")[211] are two examples that come easily to mind. It has long been clear that values enter into the interpretation of the great phrases of the federal Constitution, and in a society that has lost its faith in there being real values, the natural justificatory peg on which the Supreme Court has rested has been the "enduring," "basic," or "fundamental" values shared in our society.

---

207. Cahn, *Authority and Responsibility*, 51 COLUM. L. REV. 838 (1951). Cahn is generally critical of Hand's conventionalism.

208. For the dependence of moral reasoning upon the emotions, and thus upon some real emotional involvement, see Moore, *supra* note 17, at 1135-36 and the articles cited therein.

209. A real danger may be that many judges simply are not up to the kind of systematic moral reasoning that nonetheless pays detailed attention to the facts and circumstances of the case before them. *See* Weisburg, *supra* note 16 (describing the "scholar's heroic ideal of a deep judicial mind and spirit brooding over a rich scholar's universe," an ideal Weisburg regards as a myth). Yet, given the sensitivity of many areas of our law to supple moral distinctions, there must be some judges out there capable of the kind of realistic jurisprudence I have in mind.

210. Trop v. Dulles, 356 U.S. 86, 101 (1958).

211. Rochin v. California, 342 U.S. 165, 169 (1952).

Despite the official rhetoric, courts often do look to real values in interpreting the Constitution, and they are right to do so. Both the consequentialist and the rule of law arguments made above apply here as well. Because the arguments need to be altered a bit for constitutional interpretation, I shall readdress each below.

The democratic arguments are, if anything, strengthened for the realist when it is a constitution that is to be interpreted. It is true that there are competing conceptions (realist and conventional) of the democratic "will" that stands behind constitutions as well as statutes. A conventionalist will say that the great clauses of the Constitution were either an embodiment of the conventional morals of the time of their passage[212] or an invitation to successive generations to fill in their meaning with the conventional morals of the time.[213]

A realist will regard those clauses differently. What was done when those clauses were enacted was to name real moral qualities, such as equality, that it is the business of those interpreting the Constitution to describe. To truly follow the "will of the (super) majority" will be to seek the right answers to the questions of what process is due persons, what liberties of speech and religion are due them, what punishments are cruel, and the like. As before with statutes, one's choice of a theory of interpretation here will follow on one's choice of a theory of constitution-making. My own view is that a constitution is simply a political philosophy written down. It is a blueprint of the good society, and those who draft it should do so with just such a vision of what they are doing. The interpretive theory such a theory of constitution-making generates is a realist interpretation theory.

Apart from this constitutional analogue to my realist argument from democracy for statutes, there is of course the additional consideration that constitutional interpretation involves a court in an inherently undemocratic process, that of reviewing the decision of the people's

---

212. *See* R. BERGER, DEATH PENALTIES 66 (1982). The late Justice Black, perhaps joined by Justice Rehnquist today, also shared this view of the importance of the conventional morals accepted at the time the Constitution was adopted or amended. *See* Woodson v. North Carolina, 428 U.S. 280, 308 (1976) (Rehnquist, J., dissenting); McGautha v. California, 402 U.S. 183, 225-26 (1971) (Black, J., concurring).

213. For an example, see the language of Earl Warren in Trop v. Dulles, 356 U.S. 86, 101 (1957). Ronald Dworkin has argued in the eighth amendment context that the framers specifically chose the broader language of the eighth amendment intending that subsequent generations fill in those clauses with their own conceptions of what is a cruel and an unusual punishment. *See* R. DWORKIN, *supra* note 35.

currently elected representatives. A conventionalist has his work cut out for him in justifying judicial review in the name of conventional values; for to do this involves asserting that a court is a better surveyor of conventional values than is the legislature.[214] A realist has no similar embarrassment. The justification for judicial review is simply that people really have rights, and no consensus of the majority, even when embodied in a statute, should be allowed to trample on them. A realist can concede the antidemocratic nature of judicial review because he can justify it with higher values. A conventionalist must scurry about for some even more democratic, conventional consensus to justify the overturning of the output of the democratic process.

To the earlier consequentialist considerations should be added the idea that conventionalist interpretation leads to some very bad consequences when applied to constitutional rights. As John Ely has argued,[215] it makes little sense to use the majority's (consensus) values in determining the minority's rights against that very majority. Most people may prefer: that there be capital punishment for murder, that free speech not be exercised in an obscene or even merely bothersome way, or that a woman's liberty not extend to the right to abort her own fetus. As Ely powerfully suggests, the very idea that people have constitutional rights to be free of cruel punishments, to free speech, or to privacy, is difficult to square with the idea that the content of these rights is subject to the consensus of a majority. It is precisely when the majority does *not* want someone to exercise such rights that those rights have any importance. To have a right against the majority, good only so long as the majority values its exercise, is to have no right at all.

True, a conventionalist may find some protection here with some fancy footwork. The conventionalist may attempt the task outlined by Dworkin, as did Justice Marshall in the death penalty cases,[216] and seek to divine the deeper principles that underlie conventional morality as a whole, using those to overturn a popular judgment of a particular sort (such as how some murderers deserve death). Alternatively, the conventionalist may invoke the consensus of the past, of the future, or of some mobile combination of them, to overturn the consensus of to-

---

214. *See* J. ELY, *supra* note 1, at 67 ("As between courts and legislatures, it is clear that the latter are better situated to reflect consensus.").

215. *Id.* at 68-69.

216. *See* Gregg v. Georgia, 428 U.S. 153, 232 (1976) (Marshall, J., dissenting). Marshall's approach to the death penalty analysis is helpfully analyzed in Radin, *The Jurisprudence of Death: Evolving Standards for the Cruel and Unusual Punishments Clause,* 126 U. PA. L. REV. 989, 1039-42 (1978).

day. But these are subterfuges for what really does (and should) happen. A court protects constitutional rights best when it develops its own theory about what those rights really are. Surely Justice Marshall believes that the death penalty is everywhere and always a cruel, inhumane, and excessive punishment for anything one person can do to another; surely Marshall is not motivated by the "better" sociological insights into conventional morality that his interpretive theory demands that he claims for himself over his brethren.

Marshall, like Hand, would do better in protecting the moral rights of the litigants before him if he saw himself as protecting something real, not merely some hidden facets of the moral conventions that others accept. He would, for example, need to face a question his death penalty opinions ignore: can one person do something to another so awful that he *deserves* to die at the hands of the state? Marshall's conventionalism about value prevents him from ever seeing this as a relevant question to ask here; he addresses the retributive theory of punishment only in its bastardized, utilitarian guise whereby one punishes in order to prevent private violence against the criminal by vengeful citizens.[217] Stripped of his conventionalist blinders Marshall would see the need to be "in session with himself" on this difficult moral question of just deserts. In Marshall's case, he probably would not reach a different result with avowedly realist interpretation, but he might. In any case, he would be asking the right questions about the constitutional right to be free of cruel punishment.

V. CONCLUSION

Very generally speaking, there are two conclusions I have hoped to establish in this paper. The first is a practical thesis about the right way to go about interpreting legal texts:[218] look to the ordinary meanings of words, using a realist theory of meaning and not either of the two conventionalist theories of meaning; treat statutory definitions as having no more dignity than ordinary definitions are given on a realist theory

---

217. See citations and discussion of Justice Marshall's convention-induced blindness in Moore, *supra* note 17, at 1067-68.

218. The practical thesis does not necessarily give a decision procedure to be followed; it may in fact be better if judges simply hunched, and this would be perfectly consistent with my practical thesis. The thesis rather is a recipe for the right-making characteristics of a correct interpretation. The recipe aims, in other words, at telling us what is the correct interpretation of a legal text, not what psychological steps judges should go through to reach it. One might also think that judges ought to follow the recipe as a decision procedure but this would be a distinct and additional thesis. For the distinction between recipes for discovery and recipes for justification, see N. MAC-CORMICK, *supra* note 12.

of meaning; adjust the ordinary or statutory meanings by case law developments, using a realist theory of precedent to do so; check both meanings and precedent against one's theory of the purpose(s) the text in question serves, using "purpose" here as "function" and not as "intent"; and check meaning, precedent, and purpose with a general safety-valve question of value.

The second thesis of this article is a more theoretical one: that our interpretive practices reveal us to be both metaphysical realists and (as a special case of that) natural lawyers. As we have seen, the way we use language in both ordinary speech and in statutes presupposes a realist metaphysics about the hidden nature of natural kinds. Even when there is a special statutory definition of some word or phrase it is hard to leave our realism to the side, as the "bird" and "malice" examples show. Similarly, it is because we are realists about minds, as well as about the physical world, that we cannot have a psychological conception of legislative intent; our realist presuppositions that there really are individual intentions prevent us from accepting any of the easy constructions a conventionalist can propose as to what a legislature's intention might be. Nonetheless, our legal practices are such that we do look for a purpose behind every rule. Our realism about minds may prevent any psychological interpretation of "purpose," but our realism about morals makes possible a moral interpretation of "purpose" as just that function a statute serves in a just society.

With regard to precedent, we could practice precedent in a way that allows courts to lay down rules like a minilegislature (the classical theory), but we do not. We assume that there is a holding to be extracted from the particulars of a case. This too is possible only because we are sufficiently realist about morals that there is a right answer to the question of what facts of the precedent case are (morally and thus legally) relevant to its holding. Similarly, we could practice precedent in a way that gives absolute weight to the holding of cases but we do not. Instead, we expect our courts, in according weight to prior cases, to engage in the balancing of the real values that favor following precedents against the (equally real) values that may favor overruling them.

Finally, we could interpret legal texts without asking the safety-valve question of justice and fairness. But we do not. Despite occasional protest to the contrary, our courts do explicitly check the other ingredients of interpretation with this last, most explicit value judgment. This is because most of us, like Justice Stewart, think we "know it when we see it" when it comes to rank injustice or unfairness. Our confidence betrays our realist conviction that the moral universe is no less obvious to us at times than is the physical universe.

Such realism about morals, minds, and language results in a natural law theory of interpretation. Such a theory does not take a position on the classical natural lawyer's slogan, "An unjust law is no law at all." Rather, a natural law theory of interpretation speaks only to the question of interpretation and not to the question of how the text to be interpreted is itself to be pedigreed as authoritative. Yet even with this narrower focus a natural law theory of interpretation reminds us of something that is important: in applying the law to the facts of any case whatsoever a judge must engage in that moral reasoning that makes legal reasoning possible.

Part III
Interpretation and Application of Legal Rules, Vagueness and Defeasibility

[6]
Justification and Application of Norms*

ROBERT ALEXY

Abstract. According to the author there is no doubt that one has to distinguish between the justification and the application of norms. Problems are seen only to arise if one asks what exactly the distinction is and which consequences have to be drawn from it. Recently, Klaus Günther, in particular, has searched for this distinction and connected it with far-reaching conclusions concerning the theory of norms, arguments, and morals. His theses are the object of the author's considerations.

I.

According to Günther, there is a fundamental difference between the justification and the application of a norm (Günther 1988, 25). The justification of a norm would be concerned with its validity, and only its validity, the application with its appropriateness, and with that alone. The appropriateness of a norm could only be determined with reference to a certain situation of application. In order to find out if a norm would be appropriate in a certain situation,[1] it would be necessary to evaluate it with reference to all the situation's features and all norms which might alternatively be applied (Günther 1988, 94, 257, 271, 298). The appropriateness of a norm accordingly consists of two components: of its relation (1) to a certain situation and (2) to all other norms which might be applied in it. Günther tries to get hold of this by employing the concept of coherence (Günther 1988, 96, 304f., 307). A discourse of application would be therefore a discourse in which an attempt would be made at considering all features of a situation with respect to all norms which might be applied

---

* Paper presented at a workshop on "Justification and Application of Rules" at the European University Institute (Florence, March 1992). The author's thanks are due to Mrs Susanne Gaschke for help with the translation into English.

[1] "Appropriateness" is supposed to mean one predicate of a "norm in a situation in relation to all other features" of the situation (Günther 1988, 75).

(Günther 1988, 257ff.). Its impartiality consists in not suppressing any feature nor any norm which might alternatively be applied. Günther calls this the "applicationary meaning of impartiality" (Günther 1988, 257).

For the discourse of justification on the other hand, a "universal-reciprocal" meaning of impartiality (ibid.) should be constitutive. While the applicative impartiality is supposed to have reference to the features of the situation and to the system of norms, the universal-reciprocal impartiality is defined by its reference to persons and procedures. A norm should be neutral in this sense if all could agree with it in a discourse determined by freedom and equality (Günther 1988, 56). If this were the case, the norm should be considered universalizable and therefore justified and should consequently be valid.

A decisive step in Günther's argument is that in his opinion the discourses of justification necessarily lack the dimension of application. In discourses of justification, an evaluation of norms would be carried out which would be basically independent of any situation (Günther 1988, 257). This could not be different for two reasons. For one thing, the knowledge of the participants in the discourse was limited. It was not possible to know all features of all situations of application. On the other hand, both the knowledge about the situations of application and the interests to which the norms were referring could change (Günther 1988, 52). The result of any discourse of justification would therefore be relative in a double sense: with respect to the actual knowledge and with respect to the actual interests of all participants in the discourse.[2] Günther concludes that in discourses of justification only *prima facie* norms could be substantiated (Günther 1988, 94). With reference to Searle (1978, 88f.) he defines *prima facie* norms as "norms that are valid other things being equal" (Günther 1988, 259). Each result of a discourse of justification would therefore be equipped with a *ceteris paribus* clause (Günther 1988, 266). Günther explains this with a remark we shall come back to: "In discourses of justification its function is to exclude artificially the consideration of different situations of application" (ibid.).

The fact that discourses of application and of justification have to be strictly distinguished is but one aspect of the matter, according to Günther. Their interplay he considers quite as important. The character of the interplay becomes obvious in front of what Günther calls the "ideal of a perfect norm" (Günther 1989, 167). A norm would be perfect if it was the result of a discourse ideal in all respects.[3] Günther presents three features of such an

---

[2] Habermas has recently sharpened this reservation and made it more precise: "This *specific* reservation with which we consider well-substantiated norms of action only to be *prima facie* valid in a sense needing to be complemented, can also be explained by the limitedness of our actual knowledge, but not by its fallibility. The more far-reaching reservation of incompleteness can be explained . . . by the existential provinciality in view of the historic changes of the things themselves . . . (and) finally by the fact that the social world . . . is ontologically constructed in a different way" (Habermas 1991, 141f.).

[3] For the concept of the discourse ideal in all respects and the problems connected with this concept, see Alexy 1988, 48f.

ideal discourse: (1) unlimited free and equal participation, (2) unlimited time, and (3) unlimited knowledge. As the participants in a discourse ideal in all respects have unlimited knowledge,[4] they know all situations of application with all their features. If they also have unlimited time, they can try to substantiate norms which already consider all possible situations of application with all their features and have been set in relation to all other norms. Whether they will find exactly one solution to any case may remain open here (cf. Alexy 1988, 49ff.). Günther is right in any case when he says that under such ideal conditions a special discourse of application would be unnecessary (Günther 1988, 49f.).

Günther's idea is to compensate the fact that such an ideal discourse cannot be realized at least to some extent by the interplay of discourses of application and justification. Though it wouldn't be possible to consider all situations of application with all their features in discourses of justification, one could at first restrict the discourses of justification to the more modest task of justifying *prima facie* norms and then in the discourses of application at least consider all features of the actual case to be decided.

II.

Before examining Günther's argument by means of an example, we shall have to make some general statements. One of Günther's central arguments first for the separation and then for the connection of discourses of justification and of application is the limitedness of our knowledge, that is our inability to foresee all of a norm's possible situations of application with all their features. This fact, which is constitutive for all real discourses, leads indeed to a *prima facie* or *ceteris paribus* reservation by which a fallibilistic assessment of all results of the discourse is expressed. It is remarkable, however, that Günther only in part gives up the idea of a discourse of justification which is ideal in all respects. Only in the dimensions of empirical knowledge and time does it become a real discourse. In the dimension of participation, the discourse of justification remains ideal. Also, no compensation, like trying at least in individual cases to exhaust all features, is offered. It is certain, however, that unlimited participation, too, can only be realized approximately. From this it follows that all results of real discourses must not only be placed under reservations of knowledge and time, but also under a reservation of participation.[5] This can only be denied

---

[4] The unlimited knowledge mentioned here is just an empirical knowledge about outer and inner facts. If it was normative knowledge, too, it would directly include the correct solution to any case, and a practical discourse would become superfluous.

[5] Habermas demands that the principle of universalizability as a rule for argumentation must not demand "anything impossible." It has to "retain an operational meaning" (Habermas 1991, 139). As long as one continues to demand that the participants in a discourse are real persons (and one has to keep demanding this), the principle of universalizability as a rule of argumentation asks for something factually impossible, if it is not equipped with a reservation of participation.

by someone who considers the participants of a discourse irrelevant to its result. Proposing this thesis however would mean leaving the realm of discourse theory.

Günther's separation of discourses of justification and discourses of application is not falsified by a reservation of participation. It gives reason to suppose, though, that not the distinction between justification and application could be the decisive problem for discourse theory, but rather the distinction between ideal and real discourses.

It is noteworthy that Günther names a totally different argument besides the discourse-theoretical one outlined above for the separation of justification and application: "I want to defend the thesis that by the impartial justification of a norm's validity we *mean* something different from its impartial application in an individual case" (Günther 1989, 168). An opponent of discourse theory could also agree with this argument, for example someone who considers the application of norms a mere act of prudence, hermeneutic insight or skilled intuition. The decisive moral-theoretical problem is not yet formulated by stating that the impartial justification of a norm is something different from its impartial application. This concerns the question whether the discourse-theoretical interpretation of the impartiality of an application of norms is the best interpretation of this concept. Thus, the decisive question is defined: Does the splitting into discourses of justification and of application proposed by Günther lead to the best defence of a discourse-theoretical and therefore universalistic interpretation of impartiality in the application of norms? This can only be the case if Günther's theses concerning the distinction between discourses of justification and of application are correct.

III.

The question whether Günther's distinction is correct shall be discussed by considering the school case also used by Günther (1988, 261, 288ff.), in which *a* has promised Smith to attend his party, but hears that his friend Jones has been seriously taken ill and needs his help, before he can fulfill his promise. Help can only be given at the time when the party takes place. In this situation, which shall be called "S," two norms are applicable. They can be roughly formulated as:

N_1: Promises must be kept.
N_2: Friends in need must be helped.

In discussing the problem of justification and application it is useful to bring these norms into the following conditional form:

N_1: Someone who has promised to do something has an obligation to do it.
N_2: Someone who hears that a friend is in need and needs help, has an obligation to help this friend.

Justification and Application of Norms

If one applies these norms to S, one gets two singular or individual norms,[6] which do not as such contradict each other, but of which only one can be fulfilled in the situation S. The application of N_1 and N_2 to S has the following structure:

(I)   (1) Someone who has promised to do something has an obligation to do it. (N_1)
    (2) *a* has promised to attend Smith's party.
    (3) *a* has an obligation to go to Smith's party.

(II) (1) Someone who hears that a friend is in need and needs help, has an obligation to help this friend. (N_2)
    (2) *a* has heard that his friend Jones has been seriously taken ill and is, for that reason, in need and needs help.
    (3) *a* has an obligation to help Jones.

One has to stress that (II) has a more complicated structure than (I). Premise (2) includes the premise that someone who is seriously taken ill is in need. In a comprehensive presentation of norm application this thesis would have to be named as an independent premise (cf. Alexy 1989, 225ff.). As we are only concerned with the problem of collision and not with the problem of subsumption at this point, we shall omit this here.

For further considerations it is useful to bring into view the logical structure of the application of N_1 and N_2 to S at least in its most fundamental aspects. That of (I) can be presented in the following way (cf. Alexy 1989, 68, 222):

(I)   (1) $(x)(T_1 x \rightarrow OR_1 x)$ (N_1)
    (2) $T_1 a$
    (3) $OR_1 a$.

(1) represents the structure of N_1 as a universal norm. "T_1" represents "has promised to do h," "R_1" represents "does h." "O" is the deontic operator "it is obligatory that."[7] (2) is an empirical sentence which expresses that with reference to *a* in the situation S the feature T_1 is given. (3) is the individual norm logically following from (1) and (2), which says it is obligatory that *a* keeps his promise, which is to imply that he has an obligation to do this.

The logical structure of the application of N_2 can be presented, much simplified, in a similar way:

(II) (1) $(x)(T_2 x \rightarrow OR_2 x)$ (N_2)
    (2) $T_2 a$
    (3) $OR_2 a$.

---

[6] For the concept of the individual norm see Alexy 1985, 73.
[7] Of course the logical structure of (1) and therefore of (I) could be presented in a far more differentiated way. For a complete analysis one would also have to include variables for the receiver of the promise and for its subject, which is only possible if one uses relational predicates. For the considerations made here, however, the representation suffices.

(II) is an even more radical simplification than (I). Not only does (2) include a word usage or semantic rule (cf. Alexy 1989, 226, 234) which would have to be mentioned as an independent premise (see above), (1) also sums up various features in one. Still in this case a simplified representation suffices for the argument to be presented here.

The considerations so far lead to two simple insights. The first is that the application of norms, too, can be considered a justification of norms. In its logical form it only differs from what is generally called "justification of norms" insofar, as its object of justification is not a universal but an individual norm. This, however, has far-reaching consequences. Far more important is the second insight. It consists in the fact that with the school case considered here, problems do not arise within the application of N_1 and N_2 to S, but just because of the relationship between both applications, which, as seen for themselves, are unproblematical. Only because firstly N_1 and N_2 are valid and because secondly the situation S shows the features T_1 and T_2, do two individual norms come into existence which cannot both be fulfilled. This causes what Günther calls the "problem of collision" (Günther 1988, 267). The question is what follows from the problem of collision[8] for the distinction between discourses of justification and of application.

If one takes a look at the matter from the point of view of the result, three model solutions are possible. In the first one the collision remains unsolved. In spite of the fact that a cannot fulfil both obligations, he is subjected to both. He can do what he may, still he always violates a norm and therefore does wrong. This model can (at least with respect to cases in which someone gets into a situation like a due to no fault of his own) be called the "tragic model." I do not want to decide here whether there are cases in which the tragic model recommends itself. Anyway the present case is not of this kind. The second model is the extreme opposite of the tragic one. It is chosen if one supposes that in cases of collision there is no obligation whatever. Günther does not even consider this model and is right in not doing so. It would lead to a going free of his obligation to help his friend because he had by mere chance promised Smith to attend his party. Only the third model of solution can therefore be correct here, in which one or the other obligation remains valid. I hope to be able to say without further explanation that in the present case it is the obligation to help the friend in his difficulties.

Someone who chooses the third and the only right model of solution, can construct the relationship between the relevant norms (in this case between N_1 and N_2) and the result (in this case the obligation to help the friend (OR_2a)) in two ways. The first construction leaves the level of norms untouched by the decision in favour of OR_2a. Before and after the decision

---

[8] I do not intend to make the distinction of rules and principles a topic here. If I did so, one would have to distinguish conflicts of rules and collisions of principles (cf. Alexy 1985, 77ff.). The term "collision" is therefore used in a wider sense here, and refers to conflicts of rules as well as to collisions of principles.

it consists of N_1 and N_2 as *prima facie* norms. The decision just adds the individual norm OR_2a.

He who chooses this construction can easily separate discourses of justification and of application. The object of discourses of justification are norms of simple character like N_1 and N_2, which do not refer to each other and are in this sense isolated *prima facie* norms. Discourses of application take such norms as a starting point, but they exclusively have individual norms like OR_2a (which express definite decisions in concrete cases) as their object. Universal norms cannot be the object of a discourse of application simply because in this construction, there are no universal norms apart from N_1 and N_2 which have to be applied. This construction is advantageous to someone who wants to defend a strict separation of discourses of justification and of application, but it has great disadvantages with respect to practical rationality. A universalistic practice of decision-making is not possible with this construction. The relations between the level of the *prima facie* norms and the level of definite decisions have an *ad hoc* character. The fundamental moral demand of equal treatment runs empty because in the sparsely furnished normative universe of this construction there is nothing that could grant equal treatment. There are only definite individual norms which are completely cut out for individual situations, and simple *prima facie* norms like N_1 and N_2 which have to be evaluated anew in any new situation. Normative coherence cannot be reached in such a system.

There are some statements by Günther which suggest that he wants to choose this construction, if one looks at them isolatedly. For example he says that in discourses of application the statement "that Jones was in a helpless situation and therefore the obligation to help had to be fulfilled, gained the status of an *argument*." This argument aimed "no longer at the validity of the colliding norms but only at their *appropriateness* under consideration of all the situation's circumstances" (Günther 1989, 172). The fact that N_2 is appropriate under this condition does not mean anything other than what N_2 demands is definitely valid. Therefore one could read Günther as if he thought that there was nothing but *prima facie* norms like N_1 and N_2, definite individual norms like OR_1a and OR_2a, and a judgement of appropriateness, which prefers one of the two *prima facie* norms and consequently one of the two definite norms, in this case N_2 and OR_2a. That would equal the first construction.

If one takes a comprehensive look at all of Günther's statements, one arrives at a different impression. For example, he talks about "new interpretations of situations" leading to "change, modification, revision" of the "semantic content," "with the consequence that a norm which has been modified in such a way again has to be examined as to whether it can be accepted with reasons by all with respect to the contexts now known" (Günther 1988, 95). That does not mean anything but that the norm is changed for the solution of a case and that the changed norm can and must be justified. Günther becomes most explicit when talking about word usage or semantic rules. In the case of N_2 there are many situations in which it is not clear whether N_2 can be applied to them. The word usage rule (presupposed above) which says that someone who is seriously taken ill is in need causes relatively few problems. But how about a minor illness, say an inflammation of the tonsils? N_2's second precondition causes far more problems of interpretation. Does a friend, who is taken seriously ill, need help, if a nurse takes the necessary care of him, who is, however, extremely unfriendly, and makes him want a friend's consolation? The features of such situations can be linked in positive and negative ways to the concepts contained in N_2. After this has been done, the case can be solved by a subsumption (Alexy 1989, 224ff.).

The most simple positive case of application corresponds with the following scheme (Alexy 1989, 234):

(II') (1) $(x)(T_2 x \rightarrow OR_2 x)$ (N_2)
(2) $(x)(Mx \rightarrow T_2 x)$
(3) Ma
(4) $OR_2 a$.

Günther stresses correctly that word usage rules like (2) "need justification like a norm" (Günther 1988, 291) because a new norm (1'): $(x)(Mx \rightarrow OR_2 x)$ follows from (1) and (2). Correct is also his statement that "the task of justifying the appropriateness of a determination of meaning in relation to other variants of meaning does not differ from the task of justifying the appropriateness of a norm in relation to other applicable norms" (Günther 1988, 293). In the case of indeterminacy as well as in the case of collision the decision about appropriateness in a given situation on the level of norms includes modifications that both can be and must be justified.

To this corresponds the second construction. It is characterized by the fact that it represents the decisions made in concrete situations on the level of norms. In our case, that is, S, this can happen by adding an exception clause to N_1 (the norm which demands the keeping of promises), which refers to the norm N_2 colliding with it in S. N_1 gets the following form:

N_1^k: Someone who has promised to do something has an obligation to do it except if he hears that a friend is in need and needs help.[9]

N_1^k has the following structure:

N_1^k: $(x)(T_1 x \wedge \neg T_2 x \rightarrow OR_1 x)$.[10]

N_2 may remain as it is. Now N_1^k and N_2 can be applied to S without colliding.

---

[9] For a similar formulation see Günther 1989, 178.
[10] For this structure as the basic structure of a norm's limited applicability see Alexy 1989, 236.

IV.

If one accepts the second construction, the question arises whether the problem of application is not at heart a problem of justification. Although the situation S with the features T_1 and T_2 is the motivation to modify N_1, the important thing seems to be whether the modified norm is justified, that is, whether N_1^k can be accepted in a discourse of justification and is therefore valid. Günther answers this question in the negative. In his answer one can distinguish two reasons.

A first argument is that one must not isolatedly refer to a newly constructed norm. A discourse of justification would not be necessary as long as "the interpretation moves along the lines and within the boundaries of the meaning of the norms and principles commonly accepted as valid." What Günther means becomes clear when he adds: "Within those boundaries we strive for an *ideal coherent system* among the colliding norms. All newly constructed norms which serve the purpose of producing support relations within this ideal system still belong to the set of norms commonly accepted as valid" (Günther 1989, 181). With a view to the small universe of the case S, one can sum this up into the following thesis: N_1^k does not have to be substantiated in a discourse of justification if N_1^k serves for the production of an ideal coherent system among N_1 and N_2. I think this thesis is wrong. N_1^k is first of all a norm, and what is more, a norm that shows an additional normative content in relation to N_1 and N_2 (cf. Dwars 1992, 75f.). N_1^k contains consequences for the fulfillment of interests of the people concerned by it, which are not yet included in N_1 and N_2. Discourse theory's principle of universalizability therefore demands that N_1^k is substantiated in a discourse of justification.

Günther's thesis would only be right if one could say that N_1^k was already contained in N_1 and N_2 and therefore already belonged to "the set of norms commonly accepted as valid" (Günther 1989, 181). If one looks at N_1 and N_2 isolatedly as *prima facie* norms, N_1^k is certainly not contained in N_1 and N_2. This is simply because N_1^k does not follow from N_1 and N_2. Only with addition of a further premise could N_1^k therefore belong to the norms already accepted as valid. Günther offers such a further premise with the idea of an ideal coherent system. The idea of coherence is either a magician's hat one can draw anything out of—one likes to talk about "Gesamtschau" —or it refers to the procedure of justification in a system.[11] Günther's attempts at operationalizing the concept of coherence (Günther 1988, 299ff.) hint at his aiming at the second conception. But if producing coherence is a procedure of justification, it is not limited to discourses of application but can also be used in discourses of justification. Someone who wants to deny this has to claim that coherence is irrelevant for the justification of norms. That is why the idea of coherence does not allow for N_1^k to be taken out of the realm

[11] For the latter see Alexy and Peczenik 1990, 130ff.

of the discourse of justification as not needing to be substantiated. Günther seems to see this when he says that in all cases where a norm's like $N_1^{k'}$'s claim to validity is being debated one can find out "in a discourse of justification . . . whether the norm represents a general interest and should belong to the set of norms accepted as valid" (Günther 1989, 181). Thus he concedes that any norm like N_1^k *can* be substantiated in a discourse of justification, because it is impossible to exclude right from the beginning that a norm might be questioned. He seems to think, however, that not every norm like N_1^k *needs* to be substantiated. According to him this should not be the case if a norm like N_1^k can be shown to be an element of a coherent system, a thing that had to be done in discourses of application (Günther 1989, 188). It is not possible to agree with this.

Günther's argument, as described and criticised so far, leads to a strange shift of the concepts of discourses of application and of justification. In a discourse of application, the individual case recedes into the background. The coherence of all elements in the system of norms becomes decisive with respect to the cases already decided or still to be decided. The discourse of application in this manner turns into a discourse of coherence. This goes hand in hand with a thinning of the discourse of justification, if one takes some of Günther's statements seriously. At one point, for example, he says that "we do not accept valid norms . . . with respect to external collisions" (Günther 1989, 180). By external collisions Günther means the collision of two valid *prima facie* norms (Günther 1989, 170) like, e.g., that of N_1 and N_2. The subject matter of a discourse of justification is accepting norms as valid. If collisions of norms are no longer to be topics in discourses of justification, apart from the exclusion of norms never to be applied (like norms allowing the unlimited maximisation of individual utility (cf. Günther 1989, 169) or norms which, for example the principle of race in National Socialism, damage the interests of participants in the discourse in any situation) only the production of general arguments for discourses of application and of rules of thumb for standard cases would remain. With the rise of the discourse of application to a discourse of coherence, the discourse of justification would deteriorate to a mere discourse of *topoi*.

V.

One therefore has to question the acceptability of Günther's second argument for the independent character of the discourse of application. It says that discourses of application are concerned with the correct decision in a certain situation, discourses of justification, on the other hand, with a norm's validity. This perception is right. The question is only whether it really causes the far-reaching consequences Günther proposes.

First doubts are caused by the fact that situations of application are by no means only employed in an "illustrative" way in discourses of justification, as Günther occasionally seems to think (Günther 1989, 167). On the contrary, the reference to situations of application is also necessary in discourses of justification. Without reference to situations of application it is impossible for the participants in the discourse to find out which consequences a norm is likely to have for the interests of those who will be concerned by it. Günther notices the problem (Günther 1988, 25). He thinks, however, it can be solved with reference to the fact, that in discourses of justification referring to situations happens in a different way from in discourses of application.

In one point his thesis is doubtlessly correct. Moral[12] discourses of application have a topic directly referring to a situation which discourses of justification lack. For discourses of application the question what is the correct solution *in a certain situation* (Günther 1988, 34) is constitutive, for discourses of justification, the question which *universal norm* is right. But from the fact that those two questions have to be distinguished it does not follow that there exist two essentially different kinds of discourse. It is also possible that those two questions only set off two different operations within one form of discourse and therefore only lead to two variations of the same form of discourse.

The latter would be the case, if discourses of application and of justification started with different questions, but when answering them, found the same questions and had to answer them in the same form of argument and according to the same rules. With Günther this is exactly not the case. In discourses of justification, situations of application are supposed to have only the character of "hypothetical" or "exemplary situations" (Günther 1988, 51). Such exemplary situations should differ fundamentally from "genuine situations of application" (ibid.): "The microcosm of each individual situation is as infinite as the macrocosm of all situations to which a norm can be applied" (Günther 1988, 58). Therefore, only in discourses of application could one try to "consider all features of a situation" (Günther 1988, 95), but this claim would not be valid in discourses of justification.

Günther is right if he points out that any concrete situation shows a potentially infinite number of features. This is at least true if "feature" also means the gradation and the combination of features. His concept of a hypothetical or exemplary situation, however, demands an interpretation. In some places he seems to say that the situations of application referred to in discourses of justification have to be artificially simplified standard cases.

---

[12] In legal discourses of application this is different to a certain degree because of the institutional character of the norms to be applied. Even there, however, we are regularly faced with problems of collision (cf. Alexy 1985, 78ff.) and the question of modification arises as a problem of the development of law (cf. BVerfGE 35, 263 (278ff.); 37, 67 (81); 38, 386 (396f.); 49, 304 (318ff.); 65, 182 (190ff.); 71, 354 (362f.); 82, 6 (11ff.)). Apart from that, the justification of word usage rules created in situations of application is one of the main tasks of legal argumentation.

This can be called "standard case interpretation." We have already mentioned Günther's thesis that in discourses of justification the *ceteris paribus* clauses serve the purpose of "artificially excluding the consideration of different situations of application" (Günther 1988, 266). Elsewhere, he talks about "selective descriptions of situations" as well as that it would be sufficient to "reduce" (Günther 1989, 171) the descriptions of situations to unchanging circumstances. This interpretation of the concept of the hypothetical situation leads to what I called "discourse of *topoi*" above. If the relevant case material in discourses of justification is reduced to simple standard cases, these discourses can only produce points for weighing and rules of thumb. This would have the fatal consequence that the norms modified or newly created for the decision of a case in a discourse of application could no longer be subject matter of a discourse of justification and therefore could not be substantiated. The standard case interpretation must therefore be excluded.

The second interpretation can be called "approximation interpretation" according to which hypothetical situations of application in discourses of justification may not only but should be as manifold as possible. There is no discourse rule which forbids making up complex situations and asking whether in reference to them, too, the proposed norm is acceptable to all. The admissibility of fantasy is but one aspect of the matter. The other is the admissibility of experience. The participants in the discourse own a biography and can lean on historical experience. In this way, there is a rich "situation material" at hand. A limitation is only caused by the factual possibilities, that is, the limits of empirical knowledge, of historical experience, and of time. In Günther we find this approximation interpretation when he answers the question "according to which criterion we are supposed to distinguish an exemplary situation used in justification from a genuine situation of application" by saying that:

There must not be such a criterion as it would be irreconcilable with the meaning of the principle of universalizability . . . any limitation would have the consequence of putting certain possibilities of application under taboo and withholding them from an examination of their relevance to the interests of every individual . . . The limitation . . . lies on the subjective side. It depends on the historical status of our experience and our knowledge. (Günther 1988, 51)

If one follows this interpretation, the difference between discourses of application and of justification is reduced to two points. The first is that in both discourses, a different question is asked at the beginning and a different answer is given at the end. Discourses of justification are concerned with universal norms, discourses of application with individual ones. The second and decisive difference is that in discourses of justification one refers to many constructed or experienced situations, while in the discourse of application one is concerned with one concrete situation.

For two reasons the concrete situation of application has a genuine discourse-theoretical significance. The first is that because of its richness in features it is a touchstone of a special kind. The demand to consider all its features is an elemental postulate of rationality. For a long time it has found its expression in the formula "under consideration of all circumstances in the individual case." Each developed legal system shows how the consideration of all circumstances leads to a permanent process of making more precise, changing, rejecting and newly creating. Insofar the concrete situation of application is an irreplaceable instance of examination. But that is all. The norm which in a concrete case has been made more precise, changed or newly created must be justifiable in a discourse of justification and the rejected norm must be allowed to be proved non-justifiable.

The second reason for a genuine discourse-theoretical significance of the concrete situation of application is that by means of application the discourse comes into contact with the social world and thus with history. History keeps producing unpredictable and surprising situations and with them a rich material of fallibilistic instances, and in history the interests, preferences, and normative convictions of the participants in the discourse change. Insofar one has to agree with Habermas if he talks about "intrinsic historicity" (Habermas 1991, 142) with a view to the problem of application. All this, however, does not change the fact that one cannot exclusively react with situative, individual norms to historical experiences and changes. Rather, the existing system of norms has to be made more precise or modified because of a new historical experience, if one cannot simply react to new situations by applying norms already accepted. Those norms made more precise, changed or newly created because of a new situation can be and have to be substantiated in a discourse of justification, no matter if it is a new, but everyday case or a situation totally unknown so far. The same is valid for rejected norms. The "intrinsic historicity" is doubtlessly of great importance from the aspect of the relationship between discourse and reality. To upgrade the discourse of application so that it becomes an equal counterpart to the discourse of justification would however be a wrong conceptualization of this relationship. The fact that any discourse of application necessarily includes a discourse of justification on which its result depends, forbids contrasting discourses of application and of justification as two independent forms of discourse.

Christian Albrechts University
Faculty of Law
Olshausenstraße 40
D-2300 Kiel 1
Germany

References

Alexy, Robert. 1985. *Theorie der Grundrechte*. Baden-Baden: Nomos. (Reprint: Frankfurt: Suhrkamp, 1986.)

———. 1988. Problems of Discourse Theory. *Crítica* 20: 43–65.

———. 1989. *A Theory of Legal Argumentation*. Trans. Ruth Adler, and Neil MacCormick. Oxford: Clarendon. (1st ed. in German 1978.)

Alexy, Robert, and Aleksander Peczenik. 1990. The Concept of Coherence and Its Significance for Discursive Rationality. *Ratio Juris* 3: 130–47.

Dwars, Ingrid. 1992. Application Discourse and the Special Case-Thesis. *Ratio Juris* 5: 67–78.

Günther, Klaus. 1988. *Der Sinn für Angemessenheit*. Frankfurt: Suhrkamp.

———. 1989. Ein normativer Begriff der Kohärenz für eine Theorie der juristischen Argumentation. *Rechtstheorie* 20: 163–90.

Habermas, Jürgen. 1991. Erläuterungen zur Diskursethik. In Jürgen Habermas, *Erläuterungen zur Diskursethik*, 119–226. Frankfurt: Suhrkamp.

Searle, John. 1978. Prima Facie Obligations. In *Practical Reasoning*. Ed. Joseph Raz, 81–90. Oxford: Oxford University Press.

[7]
Critical Remarks on Robert Alexy's "Special-Case Thesis"*

KLAUS GÜNTHER

Abstract. In this paper the author criticizes the way Robert Alexy reconstructs the relationship between legal and practical reasoning. The core of Alexy's argumentation (Alexy 1978) is considered the claim that legal argumentation is a "special case" of general practical discourse. In order to question this claim, the author analyzes three different types of argument: (1) that legal reasoning is needed by general practical discourse itself, (2) that there are similarities between legal argumentation and general practical discourse, (3) that there is a correspondence between certain types of argument in general practical discourse and in legal argumentation.**

Contemporary theories on legal argumentation can be classified according to their interpretation of "what a legal reason is." There are two mainstreams both of which tend towards extreme positions. Their difference consists in the point of view from which they interpret the meaning of legal reasons. The first takes the point of view of an observer who looks on the legal system from an external position. The question "what a legal reason is" is answered by its function within the legal system as an action-system (legal realists, Luhmann, Teubner, CLS). The second position argues from a point of view which is located within the legal system. It is the point of view of a participant in legal argumentation. The question "what a legal reason is" is answered by the role legal reasons play within argumentation (hermeneutics, semantic theories, discourse theory).

As I indicated above, both positions tend toward extremes. This happens if they conceive of themselves as a totalizing view on legal argumentation. The type of argument the adherents of these extremes use can be characterized as "nothing else, but . . ."-arguments. They use different strategies: that the features which are explained by the opposite position are mere self-deceptions or contingent side-effects. One could label these extreme positions as "realism" and "idealism." The extreme position of "realism"

---
* Paper presented at a workshop on "Justification and Application of Rules" at the European University Institute (Florence, March 1992).
** Abstract by Gianfrancesco Zanetti.

argues that there is no internal perspective on legal argumentation. The extreme position of "idealism" argues just the other way round. The modest position is the methodological one, which says that both types of explanation do not exclude each other because they are made from different points of view. My critique of Alexy can be characterized roughly as follows: His position tends too much in the direction of the second extreme. This means that I put myself in a position where everybody wants to be because you can have the best of both worlds: right in the middle.

It is Alexy's merit to have introduced discourse theory into the realm of legal reasoning (Alexy 1978, 1989). For legal theory, this introduction has made it possible to demonstrate in detail what legal reasoning has to do with practical reason—which until then was more a claim than a substantiated theory. For discourse theory, this introduction showed a way to the legal sphere which was until then subsumed more or less under the concept of strategic action only. And the connection of discourse-theory with law seems to be one of the possible theoretical lines which leads to an answer to the eternal question of how practical discourse can be institutionalized in society. The following critical remarks are not aimed at a new separation of law and legal reasoning from the idea of practical reason, but at a critique of the way Alexy reconstructs the relationship between both. I shall concentrate my remarks on the argument, which seems to be most important, i.e., the claim that legal argumentation is a "special case" of general practical discourse.

In the following, I simply presuppose that Alexy's reconstruction of general practical discourse is acceptable—a presupposition which could be criticized too. What I am interested in now is only the question whether the claim of legal argumentation as a special case of general practical discourse is acceptable. Alexy bases his claim on three different types of argument. The first is a functional argument, viz., that legal reasoning is necessary to overcome the specific weakness of general practical discourse and is therefore justified (1). The second refers to some similarities and correspondences between legal argumentation and general practical discourse (2). The last one is based on the content of arguments: Some arguments which are usual in practical discourse also appear in legal argumentation (3). I start with the first, the functional argument.

1. The Functional Aspect

The specific weakness of practical discourse, which has to be compensated by legal argumentation, is its indefiniteness with respect to a final, definite decision. This weakness is a result of the manner of operation of the rules of practical discourse. The rules of practical discourse do not work like a machine that produces definite, clear-cut results. They refer to participants with different normative systems, who apply the rules and principles of discourse under certain constraints. Although there are always some results which are discursively impossible or discursively necessary, most results are only discursively possible. This means that a practical discourse on the validity of a normative proposition could lead (and in most cases does lead) to more than one result, or even to contradictory results — without violating the rules of practical discourse. This produces a sphere of "insecurity" around general practical discourse. To this case of insecurity concerning the cognitive indeterminacy with respect to the definite correctness of normative propositions, a second case is added. General practical discourse cannot guarantee that its results will be realized. It suffers from a motivational deficiency in respect of factually observing a valid norm. Both cases of insecurity justify the introduction of law.

The way in which the law and especially legal argumentation attempts to compensate this weakness consists of several steps which restrict the space of the "discursively possible" (*das diskursiv Mögliche*) successively. By legislation, norms are produced which in turn suffer from indeterminacy. So, in the next step, we need legal procedures in which legal argumentation takes place and which lead to singular normative propositions or decisions of particular cases.

Insofar as law and legal argumentation serve to remove the uncertainty of general practical discourse, they are justified by practical discourse. This relation is not only functional. As Alexy indicates in the postscript to the new edition of his "Theory of Legal Argumentation" there is also a normative relation which requires elements of discursive rationality in legislation and adjudication (Alexy 1991, 429, 433). Otherwise, one could assume that instead of legislation and adjudication, a Hobbesian "Leviathan" would be sufficient, one that decides what follows from the discursively possible. Is this relation between practical discourse and legal argumentation sufficient to justify the special-case thesis?

The indefiniteness of decision is, as Alexy indicates, an institutional problem. But Alexy puts too many different kinds of things into the concept of "decision" or "deciding." One thing is that the rules and principles of general practical discourse refer to an ideal which presupposes an indefinite and unlimited amount of time and knowledge, as well as complete transparency between all participants. Because we are able to fulfil these presuppositions only approximately here and now, we cannot definitely make up our minds about the "validity" of a normative proposition. This is the question of how ideal and real discourse are related. Another thing is the uncertainty which derives from the possibilities of different discursively possible results concerning the solution of a normative conflict. In cases of normative conflict, we need a decision about what is right or just here and now. The third problem is that the rules and principles of general practical discourse do not lead to a decision about what to do in a particular case. This is the problem of the application of general norms to concrete cases. Another problem is that even if general practical discourse led to definitive decisions, these decisions would only be morally binding and not factually.

It is obvious that all these different aspects of "indefiniteness" belong to different theoretical levels. Those deficiencies which have to do with uncertainty and with efficiency concerning rule-following are part of an institutional frame of reference. Consequently Alexy says that law is an "institutional restraint" on general practical discourse. This is the reason why law is always connected with some means of enforceability, and why every legal order consists of secondary rules that establish procedures of legislation and adjudication. Both properties together, enforceability and the establishment of institutions of law-making and law-applying, lead to definite decisions in concrete cases and to the realization of these decisions. Nevertheless, there is a difference between a decision in a concrete case, and a singular normative proposition, which could become the rational basis of a decision. Alexy often speaks about "rational legal decision" as a purpose of legal argumentation (e.g., Alexy 1991, 352, 433). But the disadvantage of general practical discourse, that it cannot guarantee a correct decision in a particular case, is not only a problem of institutions of decision-making, but also one of argumentation. If it is conceived as a problem of argumentation, its solution requires the introduction of a *different* theory of argumentation into the theory of general practical discourse, which demonstrates how singular normative propositions can be justified. If such a theory is possible, this different type of argumentation could then serve as a reconstruction of legal argumentation which is more appropriate than the special case-thesis.

(a) There are, however, good reasons to maintain the thesis that law can at least approximately solve all problems which follow from the deficiencies of general practical discourse. But the question is whether this changes the character of argumentation so fundamentally that it affects the special case thesis. The central feature of this kind of argumentation consists in its reference to law. Legal argumentation refers to law—whatever "law" means—not only institutionally, but also conceptually, i.e., by definition. The special case thesis would be correct, if "the law" consisted of norms which rank among moral norms and could therefore be justified by general practical discourse, but which are connected with institutions as compensations for cognitive and motivational deficiencies only. But this isn't true—neither for the validity claim of legal norms, nor for their procedure of justification, nor for the character of legal norms.

Concerning the validity-claim or the "claim to correctness," it is obvious that there is a fundamental difference between moral and legal norms. Moral norms claim to be valid for all those affected; their claim is universalist in the sense of it being accepted by everybody on the basis of rational deliberation. Legal norms do not claim to be valid for everyone, but only for the members of a concrete legal community. Since I shall argue about this point more extensively in a moment, I merely mention this difference here.

Concerning the procedures of justification, there is a further difference between moral and legal norms. As Alexy himself indicates, there are two different legal procedures, procedures of legislation and of adjudication, which are different from general practical discourse, because they consist of rules and mechanisms for ending a debate and for producing a decision. Again, Alexy's thesis would be true, if both legal and moral procedures had the same subject matter, but only differed in the property of possessing institutional constraints that lead to a final decision or not. Here, I think, is the most important difference between legal and moral norms.

One of the features which general practical discourse and legal argumentation have in common, according to Alexy, is the subject matter of discourse: Both are concerned with "practical questions" (Alexy 1991, 428), with norms that are permissions, prohibitions or obligations, and which raise a claim to correctness. Whether this property is enough to support the special case-thesis depends on a further specification of the term "practical questions." Alexy's characterization is true at least for moral norms, whose validity-claim should be accepted by everybody. Consequently, moral norms are accepted on the basis of a rational motivation, they are directed at the autonomous will of everybody, and they express an interest which is strictly universalizable. Legal norms are different types of norms. They are based on the acceptance of a legal community, they can be enforced by state authority against the individual will, and they do not require rational motivation. They do not express an interest which is strictly universalizable—even when human rights form a part of a constitution, their formulation is the result of an interpretation by a concrete legal community. Consequently, law consists of many norms which could not be the hypothetical result of a general practical discourse, but which express the specific values of a concrete legal community. Many legal norms do not permit or prohibit an action or sanction an omission, but they set a political goal which should be reached by legal and administrative institutions. Other legal norms are only the result of a compromise, where both sides know that their agreement is based on a "deal" and not on a mutual recognition of interests.

All these norms can be considered as "legal norms," without them being a "practical question" for a general practical discourse. For this reason, the feature of "legal validity" can be ascribed to a lot of different kinds of norms which are not the subject matter of general practical discourse—by definition. If this is true, then it becomes difficult to maintain the special case-thesis. The only rational imperative, which can be derived from an application of the theory of general practical discourse to this type of norms, is the requirement that their justification be a public and democratic procedure. But this requirement does not entail those rules and principles which are constitutive of the justification of moral norms. It would be a very abstract general theory of general discourse. Then, moral and legal discourse could both be "special cases" of this very general discourse.

Klaus Günther

(b) Following Alexy's reconstruction, it is obvious that the *decision of particular cases* is the focus of legal argumentation in general. Because legislation suffers from a problem of indefiniteness similar to general practical discourse, legal reasoning in adjudication is the next step on the way to a definite decision. "As historical experience and conceptual deliberation have shown, a legislative procedure can never lay down exactly one solution for every case from the beginning. This justifies the necessity of legal discourse."[1] The task of looking for a solution for every singular case makes legal reasoning necessary.

This task is, however, not a specific feature of legal reasoning alone. It is also true of moral reasoning. If the deficiency of cognitive indeterminacy concerning concrete cases is a problem of general practical discourse, then it arises in moral cases as well as in legal cases. And if the supplementation of general practical discourse by legal reasoning were the only possible way to overcome this deficiency, then we would have to switch into legal reasoning in every single moral case. This conclusion cannot be correct. That is why the problem of cognitive indeterminacy concerning concrete cases cannot be a reason for the necessity of legal reasoning as a special case of general practical discourse. Instead of going this way, we should ask if it makes sense to look for a procedure within general practical discourse itself, one that fulfills the task of finding a definite normative solution in concrete cases. This requires us to separate momentarily the problem of the application of norms to concrete cases from the debate about the special-case thesis.

There is a similar problem of application in general practical discourse. The rules and principles of general practical discourse, as it is conceived by Alexy, do not lead to a singular normative proposition about what ought to be done in a singular case. It only refers to "rules" (cf. Alexy 1978, 250ff.) or norms and their moral validity. Rules or norms cannot determine their own application to singular cases. This is one of the reasons for the cognitive indeterminacy of general practical discourse, and one of the cases in which contradictory norms could be accepted as a result that is discursively possible. The norm that promises should be kept, and the norm that everybody should help someone who is severely injured, are both norms which could be accepted in general practical discourse. But it is easy to imagine that they could lead to contradictory singular normative propositions in a particular case. For example, a singular normative proposition, that you should help the severely injured woman lying on the street, even if that means that you will break your promise to show up at the station at five o'clock, contradicts the norm that promises should be kept.

---

[1] "Auch durch ein Gesetzgebungsverfahren kann aber, wie sowohl historische Erfahrungen als auch begriffliche Überlegungen zeigen, niemals für jeden Fall von vornherein genau eine Lösung festgelegt werden. Das begründet die Notwendigkeit des juristischen Diskurses" (Alexy 1991, 430f.).

This problem can be solved, if one interprets the function of general practical discourse in a different way (cf. Günther 1988, 1992, 1993). Then, practical discourse does not have the function of leading to concrete results about what should be done in concrete cases—a function which can obviously never be fulfilled. Instead of this extended interpretation, I would like to suggest a more restricted one: In general practical discourse, we figure out which norms should be included in our moral deliberations on concrete cases. By "moral deliberation," I mean a rational social practice where normative reasons are used for the justification of singular normative propositions which prohibit, permit or command an action or sanction an omission in a concrete case. This practice of moral deliberation is based on the intersubjective relation of mutual recognition. Moral reasons, which are used for justification in concrete cases, shape the mutual relations between each of us as individuals and as members of a moral community. They represent the characteristic traits of our intersubjectivity, i.e., the general expectations according to which we want to treat each other and how we want to be treated. For example, we don't want to be treated as someone who could be betrayed for any reason. It is a "moral" deliberation because the reasons used for justification have to fulfil certain conditions, like those which are required by the rules and principles of general practical discourse. Among these principles, the principle of universalizability plays a prominent role because it precisely refers to these characteristic traits of our intersubjectivity. It requires us to look at the consequences of a general observance of a norm for the interests of each of us. By means of general practical discourse, then, the participants deliberate whether a norm should function as a reason for the justification of singular normative propositions. Those norms which are morally valid are constitutive of our moral practice as a whole. To this intepretation one could object that it would turn general practical discourse into a superfluous arrangement or something just for fun: Why should we think about reasons first, when the decision about what we really are obliged to do depends on the concrete case? But this objection does not sufficiently emphasize two aspects.

First, it does not pay enough attention to the function of the principle of universalizability in practical discourse. This principle only refers to cases which are alike. Its usage only makes sense if it leads to the question: What would be the consequences of a general following of the norm under *unchanging* circumstances? Only then can we figure out which interests are violated or advanced by the contested norm. This would be impossible, if the principle of universalizability required us to look at the consequences of the general following of the norm in situations which are *different*. Therefore, the principle of universalizability enables us to recognize which norm should be a characteristic trait of our moral practice. We can do this by asking what would happen if the situation in which all addressees follow a contested norm, became *typical* or *exemplary* for our moral practice. *Second*, its comprehension of "legal validity" is too shallow. Those norms which are morally valid are reasons which everybody is obliged to take into account in concrete cases. But the universal validity of a moral reason does not mean that every norm or rule justified in general practical discourse should be applied to concrete cases as a singular normative proposition about what ought to be done here and now. Otherwise, we could never accept norms like "you should keep promises" or "you ought to help your neighbour if he or she is in an emergency," as morally valid. We can imagine intuitively a lot of different cases where a singular normative proposition that expresses one of these norms conflicts with another norm. If a morally valid norm only refers to the characteristic traits of our moral practice, then it is possible to assume a multiplicity of different valid norms and *to presuppose* that they cohere in particular cases. No valid moral reason stands alone for itself; rather they cohere with other moral reasons. *Together* they form the characteristic traits of our moral practice which is continued case by case every day.

Consequently, with respect to singular cases, we need a principle which supplements the principle of universalizability in general practical discourse. If the principle of universalizability only says which norm is a morally valid reason with respect to any case, then we need a principle which says when a morally valid reason justifies a singular normative proposition in a singular case. For this reason, I have suggested introducing the concept of an "application discourse" (Günther 1988, 1993). The rules and principles of application discourses determine how the participants should operate with those morally valid reasons which they are obliged to take into account when they use them as a justification for singular normative propositions. The task of the rules and principles of application discourse is to ensure the impartiality of application. The meaning of impartial application can best be explained by two cases of the violation of this idea. The first one I shall call the case of "rigid application," the second one the case of "selective application." The first example comes from a possible (mis-)interpretation of the classical maxim "fiat iustitia, pereat mundus." One possible interpretation of this maxim is the well-known example, used by Benjamin Constant and by Kant, where an innocent man, who is persecuted by a brutal police force in a state without justice, could be protected by telling a lie about his hiding-place. Kant argues that the norm "Never tell a lie" should be taken into account here. It is possible to understand Kant's argument in a way that turns the morally valid norm directly into a singular normative proposition. Then, moral validity would mean that a morally valid norm has to be applied to every single case rigidly, i.e., without further consideration of the situation and of other relevant moral reasons, even if it is obvious that they will be violated. The other example is complementary to the first one: One can use morally valid norms for bad purposes. If the description of a concrete case is incomplete with respect to other relevant moral reasons, then it is very easy to hide one's own bad purposes behind the application of a moral reason. In the history of morality, the conscious usage of selective application was one of the reasons for the decline of scholastic casuistry. One can simply ignore the fact that the police force persecuting the innocent man is brutal and works for the interests of a bad guy, so that the innocent person will surely be killed just for nothing. Then, one concentrates on only one of the issues at stake in the concrete case: Is it correct to tell a lie? This happens also (more or less) non intentionally: The history of morality and justice is full of examples of selective applications of morally valid principles or rules. A famous example for a more intentional selective application is the refusal to extend equal rights to women, e.g., voting rights, although the principle of equality has been acknowledged as valid since the French Revolution.

The principles and rules of application discourse focus on these exemplary cases of partial application. It is only possible to overcome selectivity by a complete description of the concrete case with respect to other relevant moral reasons. And it is possible to overcome rigidity only if one realizes that moral reasons refer to each other, and therefore, need a coherent interpretation in concrete cases. For this reason, I have suggested the following two "principles of appropriateness." Everybody who uses a valid moral norm as a reason for a justification of singular normative propositions has to observe at least two principles: (1) A justification of a singular normative proposition requires a complete description of the concrete case with respect to all those moral reasons which are relevant. (2) A justification of a singular normative proposition requires a coherent interpretation of those morally valid reasons which are directly or indirectly relevant to the concrete case. The first principle refers to the case of selective application, the second one to the case of rigid application. Both principles together realize a presupposition which was made in general practical discourse, when the participants argue about the validity of moral reasons: the presupposition that valid moral reasons cohere with each other in concrete cases. It should be obvious that both principles can only be realized by discourse. Because morally valid reasons are addressed to one another, everybody has to take these reasons into account in concrete cases. Nobody may vicariously rely on a given complete description and a coherent interpretation. Everybody who can refer to a valid reason with respect to his or her complete description of the concrete case, is a participant in application discourse. Consequently, a "complete description" cannot be made from a transcendent point of view, and a coherent interpretation cannot be given by an impartial spectator.

One could object that these principles of appropriateness do not solve the problem of how the participants in a discourse can reach a singular decision. It is at this point that Alexy's argument of institutional restrictions comes into my argument. Even the application discourse cannot lead mechanically to a singular decision. Its rules and principles establish only those conditions which we have to fulfil when we justify a singular normative proposition in a concrete case—which could be *the (moral) reason for* a singular decision, but which does not necessarily *cause* it. Nevertheless, the application discourse minimizes the space of the discursively possible. The requirement to consider all those valid reasons that are relevant in the concrete case opens a sphere of argumentation where nobody can do with reasons whatever he or she wants to do. Moral (and also legal) reasons are like chess-figures; you can only move them in certain directions according to certain rules. If the proponent in the Benjamin/Kant-example referred to the norm "Don't tell a lie," the opponent, who refers to the norm of mutual help in cases where life is at stake, cannot simply say that the prohibition of lying is not a morally valid reason. He or she has to look for different arguments which lead to a coherent interpretation of both norms in this concrete case.

Now, I would like to summarize this paragraph and put both problems together again, which I have separated above. The deficiency of cognitive indeterminacy concerning concrete cases, does not require legal argumentation as such, but a different type of discourse, one which is also practical, but with reference to the application of norms in concrete cases, and not to the justification of the claim to universal validity. As I have shown, even the application discourse does not lead to singular decisions in concrete cases. At this point, law, legal procedures, and legal reasoning become relevant — not as a special case of general practical discourse, but rather as an institutionalization and — perhaps — as a special case of an application-discourse.

2. The Claim to Correctness

The last point has consequences for Alexy's claim that there is a partial coincidence of the "claim to correctness," which is raised as a validity claim for normative propositions in general practical discourse, and the "claim to correctness" in legal argumentation.

First, a partial coincidence would presuppose at least an identity of the constitutive features of the claim to correctness in general practical discourse and the claim to correctness in legal reasoning. The claim to correctness is a validity claim which is raised for regulative speech acts, and that can be substantiated by the principle of universalizability in practical discourse. The principle of universalizability is not one discursive rule among others, but the central rule of moral argumentation; it belongs indeed, as Alexy says, to the "normative core" of discourse theory (Aarnio, Alexy and Peczenik 1981, 49). But it is exactly in this respect that the validity claim in general practical discourse differs from the validity claim in legal reasoning. Whereas the moral validity claim depends on the presupposition that everybody can articulate his or her perspective on a norm, legal reasoning always refers to law which is already legally valid, i.e., whose validity as law may not be put into question in legal reasoning. Thus, Alexy admits that the claim to validity (or correctness), which is raised in legal reasoning, also depends on rational legislation. Nevertheless, I shall argue, that this claim to correctness differs fundamentally from its meaning in general practical discourse, even if we admit that one part of it cannot be fulfilled by legal argumentation alone but only by rational legislation. Alexy himself uses different characterizations for both aspects of the legal claim to correctness. "In passing a judgment a claim is necessarily raised that the law has been applied correctly."[2] He also admits that there are two different aspects to the claim to correctness (Alexy 1991, 432), one of which refers to the correctness of legal decisions "in the framework of the valid legal order" (ibid.), the other refers to the rationality or justice of positive law ("daß das geltende Recht vernünftig oder gerecht ist") (Alexy 1991, 433). Consequently, it makes sense to distinguish between two different "claims to correctness." But then he puts both aspects together in the following statement: "The claim to correctness, which is raised in legal adjudication, includes both aspects."[3]

If one introduces a second type of practical discourse, the application discourse, which is governed by the principles of appropriateness, it is easier to explain the difference between these two aspects of the claim to correctness, and one can avoid an unclear mixture. The characterization of legal reasoning as a practice which aims at decisions that are correct within the framework of a valid legal order fits much better to the conception of an application discourse. The claim to correctness, which is raised in legal reasoning, would then be a claim to legal appropriateness. Alexy himself seems to move in this direction when he discusses two examples of a performative contradiction, which occurs when a judge pronounces a verdict while admitting that he or she has violated certain constitutive rules of legal reasoning (Alexy 1991, 433). The first example was a verdict like: "You will be condemned to ten years in prison, although I know that there are no good reasons for it." This example does not clearly entail a performative contradiction because the rules which are violated could be social or legal rules only, but not a pragmatic rule. Alexy modified this example to a verdict like this: "You will be condemned to ten years in prison, although I know that this decision is based on *a wrong interpretation* of the law." Here, the pragmatic contradiction is obvious: A judge who makes a legal decision raises the claim that the decision is correct (appropriate) with reference to valid law—otherwise, it would not be a legal decision at all. But the content of the claim is the appropriateness of the interpretation.

Above, I have interpreted the function of moral validity as an obligation for everyone to take morally valid reasons into account in every justification of singular normative propositions in concrete cases. But this obligation, as a moral obligation, does not guarantee that valid reasons have a *factual relevance* in concrete cases. It's up to everybody's own conscience. Legal

---

[2] "Mit einem richterlichen Urteil wird notwendig der Anspruch erhoben, daß das Recht richtig angewandt wird" (Alexy 1991, 429).
[3] "In dem mit gerichtlichen Entscheidungen erhobenen Anspruch auf Richtigkeit sind beide Aspekte enthalten" (Alexy 1991, 433).

validity transforms this obligation into an institutional mechanism. If a reason is a legally valid reason, then there must always be some institutional means with which somebody is able to enforce the obligation to take valid reasons factually into account. This is one of the reasons why primary legal rules are always connected with secondary rules that establish certain procedures for legal adjudication. These rules establish procedures in which legal norms are applied and can lead to concrete decisions.

Obviously, this function does not exhaust the meaning of legal validity. As a result of legislative procedure, legally valid norms fix the characteristic traits of a legal community. They give "rights" to every citizen, who has the legal competence to refer to legal reasons in well-established adjudicative procedures. Legal validity also *exonerates* the citizen from demonstrating that the legal reason to which he or she refers is legitimate. Legal validity has a two-fold function: It establishes those norms as valid which express the characteristic traits of a legal community. And it puts something like a "marker" or "sticker" on legal reasons which makes it obligatory for the members of institutionalized procedures of application to take them into account.

This interpretation of the concept of legal validity could also serve as an explanation for the distinction between legislation and adjudication. In concrete cases, we should not argue about the validity of reasons as moral or legal reasons, but only whether they are relevant. In this way, the situational bias and partiality could be precluded. This is even more true for legal systems with precedents, where the principles of overruling and distinguishing with respect to a *ratio decidendi* in concrete cases play a prominent role. With this distinction, one has no problems accepting that legal norms consist of a different kind which could not be a subject matter of general practical discourse. The advantage of the conception of application discourse can best be demonstrated in this context. It enables us to interpret the rules and principles of legal reasoning as an interpretation of the principles of appropriateness with respect to different kinds of legal norms, which are applied in adjudicative procedures. This will be my last point.

3. The Correspondence-Thesis

The third argument for the special case-thesis refers to the correspondence between certain rules and forms (a), and between certain types of argument (b) in general practical discourse and in legal argumentation.

Alexy argues for this thesis in respect of both parts of legal argumentation, i.e., internal and external justification. Concerning internal justification, all those rules and forms of argument which belong to this type of justification are derivations from the principle of universalizability, as it is presented by Hare. And this principle plays a prominent role in general practical discourse. Nevertheless, this principle only demands of every speaker that he or she use language consistently. To be sure, this principle is certainly a requirement for general practical discourse. One cannot imagine any discourse without this rule, it is constitutive of our use of language. But for that very reason, it is *not* a characteristic feature of *practical* discourse because even a dictator has to use language consistently if he wants his orders to be intelligible. Our obligation, which we have as speakers, to use language consistently is a common feature of both general practical discourse and legal argumentation, because and insofar as we use language in both types of discourse.

Concerning external justification, the rules and forms of discourse, which are relevant to the special case-thesis, do not refer to the characteristic feature of general practical discourse, i.e., to the principle of universalizability. A great many of them have — at least indirectly — to do with justification of singular normative propositions in concrete cases. This is true of the canons of interpretation, which, for Alexy, serve as semantic interpretations of the legal norm with respect to the features of the case. It is also true of the establishment of legal doctrine (Alexy 1978, 322), and of the use of precedents (especially overriding and distinguishing). Although these rules and forms of argument might be necessary requirements of general practical discourse, they are not necessarily linked to it.

This could be an indication of the fact that we have to look for a different task of legal reasoning, one which gives a meaning to its rules and forms of argument that is different from the special case-thesis. Then, the logic of argumentation comes from a different task: They interpret the principle of appropriateness with respect to (a) the application of legally valid norms, and (b) to different problems of justification of singular legal norms in concrete cases. They establish rules for how to deal with legal reasons in specific contexts. They answer the question of what should be done if a singular normative proposition which is justified by a valid legal reason conflicts with other legal reasons. Legal doctrine has a special function in this context: It generalizes patterns or paradigms of coherent interpretation of legal norms with respect to a certain range of cases which have some relevant features in common.

Now, in conclusion, let me summarize the complementary functions of legal procedures and legal reasoning: "Legal validity" makes it institutionally obligatory to take certain reasons into account. In continental legal systems, legal validity is established by a legislative procedure. Litigation procedures and administrative procedures establish the procedures in which valid reasons are considered. They distribute and define the roles of the participants in legal procedure, and the way in which legal reasons are introduced into the adjudicative process. For example, in civil law cases, it is up to the litigating parties to introduce valid reasons into the adjudicative process. But once they are introduced and substantiated by "evidence," they cannot be excluded from the sphere of argumentation by means other than legally valid counter-arguments. Now, the rules and forms of legal argumentation regulate how the legal reasons, whose consideration is obligatory, should be used for the justification of singular normative propositions in concrete cases. Interpretive communities are established and enfranchised to give an authentic coherent interpretation of the law, which then leads to a definite decision.

Johann Wolfgang Goethe University
Institute for Criminology
Senckenberganlage 31–33
D-6000-Frankfurt am Main
Germany

References

Aarnio, Aulis, Robert Alexy, and Aleksander Peczenik. 1981. The Foundation of Legal Reasoning. *Rechtstheorie* 12: 133–58, 257–79, 423–48.
Alexy, Robert. 1978. *Theorie der juristischen Argumentation*. Frankfurt: Suhrkamp.
———. 1989. *A Theory of Legal Argumentation*. Trans. Ruth Adler, and Neil MacCormick. Oxford: Clarendon.
———. 1991. *Theorie der juristischen Argumentation*. 2nd ed. Frankfurt: Suhrkamp.
Günther, Klaus. 1988. *Der Sinn für Angemessenheit*. Frankfurt: Suhrkamp.
———. 1992. Universalistische Normbegründung und Normanwendung in Recht und Moral. In *Individualisierung und Generalisierung im Rechtsdenken*. Ed. M. Herberger, U. Neumann, and H. Rüssmann, 36–76. Stuttgart: Steiner.
———. 1993. *The Sense of Appropriateness*. Trans. John Farrell. Albany, N.Y.: SUNY-Press (forthcoming).

[8]
Law, Love and Computers
*Zenon Bankowski**

This article is the revised text of an inaugural lecture delivered in the Faculty of Law, University of Edinburgh, on 24 November 1994. The paper examines what it means to live under rules in general, considering first the problem of an individual up against the law, then secondly, and using a computer analogy and metaphor, what it means to place oneself under the governance of rules, and, finally, how love links the first two parts because it fulfils rather than destroys the law.

A. PREFACE

It is a great honour to be called to a chair at the University of Edinburgh. To become a senior colleague at an ancient and great European university and faculty. To take one's place among illustrious precursors and an illustrious team. I have great honour and pleasure in so doing and especially among those who have made contributions to the general field of my chair. I mention here Professor Archie Campbell, the Professor of Public Law and the Law of Nature and Nations from 1945 to 1972. A great scholar, he brought Italian legal philosophy to the attention of the English-speaking world. I remember Professors Bill Wilson and Derrick McClintock, two colleagues who sadly died in 1994. Bill Wilson, one of our pre-eminent private lawyers, was also deeply interested in the philosophy of law. His clear exposition of Hohfeld was exemplary.[1] Derrick McClintock held the first chair in Criminology at the University and was one of the founders of the Centre for Criminology and the Social and Philosophical Study of Law. Though mainly a criminologist, his work also looked at the philosophical and theological aspects of law. I recall Sheriff Gerald Gordon, one-time Professor of Scots Law here, whose magisterial work on the criminal law of Scotland combines dogmatic precision with philosophical expertise. Professor David Garland's study of punishment brilliantly shows the fruits of a Centre which seeks to combine the philosophical and the sociological. Finally, there is Professor Neil MacCormick who is, quite simply, one of the leading philosophers of law in the world today. It is with pride and humility that I take my place in such company.

---

* Zenon Bankowski is Professor of Legal Theory in the University of Edinburgh.
  For Christine.

---

1 "A note on the Hohfeld analysis", 1972 *Juridical Review* 162–169.

An inaugural lecture should give a conspectus of the subject and speak of the intellectual development of the chair-holder. For me that has never been separated from the personal. My endeavours have always been to try to see how one can lead a good life; to be able to encounter people and deal with them honestly. This has led me to be fascinated and captured by rules. My intellectual and personal life has been concerned with trying to escape the net of rules. But, as Iris Murdoch shows in *Under the Net*, that attempt can lead to disaster. The trick is to take a practically reasonable attitude to rules, to be able to step in and out of the law without throwing it away.

I can illustrate the problem by a story. When I lived in Italy I was struck by the seeming chaos on the roads. But drivers did not go out to kill pedestrians at, for example, pedestrian crossings or traffic lights. They never stopped but rather tried, with more or less success, to weave around the pedestrians who would be scared out of their wits. I then visited Germany where I was struck by how different it seemed. How at controlled pedestrian crossings, cars, when signalled to stop, always did so. If there was a green light for the pedestrian, one could boldly cross without looking out for cars. One could do something not possible in Italy, cross the road and not fear the cars. You knew they would stop. However, if you crossed the road on the red, you were dead! You would not be seen because you were crossing the road contrary to the rules. You should not be there, therefore you were not there.

I suspect that, personally and intellectually, I was always rather German. Even my earlier more anarchist work comes out of a feeling that rules are to be obeyed at all costs. If there are rules, one must obey them; you cannot bend them a bit. And so the only way one can challenge legality is to deny it *tout court*. One cannot creatively bend the rules.

I have at last learned better. The point of my lecture is to suggest that this, after all, can be done without losing the rules or the creativity of breaking them. I have to thank especially two people and a different ontological entity. The first person is Peter Young. I met him here when we were both young lecturers in the Faculty. It was through him that my crude and untutored social science gained any rigour that it might have. His wise, calm and practical counsels have always stood me in good stead. Finally I would like to thank Neil MacCormick. I have known him as teacher, senior colleague and mentor, collaborator and friend. My intellectual and personal debt to him cannot be measured.

The different ontological entity that I would like to thank is the Law Faculty. During the war, apart from the Polish Medical School, the Law Faculty ran a postgraduate Diploma in Law for Polish Students. This is how a Scottish member of that class remembers them.[2]

---

2 For the quotation which follows, see W Tomaszewski (ed), *The University of Edinburgh and Poland* (1968), 54–55.

The advent of the Poles in the Old Quadrangle in the unlovely days of wartime was a thing which seemed to bring us closer to the continental civilisation, from which we had been for some years cut off. They came in their uniforms and their immaculate appearance gave a welcome touch of distinction to the classes and to the graduations, while their struggles with the English language earned our admiration.

As graduates, already experienced in their professions, they brought a mature approach to the system of administration and practical demonstrations which they saw here, weighting them critically against those they already knew.

They kept their sorrows very much to themselves and were willing to join in the social side of University life of the time. The parties held at the home of their "professor" were memorable for the singing of members of the Polish Army choir and for individual performances by members of the "Lwowska Fala", who were enrolled at the course. One of these used to start his monologue with the words, "I am a Scottish Pole." So indeed were they all.

And this is what a Polish student then says:[3]

In order to appreciate fully the value which the Diploma course had for us Poles in the difficult and trying days of war, it is imperative to remember that we were a group of lawyers in uniform, bewildered after having lived through two catastrophes—the fall of Poland and the fall of France—and uncertain about the future.

We foresaw that, whatever the outcome of the war, it might be followed in Poland by social and economic change, which would make our legal knowledge and experience in many ways outdated. For the time being we were out of touch with legal practice and legal thinking—neither active soldiers nor active lawyers.

The medical students were lucky! The Polish School of Medicine was created. The gates of the University of Edinburgh stood open for them. We thought of the colleagues from the "other place" with envy.

And then, in the autumn of 1941, the magnificent news reached all the Polish military camps in Scotland. The Alma Mater Edinburgensis was to open its doors to us Polish lawyers.

We became *cives universitatis* again! What was more, we were invited to study for the Post-Graduate Diploma; for that purpose, our degrees in Poland were fully recognised.

Mr Ronald McLarty was our guardian, teacher and friend, a typical example of Scottish modesty, unobtrusive magnanimity and the tendency to overlook one's own efforts and difficulties, while bringing out the best in us.

Our enthusiasm was great, our English atrocious, our knowledge of the English legal vocabulary very limited.

The continental "stand to attention" attitude in personal contact with our professors and lecturers made them feel embarrassed. Our mannerism in general, and vigorous gesticulation in particular, was in striking contrast with the casual Scottish approach.

In those circumstances how could our teachers be sure that their lectures, delivered in English, would be understood? Would they succeed in reading and assessing examination papers written in "phonetic" English? Would they understand what the Polish students intended to convey during oral examinations?

They did! They succeeded all the way through! They passed their examinations in patience, perseverance, subtlety and understanding every day through all these years.

---

3 Ibid, 55–57.

Equally hearty thanks must be expressed to the servitors for their warm greetings in the morning, for their friendly attitude and for the words of encouragement at the entrance to the examination hall.

We cherish in our grateful hearts the memory of the lady [McLarty's mother] who spontaneously undertook the burden of treating and mending our sore souls at her home at 23 Abercromby Place. Our appreciation of her motherly hospitality, of her smile distributed so generously in her home, her interest in the psychological welfare of every one of us, is beyond words.

I am, of course, the son of these students. I have also, in my time here, encountered the warm, friendly and intellectual environment that the Faculty provides. The Faculty has a long tradition of doing this for those in need. In my years we have seen the successful links with the Universities of Lesotho, Botswana and Swaziland, with their students coming here for a year. I hope that the Faculty will continue this sort of help to students from all over the world and not let the call for profit detract it from that mission. The lecture that follows is my personal thanks—and a poor repayment of my debt—for the honour it has done to me and the help it gave to them.

B. INTRODUCTION

Anarchists have always distrusted law. Tolstoy says that the law is based on violence; is in the interests of the ruling class; involves mystifying through the "science of legislation". Instead of making things clear, it builds up a huge opaque apparatus of its own, comprehensible only to its acolytes. Direct responsibility is evaded. Anyone can deny responsibility for what they have done as merely carrying out the law. Two different prongs in this attack can be discerned.

The first is that law has been captured by a group of people and used for their own interests. Crudely, law is used by those who have to rob those who have not. More modern studies have indeed shown that lawyers' high-sounding phrases often mask naked self-interest.[4] That "the interests of justice" often mean my interests. Legal aid means aid for lawyers and not by lawyers. But does this mean that the Rule of Law as an idea (or ideal) is thereby flawed? In part, yes. If that is how it is in practice, then that is what the ideal actually means. All else is illusion. In part, no. For many radicals, the law has been captured by a particular group who use it for themselves and not for the good of others and society. But, it is argued, the law can be recaptured, can be used to do good. Can it? There is a strange coalition between right and left here. Both think that it cannot. Both think that is so because the law is inextricably linked with the capitalist, market society.[5] Its instrumental use will, for the former, destroy it as law. For the latter, it will merely reproduce capitalist society.

But it is the second prong of the anarchist attack that I wish to concentrate on in this lecture. That goes further. It is not concerned with law's connections to a

---

4 Z Bankowski and G Mungham, *Images of Law* (1976), ch 3.
5 C Sypnowich, *The Concept of Socialist Law* (1990), ch 3.

particular form of society. Rather, it is concerned with what is the moral meaning of legality. What it means to live under the Rule of Law. What it means to live under rules in general. It is this question that I want to take up. Neil MacCormick[6] gets at the problem when he morally defends the Rule of Law, or what he calls legalism. He gets to the heart of the problem. Legalism suggests some sort of rule-bound way of living, both personally and socially. Here we see the crux of the ethical point that I want to discuss today. Is there something wrong with surrendering our lives to rules? We are, as the phrase goes, "slaves of the law in order that we might be free". But why should we be slaves? This is not a question of who controls the society and for what reason. It is about the moral implications of placing ourselves "under the governance of rules"[7] as we try to live our lives among our fellows. What does it mean for the individual and society to organise in this way?

I will proceed as follows: first, I will outline the basis of this moral criticism of law by starting with the problem of a particular individual up against the law. I broaden this to cover the moral implications for rule-bound governance. Secondly, I will look at what it means to "place oneself under the governance of rules". I use a computer analogy and metaphor to clarify this. Finally, I turn to love. Love comes in at the end because it links the first two parts. I will show how, through this linkage, we can have what I call the law of love. Love fulfils the law and does not destroy it.

C. LAW

What, then, is it about the second prong of the anarchist attack that engages deep moral concerns? Anarchists above all oppose law because they think that it takes away decisions that should rightly be my own: that instead of my deciding what to do, I let some external force do this for me. In short, I behave *heteronomously* rather than *autonomously*. Robert Paul Wolff[8] explains this by looking at a particular individual in his confrontation with the law.

(1) Stephen's story

Wolff considers the dilemma of whether we should obey laws. He considers the story of Stephen, a young American of draft age during the period of the Vietnam War. His dilemma, as Wolff puts it, is this: under what circumstances would it be right for Stephen to go and fight in Vietnam, even though he thought it wrong to do so? Notice that the question has been put rather differently from the way we normally encounter it. We are not asking when it is right to break the law. Rather, when is it right to follow it? As we shall see, the reasons given go right to the heart of our problem.

---

6 D N MacCormick, "The ethics of legalism" (1989) 2 *Ratio Juris* 184–193.
7 L Fuller, *The Morality of Law* (1969).
8 R P Wolff, *In Defence of Anarchism* (1976), ch 1.

In what circumstances, then, should Stephen go and fight? Wolff decides that democracy must be the best answer. That seems to involve Stephen in taking part in the decision, made by the USA, to fight in Vietnam. And if this is the case, it seems clear that he must go. But how does democracy structure our participation in decision-making? Wolff goes over the options. He first of all considers representative democracy and rejects it. In such a system it is not clear that you actually take part in the decision-making. We vote for people who will represent us in the decision-making councils. They will be representatives and not delegates. It is them and not us who will decide what it is right to do. This might not necessarily be what we want. In modern democracies this often happens. How much faith can we put in the promises of the political parties? But Wolff's point is not about fraud and lying by cynical political parties and their members. It is more fundamental than that. The core of representative democracy is to elect others whom we trust to make decisions for us. Does this solve Stephen's dilemma? Can we call that participation in decision-making? Wolff says no.

He next asks whether direct democracy can be considered a system where we take part in the decision-making. Here there are no representatives. I, or someone whom I mandate to do what I say, vote. So what I want is actually put into the voting urn. But does actual voting for a decision mean that I take part in the decision-making? Consider the following case. We decide upon something in an assembly with one person dissenting. But that person by force of arms, or fraud, manages to get his view implemented. Would we say that the rest of us had participated in the decision to do what he wanted and were therefore bound? It seems not. But if this is the case, why does it appear that 51% are entitled to force the 49% to do what they did not vote for? It might still come to force. The criterion seems to be majority rule. But Wolff cannot find any principle that will sustain it. If that is the case, then it does not matter if the minority is one only. That is still no reason to force that person. We must therefore say that here as well we do not participate in the decision-making.

The conclusion for Wolff is that the only acceptable solution to "Stephen's problem" is a system of direct democracy with a unanimity rule. It is only in this case that Stephen will think himself to be rightly obligated. Here he has not acted heteronomously by virtue of a law that someone else has made. It is only in this case that Stephen has acted under a law that he made for himself. This autonomy is important. For it is the only way that morality can be constituted. On this way of looking at it, most systems of ordering society would be immoral. In following the rules, I would often be following rules not set by myself. I would be thinking it right so to do. Even if I did not particularly object to the rule, I would still not be following it by virtue of having made it myself. I would not be looking to the content of the rule but merely following it.

(2) "It's nothing to do with me"

What does this mean for our problem? At the end of our story we are left with a lone voice. It does not want to be forgotten. It does not want to be subsumed into a general rule which all must follow. It is the concrete person saying, "I'm here. I'm important." But it is not just the effect on that lone voice that anarchists have in mind. It is also what it does to those who do not know what to do with all these lone voices—all wanting different things. In despair, they decide that the only thing to do is to have a regime of rules. To introduce the Rule of Law or legalism. To treat all voices equally under general rules.

But is this not the evasion of responsibility? For are we not hiding behind the rules? Are we not denying flexibility and compromise by claiming we can do nothing about it? "It's nothing to do with me, I don't make the rules." Rules are binary. They either exist and we apply them, or they do not. There is nothing in between. Judith Shklar puts it like this:

> [T]his isolate[s] law completely from the social context within which it exists. Law is endowed with its own discrete integral history, its own "science" and its own values, which are all treated as a single "block" sealed off from general social theory, from politics, and from morality. The habits of mind appropriate, within narrow limits, to the procedures of law courts in the most stable legal systems have been expanded to provide a legal theory and ideology with an entire system of thought and values. This procedure has served its own ends very well: it aims at preserving law from irrelevant considerations, but it has ended by fencing legal thinking off from all contact with the rest of historical thought and experience.[9]

The claim here is that, no matter where the rules come from, the effect of legalism is to make them appear objective and unchangeable. Legalism does not so much deny the connection between law and values as hide it and tuck it away from view. Since it concentrates on the rules to the exclusion of everything else, the rules lose their sense of contingency. They dominate the entire moral universe. They are the islands of stability in a chaotic universe. This concentration on law and the rules has made us forget that it is we who make the rules and we who can change them. We see ourselves instead as the technicians of rules that we do not and cannot challenge. The morality of law becomes one of legalism; of the technical rational manipulation of rules. The rules have a life of their own which cannot be challenged. They control us rather than we control them. What we concentrate on is the rules themselves. We follow them and do not think about what they say.

We saw in Stephen's story that what we normally think of as participation is not enough. Responsibility is still evaded. This evasion means you lose sight of the concrete person—the lone voice of our story.

---

9 J Shklar, *Legalism* (1986), 2–3.

How might that happen? How is Stephen forgotten? How do people become invisible? G K Chesterton[10] in his detective stories makes this clear. In one he gives us the classic locked-room mystery. Someone is murdered in a locked room, the sole entrance to which has been kept under observation. No one was seen. Who did it? The answer is the postman because no one noticed him. Since he was always there, he was invisible. Think of the way some people have treated, and treat, their servants. They are people who perform certain functions and who never get in the way—never appear to be there. People would say they were alone when in fact they were surrounded by servants. Indeed this ability to treat the servant as invisible was seen as a mark of the upper-class.[11] Is this what happens when we decide what to do with people by applying rules to them?

D. COMPUTERS

To make this clearer, I introduce an analogy with, and a metaphor of, the computer. Why use this metaphor? In looking at the place of the computer in law and society, we sometimes raise the spectre of a sort of Frankenstein monster taking over. Why? Because somehow automated systems in law miss out human creativity. Miss out the flexibility that should come with human decision-making. We say of someone: "They're just not human, they've got everything calculated and worked out, they're just like a computer." Thus, computers can never model law as an expression of that creativity.

One way of answering this is to say that computers are not meant to play that role in society or the law. That they best and most accurately model another aspect of human behaviour. What then do computers model best? They best model humans who are pretending to be computers, pretending to be machines. After all, it is always easier convincingly to mimic someone who is pretending to be what you are. When, then, do humans act like machines? In many instances. When they are in the army. When they are on the assembly line. But remember what we have been saying about legalism and legality. Is that not, on the anarchist view, an example of machine-like behaviour? Where we do not think about what we should do. Where we merely follow the rules.

Why fear this? Consider the horrors of a science-fiction dystopia. Here, the world is administered by machines which always follow the program. They do not admit of exceptions however obviously they could. This generates the image of the computer judge where the rule is automatically applied without exception. Here we get an image of a world governed by a computer, where a network of cameras and highly accurate gas ejectors is erected over the world and connected

---

10 G K Chesterton, *The Father Brown Stories* (1960).
11 Bankowski and Mungham, *Images of Law*, 87–104.

to the computer.[12] They fire at anyone who breaks the rules. They do not stop to consider.

That image is fantasy. But what it means is real. Think of a simplified model of the rules for a university library system.[13] We might think of a system where there are rules which specify (1) how many books each category of user may have; (2) for how long they may keep them out; (3) the maximum number of books which may be borrowed at any one time; and (4) a prohibition on the loan of books to anyone in breach of the regulations. Imagine if the library were to be automated. Everyone would be issued with a card which would be inserted into the computer system. The system would see if you were in good standing in respect of the regulations. Only then would it let you borrow an electronic copy of the book desired which would self-destruct after the loan time allowed! Most of this is technically possible. But we are not interested in that here. What is important is that it has transformed what is happening. Before, there was the possibility of choice. But now there is none. The rules are either redundant or descriptions of what is the case. Once within the library system, the pathways that the rules set are followed. This gives us a model of machine-like behaviour. There is no room for thinking about whether it is right to do so or not. The rules are applied. The normative becomes, in a certain sense, descriptive.

In case this also seems too fantastic, consider another case. Imagine the cash machines that banks use to dispense cash to their customers. All users have a card. They insert this into the machine. They then key in their private code and the amount of money that they want. The machine checks the status of their account and the amount of withdrawals that they have made. Depending on their status, it then gives them the money or it does not. There is no argument. You cannot plead with it. You cannot show how here, for pressing and important reasons, it should read the rules differently and give you the money. The machine does not see you, the concrete human being with particular pressing needs and problems. It just sees (reads) the card. The creative human element has been factored out, just as in the library system (and remember, the machine does make bank tellers redundant). You have become that card. The card no longer represents you, it is you. You have disappeared and become invisible. The lone voice crying "What about me?" is no longer heard. It has been absorbed by the universal rules that the system applies without thinking about it.

It might be argued that this is wrong. That there is always a bank teller or librarian there who takes the decision. But it is the librarian and the bank teller who are the machine. And it is applying rules that makes them like that. We might argue that in

---

12 See M Detmold, *The Unity of Law and Morality* (1984).
13 I take this example from J Jones and M Sergot, "Deontic logic in the representation of law: towards a methodology" (1992) 1 *Artificial Intelligence and Law* 45–64.

effect they take a decision. For they must at least be held to have decided that, in any particular case, the rules are to be applied without consideration of any special pleading. But that misses the point. Of course they must be held morally responsible for their particular action. "I was only following orders" does not excuse. But it does not mean that someone took a conscious decision and looked at the case. They were after all "only following orders". They were not thinking about the particular case, only about following the rules.

That seems to be the point of applying rules. You apply the rules and you necessarily have to forget Stephen. You might decide not to apply the rules but you are not looking at Stephen. You do not see him. Your decision is based on the system logic; the rules have to be applied. Once you enter the system or institution, you only operate within that institution. When we enter into an institutional arrangement, we are guided along certain predetermined pathways which the institutional rules lay out for us. This helps us determine our rights and responsibilities. What we have to do without having to make separate and complicated decisions at each juncture. But it not only gives us this facility, it also enables others to plan their actions and determine one another's rights and responsibilities.[14]

We can see this in Sandra Dewitz's design for an electronic contracting network which would automatically generate the bills of lading used in import and export. Once the institutive rules of the system/institution have been set up, the bills are automatically generated and no one has to think what to do. Those rules are out of sight and out of mind.[15]

Law is like that.[16] Love and need are not necessary; they stand outside the system. I see a lot of money on the pavement. What do I do with it? To whom should I give it? Myself? I need a new car. The university? It needs new books. The beggar I see on the street? But which one? There are so many. But I realise that it would be against the law to take the money. It is not mine. It is not a *res nullius*. So I give it to the police. Once in the system of law, I apply the rules. Love and need stand outside.

E. LOVE

But surely they ought not to? Is not that precisely the argument of the radicals with which I started? The machine-like necessity of law cannot deal with the concrete individual. It forgets them. Normativity was turned into description and with it the chance of reacting with love to the particular needs of the individual. The social world becomes closed and constraining.

---

14 D N MacCormick and O Weinberger, *An Institutional Theory of Law* (1986).
15 Cf S Dewitz, "Using information technology as a determiner of legal facts", in Z Bankowski, I White and U Hahn (eds), *Informatics and the Foundations of Legal Reasoning* (1995), 357–370.
16 J Raz, *Practical Reason and Norms* (1975).

(1) Love and order

Is this necessarily a bad thing? Does "All you need is love" really capture how we should live? The parable of the labourers in the vineyard can help clarify this. We might say that the parable means that love is its own reason. That the love of God knows no bounds and He gives to all what they need. He cares for all and gives to each the subsistence of a day. He does not care that effectively some get paid more per hour than others, even although they are doing the same work. But the parable can also show us the danger of love without rules. For it might be that it (rightly) rigs the case. Why? The master is God and therefore a special case. He is all-knowing as well as all-good. Since God knows all, He knows what is best for everyone; being all-good, He can be trusted to will it for everyone; by being all-powerful, He can achieve it for everyone. But we are not Gods and we are defective in this respect. If we rely on love, we will inevitably get things wrong. Experience tells us that that sort of society will soon dissolve into one where the lovers are the dictators. They know what is best for you. You will be forced to do it because it is what you really want—regardless of what you say. You will be forced to be free—the road to hell is indeed paved with good intentions.[17]

This is Hayek's argument for the market and also for a régime of formal rules which apply equally to everyone. We might not know what is right to do. But at least we wrong no one. Why is that? Max Weber said that scientific rationality, in the coming of capitalism, destroyed the magic in the world. You do not see a tree and the tree-spirit inhabiting it. You see the processes of nature. You see furniture and profit. You do not see the gods angry and hurling down thunderbolts. You see climatic conditions producing a thunderstorm. The advantage is that you control the world. You use it in a way that you could not when it was magic. Science rolls over the magic of the natural world and makes it flat and predictable. You do not have to worry what the tree-fairy will do; you know what makes the wood grow. You know how to help it do so. You do not worry that the gods are angry; you know why there is a thunderstorm. The world might be more boring but it is predictable.

We can view the régime of formal rational rules in the same way. Take the library and the cash machine. They, in their turn, roll over the normative world. They take away the magic from that world. They take away the mysterious force of love. That force that makes people do so many things, good and bad but above all unpredictable. They make it predictable. The point of law is to measure up to the library and the cash machine. To enable Stephen and all the other lone voices to plan their lives in security and peace. But the price is that they are lost, and forgotten. And when they really are alone, needing something outwith the rules—nobody sees them, nobody cares. For Hayek, this is the price we have to pay for the "great society". It might

---

17 Z Bankowski, "Social justice and democracy", in R Bellamy (ed), *Theories and Concepts of Politics* (1993), 77–97.

not have the fellow feeling and warmth of the old tribal communities. It might be fragile. But it is the price we have to pay for civilisation and progress. Those who want to make rules more "creative" are only presaging a return to the old tribal communities.

Here again we can see some sort of agreement on both sides. They both use the "thin end of the wedge" argument. For Hayek any relaxation from the strict following of the rules, in the machine-like way that we saw above, means the eventual and total collapse of the rules. For the other side, the slightest indeterminacy of meaning means that the rules are always applied creatively. Even if we fool ourselves that they are not. So they argue that we should stop the fooling and come out into the open. That way we can contest the power of those who impose their version of the rules; who hide their domination behind the façade of "We have no choice".

But we do not have to choose indeterminacy or fixity. We do not need to decide for autonomy or heteronomy. Hayek, and liberalism in general, want the heteronomy of the law because for them it guarantees the autonomy of private life, i.e. morals. The law's heteronomy enables citizens to do what they want; slaves as they are to the rules which regulate the intersection between the desires of each citizen. This argument implies that autonomy and heteronomy reside in two different institutions: autonomy in morals and heteronomy in the law. I have argued against this division more fully elsewhere.[18]

But neither do I want to argue for the other side. They see this "slavery" as altogether bad. They have an epistemological and a moral argument. The epistemological one first. It is not true. The law has not got this machine-like quality. It is in, fact, plastic and changeable. It can mean more or less what one wants it to mean. Legalism, as shown earlier, means we have forgotten that. We think the computer analogy is reality. Modelling the law in this way has not meant that computers have approximated to human beings; that we have built "intelligent" legal expert systems. Rather we have become more like machines. The moral argument says that we should celebrate the plasticity that the epistemological argument proclaims. It gives us autonomy; it means that our voices need not be forgotten. It enables us to organise our lives to cope with people's needs, to respond with love. So for them, law and love need not stand opposed to each other. Law collapses into love. Into a form of morality.

I want to argue that both sides have a point. That law, and morals, consist of autonomous and heteronomous parts. They have the tensions between autonomy and heteronomy built into them. When dealing with law, then, we must view the relation between autonomy and heteronomy as something internal to law. It cannot be solved by moving the autonomy part into another, though complementary, box.

---

18 Z Bankowski, "Don't think about it?: legalism and legality" (1993) 15 *Rechtstheorie Beiheft* 45–58.

That would indeed lead us to view law as the legalism that Shklar warns us about. Law does have some of this machine-like quality. The computer analogy is apt. But that does not mean that that is all there is to law.

Let us think of Stephen again. This time as a story about democracy. About the ability of voices to be heard in managing society. Again, the tension is present. For it appears that the law needs to exclude democratic voices from its process, when its system rationality is left to itself and its acolytes. Constitutional arrangements show this well. If we have a commitment to democratic self-government in a pluralistic community, then how can the fundamental terms of that association be given to a group of "founding fathers" or some present élite? But making these terms open and subject to the democratic self-government of the rest of the society seems precisely to attack the base of that society. Thus the universalistic system rationality of the law seems to exclude the voices who want to subject it to their autonomy. Yet we need both. We must therefore try to link these two parts. The law's heteronomy, when within it people are subject to an extraneous will, to some governing legislature. And its autonomy, when acting subjects decide, after critical reflection upon information, what it is right to do.

Legality consists in the articulation of autonomous and heteronomous systems. We need heteronomy as well as autonomy. We cannot collapse the one into the other. We need to be dependent upon people; we are beings who need other people and cannot live without them. But this dependency means that we must not think of ourselves as wholly autonomous, dependent upon our will alone. Nor does it mean that we have to surrender our autonomy and live a wholly heteronomous life. We are neither slave nor lord of all. The law seems to have a universality that takes it away from that concrete case into a system rationality of its own. Here we are concerned with how the autonomy of the concrete case can break into system rationality and not be swallowed up. How we can look at system rationality and concrete autonomy without downgrading either.

(2) Love and passion

I illustrate the problem of the last section by starting with the personal and working up to the social. Take marriage as an example. We can, according to Luhmann, oppose marriage with love or passion.[19] Love is spontaneous and always questions itself. It is always in the present; the future does not exist for it. It operates in the now. It is uncoupled from external relations, it is contingent and a matter of fate. The lover does not ask how or what it will do or where it will lead. It is a grace and those questions are irrelevant. The lover is just grateful for the love. He or she does everything because of love. There is no need for duty or obligation. At the same time love consumes everything; it thematises the whole relationship. Everything

---

19 N Luhmann, *Love as Passion* (1986).

that the lovers do, all the everyday decisions that they take, even the most banal (should we have cornflakes for breakfast?), are taken as going to the roots of the relationship and questioning it. Marriage, on the other hand, loses passion or love. Marriage wants to make something eternal, not something in the present. Marriage wants to reduce spontaneity and make things simpler. It operates to "calm this grand passion", to reduce spontaneity and cut out chance. To make it possible to live because every decision does not thematise the whole of the relationship. It thus denies love. Marriage then routinises. It is boring and lacks the warmth of love. Love often transforms itself into marriage because this is the way love stabilises itself. But in so doing it loses that love and is no longer connected to it. We are doomed to be slaves or lovers.

This way of looking at it seems precisely analogous to our problem. It appears that we can be heteronomous or autonomous but not both. I want to argue the contrary. Love comes not from autonomous passion but from the articulation of that passion with the heteronomous nature of marriage. It is then that we can say that there is love. It is the way in which we join these strands. In a marriage or a long-term relationship we can recognise certain phases. Sometimes at the beginning, people are so "in love" that they do everything together, operate as a single unit. Then, realising that this is not the best way, they act autonomously but as though they were completely separate—one would be amazed to find out they were married. They only realise the relationship properly when they come to some way of yoking these together. When they move from the first stage of "undifferentiated unity" and the second stage of "differentiated disunity" to the stage of differentiated unity.[20]

Let us turn to the cash machine or the librarian. I put the card in and it tells me that I cannot get any money out. I start to argue with the machine, for my need is pressing and urgent. I beg the machine to give, out of its love, money for my need—but to no avail. Then, hearing my desperate pleas, the teller comes out. But, as we have seen, that is also a machine. He says no, for that is the way the law must operate. The teller never gets beyond the smart card. But what, if no matter what decision he comes to, he considers the matter? Then the converse is the case. For then he is jumping beyond the smart card and reaching me, the concrete voice crying out of need for love. He then breaks through the smart card. For the decision he made is particular, at a particular time in concrete circumstances. Even if he says no, he has lost touch with the smart card and is only in touch with me. On the one hand he is locked in the universality of the smart card and on the other he is locked into the particular case. This is analogous to the marriage example. How can we find the love that links them without their being locked into separate spheres?

But if we cannot do this, surely we should choose the latter: forget the smart card and touch the individual. But think of the cash-machine analogy again. Say the

20 Cf G A Cohen, "Marx's dialectic of labour", 1974 *Philosophy and Public Affairs* 235–261.

machine becomes a teller who cares. He does not see you as the cash card. Rather he sees you as someone in need. His love goes out to you and he gives you money. But if tellers keep doing this, listening to their feelings, where will all the money come from? Will the bank have any left? What about the depositors? For the sake of helping a few, they may have harmed the many. It is the rules and the machine-like activity of the law that keeps that in check. The smart card is important after all.

What one needs is a way of knowing when to stop acting like the machine and not follow the set patterns. When to let the person in the card break out. The parable of the good Samaritan is instructive. It might be interpreted as saying that by the encounter the Samaritan makes the person lying injured a neighbour. And therefore it is the particular encounter that is important. For Jesus says: that person is your neighbour to whom you act in a neighbourly fashion. But why should he make him his neighbour? I cannot act as the good Samaritan to everyone. I walk home and encounter many beggars, the sick, the ill, the poor and the drunk. I cannot help them all in the same way. I cannot give them all money. I must have some idea of whom I can, in each encounter, give money to. Surely that must be a universal question? One could then interpret the parable as giving a definition of neighbour. This is, of course, what the law does. Thus in *Donoghue v Stevenson*[21] Lord Atkin said:

> The rule that you are to love your neighbour becomes in law: You must not injure your neighbour, and the lawyer's question: Who is my neighbour? receives a restricted reply. You must take reasonable care to avoid acts or omissions which you can reasonably foresee would be likely to injure your neighbour. Who then, in law, is my neighbour? The answer seems to me to be persons who are so closely and directly affected by my act that I ought reasonably to have them in contemplation as being so affected when I am directing my mind to the acts or omissions which are called in question. This appears to me to be the doctrine in *Heaven v Pender* as laid down by Lord Esher.[22]

But then it misses the particular. Remember the parable was in answer to a question by a lawyer. And of course we do need a definition and a theory of "who is my neighbour". But we must be careful not to be trapped in that theory or definition. If we are, we lose the particular concrete person. The Israelites were enemies of the Samaritans. It would be as if I did not see a bleeding man in need of help but an enemy. I was in thrall to the definition that enemies are not neighbours.

You are therefore either locked in the universal, walking along the street missing all the beggars because they do not fit the definition of neighbour, or, and this is as bad, never getting to your destination because you stop at every beggar on the way. The image of particularity and universality that I have here is this. One is either locked in the general rules or stuck in particularity. A computer programmed to

---

21 1932 SC (HL) 31.
22 Ibid at 44.

apply a legal code will do so without reference to the outside. It will only refer to its own internal operations and ignore the reality outside. That will not impinge upon it. It will merely apply the results of its own internal operations to that reality. Rules are like that. To apply to everyone equally one has to abstract from the particularity of each person and make them legal subjects. In doing that what happens is that the actual person gets lost. The legal subject gets drawn into the referential cycle of the law and loses its connection with the real person. One can sum the point up in a phrase that people often use to express a (philistine?) view of art: "I know nothing about art but I know what I like." That person just sees the particular. Someone who, vice versa, says "I know everything about art but I don't know what I like", is someone who cannot get out of the universal. The former mistakenly thinks that you can know what you like without knowing about art. The latter mistakenly thinks that knowing everything about art determines what you like.

This is a problem that I face every day on my way to work, as I pass the beggars in my path. And it is also the problem of law. How to yoke the particular with the universal. For we cannot keep the smart card and the person behind it completely separate. We must not lose the connection. The connection between the smart card and the person must be maintained. Law, in its universalist form, takes the magic away from the social world by producing predictability and rationality. This is what the computer teller does. This is important, but the computer teller must know when the magic has to come back. When it is necessary to stop the "computer" merely repeating itself. When we should treat something as problematic or hard.

Look at it from the point of view of the library. I have presented the problem as one where the librarian has to break through the all-embracing system to encounter the concrete student without losing the system rationality of the library. I hinted that what we call love is the yoking of the routine of marriage with the passion of the lover. This is the full realisation of the relationship. Heteronomy and autonomy are yoked together. But how do we know when it is right to move from the one to the other? When is the librarian right to switch from the system rationality of the library and consider the concrete student?

(3) Love and encounter

This is just one way of stating perhaps the greatest problem of ethics. How do we know when it is right to act in a particular way? Take the good Samaritan again. It is, as I said, a parable of encounter. The theory or definition of neighbour helps us to know whom to encounter. My theory is tested in the crucible of the concrete encounter. But I have to recognise the universal in the particular encounter. I have to see how that particular person whom I help is connected with all the others. I have to see and recognise its connection to the world and to me. That will be the true test. We have to see that individual, trailing their history behind them. They are not socialised by it but rather it is part of them. This is the way we can understand

Detmold when talking of precedent. He says that it is only particulars of the particular case that give us reasons for actions. Not the universal rules that we derive from them. However when we weigh particular cases one against the other, we do so by virtue of their attached universals. We weigh particulars with certain universals "particularly attached".[23]

The judgment scene in Matthew is apposite, if we wish to put it in more religious imagery.

> Then shall the king say to them that shall be on his right hand: come ye blessed of my Father, possess you the kingdom prepared for you from the foundation of the world. For I was hungry, and you gave me to eat; I was thirsty and you gave me to drink; I was a stranger and you took me in (25:34-35)

The point here is that it is God, the expression of universal rationality, who is the concrete particular, lying injured on the street. It is He who is aided by the good Samaritan. The Samaritan sees not just the beggar, but in that beggar he sees the Divine. And it is because of that he knows what to do.

Thus far my point has been to show how law should, in general, operate in the machine-like way. But at the same time how it should know when to be creative. When to break out of the machine mode and to rethink in the encounter with the concrete. It is the joining together of these two spheres, the autonomous and the heteronomous, that is the full realisation of legality. There, law and love are not destructive of each other but are opposite sides of the same coin.

Let us now look at love as the principle that bridges the two spheres. Think of the image of the student in the face of the human/computer librarian. The librarian needs, at the correct time, to break through the system and reach the student. It is the love and the need for love that makes the librarian do it. But is that not like saying the librarian should be autonomous like the student? Should not the librarian be like Stephen in our story? Here we come to the deep intertwining of both heteronomy and autonomy. Love transforms both. It shows how autonomy must find itself in dependence and need. There is a jump and a risk to be taken by both sides. Autonomy needs love, otherwise it is mere caprice. For in a way the individual itself can become a heteronomous system. It is lost in itself. It thinks that it is looking outside. But, instead of looking through a glass, it looks through a mirror. It does everything for what it sees outside—but what it sees outside is itself. Thus Stephen, or the student in the library, must also be aware that autonomy does not mean he is the only person in the world; that everyone is only there to do his will. That form of "autonomy" is really heteronomy since you are lost in your own comfortable world. And even when he sees that, Stephen risks much for he risks losing himself in the heteronomy of the system world. The librarian jumps and risks the comfortable world where everything is predictable and known. He or she must risk love and

---

23 Detmold, *Unity of Law and Morality*, 179.

make the connection. The risk is great. Hayek was wrong when he thought the great society was fragile. Its system rationality, the relentless application of the law, protects it. That is what we risk when we make the jump. So both risk much. Both might be safe in their world but they need to jump out and connect. It is that love that transforms the system world of law into legality where law and love do not destroy one another.

Why take this risk? I finish with a fable. If all reference to the outside world is stopped by the smart card or the mirror, then the *you* I see is something that is constructed by my system. Morally that means that I do not treat you as anything other than my instrument—I make what I want of you. I am a tyrant. Why should I do otherwise? Consider God—all-powerful and all-loving. He creates us in His own image. But we are not just His creatures. He allows us autonomy, risks the introduction of caprice and will into His comfortable system world. Why? Because of His love.

[9]
On Law and Logic

CARLOS E. ALCHOURRÓN

Abstract. The main purpose of this paper is to explore the role played by logic in the legal domain. In the traditional conception which underlies the movement of codification, judges are able to find in the legal system (the Master System) a unique answer for every legal problem. This entails its completeness, consistency and the possibility of deriving from it the contents of all judicial decisions. Although the ideal model of this conception is supported by important theoretical and political ideals, it has significant shortcomings. The elements of normative systems (Master Systems) are "norms" and not mere "norm-formulations." A "norm" is the meaning attributed to normative linguistic expressions. The set of all normative expressions, such as statutes, codes, etc. forms what is called the Master Book. One of the main problems for the ideal model is the identification of a normative system behind the Master Book. Interpretative arguments are the tools designed to solve these problems. Although the requirements of the model are not totally fulfilled in actual practice, it remains as an effective ideal rational goal behind legal activities linked to adjudication and most theoretical approaches to law.

1. Introduction

The role of logic in law has sometimes been overestimated and sometimes underestimated. There are several reasons that can explain these misconceptions. One stems from the idea that logic is concerned with the laws of thought, aiming to describe and to guide the way people argue about different topics. From this perspective the function of logic in law would be the description of different forms of argument displayed to justify legal positions in order to find out how to improve these arguments. This would be a wonderful task, but unfortunately logic is not able to perform it. Logic cannot tell us how to improve our argumentative abilities. It can only show whether and how our conclusions are grounded on the premises used in our arguments. The justification of the conclusion is always a relative matter, since it depends upon the premises considered. Nevertheless, different logics can afford different kinds of justification. An invalid argument can be shown to be valid with a different logical analysis of the statements involved, or from the perspective of a different logic. From the metatheoretical point of view, logic can be used to evaluate the consistency and completeness of a legal system, even though it cannot give us any help in the task of overcoming the inconsistencies or the gaps that may be found in a legal system.

In the history of science logic is intrinsically connected with one of the scientific ideals that characterizes western scientific thought: the deductive or axiomatic organization of a field of research. In a historical perspective the evolution of this ideal is linked with the evolution of geometry. The project of Euclid was to organize the field of all geometrical truths in such a way that from a selection of some of them all others can be logically derived. The same idea is found in Aristotle's conception of a demonstrative science. The effective realization of this ideal showed how many difficulties it must overcome. It was not until the beginning of this century, in the hands of Hilbert, that Euclidean geometry was completely organized in a deductive form. One of the obstacles stems from our natural enthymematic way of thinking. We usually take for granted, without noticing, many important assumptions that logic may help to identify. Hilbert's axiomatization shows how many unconscious suppositions passed unnoticed for centuries. It is interesting to recall that the first theorem derived by Euclid from his axioms did not follow logically from them. In fact one of the aims of the axiomatic deductive method is to make explicit all the assumptions used in our natural way of arguing. A methodological strategy, closely related to the axiomatic approach, that has proved very fruitful in the history of science, is that of abstracting certain features of a complex reality to build a simplified model of it in order to work with it instead of the richer reality we are interested in. Examples of this procedure can be found in any science. In political philosophy the abstract models of those theories that work with idealized social contracts constitute instances of the abstracting procedure. The fact is that in an abstract model it proves easier to look for a deductive organization and check for implicit assumptions.

The ideal of the deductive organization is also present in the field of law as well as in legal science (legal dogmatics). In this paper I should like to comment on its possibilities, its political background, its limitations, the kind of conception attached to it as regards the nature of law, and the commitments that follow from it.

Law can be seen as a tool to organize the way of life of in a certain society. Certain general patterns of behavior are necessary to guide the actions that should or can be done. This suggests the convenience of having an explicit formulation of the rules designed to perform this guiding function. Once we have them it is assumed that the particular decisions will be taken in accordance with the relevant rules of the set. In this ideal model the set of rules are the starting points (axioms) for deriving the instructions to follow in each particular concrete situation. I will call the legal conception that stems from this ideal model the conception of the Master System. The ideal

2. The Master System

In legal history the Master System conception is naturally associated with the various codification movements, as well as with their successes and their failures. It is also associated with the rationalistic natural law school of the eighteenth century. Nevertheless, the abstract ideal model is not necessarily committed to many of the putative mistakes of these historical movements. Its impact on law can be detected in every contemporary legal system. There are several political and theoretical reasons that justify it as an effective ideal.

In contemporary society there are at least three principles that have particular significance in relation to the Master System conception. They are:

(A) *Principle of unavoidability*: Judges must resolve all the cases submitted to them within the sphere of their competence.

This requirement often appears in positive law in the form of a prohibition against declining to decide a case, and even though each judge is obliged to resolve only the cases within his competence, it is supposed that the competence of all the judges, taken together, is exhaustive. So it is assumed that for each and every possible case there is a judge with competence and the obligation to provide a solution.

(B) *Principle of justification*: A judicial decision requires a ground or reason and the judges must state the reasons for their decisions.

Not only is it the unavoidable duty of a judge to resolve all cases submitted to him within the limits of his competence; it is also required of him that his decision should not be arbitrary and that he should give reasons justifying the solution he adopts. The purpose of this principle is to eliminate one of the possible sources of the injustice which might infect judicial decisions without sufficient reasons.

This requirement is also almost universally embodied in positive law in the form of obligations imposed upon judges by rules (or codes) of procedure.

(C) *Principle of legality*: Judicial decisions must be grounded on legal norms of the State.

This principle is complementary to the previous one: It is held that every decision requires not merely grounds, but grounds of a special kind: they must be legal. The judge must not go beyond the sphere of the state's law, by appealing to the law of another state or to non-legal (e.g., moral) norms, except in cases where the law itself authorizes him to do so. And even in these cases the ultimate ground for decision will be a legal norm of the system.

The principle imposes a restriction on the selection of grounds, limiting the range of statements which may appear as acceptable grounds.

We can summarize the three principles mentioned above by saying:

(D) Judges must resolve all cases submitted to them within the limit of their competence by means of decisions grounded on legal norms of the system.

It is assumed that this principle does not impose an impossible obligation. Judges are able to fulfill its requirements. The possibility of satisfying (D) entails the truth of:

(E) In any legal system there are norms that supply grounds for solving every possible case.

This is the Postulate of Completeness (absence of gaps) of legal systems. The above argument shows how the truth of the postulate is assumed behind apparently innocent rules.

The truth or falsity of the postulate depends mainly on (i) how the notion of justification is interpreted and (ii) how the elements of a legal system are identified.

In the ideal version I am discussing, two conditions must be satisfied in order to provide an adequate justification: (1) the content of a decision should be a logical consequence of the premises that ground it, and (2) the normative premises used in the justification should be general. The only exception admitted to (1) is when the general rules give the judge discretion to take his decision within certain limits, as is the case, for example, with penalties and compensations.

The kernel of this notion of justification has suggestive analogies with Carl G. Hempel's theory of explanation of particular facts in empirical sciences. According to Hempel an explanation of an empirical event is a logical deduction whose consequence is a description of the fact to be explained (the *explanandum*) and the premises (the *explanans*) are statements of two kinds: a set of general laws and a set of singular statements describing the initial antecedent conditions. Several adequacy conditions should be fulfilled in every explanation: (i) the *explanandum* should be logically entailed by the *explanans*, (ii) the *explanans* must contain general laws and (iii) the sentences constituting the *explanandum* must be true. The explanation consists in showing that the phenomenon to be explained is a particular case of a general law. General laws supply the basic explanatory element in every explanation and logic takes the job of linking their conceptual content with what actually is the case.

Although empirical sciences do not have an explanation for every fact, the pursuit of scientific investigation is grounded on the belief that there is an explanation for every fact. The principle of universal causation (a version of the principle of sufficient reason) is the analogue of the normative principle of completeness.

As to the identification of the elements of the normative system to be used as grounds in a justification, there are different versions of the theory according to the distinct ways of making the distinction between the so called formal and material sources of law. The strictest version takes statute law as the only formal source, customs as well as other kinds of norms are considered only when statutes indicate the circumstances in which they have to be taken into account. A strict distinction between creation and application of law would make it pointless to consider precedents as a formal source of law. If a judicial decision follows from a statute, it adds nothing to it and if it does not follow it should not be taken into account because the judge has not fulfilled his duty to apply the law without modifying it. Other versions will also include precedents and customary norms in a subordinate position.

The distinction between normal and material sources of law is closely connected with the definition of positive law. The opinion of the experts, which constitutes so-called legal dogmatics, has a prominent role in some countries but only as a material source. The most controversial issue is the question whether morality is or is not a formal source of law. That it is a material source is beyond question.

The conception is supported by certain political ideals. In the first place it derives from the political doctrine of the separation of powers. More specifically, the separation of the legislative power from the judicial power supplies one of the grounds for this conception. According to this doctrine the legislative power is the main competent authority to specify the general rules to guide and to evaluate people's behavior within the community. The function of the judicial power is only to resolve particular cases according to the general rules enacted by the legislature. There are several political reasons that ground this kind of separation. In the first place we have the argument from equality. Whenever judges limit themselves to applying the general rules enacted by the parliament, all cases of the same type will receive the same solution. Thus the requirement of the political ideal of formal equality justifies the separation of powers. Then we have the argument from democracy. In those countries in which the members of the parliament are democratically elected, which usually is not the case with the members of the judiciary, a sharp separation allows democratic control of the way of solving disagreements between members of the community. Thirdly we have the argument from certainty and security. Only by means of a strict division of powers are people able to know their rights and duties *in advance* of judicial decisions. Any decision not justified as required is considered arbitrary, in the sense that the adjudicated rights or duties are fixed *ex post facto* by the judge.

Of course, even if it were possible to maintain the sharp separation in the above way, the results do not certify the intrinsic qualities of the solutions adopted. The justice of judicial decisions derives in the model from the justice of the legislated general norms. Moreover, as long as equity requires in some cases a particular solution different from the treatment of standard cases there is no place for it in this theory.

The Master System conception has been designed to give satisfaction to the political ideals of security and formal equality, but it cannot guarantee other ideals, such as justice and equity. Since this limitation restricts its importance, we need to see how much of it can be preserved in the light of the constraints of actual practice and other political requirements and look for its impact in the practice of law. The postulate of completeness is one of the conditions that the Master System should satisfy in order to offer the security and objectivity required. Nevertheless, completeness is not sufficient; the system must also be consistent.

The postulate of completeness requires the System to have a normative solution for every case. Quite often it has been said that this is an impossible demand since no one is in a position to know, nor even to imagine, the potentially infinite variety of cases that may occur in a society. In an important sense this is true, but there is an ambiguity in the legal notion of "case" that may help to understand the scope of the requirement. Thus, for example, we speak about the case of political murder as well as the case of the murder of Mahatma Gandhi or the case of the murder of J. F. Kennedy, of the case of divorce and the case of the divorce of Lady Diana. It is obvious that the word "case" does not have the same meaning in these phrases. Gandhi's and Kennedy's murders are real events, that happened in a certain place and at a certain moment of time. The expression "case of political murder" does not refer to any concrete event, it is the mere description of certain properties of a set of events. The property of being a political murder may be instantiated in an unlimited number of concrete occurrences. In order to remove the ambiguity I will introduce the expressions "individual case" and "generic case," respectively, for each concrete particular event and for a class of concrete events that have a common property.

The postulate of completeness is concerned with generic cases. But since metatheoretical notions like completeness impose different constraints in different contexts, the meaning intended here will be introduced with an example borrowed from Argentinian law. It is known as the problem of the recovery of real estate from third party holders. The problem arises when someone in possession of a real estate—which is owned not by him but by someone else—transfers it (by way of sale or gift) to a third party. Then the question arises whether (and if so, in what circumstances) the owner of the real estate may recover its possession from the third party. Or to put the question in other terms: In what circumstances does the third party have an obligation to restore it to its owner and in what circumstances (if any) may he keep it, i.e., to refuse to restore it? The legislator made a classification according to three relevant properties: the good faith of the former possessor (the transferor), the good faith of the present holder (the transferee) and the onerous character of the act of assignment (transfer). The legislator gave special provisions for several combinations of the relevant properties, but he left no indication as how to solve the generic case in which both the transferee and the transferor have acted in good faith and the transfer was onerous.

The general structure of the situation is as follows. For a certain legal problem the norms of the system select as relevant a set of properties. Taking into account the presence or absence of each of the relevant properties, it is possible to construct a set of "elementary generic cases." That is, cases in which each of the relevant properties is either present or absent. The case in which both the transferee and the transferor have acted in good faith and the transfer was onerous, is, in our example, an elementary generic case. When for each of the elementary cases there is in the system a norm giving an answer to the legal problem in question, the system is complete. When, on the contrary (as in the problem of the third party holder) no norm of the system indicates how to deal with the normative question in an elementary case, the generic elementary case is a *normative gap* in the system. The class of all elementary cases forms an exhaustive and mutually exclusive classification (a partition) of all the individual cases. Each individual case must belong to one elementary generic case and cannot belong to more than one of them. In this sense, a complete system that gives answers to all elementary generic cases indirectly provides normative solutions to all individual cases.

Although the procedure has been exemplified in relation to a specific legal problem, it should be clear how it can be generalized to take into account the class of legal problems dealt with in a legal system. It is important to emphasize that problems of completeness (as well as problems of consistency) are *relative* to a set of norms and a set of (generic) cases. This relativization allows us to isolate in a system those areas in which there is a normative gap. Gaps of this kind are called "normative" because they arise from the fact that the system lacks a general norm to deduce normative consequences for a generic case. Whether the relevant properties are more or less vague is irrelevant for this notion of completeness. Deduction of normative answers for generic cases from general norms of the system is not disturbed by the vagueness of the relevant properties involved. Vagueness can present problems only when we try to subsume an individual case under a generic case.

There is no other way to overcome a normative gap than to extend the normative system, incorporating a new norm to resolve the unprovided for case. Many well-known arguments provide different forms of filling the gap in the way that is most harmonious with other parts of a legal system. Sometimes an argument from analogy or *e contrario* is the most suitable. On other occasions an appeal to a general principle of law or the goal of the statute or the intention of the legislator may supply a more satisfactory way out of the difficulty.

The postulate of consistency requires the non-existence of incompatible normative solutions derived from a set of norms for a generic case. Normative solutions provided by the Master System for each generic case must be compatible. Although the relevant notion of compatibility is a main focus of research in deontic logic, I will not discuss the topic, since for the present purpose the intuitive pre-analytic notion is sufficient. It is possible for a generic case to be resolved inconsistently relative to a set of norms and at the same time for another generic case to be resolved consistently by the same set of norms. But in some cases the inconsistency is immediate. An example of this kind of inconsistency is found in the prescriptions of articles 97 and 112 of the Civil Code of Louisiana. According to the former "The minor of either sex, who has attained the competent age to marry, must have received the consent of his father and mother ... ." But article 112 prescribes that "The marriage of minors, contracted without the consent of the father and mother, can not for that cause be annulled ... ." Is the marriage of a minor contracted without the consent of one of his living parents annullable? According to article 112 the answer is clearly negative, but according to article 97 the marriage seems to be annullable since for its validity the consent of both parents is required.

On the standard interpretation, these articles express incompatible norms. But the fact that with a different interpretation the norms expressed by these articles may be compatible shows an important characteristic of the notion of normative consistency: It is a property of the *meanings* attached to normative texts and not of the normative texts themselves.

The postulates discussed so far are concerned with certain relations among norms contained in the Master System. The system is a set of norms, not a set of linguistic expressions. By a "norm" I understand *the meaning* that may be attached to a linguistic expression, not the linguistic expression itself.

Thus since the paragraphs of a statute, a constitution or a code are linguistic entities, they do not form part of the system. I will refer collectively to the totality of all legal texts as the Master Book. This means that when a paragraph of a statute receives two different interpretations, i.e., when it expresses two different norms, each of the norms form part of a different Master System coordinated with the same Master Book. Each of the different interpretations of the Master Book gives rise to a different Master System.

Only when a Master System is identified, that is, when we work with an interpretation of the Master Book, may we inquire after its consistency and completeness. Independently of its interpretation, it does not make sense to ask, regarding two normative expressions, whether they are consistent or not. On one interpretation they may express compatible norms but on a different interpretation they may be incompatible. A provision which may resolve a generic case under a certain interpretation may be a gap on a different understanding.

The interpretations of the Master Book should be empirical. The meanings attached to its linguistic elements must include reference to concrete situations of everyday life. This fact, which is the condition of the possibility of applying the general norms of the Master System, is also the source of most of the uncertainties that legal interpretation must overcome to approximate to the ideal model.

Since the starting point is always the Master Book, the ideal conception requires that there be one and only one clear Master System attached to it.

From a theoretical point of view, the ideal of the Master System is the ideal of maximum objectivity. For this reason it is not surprising that enormous efforts have been made to try to reach the ideal without abandoning other political goals.

Hart once called the picture of the Master System conception a "noble dream," recognizing the positive nature of the ideals that lie behind it and at the same time the unrealistic assumptions on which it is based. Most of the unrealistic assumptions derive from the interpretative difficulties of the Master Book.

3. The Master Book

In relation to an ideal such as the present one, there are several dangers. The first is the rationalist illusion of believing that the ideal is realized in some or in all normative systems. The second stems from not noticing that because there are other ideals that point in different directions, it may not even be convenient to try to maximize its requirements.

The fact that the Master Book is written in ordinary language presents the well-known difficulties derived from ambiguities and vagueness. I will now recall the standard problem of ambiguity to introduce a subject which has not been analyzed as much as it deserves: the problem of defeasibility.

Legal texts are expressed in natural language. The rules that give meaning to natural language expressions are the starting point of any interpretation. The fact that most expressions are ambiguous, i.e., that they have more than one meaning, is, in an important sense, a virtue of natural languages, since it allows speakers to express a large class of concepts with a restricted vocabulary. In most contexts the plurality of meanings of a term causes no problem in identifying the sense of the sentences in which it occurs. Nevertheless there are circumstances in which semantic or syntactic ambiguities may leave the sense of a normative expression undetermined. Moreover, some words have a technical legal sense different from their ordinary meaning, so that in some contexts it may be doubtful in which of its senses a word has been used.

In every process of linguistic communication we must analyze the situation from the point of view of the person who utters a sentence to communicate some conceptual content and from the point of view of the interpreter who tries to grasp the conceptual content communicated. When an ambiguous term occurs in a sentence it may be that the term was not used ambiguously by the utterer—the utterer may have intended to communicate a definite sense with one of the several meanings of an ambiguous term. In such a case the expression was not ambiguous from the point of view of the utterer. Nevertheless it may be ambiguous from the point of view of the interpreter for he may not have sufficient evidence for the meaning effectively used by the utterer. In this case the indeterminacy exists only from the interpreter's point of view. Of course, the ambiguity from the utterer's point of view is independent from the ambiguity of the interpreter's point of view.

This independence of the two points of view has important consequences for identifying a "creative" element in a process of legal interpretation. To know, for example, whether the interpreter has changed the norm expressed in a normative text, making it more specific or revising it, both points of view should be considered.

Whenever an expression is ambiguous from the interpreter's point of view he has, in order to overcome the indeterminacy, no other choice but to select one of the alternative meanings, making use of his evaluative perspective. Nevertheless, if the expression was not ambiguous for the legislator and the interpreter has selected the same meaning used by the legislator, then the norm expressed by the legislative text is for both, the legislator and the interpreter, the same. Although the interpreter has used in the interpretation his evaluative perspective he has not introduced any modification in the norms of the system. Any decision based on his interpretation is a logical consequence of the preexisting norms of the system. In this sense his interpretation is not "creative." In most cases this coincidence is a consequence of the existence of a common set of basic values shared by the interpreter and the legislator.

In order to know whether an interpretation has modified the law there is no other option but to compare the meanings attributed to a text by the interpreter and the meanings attributed to it by the legislator.

It is a well-known fact that more often than not it is very difficult, and in many cases practically impossible, to identify the precise meaning attached to a text by the norm-giver; in particular, when the law-giver is a corporate body. The communicative model of interpretation faces a substantial task in detecting those changes in the law introduced by judges in their task of adjudication.

Even though the linguistic phenomenon of ambiguity does not entail the introduction of an evaluative creative element, it is one of the factors that contributes to create an indeterminacy of the normative system that can be overcome only by an evaluative selective operation.

Independently of this standard notion of ambiguity there is a more complicated kind of indeterminacy which is not usually discussed. In Artificial Intelligence and in Logic the problem is known as the problem of nonmonotonicity or defeasibility.

Often, in ordinary language, conditional constructions of the form "If A then B" are used in such a way that it is not intended to assert with them that the antecedent A is a sufficient condition of the consequent B, but only that the antecedent jointly with a set of assumptions accepted in the context of utterance of the conditional is sufficient for the consequent B. Such is, for example, the case when it is asserted, in relation to a certain gas sample, that its volume will increase if the temperature rises, assuming in the context that the pressure is kept constant. The conditional assertion is defeated when some implicit assumption is not true.

A defeasible conditional can also be defined as one which has implicit exceptions. In the example, a variation in the gas's pressure is an implicit exception that defeats the conditional assertion. In relation to a defeasible conditional we may have the truth of "If A then B" jointly with the falsity of "If A and C then B." When such is the case circumstance C is an exception that *defeats* the conditional "If A then B." The above is the standard definition in logic of defeasible conditionals. That is, a conditional is defeasible if the following inference pattern (called *Strengthening of the Antecedent*) is logically invalid: From "If A then B" it follows that "If A and C then B."

Most of our ordinary language conditional statements are, in this sense, defeasible. The idea of defeasibility is connected to the notion of "normality." We make our assertions for normal circumstances, knowing that in some situations our statements will be defeated. The notion of normality is relative to the set of beliefs of the speaker and the context of utterance. What counts as normal for a person in a certain context may be abnormal for another person or for the same person in a different context.

Most, if not all, normative formulations are defeasible, i.e., they usually have implicit exceptions, i.e., circumstances that defeat the norm though they are not explicitly stated. Even a very simple and clear rule like "every driver should stop at a red traffic light" may have exceptions not explicitly formulated. For this reason Hart held that rules should be read as ending with a clause like "unless ..." intending to assert that they have an undetermined set of implicit exceptions. Usually our understanding of the rule will allow us to give a list of implicit exceptions as well as a list of circumstances which are not mentioned because they are rejected as exceptions. But the relativity of the notion of normality makes many situations ambiguous from the interpreter's point of view. The above traffic rule may be understood by someone coming from California with the tacit exception "unless turning right" which would be excluded in European countries. Unless the exceptions are made explicit the conceptual content of the normative expression is left undetermined.

But how shall we identify the implicit exceptions to a normative formulation? How shall we know what meaning is attached to a defeasible normative expression, that is, how shall we know which norm is expressed by that expression? To answer these questions I will use a dispositional notion of defeasibility. Although this is not the only way to deal with the subject, the approach is particularly suitable for the analysis of some problems of legal interpretation.

According to the dispositional approach a condition C counts as an *implicit exception* to a conditional assertion "if A then B" made by a speaker X at time

T when there is a disposition of X at time T to assert the conditional "if A then B" whilst rejecting "if A and C then B." This means that C is an exception to be included in the conceptual content expressed by the conditional, if it is the case that X at time T would have made the exception had he considered the case of having A jointly with C as antecedent of the conditional. On the other hand, a condition C counts as an *implicit non-exception* when there is a disposition of X at time T to assert the conditional "if A then B" jointly with "if A and C then B." This means that C is to be excluded as an exception in the conceptual content of the conditional if it is the case that X at time T would *not* have made the exception had he considered the case of having A jointly with C as antecedent of the conditional. It should be noticed that there may be circumstances in which a condition C is not an implicit exception nor an implicit non-exception. This is the case when at time T there is no disposition in X to include C as an exception nor a disposition to exclude C as an exception. The exceptional character of C is, in such a case, undetermined. Hence the conceptual content of the conditional is also undetermined in relation to C. So a condition C has three possibilities: It may be (i) an *implicit exception*, (ii) an *implicit non-exception* or it may be (iii) *undetermined* as an exception.

In legal contexts the dispositional account of defeasibility has some consequences that may seem paradoxical. Suppose that the legislator at the time of enacting a statute did not foresee a certain circumstance C. Of course, at that time he was not in a position to present C as an explicit exception but if it is the case that had he considered C he would have introduced it as an exception, the dispositional account considers C as an implicit exception even at the time of the enactment. In the norm expressed by the statute C is an exception. The explanation of this apparently surprising result is that since we are trying to understand the conceptual content of a speech act we must take into account the utterer's set of factual and evaluative beliefs; this amounts to taking into account his dispositions to react in different circumstances. Thus the purpose of the dispositional account is to fix the conceptual content of normative texts considering the evaluative standpoint of the legislator.

Clearly it is convenient to make explicit what is implicit. Legal science and judicial experience continually perform this task of making explicit the implicit assumptions and exceptions. This attitude follows from the same policy that requires the enactment of a clear statute instead of a customary rule with the same conceptual content. Nevertheless, since unforeseen circumstances by their very nature cannot be made explicit, it seems wise to leave open the formulation of exceptions for those abnormal cases. In this sense Neil MacCormick (1991) wrote: "Notoriously, it would be extremely difficult, perhaps impossible, and for sure the enemy of any kind of clarity or cognoscibility in law, to attempt a formulation of every conceivable precondition of validity in every statement of every rule. So general formulations of rights are apt to leave many background conditions unstated, especially those which arise only in rather exceptional cases." Nevertheless, as implicit exceptions in a normative text are often made explicit in other texts, the task has sometimes already been performed by the legislator. Systemic interpretation allows us to reconstruct, in such cases, the conceptual content of each of the norms of the system.

The relevance of defeasibility in legal argument can be illustrated by recalling the famous case *The Church of the Holy Trinity v. United States*. The Supreme Court of the United States was confronted with a legal disposition that did not make any distinction for a circumstance which was axiologically relevant for the Court. The statute made it unlawful for any person to assist or encourage the importation of any alien into the United States under a contract or agreement made prior to the importation of that alien in order for the alien to perform *labor or service of any kind*. The Church of the Holy Trinity made an arrangement with a British pastor by the terms of which he was to come to the United States and enter into the church's service as a rector and pastor. The circumstance that the contracted person was to serve as a pastor was for the Supreme Court a relevant circumstance even though it was not mentioned in the statute. The Court asserted that it has to be "presumed that the Legislature intended exceptions to its language ... The common sense of man approves the judgment mentioned by Puffendorf that the Bolognian law which enacted 'that whoever drew blood in the streets should be punished with the utmost severity' did not extend to the surgeon who opened the vein of a person that fell down in a street in a fit." This statement is a clear recognition of the defeasible nature of legal normative expressions.

It is clear that the normative *text* does not contain any exception. The important question in identifying the existence of a "creative" element in the Court's decision is whether the norm expressed in the statute's text contains, or does not contain, the exception. For this purpose we have to consider the three alternatives mentioned above.

Let us assume first that the legislator did not in fact consider the particular circumstance of the case, but let us also assume that if he had considered the circumstance he would have made the same exception that was made by the Court. In this case the exception was implicit in the legislative text, and according to the dispositional approach to defeasibility the norm expressed by the text contains the exception as one of its conditions. This means that the norm used by the Court to justify the decision is the same norm that was expressed by the legislator. Although the members of the Court made use of their evaluative perspective they did not introduce any modification in the legal system. The content of the decision follows from the existing norms.

For the second alternative let us assume that the circumstance was undetermined for the legislator. Had he noticed it he would neither include nor exclude it as an exception. Then the interpretation of the Court amounts to a change of the legislative norm. Following their evaluative perspective the members of the Court have enriched the content of the legislative norm by the addition of an exception. But since the exception was not excluded by the legislator the modification is compatible with the previous norm and amounts to supplying a more precise normative content to the statute.

Finally, if the particular circumstance of the case were an implicit non-exception for the legislator because he would have rejected an exception, the Court's interpretation has introduced a norm incompatible with the legislative norm. In the last two alternatives there would be a creative interpretation. The evaluative perspective of the Court would be the source of a new norm. Since defeasibility (or at least the kind of pragmatic defeasibility here considered) is a phenomenon that occurs in a process of human communication, it is not surprising that in legal contexts its discussion is linked to conjectures about the law-giver's intentions with all the well-known shortcomings of such references. Thus what appears to be a historical investigation hides the political preferences of the interpreter. Nevertheless this historical comparison is necessary to know the kind of fit existing between judicial and legislative interpretation. Defeasibility, more than simple ambiguity, makes the identification of the norms of a legal system very difficult. So it is one of the factors that makes it necessary, in most situations, to introduce evaluative operations and the use of axiological standards in the interpretation of normative texts.

One of the main problems that arises in the application of general norms to individual cases is the classification of an individual case as belonging to one of the generic cases. Jurists usually refer to this problem by the name of *subsumption*.

The difficulties of the classification of the individual case may arise from two sources. The first is lack of information concerning some relevant fact. Sometimes we do not know whether or not a concrete fact (individual case) belongs to a class (generic case), because we lack the necessary information; there are some aspects of the fact that we do not know, and this lack of knowledge is the cause of the difficulty in classifying the case. For example, even knowing that every case of transfer is necessarily made with or without consideration, we can very well not know whether the transfer of Peter's house to Andrew has been made with or without consideration, simply because we do not know whether Andrew has paid anything for the house or not.

But the difficulty of knowing whether Peter transferred his house with or without consideration may arise from yet another source: the semantic indeterminacy or vagueness of general words. Even with full knowledge of the facts of the case, we may not know whether the transfer was made with or without consideration because we do not know whether the amount of money Andrew gave to Peter for his house is or is not a price in the technically relevant sense. Let us suppose that the amount of money handed over is markedly less than the economic value of the house. In such a circumstance it may be doubtful whether it is a sale or a concealed gift.

Overcoming the uncertainty derived from semantic indeterminacy, which Hart calls problems of the penumbra, requires the use of evaluative standards to justify the interpreter's decision.

In a disposition like "no one shall be criminally liable for an act committed in self-defense," independently of the ambiguities that may disturb its interpretation, significant doubts may arise about whether an act of self-defense was excessive or proportionate to the aggression received. The difficulty may stem from a lack of information about the facts that occurred or, as shown above, from the vagueness of the notion of proportionality. The vagueness of general words implies that sooner or later difficulties will appear in the subsumption of a particular case under a certain category. All general words suffer from some degree of vagueness which may make it undecidable whether some object or situation falls within or outside its field of reference.

In situations of ambiguity the source of the trouble is an excess of meaning. Vagueness on the contrary stems from a lack of sufficient determination of meaning. In both situations the meaning indeterminacy forces the interpreter to perform a selection based on evaluative considerations that may go beyond the immediate linguistic information received by him.

4. Interpretative Arguments

Systemic problems (normative incompleteness and inconsistency) as well as linguistic indeterminacies (ambiguity, defeasibility and vagueness) make the use of evaluative considerations necessary in adjudication. From a broader perspective, evaluative considerations are involved in *every* process of adjudication either in the selection of the norms used to ground the decision or in the identification of the relevant "facts" of the case at hand. In this sense interpretation is always an evaluative activity. The formalist illusion of the purely deductive model has to be given up. But in order to see the force of the model as an ideal it is convenient to observe the kinds of arguments used to justify the evaluative selections, the elements included in them and the motives that lie behind their use.

There is a group of arguments which are related to the systemic nature of law. Their function is to justify evaluative selections pointing to other elements of the normative system. For example, in an argument from contextual harmonization a statutory provision is understood within a larger scope. Its meaning is identified in the light of closely related provisions of the same statute or of a set of related statutes, showing that the proposed meanings are evaluatively coherent with other sections of the statute or with related sections *in pari materia* of other statutes. Sometimes the argument is strengthened by arguments from general principles of various kinds. Some principles are related to certain institutions. The principles that supply grounds for some dispositions are used to make clear the meanings of other provisions. Behind these principles lie some inductive operations designed to extend the scope of some norms showing their common evaluative reasons, which may be used to resolve situations not explicitly regulated or whose solution remains uncertain for reasons of linguistic indeterminacy. Systematic arguments from analogy also have this inductive nature. Their function is to extend the evaluative reasons that ground some norms to circumstances that share some common properties in the identification of the generic or individual cases considered. Arguments of this kind are conceptually linked to arguments from precedent. The argument from precedent is designed to show the intersubjective character of the evaluative standpoint used in the interpretation as well as to satisfy the requirement of equality. Of a different nature are arguments from general legal or moral principles. In them, the principle often directly supplies the general norm to justify the resolution of cases unprovided for, or wrongly provided for by specific norms. In other cases the principle supplies the evaluative grounds for the justification of the norm needed for the case.

It is very difficult to make an exhaustive classification of interpretative arguments; the above is only a sample of some recurrent systemic arguments. A non-systemic argument which should be mentioned for its peculiar features is the argument from intention.

According to the argument from intention, the interpreter tries to follow the intention of the legislator. The argument has two versions: the "subjective" and the "objective." In the subjective version the decisive element is the historical intention of the author of the legal text or the intention embraced by members of the legislature in the process of legislation. The objective intention is the intention ascribed to the legislature as an ideal rational legislator responsible for enacting that set of provisions in the relevant political circumstances.

In some cases there is sufficient evidence of the subjective intention of the historical legislator. That is the case with the Argentinian Civil Code, which was written by a single man: Dalmacio Vélez Sarfield. The situation is particularly clear because he used to comment in footnotes on the contents of the various paragraphs of the Code. Of course this is not the standard case. Quite often the *travaux préparatoires* do not provide adequate evidence of any particular intention, or they contain so many conflicting statements of intention as to open again a broad range of judicial choice.

In any case, the subjective and the objective version have different purposes. The subjective argument is designed to show a substantial evaluative agreement with the original historical legislator and involves essentially empirical evidence. The objective argument is of a different nature. It is an argument designed to uphold the intrinsic value of the proposed interpretation. For this reason it is assumed that every reasonable person would adopt, in the actual interpretative circumstances, the interpretation that fulfills the objective intention. The argument from objective intention is sometimes used to give prevalence to a current interpretation of some rights instead of the original historical interpretation.

It is clear that the objective and the subjective arguments may ground different and incompatible interpretations. Moreover, the same is the case with all interpretative arguments. Two different principles may point in opposite directions, so that it is necessary to weigh their relative importance for the case at hand. Taking into account different similarities, analogical arguments may support opposite interpretations.

Frequently more than one argument is applicable in a single situation. This might on certain occasions be no more than a case of coinciding arguments, but in some situations their individual strength may be increased by a cumulative effect. Nevertheless, just the opposite may occur: The plurality of arguments may justify rival interpretations. Conflicts between interpretative arguments in relation to cases of the same type are the result of partially incompatible evaluative points of view. So in order to overcome interpretative arguments with opposite results, we need to have some set of normative principles that allows us to interpret legal materials coherently. Thus we need some pattern that allows us to select between competing results of the use of interpretative arguments. I have described so far some of the interpretative arguments used in the actual practice of adjudication to justify the identification of the required norms. But the subject looks different if we adopt a normative conception of interpretation and adjudication. If we ask not how judges usually justify their selections but how they should interpret legal texts then the answer may differ substantially. From this perspective the most interesting question is concerned with those cases in which there are systemic problems (normative gaps or inconsistencies) or linguistic indeterminacies, that is, those cases in which no explicit rule firmly decides the case either way. Perhaps some judges try to follow the hypothetical subjective intention of the legislator. But is this the right way to solve the problem of adjudication in hard cases? As is well-known, Ronald Dworkin has given a negative answer to this question. His positive alternative, in what he calls "the rights conception," is that judges should identify those norms that best fit the background moral rights of the parties. From this point of view we have a general pattern for resolving the possible conflicts that may arise from different uses of interpretative arguments. All we need to know is which of the competing answers fits the underlying moral rights better. Nevertheless conflicting answers are not completely excluded by the rights conception. Such conflicts may arise from two sources: (i) because two interpreters hold different views about the background moral rights of the citizens, that is when they do not share a common set of moral principles, or (ii) because they have different conceptions of the notion of fitting, that is, when they disagree as to the coherence of the case at hand with the moral rights. Even though moral disagreements and different notions of internal moral coherence are not, as a matter of fact, excluded in the rights conception, the fact that that conception describes an ideal that should guide any process of adjudication entails that it should postulate a privileged moral set of principles, the true moral principles, and a privileged notion of moral coherence. Hence, since in Dworkin's approach moral principles form part of the law, the completeness and consistency of the Master System appear in new clothes.

This shows the enormous force of appeal of the model of the deductive system as an ideal. In the rights conception the model contains not only the formal ideals of completeness and consistency, but also the ideal of justice. I have mentioned Dworkin's approach because it is the most categorical in its conclusions, but I think the deductive ideals of the Master System are present behind most of the theories about interpretative and practical legal arguments. That law should provide a coherent and complete set of answers for every legal case is a theoretical and practical ideal that lies behind many contemporary developments in legal philosophy.

Reference

MacCormick, Neil D. 1991. *Defeasibility*. Typescript.

Part IV
Legal Interpretation and Politics

[10]

Legal Analysis as Institutional Imagination

*Roberto Mangabeira Unger**

The arrested development of legal thought

The genius of contemporary law

To grasp the potential of legal analysis to become a master tool of institutional imagination in a democratic society we must begin by understanding what is most distinctive about law and legal thought in the contemporary industrial democracies. In this effort no contrast is more revealing than the comparison of the substantive law and legal methods of today with the project of nineteenth-century legal science and the law of nineteenth-century commercial economies.

Consider how the law and legal thought of today may look to a future student who tries to identify its deepest and most original character within the larger sequence of legal history. Suppose that we use in this endeavour less the search for recurrent doctrinal categories and distinctions Holmes pursued in *The Common Law* than the reciprocal reading of vision and detail von Jhering offered in *The Spirit of the Roman Law*. The latter method rather than the former respects the place of law between imagination and power, and connects the self-understanding of legal thought to the central tradition of modern social theory founded by Montesquieu. Viewed in this light, the overriding theme of contemporary law and legal thought, and the one defining its genius, is the commitment to shape a free political and economic order by combining rights of choice with rules designed to ensure the effective enjoyment of these rights. Little by little, and in country after country of the rich Western world and of its poorer emulators, a legal consciousness has penetrated and transformed substantive law, affirming the empirical and defeasible character of individual and collective self-determination: its dependence upon practical conditions of enjoyment, which may fail.

This conception stands out by contrast to the single most influential idea in the law and legal thought of the nineteenth century, an idea developed as much in the case-oriented discourse of American and English jurists, or the aphoristic and conclusory utterances of French lawyers, as in the relentless category-grinding of the German pandectists. According to this earlier idea a certain system of rules and rights defines a free political and economic order. We uphold the order by clinging

---

* Professor Unger, Professor of Law, Harvard University, delivered the twenty-fourth Chorley Lecture on 31 May 1995 at the London School of Economics and Political Science, when he presented ideas developed in a forthcoming book to be published by Verso entitled *What Should Legal Analysis Become?*

to the predetermined system of rules and rights by preventing its perversion through politics, especially the politics of privilege and redistribution.

A consequence of this animating idea of contemporary law has been the reorganisation of one branch of law and legal doctrine after another as a binary system of rights of choice and of arrangements withdrawn from the scope of choice the better to make the exercise of choice real and effective. The governing aim of this dialectical organisation is to prevent the system of rules and rights from becoming or remaining a sham, concealing subjugation under the appearance of coordination.

Sometimes this binary reshaping takes place by marshalling countervailing rules and doctrines within a single branch of law, as when the doctrine of economic duress and of unequal bargaining power complements and qualifies the core rules of contract formation and enforceability, or when freedom to choose the terms in a labour contract is restricted by selective direct legal regulation of the employment relation. At other times the dual structure works by assigning the choice-restricting and freedom-sustaining arrangements to a distinct branch of law, as when collective bargaining law attempts to correct the inability of individual contract to compensate for the power disparities of the employment relation. At yet other times the dual structure has taken the form of a coexistence of two legal regimes for the governance of overlapping social problems. Thus, fault-based liability may be strengthened rather than undermined by the refusal to extend it to the compensation for the actualisation of the risks inherent in a line of business, and by the development of insurance systems disregarding fault-oriented standards of compensation.

The binary structure that has reorganised private law in every industrial democracy recurs, on a larger scale, in the relation of governmental regulation to private law as a whole. The entitlements afforded by the welfare state, and the enjoyment by workers of prerogatives relatively secure against labour-market instability and the business cycle, have been understood and developed by twentieth-century lawyers as devices for guaranteeing the effective enjoyment of the public-law and private-law rights of self-determination. If the market economy, representative democracy, and free civil society have certain inherited and necessary forms, these forms must nevertheless be refined and completed so that they may provide the reality as well as the appearance of free choice and coordination to every rights-bearing individual.

The supreme achievement of this sustained exercise in correction is to make the individual effectively able to develop and deploy a broad range of capacities. He can then form and execute his life projects, including those most important ones that he may need to imagine and advance through free association with other people. Class hierarchies may nevertheless have persisted with barely diminished force. The majority of the people may be an angry and marginalised although fragmented mass of individuals, who feel powerless at their jobs and hopeless about their national politics, while seeking solace and escape in private pleasure, domestic joys, and nostalgic traditionalism. According to this mode of thought, however, these burdens of history and imperfection merely show that we must patiently continue the work of securing the effective enjoyment of rights.

The theme of the dialectic between the realm of free economic and political choice and the realm of that which is withdrawn from choice for the sake of choice is all the more remarkable because it fails to track any specific ideological position within the debates of modern politics and modern political thought. It merely excludes positions that from the vantage point of those who inhabit this imaginative world may seem extremist. It excludes the old nineteenth-century idea that a particular scheme of private and public rights will automatically secure economic and political freedom if only it can be protected against redistributive interventionism. It also repels the radically reconstructive idea that no real and widely shared experience of individual and collective self-determination will be possible unless we revolutionise the present institutional system by substituting, for example, 'socialism' for 'capitalism.' Yet while the spirit of contemporary law may seem to antagonise only unbelievable or insupportable alternatives, it generates, in detail, endless practical and argumentative work for the analyst and the reformer. Thus, it resembles, in the generality of its scope and the fecundity of its effects, the general conception that preceded it in the history of law and legal thought: the project of a legal science that would reveal the in-built legal and institutional content of a free society and police its boundaries against invasion by politics.

The limit of contemporary legal thought

There is nevertheless a riddle in the career of this idea. Until we solve this riddle, we cannot correctly understand the genius — and the self-imposed poverty — of contemporary legal thought, nor can we fully appreciate the extent to which the development of law remains bound up with the fate of democratic experimentalism. When we begin to explore ways of ensuring the practical conditions for the effective enjoyment of rights, we discover at every turn that there are alternative plausible ways of defining these conditions, and then of satisfying them once they have been defined. For every right of individual or collective choice, there are different plausible conceptions of its conditions of effective realisation in society as now organised. For every such conception, there are different plausible strategies to fulfil the specified conditions.

Some of these conceptions and strategies imply keeping present institutional arrangements while controlling their consequences: by counteracting, for example, through tax-and-transfer or through preferment for disadvantaged groups, their distributive consequences. Other conceptions and strategies, however, imply a piecemeal but cumulative change of these institutional arrangements. These structure-defying and structure-transforming solutions may in turn go in alternative directions. They may mark the initial moves in different trajectories of structural change.

Thus, the reach toward a recognition of the empirical and defeasible character of the rights of choice should be simply the first step in a two-step movement. The second step, following closely upon the first, would be the legal imagination and construction of alternative pluralisms: the exploration, in programmatic argument or in experimental reform, of one or another sequence of institutional change. Each sequence would redefine the rights, and the interests and ideals they serve, in the course of realising them more effectively. Contemporary legal theory and doctrine, and substantive law itself, almost never take this second step. Theirs is a striking instance of arrested development.

The failure to turn legal analysis into institutional imagination — the major consequence of the arrested development of legal thought — has special meaning and poignancy in the United States. For surely one of the flaws in American civilisation has been the effort to bar the institutional structure of the country against effective challenge; to see America's 'scheme of ordered liberty' as a definitive escape from the old history of classes and ideologies; to refuse to recognise that the spiritual and political ideals of a civilisation remain fastened to the special practices and institutions representing them in fact. Experimentalism has been the most defensible part of American exceptionalism; yet only under the pressure of extreme crisis have Americans brought the experimentalist impulse to bear upon their institutions. Those American thinkers have been the greatest who, like Jefferson and Dewey, tried to convince their contemporaries to trade in some bad American exceptionalism for some good American experimentalism. Those periods of American history have been the most significant when interests became entangled in ideals because both ideals and interests collided with institutional arrangements.

Structural but episodic intervention

What force arrests the development of legal thought in the move from the discovery of the institutional indeterminacy of free economies, societies, and polities to the exploration of their diversity of possible institutional forms? We can shed an oblique but revealing light on this riddle by reconsidering it from the perspective of what has come to be known in American law as the problem of complex enforcement and structural injunctions.[1] Although the procedural device has developed more fully in the United States than anywhere else, the opportunity it exploits in the relation of law to society is fast becoming universal. The new mode of procedural intervention seems like a natural extension and instrument of the central idea of contemporary law. Nevertheless, the incongruities of its theory and practice makes the arrested development of this idea all the more startling.

Alongside the traditional style of adjudication, with its emphasis upon the structure-preserving assignment of rights among individual litigants, there has emerged a different adjudicative practice, with agents, methods, and goals different from those of the traditional style. The agents of this alternative practice are collective rather than individual although they may be represented by individual litigants. The class-action lawsuit is the most straightforward tool of this redefinition of agents.

The aim of the intervention is to reshape an organisation or a localised area of social practice frustrating the effective enjoyment of rights. The characteristic circumstance of frustration is one in which the organisation or the practice under scrutiny has seen the rise of disadvantage and marginalisation that their victims are powerless to escape. Subjugation, localised and therefore remediable, is the paradigmatic evil addressed by the reconstructive intervention.

The method is the effort to advance more deeply into the causal background of social life than traditional adjudication would countenance, reshaping the arrangements found to be most immediately and powerfully responsible for the questioned evil. Thus, the remedy may require a court to intervene in a school, a prison, a school system, or a voting district, and to reform and administer the organisation over a period of time. Complex enforcement will demand a more intimate and sustained combination of prescriptive argument and causal inquiry than has been characteristic of lawyers' reasoning.

The basic problem in the theory and practice of structural injunctions is the difficulty of making sense of their limits. Once we begin to penetrate the causal background of contested practices and powers why should we stop so close to the surface? The evils of unequal education for different races, for example, may soon

---

1 See Sargentich 'Complex Enforcement' 1978 (unpub. on file, Harvard Law Library).

lead an American structural reform in one direction to question the legitimacy of local financial responsibility for public schools and in another direction to challenge the institutional arrangements, such as subcontracting and temporary hiring, that help reproduce an underclass by segmenting the labour force. The more circumscribed corrective intervention is likely to prove ineffective. If causal efficacy is the standard of remedial success, one foray into the structural background of rights-frustration should lead to another. Once we start to tinker with relatively peripheral organisations such as prisons and asylums and to reshape them in the image of ideals imputed to substantive law, why should we not keep going until we reach firms and bureaucracies, families and local governments? As we deepened the reach and extended the scope of intervention, the reconstructive activities of complex enforcement would become evermore ambitious, exercising greater powers, employing bigger staffs, and consuming richer resources.

The missing agent

None of this, of course, will happen. It will not happen because no society, not even the United States, will allow a vanguard of lawyers and judges to reconstruct its institutions little by little under the transparent disguise of interpreting the law. The mass of working people may be asleep. The educated and propertied classes are not. They will not allow their fate to be determined by a closed cadre of priestly reformers lacking in self-restraint. They will put these reformers in their place, substituting for them successors who no longer need to be put in their place.

The deepening of the reach and the broadening of the scope of complex enforcement would soon outrun the political legitimacy of the judiciary and exhaust its practical and cognitive resources. Moreover, in the name of the mandate to intervene the better to secure the effective enjoyment of rights, judges would usurp an increasing portion of the real power of popular self-government.

So what should the judges do, and what do they do in fact? Judges in the United States have sometimes seemed to want to do as much as they could get way with: better some penetration of the structural background to subjugation than none; better marginal social organisations than no organisations at all. The difficulty arises from the disproportion between the reconstructive mission and its institutional agent. Complex enforcement is both structural and episodic. The work of structural and episodic intervention seems required if we are to ensure the effective enjoyment of rights and execute the mandate of substantive law. It is a necessary procedural complement, not a casual afterthought to the genius of contemporary law. But who should execute such structural and episodic work in contemporary democratic government?

No branch of present-day presidential or parliamentary regimes seems well equipped, by reason of political legitimacy or practical capability, to do it. The majority-based government of the parliamentary system, or the executive branch of the presidential regime, cannot reinterpret rights and reshape rights-based arrangements in particular corners of social life without danger to the freedom of citizens. Moreover, they would soon find themselves distracted and demoralised by countless forms of petty anxiety and resistance. The administrative agencies or civil service might have more detachment and expertise but correspondingly less authority in the choice of a reconstructive direction or in the exercise of a power free to forge singular solutions to localised problems. Legislatures and parliaments would become both despotic and ineffective if they were to deal, in an individualised and episodic manner, with structural problems and institutional rearrangements. The judiciary lacks both the practical capability and the political legitimacy to restructure, and to manage during restructuring, the deserving objects of complex enforcement. Its unsuitability to the task will be all the more manifest if the frustration of enjoyment of rights by intractable disadvantage turns out to be a common incident of social life, and if the cure demands an increasingly invasive reach into the background of practices and institutions.

The truth is that no part of present-day government is well suited, by virtue of practical capacity or political intervention, to undertake the job of structural and episodic reconstruction. The mission lacks — as every novel and serious mission in the world does — its proper agent. The best response is then to forge the new agent: another branch of government, another power in the state, designed, elected, and funded with the express charge of carrying out this distinctive, rights-ensuring work. Such a move, however, would demand the very openness to institutional experimentalism in which contemporary law and contemporary democracies have proved so markedly deficient. It would require us, as lawyers and as citizens, to complete the move from the accomplished first step of insistence upon the effectiveness of the enjoyment of rights to the missing second step of institutional reimagination and reconstruction.

In the absence of such an extension of the cast of available agents, any of the existing, somewhat unsuitable agents might accept or refuse the work, and then, having accepted it, push it as far as it wanted or could. In the United States, the judiciary, especially the federal judiciary, has been this incongruous, sometime, and half-hearted agent. In other countries it could be any other power in the state. From this marriage of the indispensable work to the unsuitable agent there arises the implicit theory of the structural injunctions in American law. This theory requires us to split the difference between two persuasive and incompatible propositions: the maxim that we must carry out the mandate of substantive law whether or not we have available the right agents and instruments, and the contrasting maxim that the implementation of law must take place under the discipline of institutional propriety and capability.

Thus the problem of complex enforcement sheds a double light upon the arrested development of contemporary legal thought. It shows how fidelity to law and to its imputed ideals may drive, unwittingly and on a small scale, into the institutional experiments that we have refused straightforwardly to imagine and to achieve. It also demonstrates how our failure to take the second step disorients and inhibits our small-time reconstructive work. This chapter in the history of contemporary law wonderfully illustrates the combination of self-concealment and self-disclosure in a ruling vision.

The spell of rationalising legal analysis

Legal thought and social democracy

Why have law and legal doctrine failed to make the move from their characteristic focus upon the effective enjoyment of rights to the recognition and development of transformative institutional opportunity? Why have they worked in the belief that individual and collective self-determination depend upon empirical and defeasible conditions without turning more wholeheartedly to the legal analysis and construction of the contrasting practices and institutions capable of fulfilling these conditions? Why therefore have they not gone on to identify in these small and fragmentary alternatives the possible beginnings of larger alternatives: different institutional pathways for the redefinition and transformation of representative democracy, market economy, and free civil society? Why, in other words, have they failed to extend their rejection of the nineteenth-century idea that free polities and economies have a predetermined legal form, constitutive of freedom itself, into a more thoroughgoing rebellion against institutional fetishism?

The most important reasons for the arrested development of legal thought lie in the history of modern politics. Nevertheless, the simple attribution of the limits of contemporary legal thought to the constraints upon the political transformation of social arrangements is insufficient as explanation on several grounds.

The same period that saw the development of legal thought arrested also witnessed a connected series of radical reforms in the institutional and ideological context of political and economic life: the reforms labelled in Europe as social democracy and described in the United States as the New Deal. These changes had one of their points of focus and support in Keynesianism: a connected series of institutional and ideological innovations, freeing national governments from sound-finance doctrine and thus diminishing the dependence of public policy upon the level of business confidence. These were radical reforms because we cannot understand the force and shape of the major political, economic and discursive routines of the contemporary industrial democracies — such as the political-business cycle — except by reference to them. They helped set the boundary conditions within which individuals and organised groups would, in the succeeding period, understand and defend their interests.

It is nevertheless true that like any institutional settlement the social democratic compromise implied renunciation of a broader realm of conflict and controversy. National governments won the power and the authority to manage the economy counter-cyclically, to compensate for the unequalising effects of economic growth through tax-and-transfer, and to take those investment initiatives that seemed necessary to satisfy the requirements for the profitability of private firms. In return, however, they had to abandon the threat radically to reorganise the system of production and exchange and thereby to reshape the primary distribution of wealth and income in society.

The refusal of legal analysis to move from the concern with enjoyment of rights to the pursuit of institutional change may seem merely the legal counterpart to the foreclosure of broader conflict by the social-democratic settlement. The role of the practical legal reformer would be to continue and to complete the unfinished work of the social-democratic reformation. The task of the legal thinker would be to develop a theory of law that, freer of the nineteenth-century devotion to a predetermined private-law system, would do justice to social-democratic commitments. From this angle the reluctance to pass from the theme of effective enjoyment of rights to the practice of institutional criticism appears to be a consequence of the renunciation of broader institutional experimentalism. Such a renunciation represented an essential term of the social-democratic compromise. Not until that compromise gets challenged and changed could we expect legal analysis to continue on the trajectory I earlier traced. As it has been challenged if at all mainly from the right, so the argument would conclude, there is little reason to expect such a forward impulse.

The trouble with this account of the sources of institutional conservatism in the practice of legal analysis is that it relies upon too static and one-sided a picture of institutional settlements and of their relation to legal thought. For one thing, there is no watertight division between the reconstructive moment of crisis and energy and the supposedly barren sequel. Not only have problems and alternatives touching on the design of institutions continued to appear, but it is also often hard to say which of the solutions considered is more faithful to the earlier, foundational compromise. For another thing, institutional change is not just a cause of reimagination; it is also a consequence. If we have indeed renounced a functionalist and evolutionary determinism in our understanding of institutional history, we must grant to our practices of social imagination such as legal analysis some power of productive apostasy and practical presentiment. Finally, the exculpatory picture fails to acknowledge the self-subversive and self-transformative capacities of a tradition of discursive practice such as that of legal analysis. The history of legal thought over the last hundred years provides — I shall soon argue — a striking example of these capacities. Why have they fallen into disuse?

The method of policy and principle

The failure to move from the moment of attention to enjoyment of rights to the moment of institutional reimagination is more than the silent echo in law of political quiescence in society. It reveals the influence of a now canonical practice of legal analysis: one that enjoys increasing influence throughout the world but that has till now found its most elaborate development in American legal doctrine and theory. I shall call it rationalising legal analysis, giving, for the purpose, specific content to the term 'rationalising.' It is a style of legal discourse distinct both from the nineteenth-century rationalism and from the looser and more context-oriented analogical reasoning that continues to dominate, in the United States as elsewhere, much of the practical reasoning of lawyers and judges.

There is no such thing as 'legal reasoning': a permanent part of an imaginary organon of forms of inquiry and discourse, with a persistent core of scope and method. All we have are historically located arrangements and historically located conversations. It makes no sense to ask — What is legal analysis? — as if discourse (by lawyers) about law had a permanent essence. In dealing with such a discourse, what we can reasonably ask is — In what form have we received it, and what should we turn it into? I argue that we now can and should turn legal discourse into a sustained conversation about our arrangements.

Rationalising legal analysis is a way of representing extended pieces of law as expressions, albeit flawed expressions, of connected sets of policies and principles. It is a self-consciously purposive mode of discourse, recognising that imputed purpose shapes the interpretive development of law. Its primary distinction, however, is to see policies of collective welfare and principles of moral and political right as the proper content of these guiding purposes. The generalising and idealising discourse of policy and principle interprets law by making sense of it as a purposive social enterprise that reaches toward comprehensive schemes of welfare and right. Through rational reconstruction, entering cumulatively and deeply into the content of law, we come to understand pieces of law as fragments of an intelligible plan of social life.

Within such a practice, analogical reasoning is defined as the confused, first step up the ladder of rational reconstruction. The often implicit purposive judgements guiding the analogist point upward, for their authority and consistency, to more comprehensive ideas of policies and principle. The repeated practice of policy-oriented and principle-based analysis should, so the most ambitious and influential views of the practice teach, lead to ever higher standards of generality, coherence, and clarity in the rational representation of law.

The ideal conceptions representing law as an imperfect approximation to an intelligible and defensible plan are thought to be partly already there in the law. The analysts must not be thought to make them up. They are not, however, present in a single, unambiguous form, nor do they fully penetrate the legal material. Thus, legal analysis has two jobs: to recognise the ideal element embedded in law, and then to improve the law and its received understanding. Improvement happens by developing the underlying conceptions of principle and policy and by rejecting, from time to time and bit by bit, the pieces of received understanding and precedent that fail to fit the preferred conceptions of policy and principle. Too much pretence of discovering the ideal conceptions ready made and fully potent within existing law, and the legal analyst becomes a mystifier and an apologist. Too much constructive improvement of the law as received understanding represents it to be, and he turns into a usurper of democratic power. In fact, because the apologetic mystification may be so insecurely grounded in the actual materials of law, both these countervailing perversions of rational reconstruction are likely to end in an unjustified confiscation of lawmaking power by the analyst.

In what vocabulary should we think of policy and principle or to what conceptions should we resort in trying to connect policies and principles to one another, and to prefer some to others? The major schools of legal theory in the age of rationalising legal analysis can most usefully be understood as the contrasting operational ideologies of this analytic practice. Each school proposes a different way of grounding, refining, and reforming the practice. Thus, for example, one school may look to goals of allocational or dynamic economic efficiency while another may start from a view of the proper roles and responsibilities of the different institutions within a legal system. Nevertheless, the same argumentative structure recurs in all these theories: the purposive ideal conceptions of policy and principle, whatever their substance, are partly already there in the law, waiting to be made explicit, and they are partly the result of the improving work undertaken by the properly informed and motivated analyst.

The diffusion of rationalising legal analysis

The practice of legal analysis theorised in this manner now enjoys immense and increasing influence. It may dominate only a minor part of the practical discourse of lawyers and lower-court judges, preoccupied with preventing conflict, controlling violence, and negotiating compromise. It nevertheless is coming to occupy the central imaginative space in the way in which the judicial, legal-professional, and legal academic elites talk about law and develop its practical, applied understanding. At a minimum, it pre-empts an alternative imagination of law from holding this space and exercising this influence.

Given its historical specificity, this style of legal discourse spreads unevenly throughout the world, and takes on in different places characteristics shaped by an earlier history of methods and ideas. It has received its most lavish elaboration in the contemporary United States, but its worldwide influence grows steadily. In this respect it is an event characteristic of an historical situation in which humanity finds itself united by a chain of analogies, in experiences, problems, and solutions, and anxious reformers of society and culture pillage and recombine practices and institutions from all over the world. It is in this way rather than by the cruel devices through which capital becomes hypermobile while labour remains imprisoned in the nation-state — or in blocs of homogeneous nation-states — that mankind is becoming truly one. Countries in which a more analogy-bound practice of legal reasoning continues to enjoy greater respect (for in all countries such a practice enjoys actual influence), or in which the project of nineteenth-century legal science clings to a life-in-death, soon become theatres for the conflict between the old doctrinalism and the new style of rational reconstruction in law.

A familiar difference of emphasis illustrates how, as it spreads through the world, the method adapts to the idiosyncratic compulsions born of the many histories it intersects. In the United States the continuing duality of common law and statutory law has repeatedly suggested the idea that the retrospective, reconstructive, and dynamic interpretation of law under the guidance of connected policy and principle has a broader and more persistent role to play in judge-made law than in the judicial construction of statutes. Only slowly have lawyers knocked these barriers down, claiming in statutory construction the same freedom to keep on reinterpreting and reconstructing that they attribute to the internal development of the common law.

In civil law countries the path-dependent history of attitudes toward rational reconstruction in law followed a different course. The project of nineteenth-century legal science, which found its most systematic expression in the work of the German pandectists, was understood by its votaries to be the rescue and refinement of the old Roman-Christian common law of Europe. A struggle developed between two attitudes toward codification — codification as the taming of the power of the jurists by democracy and codification as the convenient summation of the jurists' doctrines. Where the first attitude prevailed, as in postrevolutionary France, there was a concerted attempt to uphold literalism in the interpretation of law. This literalism outlived its political roots and helped pre-empt pandectism, as it helps restrain today the full-fledged inauguration of rationalising legal analysis. But where, in the late democratising countries of most of Europe, private and academic jurists retained their law-shaping authority throughout the era of great codifications in the late nineteenth and the early twentieth centuries, codes were imagined by the jurists as the compressed expression of their science. Democratic institutions, where they existed, confirmed and corrected doctrines that predated them. In such a climate the road to rational reconstruction in legal analysis was open. No association between codification and literalism took hold. A long history prepared the reception of today's rationalising legal analysis.

The anti-experimentalist influence of rationalising legal analysis

As it spreads through the world, rationalising legal analysis helps arrest the development of the dialectic between the rights of choice and the arrangements that make individual and collective self-determination effective — a dialectic that is the very genius of contemporary law. The most important way in which it does so is by acquiescing in institutional fetishism. It represents the legally defined practices and institutions of society as an approximation to an intelligible and justified scheme of social life. It portrays the established forms of representative democracy, the regulated market economy, and civil society as flawed but real images of a free society — a society whose arrangements result from individual and collective self-determination. If these forms are never the only possible ones, at least they are, according to this point of view, the ones that history has validated

— a history marked by both the intractability of social conflicts and the scarcity of workable arrangements.

Rationalising legal analysis works by putting a good face — indeed the best possible face — on as much of law as it can, and therefore also on the institutional arrangements that take in law their detailed and distinctive form. It must restrict anomaly, for what cannot be reconciled with the schemes of policy and principle must eventually be rejected as mistaken. For the jurist to reject too much of the received understanding of law as mistaken, expanding the revisionary power of legal analysis, would be to upset the delicate balance between the claim to discover principles and policies already there and the willingness to impose them upon imperfect legal materials. It would be to conspire in the runaway usurpation of democratic power. Thus, deviations and contradictions become intellectual and political threats rather than intellectual and political opportunities, materials for alternative constructions.

The complex structure of legal consciousness

No style of discourse, however powerful its influence, occupies the whole of a legal culture or penetrates all of a legal mind. Even in those places where it is most articulate and effective, rationalising legal analysis gains its characteristic position from its coexistence with different ideas of law. Before turning to the roots and limits of the policy-oriented and principle-based mode of legal reasoning, consider the ordinary shape of this coexistence today. I take my examples from the legal culture that has pushed furthest beyond the limits of nineteenth-century legal science — that of the United States — and I tell the story in the form of a simplified sequence. Three moments of legal consciousness, each uniting a vision of law with a method of legal analysis, have followed one another in time. The later, however, do not fully displace the earlier. They become superimposed upon the preceding ones. This superimposition produces the complex coexistence of distinct ideas of law and practices of analysis marking the legal culture in which, increasingly, we have come to move.

The moment of nineteenth-century legal science

The first moment in this sequence is the moment of nineteenth-century legal science. The animating idea is the effort to make patent the hidden legal content of a free political and economic order. This content consists in a system of property and contract rights and in a system of public-law arrangements and entitlements safeguarding the private order. Hard law is the distributively neutral law of coordination defined by this inbuilt legal content of the type of a free society. It must be distinguished from bad, soft, political law: the product of the hijacking of governmental power by groups who use lawmaking power to distribute rights and resources to themselves.

The methodological instrument for this substantive vision of law is the repertory of techniques we now know derisively as formalism and conceptualism. We should not characterise them as a crude deductivist prejudice about language and interpretation, for they make sense in the context of the idea of a predetermined legal content to a free order. Thus, conceptualism explores the packages of rule and doctrine inherent in the organising categories of the rights system — categories like property itself — while formalism infers lower-order propositions from higher-order ones. Discursive practices designed to police the boundaries between distributively neutral, good law and redistributive, bad law complement these basic methods. The primary such policing practice is constructive interpretation, redescribing and reforming bad law, whenever persuasively possible, as good law. The back-up policing practice is constitutional invalidation, striking down those instances of redistribution through law that cannot be pre-empted through improving interpretation. By deploying all these methods, legal science carries out its fundamental mission of representing in a system of legal rules and ideas, and thereby securing against perversion, the scheme of political and economic freedom. Its scientific task matches its political responsibilities.

This approach to law suffocated social conflict. All the active interests and ideologies that wanted more from the promises of modernity, and refused to see in the institutions of their society a scheme of neutral coordination, waged war against it. The project of legal science, however, was not merely attacked from without. Like every powerful imaginative practice, it undermined itself. Its votaries discovered that at every turn in the march from relatively greater abstraction to relatively greater concreteness in the definitions of rules and concepts there was more than one plausible turn to take. Thus, a method designed to vindicate conceptual unity and institutional necessity revealed nevertheless unimagined diversity and opportunity in established law.

The single most important instance of this insight into unwanted indeterminacy was the discovery of irremediable conflict among property rights. The doctrine of *sic utere* was one of many announcing the hope that under a private property regime each right-holder could enjoy absolute discretion within the citadel of the right. So long as he did not invade anyone else's zone of right and property he could enjoy the privileges of his whims. He could treat property as an alternative not only to personal dependence but also to social interdependence. Practical lawyers, however, discovered that the conflict among rights, reasonably and conventionally exercised, was both pervasive and unavoidable. The law in practice turned out to be rife with *damnum absque iniuria* — instances of damage one right-holder could, with immunity or without liability, do to another — and with competitive injury — the infliction of economic harm resulting from the ordinary practices of economic competition.

Every initiative in the deployment of rights proved to have what the economists later called 'externalities'. To prohibit the initiatives or to make the right-holder pay for all of them ('internalising the externalities') would be to inhibit productive action and to eviscerate the force of the rights. But to allow the rights-invading use of rights and to pick and choose in the imposition of liability for the prejudicial consequences was to recognise the poverty of the pure logic of rights. There was no way to resolve the conflicts, or to make the selections, by probing more deeply into the system of categories and doctrines. It was necessary to take a stand and to justify it by reference to judgements of purpose, whether avowedly factional or allegedly impersonal. Doctrines of competitive injury and of *damnum absque iniuria* revealed the ineradicable contest among property rights, however such rights might be defined, in the law of a market economy. They marked horizontal conflicts among owners, and required policy compromises to resolve them.

Legal thought took much longer to recognise a second, vertical style of conflict: a series of unavoidable and interlocking choices about the conditions on which economic agents could run risks without incurring immediate economic death. The red line of failure and liability at which economic agents must cease to function, going bankrupt or paying for the consequences of the harms they inflict upon others, has no fixed and natural place in the legal logic of a market economy. The jurists and the legislators had to confront a connected set of dilemmas: immediate bankruptcy for failed firms or the chance for a second life through reorganisation under the control of present management (the Chapter 11 of American bankruptcy law); unlimited or limited liability in combined economic activity; the governmental monopoly of money-making or its independent creation by banks, and, with the choice of the public monopoly of money and the emergence of a central-banking system, insured or uninsured bank deposits.

The structure of these dilemmas was always the same. The impulse to contain moral hazard and to make people responsible for the uncompensated consequences of their activities had to be balanced against the need to encourage risk-taking behaviour in production and in finance. There was never a way to distinguish beforehand, and in general rule-bound terms, the good risk-bearing activities from the bad ones. Indeed, the impossibility of making such a distinction has been one of the reasons to prefer a market economy in the first place. Similarly, the existence of a class of people happy to pay a premium for the privilege of running a risk has been said to be the historical justification of 'capitalism' if by capitalism we understand not just the abstract conception of a market economy but a particular version of that economy rewarding personal success with personal wealth.

The red line was not only movable; it had to be moved all the time, and no particular way of demarcating it seemed wholly satisfactory. Once again, the choices had to be made by purposive judgements of policy that the jurists were powerless to infer from the supposed legal logic of the economic order. We still struggle to understand that assumptions about the possible institutional forms of the market economy — assumptions worked out in the detailed language of law — shape what we imagine the possible solutions to both the horizontal and the vertical conflicts among property rights to be.

It is one thing to recognise that horizontal and vertical conflicts among property rights are pervasive; that we cannot infer the solutions to them from the abstract conception of a market economy and of its legal logic; and that such localised solutions as we may adopt must rely upon fragmentary and contested compromises among policies or interests. It is another thing to identify in some of these solutions the germs of a market economy and of a system of private law distinct from the ones established in the contemporary industrial democracies.

For example, Chapter 11 style corporate reorganisation in American bankruptcy law provides an alternative to the death of a firm in the red: the management of the firm may be given a chance to borrow and to reform while the firm holds its creditors at bay. Similar provisions exist in the bankruptcy laws of all the industrial democracies. There are analogies to Chapter 11 in many fields of law, all the way from the intervention of the International Monetary Fund and of consortia of governments to rescue countries undergoing liquidity crises, to the public supervision of regional economic reconstruction when major parts of industry risk going broke, as in the selective turnaround decisions undertaken by the *Treuhandgesellschaft* in the reconstruction and privatisation of East German industry.

Suppose that we lack reliable, *ex ante* economic standards by which to identify the deserving beneficiaries of selective turnaround. Suppose, further, that the success of selective turnaround — the wisdom of the initial decisions and the support for their continuing execution in firms and communities — depends, as so many economic initiatives do, upon many interlocking forms of cooperation:

between firms and local governments, between local governments and community organisations, between investors and workers, between insiders (job-holders in the rescued enterprises) and outsiders (workers in established firms and job seekers). Under these assumptions, selective turnaround may demand a comprehensive and complex legal structure of cooperation among interests.

Such a structure may include transactions that amount to continuing discussions; reciprocal reliance and adjustment that stops short of becoming articulated contracts; property rights that violate the traditional property-right logic of the bright-line demarcation of zones of entitlement; and supervisory or coordinating associations that stand midway between governments and firms. To develop such suggestions would be to reinvent the legal form of the market economy. To begin reinventing the legal form of the market economy would be to bring pressure to bear against the inherited legal forms of representative democracy and of free civil society.

There is a difference between recognising that conflicts among property rights must be resolved by flawed, rough-and-ready compromises, and seeing in some of these compromises the possible starting points of a cumulative institutional transformation. It is, however, no more than a difference in how far we keep moving away from the original idea of a market economy with an inbuilt and determinate legal logic. Nonetheless, although legal thought has decisively done the first of these two jobs, it has just as unequivocally failed to accomplish, or even to imagine, the second.

The self-subversive work of legal thought, illustrated by the progressive discovery of the horizontal and vertical conflicts among property rights, has had two remarkable features. The first is that it has gone so far. The second is that it has nevertheless stopped where it has.

Under these restraints, legal analysis has slowly developed its insight into the political constitution and the institutional contingency of the market economy. The whole movement of legal doctrine and legal theory for the last hundred and fifty years has been a struggle to develop this insight and to understand its implications. The struggle, however, was waged by, as well as against, legal science; legal science waged war against itself.

Contemporary jurists mistakenly believe themselves to be free of the taint of this vision of law. Thus, American legal theory regularly congratulates itself on its rejection of 'Lochnerism': the fetishistic acceptance and constitutional entrenchment of a particular private rights-system against all efforts to redistribute rights and resources and to regulate economic activity. In fact, however, Lochnerism has survived as an undercurrent of later moments of legal consciousness. In this latent position it has turned out to be all the more recalcitrant to criticism. To be sure, it has enjoyed its most vigorous afterlife in economics rather than in legal thought: all but the most austere and self-denying versions of economic analysis continue to rely upon the idea of a natural legal-institutional form of the market economy, open to only minor variations.

This belated and unconfessed Lochnerism also continues to leave its mark upon law. It does, sometimes, in the form of organising doctrinal conceptions such as the state-action doctrine in American law and the functional equivalents to that doctrine in other legal systems. State-action doctrine assumes the validity of a distinction between social arrangements that are politically constituted and social arrangements that are somehow just prepolitically there. Yet that distinction rather than one of its now derided byproducts — the special authority of private-law rules and concepts to mark neutral baselines against which to judge governmental activism — was precisely the central axiom of Lochnerism. Sometimes we can identify the influence of this vision of law in a set of attitudes eluding precise doctrinal manifestation such as the willingness to accept the greater stability and rationality of the central rules of private law. This view contrasts private law to the circumstantial and controversial efforts of the regulatory and redistributive state as if the rules of property and exchange were any less artificial than the provisions for tax-and-transfer. However, the single most important demonstration of the continuing power of the project of legal science is rationalising legal analysis, the style of discourse that displaced nineteenth-century legal science while remaining dependent upon many of its assumptions and devoted to many of its ambitions.

The moment of rationalising legal analysis

The second moment in contemporary legal consciousness is the moment of rationalising legal analysis itself: the policy-oriented and principle-based style of legal analysis that, recognising the reliance of legal analysis upon the ascription of purpose, gave to the guiding purposes the content of general conceptions of collective welfare or political right. This idealising and generalising discourse about law in the language of connected principle and policy ideas was not, however, the sole successor to the earlier project of legal science. At least two different vocabularies for thinking and talking about law have flourished in the aftermath of that project: the view of law as the outcome of a series of compromises in a well-ordered conflict of organised interests — the conception sometimes labelled 'interest-group pluralism' — and the idea of law as the flawed but tentative embodiment of impersonal ideals of welfare and right. I shall soon have more to say about the paradoxical and disconcerting transactions between these two vocabularies: the one leading to an understanding of law as a series of regulated contracts among interest groups; the other producing a view of law as a partial expression of general and idealised purpose. The latter approach rather than the former has achieved canonical status in professional and academic legal culture. It is, in any event, the one closest in spirit and consequence to the legal science it displaced. The coexistence of these two vocabularies serves to introduce the central organising distinction of the new style of legal analysis.

Rationalising legal analysis puts the contrast between law as impersonal policy and principle, and law as factional self-dealing by powerful interest groups, in place of the more ambitious and inflexible contrast between law as a distributively neutral framework of coordination among free and equal individuals, and law as an illicit, redistributive intervention by the government, in this framework. Correctly understood, the parallel between these two pairs of distinctions should be too close for comfort.

What is gone is the idea of a fixed system of private and public rights implicit in the very definition of a free political and economic order. Rationalising legal analysis has rejected, together with that idea, its chief corollary: the claim of the private-law system of property and contract to provide a distributively neutral standard against which to judge the legitimacy of governmental 'intervention.' It has nevertheless rescued from the ruin of that claim the commitment to represent law as the search for a public interest capable of description in the language of policy and principle and resolutely contrasted to factional self-promotion through lawmaking.

No component of public interest seems more important than the commitment to assure people of the practical conditions effectively to enjoy the rights of free citizens, free economic agents, and free individuals. The regulatory and redistributive activity of the state gains legitimacy, and demonstrates its connection with the public interest, by having as its mission the satisfaction of the requirements for the effective enjoyment of rights.

The self-conscious task of this representation of law was to imagine as law the regulatory and redistributive activity of an activist government. This is the work in which rationalising legal analysis has been most successful. The larger task was to reimagine from the perspective of social democracy the working methods of legal reasoning and the entire body of law and legal institutions including traditional private law. In this larger work the success of rationalising legal analysis, and of its supporting cast of theories of law, has been far less certain. Indeed, the incompleteness of the larger mission has given contemporary jurists an excuse to disclaim broader intellectual or transformative ambitions; there is so much work left to do. Spellbound by the Atlas complex it has willed upon itself, legal thought halts in its journey away from the nineteenth-century project of legal science.

Once again, the combination of real social conflicts and irrepressible intellectual self-subversion have begun to expose the limitations and frailties of this now dominant way of thinking and talking about law. The endless strife over group benefits and burdens, social incorporation and exclusion, in the era of regulatory and redistributive government undermines the authority of the idea that any particular pattern of regulation and redistribution could be held up as the authoritative correction to the pre-existing social order: the one that would make real the promises of liberal democracy. More troubling yet is the discovery that the most important sources of frustration of the effective enjoyment of rights may lie in practices and institutions that the policy tools of an institutionally conservative social democracy are unable to reach and that the lawyer's discourse of policy and principle is unable to represent.

As a strategy for limiting inequality, tax-and-transfer has ordinarily had disappointing results. In few countries has it produced more than marginal increases in equality of wealth and income, and it has had an even more modest effect upon the distribution of economic power. Every major effort at redistribution through tax-and-transfer produces economic stress and crisis either directly through disinvestment and capital flight or indirectly through its corrosive effects upon public finance. This practical disappointment finds expression in a mode of discourse contrasting equity and efficiency as goals locked in a tense and often inverse relation. The alternative would be a reorganisation of the system for production and exchange, and of the relations between public power and private initiative, influencing the primary distribution of wealth and income, while affirming and extending the scope of market activity. Such an alternative, however, depends on institutional experiments, including experiments in the property regime, that the social-democratic compromise seems to have foreclosed.

As the limits of the social-democratic compromise become manifest, rationalising legal analysis finds itself pulled between two forces. On the one hand, it clings to the attempt to put the best face on the established institutional settlement, treating it not as a transitory and accidental set of compromises but as a lasting and rational framework, to be perfected rather than challenged or changed. On the other hand, however, to take seriously the view of law as an embodiment of social ideals, describable in the language of policy and principle, is to admit that these ideals may come into conflict with actual practices and organisations. Complex enforcement is the single most striking expression of this countervailing impulse in legal doctrine. Up till now, a division of domains has concealed this conflict of directions. The immunisation of institutional arrangements against close scrutiny has prevailed in the vision of substantive law. The selective probing of institutions has remained largely confined to development of procedural remedies such as those of complex enforcement. The consequence of this procedural innovation, we have seen, is to use the available roles and agents of the legal process incongruously: judges undertake complex enforcement because they want to, because the mandate of substantive law seems to require that someone undertake it, and because all other branches of government seem just as unsuited to the task as the judiciary is. Lacking the resources of authority, expertise, and funds with which to do the job, they do it haltingly and at the margins, until they run out of power and out of will. Thus, by the self-subversive logic of evolution in legal ideas, we derationalise procedure the better to vindicate the rationalisation of substantive law. At the next turn of our thinking, we might well ask why we should not derationalise substantive law the better to affirm our interests and ideals.

There are several equivalent ways in which to describe the core of weakness and self-subversion in rationalising legal analysis. On one description the focus of perplexity in rationalising legal analysis is the difficulty of sustaining the organising distinction between factional interest and impersonal policy or principle. Every particular definition of the public interest, in the idealised language of policy and principle, will seem either too indeterminate to guide judgement toward particular outcomes or too difficult to disentangle from controversial beliefs, connected, in turn, to factional interests.

The most revealing and disconcerting aspect of this discursive practice, however, becomes apparent when we focus on the relation between legal ideals and social facts. Consider, as an example, the typical form of a law-review article by an American legal academic at the close of the twentieth century. Such an article typically presented an extended part of legal rule and doctrine as the expression of a connected set of policies and principles. It criticised part of that received body of rule and doctrine as inadequate to the achievement of the ascribed ideal purposes. It concluded with a proposal for law reform resulting in a more defensible and comprehensive equilibrium between the detailed legal material and the ideal conceptions intended to make sense of that material. But why should the reform stop at one point rather than another? Why should it not advance more deeply into the stuff of social arrangements, reconstructing them for the sake of the ideal conceptions, and then, later on, redefining the ideal conceptions in the light of the actual or imagined rearrangements? An implicit judgement of practical political feasibility controls the answer to this question. Given that most of the institutional background must, as a practical matter, be held constant at any given time, proposals for institutional tinkering should remain modest and marginal. Moreover, given that the author is speaking in the impersonal voice of the quasi-judge or the quasi-bureaucrat, the reform proposals should never seem too sectarian. Thus, the practice of rationalising legal analysis comes to be shaped by implicit constraints that the analytic practice itself leaves largely unchallenged and unexplored. From this conformity to shadowy and unjustified constraints arises the sense of relative arbitrariness, of confusion between normative justification and practical strategy, that increasingly becomes part of the actual experience of doing legal analysis.

The example of the law-review article may seem limited in its significance to the situation of a jurist who, without administrative or adjudicative responsibilities, but with a desire to remain connected to the worlds of practical administration and adjudication, offers proposals to reform law. Yet the earlier example of the complex injunctions suggests that the problem reappears in many of the roles in which we practice legal analysis. The judge must revise received legal understandings, from time to time, but if he revises too many of them, or revises a few of them too radically, and if in so doing he challenges and changes some part of the institutional order defined in law, he transgresses the boundaries of the role assigned to him by rationalising legal analysis. What keeps him within these boundaries? The happy assurance that most of the received body of law and legal understanding at any given time can in fact be represented as the expression of connected policies and principles? If so, how could such a harmony between the prospective history of law as a history of conflicts among groups, interests, and visions, and the retrospective rationalisation of law as an intelligible scheme of policy and principle ever occur? Or is the restraint of revisionary power by the judge something that comes from an independent set of standards about what judges may appropriately do? If so, from where do these standards come? Whatever their content and origin, how can they escape imposing a severe and wandering constraint upon our capacity to reimagine and to reconstruct law as the expression of policy and principle?

The moment of the tactical reinterpretation of legal doctrine

Such varieties of bafflement have today become an integral part of the experience of doing policy-oriented and principle-based legal analysis. Together with the destabilising forces that come from outside — from the real politics of an activist, regulatory and redistributive government — they have given rise to a third moment in the evolution of modern legal consciousness, superimposed upon the two earlier ones. This third moment is the redefinition of the principle-based and policy-oriented style of legal discourse as a tactic deployed in the service of a distinctive family of political projects.

I shall label this family of political projects conservative reformism: the pursuit of programmatic goals, such as more economic competition or greater equality of practical opportunity and cultural voice, within the limits imposed by the established institutional order. A specially influential version of conservative reformism in the development of the tactical moment in contemporary legal consciousness has been what I shall label progressive pessimistic reformism.

Two beliefs and a commitment define progressive pessimistic reformism. The first belief is what makes it a species of conservative reformism: no institutional change is in the cards. Moreover, even if such a change were possible and desirable, we, the jurists, cannot be its legitimate and effective agents. The second belief is what makes it pessimistic: in the politics of lawmaking, the self-serving majority will regularly dump on marginalised and powerless groups. Even if we could ensure cumulative change in the formative arrangements and enacted beliefs of society, it would likely make things even more dangerous for the most vulnerable groups. Their protective rights might be swept away in the enthusiasm of a reconstructive period. The tax-and-transfer schemes of an institutionally conservative social democracy and the retrospective improvement of law by rationalising legal analysis offer the weak their best hope. Indeed, seen in this revealing light, social democracy and rationalising legal analysis are the twin instruments of the same political project. By putting the best face on the law, by representing it as impersonal policy and principle rather than as the triumph of powerful and partial coalitions of interests, the lawyer can make things better for the people who need help most. In the name of the idealising interpretation of law, he can redistribute rights and resources to the repeated victims of the lawmaking coalitions. The progressive commitment is, therefore, the determination so to use rationalising legal analysis.

From such a vantage point the canonical style of legal doctrine may be a lie, but it is a noble and a necessary lie. It gives insurance against the worst as well as the promise of modest but real improvement in the condition of those, who without its help, would stand to lose most.

The analytic practice accompanying this vision of law hardly differs from the recourse to ideal purposes in rationalising legal analysis. It is rationalising legal analysis with an ironic proviso: that although the assumptions of the method may not be literally believable they serve a vital goal. The subtlety in this conversion of vision into vocabulary and of vocabulary into strategy is that the strategic imperative requires the agent to continue speaking the vocabulary of the vision in which he has ceased to believe. In so doing, he fails fully to grasp the hidden restraints implicit in his supposedly strategic language. Rationalising legal analysis, it turns out, is not equally well-suited for all varieties of politics. It suits an institutionally conservative politics: one that renounces persistent and cumulative tinkering with the institutional structure and seeks, instead, to redistribute rights and resources within that structure.

When the major problems of society begin to require, for their solution, experimentalism about practical arrangements, this defect proves fatal. The tactic avenges itself against the tactician.

The present form of legal consciousness is not one of these moments of legal thought or another. It is, rather, the combination of all three. All three ways of thinking coexist not only in the same legal and political culture but often in the same individual minds. The result is a discursive community bound together, as discursive communities so often are, according to the principle enunciated by the narrator in Proust's novel: we are friends with those whose ideas are at the same level of confusion as our own.

Legal analysis as institutional imagination

Aims of a revised practice of legal analysis

Implicit in my discussion of rationalising legal analysis are a series of connected standards by which to guide and to assess the redirection of legal thought outside adjudication. These standards converge to yield the idea of legal analysis as institutional imagination.

Thus, the method we need should be free of the taint of institutional fetishism and structure fetishism. Institutional fetishism is the identification of abstract institutional conceptions like the market economy or representative democracy with a particular repertory of contingent arrangements. Structure fetishism is its higher-order counterpart: the failure to recognise that the institutional and imaginative orders of social life differ in their entrenchment as well as in their content: that is to say, in the relation to the structure-defying and structure-transforming freedom of action and insight they constrain. The method should help us identify and resolve the internal instability characteristic of programmatic positions in contemporary law and politics: the conflict between the commitment to defining ideals, and the acquiescence in arrangements that frustrate the realisation of those ideals, or impoverish their meaning. Consequently, it should seize upon the internal relation between thinking about ideals or interests and thinking about institutions or practices. When so doing, it can gain energy and direction from a larger conception of the democratic project as well as from more particular professed ideas and recognised interests, for the democratic project, properly interpreted, is both our most powerful family of ideals and our most promising way to reconcile our devotion to these ideals with the pursuit of our material interests.

To these ends, the method should make good on the capacity of law and legal thought to move at the level of full detail in representing the relation of practices and institutions to interests and ideals, and in connecting the realities of power to the discourse of aspiration. To mobilise these resources, it must rid itself of the anti-analogical prejudice; of the illusory belief in rational reconstruction as the necessary and sufficient antidote to arbitrariness in law; of the confusions and equivocations of conservative reformism, particularly in the variant of pessimistic progressive reformism; and of the obsession with judges and the ways they decide cases. It must elect the citizenry as its primary and ultimate interlocutor. It must imagine its work to be that of informing the conversation in a democracy about its present and alternative futures.

Mapping and criticism

These aims come together in the practice of legal analysis as institutional imagination. This practice has two, dialectically linked moments: mapping and criticism. Give the name *mapping* to the suitably revised version of the low-level, spiritless analogical activity, the form of legal analysis that leaves the law an untransformed heap. Mapping is the attempt to describe in detail the legally defined institutional microstructure of society in relation to its legally articulated ideals. Call the second moment of this analytic practice *criticism*: the revised version of what the rationalistic jurists deride as the turning of legal analysis into ideological conflict. Its task is to explore the interplay between the detailed institutional arrangements of society as represented in law, and the professed ideals or programmes these arrangements frustrate and make real.

Mapping is the exploration of the detailed institutional structure of society, as it is legally defined. It would be naive positivism to suppose that this structure is uncontroversially manifest, and can be portrayed apart from theoretical preconceptions. The crucial point of mapping is to produce a detailed, although fragmentary, legal-institutional analysis replacing one such set of preconceptions by another.

The perspective to be adopted is the standpoint of the second moment of the revised practice of legal analysis I am sketching: the moment of criticism. Thus, the two moments connect closely; they are related — to use one vocabulary — dialectically — and to use another — internally. Mapping serving the purpose of criticism is an analysis exhibiting the formative institutions of society and its enacted dogmas about human association as a distinct and surprising structure and, above all, as a structure that can be revised part by part. The established system of such arrangements and beliefs both constrains the realisation of our professed social ideals and recognised group interests and gives them much of their tacit meaning.

The preconceptions to be replaced negate the possibility or the significance of criticism. Such preconceptions present the greater part of any extended and received body of law and legal understandings as an expression of a cohesive moral and political vision, or of a set of practical necessities, or of a lawlike evolutionary sequence.

One set of such anti-critical abstractions exercising especially great influence in contemporary law and legal thought is the second-order Lochnerism explored earlier. Remember that the earlier, cruder, repudiated Lochnerism is the contrast between a law that is just there, prepolitically, as the built-in legal structure of an accepted and established type of economic and governmental organisation — call it liberal capitalist democracy or whatever — and a law that represents the unprincipled, faction-driven, redistributive intervention of government in this core legal structure. That is the Lochnerism American notables — and their European counterparts — rejected, although they still have not rejected it completely and unequivocally. The Lochnerism that survives, generating a steady stream of abstractions that prevent the work of mapping-criticism, is the Lochnerism meant to distinguish concessions to factional interest or outlook from expressions of impersonal moral and political vision or practical necessity. The expressions must be rescued from the concessions, and it is on the basis of invocations of the former and denunciations of the latter that rationalising legal analysis does its work.

The language of contemporary politics commonly superimposes such reassuring ideological abstractions, more or less directly, upon low-level promises to particular organised interests. At every turn it becomes impossible to tell whether the abstractions serve as an ideological disguise for the pursuit of the interests, or whether, on the contrary, the pursuit of the interests is being disoriented by the abstractions. What we chiefly lack is what should be the very heart of political discourse: the middle ground of alternative trajectories of institutional and policy change. To help develop this middle ground is one of the tasks of the combined practice of mapping and criticism. A requirement for the accomplishment of this task is that we resist the impulse to rationalise or to idealise the institutions and the laws we actually have.

What type of insight may one hope to develop through the practice of mapping? Consider the example of the relation of the traditional property right to the many exceptions that begin to surround it. The property right, bringing together many faculties assigned to the same right-holder, is the very model of the modern idea of right, and the central mechanism for the allocation of decentralised claims to capital. Yet we find in contemporary legal systems many areas of law and practice that settle matters in ways departing from the logic of this property entitlement. In agriculture, for example, there may be a partnership between the government and the family farmer decomposing the property right and limiting the absoluteness of the property owner's right in exchange for varieties of governmental support. In the defence-procurement industry, and even more under the conditions of war capitalism, a similar decomposition in the form of collaboration between public power and the private producer may occur. In the development of contemporary capital markets we see a continuous creation of new markets in particular faculties abstracted out of the comprehensive property entitlement. The situation then begins to look like this: the main mechanism is surrounded by a growing number of exceptions. However, even if traditional property had been eviscerated more than it in fact has been, it would continue to occupy the vital role of holding the space that any other generalised form of decentralised allocation of capital would hold. It holds the place that would be occupied by the alternative method of decentralised capital allocation already prefigured in the current exceptions to the unified property right. This is a typical example of the type of combination of sameness and variety one might hope to discover through mapping.

The second moment of this revised practice of legal analysis is criticism. Criticism explores the disharmonies between the professed social ideals and programmatic commitments of society, as well as the recognised group interests, and the detailed institutional arrangements that not only constrain the realisation of those ideals, programmes, and interests, but also give them their developed meaning.

The relation between criticism and mapping can now come more clearly into focus. Mapping provides materials for criticism, and criticism sets the perspective and the agenda for mapping. Nothing in my account of the revised practice of legal analysis defines the extent to which criticism can itself be informed or guided by a more context-independent type of moral and political argument. Rather than addressing that issue now, however, it is enough to recognise how little we need a prior and confident view of it, to begin revising the practice of legal analysis in this way and to begin practising the revision. The reoriented approach may prove compatible with a broad range of positions about our ability to connect with a less history-bound mode of judgement. Moreover, the new practice may itself have something to teach us about the relative merits of different views of authority beyond context in moral and political disputes.

Consider now some lines along which we might work out the anti-rationalising response to the circumstance of contemporary law and legal thought. The first task — the task of the mapping moment — is to understand the existing institutional situation as the complex and contradictory structure that it really is, as the strange and surprising settlement that you could never guess from abstractions like 'the mixed economy,' 'representative democracy,' or 'industrial society.' In this view, the jurist should work as an enlarger of the collective sense of reality and possibility. He must imitate the artist who makes the familiar strange, restoring to our understanding of our situation some of the lost and repressed sense of transformative opportunity.

The focus of mapping is the attempt to construct a picture of our institutions — of the government, of the economy, the family — out of the stuff of law and legal doctrine. It is a hard task; the material wears no particular picture on its face. What kind of picture do we want? First, we want a view that defines itself by contrast to the rationalising account. This account — remember — wants to present the stuff of law as tied together in a way that justifies most of it while rejecting a minor part of it. Rational reconstruction in law justifies and interprets the greater part of the law and of the received legal understandings either as the expression of an evolving system of moral and political conceptions or as the outcome of inexorable functional requirements. Affirmatively, the view we want is the view serving the purposes of the second moment of this analytic practice: the moment of criticism, when we focus on the disharmonies of the law and on the way in which the ideal conceptions, expressed in policies and principles, or the group interests represented by programmes and strategies, get truncated in their fulfilment and impoverished in their meaning by their received institutional forms.

I have already offered a number of examples of the mapping exercise: the partial alternatives to the unified property idea that we can already witness in current law and practice; the relation of traditional rights adjudication to the structural but episodic intervention of complex enforcement; and, more generally, the dialectical organisation of contemporary law in each of its branches as a duality of rights of personal choice and popular self-government and rights designed to ensure the reality of individual and collective self-determination.

Do we need a full-blown theory, a practice of social explanation, a set of programmatic ideas, and a conception of the relation between programmatic thinking and social explanation to inform mapping? The answer is yes and no. We need such ideas fully to develop and elucidate the revised practice of legal analysis. But we need not have such a theory to begin the mapping.

We already have two points of departure at hand. One starting point is the effort to radicalise the professed social ideals or party programmes, to take them beyond their existing institutional constraints, and to change their meaning in the course of doing so. Another point of departure is the negativistic work of demolishing the rationalising conceptions and interpretations of contemporary law.

Thus, this mapping involves no naive acceptance of the low-level, analogical, glossatorial picture of law as an unshaped, undigested heap. It demands a radical redrawing of that picture from the standpoint of the precommitments of criticism. The moments of mapping and criticism form a dialectical unity. We can nevertheless claim for the low-level, analogical conception of law certain advantages. It presents extant law and received legal understanding free — or freer — from the rationalising spell and from the special outlook of the Madisonian notables, ever anxious for a view of law on which, as judges or publicists, they can act with the least embarrassment.

Is criticism more likely to occur under conditions in which mapping dominates the legal culture, or in situations in which rationalisation does? To answer this question, we must begin by remembering that mapping and criticism are indissoluble; they are aspects or moments of the same practice. Just as mapping provides materials for criticism, it is already done with the interests of criticism in mind. Moreover, as a practical matter, the formation of such a transformative analytic practice is possible only in the historical circumstance in which we can rebel against runaway rationalisation. For, even as rationalising analysis in law, and in the corresponding areas of political and social thought, mythologises our institutions, it also generalises our ideals. It thus sets the stage on which the mapper-critic can go to work.

The realist and the visionary

Lawyers have pictured law as reason encoded in the doings and dreams of power just as economists have seen actual market economies and their law as approximations to a pure system of rationality and reciprocity. They have sung for their supper by singing in their chains. Hope and insight may nevertheless succeed where indignation and history worship failed, and draw the lawyers and economists into the work of giving eyes and wings to the institutional imagination.

Our interests and ideals remain nailed to the cross of our arrangements. We cannot realise our interests and ideals more fully, nor redefine them more deeply, until we have learned to remake and to reimagine our arrangements more freely. History will not give us this freedom. We must win it in the here and now of legal detail, economic constraint, and deadening preconception. We shall not win it if we continue to profess a science of society reducing the possible to the actual, and a discourse about law anointing power with piety. It is true that we cannot be visionaries until we become realists. It is also true that to become realists we must make ourselves into visionaries.

[11]

The Inertia of Institutional Imagination: A Reply to Roberto Unger

Emilios A. Christodoulidis*

Introduction

Today, as ever, Roberto Unger challenges us to place our concept of the political at risk. Much of his recent work renews his earlier call for an empowerment of politics, involving our constant alertness to the possibilities of change, the revisability of those possibilities and the removal of all that falsely presents itself as unrevisable. This call for the empowerment of politics is not, of course, couched in the vocabulary of republicanism, as so much other recent legal theory is. But neither is it an appeal to the smashing of all contexts, to the tireless resistance to the institutional; no, Unger's great novelty is that his politics are both radical and institutional.

Nothing, says Unger, compels us to reduce the political to the exclusive alternatives of 'tinkering' with the institutions or revolting against them.[1] This disjunction blinkers the very real possibility that the political may draw its inspiration from the institutions' — significantly here law's — own powerful imagination. Unger's work in legal and social theory is the constant endeavour to do just that, to tap that imagination. For him law is not rigid and confining. In a powerful statement of the 'law-as-politics' thesis, Unger vests in law the possibility to pursue radical politics and counter the 'false necessity' of the confinement of our political vision within rigid institutional assumptions. This argument has for some time now been expounded by the Critical Legal School that seeks to upset the legal system's tendency to assimilate the new to the old, its overwhelming of the innovative, its tendency to rationalise the incongruent into coherence. In his article in this journal,[2] Unger names his opponent as the school of 'rationalising legal analysis,' where 'rationalising' means the alleged 'improvement' that 'happens by developing the underlying conceptions of principle and policy and by *rejecting* bit by bit the pieces of received understanding and principle that *fail to fit* the preferred conceptions of policy and principle.'[3] Unger

---

*Lecturer in Jurisprudence, Centre for Law and Society, Faculty of Law, University of Edinburgh.
This article was written in reply to Roberto Unger's Chorley lecture, 'Legal Analysis as Institutional Imagination,' given at the London School of Economics on 31 May 1995, the revised version of it, 'Legal Analysis as Institutional Imagination' (1996) 59 MLR 1, and the informal seminar that followed the lecture the next day. The author would like to thank Beverley Brown, David Garland, Sean Smitn, Scott Veitch, the participants in the Political Theory Seminar in Edinburgh and the anonymous expert readers of the MLR for their helpful comments.

1 'In this way we can break a little further from the tedious, degrading rhythm of history — with its long lulls of collective narcolepsy punctuated by violent revolutionary seizures': *False Necessity: Anti-Necessitarian Social Theory in the Service of Radical Democracy* (Cambridge: Cambridge University Press, 1987) p 1.
2 Unger, 'Legal Analysis as Institutional Imagination' (1996) 59 MLR 1.
3 *ibid* p 9, emphasis added. Obviously, if not explicitly, Dworkin, *Law's Empire* (London: Fontana, 1986). In this context, see also Bengoextea's excellent 'Legal System as a Regulative Ideal' (1994) *ARSP Beiheft* 53, 66–80, for a different account of the 'rationalising' process.

warns that a theorist undertaking this kind of analysis 'will sooner or later become a mystifier and an apologist,' 'acquiescing to institutional fetishism' and conspiring to the impoverishment of legal analysis through its foreclosure of broader conflict. In contrast, Critical Legal Analysis is geared to restoring 'deviations and contradictions as intellectual and political opportunities rather than threats.'[4] To resist the severing of legal analysis from broader conflicts, it will draw from the system itself to reveal suppressed possibilities by showing legal dogma to be incoherent, then play up the 'dangerous supplements.' Where the law exhibits the overwhelming tendency to assimilate the 'deviant' case within already existing schemata of processing it, the critical scholar will emphasise alternative possibilities, new relevancies that upset settled patterns. There is a strong continuity in Unger's accounts of how this strategy of 'dis-entrenchment' and 're-construction' is envisaged, going back to at least his CLS manifesto,[5] and variably described as 'deviationist doctrine,'[6] 'negative capability,'[7] and 'mapping and criticism.'[8] In each case, significantly, the same political logic of disruption draws from within the institution: as Unger put it in the Chorley lecture, his Critical Legal Theory understands the institution as law but undertakes it as politics.

I will return to this later to detail, with Unger, aspects of this institutional imagination. But I want to argue that Unger invests too much in this. While he is right to say that the system's inertia can be shaken from within, the endeavour cannot carry through to those constitutive assumptions that underlie the institutional identity as such. Employing Niklas Luhmann's terms, we will see that there are certain constitutive reductions at play in law's picture of the world and to challenge those would not be to undertake law as politics but to do away with law altogether. To denote this form of unshakeable inertia, I will call it 'structural' and distinguish it from a second form, 'simple' inertia, that can indeed be successfully redressed. In effect, this is the dilemma that, I suggest, Unger has to face: either he concedes the 'structural' type of inertia in which case he *can* exploit the transformative potential of the system to combat 'simple' inertia, but within the limits dictated by the system, or he concedes nothing, undertakes law as politics, but then collapses the specific institutional achievement that is law and the possibilities *it* offers. And if Unger thus collapses law into politics, what remains of the heuristic value of the politics *of* law? Of course, Unger would contest this and argue that it resurrects the unnecessary disjunctions between what is revolutionary and thus authentic, and what is institutional and thus frozen, what is total, radical change against what is moderate and fragmentary change, etc. To some extent he must be right, but then, can he really say that there is no asking price for a politics of law? I suggest not. In fact, I will argue counter-intuitively perhaps, if law does harbour transformative opportunities it is because there are limits to law's institutional imagination that take the form of reductions which, at a deep level, cannot but remain in place. We cannot retain the opportunities if we do away with the reductions. And, as a result, law cannot but foreclose broader political conflict and, in the last instance, assimilate transformative opportunity to its own self-maintenance and assimilate the disruptive to its own controlled

---

4 *ibid* pp 9–11.
5 Unger, *The Critical Legal Studies Movement* (Cambridge, Mass: Harvard University Press, 1983).
6 *ibid* pp 15ff.
7 Unger, *Social Theory: Its Situation and Its Task* (Cambridge: Cambridge University Press, 1987) pp 81, 156–157.
8 Unger, *op cit* n 2, pp 20ff.

evolution. To this, Unger will only ever respond with a statement of faith in the infinite plasticity of law.[9]

The case of 'solidarity rights'

Throughout the article I will use one of Unger's favourite examples and turn it against him. It is an example of the interplay of the institutional on the one hand, of the imaginative, spontaneous and 'plastic'[10] on the other. It is, or so it is claimed, an interplay that allows the institutional to feed off social imagination and the imaginative to appear as something more than the mere negation of the institutional. This is precisely the moment of the overcoming of those dualisms that Unger vehemently opposes. The example is that of *solidarity rights*,[11] one of the four categories of his 'reconstructed system of rights.'[12] True to the 'generative principles' that inform Unger's programme for empowering democracy, the concept brings together the institutional — the right — with the spontaneous — solidarity — in a moment that empowers them both.

It is worth noting that Unger is more vague than usual in the discussion of the content and precise function of these rights. Of course, many of Unger's most important and valuable theoretical insights are couched in an idiom that is tentative, suggestive, declaratory, never quite concrete enough. As theory for a practice that itself plays on and tends to the unfinished, the endeavour is commendable. But one cannot help wondering if the generality of his analysis here, very much on the lines of a directive for future undertakings, is an intentional evasion. This is worrying. The connection between solidarity and law is a crucial one. Solidarity is the foundation of community, the ideal behind human association that motivates much Critical Legal Theory. Unger cannot afford to allow the argument to weaken at this point. Were a successful theory of solidarity rights to be advanced, Unger could claim to have given communities the institutional medium to achieve solidarity and to that extent a language for self-realisation; with the same token, to have transcribed at the institutional level the transformation of personal relations, his *ultima ratio* of politics;[13] and, most important for present purposes, to have pursued this political vision with the means provided by the law, to have had social experimentation flourish on the back of the institutional.

Unger has no qualms about pronouncing the importance and breadth of the project of institutionalising solidarity. 'Solidarity rights,' he says, 'form part of a set of social relations enabling people to enact a more defensible version of the communal ideal than any version currently available to them.' He accepts that these rights do not sit comfortably with the typical form of a right that remains 'devoted to the model of consolidated property.'[14] What the introduction of this

---

9 'Lawyers ... have sung for their supper by singing in their chains. Hope and insight may nevertheless succeed where indignation and history worship failed, and draw lawyers into the work of giving eyes and wings to the institutional imagination' (*ibid* p 23).
10 According to the title of vol 3 of *Politics: Plasticity Into Power* (Cambridge: Cambridge University Press, 1987).
11 Unger, *op cit* n 1, pp 535ff.
12 *ibid* pp 508ff. The other categories are 'market rights,' 'immunity rights' and 'destabilization rights.'
13 Something that Unger does not discuss fully in *Politics* but refers his reader to his 'parallel exploration' of the topic in *Passion: An Essay on Personality* (New York: Free Press, 1983): see *op cit* n 7, p 223, and *op cit* n 1, p 604.
14 Unger, *op cit* n 1, pp 535, 536.

type of right achieves is to 'prevent people from taking refuge in an area of absolute discretion[15] within which they can remain deaf to the claims others make upon them.'[16] This paves the way to solidarity. Unger also clarifies that conflict, in the context of which solidarity rights will be raised, does not erode solidarity. Solidarity, he says, is not the opposite of conflict. Rather, people should be encouraged to recognise and use the element of conflict 'that marks even the closest personal connections.'[17]

Although very little is said about the precise content of these rights, one can assume on the basis of Unger's other writings that the content would be retrieved through playing up principles already present — if sometimes suppressed — in existing law. The mechanism and logic of this have been elaborated at length elsewhere by Unger in the context of legal analysis[18] and more generally.[19] In 'Legal Analysis as Institutional Imagination,' he renews his call for a 'selective probing of institutions' through the 'dialectical exercise of mapping and criticism.'[20] Unger's suggestion in all of this is for an interpretative method of reasoning that draws on and exploits strategically existing if latent institutional possibilities. In the case of solidarity rights, reconstruction would proceed from the protection of solidarity in existing law — of contract and delict basically — such as the protection of reliance and the protection of the disadvantaged party, general clauses of good faith and of abuse of rights, etc, 'by which private law supports communal relations while continuing to represent society as a world of strangers.'[21]

But can the law fulfil the quest for solidarity? There are problems here. There is a certain incompatibility that brings out a paradox. Sacrifices made in solidarity towards fellow members of the community must be voluntary if they are to express solidarity; their enforcement, whether in court but even 'in the shadow of the law,' makes the right the opposite of solidarity.[22] Either the right is enforced, in which case it is not the expression of solidarity, or it is in solidarity, therefore *never* to be enforced and therefore not a right. Unger is aware of this and claims that 'it does not follow from the establishment of solidarity rights that they ought to be coercively enforced.' It is difficult to know what to make of this. Unger's suggestion is that 'many of the solidarity rights may best be enforced, when they are enforced at all, by more informal means of mediation.' Notwithstanding this reference to informal justice, he is happy to accept that 'many solidarity rights may best remain unenforceable, as a statement of an ideal ... because the threat [of enforcement] might fatally injure the quality of reciprocal trust they require.'[23] This is the argument I made previously about enforceability being the opposite of solidarity. But the concept cannot withstand this contradiction. These rights cannot

---

15 Through immunity rights and market rights; *ibid* pp 520–530.
16 *ibid* p 537.
17 *ibid* p 536.
18 Unger, *op cit* n 5, pp 15–22, 88–90.
19 Unger, *op cit* n 1, pp 277ff.
20 Unger, *op cit* n 2, pp 17, 23.
21 Unger, *op cit* n 1, p 537.
22 This may be too strong a statement because some part at least of taking the conflict to law involves consenting in advance to the enforcement of the decision even if one loses. One can thus speak of a 'thin' solidarity of a different level, one that involves an agreement to disagree and that upholds the solidarity of the community at some level. But can this kind of commitment ever generate the kind of solidarity Unger has in mind and which he has elsewhere described as the 'social face of love'? (See text to n 25.)
23 Unger, *op cit* n 1, pp 538, 539.

be operationalised without undercutting what they are meant to enact, that is, solidarity. A right that *must not* be enforced is no right at all, to the extent that even its symbolic value — 'as a statement of an ideal' — is undercut by the lack of willingness to enforce it, because it takes away that sanctioning that is specific to law and is therefore anterior to any symbolic value the law may have as law (not least because enforceability is the expression of the will of a society to back the rightness of its law by force if necessary).

But enforceability is not the whole problem, it is merely symptomatic of the problem. What about the content for example? The content of solidarity cannot be argued in law except in terms of claims and counter-claims, what solidarity is not. Paradoxes spring up everywhere; we will explore them systematically when we discuss later how law 'reduces' solidarity in the 'social' and 'material' dimensions. Suffice it here to indicate how uncomfortably the ideal sits with its 'realisation' in law; how the purported 'dialectic' is constantly verging on 'contradiction'; how, in Fullerian terms perhaps, the duty is undercutting the aspiration.[24] The process of reconceiving the ideal legally forces anything but the thinnest notion of solidarity to continually slip away in the face of legal assumptions that cannot be negotiated or imagined away. And it is no thin notion that Unger has in mind; as he pointed out nearly twenty years ago, for him solidarity is nothing short of:

> the social face of love; ... [and] love is neither an act nor an emotion, but a gift of self, which may fail to eventuate in acts ... There is a single reason why no set of rules and principles can do justice to the sentiment of solidarity. A legal order confers entitlements and obligations ... An individual's rights and duties resemble the forces of nature in the way they set limits to his striving.[25]

Unger is here criticising a type of legal system that exhibits formality and rigidity, so it would do his argument injustice to generalise it. But let us at least note the tension: solidarity involves a 'reaching out' to the other person, an element of suppression of the self and sacrifice towards the other, and law by its very structure as a means of litigating competing claims, its operating of dispositive concepts and the win-or-lose principle, violates the self-effacing moment underlying the encounter of solidarity.

So it may not be that surprising, but it is remarkable, that in the moment of difficulty Unger abandons the legal for the extra-legal: he says that what is required is 'an additional definition in context,' one that presumably overcomes law's rather flat picture of social relationships; then he oscillates back to law to resurrect the paradox: 'for only the specific relational context can reveal a structure of interdependence ... because it undermines rigid role systems.'[26] But how will this additional definition be worked into law if not through legal relevancies? How will notions of interdependence be worked into law if not through legal self-descriptions of positions in law (employer–employee, spouses, seller–buyer, commissioner–commissioned, producer–consumer, etc); in other words, 'role systems'? Legal self-descriptions become more varied as law becomes more 'responsive' or 'material,' but the variety is still produced by a proliferation of relevant positions that are reductions in law: points of allocation and address of subjectivity in law. The law cannot take social interdependence on board as such, since, in law, such interdependence, whether as co-operation or conflict, is staged

---

24 Fuller, *The Morality of Law* (New Haven: Yale University Press, 2nd ed, 1969).
25 Unger, *Law In Modern Society* (New York: The Free Press, 1976) pp 206–207.
26 Unger, *op cit* n 1, p 538.

through categories that pre-ordain its form and content, demarcate the problems and pre-empt what can be said about them. At the same time, other demarcations of the problem and its object are excluded. Briefly put, in the legal system solidarity is necessarily aligned to legal co-ordinates where concepts of rights, liberties, legal notions of harm and legal analogies, legal tests and legal presumptions first make sense of it. Who can allege to have suffered harm or benefited, who counts as the disadvantaged party entitled to a solidarity claim, why and when, as well as what enters the balance and what tilts the balance, to what side, all depend on a multitude of legal descriptions and conditional attributions that create the necessary relevancies and legal evaluations; in a word, all that is experienced as law. *All these relevancies allow for social interdependence selectively, they impose reductions on possible alternatives.* What remains outside the sphere of legal relevance, outwith the area of legal contingencies, appears as natural, obvious, given, inert to challenge. Unger is uncomfortable with this and designates the crucial structural feature of a solidarity right as demanding that 'the determination of where the rightholder stands along the spectrum of legal protection depends on an analysis of his pre-legal relation to the person against whom he wants to assert the right.'[27] This is unworkable, as we will see. 'Pre-legal' only resonates in law as legal. Otherwise, what criteria is law to operationalise to determine the 'pre-legal' that are innocent of their own classificatory logic?

At this point I will begin to elaborate more precisely the argument against Unger's purported unleashing of the institutional imagination. Specifically in the following section, we will ask: why is it that legal analysis gives us a limited and limiting repertoire for 'a sustained conversation about our [social and political] arrangements?'[28] I will argue against Unger that it is limiting, not because I mistake 'discourse about law [to have] some permanent essence,'[29] but because of a complexity deficit: law is a reduction from other possible political discourse. Legal institutionalisation is the entrenchment of certain reductions. Having established this, I will argue, more narrowly, that social interdependence acquires a specific form in law to the exclusion of other possibilities. One such excluded possibility is fully-fledged solidarity. For the purpose of arguing both these points, I will employ some theoretical suggestions of Niklas Luhmann's. I should say, however, that the reference here to systems theory is of necessity both sketchy and selective. It aims to explain why law is an area of reduced complexity in relation to the world it tries to account for and regulate, and what this means for the politics of law. Also, why this reduction is, contra Unger, not only inescapable but, counter-intuitively, why it is also empowering; in Luhmann's terms, 'a reduction *achievement.*' In the later sections we will explore why this reduction is tied to a certain *immunisation* from all those political possibilities that Unger invites law to remain attentive to. We will do this by returning to the example of 'solidarity rights.' In the process we will discuss the two types of inertia — simple and structural — already mentioned that present Unger with a dilemma that is no longer false.[30]

---

27 ibid.
28 Unger, *op cit* n 2, p 8.
29 ibid.
30 Following Unger (*op cit* n 7, p 4), I employ the terms 'structure,' 'context' and 'framework' interchangeably, as the associative webs that bind us and, with some qualifications, will add 'system' to the list.

Institutional imagination as reduction achievement: the contribution of systems theory

The world is infinitely complex, says Luhmann, it admits of a variety of ways it can be talked about, it possesses many aspects and possibilities of its description.[31] New perspectives relativise older ones, the false necessities of 'natural' descriptions are shaken as they do; every such new description reminds us of the world's complexity, but also increases that complexity by adding to the possibilities of describing it.

Every system restricts on its own terms the ambit of what is meaningful by filtering communication through system-relevance established by the code.[32] Competing categorisations and interpretations of events will not all find expression in the system's terms; out of the infinite possibilities of describing a person's action, for example, the legal system addresses what is relevant to deeming it legal or illegal. Only on that basis can a person's will further be thematised as intention or motive on the basis that it is conducive to a legal characterisation of his/her action. (The economic system may recast that expression of the will as economic–rational preference, the political system assesses it in terms of support or disaffection to Government or Opposition.) Each system will restrict the modes in which the world can be talked about by perceiving it in a categorically preformed way.[33] The complexity of the world is thus met from within the system through specific capacities of resonance. The system creates 'order from noise' by drawing selectively on the surplus of possibilities — the domain of high complexity — potentially available outwith it. 'Noise' is what is not yet reduced. In the process of this selective depiction, the system constructs the external world that it cannot conceive in its complexity. A system knows by simplifying, and then by choosing amongst, manipulating and combining these self-produced simplifications that stand in for that which is too complex for the system to conceive. Systems are agents of reduction, in terms of which the unbearable complexity of the world becomes meaningful. This reduction, adds Poggi, allows the system 'a simple hold upon possibly highly complex stretches of reality.'[34] Meaning is always system-specific, says Luhmann. It depends on a reduction of complexity, a reduction in the scope of possibilities of all that may be communicated.[35] A system comes about when a specific, reductive, selective way of observing a complex world, with a surplus of possibilities, is established. Put another way, in Husserl's terms perhaps, the world is a horizon; it is not yet meaningful except as a background against which certain possibilities are actualised (by the system) over against those that are not (the environment).

Luhmann is thus arguing that what Unger calls institutional imagination forces and entrenches a reduction on the 'plastic' world of political possibilities. We will return to this discussion in the next section to see how *reduction* translates into *a*

---

31 Luhmann's theory cannot be explained at length here. His theory of the autopoiesis of social systems is masterfully developed in his *Soziale Systeme* (Frankfurt: Suhrkamp, 1984).
32 For a concise account of how coding works and how it links to 'programming,' see Luhmann, *Ecological Communication* (trans J. Bednarz, Cambridge: Polity Press, 1986).
33 *ibid* p 12.
34 In his introduction to Luhmann, *Trust and Power* (Chichester: Wiley, 1979) p x.
35 'Everything which can be predicated of systems — differentiation into parts, hierarchy building, boundary maintenance, differentiation between structure and process, selective modelling of environments, etc — may be functionally analysed as a reduction of complexity' (Luhmann, *ibid* p 256).

certain redundancy of legal reasoning, a certain inertia of the system, in what it is prepared to process as information that might stretch its imagination and discover within it Unger's much emphasised 'transformative opportunities.' At this stage, let us note an important point. It is precisely this reduction that is treated by Luhmann as an achievement. Because before the system reduced it by encoding it, the world in all its complexity remained undifferentiated and thus unobservable, its wealth of possibilities still underdetermined. The world itself is not binary; through the bivalency of the code a reduction is imposed on it in a way that makes it yield information. It is for this reason that reduction is an 'achievement,' both empowering and limiting. The institutional imagination is always the imagination of something already reduced, but it is also an achievement, a source of insight. The system's cognitive openness, in fact the cognitive openness that can be nothing else except systemic, is premised on the system's closure, its ability to reduce the complexity it is faced with. Then, gradually, the system can build up internal complexity, become what Unger would call more 'plastic,' 'see' more things and cope more adequately with external reality, grasping states and events as information, 'setting up systemic boundaries, structuring a discourse, establishing a universe.'[36]

Legal institutionalisation is the entrenchment of certain reductions on the possibilities of communication; through it, social interdependence acquires a specific — 'reduced' — form in law to the exclusion of other possibilities. This in turn is in its own way empowering. Institutional imagination is indeed a reduction *achievement*. It is an achievement to be assessed in the light of the possibilities it offers people to communicate successfully, among other things, about what it means to be in a community, what solidarity requires. It is an achievement in the face of high complexity, in a world that is making it all the more urgent but at the same time all the more unlikely that such communication and the action that depends on it (political praxis significantly) will be carried out with success. Since Parsons, and Hobbes before him, the question has been traced back to how patterns of social interdependence can build up with any constancy; Parsons suggested locating the query in the context of the potentially erosive situation of *double contingency*, the problem, that is, of the potential unlikeliness that people's expectations will articulate to allow communication and interaction in the first place. Let us look at this more closely.

Interaction depends on social–cognitive concepts regarding Ego/Alter relations. Interaction requires that the social actor relate the meaningful sense of his/her action to that of others. Interaction implies that success or failure of a communicative offer oriented to Alter depends on what Alter expects. Otherwise there is no communication and neither side can orient their action, in a way either can comprehend, to the other's expectations. In order to achieve this elementary interaction with Alter, Ego not only has to predict and take account of Alter's behaviour but also Alter's expectations of Ego's behaviour. This creates a double indeterminacy that has to be settled. Parsons uses 'contingency' in the sense of 'dependence' and the term 'double contingency' to designate the double dependence of Ego's action on both Alter's behaviour and on Alter's expectation of Ego's behaviour. Because Ego's perspective on Ego/Alter relationships must take on board (is contingent on) Alter's perspective, there exists in this

---

36 Grundmann, 'Luhmann Conservative, Luhmann Progressive,' European University Institute Working Paper, Florence, 1990, p 33.

interdependence two self/other cycles that need to be co-ordinated.[37]

Having relied on Parsons to formulate the problem, Luhmann now breaks in a most significant way from the former's over-reliance on a 'shared symbolic system' — and, underlying it, a normative consensus — that, notoriously in Parsonian theory, overestimates the consensus that exists or, adds Luhmann, that is structurally necessary.[38] That which is required in order for people to interrelate their behaviour is that the complexity of the double indeterminacy be *reduced*. There are a number of levels at which this might happen; for Luhmann, a number of types of systems that may achieve it. The achievement is that of *fixing a context*. This context furnishes a background of shared expectations that will accommodate the reciprocal communicative offers. Interaction first becomes meaningful when the communicative offer is bound to a common context, a background of reciprocity, that alone allows it recognition. More precisely, Luhmann talks of a reduction of double contingency through a structuring into frameworks that have the form of *'expectations of expectations.'* The structuring first allows every single communication to surface as meaningful (therefore as communication), as the common ground where Ego meets Alter around a communication they both understand. Recognition of Alter's intended meaning must be structurally facilitated or it will remain underdetermined. What is understood as a communication depends on how the context accommodates the communicative offer, what Alter expects and what Ego expects Alter to expect, which in turn varies according to how the message is filtered into the specific framework of expectations of expectations. Systems thus become constraints that facilitate meaning. And this is no paradox: only constraints as reductions can allow intelligibility and interaction by *setting up a context* and carving out *only a certain part of the totality* (of possible communication) *as expectable*. The expectability of expectations underlies all social interaction, but acquires specific forms that are particular to systems that, as templates, impose specific reductions to the open contingency of (proto-) communication and make it structured and meaningful. What reductions structures impose has to do with how their selectivity mechanisms set up the system domain and how themes of communication develop, around which communicative offers may be organised. Taking it all back to double contingency allows Luhmann to establish that communication is only possible through reductions which are in turn premised on system selectivity. In his own words, 'Kommunikation ist koordinierte Selektivität.'[39] It is of constitutive importance for communication that communicative offers crystallise in systems around 'selective alignments of meaning selections'[40] and thus ensure the possibility of successful communication.

---

37 The *locus classicus* in Parsons for describing this interdependence is the following: 'Since the outcome of ego's action (eg success in the achievement of a goal) is contingent on alter's reaction to what ego does, ego becomes oriented not only to alter's probable overt behaviour, but also what ego interprets to be alter's expectations relative to ego's behaviour since ego expects that alter's expectations will influence alter's behaviour' (Parsons and Shils, *Toward a General Theory of Action*, Cambridge, Mass: Harvard UP, 1951, p 105).
38 Luhmann argues that neither the possibility of such consensus nor (contra Habermas) the willingness of actors to reach it can be guaranteed at the outset. Assuming it on the basis of a shared cultural background leads Parsons to overestimate the integrative function of culture which he uses as a ready for use provision, a postulate that begs the crucial question of how it came to be (Luhmann, *op cit* n 31, pp 149ff).
39 *ibid* p 212.
40 *ibid* p 192.

Contexts can be fixed at a number of levels. Simple interactions between, say, friends, lovers, colleagues, develop as contexts that allow reciprocal perspective-taking and thus expectations to articulate. Interactions in wider settings also develop elementary contexts that allow meaningful interchange. But the greatest constancy of the context of reciprocity is achieved at the level of second-order autopoiesis, in other words by functional systems like science, the economy, *law*. Law secures this constancy by narrowing the expectability of expectations, by abstracting from various 'irrelevant' contingencies of the pragmatic situation, by providing norms that involve sanctions should Alter not conform (and thus granting Ego the security of the expectation that Alter *will* conform) but, most important for present purposes, by abstracting from the 'concrete' parties involved and the reciprocal perspective-taking that in turn would involve knowledge of Alter and the contingencies that entails. Instead, the legal system generalises expectations through institutionalisation which here (in Luhmann's terms in the 'social dimension') means the introduction of the third position of the generalised co-expecting[41] other, who, by definition, could have no knowledge of the concrete people involved and could not partake in mutual perspective-taking. The law provides a constancy peculiar to it alone. This is due to the function law has in society of stabilising expectations, of controlling normativity, of guaranteeing that its expectations will not be discredited if disappointed, that Alter is bound by the legal norm and will bear the consequences if she defies it.[42] Legal institutionalisation constructs a context of expectations by reducing double contingency and at the same time renders this context independent of the indeterminacy that comes from concrete interactions: *it allows people to encounter each other as role-players, here, as legal actors.*

A system ascribes roles as descriptions of identity, it allocates roles as the points of attribution and address of Ego and Alter within the system. Roles are part of the system's selectivity mechanisms, an aspect of its reduction achievement, the means through which the system simplifies the potential indeterminacy of social interaction. Through its specific mode of reducing complexity, then, the system establishes the possibility of communication between Ego and Alter as *always-already role-players*. Motive, identity, implied reciprocities that stem from role, are always-already aligned to systems. For Luhmann, role-indeterminacy as context-indeterminacy becomes settled *by* the system but only *for* the system. Co-ordination is settled *by* the system because the system that is doing the reduction work is thereby fixing the contingency space within which the interlocutors' offers can be nothing but co-ordinated, as each takes up one of two exclusive alternatives, the yes or no option. But co-ordination is thus settled only *for* the system. In the absence of any hierarchy between systems or meta-level at which (role-taking) differences between systems could be settled, role co-ordination remains forever open to competing contingencies, competing observations as to what Ego expects of Alter and what is expected of Ego to expect Alter to expect.[43]

So, is Unger not persistently flirting with what is fundamentally erosive to his own theory? What is the meaning of his invitation to 'an institutional order that

---

41 *Normatively* co-expecting, which means that the third party's expectation of alter will *not be discredited* should alter not behave as expected, only *disappointed*.

42 For a similar argument outwith the systems framework, see Aubert, *In Search of Law* (Oxford: Martin Robertson, 1983). One of the most penetrating analyses employing Luhmann's insights here is Klaus Guenther's *Sense of Appropriateness* (Albany: SUNY Press, 1993) pp 255ff.

43 Problems of alienation, role-strain, etc, therefore come about due to the synchronicity of multiple competing systemic role ascriptions.

encourages the jumbling up of fixed roles,' his challenge to the legal to remain attentive to 'the pre-legal' and to define things 'addition[ally] in context'? What additional context? Law provides a context to settle contingencies and the constancy it gives us, Parsons' 'stability of meaning,' is at the expense of other contexts. Unger's impatient urgings to take the 'pre-legal' on board would reopen the contingency, not the empowering contingency that he has in mind, but the double contingency and the incommunicability that would come with keeping both contexts in play, the legal one and Unger's 'additional one.' To 'jumble roles' is an impossible stretching of the institutional imagination that understands interaction by disciplining it within a role; to negotiate roles resurrects the double contingency of social life.

We can now return to the dilemma facing Unger's politics of law. Keeping in mind, first, that legal institutionalisation is an achievement, but a reduction achievement; and, second, how that translates in the realm of social interdependence as a pool of encounters amongst legal actors (as role-players), we will consider how much mileage is left in law's 'transformative opportunities.'

Inertias simple and structural

A system of rights, argues Unger, is an institutionalised version of society, which is to say, a form of social life acquiring a relatively stable and delineated form and generating a *complicated set of expectations*. Luhmann, too, stresses that systems, as dynamic, reproduce themselves by projecting *expectations*, the fulfilment or disappointment of which allows the system to react, modify expectations and evolve. These expectations are of course complicated, as Unger intends them, but not as complicated as social interdependence is in all its potential expressions; legal expectations, as we saw, impose reductions on — and thus always have a complexity deficit in relation to — social expectations. There is a reduction in law from possible expectations and, with the same token, there is *immunisation* from challenge.

Why? Because reduction as simplification works to assimilate potential disruptive complexities into systemic patterns of processing it. This (immunisation or reduction) achievement, while facilitative in many ways, has its cost, a cost for the spontaneous, 'plastic' and imaginative, a cost for reflexivity, for thinking things through. The immunisation works to exclude other possible political conflict, where it is this other conflict that Unger invites as capable of shaking stale assumptions and frozen understandings. Legal expectations allow uncertainty in specific, controlled ways and immunise the system towards other uncertainties it cannot control. The legal system reduces the complexity of possible contingencies: it allows for some, and reproduces itself by responding to them. By the same token, it immunises itself against others that are precluded because expectations are not attuned to them. A system modulates its reaction to its environment by changing expectations and controlling this change at the level of expectations of expectations. There is a deep approximation of conflict to order in this and, at the same time, an impoverishment of the imagination of conflict; among other things, because conflict that is radical and dangerous is thereby silenced. Another reference to systems theory of evolution will explain why.

A system's 'openness' to the world consists in its reading disappointment or fulfilment of the expectations it itself projects. Of course, the system is neither static nor insensitive to change; to remain responsive to a changing world, the system must also vary the expectations it projects. New legal possibilities need to be projected to respond to new situations. New expectations test new patterns of conflict around new issues and their fulfilment or disappointment is fed back into the law as valid new premises for future decisions. The legal system thus varies its structures, reconstructs and alters them, and in the process 'learns' and *evolves*. It does this by providing legal answers to the conflictual expectations that face it requiring litigation. Conflict is necessary for law because it provides input into the reproductive process, without which the system of law would stagnate. But in dealing with conflict, law only achieves a new return to order. It pushes back the threat of disorganisation by conceiving and resettling disturbed practice on the basis of uncontroverted practice.[44] Law conceives of conflicts as disturbances that must be overcome. The conflictual pattern is transitory;[45] a destabilisation that allows legal evolution through successive steps of return to order. The uncertainty of expectations that face law in a situation of social conflict is fruitful ground for internal innovation and simultaneously for the genesis of legal order.[46] The system overcomes the turbulence that it sees conflict as presenting it with, by resettling disturbed practice and sanctioning the resettlement with permanence for the time being. For the legal system, the conflictual pattern is a pathology in the healing of which law evolves.

In a nutshell, the evolution of a system is structural *variation*; and what can vary depends on what already exists. This has major consequences for radical political critique. It brings already existing structural assumptions into play as preconditions to all attempts to push for change. The only way in which a claim for change may register is if it manages to surprise projections of expectations. Following the principle that we can only see what we know how to look for, perception must be based upon an already existing preconception of what is to be seen or understood. For a challenge to register, that is, the system's memory has to be tapped.[47] Law thus controls the context against which informative surprises may be articulated. Change will only always come about as structural drift, a move away from already existing structural givens. This is where I suggest locating the system's *inertia*. While both Unger's and Luhmann's theories capture this powerfully, Unger elides a distinction here that matters: a distinction that needs to be drawn between (i) simple inertia and (ii) structural inertia. It is a distinction that turns on the question of what can be meaningfully challenged within the ambit of the politics of law. It is my claim that we need to take full account of the selectivity of legal imagination, and the 'structural' inertia that comes from the reductions that underlie that selectivity, if we are to make these politics of law aware of the field in which they operate usefully.

---

44 On examples of this, see Heller, 'Accounting for Law' in Teubner (ed), *Autopoietic Law: A New Approach to Law and Society* (Berlin: de Gruyter, 1988) p 187 and n 15.
45 On the transitory nature of conflict situations in law, see also Broekman, 'Revolution and Moral Commitment to a Legal System' in MacCormick and Bankowski (eds), *Enlightenment, Rights and Revolution* (Aberdeen: Aberdeen University Press, 1989) p 318.
46 The degree to which the system is open to learning is, of course as always, an internal matter. In Luhmann's terms this would be expressed in the following way: the system itself controls the balance of redundancy and variety. It is a distinction that bears on the system's readiness to vary its structures in the face of an evolving environment. Variety is about increasing responsiveness, redundancy about suppressing the element of surprise in the system.
47 cf Neisser, *Cognition and Reality* (San Francisco: W.H. Freeman, 1976) pp 20ff. Neisser calls these preconceptions 'orienting schemata' and they orient the observer within the complexity and equivocality of the immediately available environment by constructing certain expectations about relevant information.

Simple inertia

Both Unger and Luhmann address the problem of law's simple inertia and there is a significant proximity in their approaches. For Unger, law's inertia is the product of 'formative contexts.' It is, that is, related to the embeddedness of dominant principle and dominant value in our legal system. From a systems-theoretical perspective, it is the case that, given law's function in society of stabilising expectations and the values that consequently accompany its development (rule of law), it is only congruent that 'the surprising or anomalous event is grasped as concretely as possible, so that the required structural changes can be kept limited in scope and made to proceed along predictable lines.'[48] Does this mean that one can never take to law to challenge existing structures? No, it only means that:

> a special effort and special measures within the system are required if this normalisation tendency is to be changed into a tendency for existing structures to be questioned or problematised and information evaluated as a symptom of impeding crisis, as cost, as dysfunction in the prevailing order, or somehow or other looked at as a possible source of alternatives.[49]

A 'special effort' is required because the system will always, initially at least, give a disciplining, non-random response to the random event.

Luhmann borrows from information theory the term *'redundancy'* to denote the system's tendency to reduce the element of surprise within it. Information is produced when the system is surprised in some way. On the other hand, a system is redundant 'in so far as it supports itself in processing information on what is already known ... Every repetition makes information superfluous, which means, quite simply, redundant.'[50] The problem of law's 'simple' inertia is that the legal system is paramountly a redundant order. In processing information on the basis of what is already known, it supports itself and self-referentially assimilates what is new to what already exists. Legal argumentation, says Luhmann, 'overwhelmingly reactivates known grounds.' Information becomes confirmed in subsequent operations, gradually becomes entrenched in self-descriptions, acquiring orientation value for new arguments and condensation value for the system.[51] Of course, the assimilation cannot be complete. The system needs to react to a changing environment and, to this effect, *'variety'* comes into play. Significantly, the practice of distinguishing and overruling 'occasionally invents new [grounds] to achieve a position where the system can, on the basis of a little new information, fairly quickly work out what state it is in and what state it is moving towards.'[52] The reason why it requires 'a special effort' to shake the redundancy of the system and stretch its imagination is because the system tends to 'reduce its own surprise to a tolerable amount and allow information only as differences added in small numbers to the stream of reassurances.'[53]

In an extract that could easily have been written by Critical Legal Scholars had it not preceded them by a decade, Luhmann says:

---

48 Luhmann, 'Meaning as Sociology's Basic Concept' in *Essays on Self-Reference* (New York: Columbia University Press, 1990) p 33.
49 *ibid.*
50 Luhmann, 'Legal Argumentation: An Analysis of Its Form' (1995) 58 MLR 285, 291.
51 On confirmation and condensation, see Smith, 'The Redundancy of Reasoning' in Bankowski, White and Hahn (eds), *Informatics and the Foundations of Legal Reasoning* (Dordrecht: Kluwer, 1995).
52 Luhmann, *op cit* n 50, p 291.
53 *ibid.*

suitable information ... must be specially produced, brought to light by uncovering some latent aspect of *existing order*, or retrieved from the existing decision-making process by incongruent questions.[54]

Both central elements of CLS deviationist doctrine are here: the retrieval *in* law of the dangerous supplement; and the strategy of playing it up so that what is suppressed surfaces to subvert established patterns and entrenched principle in law. Unger's declaration of war in *Politics* against all institutional 'formative contexts' is very much the logic of deviationist doctrine writ large, a strategy reactivated in his recent prescriptions for 'mapping and criticism.'[55]

The project is no doubt both intriguing and promising. It is a remarkable feat of deviationist doctrine that it forces the system to thematise the ordinary as a possible source of alternatives — Luhmann's 'redundancy' and 'variety.' But it also points to the limitations of the project that are associated, it is my suggestion, with inertia of a second type.

Structural inertia

Unger's project is premised on tapping 'the self-transformative capacities of the practice of legal analysis'[56] by feeding deviant, subversive counter-theses into law in ways that will resonate in the discourse and lead to cumulative change. But, to repeat, this has to rely on the system's structural flexibility to accommodate such strategic imputs. The strategy relies on an argumentation that must reactivate known grounds if it is to secure a surprise, let alone effects, within the system. It relies on creating, in the receiving system, what could be called an innovative dissatisfaction (or 'goal-generating dissatisfaction' to use Maruyama's formulation).[57] Although this is a powerful weapon against 'simple' legal inertia, consider the flip-side: it in turn depends on a manipulation of a systemic reduction already in place, that one is therefore prepared to leave intact if only to allow the dissatisfaction to register. That is what Luhmann means when he says '[e]volution works epigenetically. Only in this way can innovations that presuppose themselves arise.'[58] What makes this a compromise, and a debilitating one at that, is that a limitation is thus imposed on the levelling of challenges; because whatever challenge is to register in law will only make a difference in the evolution of the system on the basis of its *alignment* to already existing reductions. Something is an informative surprise against a background of settled meaning. Challenges are dealt with by the (legal) system by being so

---

54 Luhmann, *op cit* n 48, p 34.
55 Unger, *op cit* n 2, p 20.
56 Unger, *op cit* n 2, p 8.
57 Luhmann, *op cit* n 48, p 85. The problem that is being identified here is that of providing the strategically correct stimulus that may make the idiosyncratic system respond in the desirable way; desirable, that is, in terms also of how the social environment will receive the legal decision. We have learnt from Teubner how precarious the process of this 'structural coupling' between diverse fields is, how easily it can go wrong, how easily the logics of the systems can be abridged, boundaries overstepped (regulatory trilemma) (see Teubner, 'Substantive and Reflexive Elements in Modern Law' (1983) 17 LSR 239). But Teubner's departure point is from problems of regulatory failure, whereas, for us, the question is different. It is about taking our conflict to law — conflict that arises from and informs spontaneous social contexts — and deciding whether or not we must pay the price that it be compromised, normalised.
58 Luhmann, 'Law as a Social System' (1989) 83 Northwestern Univ L Rev 136, 147. In other words, it relies on 'buying into' the discourse one wishes to confront, to go back to that dilemma described by Mathiesen some twenty years ago in *The Politics of Abolition* (Oslo: Universitetsforlaget, 1974).

interpreted as to accord with already existing or accepted meaning, always-already normalised, kept within the confines of what legal expectations can read as conceivable alternatives, always hedged in, always tamed. That is why in the legal system '[t]he unknown is assimilated to the known, the new to the old, the surprising to the familiar.'[59] This is the deep 'normalising' function of the law where contingencies have already been reduced in specific ways. The events that will set off information processing within the system must play on existing redundancies, must articulate with systemic reductions if they are to make an impact at all. The possibilities of radical political change are radically circumscribed by such structural necessity that, contra Unger, is not 'false.' Challenges *to* the structure can only be accommodated *by* the structure as demands to draw new internal distinctions and boundaries. And thus, as Heller put it, 'a self-referential system's evolutionary history is one of continual internal differentiation of newly organized patterns of information out of pre-existing states.'[60] This assimilation of the extraordinary to the ordinary, of that which defies the context to that which qualifies it, places a wooden hand on the possibility to politicise and contest.

In a striking passage of his Chorley lecture, Unger points to 'two remarkable features' of 'the self-subversive work of legal thought,' of his politics of law. 'The first is that it has gone so far. The second is that it has nevertheless stopped where it has.'[61] But to some extent at least, the second feature of legal thought is not that remarkable if it is understood as a result of an inertia that is structural and thus cannot be countered from within the institution. Let me return to the example of solidarity rights to substantiate this claim.

As a test case, the concept of a 'solidarity right' serves to highlight the dilemma that haunts Unger's position: how seriously is he prepared to take law as an institutional achievement? His contention that 'a system of rights is fundamentally the institutionalised part of social life, backed up by a vision of possible and desirable human association,'[62] says very little, precisely because it does away with what is specifically institutional: the imposition and entrenchment of certain reductions in the possibilities of describing and talking about the world. Law as such an institution gives us a language to conceive of identity, interdependence, conflict, benefit and harm, concepts of risk and time, what is owned and what is due. These are precisely the kinds of reductions in the possibilities of communicating about the world that give rights and solidarity rights their specific legal nature as an institutional achievement. The selection of what is legally relevant occurs over and against the background of the possibilities 'of human association' that remain legally underdetermined, or — in systems terms — in a state of 'loose coupling.' My point is that Unger's formulation, 'backed up by a vision of possible association,' is misleading because it refers to what is *not* selected, to what is *not* actualised by the institution; it refers to what remains an environment to the system. The system actualises something over and against other possibilities — the realm of high complexity, of 'political vision' that is left behind. And that is the crux of institutionalisation, of the drawing of the legal system's boundary.

---

59 Luhmann, *op cit* n 48, p 33.
60 Heller, *op cit* n 44, p 197.
61 Unger, *op cit* n 2, p 14.
62 Unger, *op cit* n 1, p 539.

So what does the legal concept of a 'solidarity right' leave behind? A solidarity right is a problematic device because, along every axis where a reduction is effected, an uncomfortable tension is imposed. The institution must narrow down the contingency of outcomes of how solidarity may require one to act. But a relationship as complex as this — as 'the social face of love' — appears to resist its reduction to conditional rules, to role requirements; it folds every hypothesis about how one is to act back upon itself. Every action according to the rule needs to be tested as to whether it actually enhances solidarity; and the criteria cannot be provided in abstract.[63] And, ultimately, every rule as to how one should act in solidarity can be rejected in the name of solidarity itself, tested as to the appropriateness of its application in the here and now. If that is so, no reduction through rule or role can relieve the ethical responsibility as it resides in the encounter. This questioning of self, this self-referential quality inherent in solidarity, makes its reduction in law an absurdity, the reduction achievement one that collapses as it is questioned.[64] The concept of a solidarity *right* is caught up in an impossible tension, a self-undermining that is not a source of empowerment but a self-cancellation.

We see this more specifically when it comes to legal role. As we said, law secures constancy by narrowing the expectability of expectations, by abstracting from various 'irrelevant' contingencies of the real situation, by abstracting from the actual parties involved and the reciprocal perspective-taking that in turn would involve knowledge of Alter and the contingencies that entails. It sets up a context of expectations by reducing double contingency and allows people to encounter each other as role-players, as legal actors. It allows a relationship between parties meeting in a common discourse where their mutual expectations are comprehensible as pertaining to legal actors. The legal system thus generalises expectations and appends motives and implied reciprocities to the legal actor, 'always-already' aligning them to systemic selections. But solidarity cannot survive this reduction. The insertion of 'legal role' as point of address of the subject abstracts solidarity from its embeddedness in the particular encounter,[65] only in terms of which encounter it could be meaningfully owed. We can use Michael Detmold's formulation here and say that the law cannot cross the 'particularity void'[66] to realise solidarity.

Unger sees this and tries to avoid it, but now his escape route lands him in a double bind. Having inflicted on the ideal of solidarity the legal reductions that cancel it, he invites the institution itself to 'see' the reductions and to resist them. Time and again he warns against the 'failure to come to terms with the imperative of contextuality.'[67] He asks for 'additional definitions [of solidarity] in context,' definitions 'that undermine role systems' and 'encourage the jumbling up of fixed roles.' These internal challenges are both structure-dependent and structure-

---

63 Guenther's 'sense of appropriateness' as to the requirements of solidarity, and his distinction between levels of justification and application, would be particularly relevant here (*op cit* n 42).
64 I have elaborated this point more fully in 'Self-defeating Civic Republicanism' (1993) 6 *Ratio Juris* 64ff.
65 This abstraction does not, however, according to Luhmann, entail a severing or a 'solving out' ('ausloesen' in the original, *op cit* n 33, p 84) from social relations, from the interaction that generated it.
66 Detmold uses the term to denote an unbridgeable distance between — and an impossible crossing over from — the general to the particular (Detmold, 'Law as Practical Reason' (1989) 48 Cambridge LJ 436ff). See also Bankowski, 'Law, Love and Computers' Edinburgh L Rev (forthcoming).
67 Unger, *op cit* n 1, p 510.

defying. They draw this quality from the 'spirit' of law as a 'structure-denying structure.'[68] To deny law this potential would be to adhere to a disempowering 'structural' or 'institutional fetishism.'[69]

My argument against Unger is that structural reductions cannot be employed and defied at once. To see them and then to defy them as constraining involves stepping onto a different level from where one can observe the observation. But at the first-order level at which the legal achievement is effective, where complexity is reduced and where the world becomes legally observable, the reduction cannot but remain a blindspot: it cannot be at once effected and observed. Thus there can be no structure-defying structures; the institution cannot see its blindspot and shake it off.[70]

And as a result Unger has not, in fact, transcended the dilemma that has followed him all along. If he stretches the institutional imagination too far by inviting 'additional definitions in context,' legal 'jumbling of social roles' and the rest, he erodes the institutional achievement of disciplining double contingency and the definition of expectations in context (and there can be no other definition.) Unger's 'pre-legal' social relationship is incommunicable except from the legal point of view, that is, by taking on board all the constitutive assumptions; in this the pre-legal is over-determined by the legal. And it is this that makes unworkable Unger's directive to take on board the additional definition of context (social) and to remain alert to the 'pre-legal relation' of the litigants. It is a fine line that Unger needs to tread between expanding the boundaries of institutional imagination and acknowledging and respecting the existence of those boundaries. It is a fine line but it makes a world of difference. By treating the disjunction as false, eroding institutionalisation itself and defying the system's constitutive reductions, his theory ceases to be a theory about law, by giving up what is distinctive of law. The legal achievement ceases to be recognisable as such and law merges with the world.

If on the other hand he respects the institutional achievement, he can get some mileage out of its imagination, mainly by exploiting possibilities of internal differentiation. But there are things Unger cannot do.

First, he cannot institutionalise such 'strivings' as solidarity. Social solidarity always-already eludes us as legal actors, caught as we are invited to be within the institution's own imagination, looking to retrieve solidarity in a field that has no room for it, attempting to make sense of it as a legal concept in the face of what undergirds legal imagination: our operating of the legal/illegal code *tertium non datur*, our reduction to a role to which specific capacities are allocated, the rigid fixing of conditionals to consequences, our preparedness to enforce the institutional decision.

Secondly, Unger cannot make solidarity rights simultaneously context-bound and context-resistant. A system that makes sense of the world by reducing possible states cannot account for a challenge that defies those reductions, because it is those reductions that first make that challenge meaningful. And what would 'structure-defying' challenges look like, how would the structure itself accommodate their expression? The asking price for a politics *of* law is that the legal structure in the situations that it structures is not itself put to the test.

---

68 *ibid* p 575.
69 Unger, *op cit* n 2, p 19.
70 We will return to this point in the final section.

The limits of institutional imagination

In one of his more polemical moments, Unger takes issue with the 'institutional' and 'structural fetishism' of 'deep structure theory,' the unshakeable assumption that 'structures are structures.'[71] Structures, on this view, fix what can be understood as conflict into inflexible patterns. As 'formative contexts' they form routines of conflict. In 'deep structure theory' the distinction between the context that forms the routine and the routinised conflict itself is rigid and allows no dialectic. Unger queries this, as well as what results from it: that political conflict is channelled into either the routine activity that takes the context for granted or becomes a conflict over the context itself. To repeat, it is in his view narrow and disabling to present politics as the mutually exclusive possibilities of revolution or conservative tinkering.

Unger's solution to this 'false' dilemma is to loosen the distinction between context and routine. Deep-structure theory has no room for the possibility of 'revisability of the context from within.'[72] He groups the various possible strategies of disentrenchment of the formative contexts of social life as *negative capability*[73] and concludes that, given 'the range of forms of empowerment, a cumulative move toward greater revisability is possible.'[74] Formative contexts are replaceable piece-by-piece.[75] 'The fighting that goes on within a stabilized social framework is only a more truncated version of broader and more intense struggles about the framework.'[76] 'We may [thus] be able to imagine ourselves more fully as the context-bound yet context-resistant and context-revising agents we really are.'[77]

But Unger is giving us an impossible task to perform and it is because he is eliding the distinction between inertias that he cannot see that his 'disentrenching' politics cannot do the work he wants them to.[78] Let us see why more closely. Unger likens the 'more truncated' conflicts *within*, with conflicts *about* the context, he juxtaposes context-bound, context-resistant and context-revising. How could this be? The answer, for Unger, lies in the logic of piece-by-piece disentrenchment, where 'the means [themselves] of stabilization generate opportunities for destabilization.' This is not unfamiliar, it underlies the logic of deviationist doctrine that plays up 'opportunities' of deviant reconstruction from within the body itself of law. After all, stresses Unger, 'to conceive of the ideal ... is to conceive it from the standpoint of variation.'[79] But this surely is the story of simple

---

71 Unger, *op cit* n 7, p 13.
72 *ibid.*
73 'All the varieties of empowerment seem to be connected in one way or another with the mastery the concept of disentrenchment describes. I call these varieties of empowerment "negative capability"' (Unger, *op cit* n 1, p 279).
74 Unger, *op cit* n 7, p 156.
75 *ibid* p 157.
76 *ibid* p 161.
77 *ibid* p 200.
78 Of course, his suggestions re structure-denying structures, of which destabilisation rights provide the obvious example, remain problematical for other reasons too. Not only because as Yack remarks, '[i]n the end Unger does not provide a single example of a structure-denying structure,' but also because of a paradox: 'If the structure-denying structure succeeds in promoting its own subversion, then it will be replaced and will disappear as a force in our lives. If it fails to promote its own subversion, then it becomes mere constraint and needs to be evaluated as such' (Yack, 'Toward a Free Marketplace of Social Institutions' (1988) 101 Harvard L Rev 1961, 1969, 1970).
79 Unger, *op cit* n 7, p 43. That something is from the point of view of how it could be different is, of course, a central assumption of systems-theoretical structuralist observation. But variation patterns are guided by the system's constitutive reductions.

inertia. Variation involves varying certain variables, it is a movement away from the fixed, only in terms of which it *is* a movement, a variation. Shifting variables involves keeping others constant. Unger says this too: '[R]evisions typically destabilize some parts of the established framework while strengthening others.'[80] But by conceding this, Unger is conceding too much. Variation makes sense only in terms of respecting the integrity of the context, an integrity that is reinstated with each variation. And what is impossible is that 'in the contest between the incongruous insight and the established context, *the context may go under.*'[81] It is impossible because what is 'incongruous' just as what is a 'variation,' *is* such *given* the context. The contextual reduction of possible states is constitutive of the meaning of an incongruity. Were it not, what appears incongruous would not even register as such. The context does not go under, it remains there structurally inert to make sense of incongruity, challenge, resistance and conflict, contested and reinstated at the same time. Of course, things change as incongruities show up. But none of these allow for *reflexive* revisions over the context, they allow only *systemic* revisions, revisions that are, in some deep-structural way, *context-bound*. Unger's eloquent statement that 'a truth [may be revealed] in the very fields that had no room for it'[82] is fundamentally misleading, not because a field conceals the truth, but because a field organises and undergirds a certain access to truth; and what cannot be seen cannot be seen.

I have argued that Unger's emancipatory thesis is untenable because his politics sooner or later stumble on the institutional threshold. On the one hand, institutional closure cannot be altogether resisted because it is the basis of cognitive openness. On the other hand, it cannot but be confining in that it reduces possibilities. To see the closure and resist it requires a different level of observation; resistance to the context cannot be context-bound. Contra Unger, the two levels of observation do not stand in a dialectic relationship; not only can the legal system not see its closure, but it cannot see that it cannot see it. Such is the blindspot that accounts, in the last instance, for the limits of institutional imagination.

Unger himself might not be too unhappy in principle that from a systems-theoretical perspective his argument appears unconvincing. Systems theory exhibits all the features he has attributed to 'deep-structure' theory which he vehemently rejects in favour of his own 'super-theory.'[83] The difference between the two, as was said, turns on their respective attitudes toward the entrenched nature of institutional frameworks. Systems theory sees change as possible only in variation from existing formative structures that reinstate the formative context even as they challenge it. In fact they are only acknowledged as challenges, as conflicts, through the structural assumptions they are meant to challenge. Unger strongly opposes this circumscription; for him, the formed conflict may subvert the formative framework and he occasionally even talks of turning the formative structure into 'a structure of no structure.'[84] This 'transformative opportunity' I find fundamentally implausible and, with Luhmann, point again to a distinction between observers.

Where does all this leave institutional imagination, its power and reflexivity? There is, in Unger's work, an urgent emancipatory message. For him no social

---

80 *ibid* p 158.
81 *ibid* p 20, my emphasis.
82 *ibid*.
83 *ibid* p 165.
84 *ibid* p 46.

constraint is inescapable. For him 'it's all politics' because society is an artefact and all that is social is contingent, challengeable, changeable. There is no aspect of social arrangements not open to revision. Even the definitions of what can be changed and the strategies we employ to effect change are in turn open to political scrutiny. He proclaims the radical contingency of human experience and action. To understand society is to embrace that contingency, what Unger describes as 'seeing the settled from the side of the unsettled.'[85] In all this lies reflexivity, of which Unger's is a powerful and important restatement. His theory aims to keep 'the context held up to light and treated for what it is: a context rather than a natural order.' His view of a political society is one in which 'people neither treat the conditional as unconditional nor fall to their knees as idolaters of the social world they inhabit.'[86] One where the possible is not reduced to the actual,[87] where 'society is less hostage to itself.' This oscillation between context-bound (the conditional) and context-challenging (refusing to be idolaters) may present a paradox: if all activity is contextual, can all contexts be questioned? Unger's work can be seen as an attempt to expose this paradox as merely apparent. Because, according to Unger, all contexts can be questioned, disrupted, even overturned by activity that is both reflexive and contextual. I have argued against this possibility and treat the paradox as a real one.

Unger's suggestions for the imagination of law attribute to law the reflexivity that would allow it to do the job of politics. Immanent critique, deviationist doctrine, negative capability, disentrenchment, critical legal politics, are all supposed to furnish a language for political conflict that is uncompromising, that is able to institutionalise solidarity, and institutionally back any political claim without compromising it. My argument has been that while, in principle at least, Unger can thus counter simple inertia, his endeavour is less powerful than he thinks when it comes to structural inertia. In dealing with the simple inertia of law, he is correct to say that there *is* transformative potential in law, doctrine *can* be manipulated and, to that extent, transformative conflict *can* be harboured in law. But all this is only possible at the cost of cashing in on the transformative leeways the system itself provides, and thus of taking on board its main structural givens, its reduction achievements. Reflexive political contestation as such cannot be accommodated in legal indeterminacy, because what is challengeable in law is simultaneously fixed by concepts and assumptions that give rise to indeterminacies in the first place. To register as critique something must first register as information. What is contestable legally is in some part given. The improbabilities are already institutional and selections will be made within dilemmas already in place. What is context-bound is not context-resistant, what is thus fixed is not reflexive.

Our recourse to Luhmann was designed to bring the inescapable dilemma into relief. The distinction needs to be kept constantly in view, between what is inert but challengeable within the system, and what is resistant structurally and invisible to the system. As with every system there is a facilitative/confining tension here and Luhmann's redundancy/variety distinction captures precisely that tension. Unger is surely right to suggest that the facilitative/confining balance can be exploited in the direction of the former. Immanent critique makes law more aware of what is latent within it and thus less confining. But to identify the facilitative

---

85 *ibid* p 18.
86 Unger, *op cit* n 7, p 45.
87 Unger, *op cit* n 2, p 23.

with the reflexive itself either cloaks the confining moment which makes the theory ideological, or collapses law into politics, sacrifices the former to the latter and makes the theory, as a theory about *law*, self-defeating.

In an impatience to bypass what is now perceived as a totalistic theory of human emancipation, Unger has little time for the Marxist structuralist critique of legal ideology. While Unger has no problem with the Marxist argument that the law *does* conceal and its ideology *does* mask the exclusion and the compulsion of meanings, he could not accept that this compulsion is not external but *structural* and occurs at the very point of the recovery of legal meaning. And that, in effect, to treat law as interchangeable with politics as its lever and substitute, as he does, depletes the emancipatory potential of politics. I have argued against impoverishing politics in this way by pointing to the limits of legal-institutional imagination. My disagreement with Unger is that in proclaiming contingency across the board he has lost sight of what makes legal as opposed to political reflexivity possible. There is deep, structural necessity in all facets of social life and at the same time there is extreme contingency. Not because, as Unger says, constraints are falsely necessary. But because what one institutional mapping of reality compels one way, another mapping allows another way. Here reside the possibilities that systems theory has to offer, and I can only begin to allude to them here. Reflexivity involves stepping out of the institutional closure and querying from an observer's position the terms of closure and the shape of contingency. Contingencies are fixed by systems but, in the absence of meta-systems and privileged sites of observation, fixed contingencies appear contingent. That is what makes contingency an 'eigenvalue' of our society, as Luhmann recently put it.[88] To take advantage of the contingencies with which politics is fraught, one needs to probe the limits of the politics of law through the politics of theory in a way that makes visible its possibilities and inertias and makes us attentive to both; that, I believe, is how reflexive politics would be stated from the point of view of systems theory undertaken as critical theory.

---

88 Luhmann, *Beobachtungen der Moderne* (Opladen: Westdeutscher Verlag, 1992).

Part V
Interpretation and Objectivity

[12]

Law and Metaphysics

Wittgenstein on Rules and Private Language. By Saul Kripke. Cambridge, Harvard University Press, 1982. Pp. x, 150. $15.00.

Charles M. Yablon[†]

There have always been lawyers deeply attracted to philosophical discourse. It is a phenomenon at least as old as Cicero,[1] and extends to the contemporary legal academic in search of an appropriate "fancy citation."[2] Such lawyers look to philosophy as a way of connecting law with broader questions of morality and truth. They tend to view at least some legal problems as manifestations of more fundamental philosophical questions. They may even look for insight into specific legal issues in the works of the philosophical masters.

There is, however, a countertendency among many lawyers, who view philosophy with attitudes ranging from indifference to hostility. These lawyers emphasize the practical wisdom deeply embedded in the common law tradition, extol the virtues of "experience" over "logic," and stress the need for lawyers and judges to provide concrete solutions to real problems.[3] Philosophy, it is argued, with its endless debates over first principles and stratospheric levels of abstraction, can provide little insight into the problems faced by real judges and lawyers. This view of law and

---

[†] Associate Professor, Benjamin N. Cardozo School of Law, Yeshiva University. I am grateful to David Carlson, Drucilla Cornell, Jeffrey Joseph, Michel Rosenfeld, Paul Shupack and Michael Simon for their thoughtful comments and advice. An earlier version of this piece was presented at the Institute on Law and Critical Tradition jointly sponsored by the Graduate Faculty of the New School and the Cardozo School of Law.

1. "Atticus: You believe, then, that the fundamentals of justice should be deduced not from a praetor's proclamation, as many now assert, nor from the Twelve Tables of the Law, as our forefathers maintained, but from the innermost depths of philosophy?" 1 CICERO, ON THE LAWS 225 (I. Raubitschek & A. Raubitschek trans. 1948).
2. Tushnet, *Legal Scholarship: Its Causes and Cure*, 90 YALE L.J. 1205, 1217 n.51 (1981).
3. O.W. HOLMES, THE COMMON LAW 1 (1881).

philosophy also has a long and honorable history. Its proponents have often been those, like Holmes, with great familiarity and respect for the philosophical tradition.[4]

This essay is a review of a work of philosophy, Saul Kripke's *Wittgenstein on Rules and Private Language*. The book does not deal with law, or even philosophy of law, but would probably be classified as a work on philosophy of language and theories of meaning. Yet it is not only a powerful and provocative book, but it can be of great interest and use to lawyers concerned with the nature of legal knowledge.

Although Kripke's book was not written for lawyers, this review is, and must therefore deal with the two attitudes towards philosophy sketched at the beginning of this essay. Presumably, lawyers who are comfortable applying philosophical concepts to legal issues should be highly receptive to a review which commends a work of contemporary philosophy as providing insight into certain issues of legal theory. As I hope to show, the insights of such philosophically oriented lawyers as to the nature of legal interpretation and the indeterminacy of legal discourse have brought about an academic environment in which books like Kripke's are seen as relevant to lawyers. Yet it is the other category of lawyers, those who emphasize the concrete and autonomous aspects of law, who, I believe, will ultimately find Kripke's work most valuable. For them I hope to show that one of the book's most important contributions is to clarify the extent to which legal discourse, despite its indeterminacy, can constitute an independent and important field of study.

This review has two parts. The first briefly considers the relation between law and philosophy, with particular emphasis on the realist period, and describes how the realists and their predecessors used philosophy to develop and defend their critique of formalism. This part closes with an argument that the reemergence of doubts about current modes of legal explanation and methods of intepretation has created renewed interest in philosophy among lawyers. The second part considers some of the main lines of argument in *Wittgenstein on Rules and Private Language* and

---

4. *Id.* It may be rightly observed that Holmes' predilection for experience over logic was itself a reflection of his philosophical position. I am indebted to Professor Shupack for a better and more venerable expression of this view: Chief Justice Coke's response to James I's assertion, based on a claim of philosophical expertise, that as king he had the power to remove cases from the law courts and try them personally.

[T]he King said, that he thought the law was founded upon reason, and that he and others had reason, as well as the Judges: to which it was answered by me [Coke] that true it was, that God had endowed His Majesty with excellent science, and great endowments of nature; but His Majesty was not learned in the laws of his realm of England, and causes which concern the life, or inheritance, or goods, or fortunes of his subjects, are not to be decided by natural reason but by the artificial reason and judgment of law, which law is an act which requires long study and experience, before that man can attain to the cognizance of it . . . ."

12 Coke Rep. 64, 65, *reprinted in* 77 Eng. Rep. 1342, 1343 (1907).

Law and Metaphysics

the impact of Kripke's book on current debates about indeterminacy and the possibility of authoritative interpretation in law.

I.

This section begins with an expository technique beloved of both lawyers and philosophers: the analytic distinction. Philosophical writing about law may be roughly divided into two categories. One seeks to understand the interrelationship of legal and moral rules, either by trying to derive morally valid legal rules from broader ethical precepts,[5] or by presenting an account of law which differentiates between the normative force of legal and ethical rules.[6] We can describe all this work under the broad rubric used by Felix Cohen and Morris Raphael Cohen: "law and ethics."[7]

The second category of philosophical writing about law is not centrally concerned with the relation between law and morality, but with the status of law as an independent and valid field of study. Works in this category discuss the ability of legal study to yield valid and accurate knowledge of something called "law," the extent to which that study should involve deductive reasoning, empirical investigation, or some combination thereof, as well as the fundamental reality or unreality of legal concepts. Cohen and Cohen also provide a name for this category of work: "law and metaphysics."[8]

Most lawyers, when they think of legal philosophy at all, tend to equate it with "law and ethics." Most of the celebrated work of recent years, such as that of Rawls,[9] Nozick[10] and Dworkin,[11] falls in that cate-

---

5. *See* I. KANT, THE METAPHYSICAL ELEMENTS OF JUSTICE (J. Ladd trans. 1965) (part one of I. KANT, THE METAPHYSICS OF MORALS (1797)); PLATO, THE LAWS.

6. *See* H.L.A. HART, THE CONCEPT OF LAW 151-207 (1961); H. KELSEN, GENERAL THEORY OF LAW AND STATE (1945); A. ROSS, ON LAW AND JUSTICE (1959). It may strike some as odd to classify these positivists as engaging in "law and ethics" scholarship, when a better account of their scholarly program might be "law and not ethics." Yet undeniably, a significant portion of their scholarly work probes the interrelationship of legal and ethical concepts in their attempt to show that the validity of legal rules does not depend on their ethical content. H.L.A. HART, *supra*, at 181-207; A. Ross, *supra*, at 29-75 (especially 59-64).

7. M. COHEN & F. COHEN, READINGS IN JURISPRUDENCE AND LEGAL PHILOSOPHY 489 (P. Shuchman 2d ed. 1979).

8. *Id.* at 557. Defining "metaphysics" is a notoriously fruitless endeavor, but the Cohens offered at least three candidates in the introductory note on "law and metaphysics" in the first edition of their book: "the effort of a blind man in a dark room to find a black cat that isn't there," "the stubborn effort to think clearly," and "the bringing to consciousness of what is assumed in all legal argument." M. COHEN & F. COHEN, READINGS IN JURISPRUDENCE AND LEGAL PHILOSOPHY 665 (1st ed. 1951). All three definitions seem acceptable for our purpose, which is simply to differentiate work that deals primarily with ethics from that primarily concerned with the nature of legal knowledge or legal reality. This means that we classify as "metaphysics" much that others would categorize as epistemology, logic, or philosophy of language, as well as much philosophy that would be considered "antimetaphysical" in a narrower sense of that word.

9. J. RAWLS, A THEORY OF JUSTICE (1971).

10. R. NOZICK, ANARCHY, STATE, AND UTOPIA (1974).

11. R. DWORKIN, TAKING RIGHTS SERIOUSLY (1978).

gory, and the content of most law school jurisprudence courses emphasizes "law and ethics" issues.[12] This essay, however, is concerned with the issues dealt with by that more elusive form of legal philosophy, "law and metaphysics."

While most thoughtful lawyers will quickly recognize the complex interrelationship of legal and moral concepts that law and ethics seeks to understand, law and metaphysics requires a more fundamental level of doubt and detachment from legal study. It requires a willingness to reject the authority and validity of most current legal scholarship and to reconceive the subject matter of the study of law. It is not surprising, therefore, that law and metaphysics tends to be a subject of limited appeal, which gains attention only during periods of defensiveness and self-doubt within the legal profession.

There is little question that the zenith of law and metaphysics in America extended from approximately 1910 to 1935. That was, of course, a time of great questioning by many lawyers, and a fundamental redirection of legal scholarship and legal thought. It was a time when philosophically oriented lawyers argued extensively about the validity and reality of law as a field of knowledge. In so doing, they utilized concepts from metaphysics, epistemology, and philosophy of science, and works by philosophers like John Dewey and Morris Raphael Cohen appeared with some frequency in the law reviews.[13]

The role played by philosophy in these debates about legal theory changed as the critique of formal modes of legal discourse became more familiar and widely understood. In the early years, critics like Roscoe Pound and Joseph W. Bingham utilized modern philosophical ideas to discredit as "unscientific" the prevailing deductive mode of legal reasoning and explanation. They proposed instead a new, scientific study of law grounded in pragmatism. Radically empirical, it would study the actions of judges, rather than disembodied legal rules. But this identification of scientific method with strict empiricism was attacked by other lawyers, as well as philosophers like John Dewey and Morris Cohen, who, while sympathetic to the critique of law as a purely deductive study, warned against altogether banishing rules as organizing and justifying principles

---

12. Greenawalt, Book Review, 34 J. LEG. EDUC. 740 (1984) (describing "the major subjects now taught in most jurisprudence courses" as issues involving relation of morality and law).

13. *See, e.g.*, Cohen, *The Basis of Contract*, 46 HARV. L. REV. 553 (1933); Cohen, *Property and Sovereignty*, 13 CORNELL L.Q. 8 (1927); Cohen, *The Place of Logic in the Law*, 29 HARV. L. REV. 622 (1916); Dewey, *The Historic Background of Corporate Legal Personality*, 35 YALE L.J. 655 (1926); Dewey, *Logical Method and Law*, 10 CORNELL L.Q. 17 (1924) [hereinafter *Logical Method and Law*].

Law and Metaphysics

in the study of law. By the end of the period, even the most philosophically inclined lawyers had come to the view that philosophy, while it could help clear away some false logic and bad methodologies, could not provide lawyers with an affirmative path to scientific knowledge of law. The result was a new appreciation of the complexity of legal study and the kind of expertise lawyers already possessed, as well as an openness to new approaches to that study.

Pound, in his famous work *Mechanical Jurisprudence*,[14] identified his attack on the emptiness of deductive explanation in law with the attack of pragmatism on older deductive models of scientific thought:

> I have referred to mechanical jurisprudence as scientific because those who administer it believe it such. But in truth it is not science at all. We no longer hold anything scientific merely because it exhibits a rigid scheme of deductions from *a priori* conceptions. In the philosophy of to-day, theories are "instruments, not answers to enigmas, in which we can rest."[15]

Pound condemned the prevailing modes of explanation and argument used by judges and lawyers as "empty words" yielding nothing but "arbitrary results."[16] He called instead for a "sociological" jurisprudence,[17] one that would be scientific, in accordance with pragmatism's concept of science: a study that would provide workable and useful solutions for the problems of American society.

Bingham's 1912 article *What Is the Law?*[18] provided an even more extreme critique of the then prevailing view that the appropriate study of law is consideration and analysis of doctrinal rules. Bingham not only argued for a more pragmatic study of law, but also denied the objective existence of any legal rule or principle.[19]

Bingham ridiculed claims that such nonexistent rules or principles

---

14. Pound, *Mechanical Jurisprudence*, 8 COLUM. L. REV. 605 (1908).
15. *Id.* at 608 (quoting W. JAMES, PRAGMATISM 53 (1907)).
16. *Id.* at 621.
17. Pound, *The Scope and Purpose of Sociological Jurisprudence* (pts. 1 & 3), 24 HARV. L. REV. 591 (1911), 25 HARV. L. REV. 489 (1912).
18. Bingham, *What Is the Law?* (pts. 1 & 2), 11 MICH. L. REV. 1, 109 (1912).
19. Bingham wrote:
   A rule or a principle is a connected series of concepts or associations or combinations of concepts. A concept is a psychological phenomenon. It does not exist outside of the mind entertaining it. Without discussing the possible physiological causes and processes of its occurrence, we may postulate as an axiom upon the basis of common knowledge that the idea of X cannot be literally the idea of Y. Figuratively speaking, X can transmit his idea to Y. What occurs, however, is not the passage of the idea to Y, but the formation of a similar one in Y's mind because of the expression which X uses as his means of communication. Principles and rules cannot exist outside of the mind.

Id. at 4.

could have an authoritative impact in determining concrete cases. He called the claims "old superstitions" whose "wide-spread persistence in a profession which demands so much acuteness of perception and analytical power is marvelous."[20] He envisioned a science of law based on empirical study of particular judicial decisions. In such a study the rules or principles of law would be causal generalizations about judicial or other legally significant behavior (like the decisions of juries), in much the way, he said, laws in the physical sciences are causal generalizations about the behavior of physical objects.[21]

The writings of Pound and Bingham raised questions that could not be answered within the strict confines of authoritative legal materials or traditional legal discourse of the time. They were questions about the validity of the discourse itself, and the attacks were powered, in large part, by Pound and Bingham's claims that scientific knowledge about the real world could not be validly obtained through traditional legal methods. Although "science," and particularly physics, were the models to which these lawyers aspired, the concept of science they utilized was drawn from the works of philosophers, not physicists. Philosophers of the time had also been deeply impressed by the achievements of the physical sciences, and had sought to develop theories of scientific knowledge that would generalize and explain how such knowledge could be achieved.[22] Pound and Bingham consciously drew on this literature in attacking the unscientific nature of legal discourse.

By making their attack at that level of philosophical abstraction, Pound and Bingham changed the nature of the very discourse they were attacking. While their arguments engendered intense opposition from other legal scholars,[23] in order to be effective, such opponents had to engage the arguments on the same level of philosophical abstraction on which they were made.[24] Law reviews began to contain articles debating the nature of scientific truth, the validity and reality of legal rules, and the causal relationship, if any, between legal rules and judicial decisions. The development of "law and metaphysics" had become possible.

Professional philosophers began to notice the debates in the law schools. In a 1912 speech to the American Philosophical Association, Morris Raphael Cohen praised Pound's article as providing "[t]he most cogent

---

20. *Id.* at 17-18.
21. Bingham, *Legal Philosophy and the Law*, 9 ILL. L. REV. 98, 115-17 (1914).
22. *See* W. JAMES, PRAGMATISM (1907); Dewey, *Beliefs and Realities*, 15 PHIL. REV. 113, 115 (1906).
23. Even the charge of "nihilism" was leveled against Bingham. Kocourek, Book Review, 8 ILL. L. REV. 138, 138 (1913).
24. *See, e.g., id.*; Bingham, *supra* note 21.

Law and Metaphysics

argument for pragmatism or instrumentalism that I know of,"[25] and further remarked that Pound and the pragmatists in the philosophy department of Columbia University seemed unaware of each other, "a significant comment on the efficiency of our modern university organization in the making of knowledge communicable."[26]

Dewey's famous article, *Logical Method and Law*,[27] further illustrates the broad perspective philosophers were able to bring to the critique of law and legal reasoning. Dewey began by observing that he had a particular philosophical axe to grind, that his conception of logic "d[id] not represent the orthodox or the prevailing view."[28] Dewey saw logic as "an empirical and concrete discipline," a study of the way people actually reach useful decisions.[29] He believed that reasoning by syllogism is not unsound but impossible, because "[i]n strict logic, the conclusion does not follow from premises; conclusions and premises are two ways of stating the same thing."[30] Real decisions are reached, Dewey contended, by beginning with conclusions and finding statements of general import, such as rules of law, which may serve as premises. These premises then serve to explain or justify the conclusions previously reached.[31]

Dewey's article supported and generalized the attack on mechanical jurisprudence, but took a more benign view than Pound of the usefulness of traditional legal reasoning. Dewey saw all deductive processes as a means of justifying particular choices, and stated "[i]t is quite conceivable that if no one had ever had to account to others for his decisions, logical operations would never have developed."[32] At that level of generality, Dewey saw much value in legal rules. Not only do they protect judicial decisions from charges of arbitrariness by providing a means of justifying the judge's choice as rational, they also provide "members of the community a reasonable measure of practical certainty of expectation in framing their

---

25. Cohen, *Jurisprudence as a Philosophical Discipline*, reprinted in M. COHEN, REASON AND LAW 132-33 (1950).

26. *Id*. at 133. Cohen went on to recommend the study of law to philosophers, and predicted that "philosophy of law even more than the philosophy of mathematics will prove a corrective to that myopic and stingy empiricism, or sensationalism, which cannot conceive anything to be real except sensible entities that have a position in time and space." *Id*. Of course, it was precisely that "myopic" metaphysical position on which Bingham's attack on prevailing legal knowledge was based.

27. *Logical Method and Law*, supra note 13, at 17.

28. *Id*. at 18.

29. *Id*. at 19.

30. *Id*. at 23.

31. Thus, unlike Bingham, Dewey finds a use for general statements of legal rules. He says, "it is certain that in judicial decisions the only alternative to arbitrary dicta, accepted by the parties to a controversy only because of the authority or prestige of the judge, is a rational statement which formulates grounds and exposes connecting or logical links." *Id*. at 24.

32. *Id*.

courses of conduct."[33] This practical, as opposed to theoretical, certainty, Dewey saw as a legitimate and attainable goal of law.

Dewey was a more thoroughgoing pragmatist than Pound. He viewed the urge to justify choice and to guide action through general rules, not as an aberration of lawyers, but as a common and potentially useful human impulse. Accordingly, where Pound viewed deductive forms of legal reasoning as faulty and pernicious, Dewey was willing to include them, properly understood, in a broader conception of the study of law.

The rehabilitation of rules and principles in legal reasoning was carried further by Morris Cohen, whose own philosophy of science left a greater role for the "hypothetico-deductive method."[34] As he stated, "the method of beginning with hypotheses and deducing conclusions, and then comparing these conclusions with the factual world, seems to me still the essence of sound scientific method."[35] For Cohen, legal rules were not merely useful but necessary to make sense of legal phenomena, in much the way, he would claim, laws of physics are needed to make sense of physical phenomena. This view directly contradicted those of people like Bingham, who denied the objective reality of anything but particular cases.[36]

Cohen described the "present wave of nominalism in juristic science" as "a reaction by younger men against the *abuse* of abstract principles by an older generation that neglected the adequate factual analysis necessary to make principles properly applicable."[37] Cohen believed not only in the existence of rules, but that judges decide cases in accordance with them. Although well aware of the "element of discretion" in judicial decisionmaking, Cohen viewed that discretion as constrained by previous cases.[38]

---

33. *Id.* at 25.
34. M. COHEN, LAW AND THE SOCIAL ORDER (1933), *excerpted in* M. COHEN & F. COHEN, *supra* note 7, at 442.
35. *Id.* at 443.
36. *See supra* note 19. Cohen attempted to refute what he called Bingham's "nominalism":

But there is really no good reason for denying that universals as abstract predicates can denote real traits in the objective world, provided we are careful not to view these abstractions as additional things floating ghostwise in an ethereal space. They are rather the universal or repeatable abstract qualities, relations, and transformations which characterize objects and events, and constitute their objective meaning.

Cohen, *Justice Holmes and the Nature of Law*, 31 COLUM. L. REV. 352, 361 (1931).

37. M. COHEN, LAW AND THE SOCIAL ORDER (1933), *excerpted in* M. COHEN & F. COHEN, *supra* note 7, at 563.
38. *Id.* at 564.

The difficulty of seeing what rule a given case involves is partly due to the traditional way of talking about the *ratio decidendi* as if a single case by itself could logically determine a rule. Since every individual case can be subsumed under any number of rules of varying generality, it clearly cannot establish any of them. It is only because every case is related more or less to previous cases—no human situation can be altogether unrelated to all previous situations—that a decision on it tends to fix the immediate direction of the stream of legal decision. The relation between decisions and rules may thus be viewed as analogous to that between points and a line.

Id. at 564-65.

Law and Metaphysics

To those who followed the law and metaphysics literature of the 1920's and 1930's, it was becoming increasingly clear that philosophy could not provide a definitive means to make the law more scientific and certain. Indeed, there was no clear philosophical concept of what scientific knowledge was, or how it could be obtained. The debate among lawyers about the relation of legal rules to individual judicial decisions corresponded to the more abstract discussion among philosophers regarding the relation of particulars and universals.[39]

This insight, though negative, was highly important to legal scholars of the period. It meant that lawyers were free to study law in many different ways, without being subject to attack for failure to conform to a single scientific methodology. There was also an increased awareness that philosophers could provide relatively little insight into the validity or power of legal reasoning. While philosophical argument could reveal certain types of reasoning to be specious, philosophers invariably deferred to the expertise of lawyers in describing the appropriate application of principles and precedents. This helped assure lawyers that they did indeed possess a specialized expertise, which could be studied and developed.

One can see this antiphilosophical approach to legal study developing even in such philosophically oriented lawyers as Hessel Yntema and Felix Cohen. Yntema, in *The Rational Basis of Legal Science*,[40] basically took an agnostic view on the metaphysical debates between Bingham, Morris Cohen, and Mortimer Adler. He argued that the lawyer no more needs a correct theory of knowledge than the physical scientist. "[I]t is yet to be shown that a scientific demonstration is at all validated by the theory of knowledge of the scientist, any more than by his religion or the language in which the results are stated . . . ."[41] Yntema was willing to recognize that law, while "referable to experience," can also be a "logical, postulational process."[42] Thus, for Yntema, legal reasoning could proceed at various levels of abstraction. However, all such abstractions ultimately had to be empirically grounded in actual legal decisions: It is the lawyer's expertise in the actual process of legal decisionmaking that provides the raw

---

39. In his review of Jerome Frank's *Law and the Modern Mind*, Mortimer Adler attributed to the realists a "one-sided" view of scientific method based on the empirical and pragmatic tradition of "Mill, Pearson, Bridgman, Vaihinger, Barry, Dewey." Adler, *Legal Certainty*, 31 COLUM. L. REV. 91, 92 (1931). He suggested that a very different conception of science was to be found in "Whewall, Cassirer, Poincaré, Duhem, Clifford, Campbell, Meyerson, Edditson." *Id.* Similarly, the realists' acceptance of Schiller's and Dewey's approach to logic was contrasted with the alternative views of, among others, Keynes, Russell, Lewis, and the language theories of Russell, Whitehead and (early) Wittgenstein. *Id.* at 98-100.
40. Yntema, *The Rational Basis of Legal Science*, 31 COLUM. L. REV. 925 (1931).
41. *Id.* at 938-39.
42. *Id.* at 928. He was careful to add, however, that it made a significant difference "whether the [logical] propositions are deemed to be sufficiently evidenced and so are stated categorically or are unverified and so are stated hypothetically." *Id.*

material for legal abstraction. Yntema announced that the theory needed for legal science could not be derived from philosophical discourse, but had to be obtained from those familiar with "the realities of law."[43]

Even a lawyer as steeped in philosophy as Felix Cohen used philosophy and philosophical insight in an essentially negative way. In his famous article, *Transcendental Nonsense and the Functional Approach*,[44] he punctured as "nonsense" legal concepts like corporate personality, due process, and fair value, which had been "thingified" by judges and legal scholars to appear to exist in a conceptual universe unrelated to actual experience.[45]

In debunking such concepts, Cohen was, to be sure, following a modern philosophical school that was dismissing much of traditional metaphysics as similar "nonsense."[46] But the point is that Cohen, while highly attuned to current philosophical thought, was also very conscious of the limited usefulness of philosophical discourse to lawyers. To Cohen, philosophy provided a therapeutic agent to dissolve the misconceptions of previous times, but it was lawyers who had to correct those misconceptions with "facts," actual descriptions of how judges act.

Cohen's functional approach to law was one that could be pursued only by lawyers, but only by those lawyers who took an expanded view of their field of inquiry. It viewed law as a social process, and looked to lawyers to discover and elucidate the process by which economic forces, aesthetic ideals, moral principles and social conservatism were molded into judicial decisions and generalized into rules of law. Like Yntema, Cohen did not claim that his was the only valid form of legal science. He noted that his functional approach to law "is largely dependent upon the results of classificatory or taxonomic investigation, genetic or historical research, and analytical inquiries."[47] In short, Cohen's goal was to broaden the nature of legal study by looking at both the social causes and consequences of legal decisions, while not denying the role of more traditional legal scholars in classifying judicial opinions, tracing the genesis of legal doctrines, and analyzing their component parts.

In the fifty years that followed, legal scholarship developed consistently, in many ways, with the vision of Felix Cohen and Yntema. The study of

---

43. *Id.* at 934.
44. Cohen, *Transcendental Nonsense and the Functional Approach*, 35 COLUM. L. REV. 809 (1935).
45. *Id.* at 811, 820-21.
46. Cohen identifies his attack with the attack of logical positivists on traditional problems of philosophy. He quotes approvingly the observation of Wittgenstein that most propositions on philosophical matters "are not false, but senseless." *Id.* at 823 (quoting L. WITTGENSTEIN, TRACTATUS LOGICO-PHILOSOPHICUS (1922)).
47. *Id.* at 829-30.

Law and Metaphysics

law was broadened. Legal rules were often explained or justified in terms of social or economic policies they were assumed to embody.[48] The consequences of judicial opinions were studied, sometimes through empirical research,[49] sometimes through application of economic models,[50] usually with a simple presumption that careful study of judicial opinions would reveal the societal needs such rules addressed and the societal functions they were assumed to serve.[51] At the same time, doctrinal work of various kinds continued as legal scholars analyzed new decisions, synthesized or derived rules from the case law, and distinguished and classified cases according to various taxonomic formulae. These lawyers generally acted under the assumption that their work was expanding and deepening our understanding of the law, as well as providing the knowledge needed to create better laws. Law and metaphysics scholarship, which by its very nature questions those assumptions, largely disappeared.

In the last few years, this picture of legal academia has changed significantly. A new generation of legal scholars, many trained in philosophical discourse, has once again raised fundamental doubts about the established modes of legal explanation and justification. Just as Pound rejected as "arbitrary" justifications of judicial decisions expressed as formal deductions from preexisting legal rules,[52] these scholars reject as "indeterminate" arguments which seek to explain particular decisions in terms of underlying social or economic policies or embodiments of fundamental normative principles.[53] They contend that for any particular decision, counterpolicies and counterprinciples can be found within the legal system to explain and justify the contrary result. These claims cast doubt on the ability of contemporary legal scholarship to explain the law in much the way an earlier generation rejected explanations based on logical deductions from formal rules.[54]

---

48. *See* Tribe, *Policy Science: Analysis or Ideology?*, 2 PHIL. & PUB. AFF. 66 (1972).
49. *See generally* Black, *The Boundaries of Legal Sociology*, 81 YALE L.J. 1086 (1972) (discussing relation between sociological and legal scholarship).
50. *See, e.g.*, A. POLINSKY, AN INTRODUCTION TO LAW AND ECONOMICS (1983).
51. Robert Gordon has referred to this set of assumptions about the relationship of legal rules to society as "functionalism." Gordon, *Critical Legal Histories*, 36 STAN. L. REV. 57, 59 (1984); *see* Gordon, *Historicism in Legal Scholarship*, 90 YALE L.J. 1017, 1028-45 (1981).
52. Pound, *supra* note 14, at 620-21.
53. These claims are most often associated with members of the Critical Legal Studies movement, who have propounded the strongest and most generalized form of the indeterminacy critique. *See, e.g.*, Unger, *The Critical Legal Studies Movement*, 96 HARV. L. REV. 561 (1983); Gordon, *Critical Legal Histories, supra* note 51. Similar critiques regarding the indeterminacy of particular forms of legal explanation may be found in Kornhauser, *A Guide to the Perplexed Claims of Efficiency in the Law*, 8 HOFSTRA L. REV. 591 (1980); Leff, *Economic Analysis of Law: Some Realism About Nominalism*, 60 VA. L. REV. 451 (1974).
54. *See generally* Yablon, *The Indeterminacy of the Law: Critical Legal Studies and the Problem of Legal Explanation*, 6 CARDOZO L. REV. 917 (1985) (discussing problems of legal explanation raised by Critical Legal Studies theorists).

Related to this critique is the claim that it is impossible to achieve a determinate and authoritative interpretation of legal rules, including the rules set forth in the United States Constitution. Proponents of this view reject the notion that the words of legal materials have fixed and objective meanings; they deny that there is any definitive fact, such as the intention of the drafters, which can provide an authoritative interpretation of a law.[55] Such arguments require lawyers to take positions on a range of issues concerning the nature of language and its relation to knowledge. How do words acquire meaning? Is the truth of a statement determined by its correspondence to some objective reality, some community of interpretation, or is it not susceptible to determination at all?

These are now live issues among legal scholars, some of whom are turning to the works of literary theorists, semioticians, and philosophers of language,[56] just as an earlier generation turned to logicians and philosophers of science. This resurgent questioning of the validity of legal study raises the possibility of a rebirth of law and metaphysics scholarship.

II.

It is in this context that Saul Kripke's book, *Wittgenstein on Rules and Private Language*,[57] may be seen as relevant and important to contemporary lawyers. It is a powerful philosophical argument about the indeterminacy of rules and all forms of rule interpretation. Kripke demonstrates the impossibility of ever finding determinate criteria by which one can establish that a given action does or does not constitute "following a rule." Yet his argument will provide little support to those who seek to condemn legal interpretation for such indeterminacy. The indeterminacy Kripke demonstrates operates at such a high level of abstraction that it cannot function as a critique of any rule. Rather, the argument reveals a paradox that seems to discredit the very notion of following a rule. Moreover, Kripke suggests that the paradox can only be overcome by integrating its skeptical premises with our understanding of statements about rules and rule-following behavior.

Kripke's book is an elucidation of an argument he believes appears, in a more cryptic and shortened form, in Wittgenstein's *Philosophical Investi-*

---

55. *See* Brest, *The Fundamental Rights Controversy: The Essential Contradictions of Normative Constitutional Scholarship*, 90 YALE L.J. 1063 (1981); Tushnet, *Following the Rules Laid Down: A Critique of Interpretivism and Neutral Principles*, 96 HARV. L. REV. 781 (1983).

56. *See, e.g.*, Fiss, *Objectivity and Interpretation*, 34 STAN. L. REV. 739 (1982); Graff, *"Keep off the Grass," "Drop Dead," and Other Indeterminacies: A Response to Sanford Levinson*, 60 TEX. L. REV. 405 (1982); Levinson, *Law as Literature*, 60 TEX. L. REV. 373 (1982).

57. S. KRIPKE, WITTGENSTEIN ON RULES AND PRIVATE LANGUAGE (1982) [hereinafter by page number only].

Law and Metaphysics

gations.[58] As he states in the Preface, Kripke views his role "almost like an attorney presenting a major philosophical argument as it struck me."[59] While not fully embracing it, Kripke does describe the argument as "major" and "important," and concedes he found himself troubled by it.[60] Thus the argument in the book is Wittgenstein as perceived by Kripke, and the combination of perhaps the most original and subtle twentieth century philosopher with a very highly regarded contemporary logician and philosopher of language makes for an impressive one-two punch.[61]

Kripke's argument is about the indeterminacy of rules. It attempts to demonstrate that with respect to any rule and any particular action taken "pursuant to" that rule, it is impossible to state criteria that can authoritatively establish whether the rule is or is not being followed.[62] Such a demonstration might seem unexceptional as applied to such notoriously vague doctrines as due process or the parol evidence rule, but Kripke's task is more difficult. He is seeking to demonstrate the indeterminacy of the rules of arithmetic.[63]

If I say I understand or "grasp" the rule of addition, it presumably means that I know how to achieve a determinate answer to a large number of mathematical problems that I have never previously considered. As Kripke notes, this is generally what is understood by "grasping" a rule: "[M]y past intentions regarding addition determine a unique answer for indefinitely many new cases in the future."[64] Kripke then considers such a new case, a problem involving two numbers I have never added before: 68 + 57. The problem is simple, the correct answer obvious: 125.

But Kripke now introduces, as he says, a "bizarre skeptic,"[65] who challenges my result not by alleging that 68 + 57 = 125 is incorrect as a proposition of mathematics, but by challenging the assertion that, in arriving at my conclusion, I was following the rule I had previously grasped.

---

58. Pp. 1-6 (discussing L. WITTGENSTEIN, PHILOSOPHICAL INVESTIGATIONS (G. Anscombe trans. 1953) [hereinafter PHILOSOPHICAL INVESTIGATIONS]). The reworking of arguments made by earlier philosophers is a well-established philosophical tradition. It enables the writer to set forth an argument for analysis and study without endorsing it fully. Probably the most famous examples are the early and middle dialogues of Plato, in which most of the interesting philosophical ideas are presented as the thoughts of Socrates.

59. P. ix. It is interesting that Kripke perceives the ability convincingly to present an argument one does not fully believe as an attribute of the legal rather than the philosophical profession.

60. Pp. viii-ix.

61. Referring to the argument poses a bit of a problem, since it is properly neither Kripke's nor Wittgenstein's alone, and constantly referring to "Kripke's exposition of Wittgenstein's argument" is a trifle awkward. Kripke, while he believes he is elucidating an argument of Wittgenstein's, is clearly less interested in supporting that attribution than he is in the validity and coherence of the argument itself. Accordingly, for simplicity's sake, and with some awareness of inaccuracy, I refer to the argument of the book as Kripke's.

62. P. 7; *see also* PHILOSOPHICAL INVESTIGATIONS, *supra* note 58, § 201.

63. *See* pp. 7-8.

64. P. 8.

65. *Id.*

The skeptic proposes instead that the rule I had previously grasped was not addition but "quaddition," a rule which yields the same results as addition for sums up to those involving 57, but which, for sums involving 57, requires that the question be answered 5. Accordingly, by answering the question 57 + 68 as 125 rather than 5, I was not following my previously grasped rule of quaddition. I had arrived at an incorrect result, as measured by my prior intention.[66] Of course, the skeptic's argument is crazy and wrong. I know very well that the rule I learned was "addition," not "quaddition," and my knowledge of that rule somehow required me to answer 125 rather than 5. Accordingly, I should be able to demonstrate easily to the skeptic that I previously meant "addition" and not "quaddition."

The problem, Kripke argues, is that I can make no such demonstration. There is no fact that I can cite, whether it is about the world, about my previous behavior, my previous use of language or even my previous intent, which can establish that the rule I previously grasped was "addition," not "quaddition."[67] Notice that Kripke is perfectly willing to allow, as potentially dispositive facts, statements about my previous intent. He is not limiting the inquiry to objectively ascertainable facts.[68] Moreover, since we are talking about *my* intent, rather than that of the drafters or some legislative body, the problems of ascertaining intent are significantly reduced. Nonetheless, the one answer I cannot give is that "by 'addition' I meant that the correct answer to 57 + 68 would be 125." The whole premise of what it meant to grasp a rule was that my knowledge of the rule would enable me to determine infinitely many new cases and that 57 + 68 was such a new case. If I only know that 57 + 68 = 125 because I have already decided that case, I seem to be proceeding by rote memorization and not following a rule at all.[69]

Kripke next considers possible ways out of the dilemma. One possibility is to rephrase the rule in terms of the algorithm for addition. Thus the "proof" of my prior intention with respect to the rule is a statement like: "By 'addition' I meant that for any numbers x and y, the correct answer would be the result of x plus y."[70] Such an answer, however, merely rephrases the rule in terms of another rule and does not satisfy the bizarre skeptic, who merely transfers his doubts to the new rule. How do you know, he says, that by "plus" you meant the arithmetical procedure that yields 125 as the result of 57 + 68? Perhaps you meant "quus," which

---

66. Pp. 9-11.
67. P. 11.
68. P. 14.
69. *See* p. 15.
70. Pp. 15-16.

Law and Metaphysics

yields the same result for all sums not involving 57, but in which 57 quus 68 equals 5.[71] Nor will it do to say that by "plus" I meant then what I mean by "plus" now, because I am sure to be faced with the question, how do I know that by "plus" I now mean the rule that yields 125 and not 5 as the sum of 57 plus 68? To answer, "Because that is the answer I have now obtained," makes the whole justification circular.

Kripke gives considerable attention to another possible response to the skeptic, that what I acquired when I "grasped" the rule of addition was a *disposition* to respond to questions of a certain nature in a certain way. Accordingly, when I learned addition, I acquired the disposition to answer questions of the type $x + y = ?$ with the sum of x plus y, and therefore would have answered $57 + 68$ as 125.[72]

Such dispositional analysis is, of course, quite familiar to lawyers, particularly those who analyze the legitimacy of judicial decisionmaking in terms of legal process and neutral principles. While such principles are sometimes described as rules of decision yielding determinate results, they are more often analyzed as attitudes or dispositions towards the process of decisionmaking itself. By bringing to the decisionmaking process certain attributes of neutrality, rationality, and deference to prior precedent, it is argued that decisionmakers are able to "follow the rules" even when giving answers to novel legal questions.[73] Similarly, one might argue, someone with the appropriate dispositions of neutrality and rationality towards the process of addition would give the answer 125 to the sum $57 + 68$. Giving the answer 5 would reflect another disposition entirely.

Kripke's discussion, which of course makes no mention of neutral principles, focuses on the distinction between a description and a justification of my action of answering 125 rather than 5. As a description of my behavior, the statement that I am disposed to answer 125 to $57 + 68$ is entirely accurate, proven by the fact that that is the answer I actually gave. One can even concede that that is in fact the answer I would have given if I had been asked the question anytime since learning the rules of addition. Yet, Kripke says, this answer will not satisfy the bizarre skeptic, who is looking not for a description of how I will respond to the question, but for a justification that my response is the correct one pursuant to the rule. Responding in terms of the individual's own dispositions can never

---

71. P. 16.
72. Pp. 22-23. In describing my disposition by referring to the algorithm of addition, I am not claiming that what I learned was the algorithm itself, which would immediately get us back to the "plus" versus "quus" problem. Rather, I am using the algorithm as shorthand for describing my past disposition. Thus I am assuming, merely for ease of presentation, that we presently agree on the meanings of both "plus" and "quus."
73. *See* Wechsler, *Toward Neutral Principles of Constitutional Law*, 73 HARV. L. REV. 1, 10-20 (1959).

provide such a justification, unless one is willing to assume, which most of us are not, that the response the decisionmaker is disposed to give is always the correct response to the rule.[74]

The dispositions of judicial decisionmakers may provide justifications in an entirely different sense. It may be that we value the attitudes of neutrality, rationality, and deference to precedent independently of whether those attitudes achieve the correct result. Or perhaps we are willing to say, unlike Kripke and his bizarre skeptic, that any results achieved through such dispositions are, by that very fact, correct results. Kripke's analysis casts doubt on only one small part of the neutral principle concept of judicial decisionmaking. His argument makes it doubtful that any decision made by a judge pursuant to neutral principles can be justified as a correct response to any preestablished rule.

The problem that Kripke's argument elucidates does not, of course, hinge on any uncertainty or obscurity in the rules involved, or in any contradictions in the rules themselves. The problem is, quite simply, that the rules of arithmetic, like all other rules, are expressed in language. Our ability to understand and be guided by the rule depends on our ability to understand the meaning of the words in which the rule is expressed. Kripke's argument, then, is really an argument about the indeterminacy of language, a skepticism that there is any fact about our past use, intention, or attitude towards a word like "addition" that controls or restricts or limits our future uses of that word.[75]

Thus far, Kripke's argument seems to resemble those of literary theorists and legal academics who deny the existence of any objective meaning in a text. But Kripke's skepticism goes a step further, in that he appears to deny the possibility of any subjective meaning as well. When presented with an occasion to use a word whose meaning I supposedly "know," Kripke's argument maintains that there is no fact, internal or external, that can authoritatively provide the meaning of that word.[76]

Accordingly, as Kripke recognizes, the skeptical argument is not a refutation of the determinacy of rules, but a paradox about the nature of lan-

---

74. Pp. 23-24. To illustrate this point, Kripke considers another question, $57 * 68 = ?$, where the sign "*" has no number theoretic function. I can nonetheless give a response to such a question, and hereby answer it with the number 12. Presumably, a descriptive dispositional analysis of my response is quite possible. Because I gave a single determinate answer, it is probable that somewhere in my background or psyche I developed the disposition to answer 12 when asked the question $57 * 68 = ?$. The question is of course quite meaningless, and it is impossible for me or anyone else to justify my answer as the correct response to the question. The indisputable fact that I had a disposition to answer 12 does not justify that response as correct. Similarly, my equally indisputable disposition to answer 125 to the question $57 + 68$ does not justify that response as an instance of following a rule. See p. 24 & n.18.
75. Pp. 43-44.
76. P. 55.

Law and Metaphysics

guage itself. We know that words have meaning because we can use them to communicate with others. We know that we can recognize correct and incorrect uses of language and distinguish meaningful sentences from nonsense. We know that the correct answer to 57 + 68 is 125, not 5. The paradox is that although we know all this, we cannot demonstrate what it is about the words, or our relation to the words, that provides us with such knowledge.[77]

Kripke compares the skeptical paradox revealed in his argument to Hume's famous skeptical argument about causation.[78] Hume's position can also be described as a paradox in that, while I may assert that two events are causally connected, there is no fact about the two events that I can cite to justify my claim of causation. The "solution" to the paradox is to alter our assumptions about causation to include the skeptical premises of Hume's argument. There is no fact about the occurrence of two events that enables us to demonstrate that they are causally related. Rather, our assertion of a causal connection can be understood as the assertion of an invariable conjunction between certain *types* of events. Our initial assumption that causation is found in the interrelation of particular events was wrong. It is found in generalizations about categories of events.[79]

Kripke uses this discussion to prefigure the solution to his own skeptical paradox. Like Hume's, it will be a "skeptical" solution. It will not refute the skeptical premises of the paradox, but will incorporate those premises into the proposed solution. Although Hume's solution concedes that nothing about the events themselves establishes the causal relation, it nevertheless enables us to continue speaking of causation by understanding causal statements as generalizations about certain categories of events. In much the same way, Kripke's solution will concede that there is no fact about my attitude or intention towards a rule which can demonstrate whether I am following that rule. Indeed, he will argue that we can never speak of a single individual, considered in isolation, as following a rule or as meaning anything. Rather, we can continue to make statements about an individual's meaning or rule following, but understand them as involving not the relation of that individual to a text or rule, but to the behavioral interactions of that individual with the community.[80]

One of the central points of Wittgenstein's later philosophical method was his rejection of the notion that statements in language embodied "truth conditions" that described certain facts about the world and could be proven or falsified by the existence or nonexistence of such facts.

---

77. *See* pp. 60 & n.47, 62.
78. P. 62.
79. Pp. 62, 67-68.
80. Pp. 69, 87-90.

Wittgenstein instead emphasized the way statements were *used* in the linguistic interactions of the community.[81] Rather than try to define the facts that would have to exist to say of a person, "He has a toothache," Wittgenstein would ask under what circumstances it would be appropriate in our language to say "He has a toothache." Although the first question seems like an unanswerable philosophical conundrum (how can anyone ever truly know whether another is feeling pain?), the answer to Wittgenstein's question is accessible to all reasonably competent speakers of the language (if I see someone holding his jaw and grimacing, I am justified in making such a remark).[82]

Wittgenstein's method also enables us to provide an account of such linguistic utterances as "Open the door," "Can I have a quarter?," and "Wow!," all of which have meaning to a speaker of our language, but do not seem to involve any truth or falsifiability conditions.[83] Note that such an account of language and meaning looks at the role words actually play in our language. This inquiry requires reference to a linguistic community, to people who share a common set of responses to language, and who thereby share, in Wittgenstein's famous phrase, a "form of life."[84]

Kripke's skeptical paradox is an elaborate demonstration of the impossibility of providing a set of necessary and sufficient conditions for the truth of the statement "He is following a rule." The argument seeks to demonstrate that there is no fact about the rule or the individual who is trying to follow it that would render such a statement either true or false. The solution to the paradox is not to analyze the problem in terms of truth conditions, but rather to describe the conditions under which one is justified, in our language, in saying that someone is following a rule. Kripke's solution, simply put, is that we are entitled to assert that someone is following a rule when we are able to check his or her response to the rule and determine that it agrees with our own.[85]

For example, we are justified in saying that I am following the rules of addition when I add 57 + 68 and get 125 because 125 is the response that other members of the community who are recognized as competent in

---

81. PHILOSOPHICAL INVESTIGATIONS, *supra* note 58, §§ 134-142.
82. *Cf. id.* §§ 253-257. Wittgenstein makes a similar point in connection with statements about understanding words like "red" that are not definable in terms of other words. Rather than trying to determine what facts must be true of a child who "has learned the meaning of the term 'red'," we can describe the conditions under which such a statement would be justified in our language. When the child is asked to "bring the red fruit" and she hands you the apple rather than the orange, we are justified in asserting that the child "understands the meaning of the word 'red.'" If, when then asked to select the red flower, she brings the daisy rather than the rose, we would be justified in altering our conclusion. *Id.* §§ 273-274, 380-383.
83. *Id.* §§ 23, 27.
84. *Id.* §§ 19, 241.
85. Pp. 87-96.

Law and Metaphysics

following the rules of addition would give. Of course, people do not go around constantly checking each others' addition, but we do continue to check each others' responses in a negative sense. I reject the claim that someone who adds 57 + 68 and gets 5 is doing addition because I know that my response (or that of any other competent adder) would be quite different.[86] I reject the claim that someone who moves his rook diagonally is following the rules of chess (although he may *intend* to be following those rules), and I reject the claim that a city that maintains a segregated school system is complying with the Fourteenth Amendment. In each case, my assertion does not rest on the relation between the text of the rule and the individual response, but on my knowledge of the role those words play in the language of my community, in its form of life. It is, for Kripke, the "brute empirical fact that we agree with each other in our responses" that enables us to make such assertions about rule-following behavior.[87]

One can perceive the way in which Kripke's argument speaks quite directly to some current debates in law about the indeterminacy of rules and the way in which legal texts acquire meaning. His argument, like that of the deconstructionists of literary and legal texts, leads to the conclusion that there is no "superlative fact" about the text or its drafter that can provide it with a determinate meaning. Kripke's argument appears to resemble, in some respects, the argument of theorists who look both to the role of the "interpretive community" in providing such meaning and to some version of a conventionalist concept of truth.[88]

Yet Kripke's position, as set forth in his solution to the skeptical paradox, differs significantly from most versions of this argument in important respects. Such arguments often attempt to solve the problem of meaning by asserting that the meaning of a word or the application of a rule is determined by the shared understandings of a particular interpretive community. Such a position still seeks to provide determinate empirical conditions under which statements about meaning will be rendered true or false. It merely looks for truth conditions in the understandings of the community, rather than in the attitudes or past actions of the person who produced the statement. If shared community understandings can be ascertained by, for example, polling competent language speakers, it is still possible to describe statements about the meaning of words or texts as true or false.

Kripke shows, however, that conventionalist arguments that try to provide truth conditions for statements about the word "meaning" are flawed, for precisely the same reason that truth conditions cannot be prescribed

---

86. Pp. 94-95.
87. P. 109.
88. *See, e.g.*, Fiss, *supra* note 56; Fish, *Fish v. Fiss*, 36 STAN. L. REV. 1325 (1984).

for statements about "addition" or "red" or any other word. Such arguments fail to account for the complexity and creativity involved in linguistic utterance. It is certainly possible to make intelligible statements in our language about "meaning" in circumstances where the conventionalist truth conditions are not satisfied, as, for example, when a parent states: "When my one year old says 'bapu,' she means apple."

Kripke's argument, in contrast, does not seek to provide truth conditions for "meaning" or any other word, but is rather concerned with the circumstances under which statements utilizing the term "meaning" may be appropriately asserted in our language. It is a fact about our language that it is generally appropriate to assert that someone understands or knows the meaning of a word when their use of, and responses to the use of, the word are similar to the uses and responses expected of other competent speakers of the language. This is not a statement about the meaning of "meaning," but, in Wittgensteinian terms, a description of the grammar of statements about meaning, of the role these statements play in our language.[89] We do not know how to make sensible statements about meaning because we have polled the members of our interpretive community, but rather because we know how to speak our language.[90]

To lawyers, Kripke's argument is extremely important, but primarily in a negative sense. At one level, it is a powerful refutation of all lawyers who claim there is one "superlative fact"—the most popular candidate these days being the original intent of the drafters—that can provide a determinate meaning to legal rules. Such arguments are usually based on a claim that to interpret a law, lawyers must resort to the original intention of its authors because any other interpretive device is woefully indeterminate.[91] Kripke's argument demonstrates that original intent, even one's own fully knowable original intent, cannot determine any future application of a rule. Accordingly, original intent can provide no more determinate answers to questions of legal interpretation than any other hermeneutic device.[92]

Yet Kripke's argument also provides little support for the claim that the law's inability to provide determinate answers demonstrates the illegitimacy of legal rules or of their application by decisionmakers. Surely the

---

89. See PHILOSOPHICAL INVESTIGATIONS, supra note 58, § 29.
90. Id. § 381.
91. See, e.g., R. BERGER, GOVERNMENT BY JUDICIARY 363-72 (1977) (espousing original intent as basis of constitutional interpretation).
92. It would be possible to rephrase the original intent argument as a Wittgensteinian claim about the use of words in our language. It might be argued that it is only appropriate to speak of "knowing the meaning of a rule" when we have direct knowledge of the intention of the person who wrote the rule. This claim is not refuted by the skeptical paradox (although it may be indirectly refuted by rendering the notion of "direct knowledge" of someone else's intention an incoherent concept), but it does not seem to be a plausible claim about our language.

Law and Metaphysics

indeterminacy Kripke has revealed in the rules of addition does not render arithmetic illegitimate, and arithmetic teachers, by marking papers which contain the computation 57 + 68 = 5 incorrect, are not unfairly restricting their students' freedom (although they are teaching them a particular language). The philosophical demonstration of the indeterminacy of all rules does not alter the "brute empirical fact" that we continue to speak of rules and continue to distinguish between actions that follow and do not follow a rule. However, it does require us to change our understanding of the notion of rule following, to include a recognition of the social, cooperative, and even political process implicated in discussions about rules.

Probably the most important contribution Kripke's book makes to lawyers is to clarify the ways in which a rule may be indeterminate. His argument requires us to distinguish, in ways that much of the contemporary debate among lawyers does not, between two types of indeterminacy which may characterize rules. The first, which we may call "Kripkean indeterminacy," describes a rule that is indeterminate in that no particular action can ever be justified as following or not following the rule. This is quite different from a rule that is indeterminate in that a competent decisionmaker cannot arrive at a correct application of the rule in response to a particular case. We may call this "causal indeterminacy." The rules of addition provide good examples of rules which are indeterminate in the Kripkean sense (that is what the skeptical paradox demonstrates), yet fully determinate in the causal sense.

Legal rules, of course, may be indeterminate in both senses. Kripkean indeterminacy involves an observation about the nature of language and the theoretical impossibility of justifying future behavior on the basis of past uses of a word. It applies, as Kripke demonstrates, to all rules expressed in language. Causal indeterminacy, in contrast, deals with the inability of a rule to bring about what would be viewed by speakers as a correct and determinate response. Causal indeterminacy involves reference to the behavior of members of a particular linguistic community, and is highly context specific. "Dress appropriately" may be a perfectly understandable rule in certain contexts, giving rise to a single appropriate behavior. In others, it would be woefully indeterminate (in a causal sense).[93]

This distinction may help clarify some of the current debates in legal theory. For example, it sheds some light on the well-known "chain gang" exchange between Ronald Dworkin and Stanley Fish.[94] Dworkin, in

---

93. Compare Dewey's distinction between theoretical certainty and practical certainty, *supra* notes 27-33 and accompanying text.
94. Dworkin, *Law as Interpretation*, 60 TEX. L. REV. 527 (1982) [hereinafter *Law as Interpretation*]; Fish, *Working on the Chain Gang: Interpretation in Law and Literature*, 60 TEX. L. REV. 551 (1982) [hereinafter *Working on the Chain Gang*]; Dworkin, *My Reply to Stanley Fish (and Walter Benn Michaels): Please Don't Talk About Objectivity Any More*, in THE POLITICS OF INTER-

seeking to show how rules acquire determinate meaning within a legal context, argues that, as each judge in a chain of precedent decides a concrete case pursuant to a previously announced rule, the freedom of subsequent decisionmakers to act pursuant to that rule is narrowed, much as writers of a story started by someone else have their responses restricted by the preceding paragraphs.[95] Fish rejects this argument, and argues that every judge or writer in the "chain" remains totally free to add whatever he or she likes.[96] Clearly, this debate involves a confusion of the two types of indeterminacy described here. In a causal account of indeterminacy, as a behavioral fact about judges in our society, Dworkin is absolutely right. Judges' responses do tend to be more predictable—and in that sense more constrained—in areas with abundant case law. But Fish is equally right that, in a Kripkean sense, no amount of prior case law can determine or justify a judge's response in the next concrete case.[97]

Kripke's work can be extremely useful in identifying the fallacies of intentionalism and making lawyers more aware of the complexities of any claim about the indeterminancy of rules. But it also indicates that philosophy provides little help to lawyers in dealing with the societally specific rules that are the main subject matter of their study: the conflict between different social practices as manifested in legal disputes. Kripke "solves"

PRETATION 287 (W. Mitchell ed. 1983); Fish, *Wrong Again*, 62 TEX. L. REV. 299 (1983).

95. *Law as Interpretation, supra* note 94, at 542-43. Note the similarity of Dworkin's account to Morris Cohen's description of how a chain of precedent could give rise to a rule of law. *See supra* note 38. Dworkin's argument is more ambitious, however, since he is seeking to argue not only descriptively that a chain of precedent may give rise to a causally determinate rule, but also to give a prescriptive account of how judges should properly choose the correct rule out of such a chain.

96. *Working on the Chain Gang, supra* note 94, at 553-54. Fish's position is somewhat less clear than Dworkin's, since he claims that every writer in the chain is equally free and equally constrained (by their social perceptions of their own roles). But when Fish asserts that the various writers may disagree about whether the previous text is a satire, a comedy of manners, or a piece of realism, and that such a dispute cannot be resolved "by appealing to that text," it seems obvious that his claim is one of Kripkean indeterminacy.

97. An analogy may be drawn to an example used by both Wittgenstein and Kripke, the numerical series. *See* pp. 18-20. If I present you with the numerical series 2, 4 and ask you to continue it, you may be unsure as to the behavior requested. 6 seems like an appropriate answer, if you view the series as requiring the addition of 2 to the prior number. Yet 8 is an equally plausible response, since the series is equally compatible with a rule that requires doubling the prior number. However, once we are given a few more numbers in the series, say 2, 4, 6, 8 we "know" the rule and give the "correct" response. Our confidence in the correctness of the answer 10 is so great that we are willing to use such questions on standardized tests to measure a student's "mathematical aptitude."

Yet, in a Kripkean sense, both numerical series are equally indeterminate and neither has a "correct" answer. I can always come up with some possible rule that justifies any answer I choose to give to either series. The rule I am supposed to derive from the latter, more determinate series is "keep adding 2 to the prior number," but I can equally well derive the rule "keep adding 2 to the prior number until you reach 8, then add 151." Accordingly, in a Kripkean sense, 10 and 159 are equally appropriate responses to the latter series. Dworkin's chain gang is like the addition of more numbers to the series. It does indeed limit what we would consider correct behavior by subsequent judges. Yet Fish is also right that, as a purely theoretical matter, there can be no "wrong" response to such a chain. *See also* R. DWORKIN, LAW'S EMPIRE 78-85 (1986) (contrasting "internal" and "external" skepticism).

Law and Metaphysics

the skeptical paradox about rules by positing socially recognized norms of behavior, which enable a member of that society to expect and identify certain behavior as "rule following." This is certainly plausible with respect to addition, and is probably true of the vast majority of behaviors associated with legal rules as well. We drive on the right side of the street, pay our electric bills, refrain from killing each other, and have no trouble describing people who do not engage in one of these expected behaviors as violating the law.

Yet the questions which engage the attention of most lawyers involve those behaviors that, under the prevailing social and linguistic norms, may be appropriately described either as "violating" or "not violating" the law. Such ambiguities are not unique to law, but may be found throughout our language. Is a whale a fish? Is Dr. Jekyll and Mr. Hyde one person or two? Kripke's book helps us to realize that such ambiguities are not, as many lawyers assume, the result of improperly or inadequately defined words, but that under certain circumstances there is no agreement among competent speakers of the language as to appropriate responses to such well understood words as "fish," "person," or "crime." The existence of such disagreement is as much a "brute empirical fact" as the agreement in our society about the appropriate response to addition. A Kripkean analysis of language, once it recognizes such disagreement, can go no further.

Yet lawyers do go further. They argue over the appropriate response to such words as they occur in particular cases, fully aware that the resolution of such linguistic conundrums will have substantial behavioral consequences. In making such arguments, they put forth contentions about the "meaning" of the words involved, the "intention" of the entity which formulated the rule, the consequences that treating the words a certain way will have in this case and in cases to follow. From a Kripkean point of view, such arguments can never succeed in their supposed purpose of establishing the "correct" interpretation of the rule, yet they do seem to be useful, both to lawyers and judges, in helping to resolve cases. In some way that we do not understand very well, lawyers can use language to change language. More accurately, they can use legal argument to change the responses that actors within the legal system deem "appropriate" in connection with certain legal formulations. Legal discourse and legal practice themselves appear to be important mechanisms in creating or destroying shared understandings in legal language. Change in the dominant understanding of legal language has something to do with the behavior of appellate court judges, but is undoubtedly also influenced by all the other actors in the system, the lawyers, law professors, clerks, and litigants.

Trying to understand how actors within the legal system develop and modify their shared understandings of the appropriate responses to legal language is a complicated inquiry. It requires consideration of legal language and legal argument and the way both are embedded in the larger set of linguistic behaviors.

Legal argument, like language itself, is open-ended in a somewhat paradoxical way. A skilled advocate can create novel, indeed unanticipated, legal arguments, which are nonetheless coherent and "make sense" as statements about law. Concepts like Brandeis' "right to privacy" or Reich's "new property" can simultaneously invoke and change prevailing legal understandings. It is doubtful that philosophers, who do not "speak" our legal language, and rarely seek to analyze contingent facts about society, can contribute much to understanding the complex and paradoxical nature of legal discourse. Lawyers, however, considering the issues raised by Kripke's book in light of their own experience of the malleability, creativity, and indeterminacy of legal argument, the ease with which arguments about rules are formulated, and the difficulties of persuading judges, should find their understanding of what they do altered, and perhaps enriched.

[13]

KRIPKE'S CASE

Some Remarks on Rules, their Interpretation and Application

By Jes Bjarup, Århus

1. Introduction

It is, I think, a commonplace to say that judges, in any society, decide cases. Judges are there in order to settle disputes between contesting parties, imposing their decisions upon them, which can be enforced whether the loosing party accepts the judge's decision or not.

In modern societies, it has become part of the way of life that there is, as a matter of fact, a state machinery for dispute settlement with community force behind it. Judges administer justice according to law, and their decisions can, if necessary, be enforced by other state agencies.

I take it that this is not in dispute. What is in dispute is, however, the explanation and justification of how judges decide cases. That is to say, there is, on the one hand, this ordinary practice of settling disputes by appealing to judges, and there is, on the other hand, the question of giving appropriate explanations and justifications of this practice.

Clearly, the ordinary practice of judges settling disputes according to law is prior to any explanation or justification given of that practice. The practice exists independently of any theory purporting to explain or justify what judges are doing, although it must be born in mind that such theories may have some importance for the way judges do decide cases.

Nevertheless, there is a fundamental distinction between the way the world is, that is that judges decide cases, and what we say about the world, that is theories of judicial decisions.

This distinction between what judges do, and what we say that judges do or ought to do, is not isomorphic with the distinction between theory and practice. Clearly, the judges are engaged in a practice, performing judicial activities which involve ordering the lives of people. This practice does not entail that no theory is involved. The judges apply theories in the sense that they possess understanding of the legal concepts with respect to legal rules, which justify their decisions.

Theories of judicial decisions have also a theoretical as well as a practical aspect. The theoretical aspect deals with the conceptual connections among legal concepts in relation to legal rules and their application which involves the practical aspect of giving an account of how judges bring about, or ought to bring about, legal decisions.

Jurisprudence, as a branch of knowledge about the administration of law, has then a theoretical as well as a practical aspect. I have made that point in a paper, presented at the 2nd Benelux Scandinavian Symposium in Legal Theory, held in Uppsala 1986, in which I also argued that, considering statutes, theories of interpretation should be replaced by a theory of legal reasoning.[1]

2. Kripke's Case

In this paper I wish to consider another topic, that is Kripke's case concerning the understanding and following rules.

Discourse about the law includes reference to rules. According to the late Roscoe Pound, "three steps are involved in the adjudication of a controversy according to law: (1) Finding the law, ascertaining which of the many rules in the legal system is to be applied, or, if none is applicable, reaching a rule for the cause (which may or may not stand as a rule for subsequent cases) on the basis of given materials in some way which the legal system points out; (2) interpreting the rule so chosen or ascertained, that is determining its meaning as it was framed and with respect to its intended scope; (3) applying to the cause in hand the rule so found and interpreted."[2]

According to Pound's view, interpretation (2) mediates between the statute (1) on the one hand, and its application (3) on the other hand.

This is, I take it, the prevailing doctrine among legal theorists, hence the importance of offering appropriate theories of interpretation how to understand the legal language. It is this understanding, conceived as learning the meaning of legal words and sentences, which must be acquired in order to follow and obey the law. Now, various theories are put forward how to acquire the proper understanding of legal language, and what kind of interpretation is involved which bridges the gap between the statute and its application. Whatever their differences, they all, it seems to me, share the same assumption. This is the idea that to learn the meaning of a legal concept is to acquire an understanding that obliges judges and lawyers – if they

---

[1] Interpretation, Reasoning and the Law, The Structure of Law. Proceedings of the 2nd Benelux-Scandinavian Symposium in Legal Theory, Uppsala 1986 (edt. Åke Frändberg and Mark Van Hoecke), Uppsala 1987, p. 161 - 178.

[2] *Roscoe Pound*, An Introduction to the Philosophy of Law, 1922, 7th printing, London 1965, p. 48.

have occasion to apply the concept in question – to render and justify decisions in certain determinate ways, on pain of failure to obey the rules governing the meaning of legal concepts, and determining what constitutes correct and incorrect application of legal concepts.

According to Kripke, relying on the late Ludwig Wittgenstein's reflections on following a rule,[3] this idea lacks substance. "We all suppose that our language expresses concepts – 'pain', 'plus', 'red' – in such a way that once I 'grasp' the concept, all future applications of it are determined (in the sense of being uniquely justified by the concept grasped). In fact, it seems that no matter what is in my mind at a given time, I am free in the future to interpret it in different ways."[4]

Thus, Kripke presents Wittgenstein as inventing a new sceptical problem.

The sceptical problem, as Kripke sees it, is that "it appears that he (i.e. Wittgenstein) has shown all language, all concept formation, to be impossible, indeed unintelligible" (p. 62). Kripke claims that Wittgenstein's argument is that "there can be no such meaning as meaning anything by any word. Each new application we make is a leap in the dark; any present intention could be interpreted so as to accord with anything we may choose to do. So there can be neither accord, nor conflict. This is what Wittgenstein said in § 202."[5]

Kripke, following Wittgenstein, considers the sceptical problem with respect to mathematics, that is to say the calculation of mathematical functions as an example of rule-following behaviour. But, as Kripke notices, "the sceptical problem applies to all meaningful uses of language" (p. 7, cf. p. 58). Consequently, Kripke's case is relevant for law and legal theory, since after all the assumption is that there is such thing as legal language used by judges to render decisions according to legal rules which determine the decisions for indefinitely many new legal suits brought forward by litigants, and this is also the assumption made by theories concerning judicial decisions.

The purpose of introducing legal rules is to regulate and guide human conduct, and thereby legal rules also serve as standards for evaluating human conduct as right or wrong. This is the normative function of legal rules, which provides reasons for action. The assumption is that judges and lawyers follow these rules which determine that certain legal consequences follow on the performance of certain actions.

---

[3] See *Ludwig Wittgenstein,* Philosophical Investigations (transl. by G. E. M. Anscombe) Oxford 1968. Reference to this in the text as Wittgenstein followed by §.

[4] *Saul A. Kripke,* Wittgenstein on Rules, Oxford 1982, p. 107. Bare page references in the text refer to this book.

[5] *Kripke,* Wittgenstein, p. 55, the quoted reference to § 201, in Wittgenstein's Philosophical Investigations, cf. *Kripke,* op. cit. p. 7.

Now lawyers, including judges, are told by Kripke that there is no such thing as following any rule. Indeed, the problem is that there is no such thing as language. This is certainly scepticism with a vengeance. Kripke refers, in this connection, to Hume's sceptical problem concerning causation, and Hume's sceptical solution.

The lawyer, having read Hume, may answer this new sceptical challenge with Hume who writes about the sceptic that he "may throw himself or others into a momentary amazement and confusion by his profound reasonings; the first and most trivial event in life will put to flight all his doubts and scruples, and leave him the same, in every point of action and speculation, with the philosophers of every other sect, or with those who never concerned themselves in any philosophical researches. When he awakes from his dream, he will be the first to join in the laugh against himself, and to confess, that all his objections are mere amusement, and can have no other tendency than to show the whimsical condition of mankind, who must act and reason and believe; though they are not able, by their most diligent enquiry, to satisfy themselves concerning the foundation of these operations, or to remove the objections, which may be raised against them."[6]

Thus the lawyer may dismiss Kripke and his sceptical problem as conceptual nihilism, which unlike classical scepticism, is manifestly self-refuting and rather an absurdity.[7]

This dismissal is, I think, a failure. It is a failure to ignore what philosophers have to say on vital problems, such as, for example, the problem what it is to interpret, apply and follow legal rules. And it may also be worth remembering what another great philosopher, Immanuel Kant, wrote concerning the sceptical position. Kant was, after all, worried by Hume's scepticism, but according to Kant, "the sceptic is ... the task master who constrains the dogmatic reasoner to develop a sound critique of the understanding and reason. While ... the sceptical procedure cannot of itself yield any satisfying answer to the questions of reason, none the less it prepares the way by arousing reason to circumspection, and by indicating the radical measures which are adequate to secure it in its legitimate possessions."[8]

---

[6] *David Hume,* An Enquiry concerning Human Understanding, (3rd ed. rev. by P. H. Nidditch), Oxford 1975, Sec. XII, Part II, p. 160. Cf. *David Hume,* A Treatise of Human Nature, (2nd ed., ed. P. H. Nidditch), Oxford 1978, Book I, Part IV, Sec. VII, p. 269.

[7] Cf. *G. P. Baker* and *P. M. S. Hacker,* On Misunderstanding Wittgenstein, Synthese, vol. 58, 1984, p. 407 - 450 at p. 410. – Perhaps there is an analogy between this new form of scepticism with the classical scepticism of American and Scandinavian Legal Realists claiming the non-existence of legal rules, but I shall not explore this in this paper.

[8] *I. Kant,* Critique of Pure Reason (transl. by N. K. Smith) London 1976, A 769/ B 797, p. 612.

Thus I think that lawyers should enter into Kripke's speculations in order to prepare the way for theories concerning judicial decision-making. This is also the opinion of Charles M. Yablon in a recent article, reviewing Kripke's book.[9]

3. An Evaluation of Kripke's Case

In his preface, Kripke writes that "the primary purpose of this work is the presentation of a problem and an argument, not its critical evaluation. Primarily I can be read ... as almost like an attorney presenting a major philosophical argument as it struck me" (p. IX).

The problem is Wittgenstein's sceptical paradox, mentioned above, based upon the argument that there is no fact that could constitute my having attached one rather than another meaning to any word, or, in other words, nothing can accord nor conflict with a rule, because anything can be made out to do so.

The solution of the problem is to be found in Wittgenstein's 'sceptical solution'. This is the strategy to accept the sceptic's premises but denying that the sceptical conclusion follows from them. After all "the sceptical conclusion (i.e. that all language, all concept formation is impossible) is insane and intolerable." (p. 60).

So Wittgenstein, according to Kripke's understanding him, accepts that there is no fact in the world that constitutes meaning something by one's words. This, however, annihilates the possibility of meaning something by one's words and sentences only on the assumption of a realist theory of meaning. A realist theory of meaning holds that the meaning of sentences is determined by truth-conditions, that is to say correspondence between sentences and possible facts in the world. If this realist theory of meaning is replaced by an antirealist theory of meaning, which holds that meaning of sentences is determined by conditions for assertion, then there is room for language, meaning, and rules.

Thus we have to look at persons, not as single rule followers, but rather as "interacting with a wider community, others will then have justification conditions for attributing correct or incorrect rule following to the subject, and these will not be simply that the subject's own authority is unconditionally to be accepted" (p. 89).

The conclusion is, then, that meaning something by a word requires a community to supply agreement and to prevent thinking one is following a

---

[9] *Charles M. Yablon*, Law and Metaphysics. Book-review of Saul Kripke, Wittgenstein on Rules and Private Language, The Yale Law Journal, vol. 96, 1987, p. 613 - 636. Reference to this article in the text with bare page references.

rule on the one hand and following a rule on the other hand from collapsing into each other.

This is Wittgenstein's problem and solution as presented by Kripke as an attorney. Kripke, as an attorney, presents Wittgenstein's case. But his statement of this case is parasitic in relation to what is, as a matter of truth, Wittgenstein's view concerning rule-following.[10] Wittgenstein is represented as being a sceptic by Kripke, but it does not follow that Wittgenstein, in truth, is a sceptic. I cannot, in this paper, go into details concerning Wittgenstein's philosophical views. Suffice it to say that other philosophers have found Kripke to be wrong concerning his understanding Wittgenstein.[11] In effect, Kripke fails to notice that Wittgenstein claims that "there is a way of grasping of rule which is not an interpretation but which is exhibited in what we call 'obeying the rule' and 'going against it' in actual cases." (Wittgenstein, § 201).

Kripke is guilty of committing the very mistake which Wittgenstein is at pains to correct, that is to say the assumption that there must be an interpretation which mediates between an order or rule on the one hand, and an action in conformity with it, on the other hand.

Kripke's mistake is to think that understanding consists in some interpretation, i.e. some verbal or quasi-verbal formula presenting itself to the mind. That this is Kripke's view is quite clear from his own mathematical example, using the word 'plus' and the symbol '+' to denote a well-known mathematical function, that is addition. Kripke writes "by means of my external symbolic representation and *my internal mental representation*, I 'grasp' the rule for addition. One point is crucial to my 'grasp' of this rule. Although I myself have computed only finitely many sums in the past, the rule determines my answer for indefinitely many new sums that I have never previously considered. This is the whole point of the notion that in learning to add I grasp a rule: my past intentions regarding addition determine a unique answer for indefinitely many new cases in the future" (p. 7 - 8, my italics).

In this passage, Kripke reveals the misunderstanding, described by Wittgenstein in the second paragraph of § 201, which Kripke ignores in his representation of Wittgenstein.[12] And this omission is serious, because

---

[10] Cf. for a discussion of the relationship between Wittgenstein and Kripke, *Simon Blackburn*, The Individual Strikes Back, Synthese, vol. 58, 1984, p. 281 - 301.

[11] See the articles of *Baker* and *Hacker* (note 7) and *Blackburn* (note 10) as well as G. E. M. *Anscombe*, Critical Notice, Canadian Journal of Philosophy, vol. 15, 1985, p. 103 - 109; *John McDowell*, Wittgenstein on Following a Rule, Synthese, vol. 58, 1984, p. 325 - 363; *S. G. Shanker*, Sceptical Confusions about Rule-Following, Mind, vol. 93, 1987, p. 423 - 429; *Peter Winch*, Facts and Superfacts, The Philosophical Quarterly, vol. 33, 1983, p. 398 - 404.

[12] Cf. *Peter Winch*, Facts and Superfacts, p. 400.

Wittgenstein in § 201 is not presenting a sceptical problem, that is the illusion of rule-following as Kripke suggests, but rather Wittgenstein is trying to show that the act of understanding a rule cannot be conceived in terms of hitting an interpretation that will bridge the gap between the external symbolic representation and its application. The reason why this is so is that it leads to a vicious infinite regress. We may think that someone understands a rule only if he gives it a particular interpretation. However, if by 'interpretation' we mean "the substitution of one expression of the rule for another" (cf. Wittgenstein, § 201), then the particular understanding and interpretation of the rule will equally present a problem of understanding and interpreting this particular interpretation, and so on. We gain no approach to the required fact of understanding the rule by embarking on a regress of interpretations. Wittgenstein's conclusion is that an interpretation does not determine the meaning of words and sentences (cf. Wittgenstein, § 198).

Further, Kripke also commits the mistake of seeing rules as determining the indefinite totality of their own applications, as the quotation clearly reveals. But the rejoinder is, of course, that rules cannot apply themselves and determine the answers. It is us, who introduce rules, and determine what constitutes rule-following. It is not the rule which necessitates or causes me to act, but rather I who use the rule as guidance for my actions. No interpretation of a legal rule, no rule for the application of a rule, can definitely determinate, by itself, what counts as accord or conflict. This is so, because each interpretation generates the same problem, that is, has it to be applied? The answer to this problem is, I suggest, to consider reasons for actions, rather than interpretations of rules.

So Wittgenstein's point is that there can be actions which are in accord or conflict with rules. Kripke represents Wittgenstein as stating the sceptical paradox that no course of action could be determined by a rule. Kripke's representation of Wittgenstein's position does not square with what Wittgenstein says, and must therefore be rejected as an exegesis of Wittgenstein.

4. The Importance of Kripke's Case

Yablon, in his paper, takes Kripke seriously, but Yablon fails to consider whether Kripke has a case at all. On the contrary, Yablon accepts Kripke's sceptical paradox and also his sceptical solution.

Kripke's case, then, is "relevant and important to contemporary lawyers" (p. 624, cf. p. 632). In three respects.

First, Kripke's argument "is a powerful refutation of all lawyers who claim there" is one "superlative fact ... that can provide a determinate meaning to legal rules. ... Kripke's argument demonstrates that original intent, even one's own fully knowable original intent, cannot determine any future application of a rule. Accordingly, original intent can provide no more determinate answers to questions of legal interpretation than any other hermeneutic devise" (p. 632).

Is this so? Kripke's argument, applied to legal rules and their application, takes the form that there is nothing that could constitute my understanding a legal rule in a determinate way.

Yablon endorses Kripke's argument, but the argument is based upon the assumption that the understanding, on which I act when I obey a legal rule, must be an interpretation. It is, in effect, Pound's view that the act of understanding mediates between the legal rule and its application. The act of understanding, conceived in terms of hitting on an interpretation that bridges the gap between a legal statute and its application, demands to be seen as the connection between the legal words and the subsequent application. Wittgenstein rejects this idea, but it is taken seriously by Kripke, and Yablon follows suit, which leads to the absurd position that denies that there is any such thing as the correct and incorrect application of rules. If this is the case then we are faced with the paradox of conceptual nihilism: that language, including legal language, is impossible.

Besides, concerning the individual and the relation between his original intention to use words and his present intention to use them, it is important to bear in mind, as Kripke also does, that "the relation of meaning and intention to future action is normative, not descriptive" (p. 37). The importance of this is that meaning is related normatively to linguistic behaviour, which implies the need for consistency and correctness if communication is to be successful. The need for consistency, which is important also within the law, leads to the normative conclusion that I ought to use words in the same way on every occasion, that is with the same original intent, although it is important to notice the distinction, ignored by Kripke and Yablon, between (a) original intent, that is what a person means at a given time by his using words, and (b) present intent, that is whether at some later time the person isbeing consistent with his earlier use of these words.[13]

This distinction is clearly also important for the understanding of the constitution or other legal rules, since it is possible, after all, to decide to use the terms in a different way from before. In this situation there is room for a comparison between different facts, e.g. the fact what the drafters of the constitution meant by the words they used, and the fact what the Supreme Court means at some later time by those words. Surely what a judge means

---

[13] Cf. *Paul Coates*, Kripke's Sceptical Paradox: Normativeness and Meaning, Mind, vol. 95, 1986, p. 77 - 80.

by using the words presupposes that there is a legal language, in which words and sentences already have a meaning, that is a use, which the judge understands by his linguistic and legal competence to be disposed to conform or not to what the words and sentences mean.

Yablon accepts Kripke's paradox, that is that language is impossible. He also endorses Kripke's solution which leads Yablon to claim secondly that Kripke's argument "provides little support for the claim that the law's inability to provide determinate answers demonstrates the illegitimacy of legal rules or of their application by decision-makers" (p. 632).

The reason why this is so is that "the philosophical demonstration of the indeterminacy of all rules does not alter the "brute empirical fact" that we continue to speak of rules and continue to distinguish between actions that follow and do not follow a rule" (p. 633).

This remark is very much akin to Hume's remark quoted above. It is the view that scepticism does not matter for actions, which is quite contrary to classical scepticism. Leaving this aside, if the philosophical demonstration is that all rules are indeterminate, then perhaps the ordinary talk embodies error, since it is conducted as if there were facts, but Kripke has told us that there are no such facts. Consequently the error should be corrected. I do not know whether Yablon has this in mind when he writes that the philosophical demonstration "does require us to change our understanding of the notion of rule-following, to include a recognition of the social, co-operative and even political process implicated in discussions about rules" (p. 633).

Kripke's notion of rule-following is, as I have tried to show akin to Pound's notion of rule-following, so this can hardly amount to a change in our understanding of rule-following.

Thirdly, Yablon claims that "probably the most important contribution Kripke's book makes to lawyers is to clarify the ways in which a rule may be indeterminate. His argument requires us to distinguish, in ways that much of the contemporary debate among lawyers does not, between two types of indeterminacy which may characterize rules" (p. 633).

The required distinction is between "Kripkean indeterminacy" and "causal indeterminacy".

Kripkean indeterminacy is described by Yablon as "a rule that is indeterminate in that no particular action can ever be justified as following or not following the rule" (p. 633). If this is the case, no course of action can ever be determined by application of the rule by a judge, consequently there is simply no rule at all. As Kripke says "each new application we make is a leap in the dark; any present intention (Yablon's action) could be interpreted so as to accord with anything we may choose to do. So there can be neither accord, nor conflict" (p. 55).

Kripke claims that this is also what Wittgenstein says in Philosophical Investigations § 201. But what Wittgenstein actually says is that this is a mistake. The rule is empty just because it would be equally possible to show that every action could be made out to conflict with the rule. The proper conclusion to be drawn is that the rule, with its interpretation, "hangs in the air" (§ 198).

I conclude that Yablon's "Kripkean indeterminacy" also "hangs in the air". It forces Yablon to misconstrue the concepts of legal rules and rule-following to end up with that judges apply rules blindly. Surely this is not to clarify the current debate in legal theory concerning judicial decision-making, as Yablon suggests (p. 633 - 634).

Next there is "causal indeterminacy" which is described as "a rule that is indeterminate in that a competent decision-maker cannot arrive at a correct application of a rule in response to a particular case" (p. 633).

The trouble with this indeterminacy is that it suggests, wrongly, that a rule, on its own, provides the cause for its application. This is shown by Yablon's example that "the rules of addition provide good examples of rules which are indeterminate in the Kripkean sense (that is what the sceptical paradox demonstrates) yet fully determinate in the causal sense" (p. 633). But what the sceptical paradox demonstrates is that there are no rules of addition, so it is a contradiction to claim that there are such rules in the causal sense, which determine one's actions. Yablon's distinction is mistaken for the reasons set out by Wittgenstein (§ 189). It is the confusion between the use of rules which determine a mathematical function, e.g. addition, and the use of rules which determine conduct in the sense that a description is given of the practice of someone who has mastered the use of the rules of addition.

My conclusion is that Yablon's distinction between "Kripkean indeterminacy" and "causal indeterminacy" must be rejected since he is conflating the two uses of rules in the way which Wittgenstein calls a "mistake". Further, Yablon commits the error of thinking that rules can provide for their own application. Yablon thinks that the rules of arithmetic take on a certain causal efficacy when incorporated in a person's mind, whereas this is not the case with legal rules. But this is to overlook that in both cases it is not the rule which compels people, but rather that people, in the case of arithmetic, are logically committed to use the rules in order to arrive at correct answers, and in case of legal rules, judges are legally committed to use the rules in order to arrive at answers to legal questions. The fact that there is a number of possible answers to legal questions does not imply that there are no correct answers or applications of the rule by judges. And following rules is not mere regularity, as Yablon suggests (p. 634). In order to constitute rule-following, the regularity must be normative, that is to say that there is such thing as correctness and incorrectness.

The question is the conception we have of this normative regularity. Kripke suggests that the community provides the standard of correctness by "the brute empirical fact that we agree with each other in our responses" (p. 109). But this is not the case with judgements. If the community all started saying that 57 + 68 = 5, to use Kripke's example, then this "brute empirical fact" does not make me wrong when I insist that the correct answer is 125. What is the case with legal decisions is more difficult to answer. If the suggestion is that the Supreme Court provides the final answer, then their decision, as a brute empirical fact, settles the case between the parties. But whether the decision is right or wrong may still be questioned. Here there is room for a sceptical challenge.

5. Conclusion

Kripke has presented a sceptical case. The question is whether his reasoning – on its own – deserves our allegiance?

The answer by Yablon is affirmative. My answer, by contrast, is negative. The merit of Kripke's case is to question the concept of rule-following. Surely rule-following isof central importance within the law. After all we know that judges decide cases. We know, if we accept Kripke's argument, that in a community we see each other as obeying the same rules. But this fact does nothing at all, pace Kripke, to show *how* we are seeing each other when we say that we obey the rules. We know well enough what it is to see someone as a judge, because we know what judges are. But we do not know what it is to see a judge as obeying the rules, unless we know what it is to follow one. And this fact Kripke leaves unexplained.

The problem is still to clarify the criteria for describing normative conduct as a case of following rules as well as providing criteria for justification of normative conduct for following rules.

[14]

Working on the Chain Gang: Interpretation in Law and Literature

Stanley Fish

In his essay *Law as Interpretation*[1] Ronald Dworkin is concerned to characterize legal practice in such a way as to avoid claiming either that in deciding a case judges find the plain meaning of the law "just 'there'" or, alternatively, that they make up the meaning "wholesale" in accordance with personal preference or whim. It is Dworkin's thesis that neither of these accounts is adequate because interpretation is something different from both.[2] Dworkin is right, I think, to link his argument about legal practice to an argument about the practice of literary criticism, not only because in both disciplines the central question is, "What is the source of interpretative authority?," but also because in both disciplines answers to that question typically take the form of the two positions Dworkin rejects. Just as there are those in the legal community who have insisted on construing statutes and decisions "strictly" (that is, by attending only to the words themselves), so there are those in the literary community who have insisted that interpretation is, or should be, constrained by what is "in the text"; and just as the opposing doctrine of legal realism holds that judges' "readings" are always rationalizations of their political or personal desires, so do proponents of critical subjectivity hold that what a reader sees is merely a reflection of his predispositions and biases. The field is divided, in short, between those who believe that interpretation is grounded in objectivity and those who believe that interpreters are, for all intents and purposes, free. Dworkin moves to outflank both of these positions by characterizing legal and critical practice as "chain enterprises," enterprises in which interpretation is an extension of an institutional history made up of "innumerable decisions, structures, conventions and practices."[3] Interpretation so conceived is not purely objective since its results will not "wring assent from a stone" (there is still "room for disagree-

88 Meaning and Constraint

ment"), but neither is it wholly subjective, since the interpreter does not proceed independently of what others in the institution have done or said.

In general, I find this account of interpretation and its constraints attractive, in part because I find it similar in important ways to the account I have offered under the rubric of "interpretive communities" in *Is There a Text in This Class?*[4] There are, however, crucial differences between the two accounts, and in the course of explicating those differences I will argue that Dworkin repeatedly falls away from his own best insights into a version of the fallacies (of pure objectivity and pure subjectivity) he so forcefully challenges.

We can begin by focusing on the most extended example in his essay of a "chain enterprise," the imagined literary example of a novel written not by a single author but by a group of coauthors, each of whom is responsible for a separate chapter. The members of the group draw lots and the

> lowest number writes the opening chapter of a novel, which he or she then sends to the next number who adds a chapter, with the understanding that he is adding a chapter to that novel rather than beginning a new one, and then sends the two chapters to the next number, and so on. Now every novelist but the first has the dual responsibilities of interpreting and creating, because each must read all that has gone before in order to establish, in the interpretivist sense, what the novel so far created is. He or she must decide what the characters are "really" like; what motives in fact guide them; what the point or theme of the developing novel is; how far some literary device or figure, consciously or unconsciously used, contributes to these, and whether it should be extended or refined or trimmed or dropped in order to send the novel further in one direction rather than another.[5]

In its deliberate exaggeration this formulation of a chain enterprise is helpful and illuminating, but it is also mistaken in several important respects. First of all, it assumes that the first person in the chain is in a position different in kind from those who follow him because he is only creating while his fellow authors must both create and interpret. In an earlier draft of the essay Dworkin had suggested that as the chain extends itself the freedom enjoyed by the initiator of the sequence is more and more constrained, until at some point the history against which "late novelists" must work may become so dense "as to admit only one good-faith interpretation"; and indeed that interpretation will not be an interpretation in the usual sense because it will have been *demanded* by what has already been written. Dworkin has now withdrawn this suggestion (which he had qualified with words like "probably"), but the claim underlying it—the claim that constraints thicken as the chain lengthens—remains as long as the distinction between the first author and all the others is maintained. The idea is that the first author is free because he is not obliged "to read all that has gone before" and therefore doesn't have to decide what the characters are "really" like and what motives guide them, and so on. But, in fact, the first author has surrendered his freedom (although, as we shall see, surrender is exactly the wrong word) as soon as he commits himself to writing a novel, for he makes his decision under the same constraints that rule the decisions of his collaborators. He must decide, for example, how to begin the novel, but the decision is not "free" because the very notion "beginning a novel" exists only in the context of a set of practices that at once enable and limit the act of beginning. One cannot think of beginning a novel without thinking within, as opposed to thinking "of," these established practices, and even if one "decides" to "ignore" them or "violate" them or "set them aside," the actions of ignoring and violating and setting aside will themselves have a shape that is constrained by the preexisting shape of those practices. This does not mean that the decisions of the first author are wholly determined, but that the choices available to him are "novel-writing choices," choices that depend on a prior understanding of what it means to write a novel, even when he "chooses" to alter that understanding.[6] In short, he is neither free nor constrained (if those words are understood as referring to absolute states), but free *and* constrained. He is free to begin whatever kind of novel he decides to write, but he is constrained by the finite (although not unchanging) possibilities that are subsumed in the notions "kind of novel" and "beginning a novel."

Moreover, those who follow him are free and constrained in exactly the same way. When a later novelist decides to "send the novel further in one direction rather than in another," that decision must follow upon a decision as to what direction has already been taken; and *that* decision will be an interpretive one in the sense that it will not be determined by the independent and perspicuous shape of the words,

90   Meaning and Constraint

but will be the means by which the words are given a shape. Later novelists do not read directly from the words to a decision about the point or theme of the novel, but from a prior understanding (which may take a number of forms) of the points or themes novels can possibly have to a novelistic construction of the words. Just as the first novelist "creates" within the constraints of "novel practice" in general, so do his successors on the chain interpret him (and each other) within those same constraints. Not only are those constraints controlling, but they are uniformly so; they do not relax or tighten in relation to the position an author happens to occupy on the chain. The last author is as free, within those constraints, to determine what "the characters are really like" as is the first. It is tempting to think that the more information one has (the more history) the more directed will be one's interpretation; but information only comes in an interpreted form (it does not announce itself). No matter how much or how little you have, it cannot be a check against interpretation because even when you first "see" it, interpretation has already done its work. So that rather than altering the conditions of interpretation, the accumulation of chapters merely extends the scope of its operation.

If this seems counterintuitive, imagine the very real possibility of two (or more) "later" novelists who have different views of the direction the novel has taken and are therefore in disagreement as to what would constitute a continuation of "that" novel as opposed to "beginning a new one." To make the example more specific, let us further imagine that one says to another, "Don't you see that it's ironic, a social satire?," and the second replies, "Not at all, at most it's a comedy of manners," while a third chimes in, "You're both wrong; it's obviously a perfectly straightforward piece of realism." If Dworkin's argument is to hold, that is, if the decisions he talks about are to be constrained in a strong sense by an already-in-place text, it must be possible to settle this disagreement by appealing to that text. But it is precisely because the text appears differently in the light of different assumptions as to what is its mode that there is a disagreement in the first place. Or, to put it another way, "social satire," "comedy of manners," and "piece of realism" are not labels applied mechanically to perspicuous instances; rather, they are names for ways of reading, ways which when put into operation make available for picking out the "facts" which those who are proceeding within them can then cite. It is entirely possible that the parties to our imagined dispute might find themselves pointing to the same "stretch of language" (no longer the same, since each would be characterizing it differently) and claiming it as a "fact" in support of opposing interpretations. (The history of literary criticism abounds in such scenarios.) Each would then believe, and be able to provide reasons for his belief, that only he is continuing the novel in the direction it has taken so far and that the others are striking out in a new and unauthorized direction.

Again, this does not mean that a later novelist is free to decide anything he likes (or that there is no possibility of adjudicating a disagreement), but that within the general parameters of novel-reading practice, he is as free as anyone else, which means that he is as constrained as anyone else. He is constrained in that he can only continue in ways that are recognizable novel ways (and the same must be said of the first novelist's act of "beginning"), and he is free in that no amount of textual accumulation can make his choice of one of those ways inescapable. Although the parameters of novel practice mark the limits of what anyone who is thinking within them can think to do, within those limits they do not *direct* anyone to do this rather than that. (They are not a "higher" text.) Every decision a later novelist makes will rest on his assessment of the situation as it has developed; but that assessment will itself be an act of interpretation which will in turn rest on an interpreted understanding of the enterprise in general.

This, then, is my first criticism of Dworkin's example: the distinction it is supposed to illustrate—the distinction between the first and later novelists—will not hold up because everyone in the enterprise is equally constrained. (By "equally" I mean equally with respect to the condition of freedom; I am making no claims about the number or identity of the constraints.) My second criticism is that in his effort to elaborate the distinction Dworkin embraces both of the positions he criticizes. He posits for the first novelist a freedom that is equivalent to the freedom assumed by those who believe that judges (and other interpreters) are bound only by their personal preferences and desires; and he thinks of later novelists as bound by a previous history in a way that would be possible only if the shape and significance of that history were self-evident. Rather than avoiding the Scylla of legal realism ("making it up wholesale") and the Charybdis of strict constructionism ("finding the law just 'there' "), he commits himself to both. His reason for doing so becomes clear when he extends the example to an analysis of the law:

92   Meaning and Constraint

> Deciding hard cases at law is rather like this strange literary exercise. The similarity is most evident when judges consider and decide "common-law" cases; that is, when no statute figures centrally in the legal issue, and the argument turns on which rules or principles of law "underlie" the related decisions of other judges in the past. Each judge is then like a novelist in the chain. He or she must read through what other judges in the past have written not simply to discover what these judges have said, or their state of mind when they said it, but to reach an opinion about what these other judges have collectively *done,* in the way that each of our novelists formed an opinion about the collective novel so far written. Any judge forced to decide any law suit will find, if he looks in the appropriate books, records of many arguably similar cases decided over decades or even centuries past by many other judges of different styles and judicial and political philosophies, in periods of different orthodoxies of procedure and judicial convention. Each judge must regard himself, in deciding the case before him, as a partner in a complex chain enterprise of which these innumerable decisions, structures, conventions and practices are the history; it is his job to continue that history into the future through what he does. He *must* interpret what has gone before because he has a responsibility to advance the enterprise in hand rather than strike out in some new direction of his own.[7]

The emphasis on the word *"must"* alerts us to what is at stake for Dworkin in the notion of a chain enterprise. It is a way of explaining how judges are kept from striking out in a new direction, much as later novelists are kept by the terms of their original agreement from beginning a new novel. Just as it is the duty of a later novelist to continue the work of his predecessors, so it is the duty of a judge to "advance the enterprise in hand." Presumably, the judge who is tempted to strike out in "some new direction of his own" will be checked by his awareness of his responsibility to the corporate enterprise; he will then comport himself as a partner in the chain rather than as a free and independent agent.

The force of the account, in other words, depends on the possibility of judges comporting themselves in ways other than the "chain-enterprise" way. But is there in fact any such possibility? What would it mean for a judge to strike out in a new direction? Dworkin doesn't tell us, but presumably it would mean deciding a case in such a way as to have no relationship to the history of previous decisions. It is hard to imagine what such a decision would be like since any decision, to be recognized as a decision by a judge, would have to be made in recognizably judicial terms. A judge who decided a case on the basis of whether or not the defendant had red hair would not be striking out in a new direction; he would simply not be acting as a judge, because he could give no reasons for his decision that would be seen *as* reasons by competent members of the legal community. (Even in so extreme a case it would not be accurate to describe the judge as striking out in a new direction; rather he would be continuing the direction of an enterprise—perhaps a bizarre one—*other* than the judicial.) And conversely, if in deciding a case a judge *is* able to give such reasons, then the direction he strikes out in will not be new because it will have been implicit in the enterprise as a direction one could conceive of and argue for. This does not mean that his decision will be above criticism, but that it will be criticized, if it is criticized, for having gone in one judicial direction rather than another, neither direction being "new" in a sense that would give substance to Dworkin's fears.

Those fears are equally groundless with respect to the other alternative Dworkin imagines, the judge who looks at the chain of previous decisions and decides to see in it "whatever he thinks should have been there."[8] Here the danger is not so much arbitrary action (striking out in a new direction) as it is the willful imposition of a personal perspective on materials that have their own proper shape. "A judge's duty," Dworkin asserts, "is to interpret the legal history he finds and not to invent a better history."[9] Interpretation that is constrained by the history one finds will be responsible, whereas interpretation informed by the private preferences of the judge will be wayward and subjective. The opposition is one to which Dworkin repeatedly returns in a variety of forms, but in whatever form it is always vulnerable to the same objection: neither the self-declaring or "found" entity nor the dangerously free or "inventing" agent is a possible feature of the enterprise.

First of all, one doesn't just find a history; rather one views a body of materials with the assumption that it is organized by judicial concerns. It is that assumption which gives a shape to the materials, a shape that can *then* be described as having been "found." Moreover, not everyone will find the same shape because not everyone will be proceeding within the same notion of what constitutes a proper judicial

94 Meaning and Constraint

concern, either in general or in particular cases. One sees this clearly in Dworkin's own account of what is involved in legal decisionmaking. A judge, he explains, will look in the "appropriate books" for cases "arguably similar" to the one before him. Notice that the similarity is "arguable," which means that it must be argued *for;* similarity is not something one finds, but something one must establish, and when one establishes it one establishes the configurations of the cited cases as well as of the case that is to be decided. Similarity, in short, is not a property of texts (similarities do not announce themselves), but a property conferred by a relational argument in which the statement A is like B is a characterization (one open to challenge) of *both* A and B. To see a present-day case as similar to a chain of earlier ones is to reconceive that chain by finding it in an applicability that has not always been apparent. Paradoxically, one can be faithful to legal history only by revising it, by redescribing it in such a way as to accommodate and render manageable the issues raised by the present.[10] This is a function of the law's conservatism, which will not allow a case to remain unrelated to the past, and so assures that the past, in the form of the history of decisions, will be continually rewritten. In fact, it is the *duty* of a judge to rewrite it (which is to say no more than that it is the duty of a judge to decide), and therefore there can be no simply "found" history in relation to which some other history could be said to be "invented." All histories are invented in the weak sense that they are not simply "discovered," but assembled under the pressure of some present urgency; no history is invented in the strong sense that the urgency that led to its assembly was unrelated to any generally acknowledged legal concern.

To put it another way, there could be no such strongly invented history because there could be no such strong inventor, no judge whose characterization of legal history displayed none of the terms, distinctions, and arguments that would identify it (for competent members) as a *legal* history. Of course, someone who stood apart from the enterprise, someone who was not performing as a judge, might offer such a history (a history, for example, in which the observed patterns were ethnic or geographical), but to accuse such a historian of striking out in a new direction or inventing a better history would be beside the point since whatever he did or didn't do would have no legal (as opposed to sociological or political) significance. And, conversely, someone who was in fact standing within the enterprise, thinking in enterprise ways, could only put forward a history that was enterprise-specific, and that history could not be an invented one. It is true, of course, that jurists can and do accuse each other of inventing a history, but that is a charge you level at someone who has "found" a history different from yours. It should not be confused with the possibility (or the danger) of "really" inventing one. The distinction between a "found" history and an "invented" one is finally nothing more than a distinction between a persuasive interpretation and one that has failed to convince. One man's "found" history will be another man's invented history, but neither will ever be, because it could not be, either purely found or purely invented.

As one reads Dworkin's essay, the basic pattern of his mistakes becomes more and more obvious. He repeatedly makes two related and mutually reinforcing assumptions: he assumes that history in the form of a chain of decisions has, at some level, the status of a brute fact; and he assumes that wayward or arbitrary behavior in relation to that fact is an institutional possibility. Together these two assumptions give him his project, the project of explaining how a free and potentially irresponsible agent is held in check by the self-executing constraints of an independent text. Of course, by conceiving his project in this way—that is, by reifying the mind in its freedom and the text in its independence—he commits himself to the very alternatives he sets out to avoid, the alternatives of legal realism on the one hand and positivism on the other. As a result, these alternatives rule his argument, at once determining its form and emerging, again and again, as its content.

An example, early in the essay, involves the possibility of reading an Agatha Christie mystery as a philosophical novel. Such a reading, Dworkin asserts, would be an instance of "changing" the text rather than "explaining" it because the text *as it is* will not yield to it without obvious strain or distortion. "All but one or two sentences would be irrelevant to the supposed theme, and the organization, style and figures would be appropriate not to a philosophical novel but to an entirely different genre."[11] The assumption is that sentences, figures, and styles announce their own generic affiliation, and that a reader who would claim them for an inappropriate genre would be imposing his will on nature. It is exactly the same argument by which judges are supposedly constrained by the obvious properties of the history they are to continue, and it falls by the same analysis. First of all, generic identification, like continuity between cases, is not something one finds, but something one establishes, and one establishes it for a reason. Readers don't just "decide" to recharacterize a text; there has to be

96 Meaning and Constraint

some reason why it would occur to someone to treat a work identified as a member of one genre as a possible member of another. There must already be in place ways of thinking that will enable the recharacterization to become a project, and there must be conditions in the institution such that the prosecution of that project seems attractive and potentially rewarding. With respect to the project Dworkin deems impossible, those ways and conditions already exist. It has long been recognized that authors of the first rank—Poe, Dickens, Dostoyevski—have written novels of detection, and the fact that these novels have been treated seriously means that the work of less obviously canonical authors—Wilkie Collins, Conan Doyle, among others—are possible candidates for the same kind of attention. Once this happens, and it has already happened, any novel of detection can, at least provisionally, be considered as a "serious" work without a critic or his audience thinking that he is doing something bizarre or irresponsible; and in recent years just such consideration has been given to the work of Hammet, Chandler (whom Dworkin mentions), Highsmith, Sayers, Simenon, Freeling, John D. MacDonald, and Ross Macdonald. In addition, the emergence of semiotic and structural analysis has meant that it is no longer necessarily a criticism to say of something that it is "formulaic"; a term of description, which under a previous understanding of literary value would have been invoked in a gesture of dismissal, can now be invoked as a preliminary to a study of "signifying systems." The result has been the proliferation of serious (not to say somber) formalist readings of works like Fleming's *Goldfinger*.[12] Whatever one might think of this phenomenon, it is now a recognized and respectable part of the academic literary scene. At the same time the advocates of "popular culture" have been pressing their claim with a new insistence and a new rigor (prompted in part by the developments I have already mentioned), and a measure of their success is the number of courses in detective fiction now offered in colleges and universities at all levels.

Given these circumstances (and others that could be enumerated), it would be strange if a sociological or anthropological or philosophical interpretation of Agatha Christie had *not* been put forward (in fact, here we have an embarrassment of riches),[13] and as a longtime reader of her novels it has occurred to me to put one forward myself. I have noticed that Christie's villains are often presented as persons so quintessentially evil that they have no moral sense whatsoever and can only simulate moral behavior by miming, without understanding, the actions and attitudes of others. It is typical of these villains also to be chameleons, capable almost at will of changing their appearance, and one can see why: since they have no human attachments or concerns, they can clothe themselves in whatever attachment or concern suits their nefarious and often unmotivated ends. (The parallel with Shakespeare's Iago and Milton's Satan is obvious.) It would seem, then, that Christie has a theory of evil in relation to personal identity that accounts for (in the sense of generating a description of) many of the characteristics of her novels: their plots, the emphasis on disguise, the tolerance for human weakness even as it is being exposed, etc. Now, were I to extend this general hypothesis about Christie into a reading of one or more of her works, I would not be proceeding as Dworkin's pronouncement suggests I would. I would not, that is, be changing the novel by riding roughshod over sentences bearing obvious and inescapable meanings; rather, I would be reading those sentences within the assumption that they were related to what I assumed to be Christie's intention (if not this one, then some other), and as a result they would appear to me in an already related form. Sentences describing the weaknesses of characters other than the villain would be seen as pointing to the paradoxical strength of human fraility; sentences detailing the topography and geography of crucial scenes would be read as symbolic renderings of deeper issues, and so on. This interpretive action, or any other that could be imagined, would not be performed in violation of the facts of the text, but would be an effort to establish those facts. If in the course of that effort I were to dislodge another set of facts, they would be facts that had emerged within the assumption of another intention, and they would therefore be no less interpretive than the facts I was putting in their place. Of course, my efforts might very well fail in that no one else would be persuaded of my reading, but neither success nor failure would prove anything about what the text does or does not allow; it would only attest to the degree to which I had mastered or failed to master the rules of argument and evidence as they are understood (tacitly, to be sure) by members of the professional community.

The point is one that I have made before: it is neither the case that interpretation is constrained by what is obviously and unproblematically "there," nor the case that interpreters, in the absence of such constraints, are free to read into a text whatever they like (once again Dworkin has put himself in a corner with these unhappy alternatives).

98   Meaning and Constraint

Interpreters are constrained by their tacit awareness of what is possible and not possible to do, what is and is not a reasonable thing to say, what will and will not be heard as evidence, in a given enterprise; and it is within those same constraints that they see and bring others to see the shape of the documents to whose interpretation they are committed.

Dworkin's failure to see this is an instance of a general failure to understand the nature of interpretation. The distinction between explaining a text and changing it can no more be maintained than the others of which it is a version (finding vs. inventing, continuing vs. striking out in a new direction, interpreting vs. creating). To explain a work is to point out something about it that had not been attributed to it before and therefore to change it by challenging other explanations that were once changes in their turn. Explaining and changing cannot be opposed activities (although they can be the names of claims and counterclaims) because they are the same activities. Dworkin opposes them because he thinks that interpretation is itself an activity in need of constraints, but what I have been trying to show is that interpretation is a *structure* of constraints, a structure which, because it is always and already in place, renders unavailable the independent or uninterpreted text and renders unimaginable the independent and freely interpreting reader. In searching for a way to protect against arbitrary readings (judicial and literary), Dworkin is searching for something he already has and could not possibly be without. He conducts his search by projecting as dangers and fears possibilities that could never be realized and by imagining as discrete concepts entities that are already filled with the concerns of the enterprise they supposedly threaten.

One of those entities is intention. Dworkin spends a great deal of time refuting the view that interpretation in law and in literature must here concern itself with the intentions of the author. He argues, first, that the intention of a novelist or legislator is "complex" and therefore difficult to know. Second, he argues that even if the intention were known, it would be only a piece of "psychological data,"[14] and therefore would be irrelevant to the determination of a meaning that was not psychological but institutional. In short, he argues that to make intention the key to interpretation is to bypass the proper interpretive context—the history of practices and conventions—and substitute for it an interior motion of the mind. This argument would make perfect sense if intentions were, as Dworkin seems to believe them to be, private property and more or less equivalent with individual purpose or even whim. But it is hard to think of intentions formed in the course of judicial or literary activity as "one's own," since any intention one could have will have been stipulated in advance by the understanding of what activities are possible to someone working in the enterprise. One could no more come up with a unique intention with respect to the presentation of a character or the marshaling of legal evidence than one could come up with a new way of beginning a novel or continuing a chain of decisions. Simply to do something in the context of a chain enterprise is ipso facto to "have" an enterprise-specific intention, and to read something identified as part of a chain enterprise is ipso facto to be in the act of specifying that same intention. That is to say, the act of reading itself is at once the asking and answering of the question, "What is it that is meant by these words?," a question asked not in a vacuum, but in the context of an already-in-place understanding of the various things someone writing a novel or a decision (or anything else) might mean (i.e., intend).

In Dworkin's analysis, on the other hand, reading is simply the construing of sense and neither depends nor should depend on the identification of intention. He cites as evidence the fact that authors themselves have been known to reinterpret their own works. This, Dworkin asserts, shows that "[a]n author is capable of detaching what he has written from his earlier intentions . . . of treating it as an object in itself."[15] But in fact this only shows that an author is capable of becoming his own reader and deciding that he meant something other by his words than he had previously thought. Such an author-reader is not ignoring intention, but recharacterizing it; he is not interpreting in a "non-intention-bound style,"[16] but interpreting in a way that leads to a new understanding of his intention. Nor is there anything mysterious about this; it is no more than what we all do when sometime after having produced an utterance (it could be in less than a second) we ask ourselves, "What did I mean by that?" This will seem curious if intentions are thought of as unique psychological events, but if intentions are thought of as forms of possible conventional behavior that are to be conventionally "read," then one can just as well reread his own intentions as he can reread the intentions of another.

The crucial point is that one cannot read *or* reread independently of intention, independently, that is, of the assumption that one is dealing with marks or sounds produced by an intentional being, a being situated in some enterprise in relation to which he has a purpose or a point of view. This is not an assumption that one adds to an already construed sense in order to stabilize it, but an assumption without which the construing of sense could not occur. One cannot understand an utterance without *at the same time* hearing or reading it as the utterance of someone with more or less specific concerns, interests, and desires, someone with an intention. So that when Dworkin talks, as he does, of the attempt to "discover" what a judge or a novelist intended, he treats as discrete operations that are inseparable. He thinks that interpretation is one thing and the assigning of intention is another, and he thinks that because he thinks that to discover intention is to plumb psychological depths unrelated to the meaning of chain-enterprise texts. In fact, to specify the meaning of a chain-enterprise text is exactly equivalent to specifying the intention of its author, an intention which is not private, but a form of conventional behavior made possible by the general structure of the enterprise. This, of course, does not mean that intention anchors interpretation in the sense that it stands outside and guides the process; intention like anything else is an interpretive fact; that is, it must be construed; it is just that it is impossible *not* to construe it and therefore impossible to oppose it either to the production or the determination of meaning.

The fact that Dworkin does so oppose it is of a piece with everything else in the essay and is one more instance of its basic pattern. Once again he has imagined a free-floating and individualistic threat to interpretation—in this case it is called "intention"—and once again he has moved to protect interpretation by locating its constraints in a free-standing and self-declaring object—in this case "the work itself," detached from the antecedent designs of its author. And this means that once again he has committed himself in a single stroke to the extremes he set out to avoid, the objectivity of meanings that are "just there" and the subjectivity of meanings that have been "made up" by an unconstrained agent.

I cannot conclude without calling attention to what is perhaps the most curious feature of Dworkin's essay, the extent to which it contains its own critique. Indeed, a reader sympathetic to Dworkin might well argue that he anticipates everything I have said in the preceding pages. He himself says that "the artist can create nothing without interpreting as he creates, since . . . he must have at least a tacit theory of why what he produces is art,"[17] and he also points out that the facts of legal history do not announce themselves but will vary with the beliefs of particular judges concerning the general function of the law.[18] In another place he admits that the constraint imposed by the words of a text "is not inevitable," in part because any theory of identity (i.e., any theory of what is the same and what is different, of what constitutes a departure from the same) "will be controversial."[19] And after arguing that the "constraint of integrity" (the constraint imposed by a work's coherence with itself) sets limits to interpretation, he acknowledges that there is much disagreement "about what counts as integration"; he acknowledges in other words that the constraint is itself interpretive.

Even more curious than the fact of these reservations and qualifications is Dworkin's failure to see how much they undercut his argument. Early in the essay he distinguishes between simple cases in which the words of a statute bear a transparent relationship to the actions they authorize or exclude (his sample statute is "No will shall be valid without three witnesses"), and more difficult cases in which reasonable and knowledgeable men disagree as to whether some action or proposed action is lawful. But immediately after making the distinction he undermines it by saying (in a parenthesis), "I am doubtful that the positivists' analysis holds even in the simple case of the will; but that is a different matter I shall not argue here."[20] It is hard to see how this is a different matter, especially since so much in the essay hangs on the distinction. One doesn't know what form the argument Dworkin decides *not* to make would take, but it might take the form of pointing out that even in a simple case the ease and immediacy with which one can apply the statute to the facts is the result of the same kind of interpretive work that is more obviously required in the difficult cases. In order for a case to appear readable independently of some interpretive strategy consciously employed, one must already be reading within the assumption of that strategy and employing, without being aware of them, its stipulated (and potentially controversial) definitions, terms, modes of inference, etc. This, at any rate, would be the argument I would make, and in making it I would be denying the distinction between hard and easy cases, not as an empirical fact (as something one might experience), but as a fact that reflected a basic difference between cases that are self-settling and cases that can be settled only by referring them to the history of procedures, practices, and conventions. All cases are so referred (not after reading but in the act of reading), and they could not be anything but so referred and still be seen as cases.[21] The point is an important one because Dworkin later says that

102 Meaning and Constraint

his account of chain enterprises is offered as an explanation of how we decide "hard cases at law";[22] that is, his entire paper depends on a distinction that he himself suggests may not hold, and therefore, as we have seen, his entire paper depends on the "positivist analysis" he rejects in the parenthesis.[23]

One can only speculate as to what Dworkin intends by these qualifications, but whether they appear in a parenthesis or in an aside or in the form of quotation marks around a key word, their effect is the same: to place him on both sides of the question at issue and to blur the supposedly hard lines of his argument. As a result, we are left with two ways of reading the essay, neither of which is comforting. If we take the subtext of reservation and disclaimer seriously, it so much weakens what he has to say that he seems finally not to have a position at all; and if we disregard the subtext and grant his thesis its strongest form, he will certainly have a position, but it will be, in every possible way, wrong.

Notes

A version of this essay was published in the fall 1982 issue of *Critical Inquiry*, 9 *Critical Inquiry* 201 (1982), along with Ronald Dworkin's essay "Law as Interpretation," 9 *Critical Inquiry* 179 (1982). Both papers grew out of a symposium on politics and interpretation held at the University of Chicago in the fall of 1981. Essays by other participants in that symposium were also published in the same issue.

Notes 559

1 Dworkin, "Law as Interpretation," 60 *Texas Law Review* 527 (1982).
2 Id. at 528.
3 Id. at 542–43.
4 Fish, *Is There a Text in This Class?* (1980).
5 Dworkin, supra note 1, at 541–42 (footnote omitted).
6 Dworkin makes a similar but not exactly parallel point when he acknowledges that the first novelist will have the responsibility of "interpreting the genre in which he sets out to write." Id. at 541 n.6.
7 Id. at 542–43 (emphasis in original).
8 Id. at 544.
9 Id.
10 I am not saying that the present-day case comes first and the history then follows, but that they emerge together in the context of an effort to see them as related embodiments of some legal principle. Indeed, a case could not even be seen as a case if it were not from the very first regarded as an item in a judicial field and therefore as the embodiment of some or other principle. This does not mean, however, that it is to judicial principles that we must look for the anchoring ground of interpretation, for judicial principles cannot be separated from the history to which they give form; one can no more think of a judicial principle apart from a chain of cases than one can think of a chain of cases apart from a judicial principle. No one of the entities that makes up judicial reasoning exists independently, neither the present-day case, nor the chain of which it is to be the continuation, nor the principle of which they are both to be the realizations.
11 Dworkin, supra note 1, at 532.
12 Ian Fleming, *Goldfinger* (1959).
13 One hardly knows where to begin, perhaps simply with the title of David Grossvogel's study, *Mystery and Its Fictions: From Oedipus to Agatha Christie* (1979). The title of Dennis Porter's *The Pursuit of Crime: Art and Ideology in Detective Fiction* (1981) suggests a scope and a thesis somewhat less grand, but Porter does find Christie "working in the tradition of Poe, Collins, and Doyle," id. at 137, and he devotes some very serious pages to a stylistic analysis of the first paragraph of her first novel in the context of V. N. Voloshinov's *Marxism and the Philosophy of Language* (1973). Christie is taken no less seriously by Stephen Knight in *Form and Ideology in Crime Fiction* (1980). Knight speaks without any self-consciousness of Christie as a "major writer" and analyzes her "art" in terms that might well be applied to, say, Henry James: "The rigidity of the time and place structure emphasizes the obscurity of the thematic shape, challenges us all the more urgently to decide it. The dual structure enacts the central drama of the novel, a threat to order that only careful observation can resolve," id. at 126. Knight's book, like Porter's, is replete with references to Lacan, Jameson, Machery, Marx, Freud, and Barthes, and bears all the marks of sophisticated academic criticism. See also in a similarly academic mode, R. Champigny, *What Will Have Happened: A Philosophical and*

560 Notes

Technical Essay on Mystery Stories (1977); J. Palmer, *Thrillers* (1979). As this essay goes to press, I have received in the mail the most recent issue of *Poetics Today,* and find Joseph Agassi, a professor of philosophy, discussing the relationship of the novels of Christie, Chandler, Doyle, and others to the scientific theories of Francis Bacon and Thomas Kuhn. Agassi, "The Detective Novel and Scientific Method," 3 *Poetics Today* 99–108 (1982). Dworkin, it would seem, could not have chosen a worse example to support his case.

14 See Dworkin, supra note 1, at 537–39.
15 Id. at 539.
16 Id. at 542.
17 Id. at 540.
18 Id. at 545.
19 Id. at 531.
20 Id. at 528.
21 One must question, too, and for the same reason, Dworkin's distinction between "common-law" cases and cases where there is a statute, at least insofar as it is a distinction between cases whose interpretation is straightforward and cases that must be referred to the background of an institutional history. In cases where there is a statute for a judge to look at, he must still look at it, and his look will be as interpretive—as informed by the practices and conventions that define the enterprise—as it would be in a common-law case. That is, a statute no more announces its own meaning than does the case to which it is to be applied, and therefore cases where statutes figure are no more or less grounded than cases where no statute exists. In either circumstance one must interpret from the beginning and in either circumstance one's interpretation will be at once constrained and enabled by a general and assumed understanding of the goals, purposes, concerns, and procedures of the enterprise. See on these and related points two essays by Kenneth Abraham: "Three Fallacies of Interpretation: A Comment on Precedent and Judicial Decision," 23 *Arizona Law Review* 771 (1981); and "Statutory Interpretation and Literary Theory: Some Common Concerns of an Unlikely Pair," 32 *Rutgers Law Review* 676 (1979).
22 Dworkin, supra note 1, at 542.
23 In its strengths and weaknesses Dworkin's present essay is at once like and unlike his other writings. I find that in *Taking Rights Seriously* (1977), Dworkin more than occasionally falls into a way of talking that reinstitutes the positions against which he is arguing. As an example, I will consider briefly some moments in the key essay "Hard Cases" (chapter 4 of *Taking Rights Seriously*). At one point in that essay Dworkin begins a paragraph by asserting that "institutional history acts not as a constraint on the political judgment of judges but as an ingredient of that judgment." Id. at 87. The point is that what a judge decides is inseparable from his understanding of the history of past decisions, and it is a point well taken. It is, however, a point that is already being compromised in the second half of this same sentence: "because institutional history is part of the background that

Notes 561

any plausible judgment about the rights of an individual must accommodate." Id. With the word "accommodate" what had been inseparable suddenly falls apart, for it suggests that rather than having his judgment informed by the history (in the sense that his ways of thinking are constrained by it) the judge takes an independent look at an independent history and decides (in a movement of perfect freedom) to accommodate it; it suggests, in short, that he could have chosen otherwise. The notion of choice, here only implied, is explicitly invoked later in the paragraph when Dworkin discusses the situation in which "a judge chooses between the rule established in precedent and some new rule thought to be fairer." Id. But in accordance with what principle is the choice to be made? Dworkin doesn't tell us, but clearly it is a principle that stands apart from either the body of precedent or the new rule (both of which have been reified), and apart too from the judge himself, who freely chooses to employ it as a way of reconciling two independent entities.

The movement in this paragraph is from an understanding of judgment in which the judge, the context of judgment, and the principles of judgment are mutually constitutive of an understanding in which each has its own identity and can only be integrated by invoking some neutral mechanism or calculus. Later Dworkin slides into the same (mis)understanding when he says of Hercules (his name for an imaginary, all-knowing judge) that in deciding between competing theories he "must turn to the remaining constitutional rules and settled practices under these rules to see which of these two theories provides a smoother fit with the constitutional scheme as a whole." Id. at 106. Here the difficulty (and sleight of hand) resides in the phrase "smoother fit." On what basis is the smoothness of fit determined? Again, Dworkin doesn't tell us, but an answer to the question could take only one of two forms. Either the rules and practices have their own self-evident shape and therefore themselves constrain what does or does not fit with them, or there is some abstract principle by which one can calculate the degree to which a given theory fits smoothly within "the constitutional scheme as a whole." But these alternatives are simply flip sides of the same positivism. If the shape of the constitutive parts is self-evident, then no independent principle is required to decide whether or not they fit together; and by the same reasoning an independent principle of fit will be able to do its job only if the shape of the constituent parts is self-evident. For as soon as the shape of the parts becomes a matter of dispute (as it would for judges who conceived the constitutional rules or the settled practices differently), the judgment of what fits with what will be in dispute as well. In short, the criteria of fitness is no less theoretical than the theories Dworkin would have it decide between, and by claiming an independence for it he once again compromises the coherence of his position.

In general, Dworkin's confusions have the same form: he argues against positivism, but then he has recourse to positivist notions. At one point he observes that Hercules' decision about a "community morality" will sometimes be controversial, especially when the issue concerns "some contested

562 Notes

political concept, like fairness or liberality or equality," and the institutional history "is not sufficiently detailed so that it can be justified by only one among different conceptions of that concept." Id. at 127. The language is somewhat vague here, but it would seem that Dworkin is assuming the possibility of a history that *was* "sufficiently detailed": that is, a history so dense (a favorite word of his) that it was open to only one reading of the morality informing it. In relation to such a history Hercules would be in the position of the later novelists in Dworkin's imagined chain, constrained to "admit only one good-faith interpretation." But at that point Hercules would be doing what Dworkin himself says no judge can possibly do, mechanically reading off the meaning of a text that constrained its own interpretation.

I trust that I have said enough to support my contention that the errors I find in the present essay can also be found in Dworkin's earlier work. But I must also say that, at least in the case of "Hard Cases," those errors are less damaging. "Hard Cases" is primarily an argument against "classical theories of adjudication . . . which suppose that a judge follows statutes or precedent until the clear direction of these runs out, after which he is free to strike out on his own." Id. at 118. Dworkin's critique of these theories seems to me powerful and entirely persuasive, and, moreover, in its main lines it does not depend on the general account of interpretation that occasionally and (to my mind) disconcertingly surfaces. In "Law as Interpretation," on the other hand, Dworkin is concerned to elaborate that general account, and in that essay the incidental weaknesses of the earlier work become crucial and even fatal.

Part VI
Interpreting the Law

Jan M. van Dunné, Rotterdam

Normative and Narrative Coherence in Legal Decision Making

Abstract

The distinction between normative coherence and narrative coherence introduced by Neil MacCormick in 1984, the cause for a debate with Ronald Dworkin, which was joined by a number of authors, is discussed in this paper in the light of the continental jurisprudential tradition and the actual process of judicial decision making.

The normative – narrative split is difficult to advocate in a problem-oriented or dialectical approach to law and the law making process, where there is no room for the norms – facts dichotomy. Also, in a hermeneutical approach to the legal practitioner's handwork, the distinction between the normative and the factual side of decision-making is artificial and unrealistic.

To illustrate this point, three cases are presented in the fields of civil and criminal law (on standard clauses, a rental case and a squatters' case). These case stories reveal the influence of the narrative on the application of (binding) norms; the *narratio* is essential to bring a norm to life.

Finally, another illustration is found in the striking case of the *DES daughters*, a decision of the Dutch Supreme Court of 1992, where the strict rule on alternative causation in tort is applied in a liberal way, to serve the equitable protection of victims of defective drugs. In the course of interpreting the statutory rule, the narrative the legislator had in mind is changed by the Court to suit the victims' narrative.

*

1. The origins of narrativism and the law making process

1.1. The introduction of the notion of 'narrative coherence', in juxtaposition with 'normative coherence', is generally attributed to Neil MacCormick, in his 1984 Lund lecture, which gave rise to a lively discussion.[1] At its core was the debate between MacCormick and Ronald Dworkin.[2] In The Netherlands, in 1983 A.C. 't Hart emphasized the narrative structure of law in his book on criminal law *Strafrecht en beleid*, in which he found considerable support over the years.[3]

---

1   In A. Peczenik, L. Lindahl and B.C. van Roermund (eds.), *Theory of Legal Science*, Dordrecht/Boston/Lancaster, 1984, pp. 235 ff., at p. 245; see also N. MacCormick, "Coherence in Legal Justification", W. Krawietz (ed.), *Theorie der Normen*, Berlin, 1984, p. 37. Compare Bert C. van Roermund, "On 'Narrative Coherence' in Legal Contexts", *Reason in Law, Proceedings IVR Conference Bologna 1984*, Milano, 1988, p. 159; Monica den Boer, "Two in One Trolley: Reflections on the Relation between MacCormick's Institutional and Narrative Theory of Law", *International J. Semiotics of Law*, 4, 1991, p. 256.
2   R. Dworkin, "La Chaîne du droit", *Droit et Societé*, 1, 1985, p. 51; compare also his *Law's Empire*, London, 1986. See Jacques Lenoble, "La théorie de la cohérence narrative en droit. Le débat Dworkin – MacCormick", *La Philosophie du Droit Aujourdhui*, Archives de Philosophie du Droit, 33, 1988, p. 121. Another version of this article appeared in Patrick Nerhot (ed.), *Law, Interpretation and Reality. Essays in Epistemology, Hermeneutics and Jurisprudence*, Dordrecht, 1990, p. 127.
3   "Strafrecht: de macht van een verhaalsstructuur", *Strafrecht en beleid*, Zwolle/Leuven,

What then is 'narrativism'? The concept is derived from the latin *narrare*, storytelling, and *narratio*, story. Developed by philosophers as Ricoeur on the continent and Arendt in the United States, it emphasizes the functioning of the story, the plot, in science, not only in its application, but in its structure as well. It became popular in the fields of literary criticism, history, ethics, psychology, so we should not be surprised to find it in the sphere of the law too.[4]

In MacCormick's introduction of the concept it is suggested that in the realm of legal justification there are two different „tests of coherence": first the „normative coherence", having 'to do with the justification of legal rulings or normative propositions more generally in the context of a legal system conceived as a normative order'. The coherence of legal norms is considered as 'a function of its justifiability under higher-order principles or values, principles and values being extensionally equivalent; provided that the higher or highest-order principles and values seem acceptable as delineating a satisfactory form of life, when taken together'. Secondly, the „narrative coherence", having 'to do with the justification of findings of fact and the drawing of reasonable inferences from evidence', where direct proof by immediate observation is not available. The notion of „coherence" should be distinguished from „consistency": it has not to do with the non-contradiction, characterizing a set of propositions, by contrast coherence is 'the property of a set of propositions which, taken together, „makes sense" in its entirety'.

Dworkin's use of „narrative coherence" is much wider, and resembles MacCormick's „normative coherence", the coherence of a legal system in itself. As stated by Dworkin in 'La Chaîne du droit':

> 'Le principe d'unité en droit comme principe de décision s'adresse aux juges et aux autres autorités chargées d'appliquer les normes publiques de comportement d'une communauté politique. Il leur prescrit de lire et de comprendre celles-ci, dans toute la mesure du possible, comme si elles étaient l'oeuvre d'un seul auteur, la communauté personnifiée, exprimant une conception cohérente de la justice et de l'équité. Il en résulte le critère suivant de ce qui fait le droit; une proposition de droit est vraie, si elle apparaît comme la meilleure interprétation du processus juridique en son entier, comprenant à la fois l'ensemble des décisions de fond déjà prises et la structure institutionnelle, ou si elle découle d'une telle interprétation'.[5]

1983. Compare also his *Normverleggend gedrag en justitieel beleid*, with J.M. Broekman, Zwolle/Leuven, 1980. In this line of thought also: René Foqué, "Het belang van het recht. Ontwikkelingen in de continentale rechtstheorie", E.H.L. Brugmans and J.L.M. Elders (eds.), *Recht en legitimiteit*, Zwolle, 1987; 't Hart and Foqué, *Instrumentaliteit en rechtsbescherming. Grondslagen van een strafrechtelijke waardendiscussie*, Arnhem/Antwerpen, 1990; J.C.M. Leijten, "We need stories", farewell lecture Nijmegen, Zwolle, 1991.

4 For the role of narratives in ethics, see: H. Zwart, "Narratieve psychologie en narratieve ethiek", *Psychologie en Maatschappij*, 1991, p. 146. In psychology in the mid-eighties the narrative mode of thought was advocated by Jerome Bruner and others, as an addition to the paradigmatic mode of thought prevailing in cognitive psychology, see: Gerrit Breeuwsma, "Individuele ontwikkeling als narratieve structuur. 'De feiten volgens mij'", *Psychologie en Maatschappij*, 1993, p.248.

5 Op. cit., p. 51, discussed by Lenoble, at p. 128. Compare in this context also Dworkin's concept of 'law as integrity', see his *Law's Empire*, pp. 176, 225.

Leaving aside Dworkin's conception of „law as integrity", and the Dworkin – MacCormick debate, I would like to return, in a less lofty context, to MacCormick's scheme of the two coherences, and its importance for law making and decision making. In its essence, it is based on a Kantian dichotomy which is so familiar in the school of Hart and legal positivism in general: a strict separation of norms and facts. In the continental tradition, the line of thought of Josef Esser and his problem-oriented approach, that of Karl Larenz and his thinking based on dialectics, and in The Netherlands, Paul Scholten and his socio-teleological method (to drop some names), there is no room for this dichotomy. Facts are formed by norms, that is selected in anticipation of existing norms, and, vice versa, norms are formed by the facts presented for a decision. When we add Gadamer's hermeneutic inspiration so apparent in Esser's later work, the influence of the „*Vorverständnis*" (pre-consciousness) on legal decision making, we find that the selection and application of legal norms and their confrontation with the facts of the case is a combined, indivisible process. If we look for narrativism in the practice of legal decision making, a split between the normative side and the factual side of the handwork is artificial and unrealistic.[6]

1.2. This leads us to the question: how new is the narrative element in jurisprudence? A famous saying of Esser is: '*Erst die Kasuistik teilt uns mit, was Rechtens ist*', we can only know the law through the case at hand (and general principles of law are related to the '*Rechtsgedanke*', the legal thoughts, which are '*kasuistisch profiliert*').[7] Is this really different from the teaching of the Romans: *Ius in causa positum*? Or the other well-known maxim: *Da mihi facta, dabo tibi ius* ('give me the facts, then I will give you the law')? This may be covered by 19th century dust, created by dogmatists, legal positivists and other systembuilders, but also in the less distant past voices of the same message were heard. Reference is made to the *Natur der Sache* school at the beginning of this century, and revived in post-war Germany (Arthur Kaufmann, and others). An important American contribution is made by the legal realist Karl Llewellyn, and his concept of „situation sense". The source of this stream in jurisprudence is less well-known: the German „*Freirechtler*" of the 1920's and their predecessors, as Goldsmith (1874). The citation Llewellyn gives of the latter is characteristic, and still illuminating for our current topic:

> Every fact-pattern of common life, so far as the legal order can take in, carries within itself its appropriate, natural rules, its right law. This is natural law which is real, not imaginary; it is not a creation of mere reason, but rests on the solid foundation of what reason can

---

6 Van Roermund also rejects MacCormick's distinction between normative and narrative coherence, and sees narrative coherence as the very principle of the relation between facts and norms (case and decision), thereby relying on philosophical arguments. Two citations are too nice to be left unquoted. "Facts are, as Strawson put it (1964), what statements, when true, state; they are not what statements are about... i.e. they are not things or states or events, but the objectifiable contents of statements". "This definition of 'a fact' resembles ... Goodman's famous phrase: 'Facts are little theories; and true theories are big facts'" (1988, at p. 160).
7 *Grundsatz und Norm in der richterlichen Fortbildung des Privatrechts*, 2nd ed., 1964, pp. 243, 288. Esser was influenced by Viehweg's 'topical' jurisprudence.

recognize in the nature of man of the life conditions of the time and place; it is thus not eternal nor changeless nor everywhere the same, but is indwelling in the very circumstances of life. The highest task of law-giving consists in uncovering and implementing this immanent law.[8]

In other words, as the common law maxim in the field of civil liability goes: *Res ipsa loquitur*, 'the facts speak for themselves', a well-accepted principle in Dutch law of evidence in liability cases. The story the facts are telling in a legal context, the archetype in law, is what has become known lately as the *narratio*. If a court's decision does not fit well in the social context of the case, the given circumstances, usually because it felt bound to uphold an old dogmatic concept of law or an old and binding precedent, the decision is seen as a hard case, *Lex dura sed scripta*. But, as the saying goes: 'Hard cases make bad law'. Something went wrong, apparently.

The force of the factual element in the legal judgment is of course not characteristic of Western law only; in the world of non-Western law it often is the core of decision making. In Dutch literature there is the intriguing story told by Ter Haar, the specialist on the 'Adat law' of the then Netherlands East-Indies, which is Indonesia now. On one of his field trips in Java, he interviewed the local village chief and judge, and wanted to know the rule of law according to the indigenous law, say on inheritance. The chief looked blank, and told him he could not tell him. Ter Haar persisted, and repeated his question. Finally the village chief said: 'Give me a case, then I will tell you what the law is'. There was no Adat law tradition based on abstract, general rules.[9] Incidentally, in my experience legal practitioners in Europe will have the same response when asked what the substantive law in a certain field is (e.g., the rule on *force majeure* in contract law).

8   *The Karl Llewellyn Papers*, W. Twining ed., 1968, p. 122 (translation by Llewellyn), cited by W. van Gerven, *Het beleid van de rechter*, 1973, p. 56. At p. 32 this author cites Gény on 'la nature des choses', a statement of remarkable resemblance with the one just quoted. For a discussion of the jurisprudential issues raised here, with sources, reference is made to my paper "The Personality of the Judge and Legal Decision Making in Private Law", Law and Society Assoc., Toronto, 1982, in my book: *De dialektiek van rechtsvinding en rechtsvorming*, Serie Rechtsvinding, Volume 1a, Arnhem, 1984. Compare also two other papers in the same volume: "The Personality of the Judge. Some Jurisprudential Remarks" (Oxford, 1981), p. 172; "The Role of Personal Values in Legal Reasoning", (Helsinki, 1983), p. 193, also published in *Rechtstheorie*, 1986, Beiheft 10, "Vernunft und Erfahrung im Rechtsdenken der Gegenwart", p. 13.
    See also, more recently, my Erasmus University Annual lecture, "De magie van het woord", (The magic of the word), Arnhem, 1987, also published in: *De dialektiek van rechtsvinding en rechtsvorming*, Volume 1c, Arnhem, 1988, p. 125.

9   Ter Haar, *Adat Law in Indonesia*, 1948. This story is mentioned with approval by Paul Scholten, in his influential book on jurisprudence, Asser-Scholten, *Algemeen Deel*, 1931, 3rd. ed. 1974, p. 127.
    I remember a comparable story, heard from an American legal anthropologist, studying West-African law. He was interested in public law, more specifically, the rules of succession of the monarchy of an African country. He was delighted to hear, that like in Western jurisdictions, according to the law of that country, the eldest son was to be the future king. He kept inquiring however, asking if the rule also applied in the case this eldest son, by his drinking, gambling or mating habits would be less suitable for the function. The answer was, that in such case 'of course' the eldest son would not be eligible and the younger brother would become king.

One element in legal decision making which fascinates me is the role the judge (or any legal decision maker) is playing, the influence of his personality, his personality traits in his juggling with norms and facts, in the open air, watched by the public, or in back rooms, only noticed by the parties. In the words of Eugen Ehrlich, one of the band leaders of the „Freirecht" movement in the 1920s: 'There is no guaranty of justice except the personality of the judge'. If law has something to do with storytelling, the truth of this statement will meet little opposition. We find the role of the judge well characterized by Cicero: *Magistratum legem esse loquentem*, the judge is the speaking law.[10]

2. The role of narratives in legal decision making. Three case stories

2.1. So if the role of narrativism is not foreign to the realm of law, in our time and perhaps in all time, what is its role and importance for contemporary legal science? And where does 'narrative coherence' come in? In what may seem an effort to evade the last question – an observation not wholly incorrect – I would first want to give some examples of the use of the narratio, storytelling, in law, derived from English and Dutch law.

Alan Paterson, expert on decision making in the U.K. judiciary, has observed that the English appellate judicial opinions (as compared with their French counterparts) are idiosyncratic, subjective, literary, candid and nonsyllogistic. 'The English style of legal reasoning in the House of Lords until recently has laid a stress on persuasion (hence the not infrequent references to equity) rather then the assertion of authority and its greatest exponents have developed a facility for handling „difficult" precedents'.[11] A Law Lord in his opinion had to persuade his brethren to accept his view in deciding the case presented. Interestingly, in the single judgments of the House of Lords, increasing in number recently, where there is no need for persuasion, the style is more „continental", didactic language of assertion which relies on authority. Paterson gives some examples of persuasive reasoning of the justices, characterized by persuasive storytelling.

A fine example is Lord Denning's famous opinion in *Lloyds Bank v. Bundy* (1975), where he succeeded to get the majority vote of the Court of Appeal in a landslide decision setting aside the binding force of standard clauses („small print") in a case of inequality of bargaining power. It was a typical hard case, where a trusting client, the farmer Bundy, was kept to the letter of the contract by an unscrupulously operating local bank. My point is that the story Lord Denning is telling the court, his presentation of the facts of the case, and further

---

10 *De Legibus* III, 1, 2. Which reminds us of Montesquieu's 'bouche de la loi' concept. For a fresh view on this matter, see my article "Montesquieu Revisted. The Balance of Power between the Legistature and the Judiciary in a National-International Context", *Rechtstheorie*, Beiheft 15, Law, Justice and the State, 1993, p. 451 (Proceedings IVR Conference Reykjavik 1993).
11 *Appellate Decision Making in the Common Law World*, Rotterdam Lectures in Jurisprudence, Serie Rechtsvinding, Vol. 3, Arnhem, 1985, pp. 20, 27.

the presentation of the law, is so well designed to indulge his colleagues to set aside the hard and fast rule that contracts normally concluded are binding upon the parties, that the story is almost compelling the listener (reader) to follow the proposed solution. It is a good illustration of the intertwining of (hard) norms and (persuasive) facts, where recourse is sought to the principle of equity to reach a just result. The first part of Denning's opinion is following here:

> Broadchalke is one of the most pleasing villages in England. Old Herbert Bundy, the defendant, was a farmer there. His home was at Yew Tree Farm. It went back for 300 years. His family had been there for generations. It was his only asset. But he did a very foolish thing. He mortgaged it to the bank. Up to the very hilt. Not to borrow money for himself, but for the sake of his son. Now the bank have come down on him. they have foreclosed. They want to get him out of Yew Tree Farm and to sell it. They have brought this action against him for possession. Going out means ruin for him. He was granted legal aid. His lawyers put in a defence. They said that, when he executed the charge to the bank he did not know what he was doing: or at any rate that the circumstances were such that he ought not to be bound by it. At the trial his plight was plain. The judge was sorry for him. He said he was a 'poor old gentleman.' He was so obviously incapacitated that the judge admitted his proof in evidence. He had a heart attack in the witness-box. Yet the judge felt he could do nothing for him. There is nothing, he said, 'which takes this out of the vast range of commercial transactions.' He ordered Herbert Bundy to give up possession of Yew Tree Farm to the bank. Now there is an appeal to this court. The ground is that the circumstances were so exceptional that Herbert Bundy should not be held bound.
>
> *The general rule*
>
> Now let me say at once that in the vast majority of cases a customer who signs a bank guarantee or a charge cannot get out of it. No bargain will be upset which is the result of the ordinary interplay of forces. There are many hard cases which are caught by this rule.
>
> Yet there are exceptions to this general rule. There are cases in our books in which the courts will set aside a contract, or a transfer of property, when the parties have not met on equal terms – when the one is so strong in bargaining power and the other so weak – that as a matter of common fairness, it is not right that the strong should be allowed to push the weak to the wall. Hitherto those exceptional cases have been treated each as a separate category in itself. But I think the time has come when we should seek to find a principle to unite them. I put on one side contracts or transactions which are voidable for fraud or misrepresentation or mistake. All those are governed by settled principles. I go only to those where there has been inequality of bargaining power, such as to merit the intervention of the court.

Lord Denning then gives an exposition of the relevant case law, distinguished into five categories, and formulates the general principle of 'inequality of bargaining power'. Finally he refers to the facts of the case, where the bank to its benefit made use of a double function in relation to Mr Bundy, being his bank and his legal adviser.

Another example is given by Leijten, and is based on a decision of the Dutch Supreme Court in a landlord and tenant case.[12] A married man has a relationship with another woman during a considerable time. They decide to live together in a house rented by the man; the woman gives up her job. After twenty years, they have two children, the man still cannot decide for his new partner, and the woman

---

12 Op cit, p. 9. Supreme Court 13 November 1987.

puts an end to the relationship. She wishes to stay in the house with the children, however, but she is not a co-tenant of the house, and therefore lacks legal protection as such. In case of marriage she would have been co-tenant by law, in the present situation according to the law, Article 1623h of the Civil Code, a joint request is needed. This has never been done by the parties, and for reasons which may be guessed, the man now refuses to cooperate in the request. The lower courts denied the woman's request to be accepted as co-tenant without the approval of the man, as against the law.

The Supreme Court quashed that decision, with the argument that in the present case the statutory requirement of a joint request was no reason for denying the woman's request for co-tenancy, since the man's argument of the absence of his cooperation was against good faith.

In Leijten's observation, a hard and fast rule is set aside by the Court, since it would lead to such an inequitable result, that the man is refrained from relying upon it. How did this come about? Not by reducing the story to a constellation of bare facts, Leijten suggests, but by keeping the story as it stands. The legal rule is overruled by the principle of good faith (or equity) in the case at hand; the story element is precisely giving the judge room, in these exceptional cases, to decide according to the law, not in the sense of statutory law (loi), but the law based on general principles of law (droit). His conclusion is: 'We need stories for interpretation'.

Finally, in the sphere of criminal law, Van Roermund has presented a narrative of a case of squatters in his home town Tilburg in 1979, who in an effort to prevent the demolition of houses with architectural value in the course of extension of the local Health Service Office, occupied the houses.[13] The narrative is not taken from a court decision, but to the contrary, constructed as an alternative for it. Here the action of the police, the Public Prosecutor, the Mayor and the owner based on the rules of law collided with the squatters' occupation of the houses in the general interest and the protection of domestic peace. At the occasion of the eviction the squatters defended themselves with illicit means, and consequently were convicted by the District Court. Van Roermund makes clear that the events taking place lead to two completely different stories, one of the squatters and their arguments based on the general interest, the other of the public authorities and the owner, and their legal arguments. The discomforting part of it, is the world in between, a situation which is in need of correction, according to the author.

2.2. We may conclude that the role of the narratio in legal decision making is that of the go-between in the relation of norms and facts. The presentation of the facts in story form, a plot which askes for a certain (happy) end, is essential in the

---

13 "The Instituting of Brute Facts", *Internat. J. Semiotics of Law*, 4, 1991, p. 279, at p. 284. Compare also his "Narrative Coherences and the Guises of Legalism", *Law, Interpretation and Reality. Essays in Epistemology, Hermeneutics and Jurisprudence*, cit., p. 310, at p. 335. See also his *Recht, verhaal en werkelijkheid*, Bussum, 1993, p. 44, the criminal case of a doctor putting the life of an elderly patient to an end at her request. The two stories, the actual and the legal one, are printed in two columns on the same page (with many blanks in the legal column).

application of norms which are of an abstract nature by birth. In the normal situation, in bread and butter cases, the storytelling is hardly noticeable. In hard cases, storytelling is the crux, if one is to realize the bending of the hard and fast rule to suit the circumstances of the case and make a just and reasonable solution possible.

Coming back to the central question regarding the relation between normative and narrative coherence (supra, section 1), my suggestion would be that all legal norms have two faces: they are meant to function in a normative and a narrative context simultaneously. Norms are in need of a narrative to come to life: that is the life of law (which is what the courts actually do, not merely what they are meant to do according to the ideas of the legislator or jurisprudent – so much we know since Justice Holmes' famous observation). Taken from another perspective, a binding legal norm is not immune to a narrative presented in the course of its application. The examples given above, the English case on standard clauses and the Dutch rental case, both had to do with constraining norms, with nothing fuzzy or narrative about them. But the constraining citadel fell under the siege of the narrative facts. Therefore, the difference between normative and narrative coherence is distinctive at first sight only, and deceptive on closer scrutiny, as so often is the case when lawyers have to indulge in handling mundane facts (stories).[14]

In this context, it should be noted that the Dutch Supreme Court does not refrain from a liberal interpretation of the Civil Code, when looking for a just and reasonable solution, in accordance with the current societal views. Since the 1940s many legal changes have been brought under the guise of 'reasonable interpretation of the law', e.g. the introduction of legal conversion, the acceptance of strict liability in some fields, and the use of 'reasonable impu-tation' in establishing proximity in tort (causation). Sometimes the code was silent on the point in question, sometimes it contained a provision that, in a more literal interpretation, used to be read differently. Compared to the French judiciary, however, the Dutch highest civil court is less audacious; the landslide decisions rendered since the turn of the century (on tort, natural obligations, unjust enrichment and the like), often come decades later than the French counterparts.[15] This continental approach must be rather striking for the common law lawyer, used to the practice in the British courts, and the reference showed for the word of the legislator, in its plain meaning, established within its linguistic boundaries. Times are changing in the U.K., however, the teleological or 'purposive' approach is increasingly being accepted by the courts; the interpretation of Community law as implemented in British law, was an incentive here.[16]

---

14 For a foundation of this view, I refer to what was said earlier, with further references. A similar approach is that of Patrick Nerhot, see his *Law, Writing, Meaning. An Essay in Legal Hermeneutics*, Edinburgh, 1992 (orig. in Italian), especially Ch. 6, "Rule, meaning, strategy: legal rationality as a coherence of narrative type", p. 35. Nerhot denies the distinction between the legislative aspect and the applicative aspect of law: all application is creation of law. "The judge's apparently logical subsumption is nothing but creative reinstatement of an interest and value judgment that was not included 'in nuce' in the norm, but runs through the positivity of law at a given moment" (p. 37). Compare also Nerhot's contribution to the book edited by him *Law, Interpretation and Reality*, cit.
15 For a discussion of these issues, see my lecture "De magie van het woord", cit., pp. 151 ff.
16 Compare John Bell, "Policy Arguments in Statutory Interpretation", Jan van Dunné (ed.),

In the discussion of the role of narrativism, it should be borne in mind that some authors use the concept 'narrative' in a special sense, ranging from a loose advisory function to a political instrument.[17]

3. A binding norm in a narrative coherence: the rule on alternative causation and the DES daughters case (1992)

3.1. I will now give a striking example of the confrontation of normative and narrative coherence of a binding norm. Here a statutory norm, the new article on alternative causation of the Dutch Civil Code, in its application was bent to meet the narrative dimension of the facts, which was accomplished by the sheer force of the story presented to the Dutch Supreme Court. I am referring to the *DES daughters* case, Hoge Raad 9 October 1992.[18]

The central role is played here by Article 6:99 CC, which reads as follows:
Book 6: Article 99

> Where the damage may have resulted from two or more events for each of which a different person is liable, and where it has been determined that the damage has arisen from at least one of these events, the obligation to repair the damage rests upon each of these persons, unless he proves that the damage is not the result of the event for which he himself is liable.

Legal Reasoning and Statutory Interpretation, Serie Rechtsvinding, Vol. 5, Arnhem, 1989, p. 55; Zenon Bankowski and Neil MacCormick, "Statutory Interpretation in the United Kingdom", Neil MacCormick and Robert Summers (eds.), *Interpreting Statutes. A Comparative Study*, Aldershot, 1991, p. 359, at p. 371.

17 Compare Erik Jayme, "Narrative Normen im Internationalen Privat- und Verfahrensrecht", *Tübinger Universitätsreden*, Neue Folge Band 10, 1993, Tübingen. The author takes narrative norms in the sense of norm texts which only have an advisory function: they rather tell than bind. On first impression they have no concrete meaning, but give orientation by directing at other norms, or contain values which may be helpful for decision making. Examples given are preambles of statutes, titles or policy-oriented introductions to major legislative works; declarations of intention, etcetera in public international law. In private international law Jayme finds narrative norms which have little content, while they are superfluous, for instance by force of existing international treaties. These are really 'talking' norms, which should not be taken too seriously.

Another use of narrativism in law is the legal storytelling that is becoming increasingly popular in the United States, especially by contributions of feminists and critical race theorists. Here narratives are seen as central to legal scholarship, as an instrument to de-emphasize conventional analytic methods. The stories concerned are particularly 'stories from the bottom' – stories by women and colored people about their oppression; adherents are less concerned about whether stories are either typical or descriptively accurate than conventional scholars would be, and they place more emphasis on the aesthetic and emotional dimension of narration. A distinctive method of legal scholarship is claimed. See Daniel A. Farber and Suzanna Sherry, "Telling Stories Out of School: An Essay on Legal Narratives", *Stanford Law Rev.*, 45, 1993, p. 807. Many leading American law reviews have published articles on this new phenomenon, often based on symposia.

18 *TMA/ELLR (Tijdschrift voor Milieu Aansprakelijkheid / Environmental Liability Law Review)*, 1993, p. 15, note Van Dunné; in Dutch, case report and note with English Summaries.

I will first give a summary of the Supreme Court's decision, followed by my comment.

The defendants, a group of 10 pharmaceutical companies, brought the drug DES onto the market from 1953 to about 1967. DES was a drug used to prevent miscarriages during pregnancy; plaintiffs are daughters of women who took DES during pregnancy. The daughters are suffering or have suffered physical complaints, such as carcinoma of the uro-genital tract. As a result plaintiffs have sustained monetary and non-monetary damages. In this case six DES daughters allege that each defendant is liable for the entire damages, the amount of which is still to be established. The District Court and the Court of Appeal Amsterdam rejected this claim on the ground that the plaintiffs failed to identify the manufacturer of the tablets prescribed to their mothers during pregnancy. The Court of Appeal held that there could not be a definite tort against one or more DES daughters because no facts were put forward from which it would appear that specific behaviour was directed at the DES daughters. The Court also concluded that Art. 6:99 Civil Code was not applicable (joint and several liability under alternative causation), a rule which was regarded as applicable during the period 1953-1976. According to the Court of Appeal, in order for Art. 6:99 to apply the plaintiff must precisely establish who belongs to the circle of persons liable in tort.

The Court of Appeal judgment is overturned by the Supreme Court. According to the interpretation of the rule of alternative causation, based on the wording, the meaning and parliamentary history of Art. 6:99, there cannot be a requirement that specific behaviour be demonstrated. Additionally, the Court of Appeal's ruling leads to the unacceptable conclusion that the DES daughters are deprived of a remedy merely because they are unable to prove where the tablets which their mothers took originated. It is not reasonable to place the DES daughters in a worse evidentiary position than is provided in Art. 6:99, simply because there are many injured parties. In addition, the manufacturers who are liable for all the damages have recourse against each other.

Nor can the injured parties be required to establish who belongs to the circle of persons, liable in tort. In a situation such as the case at bar, such a requirement leads to an unreasonable result: the injured party must herself bear the damage if she is not able to identify all manufacturers who brought DES onto the market in the relevant period, although such an identification of all manufacturers will in fact be practically impossible. A summons directed to one liable person will suffice.

For application of Art. 6:99 it is sufficient if the injured party proves that (1) the company concerned brought DES onto the market in the relevant period, and furthermore is liable through his own fault; (2) that there are still one or more manufacturers who brought DES onto the market during the relevant period and furthermore they are liable for a defect; and (3) that the plaintiff has sustained damages and the damages are the result of the use of DES, but is it not necessary to establish from where the DES originated. Each of the pharmaceutical companies can avoid liability by proving that the damages suffered by the DES daughter are not a result of the drug which it brought onto the market.

It is possible that the DES daughters sustained their damages through agencies of the manufacturers who, because of the absence of fault, are not liable. However, this will not discharge the other manufacturers from liability for the entire damages, except that under the given circumstances, in view of the size of the chance that the damage to the DES daughter concerned was caused by a manufacturer who escapes liability, this would be unacceptable to standards of reasonableness and fairness.

(The case is remanded to the Court of Appeal The Hague for further treatment and decision with respect to the determination whether the actions of the 10 DES manufacturers were negligent).

The above decision of the Dutch Supreme Court, the first Dutch DES case, brought a surprise, compared to the American DES cases of the last years: it established joint and several liability in tort for the manufacturers. It clearly is a landmark decision in this field, but it is also of importance for environmental liability and tort liability in general, as regards multiple action.

A central theme in this litigation is the rule on 'alternative causation' of Article 6:99 CC, establishing joint and several liability for the tortfeasors involved. The issue here is the application, and therefore, interpretation of this statutory rule in regard to the case at hand. Article 6:99 CC was modelled after the famous American 'two hunters' case, *Summers v. Tice* (1948) as may be inferred from legislative history. So the „story" the legislator had in mind when drafting the article was a situation where the number of actors was restricted, actually to two persons. Therefore, it was alleged by defendants, its wording, combined with the intention of the legislator would bar its application in a situation where an unknown number of potential tort feasors is involved. The precise number of tortfeasors should be established, in order that Art. 99 be applicable. District Court and Court of Appeal Amsterdam accepted that view; the latter Court furthermore required the tort action of any defendant to be more specific, as regards the damages inflicted to plaintiffs. A general tortious act, consisting of putting a potential dangerous drug onto the Dutch market would not be sufficient in that respect.

Surprisingly, the Supreme Court takes the opposite view, although the lower Courts on this issue found support from the Attorney-General Hartkamp. The difficult position of the manufacturers in a law suit based on tort inspired the lower Courts in their decisions, whereas the Supreme Court is more concerned with the position of the victims, the DES daughters, and their formidable burden of proof. In the above decision the Court takes into consideration the wording and the parliamentary history of Article 99, but above all, its legal meaning, to wit, the support for reasons of equity of the victim in distress, not being able to prove which person caused its damage. The damage is certain, the tort is certain, but uncertain is the identity of the tortfeasor, out of a group of potential tortfeasors. The requirement of a 'specific tortious act', imposed by the Court of Appeal, therefore is rejected by the Supreme Court, as inconsistent with the rule of Article 99 according to its true meaning. The defendants' argument that in the travaux préparatoires nothing was said over a situation like that of defective DES products (and therefore, that the article is not written for such situation) was rejected by the Court, since 'it is plausible that such a situation at the time was beyond the range of vision of the drafters'.

In the Court's opinion, therefore, the story behind a legal norm should not be taken literally. The result reached by the lower court is considered unreasonable by the highest court, since victims would be left with their damages if the identity of the DES manufacturer which committed the tort can not be established by the plaintiffs. It would be unfair to restrict the application of Article 99 to damage caused by a small number of persons, which can be traced. Along the same line of thought, the Court rejected the lower court's view that the 'circle of liable persons' had to be exactly established by plaintiffs, an unreasonable requirement in the light of the virtual impossibility to trace all DES manufacturers involved.

One may conclude, that in the approach of the Supreme Court the „story" of the DES daughters counted here, in its encounter with the ratio of the legal norm involved: the equitable protection of victims. The old story out of the drafters' cabinet was set aside and replaced by the actual story presented to the court in its social context.

Opponents of joint and several liability of manufacturers in concert of action have stressed the unfair results of this approach in the case where a certain manufacturer, held liable by a victim, can not have sufficient recourse against other manufacturers. The cause may be that they can not be traced, are out of business or in a bad financial shape. I would support the view taken by the Supreme Court, that it would be even more unreasonable to lay this risk on the victims. The liability of the manufacturers should not be rejected exactly for this reason. In my opinion, for several reasons sympathy for the hardship caused to the group of DES manufacturers by the risk contribution is not well-founded. The production of DES was not protected by patent, the drug was rather easy and cheap to make and distribute, trusting on safety research done by others. The doctrine of 'creation of danger' comes to mind, developed in Germany since 1876 (Gefährdungshaftung) and introduced into Dutch jurisprudence at the beginning of the century. Incidentally, the 6 DES daughter had summoned the group of 10 DES manufacturers, which held approx. 90 % of the Dutch drugs market at the time, and an estimated share of the DES market of well over 50 %. Therefore, a substantial percentage of the DES manufacturers involved was held liable in the present lawsuit.

4. Conclusion

The best stories, at least the best liked stories, have a happy end. That goes also for this narration about normative and narrative coherence of norms. The normative and narrative elements of norms seemed at first opposing parties, belonging to different camps, as advocated by MacCormick, but in the end they proved to be quite congenial in the actual process of judicial decision making. The last story presented, about a statutory norm on alternative causation, which under influence of the strong narrative (victims knocking on the court's door) was applied in a *pur sang* narrative coherence, was told to illustrate the point I was trying to make.

And in the law making process, as always, *all is well that ends well.*

[16]

Jerzy Wróblewski and Neil MacCormick

On Justification and Interpretation

One approach to clarifying the nature of interpretation in law is to consider it in the setting of legal reasoning treated as a for of justificatory reasoning. The process of stating reasons for a decision or an opinion on the law ought to be treated as one aimed at showing how and why the decision is a justified decision in its legal context. The reasons publicly stated by courts for the decisions they give are properly to be read as stating the judges' opinion on what justifies the decision in law. They are not to be read as though they recounted or explained the heuresis or discovery of the decision. Their adequacy or lack of it as statements of justificatory reasons are wholly independent of their accuracy or lack of it as accounts of the way in the Court came to regard the decision as the one to be given in the case.

This distinction between justification and discovery (or heuresis) is taken as the basis of analysis in *Interpreting Statutes* (MacCormick and Summers, 1991). It is an often stated and now familiar distinction. Less familiar, perhaps is the strategy of investigating interpretative reasoning as an element in justification that is as one salient element within the justificatory reasonings of lawyers and legal systems. Why and how do interpretative arguments about the meaning and point of particular statutory previous count as acceptable (partial) justifying reasons for the decisions of the judges in concrete cases? The emphasis on justification gives a particular direction to explorations of the idea of interpretation.

In November 1989, while the late Jerzy Wróblewski was Carnegie Fellow in the Faculty of Law of the University of Edinburgh, he and the other present author took several days working over the conceptual connections of interpretation and justification by way of a joint reflection on the nature of the enterprise undertaken by the remarkable group of scholars whose work has, now appeared as *Interpreting Statutes*. This joint work was intended as the penultimate draft of a chapter to be worked up for inclusion in the book after thorough discussion with the other participants in the project, but fate dictated otherwise, since Wróblewski died before the final meeting of the 'Bielefelder Kreis'. Hence this text could not be revised so as to fulfil its intended function in that book. Its place was taken by a quite new chapter written by Robert Summers and myself (MacCormick and Summers 1991 chapter 13; this is a relatively concrete exploration of aspects of interpretation as justification, drawn substantially from materials thrown up in the preceding chapters). As originally written, and as now lightly revised to take account of valuable discussion at Göttingen in August 1991, the present text does, it is hoped, have some value as exploring in a relatively abstract and general way how the two concepts interrelate. At any rate, this joint work captures in a reasonably faithful way the latest thoughts of a dear distinguished colleague who made many distinctive contributions to analytical legal theory and to the work of the IVR. The present setting thus seems an emimently appropriate one for publication of these thoughts.

1. Justification in General

For any process of justification, whether in a practical or a purely theoretical context, we postulate that there is something to be justified (an action, a decision, an interpretative choice, a statement, a belief, a theory...), what we shall call a *justificandum* (JM). In respect of the *justificandum*, there have to be produced some justificatory premises (JP) by reference to which it is justified, and some justificatory reasoning (JR) which establishes the link between JP and JM. This can be summarised in model form as: JM is justified on account of JP by the reasoning JR. Where JM is a decision or other act, it is not itself derived directly from JP and JR; in this case JP and JR are properly seen as justifying the proposition that JM ought to be done or undertaken. In this case, it is justifiable by reference to those premises and that reasoning to do or to undertake JM. Reference to "justificatory reasons" (both in common parlance and in the present paper) often involves a conflation of the premises JP and the reasoning JR used to derive JM from them or otherwise support it by reference to them.

The term "justification" in ordinary language is doubly ambiguous, first as between the process of stating justificatory reasons and the reasons so stated (justification is either the activity or its result) and secondly as between reasoning or reasons offered in justification of a given JM and reasoning or reasons which actually justify it (purported justification as against sound justification).

In the legal and other practical settings, justification pertains primarily to actions and decisions; the JM of legal reasoning is paradigmatically a decision, although it can also of course be an opinion or statement about a point of law, or a thesis in doctrinal legal discourse. But in all its forms and for any JM, justification presupposes that what we do, say or believe is subject to judgement by reference to some standard or standards of correctness, rightness or propriety; a concern that one's acts or opinions be justifiable is nothing other than the concern that they be right or correct, or at least not wrong. That concern often issues in the open and public statement of a justification for one's or opinions. The practice of offering justifications is one which acknowledges that one's actions and opinions are a subject of legitimate concern to some others, and that they may be open to challenge or objection. Presenting justifications is a way of responding to such concern, and of attempting to meet challenges or objections, by showing the JM to be well founded. Schematically, as stated above, this means offering both justificatory premises (JP) and reasoning (JR) showing how JM is concerned with JP.

Justification in the practical context plainly presupposes some normative setting. Without standards discriminating between right and wrong in action, there could be no difference between the justified and the unjustified, hence no premises to adduce or oppose in the giving or contesting of justification. The question of justification is therefore open always to the further question: justification by what standards?

A special interest in legal justification obviously prompts here the answer that legal justification is justification in terms of the law's standards, or in terms of law as itself a highly systematised set of standards of action and judgement of actions. This answer, if sound, assumes a relativistic notion of justification – all justification is justification relative to some presupposed standards. Thus there can be justification in terms of law, or in terms of economic principles, or in terms of socialist values or utilitarian doctrines or liberal principles of whatever. Legal justification is one species of the genus justification, and what counts as a satisfactory or sound legal justification depends simply on the available standards of legal judgement derivable from a variety of sources such as statutory texts, precedents, legal doctrine, case notes, and other critical materials.

This, however, relates only to justificatory premises (JP), which do indeed constitute a relativistic element in justification. But the present model also stipulates an element of justificatory reasoning (JR) as distinct from the premises. This implies a conception of rationality as underlying all forms of or claims to justification. This is not simply a matter of formal logic in the narrow sense, but seems also to involve some broader notion of rational practical discourse (cf. Alexy, 1978, Wróblewski, 1992) which enables one to differentiate sound and unsound modes of reasoning. Whether any other underlying or foundational presuppositions are required is a controversial question. Some forms of cognitivism would suggest that there are ultimate substantive values, over and above formal requirements of rationality, which should be satisfied by any successful justification, and some theories of practical rationality (e.g. that of Alexy, 1978) suggest that a formal or procedural conception of rationality can generate quite strong constraints on what is substantively arguable in the context of any practical justification. For the moment, however, we make no assumptions to the effect that any particular substantive constraints are involved in the notion of justificatory rationality itself. Suffice it to say that legal or other practical justifications presuppose some, at least formal, criteria of rationality.

In law, this implies that arguments have to be made which link a decision with legal rules. Sometimes this may require no more than stating the rule in question and some findings of fact, where the facts found are considered to count unproblematically as instances of the operative facts of the rule. Deductive/subsumptive reasoning in this case connects premises satisfactorily and unproblematically to conclusion. But sometimes further premises are required in order to elucidate further the sense of the rule or the reasons for qualifying the concrete facts as instances of the operative facts stipulated in the rule. Of these further premises, some may themselves be legal rules or directives or values, concerning interpretation of rules or appreciation of facts; but sometimes they may be extra-legal, as where, for example, moral values or theories from natural science are used in a legal argument. And forms of practical reasoning of a not essentially deductive kind may be called for in working to a final conclusion in the light of all available and relevant premises.

One highly important formal feature of legal justificatory reasoning as a form of rational practical discourse is that it contains at least implicitly a requirement of universalisability of justifying reasons for decisions (Alexy, 1978; MacCormick, 1978), No purely *ad hoc* decision couned be a justified one, even though it may be possible to state justificatory reasor ing in terms particularly related to the facts of an individual case – for where this is so, the stated reasoning is impliedly universalisable, and constitutes a sound justification only if acceptable in universalised form, taking account of the other rules, principles, and values applicable within the relevant justificatory framework. In the case of interpretative justification, this implies that the norm as interpreted has the be understood as applicable universally, not only for the special facts of a given case; and this is independent of the question whether or not the interpretative decision is treated as a precedent in the formal sense within the given legal system. This feature of justificatory reasoning, and thus of interpretative justifications, is essential to the possibility of rational evaluation of competing possible interpretations. It is also itself important in the elimination of arbitrariness in decision making.

2. Justification as a Legal Requirement

It is a common feature of modern legal systems in the European tradition that those charged with the function of taking legal decisions, especially those which directly affect particular individual citizens, are required to give only such decisions as are justifiable in law. Thus does not mean that they have in every case to state reasons for their decisions, though it does mean that they usually must state them when challenged to do so. There are some striking exceptions, most spectacularly the jury in Britanno-American legal systems. At higher levels of decision-making the duty to state reasons even if not challenged to do so is almost universal, although in some cases this duty is imposed by convention rather than strict law. Moreover, the practice of stating justifications varies considerably in its style and content, as is indicated in chapters 3–11 of *Interpreting Statutes*. Particularly significant variations concern whether or not courts exercise a collegiate responsibility, issuing a single anonymous and collective statement of the reasons ("motifs") or come to a majority decision in the light of each judge's openly stated reasoning as to the best justified decision in the case, and whether or not external as well as internal justifications are openly stated. (These two ranges of variation are not unrelated).

Such variations go along with institutional differences between systems, and different ruling ideas as to the function and standing of courts and judges and their relation to other authorities. In general, however, they relate to degree of answerability of judges and courts of their decisions, and to the controllability of decisions. If reasons have to be stated, they are both checkable and correctable. No system of appeal or review can work reasonably without some legal or conventional rules or understandings as to the range and kind of reasons judges or courts must state, or at least as to the minima required by law. The discipline of stating reasons can itself have an influence on practice, even in cases which do not result in appeals. In the case of ultimate courts of appeal or review, the high public visibility of their activity makes them very open to public criticism, which can itself be a valuable control on arbitrary or ill-grounded decisions. It may be signficant that systems with a practice of relatively shorter, less explicit, and more formulaic justifications are ones which have a strong doctrine of the collegiate quality of decision-making. Here, there are controls on individual arbitrariness of a different sort than those at work in systems that allow of a higher degree of judicial individualism in the statement of reasons.

It also tends to be the case that, whether or not precedent is a recognised source of law, the decisions and reasoning of higher courts have at least an exemplary quality in relation to the decisions of other tribunals. Here, therefore, the statement of justifications for decisions may address a wider legal audience than merely the parties to a given case, or the judge or court whose decision is affirmed or corrected. The more a higher court's reasons are recognised as constituting precedents even in individual instances, the more fully and circumstantially stated the justification tends to be.

Despite all variations, it appears that the central values served by the requirement for justifiability of decisions are those of non-arbitrariness and legality. On the one hand, the requirement to state a justification (or to state one if challenged to do so) is a control upon capriciousness: on the other hand, it offers some guarantee that it will be the law rather than some other system of norms or values that will be the primary ground of decisions given by courts. Further, even allowing for differences between common law and civil law jurisdictions in respect of precedent, the statement and publication of justifications makes possible the development of a shared understanding of the meaning of legal provisions, thus further serving the values of legality and non-arbitrariness.

3. The Interpretative Dimension

The doctrine of formal sources of law (or that of the "rule of recognition", coupled with "rules of adjudication", Hart, 1961) means that courts are required to apply as law those rules and other norms or standards that are validly generated by a recognised formal source. Since it is a judge's duty to apply valid rules in making decisions, it is *ex hypothesi* a good justification for a decision to show (a) that it applies a rule belonging to the system (a "valid" rule), and (b) that this rule is not in conflict with any rule having higher or equal authority within the hierarchy of legal sources. (To a certain extent, (b) here is already included within (a), since a rule which is inconsistent with any provision higher in the hierarchy of legal sources is pro tanto invalidated; but it is often a matter of interpretation – of both the *prima facie* inconsistent provisions – to check whether and how far conflict is avoidable.) Judicial decisions are supposed to be law-applying decisions, and hence are justified on condition that they can be shown to count as applications of law.

Thus any application of law and any legal justification will involve interpretation *sensu largo*, since it calls for an understanding of the meaning of the legal rule or legal text applied in the case. Such interpretation is not perceived as problematic by the interpreter, whether or not it might be possible to problematise the meaning of the rule or raise a real doubt about it. In contested cases, however, and in other cases of difficulty, doubts or disputes may be raised by parties or judges as to the meaning properly to be ascribed to a rule. This interpretative issue may determine whether or not a given rule is applicable to the case in hand, and, if it is, in what sense and with what effect. In such a case, interpretation *stricto sensu*, operative interpretation, is called for.

Where there is doubt, a decision has to be taken to resolve the doubt and ascribe a functionally unequivocal meaning to the rule for the purpose of applying it in the case in hand. The interpretative decision is thus one part (a "fractional decision") of the justification of the decision in the case. As a (fractional) decision, it is itself susceptible of justification. Particularly in higher courts, albeit not in all jurisdictions, it is common for justifications to be given for the interpretative decisions made, as fractional parts of the overall decision of the case as a whole. The decision in the case is justified in the light of the facts as established and qualified by the court, and in the light of some legal rule or rules and other norms as interpreted by the court; where these interpretations themselves are explained and justified, a more complete justification is stated for the final decision than where they are simply enunciated as operative interpretations.

It is of course possible to proceed to a yet further level of justification, in giving a justification of the justificatory premises of the justification given for the interpretative (fractional) decision, and so on. But at some point, the ulterior grounds of justification must simply be presupposed as taken for granted (perhaps on the ground that *interpretatio cessat in claris*, and at some level matters are taken to be clear).

4. Typologies of Interpretative Argument

Our concern with interpretation as justification requires us to focus on the types of argument that are relevant to justifying interpretative decisions, as well as on the ways in which those decisions contribute to the overall justification of a decision. This section concerns typologies of interpretative arguments.

This could be discussed as a matter of the explicit formulation ("surface structure") of arguments. This is dependent on the legal requirements or conventions as to the sufficiency of a statement of justifying reasons, and as to its style and order of presentation; whether or not a plurality of judicial opinions, including dissenting opinions, is allowed for, and so on. Here, however, the concern is with underlying patterns, or "deep structure", in accordance with the guiding conception of rationality in argumentation as developed through one or another theoretical perspective. Here, there can be, and should be when possible, some matching between theoretical typology and judicial practice; in fact, there is often an interaction between judicial and scholarly discussions of these matters, to the benefit of both.

One typology, extensively used in Interpreting Statutes, is based in a semantic approach which attends to the contexts relevant to the meaning of statutory texts, namely the linguistic context, the systemic context and the teleological/evaluative context. This enables one to differentiate linguistic, systemic and teleological/evaluative argument-types. Another attends to the tradition flowing from von Savigny's analysis, assigning interpretative arguments to one or another of a set of canons of interpretation (*Interpreting Statutes*, ch 7, by R. Alexy and R. Dreier, gives some indication of this typology) Another adopts common law usage, distinguishing the plain meaning rule, the golden rule and the mischief rule, and incorporating various more detailed rules or maxims of construction such as *eiusdem generis, noscitur a sociis* and the like. Another is focussed on the types of information taken into account in interpretation, such as linguistic data, historical data, data derived from the legal system, values stated descriptively, values adopted by the interpreter, and the like. It seems probable that any one of these typologies can be matched up with any other, sometimes in such a way as to cast new light on traditional categories or types.

When one is attempting to produce a descriptive account of interpretative practice in a given legal system, one may face a certain tension between the typology most familiarly used both in established explanations of the system and in judicial usage and the typology which seems to have the greatest explanatory or analytical power for the purpose of improving understanding of interpretation as justification. A compromise may be called for, whereby traditional categories are reconciled with and recast in terms of the favoured theoretical typology (for an example, see the treatment of common law usage in *Interpreting Statutes*, ch 10 Z. Bankowski and N. MacCormick, recasting them mainly in terms of the semantic typology). In the long run, typologies which are found successful in clarifying and explaining practice may come to be adopted into it and hence to belong both to the analysis and to the subject matter, as has happened with the Savigny typology in Germany and in countries influenced by the German tradition.

If it is true, as we would suggest, that each of the typologies mentioned can be translated into any of the others, this seems to indicate that all reflect features of the deep structure, and that notwithstanding considerable differences at the level of surface structure between legal systems, there really is a common deep structure of rational interpretative reasoning.

5. Conflicts of Intrepretations and of Rules

Given the existence of a plurality of arguments and types of argument relevant to interpretation, there necessarily exist possibilities of conflict between rival readings or interpretations of a statutory text, where each of the rival interpretations can be justified by one or more of the interpretative arguments belonging to one or more of the types. Such conflicts are commonplace in legal practice. This implies that the most urgent task for a theory of interpretative justification relates to the resolution of such conflicts. The justification of decisions in cases involving conflicting interpretations of even a single statutory provision requires some sound basis for justifying the choice between rival interpretations and interpretative arguments.

All the theorists involved in the present project appear to acknowledge in some form a differentiation of two levels of argumentation: at the first level, one offers an interpretation of the relevant statutory provision, and gives an argument in support of that; but perhaps there is also a rival interpretation (which would justify a different outcome in the case in hand), and it, too, is supported by an argument of an acceptable type. Here, then, we confront a conflict between arguments at the first interpretative level. These arguments are based on what may be styled "first-level directives of interpretation" (Wróblewski), or "canons of interpretation" (Alexy, 1978) or "first order justificatory reasons" (Summers, 1978, cf. MacCormick, 1978). To resolve them, we must proceed to a second level or order of directives or rules or forms of argument or justificatory reasons. The difficult descriptive task is to ascertain how far there are standing directives or rules or criteria of preference which (e.g.) always give higher priority to one type of first order argument over another, or which always do so in a given systemic or functional context, as e.g., in favour of the widely held preference for plain meaning interpretations (based on linguistic arguments) over purposive ones (based on the mischief rule, or on functional arguments) in the interpretation of criminal statutes, because of the significance attached to the principle nulla *poena sine lege*. Other examples of special systemic or functional contexts are those of properly law, or tax law, where strict constructions are often observed on the ground of the need for certainly of title to property, or on the ground of securing the citizen's immunity from discretionary seizure of income or property.

Second level arguments not only have regard to preferences among first level arguments considered abstractly in themselves but also take account of values relevant to the particular case in which the conflict occurs – a crude possibility might be that one should choose whichever interpretation does best justice in the individual case. Less crude is the theory which directs the interpreter to have regard both to the generalised and to the particular consequences of the rival interpretations, and to evaluate these by a range of relevant values accepted in the legal community (as conceptualised by the interpreter him/herself). This would then authorise a process of weighing of relative values, and final decision a favour of those assigned greatest weight. This weighing process itself should incorporate some reference to general principles of law, and perhaps also to certain widely held moral principles.

The analysis and explanation of this second level of interpretative argumentation is plainly deeply complex and problematic. There is no reason to suppose that a single description will work for every system, and every reason to suppose that any attempted description of any system will be controversial the more detailed it is, and unhelpfully vague the less detailed it is. We believe that from the point of view of the general theory of justification, one can say no more than that at least two levels of interpretative argument, or of directives of interpretation, have to be acknowledged.

One possible issue may, however, be as to whether the matter is adequately accounted for by reference to two levels only. It may well be that if one were to establish some *prima facie* directives or principles of preference at the second level that the grounds for preference in case of conflict between these *prima facie* directives in case of their conflict could be considered as belonging to a third level, and so on. One particular point concerns the question whether one should envisage the legal system as itself complete and "autopoietic" at this level. Many theorists would aver that at some point in some particularly difficult cases one inevitably runs out of distinctively legal materials or forms or grounds or directives of argument, and is driven to have recourse to general practical argumentation or discourse as the source of one's final justification for a decision. It seems that in some for or another, all the present authors would accept this thesis, though probably differing as to the degree of determinacy of justification thereby implied.

Apart from those problems of conflict there is another significant kind of legal conflict in which interpretation has an important part to play. This arises in those situations in which the decision of a particular case would go one way if one statutory rule is applied, but another if a different statutory rule is applied. For each of the rules in question, there is a possible interpretation according to which it is applicable and determinative, and one according to which it is not applicable at all, or applicable in a different sense and to a different effect. Quite possibly one uses different argument types, or different directives of interpretation, in respect of the different rules. (One rule would apply according to its plain meaning, but not if read in some purposive way; the other could apply according to a purposive reading, but not as a matter of plain meaning.) Here again, it seems to accord with the general rationale of justification that the second level of justificatory argument should rest heavily on considerations of general axiology, that is on the relative weighing of significant values as criteria (or elements within criteria) of preference for one first-level argument over another, or for one first-level directive over another.

Rule-conflicts of this kind can occur as between different articles of a code, or between a code article and an ordinary statute, or between either and a provision of constitutional law, or between a recognised general principle of law and a statutory provision, or a code article. In common law countries, it is not uncommon to face p*rima facie* conflicts between statutory provisions and rules or doctrines of common law. No doubt, it is true in all systems of law that if the outcome of interpretation will be to discover a flat and unavoidable contradiction between the two legal provisions in question, one will have to be pronounced at least pro tanto invalid or inapplicable, according to hierarchical rules of conflict resolution. But at least as common seems to be the practice of so interpreting the norm which yields the disfavoured solution as to show it inapplicable in the given case or type-case, while one at the same time uses a justified interpretation of the other norm to justify the decision of the case. We might call the former a case of "eliminative interpretation", or "interpretative distiguishing" of the statutory rule in question: this is really the converse of "operative interpretation", where the interpretation of the rule reveals its applicability in a particular sense to the case in hand.

The prevalence in all systems of eliminative interpretation may be understood as exhibiting respect for one of the guiding values of rational interpretation of legal systems, namely a regard for the overall coherence of the system as an order of organised human conduct. No doubt, interpretative distinguishing itself looks in the first instance no farther than simple consistency among parts of the system (see MacCormick, 1978 ch 8). But the characteristic setting of the particular concern for consistency is within a broader regard for coherence (Alexy/Peczenik, 1988; MacCormick, 1984). This can in turn be taken as a feature of a legal system considered as (part of) a "form of life" in a Wittgenstein sense (Aarnio, 1988), such that different forms of life are esssentially incommensurable. Or it may be that there is some form of rational practical discourse within which, given world enough and time, all forms of life might be discussed and compared and the most satisfactory one chosen (Alexy, 1978).

One powerful contemporary version of the coherentist picture of law is Ronald Dworkin's (Dworkin, 1986), how expressed in his thesis as to the "integrity" of legal systems. This thesis represents law in its entirety as an "interpretive concept", and suggests that in every justification of any decision, the task of court is not merely to interpret and apply particular rules of statute law, case law constitutional law or whatever, but also to interpret the legal system and tradition as a whole in order to ascertain the best possible ground for deciding the instant case concerning the rights of particular parties. In broad terms, this view has much to commend it. It is, however, material to note that, in our terms, Dworkin uses the concept of interpretation equivocally. It is one thing (interpretation *stricto sensu*) to read a particular text as ambiguous or vague over a range of possible interpretations, and to advance justificatory arguments in favour of a choice of one interpretation to apply in the particular case. It is quite another thing to evaluate the overall meaning or point or implicit value-system of the entire legal system as a potentially coherent social order. To restrict an analysis of interpretation to a consideration of this mode of interpretation would be to mistake the part for the whole.

Finally, it is at this stage appropriate to pass some remarks on the possibility of determinate right answers to questions of interpretation. There is a great deal to be said for Dworkin's thesis that each interpreter should come to the task with a sufficiently rich set of interpretational directives and principles and values to be able to show within the terms of that framework of justification that the very answer given is the best available, or the right one. Whether in any given case the "internal justification" internal to a particular justificatory schema has been carried out successfully and has generated the appropriate result is intersubjectively checkable, at least in principle. This is because the issue here is one concerning whether or not the conclusion reached is rationally derivable from or supported by the premises employed.

What this does not show, however, is that there cannot be an "external critique" (e.g., by a higher court or an academic critic) which criticises the ultimate value-premises, or other premises of this justificatory schema, and proposes different ones as applicable. To contend that there is a single best theory of the legal system which overrides all others is necessarily to presuppose a single (correct) basis for such an external critique. This is an arguable proposition, but seems at odds with the view that always there is a right answer internal to the legal system.

6. Towards a General Theory of Justification

In this section we attempt to construct a general model of justification consistent with the general underlying theoretical positions of *Interpreting Statutes*. There are three possible levels of abstractness of models relevant to our purpose. Most abstractly, we need (a) a general model of the justification of practical decisions; this becomes more concrete when elaborated as (b) a general model of the justification of legal decisions; and more concrete still in the form of (c) a general model of the justification of legal interpretative decisions (that is, of "operative interpretation", in the present terminology).

As stated in section 1 of this essay, our general model of justification is in these terms: for any given *justificandum* (JM), this can be justified only by
(i) applying appropriate justificatory reasoning (JR) to show how JM is supported by or derivable from
(ii) appropriate justificatory premises (JP)

This becomes a model for practical justification in general if we stipulate that in practical reasoning JM is an action of decision, that there have to be appropriate rules or criteria for justificatory reasoning, including in this case the rule that at least one of the premises JP has to be itself practical (imperative, normative or axiological), and that normally the premises of practical justification include both epistemic and practical premises.

For practical decisions in law (hereinafter simply called "legal decisions"), JM is a legal decision, and the rules of JR require that
there be – epistemic premises comprising
(a) information about law (legal rules, etc)
(b) information about matters of fact ("evidence")
practical premises comprising
(a) values grounded in legal axiology.
(b) other values and norms appropriate to legal decision-making

Where the legal decision in issue is a "fractional" one concerning a point of statutory interpretation, we postulate the existence of some doubt or dispute about the meaning of a *prima facie* applicable rule in a given case. Such doubts often arise because of conflict or doubt over the correct conclusion of the case in which the statute has to be interpreted.

Corresponding to what were earlier called first-level arguments, we can construct "directives" or "rules" or "canons", such as that statutes should be interpreted according to their plain meaning, or should be interpreted so as to avoid absurdity, or should be interpreted so as to achieve the purpose of the historic legislator etc. These first level directives (DI1) are a subordinate form of JP, since by appropriate reasoning from them and from factual premises we are able to identify interpretations of statutes which should *prima facie* be applied. That they only indicate *prima facie* interpretations follow from the rather obvious observation that they can themselves yield conflicting conclusions. Resolution of these conflicts can only take place at a second level of reasoning, whose practical premises can again be reconstructed as what Wróblewski calls "second level directives of interpretation" (DI2).

In a highly systematic approach, by no means fully realised in most of the systems here studied, these DI2 can be subdivided into procedural directives ands preferential directives. Procedural DI2 state which DI1 should be used in what contexts, and in what order, and direct a comparison of the meanings generated by the application of DI1a, DI1b ... DI1n. Where it turns out that all first order directives confirm a single meaning, that is applicable; but where this is not so, one must have recourse to preferential DI2. These in turn constitute practical premises whereby interpretations derived from DI1a, DI1b ... DI1n should be given greater or less weight relative to others depending on a variety of rather complex axiological criteria, and that which carries greatest weight in a given context should be applied in that context. As is obvious, epistemic premises (JP) are again required here as a matter, *inter alia*, of determining relevant contexts.

How one should formulate these "directives of interpretation" depends on the legal system one is considering, and on the extent to which one wishes (as in I*nterpreting Statutes*) to give as nearly as may be a descriptive account, reconstructing criteria of preference which fit and to a degree explain current judicial practice. An alternative possibility, would be to propose a critical reconstruction aimed at improving legal interpretative practice, by for example suggesting clearer statements of rules or directives, different axiological bases for preference, and so forth. (The beginnings of an attempt at this are now to be found in the closing sections of chapter 13 of *Interpreting Statutes*.)

The present general model of justificatory reasoning in interpretative decision-making, as well as claiming a general applicability, is clearly instantiated in all that is said in *Interpreting Statutes*. In particular, in discussing types of interpretative argument and the priorities observed in cases of conflict (also, the priorities arising from special values relevant to constitutional law and other specialised legal fields), the work there presents material relevant to articulating what are here referred to as "DI1" and "DI2". It also indicates how, even (or especially) because of the descriptive bent of the work, different formulations of directives may be chosen, on account of different underlying values in different systems. It is also the case that major institutional differences, such as those between common law and civilian (codified) systems necessarily show up in formulations of DI. Also, where one school of legal theory has had a particularly influential role in legal practice, as in Sweden, this shows up in necessary differences of typology at this level.

One thing which seems very clear is the fundamental part played by value considerations as criteria of preference in applying DI2. In this light, one can discern certain rather deep divisions among grounds of preference of first-level arguments (or DI1). There is an evident dichotomy between a cluster of what might be called "static values", such as those of certainty and stability in law, security of legal expectations, and respect for the constitutional division of power as between law-maker and law-applier, and "dynamic values" concerning the importance of adjusting legal norms to common social expectations, or to the supposed needs of a changing society, or to some substantive conception(s) of justice. The value of legal coherence or integrity, discussed above, has elements of both the static and the dynamic in it, but probably belongs more to the latter category. Where distinctions are drawn in such terms as that of a contrast between "formalistic" and "purposive" approaches, whether in terms of descriptive accounts of systems, or criticism and advocacy of change in justificatory practice, we see these distinctions as reflecting the dichotomy of the static and the dynamic.

A further variable concerns the modes of weighing involved in applying second level DI. One can envisage here there ideal types:
(i) where a strict hierarchy is ordained as between DI1 ranged in invariant priority order;
(ii) where a strict hierarchy is ordained, but variably according to conditions and domain of application;
(iii) where the preference among different DI1 is made wholly or partly dependent on the circumstances of the given case (subject to universalisability).

It seems doubtful whether any contemporary system of law instantiates any one of these types in a pure form. But the greater the tendency to uphold static values, the more one would expect to find it evidenced in a favouring of (i), and the greater the tendency to dynamic values, the more one would expect (iii).

7. Variables, Comparability and Criticism

One thing is clear from our attempt at model-building, namely that a very great range of variables is involved in any system of interpretative justification. Of particular importance in our view is the dichotomy between static and dynamic values, and the range of variation among the three ideal types of preferential directive just discussed. This poses a considerable difficulty in respect of any attempt to produce a purely descriptive account of approaches to interpretation in different legal systems taken as entireties. For it is far from clear that any legal system has, or that any could have, settled firm common usages, or positive rules, governing all aspects of interpretation. There is a great range of possible variants on the idea of rational justification in the interpretative setting. Some variants, at least as to dominant styles of approach to justification over periods of time, are liable to be found in one system as against another. But on other points it is as likely as not that there will simply be internal controversy among jurists and judges internal to a given system. It will be impossible then to say much that is informative about the system as a whole.

In such areas, the role of the theorist is almost inevitably a partly critical role. One observes the ranges of possible argumentation in use among the judiciary and scholars. But to go beyond a mere reporting of the variations of approach, and to state one as the most appropriate within the system is to take on a critical role. It is to pass beyond a merely descriptive rational reconstruction of practice, or abstract modelling of possible variables, and to enter into interpretative debate as a normative and axiological enterprise.

Nevertheless, there remains work for the comparativist to do. If there are ranges of variation within as well as between systems, these are available to be studied and explained. The well-known thesis that different legal systems with characteristic differences of technique and legal ideology nevertheless tend to coincide in achieving common or similar solutions to common problems of a social or economic kind in fact requires some theory of variables in interpretation. For if there were not such variables, one would lack a basis for explanation of the convergence of interpretative results despite the difference of starting points.

References

Aarnio, Aulis 1988. *The Rational as Reasonable*, Dordrecht, Kluwer Publishing Co
Alexy, Robert 1978. *Theorie der juristischen Argumentation*, Frankfurt am Main, Suhrkamp (Now translated as *Theory of Legal Argumentation*, tr. R. Adler and N MacCormick, Oxford, Oxford University Press, 1988)
Alexy, Robert & Peczenik, Aleksander 1988. 'The Concept of Coherence and its Significance for Discursive Rationality' *Ratio Juris* 3: 130–47
Dworkin, Ronald 1986. *Law's Empire*, London, Fontana Books
Hart, H. L. A. 1961. *The Concept of Law* Oxford, Oxford University Press
MacCormick, Neil 1978. *Legal Reasoning and Legal Theory*, Oxford, Oxford University Press
MacCormick, Neil & Summers, Robert S. 1991. *Interpreting Statutes: a Comparative Study*, Aldershot, Dartmouth Publishing Co
Peczenik, Aleksander 1989. *Legal Reasoning*, Dordrecht, Kluwer Publishing Co
Summers, Robert S. 1978. 'Two Types of Substantive Reasons' *Cornell Law Review* 63: 707–88
Wróblewski, Jerzy 1992 *The Judicial Application of Law* (ed Z Bankowski and N. MacCormick) Dordrecht, Kluwer Publishing Co

Abstract

This paper originated as a piece of work done in connection with *Interpreting Statutes: a Comparative Study* (ed MacCormick and Summers, 1991). Legal interpretation is considered not as a topic apart, nor primarily from the point of view of interpretation in other (e.g. literary of historical) contexts, but in the context of legal reasoning as practical reasoning concerned with the justification of decisions. What then are the interconnections of justification and interpretation? The first part of the paper gives an analytical account of the concept of justification in terms of *justificandum*, justificatory premises, and justificatory reasoning. The justification of any *justificandum* (JM) thus requires

(i) applying appropriate justificatory reasoning (JR) to show how JM is supported by or derivable from
(ii) appropriate justificatory premises (JP)

The second part stresses the importance of justification as a legal requirement; that is, it stresses the significance of the statutory or conventional legal requirements for the statement by decision-makers of reasons for their decisions. The third explains the interpretative dimension of legal justification, as involving the ascription of specific meanings to the legal premises used in legal justificatory reasoning; but since the question which interpretation to adopt is itself a decision (a 'fractional decision') that may call for justification, there have to be statable reasons which justify one against another possible interpretation of a legal text. Interpretative reasoning is justificatory reasoning presented in a context of serious doubt or dispute about the preferable interpretation of a text. The fourth considers possible typologies of interpretative arguments, or of the 'directives of interpretation' which can be constructed in respect of the argument types. Particular stress is laid on the Wróblewskian semantic typology used as the principal typology in *Interpreting Statutes*, but the point is taken that varying typologies seem transferable across different legal systems, hence that they perhaps all reflect a common 'deep structure'. The fifth part starts from the observation that problems of legal interpretation characteristically involve conflicts between arguments of different types, where the doubt giving rise to interpretative discussion is due to the supportability of more than one interpretation by *prima facie* good arguments. Hence there have to be second level arguments justifying preference in cases of conflict at the first level. Then in the sixth part, an attempt is made to construct a general theory of justification in this context, setting up some models of possible reasoning, and accounting for the importance of values in the ultimate choices between rival good arguments for different interpretations. In conclusion, the paper raises some doubts about the possibility of any purely descriptive account given the range of variables between and within systems of law.

[17]

Aleksander Peczenik

AUTHORITY REASONS IN LEGAL INTERPRETATION AND MORAL REASONING[1]

1. An Example of Legal Thinking: Adequate Causation of Damage

Consider the following case. Silver fox females, frightened by a very noisy military aircraft, bit their new-born cubs to death. It was held that the owner of the foxes was entitled to recover compensation in torts from the State. The decision was founded on the following two sources of the law.

(a) The Air Transport Liability Act (1922:382), sec. 1, according to which the owner of an aircraft is liable for damage caused by the use of the aircraft, even if he has not been negligent (a strict liability).

(b) An unwritten principle of the Swedish law of torts which stipulates that one has to compensate a damage only if it has been an "adequate" result of the activity for which one is liable. In this context one speaks about "adequate causation", "adequate cause", "adequate damage" etc.

The decision of the case was a result of interpretation of these two sources of the law.

2. Different Kinds of Moral and Legal Reasons

In order to understand why one must consider the problem of adequacy, let us imagine a different course of events. Assume that the owner of the damaged foxes had to kill the females and then went to the town to sell their skins. On the way, his car was destroyed in an accident. Shall the owner of the aircraft be liable even for this damage? Obviously not, for several reasons. Let me, at first, mention some moral and other non-juristic reasons.

(a) He should not be liable because this would be *commonly considered* as wrong. This is a "heteronomous" authority reason. We often use such authority reasons, simply relying on what people commonly think.

(b) He should not be liable because this would "really" *be wrong*. This is an "autonomous" reason, expressing one's own prescriptive (evaluative, normative) opinion, not describing other persons' opinions. Such "autonomous" reasons can be of three kinds:

(ba) Sometimes, one utters a universal (often vague) principle covering the case under consideration, for example the principle that one should not be liable for a "too remote" result of one's action.

(bb) Sometimes, one utters a concrete moral judgment of the case under consideration (a moral intuition), for example that the owner of the aircraft ought not to pay for the car accident in question.

(bc) Sometimes, one relies upon social considerations concerning consequences of a decision of a given kind. For example, one may take into account, the following factors.[2]

(bca) The law of torts and the insurance law should minimize the social *costs* of accidents.

(bcb) Losses should be *spread* as much as possible. Nobody should be economically destroyed by an accident.

(bcc) People should be afraid of causing accidents (general *deterrence*.)

In our actual moral *practice*, we have to rely on a compromise, a "reflective equilibrium", of all these kinds of reasons, that is, authority reasons, intuitive moral principles, concrete moral judgments and consequentialist social considerations. I do not discuss here the question whether an ideal moral agent, a "Hercules" or an "Archangle", would be able to omit some components of this list, for instance to ignore authority reasons or even to base his judgment exclusively on consequentialist considerations.

Let me now move to legal problems, concerning the considered case. The *creation* of the legal principle of "adequacy" has been a result of an effort to state the principle-component (ba) of this equlibrium in a binding manner and more precisely. The legal validity (bindingness) of this principle is an additional authority reason, of a specific character, comparable to the "heteronomous" moral reasons, see item a) *supra*. It introduces a component of certainty to the fluid set of premises of moral reasoning. An increased preciseness results from the fact that one replaces the vague principle of non-liability for "too remote" damage with a more precise principle of non-liability for "non-adequate" damage, provided, of course, that the "adequacy" can be defined in a more precise manner. Legal *interpretation* of the principle of adequacy involves thus the question of finding and justifying a precise definition of, or a precise substitute for, the concept of "adequate causation".

3. On Justificatory Jumps

Let me now return to the case of female foxes and their cubs. The reasoning of the court may thus be presented, as follows:

Premise p1   The owner of an aircraft is strictly liable for a damage adequately caused by the use of the aircraft.

Premise p2   The noise of the aircraft caused a damage which consisted in the fact that fox females bit their cubs to death.

Conclusion: The owner of the aircraft is strictly liable for the damage which consisted in the fact that the fox females bit their cubs to death.

In this reasoning, there is a gap. The conclusion does not follow deductively from p1 and p2. To make the reasoning deductive, one must fill in the gap. In other words, one needs an additional premise p3. Then, one obtains the following syllogism.

Premise p1   The owner of an aircraft is strictly liable for a damage adequately caused by the use of the aircraft.
Premise p2   The noise of the aircraft caused a damage which consisted in the fact that fox females bit their cubs to death.
Premise p3   If noise of an aircraft causes a damage which consists in the fact that fox females bit their cubs to death, the causal connection between the aircraft noise and the damage is adequate.

Conclusion: The owner of the aircraft is strictly liable for the damage which consisted in the fact that the fox females bit their cubs to death.

One must say two things about the added premise p3.
1. Obviously, this premise is not so certain (evident). A rational person can doubt it. The reasoning in question contains thus a jump, that is, it cannot be made deductive by an addition of an indubitable premise.[3]
2. This premise follows from the legal principle of adequacy. More correctly, it follows from a given interpretation of this principle.

4. Complexity of Legal Concepts

In other words, premise p3 needs justification, which can consist in the fact that it follows from (1) a precise interpretation of "adequate causal connection" together with (2) a description of facts. The language admits many such precise interpretations.

Before discussing them, let me merely make the following preliminary remark. Some of these interpretations assume that the damage in question belongs to a given type, T. In the considered case, the type T is characterized as "damage by a frightened animal". When discusing the cause of this damage, one must thus assume two links in the causal chain from the cause under consideration, i.e. the noise, to the result, i.e. the loss of the cubs: the first one from the cause under consideration to the behaviour of the animal, the second one from the behaviour of the animal to the final result.

One has, *inter alia*, to make a choice between the following precise interpretations of "adequate causation".[4]

1. If a cause relevantly increases probability of a damage of the type T (to which the damage in question belongs), then the connection between this cuase and the damage is adequate.

2. If a cause belongs to a type which is generally apt to bring about a damage of the type T, then the connection between this cause and the damage is adequate.

3. If a cause makes a damage of the type T foreseeable, then the connection between this cause and the damage is adequate.

4. If a cause immediately brings about the damage in question, then the connection between this cause and the damage is adequate.

5. If a cause is a substantial factor in producing the damage in question, then the connection between this cause and the damage is adequate.

Each of the if-clauses of the statements 1–5 has been profferred as a reason for the conclusion "the connection between this cause and the damage is adequate". Although there is a controversy about these and other definitions of "adequate" causation, one may also utter the semantical proposition that most of these "if-clauses" *are* such reasons. The following propositions thus constitute such profferred reasons:

a1: the cause under consideration relevantly increases probability of a damage of the type T (to which the damage in question belongs),

a2: the cause belongs to a type which is generally apt to bring about a damage of the type T,

a3: the cause makes a damage of the type T foreseeable,

a4: the cause immediately brings about the damage in question,

a5: the cause is a substantial factor in producing the damage in question.

Let me omit the question which of these reasons are mutually independent, and which merely constitute different formulations of the same criterion or adequacy. Surely, not all of them merely are different words for one and the same thing.

Two remarks must be added in this context. First, when making a choice between the discussed criteria or definitions of adequacy, one must rely on (moral) evaluations. Second, the multiplicity of the criteria of adequacy shows that the concept "adequate causation" is vague. In some contexts, it is even ambiguous. In the modern Swedish literature, one often regards it as vague, that is, one admits many criteria of adequacy. In the older German discussion, one often considered it rather as ambigous. One expected thus that only one of the proposed criteria of adequacy was "the right one", and then tried to state precisely, which one. One may hope that, in future, some of the proposed criteria will be eliminated, as incompatible with solutions of important cases. It would be, however, too much to expect that all but one criterion will thus be eliminated. In other words, I assume that the ordinary legal (and moral) language only seldom admits "only one right answer" to "hard" questions.

A weak semantical proposition on adequacy is, as follows: Some subsets of the set of propositions a1–a5 are "effectively adequacy-making", that is, they are sufficient reasons for the conclusion "the connection between this cuse and the damage is adequate".

One may thus formulate the following scheme, illustrating the semantical connection between propositions a1–a5 and the conclusion about adequate causation.
THERE EXIST SOME SUBSETS OF THE FOLLOWING PROPOSITIONS,
a1, a2, a3, a4, a5,
SUCH THAT IF ANY OF THESE SUBSETS IS TRUE,
THEN THE CONNECTION BETWEEN THE CAUSE AND THE DAMAGE IN QUESTION IS ADEQUATE.

The propositions a1–a5 are such that it *makes sense* to proffer most of them as reasons, supporting the conclusion "the connection between this cause and the damage is adequate". A theory of linguistic use of words, belonging to the legal language, tells us that it makes sense to do so. In other words, it tells us that it is inappropriate to exclude most of the proffered criteria of adequacy on linguistic grounds alone. A *law-theorist* can test this linguistic theory, in principle in a value-free manner. A *legal dogmatician, a judge or another practically-minded lawyer* can then "pick up" some of these propositions, for example a2 and a3, and say that they constitute an "adequacy-making" subset, that is, that they jointly decide that the connection between the cause and the damage is adequate. He says thus that a cause of a damage of the type T is adequate, if two conditions have been fulfilled: (a2) the cause belongs to a type which is generally apt to bring about a damage of the type T and (a3) the cause makes a damage of the type T foreseeable. He repudiates the other criteria of adequacy, *inter alia* the the criterion a1, according to which a cause of a damage of the type T is adequate, if the cause relevantly increases probability of a damage of the type T. The fact that he "picks up" some of these propositions (a2 and a3) and repudiates the other ones (*inter alia* a1) is the same thing as the fact that he performs a kind of *interpretation* of the concept of "adequate causation". The main question to ask is, of course, *why* the lawyer "picks up" some interpretations of "adequacy" and repudiates the other ones. The main method he uses to make this selection consists of evaluating some hypothetical cases, that is, confronting them with some moral intuitions, moral principles or consequentialist social considerations.

In order to test the probability-oriented adequacy criterion a1, the lawyer may, for example ask the question, What information is to be taken into account when computing the probability of the damage? One answer to this question is, for example, Ruemelins's metod of "objective prognosis *ex post facto*," according to which the probability should be computed in view of all the information available at the time of decision-making, considering the situation at the time of the tortfeasor's action. The method leads, however, to the following unacceptable solution of a hypothetical case. Assume that A injures B. B is taken to an ambulance that later collides with a stone blocking the road. One may argue that Ruemelin would hold A liable for B's death in the collision. A's action (to injure B) relevantly increased probability of B's death and all the factors that in fact caused B's death, (*inter alia*, the position of the stone) were determined already at the time of the initial injury. Yet, such a decision would be unjust, and thus it would "falsify" Ruemelin's method.[5]

Having performed his interpretation of the concept of "adequate causation", that is, his choice of a2 and a3 instead of, for example, a1, the lawyer can present his reasoning, as follows:

Premise p1   The owner of an aircraft is strictly liable for a damage adequately caused by the use of the aircraft.

Premise p2   The noise of the aircraft caused a damage which consisted in the fact that fox females bit their cubs to death.

Premise p4   If a cause (a) belongs to a type which is generally apt to bring about a damage of the type T and (b) makes a damage of the type T foreseeable, then the connection between this cause and the damage is adequate.

Premise p5   (a) Noise of an aircraft is generally apt to frighten animals and make them to bring about the damage of type T, that is, such damage as bitting their cubs to death; (b) noise of an aircraft makes such a damage foreseeable.

Conclusion: The owner of the aircraft is strictly liable for the damage which consisted in the fact that the fox females bit their cubs to death.

5. Complexity of Moral Concepts: Theoretical Propositions As Interpretations of Value Statements

There is a striking similarity between the juristic activity, consisting in "picking up" a precise interpretation of the concept of "adequate causation", and a *moral* activity, consisting in "picking up" some theoretical propositions as good reasons for the conclusion that some object is good. Let me consider the following theory of goodness.[6] Some subsets of a given set of theoretical propositions, p1–pn, support the conclusion that x is good. For example, one may support the conclusion "B is a good person" by some of the following propositions: B usually tells the truth; B usually helps other people; B works efficiently; B shows courage; B keeps his promises, etc. Let me call each such subset a good-making subset. One may formulate the following scheme, illustrating the connection between theoretical propositions and value statements.

THERE EXIST SOME ("GOOD-MAKING") SUBSETS OF THE FOLLOWING SET OF THEORETICAL PROPOSITIONS
p1, p2, ... pn
SUCH THAT IF ANY OF THESE SUBSETS IS TRUE,
THEN x IS GOOD.

When the variables p1–pn are changed into constants, this scheme develops into a semantic proposition, or a meaning postulate, concerning the meaning of the word "good". The meaning of the word "good", and thus the content of p1–pn, is extremely complex, but one can consider the following semantical proposition, as a simple model of this content.

There exist some ("good-making") subsets of the following set of theoretical propositions,
– (p1) B usually tells the truth,
– (p2) B usually helps other people,
– (p3) B works efficiently,
– (p4) B shows courage,
– (p5) B keeps his promises, etc.,
such that if any of these subsets is true, then B is a good person.

Neither this semantical proposition nor the general scheme, presented above, is thus a value statement. The theoretical propositions, p1–pn, included in the if-clause of this scheme, are such that it makes sense to proffer most of them as reasons, supporting the conclusion "x is good". A theory of linguistic use of words tells us that it is so. In other words it tells us that it is inappropriate to exclude most of the proffered criteria of goodness on the linguistic grounds alone. A student of linguistics can test such a theory, in principle in a value-free manner. An evaluating person can then "pick up" some of these theoretical propositions, for example p1 and p2, and say that they constitute a good-making subset, that is, that they jointly decide that x is good. A value statement thus involves an answer to the question which subset of the set of theoretical propositions p1–pn is a sufficient condition of x being good. An evaluating person can then conclude, for instance, that B is a good person because he usually tells the truth and helps other people. He picks up these properties of B as good-making, and repudiates other — semantically admissible — criteria of goodness. For example, he insists that B is a good person, albeit B does not work efficiently. The evaluating person can also propose a general doctrine (a normative "theory") of moral goodness, which ascribes to some combinations of reasons the good-making character and repudiates other linguistically meaningfull reasons for x's goodness.

In both cases, one can now say that the evaluating person makes a kind of interpretation of the word "good". The interpretation consists, for example, in the fact that he regards helpfulness and truthfulness jointly as a sufficient reason for a person's goodness, whereas, for example, efficiency is repudiated as a criterion of goodness. Why does he do so? Very often, he bases his choice of interpretation on his judgment of hypothetical cases. One can imagine, for example, a saint who helps everybody as much as he can and tells only the truth but lacks efficiency at work. Would one regard this saint as a good person? Most of us certainly would do so, and for this reason, would repudiate efficient work as a criterion of goodness, either in a considered concrete case, or at all, even if the language alone had admitted this criterion.

As we have seen in the previous section, one may in a similar manner "pick up", for example, foreseeability of damage as a sufficient reason for the conclusion that the connection between an action and this damage has been adequate. In spite of its highly technical character, the kind of legal reasoning referred to shows interesting similarities to moral reasoning.

6. Complexity of Legal Reasoning Generates Additional Authority Reasons

This choice between different semantically possible conceptions of adequacy is, however, a very complex and value-loaden reasoning process. In order to simplify the reasoning, a legal dogmatician — or a deciding judge — may, instead, quote a precedent. In the fictitious case under consideration, he may quote, e.g., the following Swedish cases: NJA 1942 p. 229, NJA 1945 p. 210, NJA 1946 p. 758. One may thus reconstruct his reasoning, as follows.

Premise p1 The owner of an aircraft is strictly liable for a damage adequately caused by the use of the aircraft.
Premise p2 The noise of the aircraft caused a damage which consisted in the fact that fox females bit their cubs to death.
Premise p6 If the Supreme Court in a series of precedents states that a connection between a cause and a damage is adequate, then this connection *is* adequate.
Premise p7 The Supreme Court has stated in a series of precedents that noise of an aircraft is an adequate cause that may frighten animals and make them to bring about such damage as bitting their cubs to death.

Conclusion: The owner of the aircraft is strictly liable for the damage which consisted in the fact that the fox females bit their cubs to death.

In the Swedish legal dogmatics, one often tries as much as possible to replace the principled moral choice between several interpretations of law by the reliance upon the choice already made by some authorities, especially high courts. *Inter alia*, one has pointed out, what follows.[7] It is impossible to formulate a uniform criterion covering the evaluation of adequacy in Swedish law, unless the criterion is very vague, almost pointless. Adequacy must thus be judged in various types of cases, not generally. One must, first of all, distinguish between personal injury and property damage. One must, then, distinguish between the stage from the wrongful action up to a personal injury or property damage, and the stage from the personal injury or property damage up to economical loss in consequence of the injury or damage. One must judge each type of cases, first of all, on the basis of existing precedents. If no sufficient precedents exist, one may rely upon analogies to cases regulated by statutes, decided by courts, or in any other way already judged by some authorities. Own "autonomous" judgment of the legal dogmatician comes at the end of this reasoning process.

7. The Limits of Reliance Upon Authorities

At least in "hard cases", a judge or dogmatician should not, however, exclusively rely upon authority reasons. For instance, he should be able to state that even the Supreme Court, that established the precedents, may have been wrong. He must thus rely on a compromise, a reflective equilibrium, of the following reasons.

(a) Authority reasons
(aa) moral ("heteronomous") authority reasons, such as "people consider that this is good"
(ab) legal authority reasons , that is such sources of the law as statutes, unwritten customary principles, precedents etc.
(b) "Autonomous" moral reasons
(ba) universal principles covering the case under consideration
(bb) concrete intuitions concerning this case
(bc) "autonomous" moral reasons concerning social consequences of the considered decision
(bd) "autonomous" moral reasons concerning the choice of semantically possible interpretations of authority reasons
(bda) interpretation of moral authority reasons
(bdb) interpretation of legal authority reasons.

Since only the components ab (legal authority reasons) and bdb (interpretation of legal authority reasons) are specifically legal, one may conclude that legal reasoning is a specialized branch of moral reasoning. Its special character is, however, rather quantitative than qualitative. It includes a richer catalogue of authority reasons than moral reasoning but, on the other hand, even moral reasoning includes some authority reasons.

All this makes the following hypothesis plausible. *At least in the Western-type society, the law is necessary as a relatively certain starting point of moral reasoning. But is is not a means to eliminate moral reasoning.*

NOTES

1. I express my gratitude to Lars Lindahl for an extensive discussion of the present paper.
2. Cf. A. Peczenik, Causes and Damages, Lund 1979, pp. 10–13; J. Hellner, Skadeståndsrätt, 2 ed., Stockholm 1976, pp. 13–26.
3. Cf. Peczenik, e.g., Legal Data, in: A. Peczenik, L. Lindahl and B. van Roermund, Theory of Legal Science, Dordrecht–Boston–Lancaster 1984, pp. 114–115; Creativity and Transformations in Legal Reasoning, in: W. Krawietz, H. Schelsky, G. Winkler and A. Schramm, Theorie der Normen. Festgabe für Ota Weinberger zum 65. Geburtstag, pp. 277–298; The Basis of Legal Justification, Lund 1983, pp. 3–4 and 70–76.
4. Cf. Peczenik, Causes ... (n. 2 supra) pp. 153–205 with extensive references.
5. Ruemelin would perhaps admit that the decision would be unjust but he would answer to the objection by pointing out that A's action did not relevantly increase the probability for B's death in a traffic accident. He would thus use another description of the type T of the injury: "death in a traffic accident," instead of "death".
6. Cf. Peczenik, Why Should Legal Value Statements Be Rational?, a plenary report at the Conference on Reason in Law, Bologna, December 12–15, 1984. The Proceedings are to be published in 1987 or 1988. Similar views were presented by H. Spector, at a conference in Buenos Aires in August 1984.
7. Cf. Hellner (n. 2 supra), pp. 147–156.

[18]

TWO TYPES OF SUBSTANTIVE REASONS: THE CORE OF A THEORY OF COMMON-LAW JUSTIFICATION*

Robert S. Summers†

It is on the question of what shall amount to a justification, and more especially on the *nature of the considerations* which really determine or ought to determine the answer to that question, that judicial reasoning seems . . . often to be inadequate.

—*O. W. Holmes, Jr.*[1]

---

* Copyright © 1978, Robert S. Summers.

† McRoberts Professor of Research in Administration of Law, Cornell Law School. B.S. 1955, University of Oregon; LL.B. 1959, Harvard University.

This Article consists of modified (and tentative) versions of several chapters of a book in progress. While working on this subject, I profited from discussions with judges in seminars I conducted for members of the Washington appellate judiciary at Olympia, Washington, on April 19-20, 1977; for members of the Tennessee judiciary at Nashville on October 14-15, 1977; for New England judges at Durham, New Hampshire, on January 14-15, 1978; and for judges participating in the A.B.A. Appellate Judge's Seminar at Tucson, Arizona, on March 23, 1978.

I also benefited from discussions of the thesis of the Article while teaching at a Law for Economists Institute sponsored by the University of Miami on June 21-25, 1977.

I am indebted as well to colleagues of the Cornell law faculty who participated in a Faculty Research Seminar on this subject on September 11, 1977. I have also lectured on the subject of this Article at a number of institutions: University of Sydney, Australia National University, Monash University, MacQuarie University, University of Queensland, all in Australia; University of Auckland in New Zealand; University of Hamburg, West Germany; University of Leuven, Belgium; and the University of Tennessee, Mansfield College, and Cornell University in the United States. In each instance I profited from discussions that followed.

I am most grateful to Professor David Lyons for numerous discussions and extensive commentary. Other members of the Cornell philosophy department who kindly discussed

TABLE OF CONTENTS

INTRODUCTION 709
I. THE VARIETY OF GOOD REASONS 714
   A. Substantive Reasons 716
   B. Authority Reasons 724
   C. Factual Reasons 725
   D. Interpretational Reasons 726
   E. Critical Reasons 726
II. THE COMPLEXITY OF JUSTIFICATORY STRUCTURES ... 727
III. THE PRIMACY OF SUBSTANTIVE REASONS 730
   A. Substantive Reasons and the Intelligibility and Scope of Precedent 730
   B. Substantive Reasons and the Paucity or Plethora of Precedent 732
   C. Substantive Reasons and the Failure of Precedent: Original Error and Obsolescence 733
IV. CONSTRUCTION, EVALUATION, AND LEGITIMACY OF GOAL REASONS 735
   A. Construction 735
   B. Evaluation 743
   C. The Bearing of Institutional Reasons 749
   D. The Legitimacy of Goal Reasons 751

---

the subject of the Article with me are Richard Boyd, Carl Ginet, Richard Miller, Robert Stalnaker, and Nicholas Sturgeon.

Others to whom I am indebted for written or other extended reactions at various stages over the past three years are Professors Christopher Arnold, Patrick Atiyah, Stanley Benn, Jan Broekman, David Cass, Roger Cramton, Ronald Dworkin, Torstein Eckhoff, Michael Fisher, George Fletcher, Alan Fogg, Oscar Garibaldi, Kent Greenawalt, Peter Hacker, George Hay, Les Holborow, Ian Macneil, Geoffrey Marshall, Thomas Morgan, Kenneth Pinegar, Samuel Stojar, Brian Tierney, William Twining, and Robin Williams.

In addition, I wish to acknowledge indebtedness to the students in my course at Cornell Law School on Jurisprudence and the Legal Process for the years 1976 and 1977. The theory I offer here is the better for discussions I had with those students.

I am indebted to Mr. Leigh Kelley, a second-year Cornell law student, for valuable aid in the final stages of this Article, and to Mr. Kenneth A. Thomas, J.D. 1978, Cornell University, for valuable research assistance.

Finally, I wish to record my appreciation to Mr. Dan Coenen, Editor-in-Chief, and Mr. Stuart Altschuler, Managing Editor, of the *Cornell Law Review*, for numerous helpful editorial and substantive suggestions.

[1] Vegelahn v. Guntner, 167 Mass. 92, 105-06, 44 N.E. 1077, 1080 (1896) (dissenting opinion) (emphasis added). Holmes displayed extraordinary methodological self-consciousness in justificatory matters.

V. CONSTRUCTION, EVALUATION, AND LEGITIMACY OF
   RIGHTNESS REASONS 752
   A. Construction 752
   B. Evaluation 759
   C. The Bearing of Institutional Reasons 764
   D. The Legitimacy of Rightness Reasons 765
   E. The Need for Rightness Reasons 772
VI. DIFFERENCES BETWEEN GOAL REASONS AND RIGHTNESS
   REASONS 774
   A. Inherent Differences 774
   B. Contingent Differences 776
VII. REDUCIBILITY OF RIGHTNESS REASONS TO GOAL REASONS 778
   A. Reducibility of Rightness Reasons to "Parasitic" Goal Reasons 779
   B. Reducibility of Rightness Reasons to Independent Goal Reasons 780
   C. Differences Again 782
VIII. SIGNIFICANCE OF THE DUALITY OF SUBSTANTIVE REASONS 782
CONCLUSION 786

INTRODUCTION

Reasons are the tools of judging, for with reasons judges resolve issues and justify decisions. My topic will be reasons in common-law cases. Although I will address appellate judges, this Article should also interest theorists of judging, and of justification in general. And if of value to judges, practitioners should find it useful, too. While I will focus on the common law (including equity), I believe my central theses have wider bearing.

Appellate judges strive not only to reach the best decisions in common-law cases, but also to justify them in written opinions. Good reasons necessarily figure in justified decisions. They ordinarily figure in processes of arriving at the best decisions, too, for judges usually consider reasons supporting each alternative before reaching a decision.

But, at least in nonroutine cases, judges do not invariably reach the best decision. And even when they do, the reasons they give are not infrequently wanting.[2] When judges appeal to precedent—

---

[2] A familiar point. *See, e.g.*, Pound, *The Theory of Judicial Decision* (pt. 3), 36 HARV. L.

give "authority reasons"—the cited cases may be distinguishable or otherwise without rational bearing. When judges appeal to moral, economic, political, institutional, or other social considerations—give "substantive reasons"—these may be question-begging, insufficiently strong, or otherwise inadequate.[3]

Of course, society cannot expect perfection from mortals. Constructing reasons is not easy. Moreover, a judge often encounters special difficulties. He might have to hurry, and counsel might provide little help. But a judge might also lack the capacity to identify and deploy good authority reasons. Likewise, he might not be well equipped to give good substantive reasons.[4]

Even if a judge is good at giving substantive reasons, he might be uneasy about resorting to them. Solicitous of stare decisis, he might feel that only authority reasons are legitimate. Or he might think that to give substantive reasons is to "legislate" (retroactively at that) and thus to encroach on other agencies of government. In addition, he might believe that such reasons call for personal and subjective value judgments and are therefore inherently suspect. Yet, as I will show, a judge in our system must give substantive reasons and must make law. Indeed, the most important attributes of a judge are his value system and his capacity for evaluative judgment. Only through the mediating phenomena of reasons, especially substantive reasons, can a judge articulately bring his values to bear.[5]

REV. 940, 951 (1923). *See generally* Leflar, *Some Observations Concerning Judicial Opinions*, 61 COLUM. L. REV. 810 (1961).

[3] This is not intended as a formal definition of the phrase "substantive reasons." Rather, it is meant to reflect generally and informally an important distinction between authority reasons and substantive reasons. Although a more precise definition could be formulated, there is no need to do so here. Judges already have a working familiarity with the notion of a substantive reason as distinguished from a reason based on prior legal authority.

[4] There may be various explanations for this. For example, judging is, as I will show, complex in its own ways, and when lawyers ascend to the bench they receive almost no formal instruction in these complexities. Most educational programs for new judges focus on administrative and related matters and on recent developments in specific fields of substantive or procedural law.

[5] For a different formulation, consider these remarks:

Much of law is designed to avoid the necessity for the judge to reach what Holmes called his "can't helps," his ultimate convictions or values. The force of precedent, the close applicability of statute law, the separation of powers, legal presumptions, statutes of limitations, rules of pleading and evidence, and above all the pragmatic assessments of fact that point to one result whichever ultimate values be assumed, all enable the judge in most cases to stop short of a resort to his personal standards. When these prove unavailing, as is more likely in the case of

In my view, a comprehensive and integrated theory of justification should be highly valuable to judges, if adequate to the complexities and presented in teachable form. In this, the theorists of judging have let the judges down. It is true that there are writings on authority reasons—on precedent—a subject that necessarily figures in any theory of common-law justification.[6] There are also essays on whether courts can and should make law.[7] But, until late, theorists have done little work on substantive reasons—on their varieties, their internal complexities, the differences among them, and the significance of these differences.[8] There are virtually no writings on the capacities required to identify, construct, and evaluate substantive reasons. Essays on the general nature and ends of common-law justification are also rare. And we have no unifying theories purporting to tie all these aspects of reasons and reason-giving together.[9]

---

courts of last resort at the frontiers of the law, and most likely in a supreme constitutional court, the judge necessarily resorts to his own scheme of values. It may therefore be said that the most important thing about a judge is his philosophy; and if it be dangerous for him to have one, it is at all events less dangerous than the self-deception of having none.

Freund, *Social Justice and the Law*, in SOCIAL JUSTICE 93, 110 (R. Brandt ed. 1962).

[6] *See, e.g.*, R. CROSS, PRECEDENT IN ENGLISH LAW (1961); R. WASSERSTROM, THE JUDICIAL DECISION chs. 3-4 (1961); APPELLATE JUDICIAL OPINIONS ch. 2 (R. Leflar ed. 1974); Schaefer, *Precedent and Policy*, 34 U. CHI. L. REV. 3 (1966); Sprecher, *The Development of the Doctrine of Stare Decisis and the Extent to Which It Should Be Applied*, 31 A.B.A. J. 501 (1945).

[7] On the creative roles of judges in common-law cases, see generally R. KEETON, VENTURING TO DO JUSTICE (1969); K. LLEWELLYN, THE COMMON LAW TRADITION (1960).

[8] Perhaps the most significant recent work has been done by Dworkin, Eckhoff, Greenawalt, Hughes, and Wellington. For some of their writings, see note 27 *infra*. Wellington's effort, for example, is illuminating. Nevertheless, he does not discern that the values underlying what I call "goal reasons" may be noninstrumental. Nor does he consider the internal complexity of substantive reasons. Consequently, he misses some of the important differences between various reason types. Yet, in these respects, he is not alone.

[9] The work of the late Roscoe Pound is an exception. Pound saw the importance of general justificatory theory, and offered judges a "theory of interests" (drawn mainly from German thinkers). For a summary of his theory, see 3 R. POUND, JURISPRUDENCE chs. 14-15 (1959). In my view, Pound's theory is fundamentally misconceived; it gives controlling importance to the concept of an interest, whereas any justificatory theory must focus on the concept of a good reason. Furthermore, Pound's fundamental "decision rule"—namely, that judges should reach the decision, among the alternatives, that secures the most interests with the least friction—is deficient in at least three ways: (1) it is vacuous and hence indeterminate; (2) judges cannot possibly know enough to apply it; and (3) it incorporates a minimal theory of the good.

Pound also stressed that judges should evaluate alternative decisions in terms of their likely social effects. He thus neglected an important subset of substantive reasons—those having to do not with predicted decisional effects, but with how the case *came about*. Yet many common-law decisions are based mainly, and properly, on such reasons, which I will call "rightness reasons."

A legal periodical can provide neither space nor format for presentation of a full-scale theory of common-law justification. Here my focus must be far narrower. I will concentrate on only one facet of the theory I have underway, namely, substantive reasons.[10] As I will show, this facet must constitute the core of any comprehensive theory.[11] Yet I cannot even treat all of it here. And, because of the complexity and novelty of the topic,[12] some of my treatment will have to be schematic and tentative at that. Nonetheless, I believe that my theory of substantive reasons is sufficiently developed to invite useful criticism—it has sufficient "body" that proposed modifications need not appear arbitrary, and their consistency with the theory can be more or less readily determined. Also, the theory is now sufficiently detailed to be tested against the realities of common-law justification.[13]

Although relatively new, the theory of substantive reasons I will offer is not a personal contrivance, let alone some utopian ideal. While my effort is not exclusively descriptive, it is in large measure so. Thus, I open with a general survey of the varieties of good reasons and of the complexities of justificatory structures actually found in common-law opinions. Judges at their best actu-

---

The general lack of "reasons theory," apart from Pound's work and that of a few others, may be one of the unhappy influences of legal realism. Indeed, in their more extreme moments, some realists suggested that giving justified answers to legal issues is simply impossible. Professor Dworkin's insistence that there is almost always one right answer might be interpreted in part as a salutary overreaction to realist extremism. *See* Dworkin, *No Right Answer?*, in LAW, MORALITY, AND SOCIETY 58 (P. Hacker & J. Raz eds. 1977). For two quite different critiques of Dworkin, see Greenawalt, *Policy, Rights, and Judicial Decision*, 11 GA. L. REV. 991 (1977); Soper, *Metaphors and Models of Law: The Judge as Priest*, 75 MICH. L. REV. 1196 (1977).

[10] I will not treat here the following other facets of the theory I am developing:

(1) the nature and ends of common-law justification;

(2) the nature of the concept of "justificatory force," and how it differs from mere persuasiveness on the one hand, and logical validity on the other;

(3) the theory of precedent and its rationales, and how reasons of substance are transmuted into legal doctrine;

(4) the nature and scope of institutional reasons, including those arising from the relations among courts, legislatures, administrative agencies, and private parties as creators and appliers of law; and

(5) a decision procedure for choosing between conflicting sets of reasons, substantive and otherwise.

[11] See Part III *infra* on the primacy of substantive reasons.

[12] *See generally* Bodenheimer, *A Neglected Theory of Legal Reasoning*, 21 J. LEGAL EDUC. 373 (1969). This type of theory has not been so neglected on the continent. See, for example, C. PERELMAN, THE IDEA OF JUSTICE AND THE PROBLEM OF ARGUMENT (1963); T. VIEHWEG, TOPIK UND JURISPRUDENZ (1963).

[13] To clothe the theory it has been necessary to devise some special terminology. I have kept this to a minimum, however, and have not invented any new words.

ally work with implicit models of good substantive reasons. Many judges will, if the matter is put to them, agree on what the general features of these models are, and on the extent to which particular reasons conform to them.[14] It does not follow, however, that judges are generally self-conscious about their formulation and deployment of reasons. Of course, it is possible for a judge who is not self-conscious to give good substantive reasons. Just as an inhabitant of a city may regularly find his way about without being able to draw an adequate map of it, a judge may be generally good at giving substantive reasons without being able to describe precisely "what is going on."

It falls to the theorists and other students of judging to discover and articulate the relevant structures and models. Much of my Article will therefore be an exercise in what philosophers sometimes call "rational reconstruction."[15] I will, particularly in Parts IV and V, strive to formulate important aspects of what must be going on (justificatorily, not psychologically)[16] when judges successfully identify, construct, and evaluate substantive reasons.

To the extent my analysis is right, the theory of substantive reasons I offer here should beget better decisions and better justifications. Precisely how, and why, I will explain en route. The importance of reaching the best judicial decisions cannot be gainsaid. When a judge fails to reach the best decision, he may sacrifice justice, liberty, security, or any of a host of other significant values.

It is also important that a judge construct the best justifications. Ideally, he should construct the justification available for each alternative decision, compare these, and then choose the decision supported by the best justification. A judge who goes through this process will more likely reach the best decision.

Even when sure he is arriving at the best decision, a judge may usefully expend additional effort constructing and deploying reasons. In so doing, he may guide other judges to better decisions in future cases. And he may serve still other ends, too. He may

---

[14] I base this statement on extensive discussion with a number of judges over the course of several years.

[15] *See* Strawson, *Construction and Analysis*, in THE REVOLUTION IN PHILOSOPHY 97 (1957).

[16] For a brilliant discussion of the distinction between justification and possible accompanying psychological processes, see R. WASSERSTROM, *supra* note 6, ch. 2. Professor Wasserstrom explains how the failure to draw this distinction has badly flawed much of the literature on judicial reasoning. It may be added that the literature is deficient in other ways, too. Theorists have imported irrelevant models from formal logic, and, most important, have failed to consider a wide range of actual examples of judicial reasoning.

render the result more acceptable to the parties, thereby reducing the need for coercive enforcement (with attendant friction, waste, and loss of liberty); and he may render the resulting state of the law (1) more "law-like" and therefore consistent with "rule of law" values (including predictability), (2) more respectworthy and consequently capable of motivating higher levels of conformity generally, and (3) more readily appraisable and thus susceptible of rational revision as conditions and values change.[17]

I turn now to my theory of substantive reasons. In Part I, I will identify substantive reasons as one of several types of reasons that judges give in common-law cases. I will, in Part II, summarize the complexities of common-law justification in which substantive reasons figure. That such reasons are the most important type in the common law will be the thesis of Part III. In Parts IV and V, I will treat the construction and evaluation of the two main types of substantive reasons—what I call "goal reasons" and "rightness reasons." In Parts VI and VII, I will identify the differences between these two types of reasons and consider whether rightness reasons are inevitably reducible to goal reasons. In Part VIII, I will explain the importance of this duality of substantive reasons.

The Article as a whole outlines the core of my general theory of common-law justification. I believe that if the theory is right, it will be of significant value to judges in common-law cases. With an increased consciousness of the nature and role of substantive reasons, and with an enhanced capacity to construct and evaluate such reasons, judges should give better reasons for what they do. Better reasons should in turn beget better results and better law.

I

The Variety of Good Reasons

Common-law justification is varied and complex. Here and in Part II, I will provide an overview of the justificatory landscape. It is important to locate substantive reasons within this broader picture before focusing on their construction and evaluation. Judges who acquire a commanding view of this terrain, and of the place of

---

[17] The preceding two paragraphs do not purport to be an exhaustive specification of the ends of common-law justification, a separate topic beyond the scope of this Article. I believe that the adequacy of any particular justification cannot be determined without reference to such ends. For a different view, see T. Perry, Moral Reasoning and Truth ch. 4 (1976).

substantive reasons within it, will be better equipped to do their work.

A typology of potentially relevant reasons can help a judge in several ways. He might miss a relevant reason altogether, a less likely occurrence if he keeps an exhaustive typology of reasons in mind. In particular, it is not uncommon for judges to miss substantive reasons.[18] Missed substantive reasons frequently account for the criticism: "Right result, wrong reason."[19] Moreover, an overlooked reason might prove decisive, at least when opposing reasons are evenly balanced. Even if not determinative, the reason might strengthen the justification and provide valuable guidance in future cases. Of course, when a judge does reach the right result solely for a wrong reason, his failure to give the right reasons leaves the decision entirely without stated justification.

A judge sometimes fails to disentangle different reasons—even reasons of different types. He might run them together as if they were one.[20] Again, a judge will be less likely to make this error if he keeps a typology of good reasons in mind. Running reasons together usually makes their exact nature more difficult to grasp. This analytic confusion may obscure the force (or lack of force) of reasons and even lead judges to apply inapposite standards of evaluation.[21] It may also lead to misapplication of precedent in later cases.

A judge mindful of the typology will be more fully aware of the differences and relations between substantive reasons and authority reasons, and should thus become better at deploying authority reasons. Authority reasons can easily be misformulated and mistakenly brought to bear. It is therefore all the more important that judges take care when resorting to them. In particular, a judge

---

[18] *See, e.g.*, Boomer v. Atlantic Cement Co., 26 N.Y.2d 219, 257 N.E.2d 870, 309 N.Y.S.2d 312 (1970) (although it notes in footnote that defendant's plant employs over 300 people, court fails to articulate this as goal reason supporting denial of injunction that would shut down plant and reduce local employment).

[19] *See, e.g.*, Escola v. Coca Cola Bottling Co., 24 Cal. 2d 453, 461, 150 P.2d 436, 440 (1944) (concurring opinion, Traynor, J.) (in products liability case, majority's decision should have rested not on manufacturer's negligence, but on policies favoring absolute liability).

[20] *See, e.g.*, Groves v. John Wunder Co., 205 Minn. 163, 168, 286 N.W. 235, 237 (1939) (judge fails to set forth distinctly a rightness reason—*i.e.*, decision for defendant would favor contractual bad faith—and a goal reason—*i.e.*, decision for defendant would undermine ability to plan for future).

[21] *See, e.g.*, McConnell v. Commonwealth Pictures Corp., 7 N.Y.2d 465, 475, 166 N.E.2d 494, 500, 199 N.Y.S.2d 483, 490-91 (1960) (in attacking majority's rightness reason for denying recovery (plaintiff committed bribery in performing contract) dissenter resorts to goal reason (denial of recovery will encourage breaches of contract)).

should not invoke an authority reason without identifying and interpreting the substantive reasons "behind" the precedent or rationally attributable to it.[22]

Most judges are mindful that reasons of different types figure in their opinions. For example, a judge might claim that "reason and authority"[23] support his decision or remark that "both utility and justice" require a result.[24] But such cryptic remarks, however suggestive, cannot serve as a typology.

In my view, the typology that follows includes all basic types of good reasons found in common-law cases. Of course, not all that judges say to support their decisions can qualify as reasons. Thus, question-begging "reasons" and emotive appeals do not appear in the typology. It includes only genuine reason types: "substantive reasons," "authority reasons," "factual reasons," "interpretational reasons," and "critical reasons."

A. *Substantive Reasons*

A good substantive reason is a reason that derives its justificatory force[25] from a moral, economic, political, institutional, or other social consideration.[26] There are three main types of substantive reasons: goal reasons, rightness reasons, and institutional reasons.[27]

---

[22] *See* notes 78-84 and accompanying text *infra*.

[23] *See, e.g.*, Garrison v. Warner Bros. Pictures, Inc., 226 F.2d 354, 355 (9th Cir. 1955) (defendant's contention "not supported by any authority or reason"); Mier v. Hadden, 148 Mich. 488, 495, 111 N.W. 1040, 1043 (1907) (concurring opinion) (majority's holding supported by "reason and precedent").

[24] *See, e.g.*, Bowles v. Mahoney, 202 F.2d 320, 327 (D.C. Cir. 1952) (dissenting opinion, Bazelon, J.) ("the rule operates to defeat the interests of utility and justice").

[25] The concept of justificatory force, as I use it here, is roughly equivalent to the "essential strength of a reason." The degree of a reason's justificatory force is the reason's most important attribute. In forthcoming work, I will offer an extended analysis of this concept. Among other things, I will argue that the relevant metaphor is not "following" but "supporting." In other words, justificatory force arises not from a deductively valid derivation, but from a reason's supporting relationship to a decision.

[26] The rational bearing of such a consideration does not depend on its recognition in a precedent or other legal authority. Indeed, I contend that for almost any noninstitutional substantive reason given by a court, it is possible to identify a counterpart reason (with almost identical elements) likely to be given in parallel circumstances in daily life.

[27] Others have sought to articulate differences between types of substantive reasons, although no one, so far as I know, has differentiated them in the fashion I do here. For some of these efforts and resulting criticisms, see T. ECKHOFF, JUSTICE 19-25 (1974); E. FREUND, STANDARDS OF AMERICAN LEGISLATION ch. 2 (1917); Dickinson, *The Law Behind Law* (pts. 1 & 2), 29 COLUM. L. REV. 113, 285 (1929); Dworkin, *Seven Critics*, 11 GA. L. REV. 1201 (1977); Dworkin, *Hard Cases*, 88 HARV. L. REV. 1057 (1975); Dworkin, *Judicial Discre-*

1. *Goal Reasons*

A goal reason derives its force from the fact that, at the time it is given, the decision it supports can be predicted to have effects that serve a good social goal. The goal may or may not have been previously recognized in the law. Below are some examples of goal reasons drawn from actual cases:[28]

(a) *"General safety"*: Because the defendant railroad is financially hard-pressed and *will* improve general safety with the money it saves from not having to perform its contract with the plaintiff, the plaintiff will be denied specific performance.[29]

(b) *"Community welfare"*: Because judicial refusal to recognize the defense of retaliatory eviction *will* make it difficult to maintain decent housing standards, this defense will be recognized.[30]

(c) *"Facilitation of democracy"*: Because the flow of information about candidates for public office *will* facilitate democracy, a newspaper that publishes falsehoods may not be held liable unless the newspaper acted in bad faith.[31]

(d) *"Public health"*: Because a utility's gas reservoir *will* adversely affect the health of people living near it, the utility may be ordered to relocate it.[32]

(e) *"Promotion of family harmony"*: Because allowing this kind of intrafamily lawsuit *will* disrupt family harmony generally, the suit will not be allowed.[33]

All goal reasons are future-regarding. They derive their force from predicted decisional effects that purportedly serve social goals

---

tion, 60 J. PHIL. 624 (1963); Dworkin, *The Model of Rules*, 35 U. CHI. L. REV. 14 (1967), *reprinted in* ESSAYS IN LEGAL PHILOSOPHY 25 (R. Summers ed. 1968); Greenawalt, *Discretion and Judicial Decision: The Elusive Quest for the Fetters That Bind Judges*, 75 COLUM. L. REV. 359 (1975); Greenawalt, *supra* note 9; Hughes, *Rules, Policy and Decision Making*, 77 YALE L.J. 411 (1968); Lefroy, *The Basis of Case-Law* (pts. 1 & 2), 22 L.Q. REV. 293, 416 (1906); Linde, *Judges, Critics, and the Realist Tradition*, 82 YALE L.J. 227 (1972); Wellington, *Common Law Rules and Constitutional Double Standards: Some Notes on Adjudication*, 83 YALE L.J. 221 (1973); Winfield, *Ethics in English Case Law*, 45 HARV. L. REV. 112 (1931); Winfield, *Public Policy in the English Common Law*, 42 HARV. L. REV. 76 (1928). It is interesting to note that nearly all of the earlier writers cited here have had little or no influence on their successors.

[28] Professor Dworkin has suggested that courts do not "characteristically" give some of the reasons I call goal reasons. *See* Dworkin, *Hard Cases, supra* note 27, at 1060. The case law, however, does not seem to bear him out.

[29] Seaboard Air Line Ry. v. Atlanta, B. & C. R.R., 35 F.2d 609, 610 (5th Cir. 1929).

[30] Dickhut v. Norton, 45 Wis. 389, 397, 173 N.W.2d 297, 301 (1970).

[31] Coleman v. MacLennan, 78 Kan. 711, 741, 98 P. 281, 292 (1908).

[32] Romano v. Birmingham Ry., Light & Power Co., 182 Ala. 335, 340-41, 62 So. 677, 678-79 (1913).

[33] Campbell v. Gruttemeyer, 222 Tenn. 133, 137-40, 432 S.W.2d 894, 896-97 (1968).

in the future. While most goal reasons incorporate general welfare values (as in all of the above examples), some goal reasons are concerned with bringing about more rightness—with rightness values. The parol evidence rule, for example, rests on a goal reason rooted in such values. Consistent application of the rule, which bars the plaintiff from introducing parol evidence of alleged contract terms, supposedly induces more people to commit entire agreements to writing; this, in turn, minimizes the possibility that fraudulent oral "terms" will be enforced.[34] If this particular reason were a good one, it would qualify as a goal reason even though it concerns the achievement of more rightness.

Presently, I will identify a special class of reasons which I call "concomitant parasitic goal reasons"—goal reasons generated by decisions based on rightness reasons. But it is first necessary to introduce and exemplify the notion of a "rightness reason."

2. Rightness Reasons

A good rightness reason does not derive its justificatory force from predicted goal-serving effects of the decision it supports. Rather, a rightness reason draws its force from the way in which the decision accords with a sociomoral norm of rightness as applied to a party's actions or to a state of affairs resulting from those actions. The applicability of most such norms cannot be determined without reference to how the case *came about*. (Later, I will elaborate the differences between goal reasons and rightness reasons at length.[35])

Below are some examples of rightness reasons drawn from actual cases:

(a) *"Conscionability"*: Since the seller knowingly took advantage

---

[34] *See, e.g.*, Mitchill v. Lath, 247 N.Y. 377, 160 N.E. 646 (1928).

[35] *See* Part VII *infra*. Because some goal reasons are concerned with bringing about more rightness and so may incorporate concepts and norms of right action, the terms "goal reasons" and "rightness reasons" may mislead: they suggest that the former may never concern rightness. Nonetheless, I have used the term "rightness reasons" because such reasons *always* turn on the accordance of a decision with applicable norms of right action. What I call "goal reasons," on the other hand, *always* involve a prediction of future decisional effects. Thus, my terminology is appropriate in at least these important respects. Other pairs of terms I considered but discarded include "forward-looking" vs. "backward-looking," "consequentialist" vs. "nonconsequentialist," and "morality-regarding" vs. "welfare-regarding." These labels are less satisfactory than the terms employed here. Note that what I seek is descriptively felicitous terminology rather than abstractions such as "A-type" and "B-type" reasons. It is almost certain, however, that no single pair of ordinary terms will include and exclude with total accuracy.

of the buyer's illiteracy, ignorance, and limited bargaining capability, the price charged to the buyer must be reduced.[36]

(b) *"Punitive desert"*: Since the seller deliberately misrepresented the mileage on a used car (by turning the odometer back), the buyer may recover punitive damages.[37]

(c) *"Justified reliance"*: Since the builder reasonably relied on the owner's untrue representation of fact and thereby suffered a foreseeable loss, the owner must compensate the builder.[38]

(d) *"Restitution for unjust enrichment"*: Since the owner of a boat has been unjustly enriched by the plaintiff, who found the boat adrift and, at his own expense, took care of it for the owner, the owner must compensate the plaintiff.[39]

(e) *"Comparative blame"*: Since the plaintiff promoted a distinctively named theatrical act by deceitful means, an injunction will not be granted against another who deliberately used the act's name for gain.[40]

(f) *"Due care"*: Since the decedent was negligent, his estate may not recover for his injuries.[41]

(g) *"Relational duty"*: Since the parent brought the dependent child into the world, the parent has a duty to support it.[42]

(h) *"Fittingness or proportionality of remedy"*: Since an injunction would impose a grave burden on the polluting defendant, and the plaintiff would receive only a slight benefit in comparison, the injunction will be denied.[43]

It should be evident that rightness reasons play important roles in common-law justification. Consider, for example, the prominence of justified reliance in contract, blameworthiness in tort, unjust enrichment in the law of restitution, and interpersonal fairness in the various fields of equity.[44]

Among the variety of rightness reasons, two main types stand

---

[36] Frostifresh Corp. v. Reynoso, 52 Misc. 2d 26, 27-28, 274 N.Y.S.2d 757, 758-59 (Dist. Ct. 1966), *rev'd on other grounds*, 54 Misc. 2d 119, 281 N.Y.S.2d 964 (App. Term, 2d Dep't 1967).

[37] Boise Dodge, Inc. v. Clark, 92 Idaho 902, 907, 453 P.2d 551, 556 (1969).

[38] Mercanti v. Persson, 160 Conn. 468, 478, 280 A.2d 137, 142 (1971).

[39] Chase v. Corcoran, 106 Mass. 286, 288 (1871).

[40] Howard v. Lovett, 198 Mich. 710, 717, 165 N.W. 634, 636 (1917).

[41] Maki v. Frelk, 40 Ill. 2d 193, 195-96, 239 N.E.2d 445, 447 (1968).

[42] Commonwealth v. Ribikauskas, 68 Pa. D. & C. 336, 337-38 (Phil. Mun. Ct. 1949).

[43] Boomer v. Atlantic Cement Co., 26 N.Y.2d 219, 223, 257 N.E.2d 870, 871-72, 309 N.Y.S.2d 312, 315 (1970).

[44] For the nearest thing to a general discussion of the use of rightness reasons throughout the common law, see P. DEVLIN, THE ENFORCEMENT OF MORALS (1951).

out: "culpability" reasons and "mere fairness" reasons. The force of a culpability reason turns on the culpability of the past action of one of the parties to the case. Cases (a) and (b) above are illustrative. In those cases, the actions are culpable in light of relevant sociomoral norms of right action, and these norms require the culpable party to "make amends" for the loss or other adversity he has caused. A culpability reason might also serve to justify denial of a claim, as in cases (e) and (f).

The force of a "mere fairness" reason does not turn on the culpability of a party's past action—indeed, that action might be neutral or even meritorious. Rather, a reason of this kind depends for its force on the fairness or unfairness of leaving the resulting state of affairs between the parties "as is." Cases (c) and (d) are illustrative. According to sociomoral norms of right action (requiring compensation for justified reliance and for unjust enrichment, respectively), the resulting state of affairs between the parties in each case is unfair unless amends are made. Yet the action of each defendant might not be culpable.[45]

Case (g) illustrates another type of rightness reason—one that turns on the past occurrence of what may be characterized as a "relational" undertaking. Indeed, there is a further type of rightness reason—one that turns, as in case (h), on the fittingness or appropriate proportionality of remedy. There may be still other types, but "culpability" and "mere fairness" reasons are the most important, and there is no need to go into others here.

A judge may bring a sociomoral norm to bear through a rightness reason even though the norm has not yet found its way into a common-law decision. Today, many forms of culpability and unfairness are legally recognized, but it does not follow that basic sociomoral norms exist only by virtue of such legal recognition, or that judges have given all the rightness reasons they might give in the name of norms already recognized in the law.

All rightness reasons are either primarily past-regarding or primarily present-regarding. *Most* are primarily past-regarding; they derive their force from how the case *came about*. Cases (a) through (g) fall into this category. Case (h), on the other hand,

---

[45] Of course, under appropriate circumstances, a claim of justified reliance or unjust enrichment might also rest partly on a culpability reason. But culpability is not required for such a claim to find support in a "mere fairness" rightness reason. Note that in case (c) I am assuming that the falsity of the representation was not blameworthy.

illustrates a present-regarding rightness reason—contemporaneous equity or fairness in fashioning relief.[46]

I have said only that rightness reasons are *primarily* past-regarding or present-regarding. Actually, a rightness reason may bear on the future by generating a special type of goal reason in two ways. First, insofar as a decision based on a rightness reason is publicized beyond the immediate parties, it constitutes a symbolic, public affirmation of the relevant rightness norm and the values that norm reflects. This affirmation may have desirable socializing effects. Second, a decision based on a rightness reason constitutes a precedent; the decision may influence judges and other actors to decide or act in accordance with the relevant rightness norm in the future. The prediction that a decision will have either of these sorts of beneficial effects (symbolic-affirmational or precedential) generates a future-regarding reason that may be characterized as a "concomitant parasitic goal reason." In our system, this kind of goal reason is a potential concomitant of every rightness reason. The concomitant parasitic goal reason is not itself a rightness reason, although it envisions a resulting state of more rightness. Rather, it is a goal reason, for it contemplates a future state of affairs brought about through decisional effects. It is, nevertheless, only a *parasitic* goal reason—a reason that depends for its force on the antecedent force of the rightness reason on which the affirmation or precedent is based.

If a proposed rightness reason lacks all force, so will its concomitant goal reason. And if a rightness reason is weak, its concomitant goal reason will be weak as well. But a parasitic goal reason might also be weak because of factors unrelated to the rightness reason from which it draws force. In the particular case or realm of human activity, the affirmation or precedent might not make a real difference to future actors, especially actors other than judges. Few might learn of the case prior to acting. Those who learn of it might not understand its bearing. Others might have no incentive to follow it.[47]

---

[46] The force of a present-regarding fairness reason does not depend on how the case came about, but on what would be fair treatment of the parties now before the court. The administration of procedural rules affords many examples. That the judge should administer these rules evenhandedly is a present-regarding fairness reason.

[47] *See generally* J. GRAY, THE NATURE AND SOURCES OF THE LAW 100 (1909). Consider also Judge Jerome Frank's skepticism about the extent of actual reliance on precedent expressed in Aero Spark Plug Co. v. B.G. Corp., 130 F.2d 290, 297-98 (2d Cir. 1942) (concurring opinion).

Note that a concomitant parasitic goal reason is distinguishable from the type of goal reason that furthers rightness but which is independent of, rather than parasitic on, the antecedent force of any rightness reason. The parol evidence example given earlier is illustrative. There, a judge sacrificed rightness in the particular case, purportedly to further the social goal of bringing about more rightness (through the predicted effects of a decision adhering to the parol evidence rule).[48]

It is now possible to offer a tabular summary of the most significant varieties of substantive reasons:

SUBSTANTIVE REASONS

Goal Reasons	Rightness Reasons
(1) Nonrightness-regarding— *e.g.*, health, economic productivity, facilitation of democracy	(1) Culpability
	(2) Mere Fairness
	(3) Other
(2) Rightness-regarding (a) autonomous (*i.e.*, independent of any accompanying rightness reason) (b) concomitantly parasitic	

3. *Institutional Reasons*

An institutional reason is a goal reason or a rightness reason that is "tied" to a specific institutional role or process. It derives its force from the way in which the projected decision would serve goals or accord with norms of rightness applicable to the actions of participants (including officials) in institutional roles and processes. Below are some examples of institutional reasons drawn from actual cases:

(a) Because recognition of the plaintiff's novel claim would necessarily launch the court upon a voyage of arbitrary distinc-

---

[48] *See* text accompanying note 34 *supra*.

tion-drawing, and because courts, above all institutions, should only decide in accord with principle, the claim will be denied.[49]

(b) Because the plaintiff's claim requires a major change in the common law, a change that the legislature may wish to consider as part of a comprehensive reform of this entire field of the law, the court should abstain and leave the decision to the legislature.[50]

(c) Because the plaintiff's claim calls for a change in the law that cannot justifiably be made without access to "general social facts" that only a legislature can adequately investigate, the court ought not to make the change, but should leave it to the legislature.[51]

(d) Because the issue is now moot, the court should not decide it.[52]

(e) Because the trial judge did not give the claimant a full and fair hearing, the decision must be reversed.[53]

(f) Because it would be impossible to measure damages reliably in cases of this kind, the court ought not to recognize the proposed new cause of action.[54]

(g) Because a court could not supervise the decree, an injunction will be denied.[55]

Even this partial list amply illustrates the diversity of institutional reasons. The values they incorporate, although often hidden from view, are intrinsically no less significant than most values that figure in other substantive reasons. Institutional reasons relate to such important matters as the rational division of legal labor, the efficient workings of judicial machinery, the practicability of remedies, "process values" such as full and fair participation,[56] and even the limits of law's overall efficacy.

I have chosen to isolate institutional reasons as a separate type of substantive reason. As I will later explain, some institutional

---

[49] Tobin v. Grossman, 24 N.Y.2d 609, 618-19, 249 N.E.2d 419, 424, 301 N.Y.S.2d 554, 561 (1969).

[50] Johnson v. Oman Constr. Co., 519 S.W.2d 782, 786 (Tenn. 1975).

[51] O'Callaghan v. Waller & Beckwith Realty Co., 15 Ill. 2d 436, 440-41, 155 N.E.2d 545, 547 (1959).

[52] Excellent Laundry Co. v. Szekeres, 382 Pa. 23, 114 A.2d 176 (1955).

[53] Whitehead v. Mutual Life Ins. Co., 264 App. Div. 647, 37 N.Y.S.2d 261 (3d Dep't 1942).

[54] Zepeda v. Zepeda, 41 Ill. App. 2d 240, 260-62, 190 N.E.2d 849, 858-59 (1963).

[55] Edelen v. W.B. Samuels & Co., 126 Ky. 295, 307-09, 103 S.W. 360, 363-64 (1907).

[56] *See generally* Summers, *Evaluating and Improving Legal Processes—A Plea for "Process Values,"* 60 CORNELL L. REV. 1 (1974).

reasons figure intimately in the force of *noninstitutional* goal or rightness reasons. These reasons might therefore be incorporated into the analysis of noninstitutional reasons rather than classified separately as institutional. But, as I will explain, there are good reasons to classify them separately.

B. *Authority Reasons*

Common-law authority reasons consist primarily of appeals to precedent. In addition, judges sometimes appeal to statutes and regulations by analogy, and to restatements, treatises, and other "authorities."[57] But judges seldom resort to statutory analogy as a source of common law, and the "authority" of restatements and experts usually depends on the force of supporting reasons of substance. For purposes of this typology, it will be enough merely to indicate the major varieties of authority reasons that take the form of appeals to precedent.

First, judges sometimes appeal directly to a nondistinguishable precedent or "line of authority" that is binding on the court.[58] This kind of authority reason derives its justificatory force from two main sources: (1) the substantive reasons behind the precedent itself, and (2) the applicability of further substantive reasons that support the doctrine of precedent.

Second, a precedent might be in point but not binding because of the status or locale of the deciding court. Generally, such authority is cited solely for the intrinsic force of the substantive reasons behind it, or because of the extrinsic consideration of "uniformity."[59] Such reasons derive no force from the doctrine of *binding* precedent.

Third, judges sometimes justify decisions on the basis of analogy to or harmony with prior decisions. The precedent cited might, in light of the substantive reasons behind it, have force by analogy. Or, though not closely analogous, it might have force by virtue of its coherence and harmony with existing authority. For example, once a court has decided that acceptance of an offer by post is

---

[57] Judges sometimes even cite law review articles!

[58] Of course, theories and practices differ on what within a precedent is binding. *See generally* Bodenheimer, *supra* note 12, at 374; Simpson, *The Ratio Decidendi of a Case and the Doctrine of Binding Precedent*, in OXFORD ESSAYS IN JURISPRUDENCE 148 (A. Guest ed. 1961); Stone, *The Ratio of the Ratio Decidendi*, 22 MOD. L. REV. 597 (1959); Comment, *Diverse Views of What Constitutes the Principle of Law of a Case*, 36 U. COLO. L. REV. 377 (1964).

[59] For useful discussion of what one theorist calls "trend reasoning," see Bodenheimer, *supra* note 12, at 386-87.

effective on dispatch, it becomes more harmonious to hold that a revocation is effective only on receipt.[60]

A fourth and familiar type of authority reason consists of the formal elaboration of concepts already recognized by the common law. Without appealing to substantive reasons, a judge might argue that the internal logic or content of concepts requires a specific result. For example, he might argue in a given case that no contract could have arisen because one of the parties to the purported contract, a corporation, was not formed at the time the contract was allegedly entered into, and the existence of the relevant parties at the time of contracting is a requirement of our contract law.[61] Here the justificatory appeal is to an existing authoritative state of affairs (built up through precedent), namely, our concept of contract. Such an appeal might or might not ultimately be to binding precedent, and it might even be to precedent that is merely analogous.[62]

C. Factual Reasons

Factual reasons are reasons that support findings of fact. A judge in a common-law case may have to justify findings of either "adjudicative" or "legislative" fact.[63] When reviewing rulings on the admissibility of evidence or on motions for a directed verdict, for example, appellate judges pass on findings of adjudicative fact. The force of reasons that support such findings turns partly on whether sufficiently probative relations exist between evidentiary fact and ultimate fact.[64] Such reasoning is often far from "purely factual." It is also rationally influenced in complex ways by goals, norms of rightness, the law's limited machinery for ascertaining truth, and other factors.[65]

---

[60] Byrne & Co. v. Leon Van Tienhoven & Co., 5 C.P.D. 344, 348-49 (1880). *See generally* D. HODGSON, CONSEQUENCES OF UTILITARIANISM ch. 5 (1967).

[61] *See* Cramer v. Burnham, 107 Conn. 216, 219, 140 A. 477, 479 (1928) (absent ratification, contract with inchoate corporation unenforceable).

[62] Langdell may have given this kind of reasoning a bad name. *See, e.g.*, C. LANGDELL, A SUMMARY OF THE LAW OF CONTRACTS § 178 (2d ed. 1880). But not all such reasoning is unsound.

[63] On the distinction between legislative and adjudicative facts, see generally 2 K. DAVIS, ADMINISTRATIVE LAW TREATISE § 15.03 (1958); Davis, *An Approach to Problems of Evidence in the Administrative Process*, 55 HARV. L. REV. 364, 402-10 (1942); Hart & McNaughton, *Some Aspects of Evidence and Inference in the Law*, in EVIDENCE AND INFERENCE 48 (D. Lerner ed. 1958).

[64] For a classic treatment, see J. WIGMORE, THE PRINCIPLES OF JUDICIAL PROOF (1913).

[65] *See generally* R. SUMMERS, TEACHING MATERIALS ON JURISPRUDENCE AND THE LEGAL PROCESS ch. 25 (1977) (unpublished manuscript). The usual theory is that trial judges (and juries) engage in fact-finding while appellate judges engage in fact review. When reviewing

An appellate judge may also have to justify his own conclusions of "legislative" fact.[66] Both ordinary factual reasoning and substantive considerations may figure in this type of fact-finding, too.

D. Interpretational Reasons

In many common-law cases judges must justify one interpretation of the text of a private arrangement over alternative interpretations. Such texts include contract language, the language of corporate, partnership, and other articles of association, and the language of wills and trusts.

All of the main types of reasons so far considered—substantive, authority, and factual—may figure in interpretational reasons. But such reasons are in some ways distinctive, too.[67]

E. Critical Reasons

The various types of reasons so far listed—substantive, authority, factual, and interpretational—can all be characterized as autonomous reason types. "Critical reasons" are not of this character. Rather, a critical reason merely formulates a criticism of some element or aspect of a given autonomous reason. Critical reasons appear not only in dissents and concurring opinions, but in majority opinions as well. Examples of critical reasons (with references to their corresponding "targets") include:

(a) The proposed goal reason is unsound because it does not involve a good goal.

(b) This rightness reason is unsound because the defendant's action should not be characterized as right.

(c) This rightness reason is unsound because the underlying norm of rightness is unsound.

---

rulings on such issues as relevance and weight, appellate judges should bear in mind the extent to which such issues in the law are not purely factual, but are also to be resolved by reference to goal reasons and rightness reasons, and to purely institutional considerations such as the limited efficacy of the law's fact-finding apparatus.

[66] *Cf.* Doe v. Bolton, 410 U.S. 179, 208 (1973) (concurring opinion, Burger, C.J.) (though troubled by majority's notice of scientific data, concedes that Court did not exceed bounds of judicial notice).

[67] Distinguishing features of interpretational reasons include the importance accorded to the intention of the author of the text, and the role played by the language of the text in determining intention. For discussion of the distinctive importance of interpretational reasons, see generally Farnsworth, *"Meaning" in the Law of Contracts*, 76 YALE L. J. 939 (1967); Halbach, *Stare Decisis and Rules of Construction in Wills and Trusts*, 52 CALIF. L. REV. 921, 922 (1964).

A critical reason derives its character from the element of an autonomous reason to which it is addressed. Thus, to identify the types of critical reasons, it is necessary to isolate the various elements of autonomous reasons—a task I undertake in regard to substantive reasons in Parts V and VI.

II

The Complexity of Justificatory Structures

The structure of the justification in even a seemingly simple common-law case may be complex in several ways. Judges who understand this complexity will not be as likely to misinterpret or misapply precedent. They will also have a better grasp of available justificatory avenues.

Consider first the justificatory structure in the simplest possible case. To the extent that any law is applicable in this case, it is common law. There is only one issue—an issue of law. One reason "lines up" on each side of the issue. The two reasons are readily separable, and easily classified in terms of the foregoing typology. The reasons are of the same type and flatly contradict each other. The issue is resolvable, and the judge resolves it in all-or-nothing fashion. He does not seek to accommodate opposing reasons; one prevails and the other is sacrificed entirely. The prevailing reason bears immediately and directly upon the decision it supports, and since there is only one reason on each side of the issue, the judge need not consider the aggregate force of mutually supporting reasons.

But the usual case is more complex, and some cases are far more complex. Although there are "pure" common-law cases, many cases also involve statutes and other forms of authority that complicate their justificatory structure. Further, while there are "pure" issues of law, many issues are more complex; "mixed" questions of law and fact are illustrative.

Moreover, common-law cases often pose more than one significant issue. In many cases, the problem is not simply whether to affirm or reverse, but how to decide each of several issues in the course of deciding whether to affirm or reverse. And these issues will not always be wholly independent. For example, it is often assumed that so-called liability and remedial issues are completely unrelated. This is false. Some judges treat these issues as interdependent, and properly so. Thus, the drastic consequences of a remedy might rationally influence the court to decide for a defendant on the issue of liability.[68]

Several reasons—sometimes as many as a half-dozen significant ones—may line up on either side of each issue. Frequently, a single reason will not suffice to justify resolving the issue one way or another. Instead, the cumulative or aggregate force of several reasons will tip the balance toward a particular decision.[69]

When evaluating the bearing of a precedent, a judge often must determine the types of reasons that appear in the cited opinion. Sometimes it will be possible to construe the previous judge's formulation as either a goal reason or a rightness reason. Consider, for example, a case in which the judge dismissed the plaintiff's action because damages would impose a "crushing burden" on the defendant. Such a statement might be construed as a rightness reason—namely, that liability would impose an unfair or disproportionate burden on the defendant as judged in relation to his prior actions (or in relation to the benefit the plaintiff would realize). Alternatively, the reference to a "crushing burden" might be construed as a goal reason to the effect that courts should seek to preserve existing, ongoing economic units rather than throw them into bankruptcy. Sometimes a close look at the facts and the opinion will enable one to determine which type of reason the judge intended to employ. But, regardless of the judge's intent, *both* reasons may properly support the result.

Nor will reasons, whether mutually supporting or opposed, always be of the same type. Reasons of several varieties and subclasses will sometimes line up on each side of an issue or of several issues. In these circumstances, the judge must commensurate different reasons and aggregate the force of reasons of different types.

In addition, a conflict between reasons will not always take the form of straightforward opposition, in which one reason *counterbalances, overrides,* or *outweighs* another. The relation of reason "not-*A*" to reason "*A*" may instead be *cancellative*. For example, the defendant may have intentionally harmed the plaintiff (thus giving rise to a culpability-based rightness reason), but the plaintiff may have assented to the harm, thereby cancelling the entire force of

---

[68] *See generally* Keeton, *Rights of Disappointed Purchasers,* 32 TEX. L. REV. 1 (1953).
[69] For a general discussion of cumulative reasons, see Smith, *Cumulative Reasons and Legal Method,* 27 TEX. L. REV. 454 (1949).

the reason.[70] Or the relation of reason not-A to reason A may be *discountive*. That is, if reason not-A is a critical reason rather than an autonomous reason, it may reduce the force of reason A in some respect without cancelling it entirely. For example, the goal reason that giving priority to upstream water users "will more fully develop the region" might be criticized as resting on an improbable prediction.[71] This critical reason discounts the force of the relevant reason on the other side of the issue. The foregoing does not purport to be an exhaustive account of the possible relations between conflicting reasons, but it indicates the complexities that may arise, especially when relations between conflicting reasons vary.

Mutually supporting reasons, like conflicting reasons, give rise to complexities. The justificatory bearing of reasons may be intermediate and indirect. Thus, just as some reasons bear on a decision (the "chair") in the fashion of direct supports (the "legs"), other reasons may be one level removed and thus support the direct supports (the "platform" for the legs of the chair).[72]

The complex relationships among reasons often produce complicated results. For example, a judge might not resolve an issue or cluster of related issues in all-or-nothing terms. Instead, he might fashion a compromise in which reasons cutting one way show up in a *general doctrine*, while countervailing reasons shape *exceptions* or *provisos*.[73]

I have not sought to explore exhaustively the justificatory structures found in common-law cases.[74] I believe, however, that I have identified all but one of the principal forms of complexity—the *internal* complexities of substantive reasons. Before turning to these, and to the construction and evaluation of substantive reasons, I will argue for the justificatory primacy of such reasons.

---

[70] *See, e.g.*, Ford v. Ford, 143 Mass. 577, 10 N.E. 474 (1887).

[71] *See, e.g.*, Irwin v. Phillips, 5 Cal. 140 (1855). For a general criticism of goal reasoning as too speculative, see Aero Spark Plug Co. v. B.G. Corp., 130 F.2d 290, 295-96 (2d Cir. 1942) (concurring opinion, Frank, J.)

[72] *See, e.g.*, Gerhard v. Stephens, 68 Cal. 2d 804, 442 P.2d 692, 69 Cal. Rptr. 612 (1968).

[73] For a perceptive discussion of how reasons show up in and shape doctrinal formulations, see R. KEETON, *supra* note 7, at 65-69.

[74] The following cases are illustrative of substantial complexity in justificatory structures: Kline v. 1500 Mass. Ave. Apt. Corp., 439 F.2d 477 (D.C. Cir. 1970); Meeker v. City of East Orange, 77 N.J.L. 623, 74 A. 379 (1909); Shelley v. Shelley, 223 Or. 328, 354 P.2d 282 (1960).

III

THE PRIMACY OF SUBSTANTIVE REASONS

A specific theory of the nature and role of substantive reasons must form the core of a comprehensive theory of common-law justification. Substantive reasons, more than authority reasons, determine which decisions and justifications are best.

Why might a judge insist on or assume the primacy of authority reasons—or at least adhere to a method in which he merely matches facts and cites precedent? Today there are more than three million reported cases.[75] In almost every case that arises, one precedent will at least be relevant. Moreover, there are strong substantive rationales for following precedent. These include predictability, evenhandedness, efficiency, and the "rule of law" itself.[76] Further, the power of substantive reasons is not unlimited. There may be no strong substantive reasons on either side of an issue, or the substantive reasons on each side may stalemate each other. If so, only authority reasons can tip the balance. Nevertheless, the case for the decisional and justificatory primacy of authority reasons pales when compared with the parallel case for reasons of substance.[77]

A. Substantive Reasons and the Intelligibility and Scope of Precedent

A judge cannot apply a precedent wisely without determining which proposed application is most consistent with the substantive reasons behind the precedent.[78] This familiar fact, too frequently forgotten,[79] extends to both routine and difficult cases. Thus, to construct the usual authority reason, a judge must identify and interpret the determinative substantive reasons set forth in the pre-

---

[75] M. COHEN, LEGAL RESEARCH IN A NUTSHELL 64-65 (3d ed. 1978).

[76] For discussion of these rationales, see authorities cited in note 6 supra.

[77] Thus, the reader will find relatively little in this Article about "reasoning by analogy," an authority-oriented maneuver that has received far more attention in the literature than it merits.

[78] Courts are sometimes quite self-conscious about this approach to determining the scope of a precedent. See, e.g., Brown v. Merlo, 8 Cal. 3d 855, 506 P.2d 212, 106 Cal. Rptr. 388 (1973). For general discussion of the wisdom of this approach, see R. KEETON, supra note 7, at 64-69; W. TWINING & D. MIERS, HOW TO DO THINGS WITH RULES 113-18 (1976).

[79] The author of a useful student note persuasively contends that the draftsmen of the Uniform Commercial Code plainly intended its provisions to be applied in light of "their reasons," yet courts have repeatedly failed to do so. See Note, *How Appellate Judges Should Justify Decisions Made Under the U.C.C.*, 29 STAN. L. REV. 1245 (1977). Similarly, common-law cases abound in which judges have applied doctrine and precedent without regard to their underlying substantive reasons.

cedent. If no reasons are stated, the judge must go back to prior precedents in the line of authority and dig them out. If even this fails, he must imaginatively construct reasons that are faithful to the materials. The usual precedent ultimately consists of nothing less than facts, issues, rulings, and substantive reasons for those rulings. It is impossible to comprehend a precedent without grasping these elements. It is especially hazardous to try to analyze and interpret precedent without a sure grip on substantive reasons.[80] Of course, when judges simply lay down a rule, one can, within limits, understand its content. But this sort of understanding is significantly incomplete. Without an appreciation of the reasons for the rule, one will usually be unable to determine its justified scope.[81]

In one respect, then, the distinction between a substantive reason and the usual authority reason is misleading, for the usual authority reason cannot be launched without resort to its underlying substantive reasons. Once launched, authority reasons move under their own power, even though partly "made up of" substantive reasons.

I do not claim that the reasons originally given to support a precedent must always determine its scope. Such reasons might be weak or poorly stated. Our traditions, however, provide for this possibility by allowing judges (within limits) to "follow" precedents in light of new or different substantive reasons rationally imputable to those precedents.[82]

Substantive considerations delimit the range of authority reasons. Moreover, judges justifiably advert to the rationales that underlie the doctrine of precedent itself in deciding how far to extend a particular precedent.[83] Although these rationales govern authority reasons, they are substantive in nature, too.

---

[80] Limitations of space prohibit the extended discussion necessary to establish this truth. I will explore the question in forthcoming work.

[81] For a perceptive discussion of why the common law cannot be reduced merely to rules, see Simpson, *The Common Law and Legal Theory*, in OXFORD ESSAYS IN JURISPRUDENCE 77 (A. Simpson ed. 1973).

[82] For example, Chase v. Corcoran, 106 Mass. 286 (1871), was fictionally based on a contractual authority reason, but later came to be cited as a leading unjust enrichment case. In Gerhard v. Stephens, 68 Cal. 2d 864, 442 P.2d 692, 69 Cal. Rptr. 612 (1968), the court referred to the special nature of oil and gas deposits and associated drilling operations as a reason to follow the common-law view that perpetual *profits a prendre* are analogous to perpetual easements and, like easements, may be abandoned through nonuse.

[83] *See, e.g.*, Barnes v. Walker, 191 Tenn. 364, 234 S.W.2d 648 (1950). *See generally* Aero Spark Plug Co. v. B.G. Corp., 130 F.2d 290, 298 (2d Cir. 1942) (concurring opinion, Frank, J.).

An authority-minded judge fails to recognize the primacy of substantive reasons. He is therefore more likely to apply precedent mechanically, in light of the literal meaning of sentences or phrases, rather than in light of underlying substantive reasons.[84] As a result, he may miss relevant precedents, or may rely on precedents not in point.

In sum, judges cannot apply a precedent soundly or consistently if they do not resort to the substantive reasons behind it, and behind the doctrine of precedent itself.

B. *Substantive Reasons and the Paucity or Plethora of Precedent*

To note without more that there are more than three million precedents is to exaggerate the extent of viable case authority. Not all decisions are in common-law fields, and many common-law cases have little precedential value because they involve unique or rarely recurring issues. The precedential significance of other cases is diminished by procedural and similar factors.[85] Change, too, takes its toll on the stock of useful precedent. In short, the conditions for the rational application of precedent are satisfied less frequently than many suppose.

Even at this late date in the history of the common law, a significant number of cases of first impression arise every year.[86] Although they take many forms, cases of first impression by definition cannot be decided solely by reference to precedent. To decide such cases, judges must construct, evaluate, and choose between conflicting reasons of substance.[87]

Cases also arise in which precedents point in opposite directions.[88] Here, too, judges cannot rationally decide without compar-

---

[84] *See, e.g.*, Courteen Seed Co. v. Abraham, 129 Or. 427, 275 P. 684 (1929).

[85] For general discussion of factors that may weaken the force of a precedent, see R. CROSS, *supra* note 6, ch. 4; Aigler, *Law Reform by Rejection of Stare Decisis*, 5 ARIZ. L. REV. 155 (1964).

[86] Of course, whether a given case is truly a case of first impression will itself often be contested. At least one party will usually claim that there is a controlling precedent. For a sophisticated argument that there can be no genuine cases of first impression, see Dworkin, *supra* note 9.

[87] The "statutory" common law also generates cases of first impression. Legislatures sometimes block out areas or topics and leave it to the courts to evolve common law within the specified bounds. *See, e.g.*, U.C.C. § 2-302.

[88] Countless examples might be cited to illustrate conflicts of precedent, and these conflicts take a variety of forms. *See, e.g.*, Crenshaw v. Williams, 191 Ky. 559, 231 S.W. 45 (1921). Note also: "The foremost criticism heard today and early voiced by Kent is that the great mass of extant case law often makes it impossible or a task of considerable magnitude to discover precedents, and as often makes it possible to find precedents on both sides of a

ing substantive reasons supporting alternative results. (Of course, judges *could* decide such cases by reference to the comparative stature of the deciding courts, the ages of the precedents, or similar extrinsic factors.)

An authority-minded judge who rejects or remains oblivious to the primacy of substantive reasons will feel more comfortable with cases of conflicting precedent than with cases of first impression. In the former, he will at least have some "law" to apply, and often he will conveniently find that one of the two precedents can be distinguished away,[89] a course not open in a case of first impression.[90]

In cases of first impression, an authority-minded judge may confront a genuine crisis. For him, the law consists solely of authority, yet in such cases there is none. Rather than create a new precedent out of substantive reasons, as has been necessary since the beginning of the common law,[91] the authority-minded judge might rest his decision on precedent not truly controlling. Or he might bend or fictionalize relevant doctrine and thereby dim the lights for future judges.[92]

The vitality of a precedential system (to say nothing of the sound resolution of particular issues) requires that judges understand how important classes of cases arise in which precedents provide no answers, and why in those cases substantive reasons must control. Of course, courts should not proceed to a decision on the merits in all such cases. In some it will be appropriate to defer to the legislature.

C. *Substantive Reasons and the Failure of Predecent: Original Error and Obsolescence*

Although precedents may provide answers, those answers may be wrong. Ours purports to be not only a rule of law, but also a rule of just and good law. Tensions between these two ideals are inevitable.

---

given question." Sprecher, *supra* note 6, at 506 (footnotes omitted). *See also* Gilmore, *Legal Realism: Its Cause and Cure*, 70 YALE L.J. 1037 (1961).

[89] *See, e.g.*, White Showers, Inc. v. Fischer, 278 Mich. 32, 270 N.W. 205 (1936).

[90] I certainly do not mean to deny that there are many judges who feel a deep moral obligation to ground every decision in precedent. Although I do not think that this sweeping view is sound, I do not wish to cast doubt on the sincerity of the judges who hold it.

[91] *See* Lefroy, *supra* note 27.

[92] *See, e.g.*, Courteen Seed Co. v. Abraham, 129 Or. 427, 275 P. 684 (1929). Many examples of legal fictions are cited and discussed in Fuller, *Legal Fictions* (pts. 1-3), 25 ILL. L. REV. 363, 513, 865 (1930-1931).

Despite the long history of the common law, no one has discovered a way to prevent judges from making mistakes. Thus, at any given time there will be "originally" bad precedents. Further, given the inevitability of change, some precedents are certain to become outmoded. For similar reasons, cases will regularly arise in which judges must consider whether an exception to a precedent should be created, whether the precedent should be extended, or whether several precedents should be synthesized into a new body of doctrine.

Although a legal system might provide that only the legislature may revise precedent, that is not our system. Early on, judges undertook to overrule or otherwise revise case law.[93] The authority-minded judge who is unwilling to construct, evaluate, and choose between reasons of substance cannot perform this work. The rational revision of precedent must proceed in the name of improving the law, and this effort requires that judges give substantive reasons to justify their revisions.[94]

The authority-minded judge takes a more conservative attitude than our system calls for. He will often resist proposed changes when counsel or fellow judges argue that precedent should be overruled. In a fundamental sense, he *might not really understand* what bad or obsolete precedent is. A precedent can be bad or obsolete only in light of substantive reasons; yet an authority-minded judge might refuse to recognize such reasons, or fail to accord them sufficient weight. And even if willing to invoke reasons of substance, he might refuse to acknowledge their primacy. This, in turn, may keep him from seeing how the substantive reasons behind the challenged precedent might have originally lacked sufficient force, or how reasons initially strong might have lost their force through change.[95]

---

[93] For a perceptive study of recent judge-made changes in the common law, see R. KEETON, *supra* note 7.

[94] This is not to say, however, that a judge should never cite cases to help justify overruling a precedent.

[95] Technological change, growth in moral enlightenment, social and political developments, or other factors may explain why precedents become obsolete.

Judges have sometimes explicitly recognized the need to identify and revise erroneous or obsolete precedents. *See, e.g.*, Thurston v. Fritz, 91 Kan. 468, 138 P. 625 (1914):

"[W]ith the death of the reason for it every legal doctrine dies."

. . . .

. . . The fact that the reason for a given rule perished long ago is no just excuse for refusing now to declare the rule itself abrogated, but rather the greater justification for so declaring; and if no reason ever existed, that fact furnishes

It is one thing to grasp the primacy of substantive reasons in a healthy common-law system; it is another to comprehend their internal complexity, and to know how to construct and evaluate them systematically. In what follows, I will first take up goal reasons, then rightness reasons. I will explore their internal complexities and their construction and evaluation. Thereafter, I will consider the differences between the two types of reasons and explain the significance of these differences. My sequence of presentation reflects these simple considerations: To appreciate the significance of the differences, one must first understand the differences; and to understand these differences, one must grasp the essential nature of each reason type.

IV

CONSTRUCTION, EVALUATION, AND LEGITIMACY
OF GOAL REASONS

I define a goal reason as a reason that derives its force from the fact that, at the time it is given, the decision it supports can be predicted to have effects that serve a good social goal. Goal reasons constitute one of the main types of substantive reasons appearing in common-law opinions.

A. *Construction*

Goal reasons are internally complex, far more so than commonly supposed. Without reference to these internal complexities, judges cannot construct good goal reasons in a systematic and methodologically self-conscious fashion.[96]

There is evidence that judges need to improve their proficiency in constructing goal reasons. For example, a judge might vaguely sense the relevance of a goal reason, yet fail to formulate it *as a reason*.[97] Or he might run together a goal reason and another

---

additional justification.
Id. at 474-75, 138 P. at 627 (quoting Harrington v. Lowe, 73 Kan. 1, 21, 84 P. 570, 578 (1906)).

[96] Holmes, it will be recalled, stressed that judges must understand the "nature of the considerations" on which the adequacy of a justification depends. Vegelahn v. Guntner, 167 Mass. 92, 105-06, 44 N.E. 1077, 1080 (1896) (dissenting opinion), *quoted in* text accompanying note 1 *supra*.

[97] *See, e.g.*, Boomer v. Atlantic Cement Co., 26 N.Y.2d 219, 257 N.E.2d 870, 309 N.Y.S.2d 312 (1970) (although it notes in footnote that defendant's plant employs over 300 people, court fails to articulate this as goal reason supporting denial of injunction that would shut down plant and reduce local employment).

reason and thereby fail to set forth the two as *distinct* reasons.[98] He might mingle foreign elements in his formulation of the reason.[99] He might give a goal reason in which the posited means will fail to serve the relevant goal.[100] He might misstate a goal reason by couching it in unduly conclusory or question-begging terms.[101] Or he might give a goal reason in which the goal is simply undesirable.[102]

To construct a good goal reason a judge must take a number of steps to combine a variety of related internal elements. I will illustrate these elements and steps by using an actual case.[103] Assume that the plaintiff office-holder claims that the defendant newspaper libeled him during his campaign for reelection. At the

---

[98] *See, e.g.*, Hadley v. Baxendale, 156 Eng. Rep. 145 (Ex. 1854) (court fails to separate goal of facilitating contract planning from rationale of safeguarding defendants against liability greatly disproportionate in light of quid pro quo).

[99] *See, e.g.*, Cornpropst v. Sloan, 528 S.W.2d 188, 199 (Tenn. 1975) (dissenting opinion) (reference to irrelevant adverse effect—impact on inner cities—mingled with statement of reason in personal injury action).

[100] *See, e.g.*, Mitchill v. Lath, 247 N.Y. 377, 160 N.E. 646 (1928) (to further goal of preventing future fraud, court purports to adhere strictly to parol evidence rule although evidence overwhelmingly established extrinsic term and underlying means-goal hypothesis seems highly questionable).

It is odd that while jurisprudential literature abounds on the lawyer's prediction of judicial decisions, there is relatively little on the judge's prediction of the effects of his decisions.

[101] *See, e.g.*, Horsley v. Hrenchir, 146 Kan. 767, 73 P.2d 1010 (1937) (in denying plaintiff recovery, majority uses goal reason that allowing recovery would undermine security and certainty of title provided by written deeds; but, in concurring judge's view, majority fails to consider soundness or strength of reason's internal elements).

Note that the time and effort a judge spends in articulating a reason will often depend on the extent to which he believes that others take for granted the values implicit in the reason.

[102] Bad goals espoused by courts are often simply goals that courts have failed to specify in sufficiently narrow terms or with the necessary qualifications. For example, "promoting limited freedom of contract" is a good goal—its pursuit is rational as long as conflicting goals and rightness factors are properly taken into account. But "promoting *unlimited* freedom of contract" is a bad goal, since its pursuit would rule out the relevance of other goals and rightness considerations that may in fact be relevant. Many goals traditionally pursued by common-law courts, if described very broadly, would be universally condemned. We generally accept, for example, the goal of securing rights in private property; we reject, however, the goal of facilitating slavery, which many antebellum courts pursued under an overly broad, illegitimate definition of "property." A contemporary example of a bad general goal that some common-law courts have adopted is the goal of recognizing and facilitating unionization in public employment. *See, e.g.*, Chicago Div. of Ill. Educ. Ass'n v. Board of Educ., 76 Ill. App. 2d 456, 222 N.E.2d 243 (1966). For the arguments that this goal is, indeed, bad, see R. SUMMERS, COLLECTIVE BARGAINING AND PUBLIC BENEFIT CONFERRAL: A JURISPRUDENTIAL CRITIQUE (1976).

[103] Coleman v. MacLennan, 78 Kan. 711, 98 P. 281 (1908). I am not unmindful that there is post-1908 law on the issues posed in this case.

close of the trial, the evidence supported a finding that the defendant libeled the plaintiff, but only negligently, not recklessly or deliberately. The trial judge instructed the jurors that if they reached this finding, they should return a verdict for the defendant. The plaintiff duly excepted, the jury found for the defendant, and the plaintiff appeals. Assume that this is a case of first impression. The appellate court is now thinking about what substantive reasons support affirmance or reversal.

The following outline sets forth the steps (though not necessarily in prescribed sequence) that a methodologically self-conscious judge might take to construct a good goal reason bearing on this decision. At each step I will identify the relevant internal element of the reason.

(1) The judge must determine from the proceedings below and the general decisional context all facts relevant to the goal-serving potential of alternative decisions: Who did what to whom? With what results? Why? In what context? For example, was the defendant newspaper carrying news of political campaigns? Does it usually? Do newspapers generally?[104]

(2) The judge must then predict the effects that alternative decisions will have on the parties to the case, on at least those third parties within the zone of immediate effects, and on parties in similar situations in the future. For example, if courts impose liability on newspapers for merely negligent libel, what will be the added expense to newspapers of continuing their business? Will newspapers be able to pass on this added expense to readers and advertisers through increased prices? If not, will newspapers choose to provide less information about candidates? Will this, in turn, lead to a decrease in the number of voters going to the polls?

Alternatively, will a refusal to impose liability deter potential candidates from seeking office for fear of being negligently maligned?

Finally, what is the degree of likelihood of any of these predictions?

---

[104] Of course, in one sense, a judge cannot identify facts relevant to a particular goal without first identifying or positing that goal; otherwise, all facts would have to be considered relevant. Still, a judge can survey the facts and decisional context of a case to determine which alternative goals are at least in the ballpark—*i.e.*, which goals might conceivably be served or disserved by a particular decision in the case. In a sale-of-goods case, for example, one possibly relevant goal would be furthering certainty in commercial transactions. Furthering exploration of outer space, on the other hand, would probably not be relevant.

Note that rules imposing liability for negligent libel might apply in other jurisdictions, and that the resulting states of affairs might shed light on the foregoing questions.

(3) Next, the judge must characterize the resulting states of affairs predicted for each alternative. In the present example, is it appropriate to say that a decision leading to a decrease in voter participation (or leading to an increase in the number of political candidacies) diminishes or enhances "democracy"? What is the essential nature of democracy anyway? It is one thing to predict the "brute facts" of a state of affairs, and quite another to characterize that future state of affairs in appropriate conceptual (perhaps even evaluative) terms. Thus, predicting that a reduced flow of information about candidates will decrease voter turnout is not necessarily the same as concluding that democracy will be diminished.

(4) The judge must next determine whether any of the alternative predicted states of affairs either affect public interests or represent particular instances of such interests, and therefore qualify as *social* goals. As I will explain, merely personal goals of a party or of the judge that neither affect nor instantiate public interests cannot qualify as social goals. The interest must be fairly attributable to the relevant community as a whole or to a significant segment thereof.[105]

In giving a reason that serves a social goal, a judge may think of at least one of the parties to the case as a kind of "social agent" whose actions affect relevant public interests. For example, a newspaper's political coverage may affect public interests by informing citizens of the quality of candidates for public office, or by deterring good candidates from running for fear of being maligned.

In other cases, predicted states of affairs will merely constitute instances of public interests. While such decisions might have substantial impact on a party and perhaps on a few related persons as well (*e.g.*, his family, neighbors, or business associates), they might not otherwise have significant community effects. For example, protecting the personal health of several families in a neighborhood might count as an instance of a public interest, even though it will not significantly affect the community as a whole. Because the community *does* have an interest in the health of its members, however, it has an interest in the health of these individual families. Similarly, an individual's desire to engage in a particular business,

---

[105] I do not postulate a solidarity of interests; interests commonly conflict.

although likely to have limited impact on the community, still qualifies as an instance of a public interest; the community has an interest in allowing people to determine the course of their own lives and careers within the limits of social tolerance.

Certain types of merely personal ends, however, neither affect nor instantiate public interests. A judge's desire to be reelected, for example, cannot qualify as a valid reason for deciding a case one way or the other. Likewise, providing one business with an advantage over competitors usually cannot qualify as affecting or instantiating a public interest, although desired by a party to the case. Society has no interest in seeing a particular judge reelected, *especially* if he decides cases on the basis of his political ambitions. Nor does society ordinarily have an interest in merely giving one business a competitive advantage over others. These interests are merely personal. They cannot qualify as *social* interests and, therefore, cannot figure in goal-serving reasons.[106]

(5) If the predicted results of a decision affect or instantiate a public interest and thus qualify as *social*, further questions arise. Which of the effects, if any, are *generally good*? Which are *generally bad*? Only effects that serve a good social goal can qualify as generally good.[107] Thus, if imposing liability on newspapers for negligent libel will encourage more good candidates to run for office by reducing their fears of negligent malignment, the state of affairs resulting from a decision to impose liability might be independently appraised as good (on the ground that it facilitates democracy, a good thing). As such, the state of affairs qualifies as a good social goal, and may generate a "positive" goal reason—one favoring liability in our example.

---

[106] I am indebted to Mr. Leigh Kelley for assistance in the formulation of the distinction between social and nonsocial goals. This distinction is particularly elusive and I welcome suggestions. In fact, an alternative approach could be taken here: Eliminate step (4) and collapse it into step (5) on the general goodness or badness of the goal. Some factors or considerations relevant to step (4) and not fully reflected in step (5) might generate institutional reasons bearing on whether a *court* ought to adopt the particular goal in question. The nature, variety, and interrelatedness of the goals that figure in goal reasons are themselves complex topics that call for considerable research. *See generally* Summers, *Naive Instrumentalism and the Law*, in LAW, MORALITY, AND SOCIETY 119, 120-24 (P. Hacker & J. Raz eds. 1977).

[107] Note that the same effects that constitute the brute facts of a predicted state of affairs may be susceptible to characterization in terms of more than one goal. For example, the same state of affairs that will result from imposing liability in our illustrative case might be characterized in terms of increased information, more voting, or greater social solidarity resulting from a wider dispersal of information.

But some predicted effects of a decision might disserve a good social goal. For example, imposing liability might cause newspapers to reduce their campaign coverage; this might lead to a decrease in the flow of information about candidates and a decline in voter turnout. These effects might be viewed as inconsistent with the goal of facilitating democracy and therefore characterized as bad. As such, they could only generate a "negative" goal reason—one opposing liability in our example.

In this fifth step, the judge must appraise predicted decisional effects and determine, in light of independent values, whether the effects serve or disserve good social goals. Even if the judge has appropriately characterized the brute facts of a predicted state of affairs (in step (3)) and has properly concluded that the state of affairs affects or instantiates a public interest (in step (4)), it does not necessarily follow that producing that state of affairs will serve or disserve a good social goal. Furthermore, even if the goal purportedly served by the predicted state of affairs is widely accepted in the community, the judge must, in this fifth step, appraise the goal in light of independent values.[108] If he constructs a reason in which the goal, although widely shared, is bad in light of these values, the justificatory force of the reason cannot be fully genuine, but must to a large extent be merely conventional. In our example, of course, facilitating democracy is not merely a conventional goal, but is also independently appraisable as good.

(6) Moreover, the judge must consider not only whether the predicted effects of alternative decisions *generally* serve or disserve a good social goal, but also whether any predicted increase in goal subservience is really needed, or whether any predicted reduction in goal subservience is really prejudicial. He must inquire more particularly into the desired level of goal subservience and the impact of projected decisions on that level.

A "positive" goal reason—for example, a reason that favors imposing liability in our case because this would reduce potential candidates' fears of negligent malignment and encourage more of them to run—is not a good goal reason if this additional encouragement is unnecessary. That is, if enough good candidates will run regardless of whether newspapers are subject to liability for negligent libel, the further encouragement attributable to imposing

---

[108] For another discussion of the need to evaluate goals, see Bodenheimer, *supra* note 12, at 394.

liability is not desirable, despite the goodness of the *general* goal of facilitating democracy by encouraging qualified persons to run.

Similarly, a "negative" goal reason—for example, a reason opposing liability in our case because such liability would cause newspapers to cut back on their campaign coverage and thus lead to a diminished flow of information and decreased voter turnout—is not a good goal reason if diminished information and reduced voter turnout are not really prejudicial. That is, if enough information will still be provided and enough voting will still occur regardless of whether newspapers are subject to liability for negligent libel, the decrease in information or voting attributable to imposing liability will not be undesirable. This holds true despite the goodness of the *general* social goal of facilitating democracy by publishing political information and stimulating voter turnout.

In sum, judges must not only consider whether the goals served or disserved by alternative decisions are generally good in themselves; judges must also consider what levels of goal subservience are desirable, and what impact changes in legal rights and duties (with their attendant costs) will have on those levels. Note that this inquiry reintroduces in part the predictive element of step (2). But here the judge predicts not just the decision's effects as such, but the extent to which those effects serve or disserve a desired level of goal realization.

(7) Finally, the judge must formulate the reason clearly, and in appropriate general terms.[109] For example: "Defendant should not be held liable for merely negligent libel because such liability would cause this newspaper and other newspapers to become unduly cautious in providing information about candidates for public office, and this in turn would reduce voting and thus significantly diminish democratic governance. Judgment affirmed."[110]

---

[109] On the appropriate generality of reasons, see the exchange between Dean Edward Levi and Professor Herbert Wechsler: Levi, *The Nature of Judicial Reasoning*, and Wechsler, *The Nature of Judicial Reasoning*, in LAW & PHILOSOPHY 263, 290 (S. Hook ed. 1964). See also the perceptive essay by MacCormick, *Formal Justice and the Form of Legal Arguments*, 6 ETUDES DE LOGIQUE JURIDIQUE 103 (C. Perelman ed. 1976).

[110] In the foregoing illustration, the judge proceeds from the construction and articulation of one available goal reason directly to his conclusion, namely, affirmance of the judgment below. While this fulfills my illustrative aim, the judge in an actual case must usually go much further. He must also (1) formulate any opposing goal reasons, again using the procedure I have just outlined in the text; (2) formulate any opposing rightness reasons, using the procedure outlined in Part V *infra*; (3) formulate any other supporting goal reasons and rightness reasons; and (4) resolve the conflicts between opposing reasons

The foregoing account of the steps and the elements involved in the construction of a good goal reason is necessarily schematic. I have not stopped to describe any of the elements in detail. Nor have I considered where they come from or how they are related. I have not explored the complexities and difficulties of each step (including the ways in which each might go awry). Nor have I discussed the value sensitivities, skills, and capacities required of a judge in performing each step (including the capacity for sound judgment). Although I will eventually treat all of these topics, the foregoing must suffice for purposes of this Article.

Although schematic, the account I have given qualifies as a general analysis of the anatomy and physiology of a goal reason. As such, it represents an effort to unpack "public policy," a phrase judges often use, yet rarely analyze. Furthermore, the analysis explains how and why a good goal reason has justificatory force. In terms of suggestive metaphors, it identifies those "organs" of a goal reason that make it "function"; the "internal mechanisms" of a goal reason that make it "fire"; the "blueprint" and the "materials" from which a goal reason is successfully "constructed."[111]

A judge need not consciously go through each step in the analysis to come up with every goal reason relevant to a case. Some goal reasons are easier to construct than others, and even a judge who is not methodologically self-conscious may get such reasons right. Moreover, counsel will often construct relevant goal reasons for the judge. Even here, however, the judge must evaluate proffered reasons, and this will frequently require reviewing at least some of the relevant steps.

On the other hand, the judge who does go through all the steps consciously and systematically will not necessarily come up with any or all relevant goal reasons. Other things might go amiss. Certain value sensitivities, skills, and capacities are called for, and no judge always commands them all, no matter how qualified. Furthermore, the justificatory resources might simply fail to provide

---

to reach a final decision. This fourth step is especially important, but I have chosen not to address it in this already extended Article.

[111] I do not claim that the justificatory resources afforded by the facts and decisional context of a case may only generate one good goal reason. They may generate more than one, and these may be mutually supporting or in conflict. If in conflict, the reasons may incorporate the same goal or two different goals. In the libel illustration, for example, it might be argued that liability for merely negligent libel would facilitate democracy more than nonliability, since nonliability discourages worthy potential candidates who wish to avoid exposing themselves even to negligent malignment.

the materials needed to construct a good goal reason. Nonetheless, I claim that, given the necessary resources, the judge who conducts the analysis I have outlined above will, in general, construct and articulate reasons more successfully than judges who do not so proceed.

Whether the process of constructing goal reasons of the kind found in common-law cases is equivalent or reducible to what economists call "cost-benefit analysis" is an interesting and important question, but I cannot explore it here.[112]

B. *Evaluation*

Of course, in performing their decisional and justificatory tasks judges must not only construct goal reasons but evaluate and grade them as well. In fact, construction and evaluation are intimately related, for judges must evaluate each element of a potential reason *in the course of constructing it*. Judges must also evaluate the reasons presented by their brethren in chambers, in conference, and in draft opinions. They must evaluate reasons given by judges in prior cases cited by counsel. And they must evaluate reasons proposed by counsel and by law clerks.[113]

There is evidence that judges need to improve their proficiency in evaluating goal reasons. For example, a judge might purport to give a good goal reason when he lacks the required facts or some other element necessary to construct the reason.[114] Or a judge might discard or deemphasize a goal reason that should figure prominently in his opinion.[115] Indeed, he might fail to select and stress the best reason of all supporting his decision. He might

---

[112] For articles and bibliography on cost-benefit analysis as used by economists, see JOINT ECONOMIC COMM., 91ST CONG., 1ST SESS., THE ANALYSIS AND EVALUATION OF PUBLIC EXPENDITURES: THE PPB SYSTEM (Comm. Print 1969). For an effort to apply such analysis to common-law issues, see R. POSNER, ECONOMIC ANALYSIS OF LAW (2d ed. 1977). The *Journal of Legal Studies* and the *Journal of Law and Economics* often publish studies that apply cost-benefit analysis of one form or another to resolve legal questions or to explain and justify those resolutions. For an interesting discussion of one of Posner's main theses, see Rubin, *Why Is the Common Law Efficient?*, 6 J. LEGAL STUD. 51 (1977).

[113] Evaluation of a reason offered by someone else calls for recognition and appraisal of the elements that would have been used in its construction.

[114] *See, e.g.*, Irwin v. Phillips, 5 Cal. 140 (1855) (decision to allow miners' construction of dams justified by court as furthering development of public mineral lands; court evidently failed to consider that decision might have opposite result, since dams might render downstream areas unworkable by conventional mining methods).

[115] *See, e.g.*, Mercanti v. Persson, 160 Conn. 468, 280 A.2d 137 (1971) (court neglects goal of efficient protection of property against fire loss).

give a weak goal reason or even a nonreason.[116] Or he might give a goal reason likely to grow into a legal weed.[117]

I believe my analysis of the "building-blocks" of a good goal reason identifies all relevant focal points of evaluation—all respects in which a goal reason might be strong or weak. The fusion of these elements accounts for the force of a good goal reason. If a required element is missing, construction of a good goal reason will not be possible. And if a required element is weak—such as an improbable effect or an uncertain fact—the strength of the reason will diminish. Thus, to evaluate a goal reason systematically, the judge must both identify and assess the various elements that figure in its construction.

To illustrate, let us hypothesize a judge, Judge Endz, who in our libel example proposes to hold the defendant newspaper not liable for merely negligent libel. His draft opinion reads: "Because imposing liability for merely negligent libel would cause this newspaper and other newspapers to become unduly cautious in providing information about candidates for public office, and this in turn would reduce voting and thus significantly diminish democratic governance, the defendant is not liable."

Let us also imagine a dissenting judge who attempts to formulate a comprehensive set of criticisms of the proposed goal reason—a criticism for each element. Perhaps no proposed reason would ever have to undergo such an all-out attack, but hypothesizing a point-by-point critique will sharpen the illustration. Some of the specific criticisms formulated by the dissenter will be unconvincing, but they will serve to illustrate the relevant types of criticism a judge might convincingly offer with respect to other goal reasons. Note, too, that the following arguments are not autonomous substantive reasons, but are criticisms of one or more elements of the autonomous goal reason offered by Judge Endz.

(1) The evidence supplied by the record and other permissible sources might fail to establish that the party whose activity supposedly serves a social goal was in fact engaging in this activity when the case arose, or even that the party stands as a representa-

---

[116] *See, e.g.,* Monge v. Beebe Rubber Co., 115 N.H. 130, 133, 316 A.2d, 549, 551 (1974) (court concludes that employers' malicious or bad-faith dismissals will adversely affect "economic system," although result appears highly improbable).

[117] *See, e.g.,* Rowland v. Christian, 69 Cal. 2d 108, 120-21, 443 P.2d 561, 569, 70 Cal. Rptr. 97, 105 (1968) (dissenting opinion) (majority's "enhanced safety" reason for abolishing common-law distinction between tort liabilities to trespassers and to invitees will open door to unlimited liability and generate uncertainty).

tive of those who engage in such activity. Thus, the dissenter might be warranted in saying: "This newspaper was not carrying campaign news, and it almost never does. In fact, newspapers generally do not. Thus, we do not have before us the public goal-serving 'agent' that Judge Endz requires if his goal reason is to have the force he envisions."

This kind of criticism is fundamental. It questions the facts upon which the challenged reason rests, including the very facts that apparently generated the case.

(2) Even if the proposed reason survives criticism (1), there might be no reliable basis for predicting the relevant effects of the decision it supports. For example, the dissenter might be able to argue: "Judge Endz predicts that newspapers will refrain from covering campaigns if they are subject to liability in cases of this sort. No evidence supports this conclusion; it is mere conjecture. On the contrary, in other states that have imposed liability for negligent libel, newspaper coverage of campaigns continues to be extensive and vigorous. But even if imposing liability will reduce the coverage of campaigns, this might still enhance democracy. The threat of liability might induce newspapers to focus on the issues rather than on personalities, and might encourage qualified persons to run for office who would otherwise refrain from doing so for fear of negligent malignment."

Or the dissenting judge might be in a position to argue: "Although Judge Endz's prediction is more probable than not, it is only barely so. His reason, although not devoid of force, is therefore extremely weak."

(3) Even if the reason survives criticism of types (1) and (2), it might incorporate a mischaracterization of some significant aspect of the predicted state of affairs. It is one thing to predict that a decision will bring about a new and different state of affairs; it is quite another to be sure of the *essential character* of that state of affairs. For example, our dissenting judge might say: "Judge Endz characterizes the predicted state of affairs inaccurately. He argues that imposing liability on newspapers for negligent libel will reduce the flow of information about candidates, and this in turn will reduce voter participation in the electoral process. This, Judge Endz says, should be characterized as diminished democratic governance. I do not agree. Factors other than mere numbers, such as the education of our voters, may be more important to democracy. After all, we don't let children vote."

(4) Even if none of the preceding criticisms is valid, analysis

might still show that the contemplated goal fails to qualify as a *social* goal, because it does not affect or instantiate a public interest. Our dissenter therefore might say: "The purportedly democratic goal cited by Judge Endz is not a social goal, but rather a personal goal of those who own newspapers. Successful pursuit of this goal will simply give publishers more interesting items to write about and thus more to sell, thereby merely furthering their own economic ends. Democracy so conceived simply cannot be a *social* goal."

This criticism obviously lacks "bite" because the reason tendered by Judge Endz incorporates a goal that inherently bears on public interests rather than on merely personal concerns. Nevertheless, not all purported goal reasons involve goals that are immune to this type of criticism.

(5) Even if the proposed goal affects or instantiates a public interest, the purported reason might still fail because the goal it incorporates proves undesirable in light of independent values. Just because pursuit of a goal is appropriately characterized and bears upon a public interest, it does not follow that the goal is good. Thus, our dissenting judge might take a dim view of democracy and argue that, although pursuit of the goal of democratic governance cited by Judge Endz affects a public interest, it still does not qualify as a good goal, because democracy is bad for society. Again, this criticism is unconvincing as formulated for the present context, but this general type of criticism might, in a particular case, easily apply.

The pursuit of a goal, then, might affect a public interest, yet the goal itself might not be good. Indeed, a goal might be intrinsically bad, or its pursuit might lead to undesirable effects.

(6) Assuming that the proposed goal reason survives up to this point, it might still fail or lose considerable force because, for example, the community already has enough subservience of the goal, either from the means envisioned in the reason or from other means. Our dissenting judge might argue: "Even if newspapers stop covering political campaigns altogether, other news media will not stop, and their coverage will be sufficient." Regardless of the probability of this particular prediction, this type of criticism will sometimes undermine proposed goal reasons.

(7) Finally, if a proposed goal reason is not well stated, whatever force it has might not be apparent and, on this basis alone, the reason might fail to support the decision.

In sum, a proposed goal reason might fail or lack force in any of the foregoing respects. But if it withstands the attack of every type of criticism outlined above—even to the slightest degree—the reason necessarily has some force.

A judge who is proficient in evaluating goal reasons will understand, at least intuitively, how each of its constituent elements may be strong or weak, depending on relevant factors.[118] A judge must also be able to evaluate a goal reason overall—as strong or weak, or something in between. This general evaluation will take the form of a two-stage process.[119] Of course, some goal reasons will not call for such elaborate evaluation.

First, the judge must evaluate each *internal* element of the reason as strong, weak, or something in between. For every type of element (except perhaps the last), the judge might imagine a continuum from the strongest element of that type at one end (*e.g.*, highest probability of the prediction), to the weakest element of that type at the other (*e.g.*, lowest probability of the prediction). Thus, the judge might readily imagine cases in which a prediction would be quite strong, quite weak, or something in between, depending on the circumstances. At this first stage of evaluation, the judge would place each element of the reason in the appropriate place on its own special continuum. At the end of this stage, the judge will have characterized each of the reason's elements as relatively strong, relatively weak, or something in between.

With these rough characterizations in mind, the judge would then turn to the second evaluational stage. First, he would imagine a "summary" continuum stretching from the strongest possible goal reason (all elements combined) to the weakest (all elements combined). He would then summarize his specific judgments arrived at in the first stage, and place the reason, evaluated as a whole, at the appropriate point on the summary continuum. The judge would thus arrive at a judgment about the overall strength of the proposed goal reason.

This overall judgment would not be comparative. It would not lead to the conclusion that the reason is stronger or weaker than some other goal reason. An extremely strong goal reason might

---

[118] Discharge of the evaluative task with respect to most elements calls for still further analysis, which cannot be attempted here.

[119] I do not claim that my account of this process is entirely a rational reconstruction of actual practice; but I believe it is consistent with that practice and accurately reveals it in many significant respects. Holmes, for example, consciously practiced something similar to the "continuum" evaluation I reconstruct here. *See, e.g.*, Noble State Bank v. Haskell, 219 U.S. 104, 112 (1911); Haddock v. Haddock, 201 U.S. 562, 631-32 (1906) (dissenting opinion); Commonwealth v. Rogers, 181 Mass. 184, 186, 63 N.E. 421, 423 (1902).

still be weaker than a competing goal reason; the latter, for example, might incorporate a goal of more importance to the community, or might promise more long-term goal realization.

Implicit in this analysis is a general model of the ideal goal reason. The features of this ideal reason can now be meaningfully rendered explicit:

(1) All facts relevant to the construction and evaluation of the reason are indisputably true.

(2) The judge has an unquestionably reliable basis for predicting decisional effects, and the prediction itself is highly certain.

(3) The judge accurately characterizes the predicted state of affairs in all relevant respects.

(4) The predicted state of affairs affects or instantiates public interests—not merely the personal interests of the parties or of the judge; thus, the future state of affairs clearly serves (or disserves) a possible *social* goal.

(5) The predicted state of affairs serves (or disserves) a social goal that is without doubt generally good in light of all relevant values.

(6) The predicted increase in goal subservience is plainly needed in the community (or the predicted decrease in goal subservience is plainly prejudicial to the community).

(7) The reason is well formulated.

Although it is abstract and idealized, this model is not a personal or utopian contrivance that I have conjured up without reference to the realities of common-law decisionmaking. Most aspects of the model are derived from the goal-reasoning practices of common-law judges. In this respect, the model represents a rational reconstruction of actual judicial practice. I do not say that judges are methodologically self-conscious about this process. Indeed, their general lack of self-consciousness makes it necessary to *reconstruct* the steps in their reasoning and the elements that correspond to each of those steps. Nevertheless, most judges are to some extent aware of most features of the model. This is especially evident from the types of critical reasons found in dissents and concurring opinions.[120]

The model is also ideologically neutral, except insofar as any form of goal rationality might be considered ideological. It can

---

[120] *See generally* APPELLATE JUDICIAL OPINIONS, *supra* note 6, ch. 8; Stephens, *The Function of Concurring and Dissenting Opinions in Courts of Last Resort*, 5 U. FLA. L. REV. 394 (1952).

therefore accommodate both a wide variety of goals and evolutionary changes in goals. Judges of earlier times and different places could and may have used it.

I believe that judges would perform their evaluational work more successfully if they consciously followed this model and evaluated each element of a proposed goal reason, and each reason as a whole, in terms of its proper place on a continuum—at least when the nature of the particular reason calls for such systematic evaluation. Judges who proceed in this manner should be taken in less often by a bad goal reason, and should more often recognize when one reason is stronger than another.

The process, however, cannot be mechanically employed. Several evaluative steps are complex and often controversial. This is true, for example, of prediction and goal evaluation. Moreover, adherence to the procedure cannot guarantee that a judge will always evaluate a reason well. But, at minimum, the model provides a way to structure the exercise of judgment systematically, pointedly, and comprehensively. Many evaluations made by judges who follow the procedure will inevitably be rough, but they are likely to be more refined than those arrived at by judges who follow no systematic method at all.

It may be objected that judges who strive to structure their judgment in this way will become so self-conscious that they will end up unable to give any good goal reasons at all; just as the proverbial centipede lost all capacity for forward motion when he started watching his legs, the judge might lose his capacity for reasoning and deciding. Justificatory activities, however, are quite different from bodily movements, the coordination of which may be diminished by too much self-conscious attention. Unlike walking, which becomes completely second nature, the construction of a legal justification must remain to a great extent a formal and deliberative process—something that cannot be done well without reflection and the conscious exercise of judgment.[121]

C. *The Bearing of Institutional Reasons*

I have so far said nothing about the bearing of institutional reasons on the construction and evaluation of goal reasons. Institutional reasons are goal reasons or rightness reasons that relate to how judicial roles and processes bear on the decisional and jus-

---

[121] On thinking about thinking, see A. FLEW, THINKING ABOUT THINKING (1975).

tificatory jobs of judges. Examples include: "This is not the kind of goal that courts ought to adopt and implement without legislative approval"; or, "Since courts cannot readily measure the damages resulting from this type of alleged wrong, we will not recognize it as a wrong."

Some types of institutional reasons might be conceptualized either as internal elements of goal reasons or as autonomous institutional reasons. Suppose, to take an extreme example, that our newspaper libel case arises during a labor shortage that is seriously affecting the city's economy. One judge might argue in support of imposing liability that the decision would force the newspaper into bankruptcy, and would thus free its employees to make needed repairs on an important bridge. Other judges would certainly object that this reason does not embody the kind of goal that a court ought to adopt. Courts, they will argue, are not in the business of managing the economy generally, let alone the local labor market.[122] These judges might readily concede that the reason would qualify as a good goal reason "if we were a legislature." But courts are not legislatures; they are institutionally limited in function.[123]

Perhaps we should conceptualize the foregoing criticism as an attack on an internal, institutional element of the proposed goal reason, which weakens or annihilates the reason *on its own terms*. If so, we might add to my earlier account of the various elements of a goal reason a further element—namely, the goal incorporated in the reason must be one that a court may properly adopt. On the other hand, the objection might be conceptualized not as an attack on an internal element of the goal reason, but rather as an independent reason going to the institutional propriety of proposed judicial action. Regardless of how it is conceptualized, however, the force of this institutional consideration as an argument against exclusively judicial adoption of the proposed goal should be apparent.

Why, then, do I treat all considerations of institutional propriety as a separate type of reason? Such treatment is, I think, more faithful to current judicial practice. On the whole, judges appear to categorize institutional reasons separately. Moreover, this approach

---

[122] *Cf.* Muskopf v. Corning Hosp. Dist., 55 Cal. 2d 211, 224, 359 P.2d 457, 464, 11 Cal. Rptr. 89, 96 (1961) (dissenter argues that court should leave abolition of governmental tort immunity to state legislature).

[123] In addition, the objecting judges might argue that the proposed goal reason incorporates a faulty means-end hypothesis: even though the newspaper's demise will free its employees to work elsewhere, it is highly unlikely that they will have the desire or the qualifications to work on the bridge.

avoids the intermingling of institutional and noninstitutional concerns, and thus increases the likelihood that each type of concern will receive due consideration. After judges construct and evaluate goal reasons on their own terms (as I have now narrowly conceptualized them), they should always go on to consider the institutional appropriateness of giving them. In pursuing this strategy, judges may bring to bear autonomous institutional reasons that weaken or nullify proposed goal reasons.

D. *The Legitimacy of Goal Reasons*

A skeptic might argue that goal reasons are not really reasons at all because they do not bring genuine values into play. Judges rarely challenge the legitimacy of goal reasons on this ground, however, presumably because goal reasons so often implicate such tangible, "real-life" values as safety, health, peace and quiet, clean air, and voter participation.

Nevertheless, judges and others do sometimes question the legitimacy of goal reasons on the ground that they necessarily sacrifice the individual to the common good.[124] It might be argued, for example, that the refusal to impose liability for negligent libel in the name of preserving sources of information and voter participation, in effect, sacrifices the claim of an injured party to the perceived good of the community. In my view, however, this is not a decisive objection to the legitimacy of goal reasons as such. How much force they have in particular cases is one thing; whether they have any force at all is quite another. Perhaps some courts accord them too much force. In a given case, a goal reason with some force might still justifiably give way to a conflicting rightness reason that favors the individual's interests.

Furthermore, some judges and commentators argue that goal reasons are inappropriate bases for common-law decisionmaking because resort to such reasons always calls for an exercise of the democratic will—solely a legislative function.[125] But judges regularly give goal reasons in common-law cases, and, in my view, this practice is legitimate. Not all goal reasons call for an exercise of the democratic will. Of course, judicial reliance on a particular goal reason in a given case might be institutionally inappropriate.

---

[124] Judges have argued this in conversation with me. *See also* Fletcher, *Fairness and Utility in Tort Theory*, 85 HARV. L. REV. 537, 567 (1972).

[125] *See, e.g.*, Dworkin, *Hard Cases, supra* note 27; Winfield, *Public Policy in the English Common Law, supra* note 27.

Note, finally, that goal reasons also play important justificatory roles in daily life. It might be thought that, while judges must always decide with society's interests in mind, the goal reasoning of individuals outside the law is inherently egoistic and self-regarding. But this is clearly untrue; some private goal reasoning is purely altruistic, and much is both altruistic and egoistic at the same time. If we abandoned goal reasons entirely, we would drastically diminish our justificatory resources both inside and outside the law.

V

CONSTRUCTION, EVALUATION, AND LEGITIMACY
OF RIGHTNESS REASONS

Rightness reasons constitute the second basic variety of substantive reasons found in common-law cases. A rightness reason derives its justificatory force not from predicted goal-serving effects of the decision it supports, but from the applicability of a sound sociomoral norm to a party's actions or to the state of affairs resulting from those actions. Reasons of this type do not derive their force from what the future will bring. Rather, most rightness reasons derive their force from how the past came about.[126]

The facts and decisional context of a case might generate only a rightness reason or only a goal reason. On the other hand, reasons of both types might be available, and these might conflict or be mutually supporting.

I now turn to the construction and evaluation of rightness reasons. I will treat these reasons in the same basic fashion as I treated goal reasons. This will call for some restatement. But there will be significant variations, too, which reflect the fundamental differences between these two types of reasons.

As I have already explained, there are two main subspecies of rightness reasons: (1) those that depend for their force on the culpability or nonculpability of a party's past actions; and (2) those that depend for their force on the fairness or unfairness of leaving the parties "as is" in light of their past interaction.

A. *Construction*

Rightness reasons are internally complex, far more so than commonly supposed. Judges cannot construct rightness reasons in

---

[126] For discussion of rightness reasons that are not past-regarding, see note 46 and accompanying text *supra*.

a systematic and methodologically self-conscious fashion without reference to these complexities. There is evidence that judges need to improve their capacity to construct good rightness reasons. For example, a judge might overlook a rightness reason entirely, even though the facts and decisional context make it readily available.[127] Or he might undertake to construct a rightness reason as if it were a goal reason.[128] Or he might fail to incorporate all the necessary elements of a rightness reason, by failing, for example, to bring the relevant rightness concept to bear.[129] Or he might formulate a potentially good rightness reason in conclusory terms.[130]

There are indications that some judges and lawyers do not understand rightness reasons as well as they understand goal reasons. Indeed, even some of the most thoughtful scholars only dimly understand the internal complexities of rightness reasons.[131] And I fear that my own efforts have not unraveled all knots. Thus, the analysis I offer is only tentative.

To construct a rightness reason a judge must take a series of steps to combine a variety of elements. Once again, I will use an actual case to illustrate this process.[132] Assume that the plaintiff contracts to build a mast for the defendant's boat on the plaintiff's premises. Before he finishes, the plaintiff becomes worried about the possibility of fire and proposes to buy insurance. The defendant,

---

[127] *See, e.g.*, Oscar Schlegel Mfg. Co. v. Peter Cooper's Glue Factory, 231 N.Y. 459, 132 N.E. 148 (1921) (court neglects to formulate and stress following rightness reason: where price of glue rose sharply during period covered by requirements contract and plaintiff's purchase orders rose by 2500%, granting plaintiff damages for nondelivery of larger orders would be unfair, since increased requirements were neither expected nor foreseeable by defendant).

[128] *See, e.g.*, Cornpropst v. Sloan, 528 S.W.2d 188, 199-200 (Tenn. 1975) (dissenting judge begins to construct rightness reason based on fairness of imposing tort duty on shopping centers, but ultimately formulates goal reason that imposition of duty would serve "best interests of the consuming public," without fully articulating original and independent rightness reason).

[129] *See, e.g.*, International Milling Co. v. Hachmeister, Inc., 380 Pa. 407, 414, 110 A.2d 186, 189 (1955) (court uses fraud concept where bad-faith concept more appropriate).

[130] *See, e.g.*, Groves v. John Wunder Co., 205 Minn. 163, 168, 286 N.W. 235, 237 (1939) (in choosing "cost of completion" over "difference in value" as measure of damages in construction-contract case, court states as rightness reason merely that plaintiff should have benefit of "lost" bargain).

[131] *Compare* Rosenberg, *Methods of Reasoning and Justification in Social Science and Law: Comments*, 23 J. LEGAL EDUC. 199, 202 (1970) (brilliant law professor analyzes rightness reason as "position based on value preferences"), *with* Miller & Barron, *The Supreme Court, the Adversary System, and the Flow of Information to the Justices: A Preliminary Inquiry*, 61 VA. L. REV. 1187, 1199 (1975) (almost as brilliant professor quoted in survey analyzes rightness reasons as requiring "very little data—only a strong ethical idea").

[132] Mercanti v. Persson, 160 Conn. 468, 280 A.2d 137 (1971).

after carelessly checking his own policy, says to the plaintiff: "I'm sure I have coverage already." The plaintiff relies on the defendant's careless representation and does not procure insurance. A fire for which neither party is responsible destroys the boat and mast when the work is nearly completed, and the defendant's policy does not cover the loss. The defendant refuses to pay for the pile of ashes, and the plaintiff sues for the contract price.

Assume that the Uniform Commercial Code would impose the loss on the plaintiff, subject to section 1-103 which authorizes judges to resort to any "general equitable principles."[133] Let us suppose, too, that the plaintiff introduced evidence of the foregoing facts, and the trial judge instructed the jury that if they found the facts as the plaintiff had alleged, they must, under section 1-103, find for the plaintiff on a theory of "estoppel by negligence." The defendant excepts to this instruction, the jury returns a verdict for the plaintiff, and the defendant appeals. The case is one of first impression, and the appellate court must now decide whether to affirm or reverse.

I will now sketch (though not necessarily in sequence) the steps that a methodologically self-conscious judge might take in constructing a "culpability" rightness reason that supports the trial judge's instruction. I will also identify the internal element of the reason that figures in each step.

(1) First, the judge must determine from the proceedings below and the general decisional context all facts relevant to the culpability of the defendant's action: Who did what to whom? With what results?[134] Why? In what type of situation? In the present case, for example, did the defendant make a representation? What facts bear on the ease with which the defendant could have determined the actual extent of his insurance coverage? Did the defendant's statement cause a loss to the plaintiff? Did the plaintiff rely? What circumstances bear on the possible foreseeability to the defendant of the plaintiff's reliance? (Note that such questions might necessitate inquiry into the parties' states of mind.[135])

---

[133] For a general discussion of this section, see Summers, *General Equitable Principles Under Section 1-103 of the Uniform Commercial Code*, 72 Nw. L. REV. 906 (1978).

[134] Note that concepts of causality play important roles in both goal reasons and rightness reasons. In goal reasons, however, *decisional* effects play a distinctive role.

[135] In contrast, a judge might also inquire into state of mind when he formulates a goal reason, but not for the purpose of determining culpability. Instead, the judge will typically seek to determine the likely effects of the decision on persons acting subsequently with the same state of mind.

(2) In light of the facts ascertained in step (1), and in light of an inventory of *possibly* relevant concepts of culpability (provisionally identifiable also in step (1)), the judge must determine, intuitively or otherwise, which concepts of culpability are in fact relevant to characterizing the defendant's action. This will often require sensitive analysis of the potentially relevant concepts and their careful particularization. Thus, in our example, concepts of negligence and responsibility for one's careless statements would seem to be most relevant in characterizing the defendant's action.

(3) The judge must then determine, in light of relevant rightness values, whether it is possible to formulate a sociomoral norm of rightness that incorporates the concepts identified in step (2), and would, if applicable to the facts, require (or not require) the party who caused the loss to make amends. Thus, a judge in our case might tentatively formulate the relevant norm (including an "amends-making" aspect) as follows:

> A person should not carelessly induce another to rely on a false representation when the representor can readily ascertain the falsity of his representation and can reasonably foresee the other party's reliance. One who does so, without more, should bear the foreseeable loss caused to the relying party.[136]

(4) Having formulated the norm, the judge must go on to evaluate its soundness in light of independent rightness values. The norm formulated in step (3), for example, might or might not be widely shared in society. If it is widely shared, but in light of independent values the court ought not to recognize it, then the justificatory force of any rightness reason that incorporates the norm cannot be fully genuine; much of this force must be merely conventional.[137] Evaluation of a norm must be distinguished from

---

[136] Norms formulated at this step might warrant injunctive relief as well. In such cases, the judge would consider whether the projected action against which the relief is sought *would be* culpable.

Although I focus in this Article on damages and injunctions, the remedial apparatus of the common law extends beyond these devices. Furthermore, while I concentrate on cases involving past interaction of the parties, not all common-law cases involve such interaction.

[137] I do not claim that when the law recognizes a culpability concept embedded in a rightness norm (through a court's reasons for decisions and doctrinal formulations), the concept or the norm never undergoes alteration. Indeed, the culpability concept employed by the law may differ significantly from the concept that a moral spectator would employ in judging the same action in a nonlegal setting for a nonlegal purpose. *See generally* W. PROSSER, HANDBOOK OF THE LAW OF TORTS § 1, at 6 (4th ed. 1971); *id.* § 4, at 18. Nor do I claim that social morality is monolithic; on some issues it is clearly pluralistic.

its formulation, if only because judges (and others) tend to take the soundness of a formulated norm for granted if it is widely shared in the community.[138]

The rightness reason now taking shape in our example might be stated as follows: "Since the plaintiff relied on the defendant's careless misrepresentation and the defendant could reasonably have foreseen this reliance, the defendant should bear the resulting loss." In my view, the rightness norm generating this reason is not only widely shared in our society, but is also worthy of judicial recognition in light of rightness values that are independent of community acceptance. Thus, if the reason holds up through the remaining steps, it will have genuine justificatory force.[139]

(5) Next, the judge must evaluatively characterize the relevant facts—here the action of the party against whom relief is sought—in light of the concepts of culpability identified as relevant in step (2) and embodied in the norm formulated in step (3). In the present case, for example, the judge must ask: Did the defendant actually exercise due care in determining the extent of his coverage? Could the defendant have reasonably foreseen the plaintiff's reliance?

Note how this step differs from steps (2) and (3). It is one thing to survey the facts in order to identify which concepts of culpability are relevant and to determine whether a norm can be formulated that incorporates these concepts. It is another to evaluatively characterize the facts by applying the relevant culpability concepts (itself often a complex act of judgment).[140]

(6) The judge must then apply the rightness norm formulated in step (3) to the facts as characterized in step (5), and decide which disposition of the legal issue *most accords* with the norm as applied to the facts. Thus, in our example, if the defendant through lack of

---

[138] *See* H. L. A. HART, LAW, LIBERTY AND MORALITY 17-24 (1963).

[139] Norms themselves may be highly complex, but I will not consider this here. For the growing literature on norms, see, for example, H. KELSEN, ESSAYS IN LEGAL AND MORAL PHILOSOPHY 83-94 (O. Weinberger ed. 1973); J. RAZ, PRACTICAL REASON AND NORMS (1975); A. ROSS, DIRECTIVES AND NORMS 78-138 (1968); R. SARTORIUS, INDIVIDUAL CONDUCT AND SOCIAL NORMS (1975); E. ULLMANN-MARGALIT, THE EMERGENCE OF NORMS (1977).

[140] Appellate judges sometimes confront a clean slate, and have the opportunity to formulate every element in the construction of a reason. *See, e.g.*, Pavesich v. New England Life Ins. Co., 122 Ga. 190, 50 S.E. 68 (1905). At other times, they must share this work with the trial judge or jury in accordance with a division of functions specified in the law. For example, a factfinder may, when the law considers a question to be one of fact, perform a characterization function (as in negligence cases), and the appellate judge may lack the authority to recharacterize the relevant facts.

due care induced foreseeable detrimental reliance, then, without more, we might conclude that the instruction of the trial judge in the illustrative case should be upheld and the judgment affirmed.

(7) Finally, the judge must formulate the reason clearly, and in appropriately general terms. For example: "Since the plaintiff relied on the defendant's careless misrepresentation and the defendant could have reasonably foreseen this reliance, the defendant should pay damages for the loss he caused. Judgment affirmed."[141]

In the foregoing account, the reason ultimately given will have force if elements (1) through (7) are appropriately combined. I cannot treat here the various elements in detail, or explore the distinctive capacities required of a judge who sets out to construct a rightness reason. I must omit subtleties and complexities. Whole books and articles have been devoted to the culpability concepts that figure in rightness reasons; these include such wide-ranging and complex notions as due care, desert, and good faith.[142] To identify and particularize these concepts, specify their content, and apply them to the facts, judges must rely on moral intuition and exercise sensitive judgment. The very question of whether a court ought to recognize a particular rightness norm may be highly controversial. What types of argument and evidence are relevant to the recognition of a norm has not yet been the subject of extended study, although judges regularly engage in such argument and marshall such evidence. My account also omits discussion of the capacities required for the faithful evaluative characterization of facts and states of affairs.[143] For purposes of this Article, what I have already said must suffice.

I have so far illustrated only the construction of a culpability-based rightness reason. The foregoing analysis applies equally, however, to rightness reasons based on mere fairness. Thus, even if the defendant did not carelessly misrepresent the facts, he might still be held responsible if it would be unfair to leave the resulting loss on the relying plaintiff. Construction of this reason would fol-

---

[141] As I noted with respect to my outline of the construction of a goal reason (*see* note 110 *supra*), my aim here is simply to illustrate the construction of one available rightness reason. Before reaching a final decision in an actual case, the judge must usually proceed to formulate any other supporting or opposing rightness reasons and goal reasons and then resolve the conflicts.

[142] *See, e.g.*, Summers, *"Good Faith" in General Contract Law and the Sales Provisions of the Uniform Commercial Code*, 54 VA. L. REV. 195 (1968).

[143] For a perceptive discussion, see J. FRANK, COURTS ON TRIAL 37-61 (1966).

low the same seven steps, except that the judge would formulate and apply a rightness norm embodying a particular concept of unfairness. In legalistic terms, "estoppel by negligence" is not the only rationally recognizable form of estoppel. Here, mere "estoppel in pais" might suffice, even if the defendant was not negligent.[144]

Analysis of rightness reasons merely in terms of "justice and equity between the parties" is really no analysis at all. Yet judges and others frequently offer little more than this familiar phrase.[145] My account of rightness reasons qualifies as an analysis of their anatomy and physiology. Moreover, because my analysis breaks rightness reasons down into elements that provide subjects for reasoned argument, the analysis can be used to rebut the charge that rightness reasons are merely "conclusory" and thus without legitimacy.[146]

The seven steps and their corresponding elements also provide a schematic "blueprint," with specifications of required materials, that a methodologically self-conscious judge might follow to construct a good rightness reason. The analysis enables us to see just how a rightness reason has force—in metaphorical terms, how it "fires," "functions," or "goes through." Of course, step-by-step adherence to the blueprint will not always generate a good rightness reason. The required resources might be unavailable, or the judge might lack the necessary skills and judgment.[147]

Rightness reasons should not be equated with what some theorists call "rights" reasons—reasons based upon moral rights.[148] Similarly, rightness reasons should not be identified with "natural law." Nor does the distinction between goal reasons and rightness reasons closely parallel the distinction between so-called teleological and deontological reasons.[149] Rightness reasons are also different

---

[144] *See generally* M. BIGELOW, A TREATISE ON THE LAW OF ESTOPPEL ch. 18 (6th ed. J. Carter rev. 1913); Jackson, *Estoppel As a Sword*, 81 L.Q. REV. 84 (1965).

[145] *See, e.g*, Mercanti v. Persson, 160 Conn. 468, 479, 280 A.2d 137, 142 (1971).

[146] *See* text accompanying notes 169-70 *infra*.

[147] I do not claim that the facts and decisional context of a case can generate only one rightness reason. In the illustrative case, there might have been a further rightness reason flatly contrary to the decisive one—namely, that the plaintiff did not justifiably rely, and therefore really brought the loss on himself. Formulation of this reason would again involve following the seven-step procedure outlined above. But this would not necessarily require formulating a further and distinct rightness norm from scratch. The norm already stated in step (3) could be explicitly revised to allow for the possibility that a competing reason of this sort might arise in a particular case.

[148] *See, e.g.*, Dworkin, *Hard Cases, supra* note 27.

[149] Discussions of teleological and deontological theories can be found in almost any elementary text. *See, e.g.*, W. FRANKENA, ETHICS 15-17 (2d ed. 1973).

from most reasons of "equity" that interest economists.[150] These topics, although of great importance, lie beyond the scope of this Article.

B. *Evaluation*

Judges must not only construct rightness reasons but also evaluate and grade them, and judges do not always perform these tasks well. For example, a judge might purport to give a good rightness reason when he lacks the required facts or some other necessary element.[151] Or a judge might discard or deemphasize a rightness reason that should figure prominently in his opinion.[152] Indeed, he might fail to select and stress the best reason of all supporting his decision.[153] Or he might evaluate a rightness reason as if it were a goal reason, and so employ inappropriate standards.[154] Or he might give a rightness reason likely to grow into a legal weed.[155]

A judge should bear in mind that the internal complexities and the potential strengths and weaknesses of rightness reasons differ

---

[150] In various contexts, economists use the term "equity" to refer to a property interest, to equality of income distribution, to a fair distribution of costs, and to a variety of other concepts.

[151] Failure to recognize that a purported rightness reason lacks the necessary factual foundation is perhaps the most egregious form of misevaluation. *See, e.g.*, Gerhard v. Stephens, 68 Cal. 2d 864, 892-95, 442 P.2d 692, 714-16, 69 Cal. Rptr. 612, 634-36 (1968) (one element of court's rightness reason was reasonableness of party's expectation that unused mineral rights might someday prove valuable, but party apparently lacked any basis for expectation). A more subtle form of misevaluation takes place when the judge mischaracterizes the facts and as a result applies an inappropriate rightness norm. *See, e.g.*, Marks v. Gates, 154 F. 481, 483 (9th Cir. 1907) (in suit for specific performance of "grubstake" contract, court characterizes parties' transaction as simple quid pro quo exchange, rather than as investment in uncertain venture; consequently, court applies inappropriate fairness norm of gross inadequacy of consideration and denies relief).

[152] *See, e.g.*, Mitchill v. Lath, 247 N.Y. 377, 160 N.E. 646 (1928) (court fails to appreciate fully that decision will result in patent injustice to losing party).

[153] *See, e.g.*, Monge v. Beebe Rubber Co., 114 N.H. 130, 316 A.2d 549 (1974) (court gives dubious goal reason—promotion of economic system—yet fails to articulate robustly independent and conclusive rightness reason—employer's gross bad faith and overreaching).

[154] *See, e.g.*, McConnell v. Commonwealth Pictures Corp., 7 N.Y.2d 465, 475, 166 N.E.2d 494, 500, 199 N.Y.S.2d 483, 490-91 (1960) (dissenting judge appears to attack rightness reason given by majority on ground that decision will have bad consequences).

[155] *See, e.g.*, Greenspan v. Slate, 12 N.J. 426, 439, 97 A.2d 390, 396-97 (1953) (court holds that "normal instincts of humanity and plain common honesty" require that parents compensate others for "necessaries" furnished their children in emergency even in absence of express or implied contract, but court fails to provide clear guidelines for determining, *e.g.*, what counts as "emergency" and what notice must be given, thus opening door to undesirable forms of intermeddling by third persons).

from those of goal reasons. Thus, the evaluation of rightness reasons requires a different analysis, and calls for the exercise of different skills and sensibilities. To evaluate a proposed rightness reason systematically, a judge must advert to each of the various elements that figure in its construction and consider their interrelation. To illustrate, suppose that a judge in our boat-mast case, Judge Normz, proposes to hold the boat owner liable to the builder for the contract price. In support of this decision, he offers the following reason: "The plaintiff foreseeably relied on the defendant's careless misrepresentation as to insurance coverage."

Now, let us imagine a dissenting judge who attempts to formulate a comprehensive set of criticisms of the proposed rightness reason—a criticism for each element. Although some of the imagined criticisms will be unsound with respect to the specific reason offered by Judge Normz, they nonetheless illustrate the relevant types of criticism that might figure prominently in other cases.

(1) The evidence supplied by the record and the decisional context might fail to establish that the defendant acted under the circumstances and with the state of mind (if any) required for the reason. For example, the dissenting judge might be in a position to say: "Judge Normz does not have the facts straight. The defendant never really made a representation about insurance coverage. In fact, the statement attributed to him was not a representation—it was only a guess." The critic thus challenges the brute facts of the episode, and seeks to show that the proposed reason lacks the factual basis upon which its force depends. Rightness reasons, it must be remembered, are generated by applying sociomoral norms to facts, and norms of this nature have their own discrete ranges of factual application.

(2) Even if the necessary facts are established, the rightness concept brought to bear might be irrelevant or misparticularized. For example, the dissenting judge might say: "The relevant concept here is that of ill desert or nondesert, not want of due care, as Judge Normz would have it."

(3) Although the rightness concept might be relevant and appropriately particularized, it might be impossible to formulate a norm that incorporates the concept *and* calls for the making of amends (or the recognition of a defense) in the type of case at hand. In our hypothetical case, for example, Judge Normz formulated the following norm:

> A person should not carelessly induce another to rely on a false representation when the representor can readily ascertain the

falsity of his representation and can reasonably foresee the other party's reliance. One who does so, without more, should bear the foreseeable loss caused to the relying party.

Our dissenter might concede that the norm aptly embodies the relevant rightness concept, but argue that the formulation is too broad and authorizes relief in cases where relief would be unjustified (or supports a defense in cases where the defense should not be recognized). Although this criticism appears unconvincing in the context of the present case, it illustrates a type of criticism that may have force in other cases.[156]

(4) Even if the norm is aptly formulated to authorize relief (or the recognition of a defense) in the type of case at hand, the norm might not be one that, in light of relevant values, the court ought to recognize.[157] For example, in opposition to the norm formulated by Judge Normz, our dissenter might argue for a "caveat relier" principle—*i.e.*, a person should be allowed to represent whatever he wants, and those who intend to rely on his representations should bear the burden of determining their accuracy.

(5) Although the proposed reason survives the first four types of criticism, the action of the party against whom relief is sought might not be susceptible to the evaluative characterization required to bring the rightness norm into play. For example, the dissenting judge might say: "Judge Normz evaluatively mischaracterizes what happened here. The defendant boat owner was not really careless, for the reasonable man cannot be expected to understand an insurance policy. Such policies use ordinary words in very odd ways. As a matter of law, the defendant cannot have failed to exercise due care."[158]

(6) Even if the proposed reason survives to this point, it might still lose force because the decision it purportedly supports is not the decision, among the alternatives, that *most accords* with the

---

[156] For a case in which the majority agreed that the rightness concept embodied in a norm was infringed but did not agree that the infringement warranted relief, see Zepeda v. Zepeda, 41 Ill. App. 2d 240, 190 N.E.2d 849 (1963).

[157] For an example of a controversial rightness norm, see *id.* (couple should not bring illegitimate child into world). *See also* Meinhard v. Salmon, 249 N.Y. 458, 164 N.E. 545 (1928) (Cardozo, C.J., speaking for majority, and Andrews, J., dissenting, disagree on whether joint venturer ought to bear absolute duty to inform coventurer of any offers made by third persons regarding property involved in joint-venture agreement, even though offer concerns development of property after agreement expires and clearly falls beyond agreement's scope). For a discussion of the necessity to evaluate such norms, see Bodenheimer, *supra* note 12, at 394.

[158] *See generally* note 140 *supra*.

applicable norm. Thus, the dissenter might argue: "Judge Normz has failed to see what his reason is a reason *for*. He says it best supports a decision holding the owner fully liable to the builder, but I say it best supports a decision apportioning the loss between the parties."

This criticism might seem to be aimed more directly at the use of a reason than at the reason itself. The justificatory force of a rightness reason, however, depends partly on the degree of accordance between decision and norm (as applied to the actions of the parties). Reasons for decisions cannot have force in a void. They have force only in relation to decisions, and have more force in relation to some decisions than to others.

(7) Finally, if the proposed reason is not well stated, whatever force it has might not be apparent and, on this basis alone, might fail to support the decision.

A proposed rightness reason might be evaluated in each of the foregoing respects. But a judge must also evaluate reasons as a whole—as strong or weak, or something in between. Again, using the tentative analysis I propose in this Article, a judge might systematically evaluate a rightness reason as a whole in a two-stage process. Of course, many rightness reasons will not call for such elaborate evaluation.

At the first stage, the judge must evaluate each of the seven elements as strong, weak, or something in between. For each type of element (except perhaps the last), he might imagine a continuum from the strongest element of that type at one end (*e.g.*, an appropriate evaluative characterization of a clearly careless misrepresentation), to the weakest element of that type at the other (*e.g.*, a highly questionable characterization of a statement as a careless misrepresentation). Thus, the judge might readily imagine cases in which an evaluative characterization would be highly appropriate, not appropriate at all, or something in between. At this first stage of evaluation, the judge would place each element of the reason in the appropriate place on its own special continuum. At the end of this stage, the judge will have characterized each of the reason's elements as relatively strong, relatively weak, or something in between.

The judge would then turn to the second evaluational stage. He would begin by imagining a "summary" continuum stretching from the strongest possible rightness reason (all elements combined) to the weakest (all elements combined). He would then summarize his specific judgments arrived at in the first stage, and place the reason, evaluated as a whole, at the appropriate point on the summary continuum. The judge would thus arrive at a judgment about the overall strength of the proposed rightness reason.

This overall judgment would not be comparative. It would not lead to the conclusion that the reason is stronger or weaker than some other reason. An extremely strong rightness reason might still be weaker than a competing rightness reason which, for example, incorporates a rightness concept that is more significant.

Implicit in the foregoing analysis is a general model of the ideal rightness reason. The features of this ideal reason are:

(1) All facts relevant to the construction and evaluation of the reason are indisputably true.

(2) The rightness concepts brought into play are indisputably relevant and appropriately particularized.

(3) A rightness norm can be formulated that clearly embodies the relevant rightness concepts *and* authorizes relief (or the recognition of a defense).

(4) The rightness norm is one that the court plainly ought to recognize in light of relevant values.

(5) The evaluative characterizations that apply the concepts embodied in the norm to the facts are indisputably appropriate.

(6) The decision supported by the reason is the one most clearly in accordance with the applicable norm.

(7) The reason is well formulated.

Note that this model is "norm-neutral"; it can accommodate both a wide variety of norms and evolutionary changes in norms.[159] Thus, judges of earlier times and different social outlooks could and may have used the model.

I believe that judges who systematically follow the model to construct and evaluate rightness reasons will generally do their work better than judges who do not. Certainly judges must exercise judgment; they cannot apply the model mechanically, or expect that step-by-step adherence will guarantee the best results. At minimum, however, the model provides a blueprint for structuring the exercise of judgment systematically, pointedly, and comprehensively. Although many of the judgments reached by judges who follow the model will inevitably be rough, they are likely to be more refined than those arrived at by judges who follow no systematic method at all.

---

[159] For an example of an evolving norm, see Florida Publishing Co. v. Fletcher, 340 So.2d 914 (Fla. 1976), *cert. denied*, 431 U.S. 930 (1977).

C. The Bearing of Institutional Reasons

My approach in this Article is to treat institutional reasons distinctly. An institutional reason, it will be recalled, is a goal reason or a rightness reason that relates to the bearing of judicial roles and processes on judicial decisions and justifications. For example, a judge might say: "A decision for the plaintiff would require us to recognize a wholly new rightness norm so controversial that we should leave it to the legislature to enact a statute that incorporates it." Or a judge might say: "In particular cases, courts will be unable to ascertain the adjudicative facts necessary to determine whether the proposed rightness reason applies; thus, a decision based on this reason would be unsound because it would introduce a rudderless precedent."[160]

As already noted with respect to institutional reasons and goal reasons, we might conceptualize some types of institutional reasons as internal elements of rightness reasons. But the considerations that militated against incorporating institutional reasons into goal reasons[161] militate against their incorporation into rightness reasons as well. Thus kept distinct, a rightness reason may be good on its own terms, yet an institutional reason may come into play to override, diminish, or nullify it. Moreover, an institutional reason may independently influence the way in which a court implements or gives legal effect to a rightness reason and its underlying sociomoral norm; as a result, the *legal* embodiment of the norm may differ significantly from corresponding manifestations in moral or other nonlegal contexts. For example, institutional considerations account in large part for the law's definition of negligence in objective rather than subjective terms, although the values and norms of daily life in which the legal concept of negligence is rooted often take subjective factors into account.[162]

D. The Legitimacy of Rightness Reasons

Judges and others sometimes challenge rightness reasons as illegitimate. Although most judges do not appear to be generally

---

[160] *See, e.g.*, Li v. Yellow Cab Co., 13 Cal. 3d 804, 823-24, 532 P.2d 1226, 1240, 119 Cal. Rptr. 858, 872 (1975) (court notes that adjudicative facts required for allocation of fault are frequently indeterminable).

[161] *See* text accompanying notes 122-23 *supra*.

[162] Thus, for various institutional reasons, a court might adopt an objective test of negligence that does not recognize subjective differences in skill or intelligence, although these might be highly relevant in determining an actor's degree of *moral* fault. The difficulties that would arise if courts gave full recognition to such differences are readily apparent. *See generally* O.W. HOLMES, THE COMMON LAW 107-11 (1938).

skeptical of rightness reasons, those who have expressed such skepticism include some luminaries.¹⁶³ Of course, a judge who is skeptical of rightness reasons because, for example, he considers them conclusory, and who is also skeptical of goal reasons because he thinks only legislators may resort to them, is likely to suffer paralysis in a case of first impression.

What are the sources of skepticism about rightness reasons, and what should be said in response? These questions merit consideration,¹⁶⁴ but they also lead into waters turbulent with philosophical controversy, which I cannot enter here. Instead, I will follow, and at times even intermingle, several strategies. I will propose explanations for the skeptic's stance—explanations designed not to refute him, but to liberate him. I will offer some counterarguments. I will appeal to the usual willingness even of skeptics to embrace goal reasons. (Judges, lawyers, and law professors who are skeptical of rightness reasons are rarely skeptical of *all* substantive reasons.) Finally, I will let the burden of proof with respect to the legitimacy of rightness reasons fall where it should —on the skeptic. In the following discussion I address each of a variety of skeptical positions.

1. *"Rightness Reasons Are Not 'Real' Reasons"*

Some who are skeptical of rightness reasons not only favor goal reasons, but apparently think that goal reasons are the only *real* reasons.¹⁶⁵

Some might think that a real reason must somehow involve the court in *doing* something. On this view, goal reasons clearly qualify as real reasons because they hypothesize decisional effects. Since rightness reasons do not contemplate such effects, they cannot be real reasons.

Similarly, some will argue that a goal reason qualifies as a real

---

¹⁶³ Several passages in Holmes's most famous essay strongly suggest a bias in favor of "considerations of social advantage," which I take to mean goal reasons. *See* Holmes, *The Path of the Law*, 10 HARV. L. REV. 457, 467-69, 474 (1897). Similarly, in Vegelahn v. Guntner, 167 Mass. 92, 105-06, 44 N.E. 1077, 1080 (1896) (dissenting opinion), Holmes stated that the "true grounds of decision are considerations of policy and of social advantage"— again an apparent reference to goal reasons.

¹⁶⁴ It is important to confront skepticism about rightness reasons if only because it might sometimes adversely affect judges in the performance of their regular tasks. Although such skepticism rarely appears in judicial opinions, judges occasionally voice it in other settings.

¹⁶⁵ *See* note 163 *supra*. Roscoe Pound, who was himself a judge for a time, evolved his theory of interests without according an appropriately distinctive place to rightness reasons. *See* note 9 *supra*.

reason because it is instrumentalist in character. A goal reason "operates" through an intervening mechanism—a decision that produces effects. Thinkers brought up in our technological age as "social engineers" and "instrumentalists" naturally sense the genuineness of goal reasons, because such reasons envision future effects. Rightness reasons, on the other hand, cannot qualify as real reasons because they are noninstrumentalist—they look only to the past or to the present.

In this scientific age, the goal-minded individual is also likely to be an "empiricist." For him, a reason must turn on facts—not just the facts of a particular case, but general facts of social causality. Rightness reasons are not real to the empiricist, since they typically do not turn on such general facts. Rather, they depend on facts about the actions of the parties, or states of affairs resulting from those actions—facts of the particular case.

Further, a skeptic might think that a real reason, or at least one that a public official may appropriately give, must concern the "public interest." Goal reasons meet this test because they serve social goals—goals that affect or instantiate the interests of the community. Because rightness reasons regard only what is right between the parties, they cannot be real reasons.

Finally, to some skeptics at least, goal reasons seem to involve something like what economists call cost-benefit analysis, a kind of calculational rationality that eminently qualifies them as reasons. Since rightness reasons involve nothing of the sort, they cannot, on this view, be real.

Some of these forms of skepticism rest on invalid factual assumptions. It is untrue, for example, that the recognition of rightness reasons only has significance as between the parties.[166] But even if all of the foregoing skeptical propositions are true, none of them counts as an *argument* for the thesis that only goal reasons are legitimate. They boil down to little more than the bare assertion that nothing can be a reason unless it has the essential attributes of a goal reason. As such, they beg the question or merely express a prejudice.

As between the skeptic and the true believer in rightness reasons, who ought to bear the burden of persuasion? Who ought to produce arguments denying or affirming that reasons other than goal reasons have justificatory force? For several reasons the

---

[166] *See* text following note 46 *supra*.

burden should fall on the skeptic. First, the skeptic has to explain away far more than the true believer. He must explain away: (1) the fact that many common-law cases rest partly or primarily on rightness reasons; (2) the apparent assumption of many judges that, even though a given goal reason sufficiently justifies a proposed decision, a further rightness reason reinforces the justification; and (3) the sense of sacrifice that many judges feel when they let a goal reason override a rightness reason.

Furthermore, the skeptic must explain away not only many features of the common law, but also many corresponding features of daily life, since judges often resort in common-law cases to rightness reasons that people give regularly in nonlegal contexts. Genuine rightness reasons are not just ritualistic or technical justifications conjured up by a priesthood clad in judicial robes. Wholesale abandonment of rightness reasons would vastly diminish our justificatory resources outside, as well as inside, the law. It would rule out, at least in giving reasons, such familiar concepts as desert, good faith, fair reliance, fault, and inequity. Dispensing with such concepts would, in fact, make us quite different people, for concepts so fundamental help to define our very nature.

With the burden of persuasion cast upon his shoulders, the skeptic must produce genuine arguments that rightness reasons cannot serve as justifications of common-law decisions. I now turn to what some of those arguments might be.

2. *"Rightness Reasons Are Too Personal and Subjective To Count as Legal Reasons"*

This form of skepticism is of ancient lineage. And it is not unusual to encounter it today. Decisions explicitly based on rightness reasons in the old Court of Chancery sometimes drew the criticism that they varied with the "length of the lord chancellor's foot."[167] More modern versions of this skepticism are usually expressed in less colorful terms: "The judge based his decision on personal preferences," or "The judge relied on subjective value judgments." Note that the skeptic does not deny the genuineness of relevant values. He merely asserts that invoking these values to

---

[167] TABLE TALK OF JOHN SELDEN 43 (F. Pollock ed. 1927). For a recent allusion to the chancellor's foot in a skeptical vein, see Stream v. CBK Agronomics, Inc., 79 Misc. 2d 607, 608, 361 N.Y.S.2d 110, 112 (Sup. Ct. 1974) ("But, as has oft been seen, there is little room for the Chancellor's foot to rotate in the law of bills and notes."), *modified on other grounds*, 48 App. Div. 2d 637, 368 N.Y.S.2d 20 (1st Dep't 1975).

decide cases is a matter of subjective preference.[168] This subjectivist form of skepticism may be subdivided into several strands.

One strand might be called the "value plurality" thesis. On this view, judges who rely on rightness reasons bring into play a nearly infinite variety of rightness values in judging actions or states of affairs, and decisions in given cases will differ depending on which values the particular judges prefer. Hence, any decision is "subjective" to the extent that it rests on rightness reasons. Two aspects of this thesis are questionable. First, it is simply untrue that an infinite variety of values will be relevant to the decision of every case. The potentially significant values are usually quite limited. It is impossible to prove this without inordinately extended discussion of a wide range of cases, and I cannot enter upon that here. I will rest instead on a familiar truth—namely, that *facts govern and circumscribe the relevance of values*. Not just any value will be relevant to any set of facts; every value has a limited factual "range." Furthermore, it is simply untrue that judges cannot agree on which values are relevant to given actions and states of affairs. Judges commonly agree at least on the legal issue, and such agreement also narrows the set of potentially relevant values. For example, most judges "know" when a case involves unjust enrichment rather than justified reliance. The existence of ready agreement in most cases is something the "value pluralist" must explain away.

A second strand of subjectivist skepticism might be called the "no-shared-values" thesis. This view can be stated as follows: "Even if rightness values are not infinitely plural, and even if judges can at least generally agree on which values are relevant to particular actions or states of affairs, the resulting decisions must still be highly subjective because judges simply do not agree on which values should control." This form of skepticism vastly overstates the extent of disagreement among judges; it probably springs from a preoccupation with difficult or borderline cases that present close questions of conflicting values. But not all or even most cases, actual and imaginable, fall into this category. It is possible to pose a wide range of cases that virtually all would agree should be decided in the same way on rightness grounds. Clear cases of deserving conduct, clear cases of want of due care, clear cases of justified reliance, clear cases of unjust enrichment, and so on, are not difficult to imagine. Indeed, they constantly arise.

---

[168] Thus, the skeptic might concede the intrinsic goodness or desirability of values, and deny only their legitimacy as bases for judicial decisions.

A related strand of subjectivist thought might be characterized as the "value indeterminacy" thesis: "Even if rightness values are not infinitely plural and judges can generally agree on their relevance, and judges share such values and weigh them similarly, the choice of reasons (and the resulting decisions) must still be highly subjective because the relevant values are inherently indeterminate." Stated a bit differently, this thesis holds that value concepts such as "desert," "justified reliance," and "inequitable overreaching" are so extraordinarily vague, ambiguous, essentially contested, or otherwise indeterminate, that judges who apply them to characterize actions or states of affairs will inevitably make highly subjective judgments. But again, it appears that judges *do* commonly agree on the evaluative characterization of particular actions and states of affairs. This at least indicates that such concepts are susceptible of determinate application.

Admittedly, when judges give rightness reasons they rely on the values they have personally come to hold. But this does not necessarily render their decisions unreasonably subjective. Judges cannot give *any* type of substantive reason without bringing values into play. Where should judges get those values? They cannot conduct public referenda; to do so would be to abdicate the office of judging as we know it, and to risk exalting merely conventional over genuine values. In their own daily lives judges participate in society's shared stock of values; indeed, individuals are selected to be judges partly because their values are thought to coincide with those of many in the community. Some values, of course, may be appropriately characterized as "merely personal." But conscientious judges take care not to bring such values into play, and the multijudge character of our appellate courts limits the effect of purely personal notions of rightness.

Skeptics who dismiss rightness reasons are usually quick to embrace goal reasons, since goal reasons clearly qualify as "policy" reasons. Presumably, skeptics simply cannot imagine that reasons of policy might also be subjective. Of course, most of these skeptics realize that judges must frequently give substantive reasons to reach a decision in a case, and that it is therefore important that some such reasons count. Yet most, if not all, subjectivist theses can also be directed against goal reasons. Consider, for example, the claim that rightness reasons are unreasonably subjective because the judge who gives them consults only his own personal values. Does a judge giving goal reasons proceed any differently? In setting goals, judges can sometimes consult legislative or other official pronouncements, but these guideposts will not always point the way. Judges must then appraise purported goals as good or bad, or as better or worse than conflicting goals to be served by alternative decisions. How are they to do this? Again, they cannot hold public referenda, nor should they. Instead, judges must consult their own values and debate those values with counsel and other members of the court.

3. "Rightness Reasons Are Conclusory or Question-Begging"

One form of skepticism about rightness reasons apparently rests on the view that such reasons are inevitably conclusory or question-begging.[169] Of course, a conclusory or question-begging "reason" is no reason at all, and therefore cannot justify decisions. A genuine reason must appeal to something independent of the decision to be justified.[170] In contrast, a conclusory or question-begging reason merely characterizes the decision to be justified, or restates some point in issue along the way to the decision.

A good rightness reason appeals to a number of elements independent of the decision to be reached. A rightness reason must appeal to an applicable norm of right action. Thus, to justify a decision for the plaintiff boat-mast builder in our earlier case, a judge might appeal to what lawyers call estoppel—a rightness norm. But the content and soundness of such norms are independent of particular rulings or decisions. Moreover, the justificatory force of a rightness reason depends on the combination and strength of the reason's internal elements. These factors cannot be characterized as a "mere restatement" of the legal conclusion that the reason supports.

4. "Rightness Reasons, Even If Not Immediately Conclusory or Question-Begging, Are Ultimately So"

The rightness skeptic might also deploy a kind of "normative regress" argument. Consider this imaginary dialogue:

True Believer: Let's take a hypothetical case. Suppose Edgar

---

[169] Such skepticism is of ancient lineage, too. *See, e.g.*, Millar v. Taylor, 98 Eng. Rep. 201 (K.B. 1769). A colleague, Professor Alan Gunn, has suggested to me that one reason some tort theorists so vigorously pursue economic analysis today may be that they think all rightness reasons are merely conclusory. But see the important writings of Richard Epstein and George Fletcher, tort theorists who are not skeptical of rightness reasons. *E.g.*, Epstein, *Intentional Harms*, 4 J. LEGAL STUD. 391 (1975); Fletcher, *supra* note 124.

[170] "[J]ustification consists in appealing to something independent." L. WITTGENSTEIN, PHILOSOPHICAL INVESTIGATIONS § 265 (G. Anscombe trans. 1953).

knows his dog will bite, yet he carelessly lets the dog loose and it bites Betsy, an innocent victim. I think Edgar deserves to compensate Betsy. Stated in these terms, this is a rightness reason.

Skeptic: I see. But isn't your reference to the concept of desert *immediately* conclusory or question-begging?

True Believer: No. In stating a reason, one typically dispenses with a full exposition of all that goes into its formulation. In my example, I implicitly appealed to an independent norm calling for reparation whenever it is said that a person deserves to be held responsible.

Skeptic: I think I follow you, and perhaps agree up to this point. But at some *ultimate* point your reasoning becomes conclusory or question-begging, doesn't it?

True Believer: How so?

Skeptic: Well, why is it a reason to decide that Edgar deserves to pay Betsy, even assuming that he was at fault and she was an innocent victim?

True Believer: Because this would give Betsy her just due.

Skeptic: So what?

True Believer: Well, interpersonal decency is worth having in itself.

Skeptic: Why?

True Believer: It won't do for you to stand there and keep asking "so what?" or "why?"; you doubtless subscribe to some values yourself, don't you?

Skeptic: Well, yes, I do.

True Believer: Name one.

Skeptic: Well, I've decided some pollution cases on the ground that my decision would bring more health to the community. Now there's a *real* value for you.

True Believer: Human health?

Skeptic: Yes.

True Believer: But so what?

Skeptic: What do you mean "so what?" Can't you see that health is valuable?

True Believer: Oh, I see! So you *do* think there must be some stopping point? But if so—if there must be some stopping point in this kind of exercise—then, provided it is not merely arbitrary, our arrival at that point in regard to a given reason should not make that reason "ultimately" conclusory or question-begging, should it?

Skeptic: Well . . . .

This exchange shows that the skeptic's "normative regress" argument is a two-edged sword; it can be effectively turned against him. Any such regress must stop somewhere. Thus, if no reason can be a "real" reason unless it is always possible to give a satisfactory "reason behind the reason," then nothing will ever count as a reason. Admittedly, the true believer would be expected to say a great deal more about the nature of interpersonal decency in the foregoing dialogue. But the skeptic would be subject to the same demand in asserting that human health is a value.

5. *"Rightness Reasons Are Moralistic or Judgmental, and Involve 'Playing God' "*

Some judges seem reluctant to give rightness reasons because they view those who give such reasons as moralistic or judgmental and thus willing to impose their moral code on others. The solution to this problem (to the extent that it *is* a problem) is to avoid giving bad rightness reasons. It is sobering to recall that goal reasons, too, can be badly formulated, misconstrued, or misapplied. Yet, presumably, the skeptic would not consider this an argument against resorting to goal reasons.

In this secular age, some judges probably approach rightness reasons cautiously or even skeptically because they associate some of these reasons with specific religious origins. Judges who take this attitude, however, fall victim to the genetic fallacy. Even if all rightness reasons could be traced to specific religious teachings, this should not taint those reasons, even for the nonreligious. Reasons must be judged by their intrinsic worth, not by their origins.

In summary, the skeptics have yet to prove their case against rightness reasons.[171] At the very least, enough has been said to take some wind out of their sails. Judges who feel uneasy about rightness reasons should put aside many of their misgivings. By doing so, judges can bring more tools to their work. This should make for better decisions and better justifications.

E. *The Need for Rightness Reasons*

Some skeptics might concede the legitimacy of rightness reasons, yet claim that they are unnecessary. These skeptics might

---

[171] A further complex source of skepticism about rightness reasons is the view that when a rightness reason apparently has force, this is really because a goal reason has also been set forth or is lurking in the background. This "reducibility" thesis is discussed in Part VII *infra*.

think that judges can always give sufficient goal reasons for a decision, since every decision has effects which will always serve, directly or indirectly, some social goal. Only the unimaginative judge, such skeptics will argue, cannot "harness" causal relations to the framework of goal reasons that are sufficient to decide a case.

But is this so? It is true that both a goal reason and a rightness reason may be available to justify a decision. Thus, a decision might subserve a good end *and* accord with a sound rightness norm. In the boat-mast illustration, for example, a decision for the relying plaintiff would facilitate future economic exchange by encouraging people to participate in relationships in which they cannot obtain perfect information and must rely on the representations of others. At the same time, such a decision would compensate the party who justifiably relied upon another's carelessly chosen words.

In some cases, however, a good goal reason will be unavailable. There might be no relevant social goal, or the causality might be far too speculative, or the community might already have enough fulfillment of the goal. Indeed, any of a goal reason's necessary elements might be lacking. When a judge reaches the bottom of the goal-reason barrel, however, he has not necessarily run out of reasons.[172] One or more rightness reasons may still be available.

Even when the justificatory resources of a case generate both a goal reason and a rightness reason and both support the same decision, it still does not necessarily follow that the rightness reason lacks justificatory significance. Standing alone, the goal reason might be too weak to provide sufficient justification for the proposed decision; the judge must then add the force of the rightness reason. The rightness reason, if well articulated, will not only strengthen the justification, but also make the precedent more intelligible, and thus easier to interpret and follow in future cases. In the latter respect, the rightness reason will not be superfluous even when the goal reason alone suffices to justify the decision.

Furthermore, the justificatory resources might generate conflicting goal reasons, and the judge might need a rightness reason to break the resulting stalemate. Similarly, the case might generate a goal reason and a countervailing rightness reason. Here the judge might resolve the conflict by resorting to differences in

---

[172] There are numerous cases in which judges give only rightness reasons. *See, e.g.,* Goodman v. Dicker, 169 F.2d 684 (D.C. Cir. 1948); Sidis v. F-R Publishing Corp., 113 F.2d 806 (2d Cir. 1940).

the strength of the reasons or by invoking further rightness reasons.[173]

VI

DIFFERENCES BETWEEN GOAL REASONS AND RIGHTNESS REASONS

It is possible and worthwhile to study goal reasons and rightness reasons separately, each on their own terms. Judges must regularly construct and evaluate both types of reasons, and they are likely to do this better if they understand the internal complexities of each reason type. There are, however, important differences between these two types of reasons. I have yet to confront these differences directly and draw them together in one place. But it is important that judges grasp these differences. A judge cannot fully understand the internal workings of each type unless he understands what sets one apart from the other. In addition, the judge who grasps these differences will be less likely to confuse the two types of reasons in his decisional and justificatory labors.[174] The differences are important in other ways, too, which I will indicate en route. But the significance of many of the differences will be best understood only after setting forth what they are, and after considering whether rightness reasons are ultimately "reducible" to goal reasons.[175]

A. Inherent Differences

Some differences between goal reasons and rightness reasons are more or less "inherent." These contrast with "contingent" differences, which I will treat in the following section. Several inherent differences are related, some rather closely.

---

[173] Of course, goal reasons and rightness reasons frequently conflict. In forthcoming work, I will consider the possibility of devising a systematic decision procedure for resolving such conflicts.

[174] Even sophisticated judges who have thought and written about justification have confused the reason types. For example, it has been suggested that all judicial reasoning is a matter of pragmatic "trial and error," a characterization that does not felicitously apply to rightness reasons. *See generally* B. CARDOZO, THE NATURE OF THE JUDICIAL PROCESS 98-99 (1921). See also Dewey, *Logical Method and Law*, 10 CORNELL L.Q. 17, 26-27 (1924), in which all reasons are characterized as consequentialist.

[175] I am indebted to Mr. Leigh Kelley for discussion and assistance in preparing this Part and Part VII *infra*.

1. Sources of Justificatory Force

A goal reason derives its force from the fact that, at the time it is given, the decision it supports can be predicted to serve a good social goal. A rightness reason, however, derives its force from the fact that the decision it supports accords with a sound rightness norm applicable to a party's past action or to the state of affairs resulting from that action.

A goal reason thus requires an appropriate prediction—a causal relation between the supported decision and desired social effects. A rightness reason, on the other hand, requires an accordance between the supported decision and an applicable sociomoral norm—a noncausal relation. A goal reason involves a means-goal hypothesis. Theoretically, this hypothesis can be verified; in time, the predicted decisional effects—effects entirely *external* to the decision—either will or will not have occurred. Rightness reasons are fundamentally different. The reason-giver does not purport to predict the future effects of a decision that implements the reason. Rather, the essential relation of accordance between decision and norm either exists or does not exist at the time of decision. Any prediction that a state of affairs will result from the decision is irrelevant to the force of a rightness reason.[176] If a judge sets out to construct a rightness reason but then raises the prospect of desirable decisional effects, he is in fact undertaking to construct a goal reason, and his labors must take on a different character.

If the prediction on which a particular goal reason rests proves erroneous, it does not necessarily follow that the reason had no force at the time of decision. Of course, if a prediction fails repeatedly, this would bear on the force of the goal reason when given in future decisions. Similarly, events subsequent to a decision based on a rightness reason—*e.g.*, newly discovered evidence or a growth in moral enlightenment—might also lead the judge to revise his earlier judgment that his decision accorded with an applicable norm. But this has nothing to do with the failure of a prediction.

Hence, proficiency in constructing and evaluating the two

---

[176] Admittedly, judicial authorization of some process for implementing the decision in the future must figure in a rightness reason. (This may involve, for example, a money judgment, an injunction, or a judgment denying both.) But authorization of such process is simply part of what is meant by a judicial decision in the first place. Hence, nothing specific to a rightness reason itself qualifies as a goal external to the decision.

types of reasons calls for different knowledge and capacities. For example, a judge might be skillful in making the predictions required for goal reasoning, but lack the moral intuition, the conceptual sophistication, or the sensitivity to the meaning and significance of norms necessary for rightness reasoning.

2. *Objects of Evaluation*

The construction of a substantive reason requires evaluation of its internal elements. Since these elements differ, the objects of evaluation in the two types of reasons will differ as well. The construction of goal reasons requires a determination of whether posited goals are good, and whether predicted decisional effects serve the posited goals. The construction of rightness reasons, on the other hand, requires the evaluative characterization of past actions or the states of affairs resulting from those actions. This in turn calls for the exercise of the intuitive and conceptual skills needed to select, particularize, and apply relevant evaluative concepts. A judge engaged in this process must also evaluate the accordance between alternative decisions (including the methods of their implementation) and applicable rightness norms. Often he will have to evaluate the soundness of rightness norms themselves. Of course, this last form of evaluation is not limited to rightness reasons, since some goal reasons contemplate more rightness. In the construction of rightness reasons, however, it is *always* required.

3. *Effectiveness of Implementation—Its Bearing on Justificatory Force*

A good rightness reason that favors a decision for the plaintiff does not lose its force even though, at the time of decision, the defendant has no money to pay damages or will be unable to comply with an injunction. A rightness reason will always have force, regardless of whether an effective remedy is available, if a decision for the wronged party accords with the applicable rightness norm —a relation of accordance unrelated to cause and effect. If a judge knew at the time he gave a goal reason, however, that the decision it supported could not be implemented, this would nullify or reduce the force of the reason, since the essential prediction of decisional effects would fail, at least in the particular case.

B. *Contingent Differences*

Some features only "contingently" differentiate goal reasons and rightness reasons. These differences emerge only when specific instances of goal reasons and rightness reasons are compared.

1. Nature of Values

The values that figure in specific instances of the two types of reasons do not necessarily differ in character. Most goal reasons look to the realization of welfare values or "public goods"—e.g., more productive uses of resources, more economic exchange, more health, more peace and quiet, more safety, more clean air. Other goal reasons, however, look to the realization of more rightness.

Rightness reasons, on the other hand, necessarily regard rightness—specific conceptions of what is just, equitable, fair, deserving, faithful, etc. It follows that *most* goal reasons differ from *all* rightness reasons in that most goal reasons look to the realization of values other than rightness in and of itself.

2. "Achievability"

Although it rarely happens in practice that a goal is fully achieved, in principle most goals that look to the realization of welfare values or "public goods" are achievable. If a goal has been sufficiently achieved, it is no longer appropriate to give a reason in the name of that goal. Thus, judges sometimes abandon a goal and refuse to decide in its name because "we have had enough fulfillment of that goal."[177] The same is not true of norms. That judges should at some point stop giving a particular type of rightness reason "because we have had enough fulfillment of the relevant norm" smacks of the absurd, since rightness norms, unlike most goals, are incapable of such fulfillment.

3. Factual Requirements

Judges can usually give rightness reasons without inquiring into facts outside the record. But goal reasons call for predictions, and thus frequently take judges into the realm of general social facts, including the causes and cures of social ills. Frequently such facts will not appear in the trial transcript, which contains "adjudicative facts"—for the most part, facts of the specific case.[178]

Occasionally, however, a judge giving a rightness reason must also go beyond the adjudicative facts. For example, equality of

---

[177] *See, e.g.*, Siragusa v. Swedish Hosp., 60 Wash. 2d 310, 318, 373 P.2d 767, 773 (1962) (court abandons goal of protecting fledgling industry).

[178] For the distinction between adjudicative and legislative facts, see authorities cited in note 63 *supra*.

access to the media might be a rightness consideration bearing on the decision in a libel case, and general social facts relevant to media access might not appear in the record.[179] The judge in this case would have to undertake an inquiry similar to that called for by most goal reasons.

4. *Necessity of Reference to the Past*

Since rightness reasons call for an evaluative characterization of past actions or the states of affairs resulting from past actions, some might think that only rightness reasons look to the past. Goal reasons, however, also direct a judge's attention to past facts: those that make up our accumulated knowledge of social causation.

Even so, the past plays significantly different roles in the construction of the two types of reasons. In giving a goal reason the judge looks back merely to "draw a bead on the future"—to "line up his sights" on what lies ahead. In contrast, the judge who gives a past-regarding rightness reason *must* look back to identify and apply the relevant rightness norms. He is not concerned with the past for the light it may shed on the future; instead, the past provides the essential reference point for bringing his values to bear. Thus, in giving rightness reasons a judge cannot dismiss the past as "sunk costs" or "spilled milk."

In sum, particular instances of the two types of reasons may differ in a substantial number of respects. There is no one, simple "distinction" between the two types, but a variety of differences.

VII

REDUCIBILITY OF RIGHTNESS REASONS TO GOAL REASONS

In previous sections I have discussed the two basic types of substantive reasons, their internal elements, the manner in which these elements are combined, and a variety of important respects in which goal reasons and rightness reasons differ. I have also responded to arguments challenging the need for and legitimacy of rightness reasons. If I am right, the differentiation of the two types of reasons cannot be merely formal—*i.e.*, merely a matter of whether a judge chooses to formulate a reason as one type or the other. Instead, the two types must be substantively distinct and mutually exclusive.[180]

---

[179] *See, e.g.*, Taskett v. King Broadcasting Co., 86 Wash. 2d 439, 546 P.2d 81 (1976).

[180] Nevertheless, a few judges, lawyers, and two law professors have insisted in discussions with me that "the distinction" is "merely formal."

Yet the claim is made, occasionally by judges and more often by law professors, that the justificatory force of a rightness reason is always "reducible to" or "derivable from" the justificatory force of an available goal reason.[181] If some version of this reducibility thesis is true, judges should recognize it, for only then would they fully understand the complex justificatory practices in which they participate. Furthermore, judges who thus came to understand these practices could, once they constructed a relevant rightness reason, always go on to identify and articulate the goal reason on which it "rests." Having thus laid bare the true basis of justification, judges would be better able to reach the best results and better able to justify them.

I cannot thoroughly explore here the complex issue of reducibility. I will identify and rebut only two forms of the reducibility thesis. I will then briefly explain why, even if some version of the thesis is true, my theory of substantive reasons survives almost unscathed.

A. *Reducibility of Rightness Reasons to "Parasitic" Goal Reasons*

A parasitic goal reason derives its justificatory force primarily from the conjunction of two factors: the rightness reason that justifies an original, precedent-setting decision, and the doctrine of precedent itself.[182] For example, a decision based primarily on a "good faith" rightness reason generates, in a precedent system, a further goal reason: it is predictable (or so it is said) that similarly situated parties will follow the precedent and act in good faith. Thus, because precedential consequences qualify as goal-serving effects of the precedent, its underlying rightness reason becomes ultimately goal-serving, however rightness-oriented it might originally be.

This form of the reducibility thesis is unpersuasive. Even if precedential consequences are goal-serving in this way, they only *add* to the justification for the decision. This added force stems from the doctrine of precedent, not from any goal-subservience of the decision itself. Furthermore, whether a precedent-setting decision will produce more rightness in the future depends on whether the decision accords with rightness in the first place. Thus, even if an original rightness-based decision always gives rise, through the doctrine of precedent, to a further goal-serving reason ("bring about more such rightness"), if the original decision rested on a

---

[181] Again, such claims have been made to me in discussion.
[182] *See* text accompanying notes 46-48 *supra*.

rightness reason that had no justificatory force, the corresponding goal reason would itself lack force, since it could not involve bringing about *more rightness*.

Moreover, without a system of precedent, a rightness reason would still have force in the particular case. At least there is no reason to suppose that its force necessarily depends on projected precedential effects. On the contrary, if the theory of rightness reasons I offer is correct, the force of such reasons derives from the applicability of rightness norms that are primarily past-regarding or present-regarding.

Even under a system of precedent, it is often predictable that a decision based on a rightness reason will influence few, if any, parties in the future. Indeed, there might be no relevant "future," for the decided case might be the last one in the pipeline before the effective date of a statutory reform. Or the decided case might involve factual peculiarities that make it virtually impossible that a similar case will ever occur. But even if the decision does have a "future," many if not most persons whose activities fall within its scope might fail to learn of the decision or grasp its bearing. They might fail to act on the decision because they lack sufficient incentives, because they disagree with it, because the law itself provides that compliance is optional, or for a host of other reasons. Yet even if such factors limit or nullify the future impact of a decision, this does not mean that the decision is poorly justified. Our reducibility proponent, however, would have to say as much.

B. *Reducibility of Rightness Reasons to Independent Goal Reasons*

Below are several illustrative claims that a reductionist might make when confronted with cases in which the judge explicitly set forth only a rightness reason. In responding to each example, the reductionist might assert that a goal reason is available either in the particular case or generally in such cases.[183]

(1) "Behind justified reliance (concededly a rightness reason) I see the facilitation of economic exchange."

(2) "Behind punitive desert (concededly a rightness reason) I see the deterrence of socially undesirable conduct."

(3) "Behind due care (concededly a rightness reason if confined to basic respect for persons and property) I see community safety for persons and property."

---

[183] Although a goal reason might be unavailable in a particular case, it does not necessarily follow that goal reasons are generally unavailable for cases of the same general sort.

(4) "Behind doing equity as between the parties (concededly a rightness reason) I see the prevention of disorderly self-help."

In the foregoing examples, the reductionist does not claim that the rightness reason derives whatever force it has from the decision's precedential effects of bringing about more rightness. Rather, he claims that whatever force the rightness reason has derives from an implicit yet independent goal reason available in that very case or generally available in such cases. This type of reductionist views the implicit goal reason not as a parasitic reason concerned with bringing about more rightness (through stare decisis), but as an independent goal reason purportedly securing values wholly apart from rightness—values such as increased productivity, deterrence of dangerous actions, protection of persons and property against inadvertent hazards, and fostering peaceful settlement of disputes.

Two considerations cast doubt on this view. First, it seems odd, or at least incongruous, that different pairs of reasons in which such different values figure could be reducible, one to another. How can "protection of justified reliance" be reduced to "facilitation of economic exchange"? How can "punitive desert" be reduced to "deterrence of socially undesirable conduct"? How can "respect for persons and property" be reduced to "general safety," or "equity" to "prevention of disorderly self-help"? Yet the reducibility thesis calls for the assimilation of such disparate values, and for the anomalous equation of reasons that turn on such disparate concerns. Each of the rightness reasons listed above apparently incorporates all of the required elements of a rightness reason. And, at least to judges, the values that figure in these reasons apparently qualify as intrinsic values, desirable for their own sake and not necessarily instrumental to the realization of other values allegedly "behind" them. Why then should these reasons not be considered autonomous?

Furthermore, judges commonly give rightness reasons as the primary grounds for their decisions. Often they do not even refer to goal reasons.[184] These judges apparently intend that their opinions be taken at face value, and they are usually so taken. In all such cases, the reductionist must argue that the rightness reason really derives its force from some implicit goal reason (available in the particular case, or generally). Yet even where a judge has found and explicitly referred to such an "underlying" goal reason,

---

[184] *See* illustrative cases cited in note 172 *supra*.

I know of no instance where he has acknowledged that it provides the sole support for the decision. Can we dismiss widespread and long-standing justificatory practices, common both inside and outside the law, as fragmentary and essentially unsophisticated? The reductionist seems to take this view.

C. *Differences Again*

The arguments I have considered here for the reducibility thesis are at best inconclusive. Whether rightness reasons are reducible to goal reasons is a complex question to which we do not have an answer. But it is undeniable that rightness reasons figure prominently in judicial justification and differ in substantial ways from goal reasons.

Nevertheless, even if the justificatory force of rightness reasons ultimately derives entirely from accompanying or implicit goal reasons, it still would not follow that judges could always dispense with constructing and evaluating any available rightness reasons, and concern themselves solely with goal reasons. For example, there might be a certain type of goal reason that only has justificatory force if it incorporates or is accompanied by a rightness reason. If so, the rightness reason would be an essential component or concomitant of the goal reason, and if any internal element of the rightness reason itself were absent or seriously deficient, the goal reason would accordingly lack force as well. Thus, if rightness reasons necessarily figure in at least some goal reasons, judges must understand the character of rightness reasons in order to construct and evaluate those goal reasons.

VIII

Significance of the Duality of Substantive Reasons

I have differentiated two basic types of substantive reasons and noted the possible importance of some specific differences between them. I now take up the general significance of this duality.

In the many cases that require resort to substantive reasons—*e.g.*, cases of first impression and cases that overrule precedent—judges must recognize and remain aware of this duality. The essential elements of good goal reasons and good rightness reasons are not identical. Moreover, the facts and decisional context of a case might generate one type of reason but not the other. The duality directs the attention of judges (and readers of opinions) to quite different facets of each case—those potentially relevant to the construction and evaluation of goal reasons (future-regarding aspects), and those potentially relevant to the construction and evaluation of rightness reasons (usually, past-regarding aspects). Judges who focus separately on these different justificatory source-beds are more likely to discover all available reasons, to incorporate all the necessary elements in their construction (while excluding all extraneous elements), and to evaluate correctly the strengths and weaknesses of each reason.

I have already noted that precedents are not self-defining and self-applying.[185] To apply a precedent rationally, judges must advert to the substantive reasons behind it. Sometimes the precedent fails to state these reasons, or fails to state them clearly. Or it might be possible to formulate new and better reasons for the precedent. If judges remain conscious of the duality of substantive reasons and choose the appropriate model, they are likely to be more faithful in reconstructing and interpreting reasons that are only implicit or poorly expressed. Similarly, they should do a better job of constructing reasons from scratch.

Furthermore, the rationales for following precedent are themselves susceptible to analysis in terms of rightness norms and goals.[186] The doctrine of stare decisis varies in force and effect depending on which type of rationale supports it most strongly in a given case.

Courts regularly reevaluate precedents in deciding whether to follow, modify, or overrule them. Yet courts cannot undertake this task without applying evaluative standards. These standards fall into two categories; precedents should be judged not only by relevant goal standards but by rightness standards as well. In addition, judges should recognize that time can take different tolls on the two types of reasons. The continued force of a good goal reason depends, for example, on the continued validity of particular hypotheses of social cause and effect—hypotheses that technological developments can undermine. The force of rightness reasons is also subject to decline. For example, growing sociomoral enlightenment may lead to the alteration or abandonment of the norm on which a rightness reason depends.

Good substantive reasons also have factual requirements that vary according to type. As a result, there may be areas of the law in which one type of reason should figure more prominently

---

[185] *See* Part III *supra*.
[186] I will consider this topic in forthcoming work.

than the other. For example, a "due care" rightness reason can support a course of decision only if certain "adjudicative" facts are regularly determinable. Yet many, perhaps most, high-speed accident cases suffer from a paucity of evidence relevant to the issue of due care, and consequently degenerate into "negligence lotteries."[187] This at least weakens the general case for resolving high-speed accident cases on due-care rightness grounds. Similarly, judges sometimes seek to base their decisions in water-law cases on goal reasons such as "development of regional productivity," yet frequently know too little about relevant causality to justify such reasoning.[188] Again, the introduction of sealed containers, preventing consumers from inspecting the contents, has largely undermined the factual basis for the familiar rightness principle of caveat emptor. Thus, a general failure to satisfy the factual requirements of a reason type argues against basing a course of decision on reasons of that type. Since judges in subsequent cases will be unable to determine reliably whether the resulting doctrine is applicable, the values to be served by that doctrine cannot be realized with regularity.

In deciding whether to alter the common law, judges sometimes find it relevant, in the name of uniformity, to consider trends across the country. The duality of substantive reasons provides a useful framework for identifying and interpreting trends. A judge might note that a particular rightness norm has gained or lost acceptance, or that courts have started to recognize and implement a particular goal, or that an increasing number of courts have concluded that a long-standing goal has been sufficiently realized.

The duality is also relevant when judges consider whether they should defer to the legislature.[189] For example, institutional reasons argue more strongly for deference to the legislature when a judge proposes to overrule a precedent for goal reasons alone. Rightness reasons, on the other hand, tend not to be politically controversial and so call less strongly for adoption solely by democratic bodies. In addition, rightness reasons rarely require factual inquiries beyond the fact-finding machinery of the courts. In most cases, courts also have sufficient powers to implement the values that typically figure in rightness reasons. Moreover, when judges

---

[187] See generally Franklin, *Replacing the Negligence Lottery: Compensation and Selective Reimbursement*, 53 VA. L. REV. 774 (1967).

[188] See, e.g., Irwin v. Phillips, 5 Cal. 140 (1855).

[189] I will deal in forthcoming work with this topic as well.

decide cases of first impression on the basis of genuine (as opposed to *merely* conventional) rightness reasons, litigants relying on old law can claim unfair surprise with far less credibility, at least when the rightness norms involved are widely shared in society.

The duality might even enhance the faith of some judges in the power of reason. Secure that they can resort to at least two legitimate wellsprings of reason, not just one, judges might refrain from watering down their opinions and generalizing their reasons simply to gain the votes of colleagues. Instead, more judges might write dissents or concurring opinions, which in the long run might well make for a better reasoned body of law.

Furthermore, a judge who recognizes the duality of substantive reasons will be a more effective advocate of his views. He will be better equipped not only to formulate reasons of his own, but also to predict what types of reasons his colleagues on the bench will marshall to support *their* positions in a case; for among the many judges who are willing to resort to substantive reasons, some may be primarily rightness-minded, some primarily goal-minded, and some a mixture of the two.[190] A judge who can anticipate the differing priorities and opposing arguments of his brethren stands in a better position to begin formulating counterarguments to win them over to his side. (This predictive capability, of course, will also aid trial and appellate advocates.)

Indeed, the duality provides a framework for analyzing the entire judicial philosophy of an individual judge. To develop this analysis we would ask not only whether the judge favored goal reasons, rightness reasons, or a combination of the two, but also: Which goals and rightness concepts figure in the judge's reasoning, which are most prominent, and how are they related?[191] (Judges

---

[190] For example, a preliminary analysis of the opinions written by Judge MacKinnon of the United States Court of Appeals for the District of Columbia Circuit suggests that he is predominantly a "rightness-minded" judge. *See, e.g*, Hooks v. Southeast Constr. Corp. , 538 F.2d 431 (D.C. Cir. 1976) (in determining scope of subcontractor's duty to insure and indemnify, emphasizes contract language and nature of parties' relationship, while ignoring possible goal question of appropriate allocation of risk); Berger v. Board of Psychologist Examiners, 521 F.2d 1056 (D.C. Cir. 1975) (focuses upon fairness in particular case; downplays social goals of reducing fraud and maintaining high professional standards); Kline v. 1500 Mass. Ave. Apt. Corp., 439 F.2d 477, 488 (D.C. Cir. 1970) (dissenting opinion) (attacks majority's risk-allocation goal reason by emphasizing rightness reason that decision imposes crushing economic burden on defendant).

[191] To complete the analysis, we would also have to study the judge's use of institutional reasons and the extent to which he relies on authority reasons. This would provide far more insight into a judge's attitude and philosophy than the mere application of such labels as "activist" or "passivist."

themselves might subject their opinions to this analysis to achieve a heightened self-awareness.) Having analyzed the philosophy of a particular judge, we might consider further whether this philosophy constitutes a recognizable type, and whether this type correlates with factors in the personal backgrounds of judges who espouse it. A great judge must be a giver of good reasons and a good critic of reasons. The duality helps to explain what these complex attributes entail.

Finally, the duality represents not just an accidental but, in my view, an essential feature of the ideal conception of common law. Thus, the theory of common-law justification I offer here serves not only as a descriptive account, but also as a justification of the common law itself. Both goal reasons and rightness reasons must thrive in a healthy and resourceful system of common law.

Conclusion

I have set forth in this Article—tentatively and schematically—the core of a general theory of common-law justification. I have addressed myself to judges, and have focused on those reasons that have primacy in the common law—reasons of substance. But the potential ramifications of my theory extend beyond common-law justification, and, in some respects, beyond the law itself.[192] By way of conclusion, I will suggest some of the broader jurisprudential and theoretical implications.

(1) Judicial resort to substantive reasons may keep the common law more or less continuous with the morality of a society. Most substantive reasons have counterparts in daily life. That these show up in common-law justification should not be surprising. By attending to substantive reasons in the law one can discern specific and fundamental ways in which the law accommodates moral considerations (without necessarily becoming moralistic). One can thus avoid the temptation to *identify* law with morality in order to account for the bearing of morality on law.

(2) It is often said that the reasoning of judges and lawyers is esoteric or "artificial"—the province of an elite legal priesthood. But to the extent that substantive reasons spring from justificatory practices in daily life, they show themselves to be neither artificial nor the exclusive province of those trained in the law.

---

[192] The theory might even have certain educational implications. Why not require a fall-semester, first-year course entitled "Reasons"? (Holmes stressed that students should strive to "get to the bottom of their subject." What better way?)

(3) Most ideas of "justice" and "injustice" found in common-law cases appear in the work clothes of rightness reasons. By studying these reasons, we should achieve a fuller understanding of justice as a distinct standard for evaluating decisions. (Note, however, that not all rightness reasons embody concepts of justice or injustice.)

(4) Rightness reasons do not fit forward-looking instrumentalist theories of law, and thus do not sit well with most "social engineers." Such theories ignore the justificatory significance of the past, except insofar as it is relevant to shaping the future through goal subservience. A sufficiently detailed account of rightness reasons might therefore serve as a corrective to the myopias of crude utilitarianism as well. Bentham was wrong to think that "thank you" means "more, please."

(5) A faithful reconstruction of the justificatory practices of judges must, in large part, map the workings of the so-called "legal mind." How judges and lawyers think when they seek to justify common-law decisions is only one facet of the "legal mind," but it is an important one.

(6) By studying substantive reasons, and particularly goal reasons, we can see precisely where and how economics, sociology, and other "policy sciences" bear on the common law. Of course, contrary to what some practitioners of these sciences believe, not all reasons are "policy" reasons, and courts can make new law without "making public policy."

(7) If my theory of substantive reasons is basically right, the very integrity, tone, and spirit of a legal order intimately depend on the way in which judges view and use rightness reasons. A legal system without decisions based on rightness reasons is imaginable but, in my view, abhorrent.

(8) Although the law is only one field within which justificatory practices occur, it is a field of distinctive significance. Judges take pride in their ability to give good reasons and correctly view reason-giving as a basic judicial function. In addition, legal records and case reports provide unusually good sources for analyzing justificatory processes. Thus, students of justification will find substantive reasons articulated in common-law cases an extraordinarily rich quarry from which to extract materials for the construction of more general theories.

(9) Common-law reasons of substance should also interest value theorists, for, among other things, such reasons invoke a wide range of evaluative notions, including some that to date have

received only scant attention. Moreover, value theorists may well conclude from their study of substantive reasons that the categories of "justice" and "utility" are not really exhaustive or sufficiently refined.

(10) The theory should also cast light on our very concept of a "reason for deciding," as distinguished from a "reason for believing." Certainly we can no longer say that having a reason for deciding is merely a matter of knowing some facts, or of bringing values into play. Furthermore, there might be something distinctive about reasons for deciding as a separate subclass of reasons for acting.[193]

My ambitions, then, for the theory I offer are considerable. And the theory itself is ambitious. Bits and pieces of it may well fall at the hands of thoughtful scholars. Indeed, fundamentals of the theory might not survive.[194] But even so, the task will have been worthy of the effort. A general theory of common-law justification is long overdue. Any failure of mine can hardly signify that a theory of this nature lies beyond us.

---

[193] Note that a particular reason may have significance on three different levels, or from three separate points of view: (1) as a motive for an actor on the front line of human interaction; (2) as a reason for a judge's decision of a case; and (3) as a standard for evaluating the action taken in situations (1) and (2).

[194] Criticism of my theory of substantive reasons is, of course, invited. Such criticism might be addressed to at least the following issues:

(1) With respect to the two types of substantive reasons: (a) Does the theory account for and appropriately characterize each type's essential elements? (b) Are any of the listed elements unnecessary or readily collapsible into others? (c) Is the manner of their combination appropriately described? (d) How appropriate is it to conceptualize the evaluation of substantive reasons and their individual elements in terms of bi-polar continua? (e) Does the theory account for all the major forms of criticisms or weaknesses to which substantive reasons are subject?

(2) Are there major types of substantive reasons in the common law that the theory omits?

(3) Are institutional reasons appropriately accounted for?

(4) How genuine are the claimed differences between goal reasons and rightness reasons? Are there other differences?

(5) Are there major forms of the reducibility thesis other than the two considered here? Are there other responses to the thesis?

(6) Does the theory overstate the significance of the duality of substantive reasons? Does this duality have other forms of significance?

[19]

REASONABLENESS AND OBJECTIVITY

*Neil MacCormick**

I. Introduction

Law and Objectivity[1] is a work of rare distinction. It accounts lucidly for the elements of objectivity and of subjectivity in legal thought, whether in relation to the elements required by the law for liability, civil or criminal, or in relation to the objectivity, intersubjectivity, or even pure subjectivity found in the weighing of legal arguments. In relation to the former topic, Kent Greenawalt reminds us that liability judged by the foresight of the reasonable person is objective, by contrast with liability grounded in the actual intentions of an acting person.[2] In relation to the latter, while he acknowledges a measure of objective rightness and wrongness and a considerable degree of intersubjective checkability in the weighing and balancing of arguments, he nevertheless concludes that, on any fine point of balancing, reasonable people can differ. These differences are not objectively corrigible. To that extent, there remains an element of apparently irreducible subjectivity in the inevitable leeways of legal judgement.[3]

In deep respect for a distinguished colleague, whom it is a very real honor to join in honoring, I should like to offer some thoughts on the concept of the "reasonable" in response to the two points I have just highlighted. On the latter in particular, now as in the past, I find myself very much of the Greenawalt camp. In doing so, I am partly restating and partly rethinking some ideas I published a few years ago.[4]

From the beginnings of my study of law, I have been both fascinated and troubled by the concept of the "reasonable" so frequently used in such diverse contexts by lawyers and legislators in the legal

---

* Leverhulme Personal Research Professor and Regius Professor of Public Law, University of Edinburgh.
1 Kent Greenawalt, Law and Objectivity (1992).
2 *See id.* at 100–08.
3 *See id.* at 216–28. I hope this is a reasonable summary of a careful and sensitive argument.
4 *See* Neil MacCormick, *On Reasonableness, in* Les Notions à Contenu Variable en Droit 131–56 (Ch. Perelman & Raymond Vander Elst eds., 1984).

traditions with which I am most familiar. In the spectrum from purely descriptive to purely evaluative, "reasonable" seems to belong more toward the evaluative than the descriptive pole, not that there is no element of the descriptive in it. If I say that the care manufacturers took in manufacturing some article fell short of the care it would have been reasonable for them to take in the given setting, I am not describing the care they took or failed to take, I am evaluating the care they took. I am comparing what was done with what could have been done, and assessing whether a reasonable evaluation of the risks would have left an actor in that situation satisfied with the degree of care that was taken, or not so satisfied.

In my youth, evaluation of that sort seemed to me to involve a high degree of subjectivity. Yet I found my elders and betters unanimous in the opinion that the standard in question was (as Greenawalt also points out) an "objective" one. This puzzled me, and to some extent still does. I am puzzled even though I know that there is no strict contradiction between the two points in view. If a person is held liable for failing to do what a reasonable person would have done in a given context concerning a given misadventure that has occurred, we all acknowledge that there need have been no real guilty intention on the agent's part concerning the misadventure, no wilful intention to bring it about. We are even ready to acknowledge that there need have been no real fault on the agent's part, for he may have been striving to the best of weak abilities to prevent the accident that happened. The point is that a common standard is set for all persons, and all must meet that standard or be held liable in the event of mishaps occurring. And this may well be fairer from the point of view of accident victims, so far as concerns compensation, than any attempt to grade fault according to the different capabilities of different actors.[5] Clearly enough, this is, from the duty-bearer's point of view, something other than a subjective standard of achievement. The law's exhortation is not simply to do your best or to avoid acting with evil intentions toward others; it is to act according to the common standard of the community, as a "reasonable person" would.

That standard could be objective vis-à-vis the acting subject, and yet have to be applied only as mediated through the subjectivity of the judge who decides after the fact whether reasonable care was shown. There is nothing a bit surprising in the thought that objective standards are applicable only through adjudicative subjectivity. It is an

---

[5] *See* Neil MacCormick, *The Obligation of Reparation, in* NEIL MACCORMICK, LEGAL RIGHT AND SOCIAL DEMOCRACY: ESSAYS IN LEGAL AND POLITICAL PHILOSOPHY 212-31(1982).

objective question as to who crossed the line first, but it has to be judged by the line-judge, the photo-finish adjudicator, or the like.

But by reference to Greenawalt's second point which was cited above, it seems that it is not just the necessary subjectivity of appreciation that is engaged here, but something in the very idea of the reasonable that calls for a weighing of more than one factor, more than one variable. There may then only be limited intersubjective controllability in evaluation, even when everyone acts in the best of good faith and tries to judge the matter fairly and correctly. Is there really an "objective" answer to the question when this "objective" criterion of liability is satisfied?

Turning now to proceed with the inquiry, I want at once to abjure any narrowness of concern, as though reasonableness were in issue only in tort law, important though that is as one context for deploying it in the law. For there are many legal settings in which the question arises of what it is reasonable to do, to say, to conclude, or to doubt in a given context. A value like "reasonable" may be very context-sensitive, and always the judgement is going to be a concrete one in a concrete context, as the late Chaim Perelman was wont to stress.[6] As we shall see, there may be many factors which in any given situation have to be considered and assessed in judging the reasonableness of an act or an omission to act or a decision in its concrete context. For this reason and in this sense, "reasonableness" taken out of context is what Julius Stone called a "legal category of indeterminate reference."[7] Whether or not it remains quite as indeterminate in context is less clear. Anyway, when we think of legal reasoning in the common law systems or in mixed systems such as Scots law, the category of the reasonable has great importance and many uses. The same, no doubt, is true of civilian legal systems also. In many branches of the law, "reasonableness" is the standard set by the operative principles and rules of conduct and of judgement, as we may see from the following illustrations.

---

6 See CH. PERELMAN, L'EMPIRE RHETORIQUE: RHETORIQUE ET ARGUMENTATION 40 (1977) ("En fait, ces valeurs font l'objet d'un accord universel dans la mesure où elles restent indeterminées; dès qu'on tente de les préciser, en les appliquant à une situation, ou à une action concrete, les desaccords . . . ne tardent pas à se manifester."). For the English translation, see CH. PERELMAN, THE REALM OF RHETORIC 27 (William Kluback trans., 1982) ("These values are the object of a universal agreement as long as they remain undetermined. When one tries to make them precise, applying them to a situation or to a concrete action, disagreements . . . are not long in coming.").

7 JULIUS STONE, LEGAL SYSTEM AND LAWYERS' REASONINGS 263–67, 301–37 (1964).

Within public law, it is a general principle that the powers of public authorities must not be exercised unreasonably.[8] Within the criminal law, the standard required in trials for the proof of an accused person's guilt is proof "beyond a reasonable doubt," this being a more exacting standard of proof than the proof "on balance of probabilities" required in most issues of civil litigation.[9] In the private law of reparation of injuries, the standard of care which each person owes to every other is the care which a "reasonable man" would take for the safety of his neighbours in the given circumstances.[10] The extent of liability for negligent wrongdoing is likewise limited by the consequences of a course of conduct so far as, at the time of action, these would have been foreseeable by a reasonable person.[11] This duty of reasonable care, although originally elaborated in the jurisprudence of the higher courts, is now also confirmed in certain more particular instances by statutory law.[12] In the law of contract, there is a general common law principle under which contracts in restraint of trade are invalid if they set restraints which go beyond what is reasonable in the interest of the parties and in the public interest.[13] Furthermore, damages for breach of contract are restricted to losses reasonably foresee-

---

8 *See* Westminster Corp. v. London & N.W. Ry. Co. [1905] App. Cas. 426, 430 (appeal taken from Eng.). Lord Macnaghten noted,

"[A] public body invested with statutory powers . . . must take care not to exceed or abuse its powers. It must keep within the limits of the authority committed to it. It must act in good faith. And it must act reasonably. The last proposition is involved in the second, if not in the first."

Id. (quoting Lord Macnaghten).

Some commentators have doubted the utility of this wide sense of reasonableness. *See* STANLEY A. DE SMITH, JUDICIAL REVIEW OF ADMINISTRATIVE ACTION 346–54 (J.M. Evans ed., 4th ed. 1980).

9 *See* COLIN TAPPER, CROSS AND TAPPER ON EVIDENCE 162–63 (8th ed. 1995). Some English judges have tended to discourage the "reasonable doubt" formula, but the Scots have held to it. *See* ALLAN GRIERSON WALKER & NORMAN MACDONALD LOCKHART WALKER, THE LAW OF EVIDENCE IN SCOTLAND (1964) (noting chapters seven and eight, and especially page 76). At page seventy-six, the authors state: "It is for the Crown to prove the accused's guilt beyond reasonable doubt . . . . The doubt must be reasonable in that it must not be a strained or fanciful acceptance of remote possibilities." *Id.* at 76; *see also* Shaw v. H.M. Advocate, 1953 J.C. 51.

10 *See, e.g.*, Donoghue v. Stevenson, [1932] App. Cas. 562 (appeal taken from Scot.). "Reasonable man" is gradually giving way to "reasonable person," and this is much to be welcomed. See Greenawalt's wise words in GREENAWALT, *supra* note 1, at 145–46.

11 *See, e.g.*, Overseas Tankship (U.K.) Ltd. v. Morts Dock & Eng'g Co. (The Wagon Mound), [1961] App. Cas. 388 (P.C.) (appeal taken from N.S.W.).

12 *See, e.g.*, Occupiers' Liability Act, 1957, 5 & 6 Eliz. 2, ch. 31 (Eng.); Occupiers' Liability (Scotland) Act, 1960, 8 & 9 Eliz. 2, ch. 31 (Scot.).

13 *See* J.D. HEYDON, THE RESTRAINT OF TRADE DOCTRINE (1971).

able as of the date of contracting, and there are other instances where rules of statutory law enable courts to set aside contractual provisions which are unreasonable.[14] In relatively recent divorce law, we find provisions whereby unreasonable conduct by one spouse towards the other may be a ground for judicial dissolution of marriage.[15]

As everyone is well aware, these are merely illustrations of a very general tendency in the law to rely upon the standard of reasonableness as a criterion of right decisionmaking, of right action, and of fair interpersonal relationships within the law of property, the law of obligations, and family law. Even as a few illustrative examples, they suffice to ground the thesis that reasoning about reasonableness is a matter of great moment within the operations of the law. If we did not understand how to work with such a notion, we would fail to understand an essential and central feature of contemporary legal reasoning. How then are we to understand it?

The first point to make is that the "reasonableness" the law has in view must be practical reasonableness,[16] not an abstract capacity for reason upon theoretical issues. The reasonable person has the virtue of *prudentia* and uses this in action. It is a virtue that is incompatible with fanaticism or apathy, but holds a mean between these, as it does between excessive caution and excessive indifference to risk. Reasonable people take account of foreseeable risks, but with regard to serious possibilities or probabilities, not remote or fanciful chances. They do not jump to conclusions, but consider the evidence and take account of different points of view. They are aware that any practical dilemma may involve a meeting point of different values and interests, and they take the competing and converging values seriously, seeking a reconciliation of them or, in cases of inevitable conflict, acting for whatever are the weightier or the overriding values.

Reasonable persons resemble Adam Smith's "impartial spectator."[17] (Indeed, it might be better to say that they themselves exhibit

---

14 *See, e.g.,* Unfair Contract Terms Act, 1977, ch. 50 (U.K.).

15 *See* Matrimonial Causes Act, 1973, ch. 18, § 1(2)(b); Divorce (Scotland) Act, 1976, ch. 39, § 1(2)(b).

16 In what follows, I am profoundly indebted, not only to Greenawalt, *see* GREENAWALT, *supra* note 1, but also, and even more, to John Finnis, *see* JOHN FINNIS, NATURAL LAW AND NATURAL RIGHTS 100-33 (1993), though in relying as I do on Adam Smith and Robert Alexy, I fall well short of Thomistic value-realism.

17 *See* ADAM SMITH, THE THEORY OF MORAL SENTIMENTS 129-37 (D.D. Raphael & A.L. MacFie eds., 1976); *cf.* KNUD HAAKONSSEN, THE SCIENCE OF A LEGISLATOR: THE NATURAL JURISPRUDENCE OF DAVID HUME AND ADAM SMITH 47-52 (1981). I have never found myself persuaded by the "rational choice" version of reasonableness that prevails in the contemporary "economic analysis of law" and commend economists to other aspects of Adam Smith's thought. I gratefully endorse the argument of Heidi Li

recourse to "spectator" reasoning.) For they seek to abstract from their own position to see and feel the situation as it looks and feels to others involved, and they weigh impartially their own interests and commitments in comparison with those of others. They are aware that there are different ways in which things, activities, and relationships can have value to people, and that all values ought to be given some attention, even though it is not possible to bring all to realisation in any one life, or project, or context of action. Hence they seek to strike a balance that takes account of this apparently irreducible plurality of values. In this way reasonable people are objective: they are not so consumed with passion for their own interest or project (though they may indeed be very committed to it) as to be unable to stand back momentarily and see the situation from other persons' points of view. Having done that, they are able to judge their own interests in competition with others' in an at least partly objective way. They will recognise that a greater interest or deeper value of another can properly take priority over the interest they pursue and the values they seek to realise, so far as conflict is inevitable. Reasonable people cultivate the Smithian virtue of self-command and apply it in self-restraint when others have legitimate priority over them.

Perfectly reasonable people would doubtless be unreal paragons of virtue. There are few to be found. Ordinary people are not; but most are reasonable some of the time and some are reasonable most of the time. And on all of us the law imposes the requirement that we act reasonably or, at any rate, act, whether by luck or by judgement, up to the standard of the reasonable in a variety of settings such as those noted. But contexts differ. As a juror in a criminal trial, I must look at the prosecution evidence with a critical eye, especially having regard to any competing evidence offered by the defence, and considering whatever grounds of doubt have been put before me by the defence. Certainty is impossible in relation to contingent assertions about the past, such as are involved in every criminal trial. Some doubt (or possibility of doubt) must always be present, but not all doubt rises above the threshold of doubt that a reasonable person would act on. Some points of doubt are properly ignored or treated as remote and unrealistic, fanciful, even, set against a powerful weight of credible evidence. As an administrative decisionmaker, I must be careful to review the whole scheme within which I exercise discretion and be sure to ground my decision on a weighing only of factors relevant to the scheme, taking no note of irrelevant matters. As a driver, I

Feldman. *See* Heidi Li Feldman, *Science, Reason, and Tort Law: Looking for the Reasonable Person*, 1 CURRENT LEGAL ISSUES 35, 39-43 (1998).

must always bear in mind that, however pressing my reasons for haste may be, and whatever burdens of worry and concern beset me, there are other road-users whose safety in life and limb ranks higher on a just scale of value than my urgent need to keep an appointment. And so on. Reasonable doubt is not the same as reasonable decisionmaking nor is either the same as reasonable care in driving. But there is a common thread that links the appellation "reasonable" in these and other instances of its use. That common thread, I would submit, lies in the style of deliberation a person would ideally engage in, and the impartial attention he would give to competing values and evidences in the given concrete setting. The ideal deliberator is the "reasonable person," and actual human agents achieve reasonableness to the extent that their decisions or actions or conclusions match those that would result from ideal deliberation. Naturally, where issues arise for decision in a court after the fact that gives rise to criminal charge or asserted civil liability, the court's deliberation, the heat of the moment being long past, can more probably replicate the ideal deliberation than can the individual human response to the heated moment.

It is a common saying that there are many questions on which reasonable people can reasonably differ. Some of these are simple differences of personal taste—baseball is for one person a more exciting game than cricket, but another prefers cricket for the long, slow build up of expectation and tension by contrast with the more explosive action in the baseball game. *De gustibus non est disputandum*; it is foolish to treat differences of taste as occasions for disputation. But this is not the only kind of difference there is. In any question that involves weighing much evidence or many interests and values and coming to a conclusion on what may seem a relatively fine balance, it does not surprise us to find others reaching a conclusion different from our own. There can here be a real difference of judgement about what is right and what ought accordingly be done. Such a difference of judgement is no mere difference of taste. And it matters to us, because a decision must be made according to one or the other view, whereas in most differences of taste it is sufficient for different persons each to go his own way. Such differences of judgement, as Greenawalt notes, are typical of so-called "hard cases" as these have been discussed in the jurisprudence of the last thirty years.[18]

The problem may have to do with the "procedural"[19] character of reasonable deliberation. In the light of human values, interests, and

---

18 *See* GREENAWALT, *supra* note 1, at 207–31.
19 *See* ROBERT ALEXY, A THEORY OF LEGAL ARGUMENTATION: THE THEORY OF RATIONAL DISCOURSE AS THEORY OF LEGAL JUSTIFICATION 177–208 (Ruth Adler & Neil

purposes, one must consider all that is relevant, and assume an impartial stance in assigning relative weight or importance to different contextually relevant values or interests. But different people may differ in how exactly they assign such weights and carry out balancing. There may be obvious errors of partiality or gross anomalies in differential weighting, but beyond that, it is difficult or impossible to show that one approach is superior to another. Provided people avoid fickleness or capriciousness and observe a decent constancy in judgement over time, while remaining open to revision of their opinion in the light of reasoned arguments, they are not unreasonable just because they take a view different from mine or yours.

It follows that on some questions, or in relation to some decisions, there may be more than one reasonable answer or, at least, a range of answers that cannot be shown to be, or dismissed as, unreasonable. That is compatible with the fact that those who hold to any of the reasonable answers can readily dismiss other approaches, on good grounds, as unreasonable ones. The absence of a single reasonable answer is not proof that there is no such thing as an unreasonable one. This is itself strongly persuasive in favour of establishing authorities charged with decisionmaking. Provided those holding authority are wise and reasonable persons, and provided there is some way of controlling or checking their decisions (e.g., by appeal, or by answerability before some representative body, or the like), there seems to be no better way than this of dealing with the problem of the nonunivocality of the reasonable. It is not surprising that constitutional states are marked by the practice of appointing decisionmakers to exercise restricted discretions by the use of proper procedures. Sometimes, moreover, to ensure the discursive and deliberative quality of the search for final decision or answer, authority is granted to a group, committee, assembly, or bench of several persons; and then there have to be voting procedures to make possible final decisions on finely balanced questions. Again, this is an unsurprising feature of contemporary constitutional landscapes.

These reflections may suffice by way of an introductory attempt to analyse and to flesh out in general terms an understanding of the idea of the "reasonable." Next, I wish to pursue this in relation to positive law, to check how far the ideas put forward here find illustration, if not proof, in the materials of the law. I shall do this in three stages, considering first the reasons that might be advanced to justify use of the standard of reasonableness in law, second the ways there are of

---

MacCormick trans., 1988). Alexy's proceduralist approach follows, but refines, that of Jürgen Habermas.

interpreting the factors relevant to reasonableness in different branches of the law, and finally concrete decisions about reasonableness where what is reasonable is (sometimes, at least) said to be a "question of fact."

II. WHY "REASONABLENESS"?

There has been a fair amount of writing on what justifies the law's resort to prescribing "reasonableness" as a guiding standard in a given general context. Early in the field was H.L.A. Hart's discussion of the reasons that sometimes militate against a legislative strategy of laying down specific and detailed rules of conduct. "Sometimes," he says, "the sphere to be legally controlled is recognized . . . as one in which the features of individual cases will vary so much in socially important but unpredictable respects, that uniform rules to be applied from case to case without further official direction cannot usefully be framed by the legislature in advance."[20] In such a case, suggests Hart, a legislature may prescribe general principles and set up a subordinate rulemaking authority to issue by way of delegated legislation more specific rules for the guidance of the general public or some section thereof.[21] Alternatively, it may resort to the "similar technique" of requiring persons in general "to conform to a variable standard *before* it has been officially defined. . . ."[22] In this case "they may learn from a court only *ex post facto* when they have violated it, what, in terms of specific actions or forbearances, is the standard required of them."[23] The prime example in Hart's view of such a "variable standard" in Anglo-American law is the standard of reasonable care as it applies in the civil and criminal law for defining actionable or punishable forms of negligence.[24]

This way of depicting recourse to the "reasonable" as an operative standard in law assimilates it to delegated legislation. The law as it leaves the legislator's hand is incomplete, and it falls to the judge who applies the law to supply a more detailed rule within the partially incomplete framework laid down. Hence the judge participates in the legislative process in a subordinate way, exercising the kind of strong discretion legislatures have in liberal democracies.

In the light of our introductory discussion of reasonableness, this seems to exaggerate the purely decisionist element in judgement con-

---

20 H.L.A. HART, THE CONCEPT OF LAW 127 (1961).
21 *See id.* at 127–28.
22 *Id.* at 128–29.
23 *Id.* at 129.
24 *See id.*

cerning the reasonable. There must indeed be a decision after a balancing of relevant considerations, but this really is a kind of judging, not a kind of legislating. A scintilla of evidence in favour of the present view against Hart's is that Hart's clashes with the lawyers' view (discussed further below) that what is reasonable in any case is a "question of fact." Moreover, it fails to square with the possibility that lay persons and businesses can perfectly well guide their own conduct with some confidence by reference to such guidelines as "reasonable care," "reasonable notice," and "reasonable conformity of goods to sample." They can do so without waiting for decisions to be laid down by the authorities. But that is what must often be done when delegated legislation is awaited to complete an imperfect statutory scheme.

To say this is to pick up a point from Ronald Dworkin's critique of the theory of "strong discretion" to which he considers Hart committed.[25] Dworkin considers Hart's whole approach to be vitiated through ignoring the role principles play in interaction with rules, with the upshot that concrete legal questions always involve appraisal of the overall balance in a constellation of principles as one interprets a legal problem involving the contested application of rules to facts.[26] Rules that incorporate standards, he suggests, function much as do principles, in that they call for a measure of balancing.[27]

As will be seen in what follows, I agree with Dworkin in rejecting the "delegated legislation" model, though I do not accept the full implications of Dworkinian interpretivism. Nevertheless, we can take up some of what Hart says. As he points out, we face a standing possibility of conflicts of interests or of values; the case of negligence in tort law is a case in point.[28] On the one hand, we set value upon the security of persons and their property and their economic interests from damage resulting from others' acts.[29] On this account, we think it right and proper that each person take care to avoid inflicting bodily harm on others or damaging their property or economic well-being. On the other hand, we set value upon the freedom of individuals to pursue their own activities and way of life without having to undertake an intolerable burden of precautions against the risks of damage to others.[30] The law has to express a balance between these values in

---

25 *See* RONALD DWORKIN, TAKING RIGHTS SERIOUSLY 14–45 (1978) [hereinafter DWORKIN, TAKING RIGHTS SERIOUSLY]; *see also* RONALD DWORKIN, LAW'S EMPIRE 280–82 (1986).
26 *See* DWORKIN, TAKING RIGHTS SERIOUSLY, *supra* note 25, at 44.
27 *See id.* at 43–45.
28 *See* HART *supra* note 20, at 129–30.
29 *See id.*
30 *See id.*

general terms, and it expresses this balance by prescribing that such care has to be taken as would be taken by a reasonable and prudent person. But just as this implies in general terms the striking of a balance between the two values of relative security from harm and relative liberty to do as you like, so it points in particular situations to a balancing of relevant values in their particular manifestations.

Judicial dicta are readily available to back this up. In *Read v. J. Lyons & Co.*,[31] the plaintiff, a government inspector working in a munitions factory in wartime, was injured by an explosion in the shell-filling shop of the factory. She sued for damages, arguing that the factory proprietor was subject to *Rylands v. Fletcher*[32] strict liability, and accordingly that she was entitled to compensation without proof of any fault in the conduct of the operations of manufacturing shells. The House of Lords rejected this argument. Lord Macmillan stressed,

> The process of evolution [of English law] has been from the principle that every man acts at his peril and is liable for all the consequences of his acts to the principle that a man's freedom of action is subject only to the obligation not to infringe any duty of care he owes to others.[33]

In the particular case, indeed, it was argued that an exception to the modern principle existed in the case of "things and operations dangerous in themselves," but as to this Lord Macmillan observed,

> [I]n the case of dangerous things and operations the law has recognized that a special responsibility exists to take care. But I do not think that it has ever been laid down that there is absolute liability apart from negligence where persons are injured in consequence of the use of such things or the conduct of such operations. In truth it is a matter of degree. Every activity in which man engages is fraught with some possible element of danger to others. Experience shows that even from acts apparently innocuous injury to others may result. The more dangerous the act the greater is the care that must be taken in performing it.[34]

Here is a pretty straightforward judicial exposition both of the standard argument in favour of upholding a requirement of "reasonable care" rather than "strict liability" and of the argument acknowledging that the degree of care required as "reasonable" must vary according to the risks at stake. This is indeed "a matter of degree." Since no legislature either can or should try to foresee all particular situations

---

31 [1947] App. Cas. 156 (appeal taken from Eng.).
32 3 L.R.-E. & I. App. 330 (1868).
33 *Read*, [1947] App. Cas. at 171.
34 *Id.* at 172.

of risk, it neither can nor should seek to make for all purposes detailed rules about precautions to be taken. It is sufficient that the law prescribe the standard of care as that which is reasonable, and defer the evaluation of particular risks to particular cases.

Still, the question of reasonableness as a matter of due care in the law of civil liability for harm negligently caused is merely one illustration of the general point. It can be made no less vividly with regard to the use of "reasonableness" in public law as a criterion for good decisionmaking by public authorities. One can summarise, and inevitably oversimplify, the relevant body of law[35] as follows. Every public power of decisionmaking, whether judicial, quasi-judicial, or administrative, must be exercised reasonably, that is, with proper regard to relevant considerations, and without any regard to irrelevant considerations.[36] The test of relevance in this case is governed by the terms in which and the objects for which the power of decisionmaking is granted by law.[37] Provided that the decisionmaker has grounded his decision upon a general appraisal of all the relevant factors and has not acted upon any irrelevant considerations, the decision cannot be quashed by the courts merely on the ground that it is erroneous "upon the merits." Only if the decision is one that no reasonable person could have reached upon any reasonable evaluation of the relevant factors, may the decision be reviewed and quashed in a court.[38]

Again, what justifies resort to the requirement of reasonableness is the existence of a plurality of factors that must be evaluated in respect of their relevance to a common focus of concern (in this case a decision to be made by a public body for public purposes). Unreasonableness consists in ignoring some relevant factor or factors, in treating as relevant what ought to be ignored. Alternatively, it may involve some gross distortion of the relative values of different factors. Even though different people can come to different evaluations in such questions of balance, and a variety of evaluations could be accepted as falling within the range of reasonable opinions about that balance,

---

35 *See* Lord Irvine of Lairg, Q.C., *Judges and Decision-Makers: The Theory and Practice of* Wednesbury *Review,* 1996 PUB. L. 59.

36 *See, e.g.,* Anisminic v. Foreign Compensation Comm'n, [1969] 2 App. Cas. 147 (appeal taken from Eng.).

37 *See, e.g.,* Padfield v. Minister of Agric., [1968] App. Cas. 997 (appeal taken from Eng.).

38 *See, e.g.,* Associated Provincial Picture Houses, Ltd. v. Wednesbury Corp., [1948] 1 K.B. 223 (Eng. C.A.); Secretary of State for Educ. & Science v. Tameside Metro. Borough Council, [1977] 1 App. Cas. 1014 (appeal taken from Eng.); Malloch v. Aberdeen Corp. (No. 2), 1974 S.L.T. 253.

the range has some limits. Some opinions are so eccentric or idiosyncratic that they are not accepted as valid judgements at all.

As Kent Greenawalt and Duncan Kennedy have shown,[39] what is presupposed in any resort to reasonableness as a standard is that there is some topic or focus of concern to which, in accordance with variable circumstances, various factors are relevant, these having to be set in an overall balance of values one way or the other. Kennedy observes that legal standards typically embody a relatively specific subset of social values, and one would be inclined to concur for values like "fairness," "due care," "due process," "natural justice," or the like.[40] But in the case of the "reasonable," there is not the same degree of localisation of values. What is reasonable in the particular circumstances depends upon an evaluation of the competing factors of decision, and what factors of decision are relevant (and thus in competition) is highly context-dependent. The very thing that justifies the law's recourse to such a complex standard as reasonableness in the formulation of principles or rules for the guidance of officials or citizens is the existence of topics or foci of concern to which a plurality of value-laden factors is relevant in a context-dependent way.

III. Interpreting "Reasonableness"

There must be at least two ranges of variation within the variables to which any question of reasonableness relates. The topics to which reasonableness connects are variable, and the factors relevant to judgement vary according to the topic. The topic, as noted several times already, may be decisions by public authorities, or decisions about guilt in criminal trials, or activities of persons which are potentially harmful to other individuals, or contractual relationships, or marital relationships, or any of many others determined by legislators or judges.

Given this variability of topic, there are necessarily certain questions about reasonableness which are pure questions of law, that is, of the proper interpretation of the law. What are properly to be treated as the factors and values relevant to a given topic? That is a question of the correct interpretation of the law as it bears upon the topic. It is quite common that statutes prescribing a standard of reasonableness explicitly indicate relevant factors. Thus, for example, the 1957 Occupiers' Liability Act requires that every occupier of premises "take

---

39 *See* GREENAWALT, *supra* note 1, at 144–45 (quoting Duncan Kennedy, *Form and Substance in Private Law Adjudication*, 89 HARV. L. REV. 1685, 1688 (1976)); *see also* DUNCAN KENNEDY, A CRITIQUE OF ADJUDICATION: *Fin de Siècle* 139 (1997).

40 *See* Kennedy, *supra* note 39, at 1688.

such care as in all the circumstances of the case is reasonable to see that the visitor will be reasonably safe in using the premises for the purposes for which he is invited or permitted by the occupier to be there."[41] Then the Act further provides as follows:

> The circumstances relevant for the present purpose include the degree of care, and of want of care, which would ordinarily be looked for in such a visitor, so that (for example) in proper cases—
>
> (a) an occupier must be prepared for children to be less careful than adults; and
>
> (b) an occupier may expect that a person, in the exercise of his calling, will appreciate and guard against any special risks ordinarily incident to it, so far as the occupier leaves him free to do so.[42]

Again, the 1977 Unfair Contract Terms Act[43] makes provision whereby the courts can control exemption clauses in contracts between suppliers and consumers of goods and services. Any contractual term which seeks to exempt a party from his normal legal liabilities may be struck down if it is not reasonable, as to which the Act makes the following further provision: "In determining . . . whether a contract term satisfies the requirement of reasonableness, regard shall be had in particular to the matters specified in Schedule 2 to this Act."[44] Schedule 2 provides that "regard is to be had in particular [to] . . . any of the following [matters] which appear to be relevant":[45]

> (a) the strength of the bargaining positions of the parties relative to each other, taking into account (among other things) alternative means by which the customer's requirements could be met;
>
> (b) whether the customer received an inducement to agree to the term, or, in accepting it, had an opportunity of entering into a similar contract with other persons, but without having to accept a similar term;
>
> (c) whether the customer knew or ought reasonably to have known of the existence and extent of the term (having regard, among other things, to any custom of the trade and any previous course of dealing between the parties);
>
> (d) where the term excludes or restricts any relevant liability if some condition is not complied with, whether it was rea-

---

41 Occupiers' Liability Act, 1957, 5 & 6 Eliz. 2, ch. 31, § 2(2) (Eng.).
42 *Id.* at § 2(3).
43 Unfair Contract Terms Act, 1977, ch. 50 (Eng.).
44 *Id.* at ch. 50, § 11(2).
45 *Id.* at ch. 50, § 11(2), sched. 2.

sonable at the time to expect that compliance with that condition would be practicable;

(e) whether the goods were manufactured, processed or adapted to the special order of the customer.[46]

In both the instances quoted, the legislature has given explicit, but nonexclusive guidance as to factors which are relevant to a judgement of reasonableness in respect of the topic in question. Similar attempts to give a partial definition of factors relevant to judgements about reasonableness in particular contexts are commonly and regularly to be found in judicial dicta. The High Court of Australia has attempted to clarify the extent of the duty to take reasonable care in giving information or advice, the following being a useful dictum by Chief Justice Gibbs:

> It would appear to accord with general principle that a person should be under no duty to take reasonable care that advice or information which he gives to another is correct, unless he knows, or ought to know, that the other relies on him to take such reasonable care and may act in reliance on the advice or information which he is given, and unless it would be reasonable for that other person so to rely and act. It would not be reasonable to act in reliance on advice or information given casually on some social or informal occasion or, generally speaking, unless the advice or information concerned "a business or professional transaction whose nature makes clear the gravity of the inquiry and the importance and influence attached to the answer . . . ."[47]

In this case of *Shaddock & Associates v. Parramatta City Council*, the High Court was deciding whether to override a restriction upon the range of liability for negligent misstatements established by the Judicial Committee of the Privy Council in an earlier Australian case,[48] in which the class of persons that would have a duty of care would be those persons who have, or hold themselves out as having, professional skills, and who give advice regarding those skills. As Justice Mason observed in the *Shaddock* case,[49] the justifying ground for such a restriction is some such policy ground as that indicated in the American *Restatement (Second) of Torts*, namely that: "[w]hen the harm that is

---

46 *Id.*

47 Shaddock & Assoc. Proprietary, Ltd. v. Parramatta City Council, (1981) 150 C.L.R. 225, 231 (quoting Lord Pearce in Hedley Byrne & Co. v. Heller & Partners, [1964] App. Cas. 465, 539 (appeal taken from Eng.)). *Compare with* Caparo Indus. v. Dickman, [1990] 1 All E.R. 568, 574 (opinion by Lord Bridge of Harwich).

48 *See* Mutual Life & Citizens' Assurance Co. v. Evatt, [1971] App. Cas. 793 (appeal taken from Eng.).

49 *See Shaddock*, (1981) 150 C.L.R. at 249–50.

caused is only pecuniary loss, the courts have found it necessary to adopt a more restricted rule of liability, because of the extent to which misinformation may be, and may be expected to be, circulated, and the magnitude of the losses which may follow from reliance on it."[50] But Justice Mason rejected this as sufficient justification for the restriction envisaged, because:

> In the first place, it denies a remedy to those who sustain serious loss at the hands of those who are not members of the class and whose conduct is negligent. Secondly, it ignores the availability of insurance as a protection against liability. Thirdly, there is no logic in excluding from the class of persons liable for negligent mis-statement persons who, though they may not exercise skill and competence, assume a responsibility to give advice or information to others on serious matters which may occasion loss or damage. Finally, the rule, recently established by *Caltex Oil (Australia) Pty. Ltd. v. The Dredge "Willemstad"* (1976)136 C.L.R. 529, is that economic loss, not consequential upon property damage, may be recoverable from those whose negligence occasions it.[51]

Here we have, in small bulk, what I have elsewhere[52] argued to be a characteristic mode of common law argumentation. In arguing in favour both of the more extended interpretation of "reasonable reliance" and thus of the more extensive view of liability for negligent misstatement, Justice Mason is advancing in his first and second points consequentialist grounds for favouring the given interpretation, and in his third and fourth points arguments of coherence.

Nor is this an unusual feature of such arguments concerning the interpretation of what is reasonable. Consider the New York case of *American Book Co. v. Yeshiva University Development Foundation, Inc.*[53] concerning the interpretation of a covenant in a lease under which the tenant of commercial premises was restricted from subletting the premises without the written consent of the landlord, such consent not to be "unreasonably withheld." American Book Company wished to sublet to an organisation called "Planned Parenthood Federation of America."[54] Yeshiva University, as successor in title to the landlord with whom the lease had originally been made, withheld consent on the ground of "philosophical and ideological 'inconsistencies' between itself and the proposed subtenant, [and] the 'controversial' na-

---

50 *Id.* at 250 (quoting RESTATEMENT (SECOND) OF TORTS § 552 cmt. a (1977)).
51 *Id.* at 250–51.
52 *See* NEIL MACCORMICK, LEGAL REASONING AND LEGAL THEORY 100–51 (rev. ed. 1994).
53 297 N.Y.S. 2d 156 (1969).
54 *See id.* at 158.

ture of the subtenant."[55] (The controversial nature in question was Planned Parenthood's character as a propagandist for contraception.) Judge Greenfield ruled that only "objective" grounds for refusal of consent were acceptable as grounds for "reasonable" refusal, that is,

> [s]tandards which are readily measurable criteria of proposed subtenant's or assignee's acceptability from the point of view of *any* landlord:
>
> (a) financial responsibility; (b) the "identity" or "business character" of the subtenant—i.e., his suitability for the particular building; (c) the legality of the proposed use; (d) the nature of the occupancy—i.e., office, factory, clinic or whatever.[56]

This denied recourse to "subjective" grounds of objection based on the particular likes and dislikes or philosophical, religious, or ideological convictions of the landlord. For the learned judge's ruling on the interpretation of "reasonableness" as here implying an objective standard, we find very characteristic reasoning pointing to the inexpedient and unjust consequences of adopting the subjective standard:

> If indeed the potentiality for controversy were a serviceable standard for measuring the acceptability of a subtenancy, many of our most socially useful institutions would be homeless vagrants on the streets, and our buildings would be tenanted by bland, unexceptionable models of propriety and dullness. Even proponents of unpopular ideas are entitled to a roof over their heads.[57]

The point just considered deals with one of the most important general aspects of the interpretation of "reasonableness" as a standard, namely its typically objective character, to which we have already alluded. Even here, though, the question can sometimes be an open one whether, for a given topic, the reasonable has to be construed as that which is objectively reasonable, without regard to personal peculiarities or predilections of individuals in a particular relationship. Cannot "reasonable" signify what is subjectively reasonable, reasonable for a particular individual in a particular setting?

On grounds which have been classically expressed by Justice Holmes[58] and by Lord Reid,[59] the ordinary presumption is that the test of reasonableness is, in the sense indicated, an objective test. The rights of persons against others in society ought to be fixed by com-

---

55 *Id.* at 159.

56 *Id.* at 159–60.

57 *Id.* at 162.

58 *See* OLIVER WENDELL HOLMES, JR., THE COMMON LAW 88–89 (Mark DeWolfe Howe ed., Harvard Univ. Press 1963) (1881).

59 *See* Lord Reid, *The Law and the Reasonable Man*, *in* PROCEEDINGS OF THE BRITISH ACADEMY, 1968, at 189, 200–01.

mon intersubjective criteria, not by reference to particular peculiarities of individuals. At least in all matters affecting the rights of persons in civil law or in public law, there should normally be an objective grounding of the rights established. On the other hand, as Lord Reid once pointed out,[60] in matters of criminal liability, at least for serious crimes, we should always apply a very strong presumption in favour of subjective mens rea or at least subjective culpability on the part of the person accused.

Once we see the matter in this light we can, however, see ground for a different judgement in such an area as family law, given the intensely personal quality of relationships (e.g., between spouses). Lord Reid himself once remarked that "[i]n matrimonial cases we are not concerned with the reasonable man, as we are in cases of negligence. We are dealing with this man and this woman and the fewer *a priori* assumptions we make about them the better."[61] This statement was in turn adopted by the Court of Appeal in England in ruling on the proper interpretation of the "reasonable" in the context of divorce law. The statute provided that divorce might be granted if a marriage had irretrievably broken down on the ground that, inter alia, one spouse behaved toward the other in such a way that the other "cannot reasonably be expected" to go on living with this spouse. The test to be applied must take account of the subjective propensities and characters of the two individuals in the relationship of marriage:

> Would any right-thinking person come to the conclusion that this husband has behaved in such a way that this wife cannot reasonably be expected to live with him, taking into account the *whole* of the circumstances and the characters and personalities of the parties?[62]

This stress on the subjectivity of the spouses, and the related subjectivity of the test for reasonableness as between them, appears at first sight to go against the general requirement of universality or universalisability in rulings upon the law and its interpretation.[63] Obviously,

---

60 *Id.* at 201. *See also* Warner v. Metropolitan Police Comm'r, [1968] 2 All E.R. 356 (noting Lord Reid's dicta).

61 Collins v. Collins, [1964] App. Cas. 644, 660 (appeal taken from Eng.).

62 Livingstone-Stallard v. Livingstone-Stallard, [1974] Fam. 47, 54 (quoting Justice Dunn) (cited with approval by Lord Justice Roskill in O'Neill v. O'Neill, [1975] 3 All E.R. 289, 295) (emphasis added).

63 For a discussion of the requirements of universality in legal rulings, see MACCORMICK, *supra* note 52, at 71–86. On the point of present difficulty, it is worth remembering that, as R. M. Hare argues, a principle may be universal even though it contains reference to "bound variables." *See* R.M. HARE, MORAL THINKING: ITS LEVELS, METHOD, AND POINT 140 (1981). An example would be if we were to say that "every married person ought to treat his or her spouse in a way that his or her spouse finds

there must between each set of marriage partners be a different "personal equation," so that what is reasonable as between any one pair may not be reasonable for any other, and we shall lose all view of the universal in a thicket of particulars. But on reflection, this doubt is groundless. We may make it a universal rule always to apply an objective test of reasonableness, for example, in negligence cases (and we may have good justifications for so doing), and yet make it an equally universal rule always to apply a subjective test of what is reasonable for any particular spouse in relation to his partner in matrimonial cases, having here a sound justification for applying the subjective test, precisely because of the type of relationship in view in any such case.

What would be objectionable would be to vary the interpretation of "reasonable" as between subjective and objective within a single type of case having a single common topic. In public law, the much criticised war-time case of *Liversidge v. Anderson*[64] ruled that a Minister might be held to have "reasonable cause to believe" that a person had hostile origins or associations, and therefore to be acting lawfully in causing him to be detained under the Defence (General) Regulations, 1939,[65] provided only that he honestly believed that he had reasonable cause for his belief. In this branch of law, there are the most powerful reasons for treating criteria of reasonableness as being objective, not subjective. Hence even the special exigencies of wartime can hardly be pled in aid to justify giving a special subjective interpretation to that criterion. In fact, the decision in *Liversidge* has been so generally disapproved as to be of practically no weight as a precedent. It is an unjustified exception to a well-justified, general rule for the interpretation of reasonableness as an objective standard in public law.[66]

Let it be remarked again that the legitimate variability as between objective and subjective grounds of reasonableness, dependent in turn on variations of topic or of focus of concern, is only one of the elements of variability in the interpretations which may properly be given of the criterion or standard of "reasonableness." What the present discussion has shown is that "reasonableness" is not itself a first-order value, but a higher-order value which we exemplify in considering a balance of first-order, or anyway lower-order values, and coming to a conclusion about their application. The task of interpretation of

---

reasonable." *See also* GREENAWALT, *supra* note 1, at 141–62 (discussing "The Generality of Law").

64 [1942] App. Cas. 206 (appeal taken from Eng.).
65 Defence (General) Regulations, 1939, reg. 18B, § 1.
66 *See* Nakkuda Ali v. Jayaratne, [1951] App. Cas. 66, 76–77 (appeal taken from Eng.).

"reasonable" in a given context is that of identifying the values, interests, and the like that are relevant to the given focus of attention. This in turn depends on the types of situation or relationship that are in issue, and on a view of the governing principle or rationale of the branch of law concerned.

IV. WHAT IS REASONABLE, AND IS THIS A QUESTION OF FACT?

It is worth observing at the outset of this Section how strange it appears on the face of things to call questions of reasonableness questions of "fact" at all. To conclude in a given case that a person has acted or decided reasonably or unreasonably is surely to make a value judgement rather than a judgement of fact. Yet "questions of fact" are what Scots lawyers and common lawyers call such judgements. Lord Denning once said the following about the analogous case of judicial determination of an employer's duty to take reasonable care for the safety of his employees:

> What is "a proper system of work" is a matter for evidence, not for the law books. It changes as the conditions of work change. The standard goes up as men become wiser. It does not stand still as the law sometimes does.[67]

It is important that we appreciate Lord Denning's point about the mutability-through-time of judgements concerning what is proper or reasonable given changing facts and circumstances. Precautions at work which were once treated as unusual or extravagant may come to be accepted as normal and proper.[68] Advances in medical knowledge may reveal risks in simple procedures such as the administration of injections, risks avoidable by the taking of new precautions; then the reasonableness of taking such precautions changes and is governed by the new state of available knowledge in the profession.[69] What can reasonably be expected of a marriage partner may change with changes in the social milieu—what husband in the present day could think unreasonable an expectation that he participate in domestic chores which even thirty years ago were firmly identified as women's work?

But that is not the only point to be taken from Lord Denning's remark. For it reminds us also of two particular features of decision-making in the common law context. First, we must remember the

---

67 *See* Qualcast (Wolverhampton), Ltd. v. Haynes, [1959] App. Cas. 743, 760 (appeal taken from Eng.).
68 *See id.*; *cf.* General Cleaning Contractors v. Christmas, [1953] App. Cas. 180 (appeal taken from Eng.).
69 *See, e.g.*, Roe v. Minister of Health, [1954] 2 Q.B. 66.

division of legal labour that makes judges masters of the law, but juries of the facts. It is for the judge to give authoritative guidance on questions of law and of its interpretation, including interpretations of the criteria of reasonableness such as were discussed above in Section II. It is for the jury to decide whether these criteria are satisfied by the facts of the given case. Most obviously, in a criminal trial, it is for the judge to explain to the jury that the prosecution must prove its case "beyond reasonable doubt," and what that means. But it is for the jury to decide whether that standard of proof has been satisfied in the case before it.

Secondly, even though (outside the sphere of criminal law) resort to jury trial is on the decline, the distinction remains between questions of law and questions of fact on the basis of how these would be apportioned between judges and juries, even where a professional judge or judges are deciders of both sorts of question. This has an obvious bearing on the doctrine of precedent. Later courts and lower courts are obliged to respect decisions by earlier courts or higher ones on questions of law (including, therefore, questions as to the proper interpretation of, for example, criteria of reasonableness). The same obligatory force, however, does not attach to decisions on the facts of particular cases, including the question whether, in a given case, a person acted reasonably.

The latter point was the one most at issue in the case from which Lord Denning's remarks above were quoted. His argument was aimed at stressing that a court's judgement as to what is, for example, a "proper system of work" in all the circumstances of one case does not constitute a binding precedent of direct applicability to other cases. Hence the importance of his stress on the possibility that social standards may change and with them conclusions as to "proper system of work," "reasonable care," and the like.

These considerations are of importance in understanding why lawyers include questions about reasonableness as falling within what they classify as "questions of fact," although they are also in part at least questions of value. Certainly, on any view they are, as Lord Denning put it, "matters for evidence." We must know in any case what was done and what was not done, and for what reasons, and what might otherwise have been done or omitted, and what is normal practice in such matters, before we can judge the reasonableness of the actings and omissions in view. Analytically, at least, the process of judgement is one which has two phases—the phase of discovering what happened and why, and the phase of appreciating that which happened in the light of the relevant value-factors.

In a famous essay,[70] John Wisdom once drew attention to what he took to be a special peculiarity of legal reasoning, in the light of which it could not be classified either as deductive or as inductive reasoning in the ordinary sense of these terms, but was in effect sui generis. He pointed out that the reasoning process in law is not like a chain of mathematical reasoning, where each step follows from the preceding one, and where any error at any step invalidates all that follows. Rather, legal reasoning is a matter of weighing and considering all the factors which "severally co-operate" in favour of a particular conclusion, and balancing them against the factors which tell against that conclusion.[71] In the end, the conclusion is to be reached rather on a balance of reasons than by inference from premises to conclusions or from known to unknown facts. The reasons for a conclusion are commonly mutually independent, offering a set of supports for the conclusion, so that failure in one of them does not leave the conclusion unsupported; such reasons are, in Wisdom's vivid phrase, "like the legs of a chair, not the links of a chain."[72]

To accept Wisdom's thesis as a complete account or description of legal reasoning would, I believe, be to mistake the part for the whole. But the part to which it applies, and with which his essay explicitly dealt, is the very part under review at the moment. As to that, Wisdom captures exactly and vividly the way in which we must bring a plurality of factors together into consideration when, as a "matter for evidence," we seek to pass judgement upon the reasonableness of some decision, or action, or omission, or choice to rely upon advice, or contractual provision, or matrimonial expectation, or whatever. What is necessary now is, however, to move beyond general description of the process to the scrutiny of particular cases in a variety of fields to see if we can establish how exactly the process of "weighing" or "balancing" the various factors of judgement may be understood.

We may start with problems of public law. How do we find judges evaluating the "reasonableness" of public authorities' decisions? The answer here seems to be that the grounds for the decision made have to be evaluated for their relevancy to the making of the decision in the light of the aims and purposes of a statutory power of decision-making. Thus in *Padfield v. Minister of Agriculture*[73] the Minister had refused to exercise his statutory power to appoint a committee to in-

---

70 John Wisdom, *Gods*, in PROCEEDINGS OF THE ARISTOTELIAN SOCIETY, 1944–1945, at 185, *reprinted in* JOHN WISDOM, PHILOSOPHY AND PSYCHO-ANALYSIS 149–68 (1957).
71 WISDOM, *supra* note 70, at 157.
72 *Id.*
73 [1968] App. Cas. 997 (appeal taken from Eng.).

vestigate complaints made by members of the Milk Marketing Board about the scheme established for fixing the price of milk. Each of the reasons stated by the Minister was reviewed in terms of its relevance to the statutory milk marketing scheme. The House of Lords concluded that the Minister's stated reasons showed his refusal to have been motivated by irrelevant reasons and thus to have been calculated to frustrate rather than promote the purposes of the legislation. On that ground, the Minister was ordered "to consider the complaint of the appellants according to law." Such a case has to be distinguished from one in which a public authority's decision is based on a genuine review of relevant grounds for decision and is not motivated by any irrelevant grounds, but is complained against on the ground of having come to a false judgement on the relative merits of relevant reasons for and against a particular course of action. Within this area, the public authority's conclusion as to what is right or reasonable must be taken as conclusive.[74]

In such cases on the relevancy of grounds of decision, it obviously makes sense to say that among the plurality of grounds offered, each may "severally co-operate" with every other in favour of the decision made and as showing it to be relevantly grounded. Yet the attack made upon the decision will seek to isolate some one or more of the grounds as having been both irrelevant and determinative of the decision. If a dominant motive for a decision is a wrong one, that may be fatal to it even though there are, or might be, perfectly acceptable other reasons for the same decision.[75] While "reasonableness" may arise from a plurality of grounds, it may be that the presence of a single improper or irrelevant consideration is sufficient to "tilt the balance" the other way.

The same may apply in relation to other legal topics of "reasonableness." For example, in tort law, the central question is commonly whether some harm suffered by the plaintiff resulted from a want of "reasonable care" on the defendant's part. It is worth remembering that in such cases the burden rests upon the plaintiff to show that the defendant did not take reasonable care. So for example, it must be proved both that harm was suffered by the plaintiff as a result of some act or event or state of affairs within the defendant's control and that it was open to the defendant to have taken some precaution which would have prevented the occurrence of the harm. In one case, a bus

---

[74] *See* Secretary of State for Educ. & Science v. Tameside Metro. Borough Council, [1977] App. Cas. 1014 (appeal taken from Eng.).

[75] The case of *Padfield v. Minister of Agriculture*, [1968] App. Cas. 997 (appeal taken from Eng.), itself indicates this point.

passenger fell out of the open door of a bus while making his way towards the door with a view to alighting at the next stop.[76] It was argued that this accident need not have happened if either the door had been kept closed or a central pillar (in addition to nine other hand holds) had been provided as a handhold on the bus platform.[77] Failure to take one or other such precaution, it was contended, amounted to a failure to take reasonable care. As against this, it was shown that (a) buses of this type had been run for several years without such accident occurring, and that (b) either of the possible precautions would have required great expense and caused great inconvenience in the use of the buses.[78] So the precaution, lack of which was alleged to be unreasonable, was in the House of Lords' view, one which it was reasonable not to take given the value to be set on general convenience in the use of the buses and the low degree of risk established by the evidence. By contrast, where window-cleaning employers failed to require employees to take any precautions in cleaning windows while balancing on window ledges, this was held to be unreasonable even though it had been shown that two of the possible safety systems would be impracticable in some cases, and prohibitively costly in others. Provided there was some precaution that could practicably be taken to diminish the obviously high risk of falling from window ledges, it was unreasonable not to take it.[79]

That in such cases there is necessarily a weighing or balancing of factors for and against is very obvious, and well illustrated by *Bolton v. Stone*.[80] A woman walking along a street outside a cricket ground was injured by a cricket ball struck out of the ground by a batsman. Such

---

76 *See* Wyngrove's Curator Bonis v. Scottish Omnibuses, Ltd., 1966 Sess. Cas. (H.L.) 47. Nowadays, buses have automatically opening and closing doors, and the standard of "reasonable precautions" for passengers' safety has surely risen, in the manner mentioned in connection with Lord Denning's opinion. *See supra* note 67 and accompanying text.

77 *See Wyngrove*, 1966 Sess. Cas. at 52.

78 *See id.* at 85.

79 *See* General Cleaning Contractors v. Christmas, [1953] App. Cas. 180 (appeal taken from Eng.). A more up-to-date example, this one concerning duties of disclosure in an insurance context, is the following holding of Justice Potter: "[I]t was the duty of PUM as prudent managing agents seeking unlimited protection . . . to consider with care what required to be disclosed to a prospective reinsurer . . . in particular, the mounting claims for asbestosis and DES which were the reason why the reinsurance was sought in the first place. Further, that duty extended to disclosure of facts which were arguably material *so as to avoid unnecessary risk of avoidance.*" Aiken v. Stewart Wrightson Members' Agency, [1995] 3 All E.R. 449, 481 (quoting Justice Potter).

80 [1951] App. Cas. 850 (appeal taken from Eng.).

mighty hits of the ball were naturally rare, but did happen from time to time. To guard against the risk of injury to pedestrians, it would have been necessary to erect a fence of some height all around the ground. It was argued that failure to take this precaution amounted to a breach of duty on the part of the cricket club.

> Those being the facts, a breach of duty has taken place if they show the appellants guilty of a failure to take reasonable care to prevent the accident. One may phrase it as "reasonable care" or "ordinary care" or "proper care"—all these phrases are to be found in decisions of authority—but the fact remains that, unless there has been something which a reasonable man would blame as falling beneath the standard of conduct that he would set for himself or require of his neighbour, there has been no breach of legal duty. And here, I think, the respondent's case breaks down. It seems to me that a reasonable man, taking account of the chances against an accident happening, would not have felt himself called upon either to abandon the use of the ground for cricket or to increase the height of his surrounding fences. He would have done what the appellants did: in other words, he would have done nothing.[81]

Here we have to set, on the one hand, the (implicit) value to be attached to the traditional English game of cricket, the cost of fencing the ground, and the low risk of pedestrians actually being hit against, on the other hand, the value of personal security from bodily injury. The House of Lords concluded that the former values in this case overrode the latter. The plaintiff had pointed to a failure of precautions—but this failure was not evaluated as unreasonable set against the other values at stake. Likewise, in cases where risks are taken in situations of emergency, the degree of risk which it is held reasonable to take is greater than in ordinary circumstances. If you are trying to save lives, you may reasonably have to take some quite serious risks in doing so.

In all such cases, it is up to one party to show a failure of reasonableness and identify the alleged lack of reasonable care; but then the other party counters this by showing the difficulty or impracticality or excessive costliness in terms of relevant values of that which it is al-

---

[81] *Id.* at 868. For a criticism of this line of reasoning, on the ground that in fact the cricket club and other cricket clubs would have had to pay for insurance, not pay for new fencing, had the decision gone the other way, see P. S. ATIYAH, ACCIDENTS COMPENSATION AND THE LAW 467–69 (1970). The most recent edition of Atiyah's book drops this point, see PETER CANE, ATIYAH'S ACCIDENTS COMPENSATION AND THE LAW (5th ed. 1993), but retains the discussion concerning the weighing of rival values, *see id.* at 35. *See also id.* at 150 (suggesting that there might be liability here without negligence).

leged he should have done. It is in that process of countering an allegation of failure to do what is reasonable that we find recourse to Wisdom's plurality of grounds severally co-operating to cancel out the allegation.

The same applies in other spheres, for example the contractual or proprietary. We saw earlier how in *American Book Co.*, Justice Greenfield ruled that relevant criteria for reasonable objection to a subtenant of leased property must be "objective."[82] That being so, on the facts of the particular case it was fatal to the landlord's objection that the proposed subtenant of the premises did satisfy all the objective criteria under scrutiny. The substantial ground of objection, the subjective hostility of the landlord to the subtenant's activities as an advocate of contraception, fell to be dismissed as an unreasonable objection.

We can find similar reasoning in the cases on contracts in restraint of trade; at common law, contractual provisions which fetter a person's freedom to trade as he wishes are illegal except where they constitute a reasonable protection for the other party and are reasonable in the public interest. In *Dumbarton Steamboat Co. v. MacFarlane*,[83] the pursuers had bought over the carriers' business of the defender and his partner, who were to be employed by the pursuer company and who undertook to procure for the company the benefit of their own previous business and also not to "carry on or be concerned in any separate business of a like or similar kind in the United Kingdom" for a period of ten years.[84] Three years after the agreement had been made, the defender was dismissed by the company and then recommenced business as a carrier in the Dumbarton area.[85] It was established that in his new business he had been actively canvassing former customers of himself and of the company, in breach of his agreement. Upon this point, the pursuers were granted an interdict to prevent him from infringing a provision perfectly reasonable in the context of the sale of a business and its goodwill.[86] By contrast, on the other point, Lord Moncrieff said:

> [A]s the business which was sold by the defender to the pursuers was of a very limited character, the restriction which would prevent him from carrying on the business of carrier in any part of the United Kingdom, however remote from Dumbarton and uncon-

---

82   See *supra* text accompanying notes 53–57.
83   1 Fr. 993 (1899).
84   *Id.* at 994.
85   See *id.*
86   See *id.* at 995.

nected with the Dumbarton trade, is excessive, and should not receive effect.[87]

In the matrimonial cases, where one of the modern grounds for divorce as following from irretrievable breakdown of marriage is "that the respondent has behaved in such a way that the petitioner cannot reasonably be expected to live with the respondent,"[88] the criteria of what is reasonable, as we saw earlier, are subjective rather than objective. But there is a matter of weighing the evidence, and of seeing whether things have been done by one to another which go beyond what that person with his character can reasonably accept. For this purpose, the petitioner must establish something seriously objectionable to himself about the other spouse's behaviour. Hence the case put by the petitioner husband in *Pheasant v. Pheasant* was necessarily an insufficient one, as appears from Justice Ormrod's summary of it:

> The husband was unable to establish . . . anything which could be regarded as a serious criticism of the wife's conduct or behaviour. His case, quite simply is that she has not been able to give him the spontaneous, demonstrative affection which he says that his nature demands and for which he craves. In these circumstances he says that it is impossible for him to live with the wife any longer and that in consequence he cannot reasonably be expected to live with her.[89]

There is a sharp contrast between such a case and that of *O'Neill v. O'Neill*.[90] After eighteen years of somewhat mobile married life, the husband having been an airline pilot and having been forced to retire for medical reasons, the O'Neills bought an apartment in which to settle down. For two years the husband worked single-handed on trying to renovate the flat, a process which involved the removal of the lavatory door and the lifting of most of the floorboards in the house. His wife found this intolerable due to the loss of privacy and the impossibility of having guests at home in the circumstances. Eventually she left with the two children of the marriage. The husband responded by writing her a letter casting doubt on the legitimacy of the children. She petitioned for divorce on the ground of his behaviour having been such that she could not reasonably be expected to live with him. The husband argued that her objection was in effect to his character rather than to his behaviour. But the Court of Appeal re-

---

87 *Id.* at 998.
88 Matrimonial Causes Act, 1973, ch.18, § 1(2)(b); Divorce (Scotland) Act, 1976, ch. 39, § 1(2)(b).
89 [1972] 1 All E.R. 587, 588.
90 [1975] 3 All E.R. 289.

jected this. As a woman who had for long desired a settled home with neighbours and friends, Mrs. O'Neill had much to object to in her husband's conduct in trying to renovate the house, on top of which there was the unacceptable act of suggesting that the children were illegitimate. What is at issue is whether in the behaviour or conduct of one spouse there has been something objectionable to the other, which can be alleged to go beyond what it is reasonable for him to tolerate. Whether it does go beyond that limit is to be assessed in the light of allegedly counteracting considerations advanced by that other.

That is, in sum, the dialectic of debate upon the reasonable. Starting from a view, most probably an open-ended or nonexclusive view as to the criteria or factors relevant to a given topic, an allegation must be made as to one or more failures under one or more criteria or factors. It is then for the other side to counter this alleged failure by reference to positive values under the same or other criteria or factors. In this sense the final judgement is one attained by "weighing" and "balancing" to decide whether, all things considered, they constitute not merely good and relevant reasons in themselves for what was done, but adequate or sufficient reasons for so doing even in the presence of the identified adverse factors.

It may seem unsatisfactory that at the end of the day, even after examining, or at least sketching, a set of more or less random examples of such judgements from various branches of the law having quite different foci of concern, we have to rest with the metaphor of "weighing" or "balancing" reasons pro and contra. For this is a metaphor. Reasons do not have weights as material objects do. To say that some reasons for action or value-factors bearing on action "outweigh" others is almost to restate the initial problem rather than to solve it. For at best we ascribe greater or less weight to some reasons or factors than others, and the question is what are the grounds of such ascription.

Perhaps the answer to this question is best given by referring back to the "procedural" aspect of reasoning. What is required is attention to, and deliberation over, the relative human importance of the different factors that enter judgement in any given case. Wherein lies relative importance? One important thing is how much people care about one thing rather than another, and surely there is no reason to leave out sense and sentiment, nor the actual psychological make-up of real people.[91] But bringing one's reflections beyond raw feeling

---

91 Heidi Li Feldman's article is an important and path-breaking work. *See* Feldman, *supra* note 17. She brings to our attention the empirical psychological work of

and into the realm of the reasonable calls for something like Adam Smith's "impartial spectator" procedure considered above.[92] A measure of weight is found in the sympathetic or empathetic response of the deliberator to the feelings of persons involved, after making adjustments for impartiality and adequate information. If this is so, there is bound to be for each of us an element of the subjective in every one of our best efforts at pure objectivity. This conclusion, I suspect, merely replicates that of Kent Greenawalt.

NB. The publisher bears responsibility for any errors which have occurred in reprinting or editing.

Daniel Kahneman and others to show how far the construct of the "reasonable man" can be rooted in ordinary people's attitudes to risk and risk-taking, and why this differs from the hypotheses built into rational choice theory. Feldman is now embarked on an "Ethico-Psychological" project, aimed at further fleshing out the evaluative as well as descriptive components of "reasonableness." The present work is confessedly longer on ethics and shorter on psychology, but I am sure Feldman is right concerning the need to incorporate findings such as Kahneman's.

92 See SMITH, supra note 17 and accompanying text.

Name Index

Aarnio, Aulis 260, 429
Acton, Lord 150
Adler, Mortimer 359
Alchourrón, Carlos E. xvii, xviii, 283–300
Alexy, Robert xix, xx, 86, 87, 88, 89, 99, 237–500, 251–64 *passim*, 423, 426, 427, 429
Allen, C.K. 48
Arendt, Hannah 410
Aristotle 64, 68, 69, 284
Atkin, Lord 279
Atria, Fernando xi, xiv, xv, xvi, 71–111
Austin, John 5
Austin, J.L. 129

Baker, G.P. xvii
Bankowski, Zenon xx, xxi, 265–82, 426
Beethoven, Ludwig von 19
Bice, Scott 187
Bingham, Joseph W. 354, 355–6 *passim*, 359
Bjarup, Jes xxv, xxx, 375–85
Brandeis, Louis 374
Brendel, Alfred 20, 21
Brest, Paul 174, 176, 178, 180, 214
Brod, Max 118
Bundy, Herbert 413, 414

Campbell, Archie 265
Cardozo, Judge 4, 197, 198
Chandler, Raymond 396
Chesterton, G.K. 272
Christie, Agatha 395, 396–7 *passim*
Christodoulidis, Emilios A. xxi, xxiii, xxiv, 327–47
Cicero 351, 413
Cohen, Felix 353, 359, 360
Cohen, Morris R. 353, 354, 356, 358, 359
Coke, Sir Edward 36, 41–9 *passim*,
Collingwood 183
Collins, Wilkie 396
Conan Doyle, Arthur 396
Constant, Benjamin 258, 260
Cromwell, Thomas 49

Davidson, Donald 12
Denning, Lord 413, 414, 546, 547
Descartes, Rene 146

Detmold, Michael J. xii, xiv, xv, xvi, xxi, 35–70, 281, 342
Devlin, Lord 215, 225
Dewey, John 306, 354, 357–8 *passim*
Dewitz, Sandra 274
Dicey, A.V. 48, 50, 52, 62
Dickens, Charles 396
Dostoyevski, Fedor M. 396
Drier, R. 426
Dworkin, Ronald xi, xii, xiii, xiv, xvi, xxv, xxxvi, 3–15, 71, 185, 188, 199, 201, 209, 231, 299, 300, 353, 371, 372, 387–8 *passim*, 389, 390, 391–3 *passim*, 395, 396, 397, 398–402 *passim*, 409, 410, 411, 429, 536

Edward I, King 65
Edward III, King 46, 47
Ehrlich, Eugen 413
Ely, John 214, 215, 216, 217, 231
Esher, Lord 279
Esser, Josef xxvii, 411
Euclid 284

Finnis, John 35, 56, 63, 64, 68, 69
Fish, Stanley xxv, xxvi, xxvii, 371, 372, 387–406
Fiss, Owen 145
Fleming, Alexander 396
Fodor 126
Frankfurter, Felix 208, 229
Freeling, Nicholas 396
Freud, Sigmund 117–18 *passim*
Fuller, Lon L. 153, 220

Gadamer, Hans H. xxvii, 149, 411
Gandhi, Mahatma 288
Garland, David 265
Goldsmith 411
Goodhart 195
Goodman, Nelson 205
Gordon, Gerald 265
Gough, J.W. 43–4, 45, 48, 49
Gould, Glenn 19
Greenawalt, Kent 527, 528, 529, 533, 539, 555
Greenfield, Justice 543, 552
Grey, Tom 142
Günther, Klaus xviii, xix, 237–40 *passim*, 242–8 *passim*, 251–64

, Ter 412
,abermas, Jürgen xx, 249
Halsbury, Lord 35, 55
Hammet, Dashiel 396
Hand, Learned 228, 229, 232
Hare, Richard O. 206, 262
Hart, H.L.A. xi, xiv, xv, xvi, xxi, xxvii, 5, 56–7, 67, 68, 71, 72–81 passim, 84, 85, 89, 91, 92, 94, 97, 98, 131, 132, 143, 173, 174, 220, 291, 293, 425, 535–6 passim
Hartkamp, Attorney-General 419
Hayek, Friedrich W. xxi, 275, 276, 282
Heller, Joseph 341
Hempel, G. 286
Henry II, King 66
Henry VIII, King 43
Herle 46, 47
Highsmith, Patricia 396
Hilbert, David 284
Hitler, Adolf 13
Hobbes, Thomas 334
Holdsworth 48
Holmes, Oliver W. 303, 352, 416, 445, 543
Horøwitz, M. xxii
Hume, David 367, 378, 383
Husserl, Edmund 333

Ihering, R. von 110, 303

Jenks 43
Jennings, 60–61, 62
Jefferson, Thomas 306

Kafka, Franz 118
Kant, Immanuel 206, 258, 260, 378
Katz, J. 126
Kaufmann, Arthur 411
Kelman, M. xxiii
Kelsen, Hans xi, 82–3, 91, 92
Kempff, Wilhelm 19
Kennedy, Duncan 539
Kennedy, John F. 288
Kripke, Saul xxiv, xxv, 351, 352–3 passim, 362–74 passim, 375, 376, 377–85 passim

Landis, James 191
Larenz, Karl 411
Leach, W. Barton 165, 166
Leavis, F.R. 12
Leijten, J.C.M. 414, 415
Levinson, Sanford 146, 149
Lewis, Justice 92
Liszt, Franz 20
Llewellyn, Karl N. 121, 411–12

Luhmann, Niklas 251, 277, 328, 332, 333, 334, 335, 336, 338, 339–40, 345, 346

MacCallum, Gerald 185
McClintock, Derrick 265
MacCormick, D. Neil xii, xiv, xvi, xvii, xviii, xxvii, xxviii, xxix, xxx, xxxi, 57, 58, 71, 72, 75, 83, 84, 86, 87, 88–100 passim, 265, 266, 269, 294–5, 409, 410, 411, 420, 421–34, 527–55
MacDonald, John D. 396
Macdonald, Ross 396
McIlwain, C.H. 42–4 passim, 44, 46–7, 49
McLarty, Ronald 267, 268
Macmillan, Lord 537
Maitland, J.P. 43, 66
Marmor, A. 82, 83, 84, 85
Marshall, Justice 44, 231, 232
Maruyama 340
Mason, Justice 541–2
Miller, Jonathan 25
Milton, John 397
Monaghan, Henry 207, 208
Montague, Chief Justice 45–6
Moore, Michael S. xvi, xvii, xxvi, 113–234
Moncrieff, Lord 552–3
Montesquieu, Charles de Secondat 303
Mosk, Justice 191
Munzer 201, 209, 210
Murdoch, Iris 266

Nickel 201, 209, 210
Nozick, Robert 353

Ormrod, Justice 553
Osmond, Marie 214

Parsons, Talcott 334, 335
Paterson, Alan 413
Peczenik, Aleksander xxviii, xxix, xxxi, 260, 429, 435–43
Perelman, Chaim 529
Plato 64
Poe, Edgar Allen 396
Poggi 333
Pollock 46, 66
Postema, Gerald J. 109
Pound, Roscoe 354, 355–6 passim, 361, 376, 382
Powell, Justice 169
Proust, Marcel 321
Pufendorf, Samuel 82, 96, 295

Quine, Willard V.O. 12, 148
Quinlan, Karen 144, 145

Radin, Max 190, 192, 221
Rawls, John 353
Raz, Joseph xii, xiii, xiv, xvi, 17–31, 35, 36, 50–52 *passim*, 53, 57, 61, 66, 71, 77, 79, 88, 100–10 *passim*
Reich 374
Reid, Lord 543, 544
Richter, Sviatolslav 20, 21
Ricoeur, David 410
Rorty, Richard 145, 146, 149
Ruemelin 439

Sarfield, Dalmacio V. 298
Sayers, Dorothy 396
Scholten, Paul 411
Sellars, Peter 25
Shakespeare, William 12, 397
Shklar, Judith 271
Simenon, Georges 396
Simpson 195
Smith, Adam xxviii, 58, 531, 555
Socrates 62
Spencer, Lady Diana 288
Stalin, Josef 7
Stewart, Justice Potter 131, 233
Stone, Julius 529
Summers, Robert S. xxix, xxx, xxxi, 421, 427, 433, 445–526

Teubner 251
Tolstoy, Leo 268

Tregor, Thomas 46

Unger, Roberto M. xxi, xxii, xxiii, 216, 217, 303–25, 327–32 *passim*, 334, 336–7 *passim*, 338, 339–41 *passim*, 342, 343–7 *passim*

van Dunné, Jan M. xxvii, 409–20
van Roermund, B.C. 415
von Savigny, Friedrich C. 426

Waisman, F. 72
Warren, Earl 229
Weber, Max 275
Wellington, Harry 215
Wellmer, A. xix
White, Dan 170, 171
Willes, Justice 50
William of York 65
Williston 173
Wilson, Bill 265
Wisdom, John 548
Wittgenstein, Ludwig xxiv, xxv, 58, 62, 63, 352, 362, 363, 367, 368, 370, 377, 379, 380–81 *passim*, 382, 384
Wolff, Robert P. 269–70 *passim*
Wróblewski, Jerzy xxx, xxxi, 421–34

Yablon, Charles M. xxiv, xxv, 351–74, 381–4 *passim*, 385
Yntema, Hessel 359, 360